Violence against Women

Classic Papers

Raquel Kennedy Bergen
St. Joseph's University

Jeffrey L. Edleson
University of Minnesota

Claire M. Renzetti
St. Joseph's University

Boston New York San Francisco
Mexico City Montreal Toronto London Madrid Munich Paris
Hong Kong Singapore Tokyo Cape Town Sydney

Series Editor: *Jennifer Jacobson*
Editorial Assistant: *Emma Christensen*
Senior Marketing Manager: *Krista Groshong*
Editorial-Production Service: *Omegatype Typography, Inc.*
Manufacturing Buyer: *Megan Cochran*
Composition and Prepress Buyer: *Linda Cox*
Cover Administrator: *Joel Gendron*
Electronic Composition: *Omegatype Typography, Inc.*

For related titles and support materials, visit our online catalog at www.ablongman.com.

Library of Congress Cataloging-in-Publication Data

Violence against women : classic papers / editors, Raquel Kennedy Bergen, Jeffrey L. Edleson, Claire M. Renzetti.
p. cm.
Includes bibliographical references and index.
ISBN 0-205-39263-6
1. Women—Violence against. 2. Wife abuse. 3. Rape. 4. Abusive men. I. Bergen, Raquel Kennedy. II. Edleson, Jeffrey L. III. Renzetti, Claire M.

HV6250.4.W65V563 2005
362.88—dc22

2004054744

Credits appear on pages 401–402, which constitute a continuation of the copyright page.

Printed in the United States of America

10 9 8 7 6 5 4 3 2 1 09 08 07 06 05 04

This book is dedicated to the memory of Susan Schechter, one of the authors represented here and a pioneer in services to battered women and their children. One of the last pieces Susan wrote before she died in 2004 was the reflection piece that appears in this volume.

CONTENTS

PREFACE

As with every book, *Violence against Women: Classic Papers* has been an adventure. This adventure began one day with an e-mail from Jeff Edleson with the brilliant idea of collaborating for a second time on a book. Our first collaborative effort, *The Sourcebook on Violence against Women* (2001), had been such a rewarding experience that we were eager for a second project. This new project was inspired by two existing books. One was M. Patricia Golden's (1976) *The Research Experience,* in which she reprinted a wide variety of research papers that were accompanied by reflections from the original authors. Although Golden's book is now out of print, it was a model on which we based this work. The second book was the much more recent *Classic Papers in Child Abuse* (2000), edited by Anne Cohn Donnely and Kim Oates. Here the editors brought together the key papers in the field of child abuse from 1946 to 1989. Our goal with *Violence against Women* was to assemble some of the classic works in the field of violence against women so that new generations of students, practitioners, and researchers would have a collective understanding of the work that has shaped the field. Our aim was also to include commentaries from the original authors reflecting on why they authored the work when they did and the influence of their work on the field. We believed that such a collection would be useful given how much the field has grown in the past three decades.

Contemporary efforts to end violence against women are entering a fourth decade. From meager beginnings in the early 1970s, a grassroots network that focused on assisting battered women and rape victims has expanded exponentially to encompass policy and practice at all levels of society. The disparate areas of adult domestic violence, rape, sexual assault, sexual harassment, and the like, have increasingly been referred to as violence against women. Examples of developments in the field of violence against women can be seen everywhere. In 2000, the U.S. government renewed the Violence against Women Act and doubled funding to $3 billion over five years to support intervention efforts. Where once small refuges housed battered women and their children in converted apartments, now newly-built facilities extend their services to include second stage housing, therapeutic services, advocacy and economic justice initiatives, child education, primary prevention, and collaboration with a wide array of other social institutions including police, courts, hospitals, and schools. Services are not just for women but also for their children and their abusive partners.

The proliferation of rape crisis centers also began in the 1970s, largely through the grassroots efforts of survivors who organized hotlines to provide emotional support to other women who had been victimized. Today, there are more than 1,200 programs in the United States offering medical and legal advocacy and mental health services to survivors of many forms of sexual violence. Over the years, the definition of violence against women has expanded to include a variety of forms of sexual and physical violence as well as emotional abuse, sex trafficking, and pornography.

There is also extensive evidence that the practices developed within the battered women's shelters and rape crisis centers over the past decades have expanded well beyond these particular services. Many hospitals, schools, police departments, courts, and places of worship and work now have prevention and intervention programs aimed at violence against women.

The publication of scholarly papers on the subject of violence against women has also grown tremendously over the years. Hundreds of books and a number of major journals are now devoted to examining violence against women in all its aspects. The field of violence against women has now matured to the point where many current publications commonly give reference to a series of papers that initially established a topical domain or sub-area. However, in teaching about violence against women, we have found that many of those new to the field (and some not so new to the field) have never read some of the classic statements on violence against women. Consequently, the goal of this anthology is to assemble into one edited volume many of the classic, groundbreaking pieces that have shaped the field of violence against women. A critical aspect of achieving this goal was to identify which pieces of work constituted "classic papers."

We began with the understanding that this anthology would focus primarily on feminist scholarship, given the influence of feminist thinking and practice on the field of violence against women and on our own work. Our criteria for selection of classic papers were that the paper was published early in the development of the field (there is only one paper originally published in the 1990s) and that the work was groundbreaking in that it drew attention to a new domain in the field or that it framed the issue in such a way as to subsequently reorient policy, practice, or research. We knew from the outset that not everyone would agree with our choice of what to include as classic. This field has benefited from the work of many people with strong and varied opinions, so we certainly did not expect complete consensus. To ensure that we considered a variety of works from many topical areas in the field of violence against women, we formed an advisory board of practitioners and researchers. We invited people who were diverse in terms of professional and personal backgrounds to comment on a tentative table of contents we had developed and to suggest other classic works that had influenced their own work along with a rationale for why a work should or should not be included. We are grateful to the following ten people for responding and serving as members of the advisory board: David Finkelhor, Anne Flitcraft, David Ford, Ed Gondolf, Peter Jaffe, Mary Koss, Phoebe Morgan, Jody Raphael, Susan Schechter, and Meiko Yoshihama. Their suggestions were much appreciated and carefully considered, and there was a considerable amount of agreement about the most influential works in the field.

The table of contents reflects the suggestions of the advisory board and our own perspectives about the classics that have influenced our work. Importantly, there were many original articles or book chapters that we wanted to include as classics but could not. Part of the adventure of assembling *Violence Against Women* was obtaining permission to reprint works that were published so long ago. Some of the works could not be included because we could not obtain permission from copyright holders or original authors and, in some cases, permission costs were prohibitive. Despite these challenges, we believe that the twenty-three classic papers that are included in this book reflect some of the most important early works in the field of violence against women.

Some of these classics, such as Diana Russell's *Rape in Marriage* (1982) and Del Martin's *Battered Wives* (1976) were groundbreaking in identifying women's experiences of violence that had been largely ignored. The works of Gail Wyatt in *The Sexual Abuse of Afro-American and White-American Women in Childhood* (1985), Barbara Hart's *Lesbian Battering: An Examination* (1986), and Kimberle Crenshaw's *Mapping the Margins: Intersectionality, Identity Politics and Violence against Women of Color* (1994) focused much-needed attention on marginalized groups of women. Importantly, works such as Diana Scully and Joseph Marolla's *"Riding the Bull at Gilley's": Convicted Rapists Describe the Rewards of Rape* (1985) and Edward Gondolf's *The Effect of Batterer Counseling on Shelter Outcome* (1988) called our attention to those who perpetrate acts of violence against women. Other works, such as Murray Straus's *Measuring Intrafamily Conflict and Violence: The Conflict Tactics (CT) Scales* (1979) and Lenore Walker's *The Battered Woman* (1979) are important not only for their content but also because these works have sparked productive dialogue and debate within the field. We believe that each classic paper in this book has played a critical role in shaping the work of subsequent generations of researchers and practitioners.

The works in this book are broadly inclusive of the domains that most authorities would consider violence against women. We have divided the classics into three general areas: Sexual Violence against Women; Physical Violence against Women; and Perpetrators of Violence against Women. Following each chapter, we have included commentaries by original authors (whenever possible) about their own work. We invited the authors of these classic papers to write reflections about their work and to specifically address why they decided to study and write about their particular issue at the time and to consider the impact that their work has had on the field of violence against women. We attempted to contact each original author for a reflection; however, several authors either could not be reached or were not able to write a commentary due to time constraints. When this occurred, we invited other experts in the particular sub-field to reflect on the importance of the classic paper and how it has influenced their own work in the field.

The commentaries that are included here are considerably varied. Some authors reflect on the personal reasons that drove them to their research, such as their own victimization or the overwhelming feeling that "something had to be done." Other reflections reveal information about the authors' perceptions of the impact of their work, including how they have influenced other researchers and how their work has often been misunderstood. Many of the commentaries reflect the policy implications of doing work in the field of violence against women and offer reflections on what still needs to change. Taken together, these twenty-three commentaries are empowering—they force us to remember the passion of those who have done this challenging work for decades. They are an amazing group of people! Reading these commentaries is also empowering in that we are reminded of the work that still must be done and the need to continue the struggle against all forms of violence.

Acknowledgments

This adventure would not have been possible without the work and support of so many people. This book would certainly not have been possible without the hard work of those colleagues who authored the classic papers and shaped this field of research and practice. We are deeply grateful for their legacy. We are particularly indebted to the members of our Advisory Board and all of those who took the time to write commentaries for this book. Their insights and work in the field are extraordinary. Special thanks to Dana Ferrell, graduate assistant extraordinaire, for her diligence and hard work. We are very appreciative of Denise Shaw for her organizational and clerical skills. The folks at Allyn and Bacon have been wonderful in offering guidance and technical expertise on this book. We owe Jennifer Jacobson, our editor, a hearty thank you for her support of this book from the very beginning and her patience and expertise throughout. We would like to thank the team at Omegatype Typography, especially Shannon Foreman and Kathleen Shigeta, for their editorial production work. We also want to thank Steve Rutter, now an editor at McGraw-Hill and formerly president of Pine Forge Press, for introducing us to Golden's (1976) book. Last but certainly not least, we are thankful to our family members, Mike Bergen, Michael Ryan Bergen, Devon Bergen, Sudha Shetty, Leah Edleson, Daniel Edleson-Stein, Eli Edleson-Stein, Dan Curran, Sean Curran, and Aidan Curran, for their encouragement and never-ending patience. And we thank each other—for support, diligence, and a lot of laughs along the way.

References

Cohn Donnelly, A., & Oates, K. (2000). *Classic papers in child abuse.* Thousand Oaks, CA: Sage.

Golden, M. P. (1976). *The research experience.* Itasca, IL: F. E. Peacock Publishers.

Renzetti, C. M., Edleson, J. L., & Bergen, R. K. (Eds.). (2001). *Sourcebook on violence against women.* Thousand Oaks, CA: Sage.

PART ONE

Sexual Violence against Women

The classic papers in this section focus on various types of sexual violence commonly experienced by women, including rape in intimate partnerships, childhood sexual assault, sexual harassment, and sexual slavery. These papers are linked by a common thread; each was groundbreaking in calling attention to a particular form of sexual violence and its effects on women. The importance of these classic papers is how they raised awareness about sexual violence and how each influenced researchers, practitioners, policy makers, and the general public to think about issues that had previously remained veiled in secrecy. This was critical given that, historically, sexual violence was an issue that was largely ignored, and many women did not even have the language to name their experiences of rape, childhood sexual abuse, and harassment. These classic papers helped to establish a framework within the anti-rape movement where women's experiences of sexual violence were not only identified and named, but also where we began to understand the horrible consequences of sexual violence for survivors and all of society.

Importantly, many of these papers are similar in that they provided critical data about the prevalence of sexual violence in the family and within women's intimate relationships. No longer could sexual violence be seen as a crime that only occurs between strangers. Taken together, these classic papers provide powerful testimony to the fact that sexual violence is a serious and pervasive problem for all women in our society—inside of the home, on the street, on college campuses, and in the workplace.

The first two classic papers presented in this section emerged early within the anti-rape movement and were instrumental in raising awareness about the widespread reality of rape and the serious consequences of sexual violence in the lives of women. In 1975, Susan Brownmiller's book, *Against Our Will: Men, Women and Rape,* was published and, as Claire Renzetti writes in her reflection, this book became the "manifesto of the anti-rape movement." What was groundbreaking about this book was Brownmiller's documentation of the historical reality of rape in the lives of women and her powerful feminist analysis of rape as a form of control by men over women. The first chapter is excerpted from chapter one of *Against Our Will,* in which Brownmiller argued that rape has played a "critical function" in lives of men and women since prehistoric times. In this chapter, Brownmiller wrote that rape "is nothing more or less than a conscious process of intimidation by which *all* men keep *all* women in a state of fear." While this statement has generated a great deal of debate and controversy, few can deny that the fear of rape is a daily occurrence for many (if not most) women and that far too frequently, what women most fear becomes a reality.

In the second paper, Ann Wolbert Burgess and Lynda Lytle Holmstrom consider the effects of rape on the lives of women and their families. In this classic piece, Burgess and Holstrom coined the phrase "Rape Trauma Syndrome" to explain the both acute and long-term reorganization process that women undergo after a rape. This paper is a classic in that it explored the serious effects of rape from a "health standpoint," as Burgess writes in her reflection. Not only were the short-term and long-term emotional and physical effects of rape considered, but so too were women's coping strategies and how they respond to the traumatic and life-changing event of rape. At an early stage in the anti-rape movement, this paper highlighted the need for a coordinated, comprehensive response to rape survivors to minimize the long-term effects.

The next three works in this section focus not on sexual violence against adult women, but on sexual violence against children. In their classic paper, *Father-Daughter Incest,* Judith Herman and Lisa Hirschman provided a feminist analysis of the deeply hidden problem of incest. Writing at a time when few researchers or practitioners believed that incest was a problem, Herman and Hirschman had the courage to give voice to the stories that they were hearing with alarming regularity among their clients. Importantly, Herman and Hirschman asked the question, "Why does incest between fathers and daughters occur so much more frequently than incest between mothers and sons?" In providing an answer to this question, they pointed to male dominance and argued that incest cannot be understood without a focus on its patriarchal roots. Furthermore, Herman and Hirschman provided a powerful critique of the social attitudes within clinical literature at a time when much of the literature denied the reality of incest, blamed the victims themselves, and minimized the effects of incest on victims. A work that started with "two women talking," as Herman writes in her "Aflerword, 2000: Understanding Incest Twenty Years Later," has had the far-reaching consequence of changing the way researchers understand incest.

In *Sexually Victimized Children,* David Finkelhor explored the prevalence of the sexual victimization of both male and female children. Like Herman and Hirschman, Finkelhor challenged the assumptions that children are to blame for their own sexual abuse by adults and his work was critical in raising awareness about a much-understudied form of violence. In his excerpted chapter, Finkelhor offered a rich theoretical analysis of the various perspectives of childhood sexual abuse. Importantly, he also took on the much-debated issue of the consequences of childhood sexual victimization. In this classic piece, Finkelhor created the framework for the following generation of researchers to explore critical questions about the causes, consequences, and prevalence of child sexual abuse.

With the publication of *The Sexual Abuse of Afro-American and White American Women in Childhood,* Gail Wyatt too influenced the ways in which researchers conceptualized childhood sexual abuse by considering the importance of race. In this classic paper, Wyatt questioned the prevailing assumption that black women were more likely to be sexually victimized, arguing that most research had been conducted with white women. When African American women were included in studies of child abuse, they were primarily drawn from clinical samples. By using a diverse sample of African American and white women, Wyatt found that rates of sexual abuse were similar for both African American and white women; however, some differences existed, including the age of onset of sexual violence and perpetrator characteristics. While these findings were significant, the true legacy of Wyatt's work is her model of research and the fact that African American women were not treated as a monolithic group. As Carolyn West writes in her commentary, Wyatt's work is significant because "she critically examined racial differences, rather than ignoring or minimizing them."

The next three classic papers were groundbreaking in that each work established a new topical domain in the field of violence against women. In 1979, Catharine MacKinnon published *The Sexual Harassment of Working Women,* and with this important book, she opened up a new terrain of inquiry for those working in the field of violence against women. As Phoebe Morgan so aptly argues in her commentary, this "book accomplishes what subsequent scholars have attempted to do but failed: in everyday language MacKinnon connects sexual violence with male domination, and then locates that nexus squarely in the workplace." In the excerpted work, MacKinnon explored the definition of sexual harassment and its impact on women. While considerable controversy has surrounded the question of what legally constitutes sexual harassment (a question that is still being hashed out in workplaces and universities today), MacKinnon's lasting contribution is that she called attention to this problem and provided ample evidence of the mistreatment of women and the serious effects on their work and lives.

Diana Russell's *Rape in Marriage* was also a book that carved out a new path in the field of violence against women and has had a profound impact on those in the field who study sexual violence in intimate partnerships. As Russell stated in the excerpted chapter in this section, her book was the first to be published in English on the problem of women's violent experiences of rape by their husbands. Writing at a time where forcible sexual intercourse was seen as a marital privilege and not legally rape in many states, Russell's research documented how widespread women's experiences of sexual violence in marriage were. More importantly, in her thorough treatment of the subject and powerful quotes by survivors, Russell legitimized the experiences of millions of women who had been raped by their husbands but lacked the language to call their unwanted sexual experiences with their partners rape.

Diana Russell's study of wife rape and the national study of sexual victimization by Mary Koss and her colleagues, Christine Gidycz and Nadine Wisniewski, were both groundbreaking in that each laid the methodological foundation on which the following generation of researchers would build. Both classics were grounded in strong empirical evidence that revealed the prevalence of women's experiences of sexual violence and the reality that women are not only raped by strangers, but also by men who are their partners, dates, and acquaintances. In *The Scope of Rape,* Koss, Gidycz, and Wisniewski discussed the findings of their national survey of more than 6,000 college students who completed their Sexual Experiences Survey. Their most startling finding, that 27 percent of college women reported experiencing some form of sexual victimization since the age of 14, received widespread media attention and continues to be the source of much debate. Importantly, this classic paper and the research on which it was grounded put the term "date rape" into the American vocabulary. The legacy of this classic work is that fifteen years after its publication, researchers and practitioners continue to explore the pervasive problem of date rape, and the Sexual Experiences Survey continues to be the most frequently used survey instrument to assess the prevalence of sexual violence.

In the next paper, *Sexual Violence: The Unmentionable Sin,* Marie Fortune explores the response of clergy members to the problem of sexual violence. As a Methodist minister herself, Fortune was in a unique position to challenge clergy members to become a resource for survivors of sexual violence and to challenge beliefs that fail to hold perpetrators accountable for their actions. At the time of its publication, this paper served as a call to action for religious leaders to respond to the pervasive problem of sexual violence against women. This call to action is still necessary today, particularly in light of the recent crisis within the Roman Catholic Church. As Fortune writes in her reflection, there is still a need for religious leaders to "take appropriate leadership to change our society's response to sexual violence."

The final paper in this section also served as a call to action on both the national and international levels. In 1979, Kathleen Barry published *Female Sexual Slavery,* which provided a feminist analysis of prostitution and the sexual trafficking of women. This work focused on a field of sexual violence that had been largely ignored, even within the anti-rape movement. Rather than looking at prostitutes as deviants (as had been historically done in a variety of disciplines), Barry asked the question, "What are the objective conditions which bring many women into prostitution?" Her response and the descriptions of women's horrific experiences of sexual slavery led to heightened awareness about this problem and served as the impetus for national and international efforts to end the sexual trafficking of women. As Barry describes in her reflection, efforts to end this serious form of sexual victimization continue today.

CHAPTER

1 Against Our Will

Men, Women and Rape

SUSAN BROWNMILLER

Krafft-Ebing, who pioneered in the study of sexual disorders, had little to say about rape. His famous *Psychopathia Sexualis* gives amazingly short shrift to the act and its doers. He had it on good authority, he informed his readers, that most rapists were degenerate, imbecilic men. Having made that sweeping generalization, Krafft-Ebing washed his hands of the whole affair and turned with relish to the frotteurs and fetishists of normal intelligence who tickled his fancy.

Sigmund Freud, whose major works followed Krafft-Ebing's by twenty to forty years, was also struck dumb by the subject of rape. We can search his writings in vain for a quotable quote, an analysis, a perception. The father of psychoanalysis, who invented the concept of the primacy of the penis, was never motivated, as far as we know, to explore the real-life deployment of the penis as weapon. What the master ignored, the disciples tended to ignore as well. Alfred Adler does not mention rape, despite his full awareness of the historic power struggle between men and women. Jung refers to rape only in the most obscure manner, a glancing reference in some of his mythological interpretations. Helene Deutsch and Karen Horney, each from a differing perspective, grasped at the female fear of rape, and at the feminine fantasy, but as women who did not dare to presume, they turned a blind eye to the male and female reality.

And the great socialist theoreticians Marx and Engels and their many confreres and disciples who developed the theory of class oppression and put words like "exploitation" into the everyday vocabulary, they, too, were strangely silent about rape, unable to fit it into their economic constructs. Among them only August Bebel tried to grasp at its historic importance, its role in the very formulation of class, private property and the means of production. In *Woman Under Socialism* Bebel used his imagination to speculate briefly about the prehistoric tribal fights for land, cattle and labor power within an acceptable Marxist analysis: "There arose the need of labor power to cultivate the ground. The more numerous these powers, all the greater was the wealth in products and herds. These struggles led first to the rape of women, later to the enslaving of conquered men. The women became laborers and objects of pleasure for the conqueror; their males became slaves." He didn't get it quite right, making the rape of women secondary to man's search for labor, but it was a flash of revelation and one that Engels did not achieve in his *Origin of the Family.* But Bebel was more at ease researching the wages and conditions of working-women in German factories, and that is where his energies went.

It was the half-crazed genius Wilhelm Reich, consumed with rage in equal parts toward Hitler, Marx and Freud, who briefly entertained the vision of a "masculine ideology of rape." The phrase hangs there in the opening chapter of *The Sexual Revolution,* begging for further interpretation. But it was not forthcoming. The anguished mind was in too great a state of disarray. A political analysis of rape would have required more treachery toward his own immutable gender than even Wilhelm Reich could muster.

And so it remained for the latter-day feminists, free at last from the strictures that forbade us to look at male sexuality, to discover the truth and meaning in our own victimization. Critical to our study is the recognition that rape has a history, and that through the tools of historical analysis we may learn what we need to know about our current condition.

No zoologist, as far as I know, has ever observed that animals rape in their natural habitat, the wild. Sex in the animal world, including those species that are our closest relations, the primates, is more properly called "mating," and it is cyclical activity set off by biologic signals the female puts out. Mating is initiated and "controlled," it would seem, by the female estrous cycle. When the female of the species periodically goes into heat, giving off obvious physical signs, she is ready and eager for copulation and the male becomes interested. At other times there is simply no interest, and no mating.

Jane Goodall, studying her wild chimpanzees at the Gombe Stream reserve, noted that the chimps, male and female, were "very promiscuous, but this does not mean that every female will accept every male that courts her." She recorded her observations of one female in heat, who showed the telltale pink swelling of her genital area, who nevertheless displayed an aversion to one particular male who pursued her. "Though he once shook her out of the tree in which she had sought refuge, we never saw him actually 'rape' her," Goodall wrote, adding, however, "Nonetheless, quite often he managed to get his way through dogged persistence." Another student of animal behavior, Leonard Williams, has stated categorically, "The male monkey cannot in fact mate with the female without her invitation and willingness to cooperate. In monkey society there is no such thing as rape, prostitution, or even passive consent."

Zoologists for the most part have been reticent on the subject of rape. It has not been, for them, an important scientific question. But we do know that human beings are different. Copulation in our species can occur 365 days of the year; it is not controlled by the female estrous cycle. We females of the human species do not "go pink." The call of estrus and the telltale signs, both visual and olfactory, are absent from our mating procedures, lost perhaps in the evolutionary shuffle. In their place, as a mark of our civilization, we have evolved a complex system of psychological signs and urges, and a complex structure of pleasure. Our call to sex occurs in the head, and the act is not necessarily linked, as it is with animals, to Mother Nature's pattern of procreation. Without a biologically determined mating season, a human male can evince sexual interest in a human female at any time he pleases, and his psychologic urge is not dependent in the slightest on her biologic readiness or receptivity. What it all boils down to is that the human male can rape.

Man's structural capacity to rape and woman's corresponding structural vulnerability are as basic to the physiology of both our sexes as the primal act of sex itself. Had it not been for this accident of biology, an accommodation requiring the locking together of two separate parts, penis into vagina, there would be neither copulation nor rape as we know it. Anatomically one might want to improve on the design of nature, but such speculation appears to my mind as unrealistic. The human sex act accomplishes its historic purpose of generation of the species and it also affords some intimacy and pleasure. I have no basic quarrel with the procedure. But, nevertheless, we cannot work around the fact that in terms of human anatomy the possibility of forcible intercourse incontrovertibly exists. This single factor may have been sufficient to have caused the creation of a male ideology of rape. When men discovered that they could rape, they proceeded to do it. Later, much later, under certain circumstances they even came to consider rape a crime.

In the violent landscape inhabited by primitive woman and man, some woman somewhere had a prescient vision of her right to her own physical integrity, and in my mind's eye I can picture her fighting like hell to preserve it. After a thunderbolt of recognition that this particular incarnation of hairy, two-legged hominid was not the Homo sapiens with whom she would like to freely join parts, it might have been she, and not some man, who picked up the first stone and hurled it. How surprised he must have been, and what an unexpected battle must have taken place. Fleet of foot and spirited, she would have kicked, bitten, pushed and run, *but she could not retaliate in kind.*

The dim perception that had entered prehistoric woman's consciousness must have had an equal but opposite reaction in the mind of her male assailant. For if the first rape was an unexpected battle founded on the first woman's refusal, the second rape was indubitably planned. Indeed, one of the earliest forms of male bonding must have been the gang rape of one woman by a band of marauding men. This accomplished, rape became not only a male prerogative, but man's basic weapon of force against woman, the principal agent of his will and her fear. His forcible entry into her body, despite her physical protestations and struggle, became the vehicle of his victorious conquest over her being, the ultimate test of his superior strength, the triumph of his manhood.

Man's discovery that his genitalia could serve as a weapon to generate fear must rank as one of the most important discoveries of prehistoric times, along with the use of fire and the first crude stone axe. From prehistoric times to the present, I believe, rape has played a critical function. It is nothing more or less than a conscious process of intimidation by which *all men* keep *all women* in a state of fear.

Reflection

CLAIRE M. RENZETTI

I remember the first time I read *Against Our Will.* I was in college, nurturing a budding feminism, but still uncertain what it meant to be a "feminist." Reading *Against Our Will* was a consciousness-raising experience that, at the end, provided me one of those glorious "aha!" moments: So *this* is what feminism is.

Against Our Will provided me and, no doubt, countless other women with an analytical framework for understanding gender oppression. In her meticulously documented history of rape, Susan Brownmiller described, as no one before her had, how the penis could be used as a weapon and, even more significant, how rape epitomized the nature of gender relations. Rape and the threat of rape, Brownmiller told us, are effective ways for men to intimidate and control women. It is women's, not men's, behavior that is changed by the threat or the act of rape. But men can also use rape as a way to punish other men: to emasculate them by "using" them "like a woman," to establish dominance by "taking" *their* women (i.e., their sexual property). In fact, it was Brownmiller's analysis of rape as a weapon of war that most moved me when I read it in 1975, and I continue to marvel at its relevance today.

Of course, any groundbreaking book will become the focal point of intense debate, and *Against Our Will* was hardly an exception in this respect. The book elicited hyperbolic praise and criticism when it was first published and long afterward. Even ardent supporters of Brownmiller's analysis, however, often tried to tone it down a bit by conceding that not *all* men are potential rapists. But whether you agreed or disagreed, in whole or in part, with Brownmiller's argument, once *Against Our Will* was published, no one could write or talk about rape without reference to this book. Indeed, perhaps the greatest contribution Brownmiller made with *Against Our Will* was putting rape in the public spotlight, making it a topic people could no longer ignore, try to hide, or speak about in only hushed tones.

When I read *Against Our Will* the first time, it made me at once sad and furious. The numerous stories of mass and individual rapes of women and girls in so many different cultures at so many different points in time often made me cry, but the repetitious details were never numbing. *Against Our Will* was—and remains—a feminist call to action. Seeing the "facts" about rape in print was empowering. It helped thousands of women overcome the intimidation that the threat of rape imposed and inspired them to act collectively to bring about social change. After reading *Against Our Will,* I didn't sit paralyzed with fear; I became a feminist activist. And isn't that one of the true measures of a classic: that it motivates us not to just *talk* about a problem, but to *act* in response to the problem? Although today we may question to what extent our activism has been successful in bringing about positive changes in society's responses to rape victims, there is no denying that the anti-rape movement has brought about significant change. And *Against Our Will* was, in essence, the manifesto of the anti-rape movement. We are indebted to Susan Brownmiller for her courage to speak out when many of us could not or didn't know the words that would make a difference.

CHAPTER

2 Rape Trauma Syndrome

ANN WOLBERT BURGESS AND
LYNDA LYTLE HOLMSTROM

Rape affects the lives of thousands of women each year. The Uniform Crime Reports from the Federal Bureau of Investigation indicated a 121-percent increase in reported cases of rape between 1960 and 1970. In 1970, over 37,000 cases were reported in the United States (1). A District of Columbia task force studying the problem in the capital area stated that rape was the fastest growing crime of violence there (2).

The literature on sexual offenses, including rape, is voluminous (3–5), but it has overlooked the victim. There is little information on the physical and psychological effects of rape, the therapeutic management of the victim, and the provisions for protection of the victim from further psychological insult (6–9).

In response to the problem of rape in the greater Boston area, the Victim Counseling Program was designed as a collaborative effort between Boston College School of Nursing and Boston City Hospital to provide 24-hour crisis intervention to rape victims and to study the problems the victim experiences as a result of being sexually assaulted.

The purpose of this paper is to report the immediate and long-term effects of rape as described by the victim.

Method

Study Population

The study population consisted of all persons who entered the emergency ward of Boston City Hospital during the one-year period July 20, 1972, through July 19, 1973, with the complaint of having been raped. The resulting sample was made up of 146 patients: 109 adult women, 34 female children, and 3 male children.

We divided these 146 patients into three main categories: 1) victims of forcible rape (either completed or attempted rape, usually the former); 2) victims in situations to which they were an accessory due to their inability to consent; and 3) victims of sexually stressful situations—sexual encounters to which they had initially consented but that went beyond their expectations and ability to control.

The rape trauma syndrome delineated in this paper was derived from an analysis of the symptoms of the 92 adult women in our sample who were victims of forcible rape. Future reports will analyze the problems of the other victims. Although not directly included in this paper, supplementary data were also gathered from 14 patients referred to the Victim Counseling Program by other agencies and from consultation calls from other clinicians working with rape victims.

A major research advantage in the location of the project at Boston City Hospital was the fact that it provided a heterogeneous sample of victims. Disparate social classes were included in the victim population. Ethnic groups included fairly equal numbers of black and white women, plus a smaller number of Oriental, Indian, and Spanish-speaking women. In regard to work status, the victims were career women, housewives, college students, and women on welfare. The age span was 17 to 73 years; the group included single, married, divorced, separated, and widowed women as well as women living with men by consensual agreement (see Table 2.1). A variety of occupations were represented, such as schoolteacher, business manager, researcher, assembly line worker, secretary, housekeeper, cocktail waitress, and health worker. There were victims with no children, women pregnant up to the eighth month, postpartum mothers, and women with anywhere from 1 to 10 children. The women ranged in physical attractiveness from very pretty to very plain; they were dressed in styles ranging from high fashion to hippie clothes.

Interview Method

The counselors (the coauthors of this paper) were telephoned when a rape victim was admitted to the emergency department of Boston City Hospital; we arrived at the hospital within 30 minutes. We interviewed all the victims admitted during the one-year period regardless of time of day or night. Follow-up was conducted by use of telephone counseling or home visits. This method of study provided an 85-percent rate of direct follow-up. An additional 5 percent of the victims were followed indirectly through their families or reports by the police or other service agencies who knew them. Detailed notes of the interviews, telephone calls, and visits were then analyzed in terms of the symptoms reported as well as changes in thoughts, feelings, and behavior. We accompanied those victims who pressed

TABLE 2.1 Distribution of Marital Status by Age ($N = 92$)

	Age (in Years)				
Marital Status	*17–20*	*21–29*	*30–39*	*40–49*	*50–73*
Single	29	25	0	2	1
Married	2	1	2	2	0
Divorced, separated, or widowed	2	6	7	2	2
Living with a man by consensual agreement	4	5	0	0	0

charges to court and took detailed notes of all court proceedings and recorded the victims' reactions to this process (10, 11). Contact with the families and other members of the victims' social network was part of the assessment and follow-up procedure.

Manifestations of Rape Trauma Syndrome

Rape trauma syndrome is the acute phase and long-term reorganization process that occurs as a result of forcible rape or attempted forcible rape. This syndrome of behavioral, somatic, and psychological reactions is an acute stress reaction to a life-threatening situation.

Forcible rape is defined in this paper as the carnal knowledge of a woman by an assailant by force and against her will. The important point is that rape is not primarily a sexual act. On the contrary, our data and those of researchers studying rapists suggest that rape is primarily an act of violence with sex as the weapon (5). Thus it is not surprising that the victim experiences a syndrome with specific symptomatology as a result of the attack made upon her.

The syndrome is usually a two-phase reaction. The first is the acute phase. This is the period in which there is a great deal of disorganization in the woman's lifestyle as a result of the rape. Physical symptoms are especially noticeable, and one prominent feeling noted is fear. The second phase begins when the woman begins to reorganize her lifestyle. Although the time of onset varies from victim to victim, the second phase often begins about two to three weeks after the attack. Motor activity changes and nightmares and phobias are especially likely during this phase.

The medical regimen for the rape victim involves the prescription of antipregnancy and antivenereal disease medication after the physical and gynecological examination. The procedure usually includes prescribing 25 to 50 mg. of diethylstilbestrol a day for five days to protect against pregnancy and 4.8 million units of aqueous procaine penicillin intramuscularly to protect against venereal disease. Symptoms reported by the patient need to be distinguished as either side effects of the medication or conditions resulting from the sexual assault.

The Acute Phase: Disorganization

Impact Reactions

In the immediate hours following the rape, the woman may experience an extremely wide range of emotions. The impact of the rape may be so severe that feelings of shock or disbelief are expressed. When interviewed within a few hours of the rape, the women in this study mainly showed two emotional styles (12): the expressed style, in which feelings of fear, anger, and anxiety were shown through such behavior as crying, sobbing, smiling, restlessness, and tenseness; and the controlled style, in which feelings were masked or hidden and a calm, composed, or subdued affect was seen. A fairly equal number of women showed each style.

Somatic Reactions

During the first several weeks following a rape many of the acute somatic manifestations described below were evident.

1. *Physical trauma.* This included general soreness and bruising from the physical attack in various parts of the body such as the throat, neck, breasts, thighs, legs, and arms. Irritation and trauma to the throat were especially a problem for those women forced to have oral sex.
2. *Skeletal muscle tension.* Tension headaches and fatigue, as well as sleep pattern disturbances, were common symptoms. Women were either not able to sleep or would fall asleep only to wake and not be able to go back to sleep. Women who had been suddenly awakened from sleep by the assailant frequently found that they would wake each night at the time the attack had occurred. The victim might cry or scream out in her sleep. Victims also described experiencing a startle reaction—they become edgy and jumpy over minor incidents.
3. *Gastrointestinal irritability.* Women might complain of stomach pains. The appetite might be affected, and the victim might state that she did not eat, food had no taste, or she felt nauseated from the antipregnancy medication. Victims described feeling nauseated just thinking of the rape.
4. *Genitourinary disturbance.* Gynecological symptoms such as vaginal discharge, itching, a burning sensation on urination, and generalized pain were common. A number of women developed chronic vaginal infections following the rape. Rectal bleeding and pain were reported by women who had been forced to have anal sex.

Emotional Reactions

Victims expressed a wide gamut of feelings as they began to deal with the aftereffects of the rape. These feelings ranged from fear, humiliation, and embarrassment to anger, revenge, and self-blame. Fear of physical violence and death was the primary feeling described. Victims stated that it was not the rape that was so upsetting as much as the feeling that they would be killed as a result of the assault. One woman stated: "I am really mad. My life is disrupted; every part of it upset. And I have to be grateful I wasn't killed. I thought he would murder me."

Self-blame was another reaction women described—partly because of their socialization to the attitude of "blame the victim." For example, one young woman had entered her apartment building one afternoon after shopping. As she stopped to take her keys from her purse, she was assaulted in the hallway by a man who then forced his way into her apartment. She fought against him to the point of taking his knife and using it against him and in the process was quite severely beaten, bruised, and raped. Later she said:

> I keep wondering maybe if I had done something different when I first saw him that it wouldn't have happened—neither he nor I would be in trouble. Maybe it was my fault. See, that's where I get when I think about it. My father always said whatever a man did to a woman, she provoked it.

The Long-Term Process: Reorganization

All victims in our sample experienced disorganization in their lifestyle following the rape; their presence at the emergency ward of the hospital was testimony to that fact. Various factors affected their coping behavior regarding the trauma, i.e., ego strength, social network support, and the way people treated them as victims. This coping and reorganization process began at different times for the individual victims.

Victims did not all experience the same symptoms in the same sequence. What was consistent was that they did experience an acute phase of disorganization; many also experienced mild to moderate symptoms in the reorganization process, as Table 2.2 indicates. Very few victims reported no symptoms. The number of victims over age 30 was small, but the data at least suggest that they might have been more prone to compounded reactions than the younger age groups.

Motor Activity

The long-term effects of the rape generally consisted of an increase in motor activity, especially through changing residence. The move, in order to ensure safety and to facilitate the victim's ability to function in a normal style, was very common. Forty-four of the 92 victims changed residences within a relatively short period of time after the rape. There was also a strong need to get away, and some women took trips to other states or countries.

TABLE 2.2 Severity of Symptoms During Reorganization Process by Age ($N = 92$)*

	Age (in Years)				
Severity of Symptoms	*17–20*	*21–29*	*30–39*	*40–49*	*50–73*
No symptoms: no symptoms reported and symptoms denied when asked about a specific area	7	4	2	0	0
Mild symptoms: minor discomfort with the symptom reported: ability to talk about discomfort and feeling of control over symptom present	12	16	0	2	1
Moderate to severe symptoms: distressing symptoms such as phobic reactions described: ability to function but disturbance in lifestyle present	12	5	1	1	2
Compounded symptoms: symptoms directly related to the rape plus reactivation of symptoms connected with a previously existing condition such as heavy drinking or drug use	7	5	3	3	0
No data available	0	5	4	0	0

*At time of telephone follow-up.

Changing one's telephone number was a common reaction. It was often changed to an unlisted number. The woman might do this as a precautionary measure or as the result of threatening or obscene telephone calls. The victim was haunted by the fear that the assailant knew where she was and would come back for her.

Another common response was to turn for support to family members not normally seen daily. Forty-eight women made special trips home, which often meant traveling to another city. In most cases, the victim told her parents what had happened, but occasionally the victim contacted her parents for support and did not explain why she was suddenly interested in talking with them or being with them. Twenty-five women turned to close friends for support. Thus 73 of the 92 women had some social network support to which they turned.

Nightmares

Dreams and nightmares could be very upsetting. Twenty-nine of the victims spontaneously described frightening dreams, as illustrated in the following statement.

> I had a terrifying nightmare and shook for two days. I was at work and there was this maniac killer in the store. He killed two of the salesgirls by slitting their throats. I'd gone to set the time clock and when I came back the two girls were dead. I thought I was next. I had to go home. On the way I ran into two girls I knew. We were walking along and we ran into the maniac killer and he was the man who attacked me—he looked like the man. One of the girls held back and said, "No—I'm staying here." I said I knew him and was going to fight him. At this point I woke with the terrible fear of impending doom and fright. I knew the knife part was real because it was the same knife the man held to my throat.

Women reported two types of dreams. One is similar to the above example where the victim wishes to do something but then wakes before acting. As time progressed, the second type occurred: the dream material changed somewhat, and frequently the victim reported mastery in the dream—being able to fight off the assailant. A young woman reported the following dream one month following her rape.

> I had a knife and I was with the guy and I went to stab him and the knife bent. I did it again and he started bleeding and he died. Then I walked away laughing with the knife in my hand.

This dream woke the victim up; she was crying so hard that her mother came in to see what was wrong. The girl stated that in her waking hours she never cries.

Traumatophobia

Sandor Rado coined the term "traumatophobia" to define the phobic reaction to a traumatic situation (13). We saw this phenomenon, which Rado described in war victims, in the rape victim. The phobia develops as a defensive reaction to the circumstances of the rape. The following were the most common phobic reactions among our sample.

Fear of Indoors. This occurred in women who had been attacked while sleeping in their beds. As one victim stated, "I feel better outside. I can see what is coming. I feel trapped inside. My fear is being inside, not outside."

Fear of Outdoors. This occurred in women who had been attacked outside of their homes. These women felt safe inside but would walk outside only with the protection of another person or only when necessary. As one victim stated, "It is sheer terror for every step I take. I can't wait to get to the safety of my own place."

Fear of Being Alone. Almost all victims reported fears of being alone after the rape. Often the victim had been attacked while alone, when no one could come to her rescue. One victim said: "I can't stand being alone. I hear every little noise—the windows creaking. I am a bundle of nerves."

Fear of Crowds. Many victims were quite apprehensive when they had to be in crowds or ride on public transportation. One 41-year-old victim said:

> I'm still nervous from this, when people come too close—like when I have to go through the trolley station and the crowds are bad. When I am in crowds I get the bad thoughts. I will look over at a guy and if he looks really weird, I will hope something bad will happen to him.

Fear of People Behind Them. Some victims reported being fearful of people walking behind them. This was often common if the woman had been approached suddenly from behind. One victim said:

> I can't stand to have someone behind me. When I feel someone is behind me, my heart starts pounding. Last week I turned on a guy that was walking in back of me and waited till he walked by. I just couldn't stand it.

Sexual Fears. Many women experienced a crisis in their sexual life as a result of the rape. Their normal sexual style had been disrupted. For the women who had had no prior sexual activity, the incident was especially upsetting. For the victims who were sexually active, the fear increased when they were confronted by their husband or boyfriend with resuming sexual relations. One victim said:

> My boyfriend thought it [the rape] might give me a negative feeling to sex and he wanted to be sure it didn't. That night as soon as we were back to the apartment he wanted to make love. I didn't want sex, especially that night. . . . He also admitted he wanted to know if he could make love to me or if he would be repulsed by me and unable to.

This victim and her boyfriend had considerable difficulty resuming many aspects of their relationship besides the sexual part. Many women were unable to resume a normal sexual style during the acute phase and persisted with the difficulty. One victim reported, five months after the assault, "There are times I get hysterical with my boyfriend. I don't want him near me; I get panicked. Sex is OK, but I still feel like screaming."

Clinical Implications

Management of Rape Trauma Syndrome

There are several basic assumptions underlying the model of crisis intervention that we used in counseling the rape victim.

1. The rape represented a crisis in that the woman's style of life was disrupted.
2. The victim was regarded as a "normal" woman who had been functioning adequately prior to the crisis situation.
3. Crisis counseling was the treatment model of choice to return the woman to her previous level of functioning as quickly as possible. The crisis counseling was issue-oriented treatment. Previous problems were not a priority for discussion; in no way was the counseling considered psychotherapy. When other issues of major concern that indicated another treatment model were identified by the victim, referrals were offered if the woman so requested.
4. We took an active role in initiating therapeutic contact as opposed to more traditional methods where the patient is expected to be the initiator. We went to the hospital to see the victim and then contacted her later by telephone.

Management of Compounded Reaction

There were some victims who had either a past or current history of physical, psychiatric, or social difficulties along with the rape trauma syndrome. A minority of the women in our sample were representative of this group. It became quite clear that these women needed more than crisis counseling. For this group, who were known to other therapists, physicians, or agencies, we assumed a secondary position. Support was provided for the rape incident, especially if the woman pressed charges against the assailant, but the counselor worked closely with the other agencies. It was noted that this group developed additional symptoms such as depression, psychotic behavior, psychosomatic disorders, suicidal behavior, and acting-out behavior associated with alcoholism, drug use, and sexual activity.

Management of Silent Rape Reaction

Since a significant proportion of women still do not report a rape, clinicians should be alert to a syndrome that we call the silent reaction to rape. This reaction occurs in the victim who has not told anyone of the rape, who has not settled her feelings and reactions on the issue, and who is carrying a tremendous psychological burden.

Evidence of such a syndrome became apparent to us as a result of life history data. A number of the women in our sample stated that they had been raped or molested at a previous time, often when they were children or adolescents. Often these women had not told anyone of the rape and had just kept the burden within themselves. The current rape reactivated their reaction to the prior experience. It became clear that because they had not talked about the previous rape, the syndrome had continued to develop, and these women had carried unresolved issues with them for years. They would talk as much of the previous rape as they did of the current situation.

A diagnosis of this syndrome should be considered when the clinician observes any of the following symptoms during an evaluation interview.

1. Increasing signs of anxiety as the interview progresses, such as long periods of silence, blocking of associations, minor stuttering, and physical distress.
2. The patient reports sudden marked irritability or actual avoidance of relationships with men or marked change in sexual behavior.
3. History of sudden onset of phobic reactions and fear of being alone, going outside, or being inside alone.
4. Persistent loss of self-confidence and self-esteem, an attitude of self-blame, paranoid feelings, or dreams of violence and/or nightmares.

Clinicians who suspect that the patient was raped in the past should be sure to include questions relevant to the woman's sexual behavior in the evaluation interview and to ask if anyone has ever attempted to assault her. Such questions may release considerable pent-up material relevant to forced sexual activity.

Discussion

The crisis that results when a woman has been sexually assaulted is in the service of self-preservation. The victims in our sample felt that living was better than dying and that was the choice which had to be made. The victims' reactions to the impending threat to their lives is the nucleus around which an adaptive pattern may be noted.

The coping behavior of individuals to life-threatening situations has been documented in the work of such writers as Grinker and Spiegel (14), Lindemann (15), Kübler-Ross (16), and Hamburg (17). Kübler-Ross wrote of the process patients go through to come to terms with the fact of dying. Hamburg wrote of the resourcefulness of patients in facing catastrophic news and discussed a variety of implicit strategies by which patients face threats to life. This broad sequence of the acute phase, group support, and the long-run resolution described by these authors is compatible with the psychological work rape victims must do over time.

The majority of our rape victims were able to reorganize their lifestyle after the acute symptom phase, stay alert to possible threats to their lifestyle, and focus upon protecting themselves from further insult. This latter action was difficult because the world was perceived as a traumatic environment after the assault. As one victim said, "On the exterior I am OK, but inside [I feel] every man is the rapist."

The rape victim was able to maintain a certain equilibrium. In no case did the victim show ego disintegration, bizarre behavior, or self-destructive behavior during the acute phase. As indicated, there were a few victims who did regress to a previous level of impaired functioning four to six weeks following the assault.

With the increasing reports of rape, this is not a private syndrome. It should be a societal concern, and its treatment should be a public charge. Professionals will be called upon increasingly to assist the rape victim in the acute and long-term reorganization processes.

REFERENCES

1. Federal Bureau of Investigation: Uniform Crime Reports for the United States. Washington, DC, US Department of Justice, 1970
2. Report of District of Columbia Task Force on Rape. Washington. DC, District of Columbia City Council, 1973, p 7 (processed)
3. Amir M: Patterns of Forcible Rape. Chicago. University of Chicago Press, 1971
4. Macdonald J: Rape: Offenders and Their Victims. Springfield, Ill. Charles C Thomas, 1971
5. Cohen M, Garofalo R, Boucher R, et al: The psychology of rapists. Seminars in Psychiatry 3:307–327, 1971
6. Sutherland S, Scherl D: Patterns of response among victims of rape. Am J Orthopsychiatry 40:503–511, 1970
7. Hayman C, Lanza C: Sexual assault on women and girls. Am J Obstet Gynecol 109:480–486, 1971
8. Halleck S: The physician's role in management of victims of sex offenders. JAMA 180:273–278, 1962
9. Factor M: A woman's psychological reaction to attempted rape. Psychoanal Q 23:243–244, 1954
10. Holmstrom L L, Burgess A W: Rape: the victim goes on trial. Read at the 68th annual meeting of the American Sociological Association, New York, NY, Aug 27–30, 1973
11. Holmstrom L L, Burgess A W: Rape: the victim and the criminal justice system. Read at the First International Symposium on Victimology, Jerusalem, Sept 2–6, 1973
12. Burgess A W, Holmstrom L L: The rape victim in the emergency ward. Am J Nursing 73:1741–1745, 1973
13. Rado S: Pathodynamics and treatment of traumatic war neurosi: (traumatophobia). Psychosom Med 4:362–368, 1948
14. Grinker RR, Spiegel JP: Men Under Stress. Philadelphia. Blakiston, 1945
15. Lindemann E: Symptomatology and management of acute grief. Am J Psychiatry 101:141–148, 1944
16. Kübler-Ross E: On death and dying. JAMA 221:174–179, 1972
17. Hamburg D: A perspective on coping behavior. Arch Gen Psychiatry 17:277–284, 1967

Reflection

ANN WOLBERT BURGESS

The fact that rape occurred and was an act of conquering has been documented in the Bible as well as war annals. But in 1972 when Lynda Lytle Holmstrom and Ann Wolbert Burgess launched their research, there were very few clinically-based articles that dealt with the incidence of rape or the impact of rape on the victim and family. And there was little information on the offender.

Holmstrom, in the early 1970s, was searching for a topic to study that had some impact on women's lives and on the relationship between the sexes. She remembered having heard many reports by women at consciousness-raising groups in the late 1960s about physical assaults that had been made on them by men. And yet, it seemed that despite its common occurrence and its apparently strong impact on the people involved, researchers seldom picked up on this assaultive behavior as a research topic. Thinking about this phenomenon led Holmstrom to the idea, initially only vaguely formulated, of studying rape and especially rape victims. The next step was to meet with Burgess, with whom she had done some interdisciplinary teaching, to discuss how to go about such a study. Burgess's immediate response was to suggest that, if Holmstrom added a counseling aspect to the study, she would be interested in going in on it with her. They discussed how the academic skills of a sociologist and the clinical skills of a nurse psychotherapist might well complement each other and decided to form a team.

Although the violent acts and the suffering of women and children had been noted since the origins of humankind, few considered it from a health standpoint. Little existed in the scholarly literature on rape victims and little existed in the way of counseling services for victims. There was literature on sexual offenses, including rape, but it had overlooked the victim.

Our access to a sample was provided by the nursing hierarchy at a large municipal hospital where a percentage of rape victims were taken, Boston City Hospital. Anne Hargreaves, Executive Director of Nursing Services and Nursing Education of the Department of Health and Hospitals for the City of Boston, paved the way for us to be put "on call" every time a rape victim was admitted to the Emergency Services of the hospital. Our primary sample consisted of 146 persons who were admitted to the emergency wards of Boston City Hospital during a one-year period from July 1972–July 1973 with a complaint of rape.

The study that began at Boston City Hospital in July of 1972 sought to document the "career" of the rape victim through institutional systems: the police, the hospital, and the courts. And while psychosocial research of this type was unfunded in those days, the important act that opened the door to begin to educate the professional community about rape was the publication in the American Journal of Psychiatry on rape trauma syndrome. That article established the impact of rape as having psychiatric sequelae and supported the idea of crisis intervention being effective as a first step in reducing the consequences of a violent act. The identification of the trauma of rape linked with a plausible intervention launched the creation and activities for further research at the Center for the Prevention and Control of Rape. This research was followed by publications and the creation of not only interest and additional research questions, but challenged the need for instrumentation and clarity of definitions and contributed to the establishment of traumatology and the general investigation of traumatic life events.

What started as an isolated experience in the emergency room of a large city hospital has now become one piece in this huge unfortunate tapestry of human indiscretions and the joining together of science, clinical practice, and human social organization to take account of and for human acts of violence and their ultimate impact on society.

CHAPTER

3 Father-Daughter Incest

JUDITH LEWIS HERMAN AND LISA HIRSCHMAN

A Feminist Theoretical Perspective

The incest taboo is universal in human culture. Though it varies from one culture to another, it is generally considered by anthropologists to be the foundation of all kinship structures. Lévi-Strauss describes it as the basic social contract; Mead says its purpose is the preservation of the human social order.[1] All cultures, including our own, regard violations of the taboo with horror and dread. Death has not been considered too extreme a punishment in many societies. In our laws, some states punish incest by up to twenty years' imprisonment.[2]

In spite of the strength of the prohibition on incest, sexual relations between family members do occur. Because of the extreme secrecy which surrounds the violation of our most basic sexual taboo, we have little clinical literature and no accurate statistics on the prevalence of incest. This paper attempts to review what is known about the occurrence of incest between parents and children, to discuss common social attitudes which pervade the existing clinical literature, and to offer a theoretical perspective which locates the incest taboo and its violations within the structure of patriarchy.

The Occurrence of Incest

The Children's Division of the American Humane Association estimates that a minimum of 80,000–100,000 children are sexually molested each year.[3] In the majority of these cases the offender is well known to the child, and in about 25 percent of them, a relative. These estimates are based on New York City police records and the experience of social workers in a child protection agency. They are, therefore, projections based on observing poor and disorganized families who lack the resources to preserve secrecy. There is reason to believe, however, that most incest in fact occurs in intact families and entirely escapes the attention of social agencies. One in sixteen of the 8,000 white, middle-class women surveyed by Kinsey et al. reported sexual contact with an adult relative during childhood.[4] In the vast majority of these cases, the incident remained a secret.

A constant finding in all existing surveys is the overwhelming predominance of father-daughter incest. Weinberg, in a study of 200 court cases in the Chicago area, found

164 cases of father-daughter incest, compared with two cases of mother-son incest.[5] Maisch, in a study of court cases in the Federal Republic of Germany, reported that 90 percent of the cases involved fathers and daughters, step-fathers and step-daughters, or (infrequently) grandfathers and granddaughters.[6] Fathers and sons accounted for another 5 percent. Incest between mothers and sons occurred in only 4 percent of the cases. Incest appears to follow the general pattern of sexual abuse of children, in which 92 percent of the victims are female, and 97 percent of the offenders are male.[7]

It may be objected that these data are all based on court records and perhaps reflect only a difference in complaints rather than a difference in incidence. The Kinsey reports, however, confirm the impression of a major discrepancy between the childhood sexual contacts of boys and girls. If, as noted above, more than 6 percent of the female sample reported sexual approaches by adult relatives, only a small number of the 12,000 men surveyed reported sexual contact with any adult, relative or stranger. (Exact figures were not reported.) Among these few, contact with adult males seemed to be more common than with adult females. As for mother-son incest, the authors concluded that "heterosexual incest occurs more frequently in the thinking of clinicians and social workers than it does in actual performance."[8] None of the existing literature, to our knowledge, makes any attempt to account for this striking discrepancy between the occurrence of father-daughter and mother-son incest.

Common Attitudes toward Incest in the Professional Literature

Because the subject of incest inspires such strong emotional responses, few authors have even attempted a dispassionate examination of its actual occurrence and effects. Those who have approached the subject have often been unable to avoid defensive reactions such as denial, distancing, or blaming. We undertake this discussion with the full recognition that we ourselves are not immune to these reactions, which may be far more apparent to our readers than to ourselves.

Undoubtedly the most famous and consequential instance of denial of the reality of incest occurs in Freud's 1897 letter to Fliess. In it, Freud reveals the process by which he came to disbelieve the reports of his female patients and develop his concepts of infantile sexuality and the infantile neurosis: "Then there was the astonishing thing that in every case blame was laid on perverse acts by the father, and realization of the unexpected frequency of hysteria, in every case of which the same thing applied, though it was hardly credible that perverted acts against children were so general."[9]

Freud's conclusion that the sexual approaches did not occur in fact was based simply on his unwillingness to believe that incest was such a common event in respectable families. To experience a sexual approach by a parent probably *was* unlikely for a boy: Freud concluded incorrectly that the same was true for girls. Rather than investigate further into the question of fact, Freud's followers chose to continue the presumption of fantasy and made the child's desire and fantasy the focus of psychological inquiry. The adult's desire (and capacity for action) were forgotten. Psychoanalytic investigation, then, while it placed the incest taboo at the center of the child's psychological development, did little to dispel the secrecy surrounding the actual occurrence of incest. As one child psychiatrist commented: "Helene Deutsch and other followers of Freud have, in my opinion, gone too far in the direction of conceptualizing patients' reports of childhood sexual abuse in terms of fantasy. My own experience, both in private practice and with several hundred child victims brought to us . . . [at the Center for Rape Concern] . . . in Philadelphia, has convinced me that analysts too often dismissed as fantasy what was the real sexual molestation of a child. . . . As a result, the victim was isolated and her trauma compounded."[10]

Even those investigators who have paid attention to cases of actual incest have often shown a tendency to comment or make judgments concerning the guilt or innocence of the participants. An example:

> These children undoubtedly do not deserve completely the cloak of innocence with which they have been endowed by moralists, social reformers, and legislators. The history of the relationship in our cases usually suggests at least some cooperation of the child in the activity, and in some cases the child assumed an active role in initiating the relationship. . . . It is true that the child often rationalized with excuses of fear of physical harm or the enticement of gifts, but there were obviously secondary reasons. Even in the cases where physical force may have been applied by the adult, this did not wholly account for the frequent repetition of the practice.
>
> Finally, a most striking feature was that these children were distinguished as unusually charming and attractive in their outward personalities. Thus, it was not remarkable that frequently we considered the possibility that the child might have been the actual seducer, rather than the one innocently seduced.[11]

In addition to denial and blame, much of the existing literature on incest shows evidence of social and emotional distancing between the investigators and their subjects. This sometimes takes the form of an assertion that incestuous behavior is accepted or condoned in some culture other than the investigator's own. Thus, a British study of Irish working-class people reports that father-daughter incest, which occurred in 4 percent of an unselected outpatient clinic population, was a "cultural phenomenon" precipitated by social isolation or crowding, and had "no pathological effects."[12] The several investigators who have also reported instances where children, in their judgment, were not harmed by the incest experience do not usually state the criteria on which this judgment is based.[13] Still other investigators seem fearful to commit themselves to an opinion on the question of harm. Thus, for example, although 70 percent of the victims in Maisch's survey showed evidence of disturbed personality development, the author is uncertain about ascribing this to the effects of incest per se.

A few investigators, however, have testified to the destructive effects of the incest experience on the development of the child. Sloane and Karpinski, who studied five incestuous families in rural Pennsylvania, conclude: "Indulgence in incest in the post-adolescent period leads to serious repercussions in the girl, even in an environment where the moral standards are relaxed."[14] Kaufman, Peck, and Tagiuri, in a thorough study of eleven victims and their families who were seen at a Boston clinic, report: "Depression and guilt were universal as clinical findings. . . . The underlying craving for an adequate parent . . . dominated the lives of these girls."[15]

Several retrospective studies, including a recent report by Benward and Densen-Gerber, document a strong association between reported incest history and the later development of promiscuity or prostitution.[16] In fact, failure to marry or promiscuity seems to be the only criterion generally accepted in the literature as conclusive evidence that the victim has been harmed.[17] We believe that this finding in itself testifies to the traditional bias which pervades the incest literature.

Our survey of what has been written about incest, then, raises several questions. Why does incest between fathers and daughters occur so much more frequently than incest between mothers and sons? Why, though this finding has been consistently documented in all available sources, has no previous attempt been made to explain it? Why does the incest victim find so little attention or compassion in the literature, while she finds so many authorities who are willing to assert either that the incest did not happen, that it did not harm her, or that she was to blame for it? We believe that a feminist perspective must be invoked in order to address these questions.

Incest and Patriarchy

In a patriarchal culture, such as our own, the incest taboo must have a different meaning for the two sexes and may be observed by men and women for different reasons.

Major theorists in the disciplines of both psychology and anthropology explain the importance of the incest taboo by placing it at the center of an agreement to control warfare among men. It represents the first and most basic peace treaty. An essential element of the agreement is the concept that women are the possessions of men; the incest taboo represents an agreement as to how women shall be shared. Since virtually all known societies are dominated by men, all versions of the incest taboo are agreements among men regarding sexual access to women. As Mitchell points out, men create rules governing the exchange of women; women do not create rules governing the exchange of men.[18] Because the taboo is created and enforced by men, we argue that it may also be more easily and frequently violated by men.

The point at which the child learns the meaning of the incest taboo is the point of initiation into the social order. Boys and girls, however, learn different versions of the taboo. To paraphrase Freud once again, the boy learns that he may not consummate his sexual desires for his mother because his mother belongs to his father, and his father has the power to inflict the most terrible of punishments on him: to deprive him of his maleness.[19] In compensation, however, the boy learns that when he is a man he will one day possess women of his own.

When this little boy grows up, he will probably marry and may have a daughter. Although custom will eventually oblige him to give away his daughter in marriage to another man (note that mothers do not give away either daughters or sons), the taboo against sexual contact with his daughter will never carry the same force, either psychologically or socially, as the taboo which prohibited incest with his mother. *There is no punishing father to avenge father-daughter incest.*

What the little girl learns is not at all parallel. Her initiation into the patriarchal order begins with the realization that she is not only comparatively powerless as a child, but that she will remain so as a woman. She may acquire power only indirectly, as the favorite of a powerful man. As a child she may not possess her mother *or* her father; when she is an adult, her best hope is to *be* possessed by someone like her father. Thus, according to Freud she has less incentive than the boy to come to a full resolution of the Oedipus complex.[20] Since she has no hope of acquiring the privileges of an adult male, she can neither be rewarded for giving up her incestuous attachments, nor punished for refusing to do so. Chesler states the same conclusion more bluntly: "Women are encouraged to commit incest as a way of life. . . . As opposed to marrying our fathers, we marry men like our fathers . . . men who are older than us, have more money than us, more power than us, are taller than us, are stronger than us . . . our fathers."[21]

A patriarchal society, then, most abhors the idea of incest between mother and son, because this is an affront to the father's prerogatives. Though incest between father and daughter is also forbidden, the prohibition carries considerably less weight and is, therefore, more frequently violated. We believe this understanding of the asymmetrical nature of the incest taboo under patriarchy offers an explanation for the observed difference in the occurrence of mother-son and father-daughter incest.

If, as we propose, the taboo on father-daughter incest is relatively weak in a patriarchal family system, we might expect violations of the taboo to occur most frequently in families characterized by extreme paternal dominance. This is in fact the case. Incest offenders are frequently described as "family tyrants": "These fathers, who are often quite incapable of relating their despotic claim to leadership to their social efforts for the family, tend toward abuses of authority of every conceivable kind, and they not infrequently endeavor to secure their dominant position by socially isolating the members of the family from the world outside. Swedish, American, and French surveys have pointed time and again to the patriarchal position of such fathers, who set up a 'primitive family order.' "[22] Thus the seduction of daughters is an abuse which is inherent in a father-dominated family system; we believe that the greater the degree of male supremacy in any culture, the greater the likelihood of father-daughter incest.

A final speculative point: since, according to this formulation, women neither make nor enforce the incest taboo, why is it that women apparently observe the taboo so scrupulously? We do not know. We suspect that the answer may lie in the historic experience of women both as sexual property and as the primary caretakers of children. Having been frequently obliged to exchange sexual services for protection and care, women are in a position to understand the harmful effects of introducing sex into a relationship where there is a vast inequality of power. And, having throughout history been assigned the primary responsibility for the care of children, women may be in a position to understand more fully the needs of children, the difference between affectionate and erotic contact, and the appropriate limits of parental love.

A Clinical Report

The following is a clinical case study of fifteen victims of father-daughter incest. All the women were clients in psychotherapy who reported their incest experiences to their therapists after the fact. Seven were women whom the authors had personally evaluated or seen in psychotherapy. The remaining eight were clients in treatment with other therapists. No systematic case-finding effort was made; the authors simply questioned those practitioners who were best known to us through an informal network of female professionals. Four out of the first ten therapists we questioned reported that at least one of her clients had an incest history. We concluded from this admittedly small sample that a history of incest is frequently encountered in clinical practice.

Our combined group of six therapists (the authors and our four informants) had interviewed close to 1,000 clients in the past five years. In this population, the incidence of reported father-daughter incest was 2–3 percent. We believe this to be a minimum estimate, since in most cases no particular effort was made to elicit the history. Our estimate accords with the data of the Kinsey report,[23] in which 1.5 percent of the women surveyed stated that they had been molested by their fathers.

For the purposes of this study, we defined incest as overt sexual contact such as fondling, petting, masturbation, or intercourse between parent and child. We included only those cases in which there was no doubt in the daughter's mind that explicit and intentionally sexual contact occurred and that secrecy was required. Thus we did not include in our study the many women who reported seductive behaviors such as verbal sharing of sexual secrets, flirting, extreme possessiveness or jealousy, or intense interest in their bodies or their sexual activities on the part of their fathers. We recognize that these cases represent the extreme of a continuum of father-daughter relationships which range from the affectionate through the seductive to the overtly sexual. Information about the incest history was initially gathered from the therapists. Those clients who were willing to discuss their experiences with us in person were then interviewed directly.

The fifteen women who reported that they had been molested during childhood were in other respects quite ordinary women. Nothing obvious distinguished them from the general population of women entering psychotherapy (see Table 3.1). They ranged in age from fifteen to fifty-five. Most were in their early twenties at the time they first requested psychotherapy. They were all white. Four were single, seven married, and four separated or divorced. Half had children. The majority had at least some college education. They worked at common women's jobs: housewife, waitress, factory worker, office worker, prostitute, teacher, nurse. They complained mostly of depression and social isolation. Those who were married or recently separated complained of marital problems. The severity of their complaints seemed to be related to the degree of family disorganization and deprivation in their histories rather than to the incest history per se. Five of the women had been hospitalized at some point in their lives; three were or had been actively suicidal, and two were addicted to drugs or alcohol. Seven women brought up the incest history among their initial complaints; the rest revealed it only after having established a relationship with the therapist. In some cases, the history was not disclosed for one, two, or even three years after therapy had begun.

The incest histories were remarkably similar (see Table 3.2). The majority of the victims were oldest or only daughters and were between the ages of six and nine when they were first approached sexually by their fathers or male guardians (nine fathers, three stepfathers, a grandfather, a brother-in-law, and an uncle). The youngest girl was four years old; the oldest fourteen. The sexual contact usually took place repeatedly. In most cases the incestuous relationship lasted three years or more. Physical force was not used, and inter-

TABLE 3.1 Characteristics of Incest Victims Entering Therapy

Characteristic	Victims (*N*)
Age (years):	
15–20	3
21–25	7
26–30	2
30+	3
Marital Status:	
Single	4
Married	7
Separated or divorced	4
Occupation:	
Blue collar	4
White collar	4
Professional	3
Houseworker	1
Student	3
Education:	
High school not completed	4
High school completed	2
1–2 years college	3
College completed	5
Advanced degree	1
Presenting complaints:	
Marital problems	5
Depression	3
Anxiety	3
Social isolation	4
Drug or alcohol abuse	4
Suicide attempt	2

course was rarely attempted with girls who had not reached puberty; the sexual contact was limited to masturbation and fondling. In three cases, the relationship was terminated when the father attempted intercourse.

> **LENORE:** I had already started to develop breasts at age nine and had my period when I was eleven. All this time he's still calling me into bed for "little chats" with him. I basically trusted him although I felt funny about it. Then one time I was twelve or thirteen, he called me into bed and started undressing me. He gave this rationale about preparing me to be with boys. He kept saying I was safe as long as I didn't let them take my pants down. Meantime he was doing the same thing. I split. I knew what he was trying to do, and that it was wrong. That was the end of the overt sexual stuff. Not long after that he found an excuse to beat me.

TABLE 3.2 Characteristics of the Incest History

Characteristic	Incidence
Daughter's place in sibship:	
Oldest daughter	9
Only daughter	3
Middle or youngest daughter	1
Unknown	2
Daughter's age at onset of incestuous relationship (years):	
4	1
5	0
6	2
7	3
8	4
9	2
10	0
11	1
12	0
13	0
14	1
Unknown	1
Duration of incestuous relationship (years):	
Single incident	1
1–2	1
3–4	3
5–6	5
7–10	2
Unknown	3

In all but two of these fifteen cases the sexual relationship between father and daughter remained a secret, and there was no intervention in the family by the courts or child-protection authorities. Previous studies are based on court referrals and therefore give the erroneous impression that incest occurs predominantly in families at the lower end of the socioeconomic scale. This was not the case in the families of our victims. Of these, four fathers were blue-collar workers, two were white-collar workers, six were professionals, and the occupations of three were not known. The fathers' occupations cut across class lines. Several held jobs that required considerable personal competence and commanded social respect: college administrator, policeman, army officer, engineer. Others were skilled workers, foremen, or managers in factories or offices. All the mothers were houseworkers. Five of the fifteen families could certainly be considered disorganized, with histories of poverty, unemployment, frequent moves, alcoholism, violence, abandonment and foster care. Not surprisingly, the women who came from these families were those who complained of the most severe distress. The majority of the families, however, were apparently intact and maintained a façade of respectability.

The Incestuous Family Constellation

Both the apparently intact and the disorganized families shared certain common features in the pattern of family relationships. The most striking was the almost uniform estrangement of the mother and daughter, an estrangement that preceded the occurrence of overt incest. Over half the mothers were partially incapacitated by physical or mental illness or alcoholism and either assumed an invalid role within the home or were periodically absent because of hospitalization. Their oldest daughters were often obliged to take over the household duties. Anne-Marie remembered being hidden from the truant officer by her mother so that she could stay home and take care of the younger children. Her mother had tuberculosis. Claire's mother, who was not ill, went to work to support the family because her father, a severe alcoholic, brought home no money. In her absence, Claire did the housework and cooking and cared for her older brother.

At best, these mothers were seen by their daughters as helpless, frail, downtrodden victims, who were unable to take care of themselves, much less to protect their children.

ANNE-MARIE: She used to say, "give with one hand and you'll get with the other" but she gave with two hands and always went down. . . . She was nothing but a floor mat. She sold out herself and her self-respect. She was a love slave to my father.

CLAIRE: I always felt sorry for her. She spent her life suffering, suffering, suffering.

Some of the mothers habitually confided in their oldest daughters and unburdened their troubles to them. Theresa felt her mother was "more like a sister." Joan's mother frequently clung to her and told her, "You're the only one who understands me." By contrast, the daughters felt unable to confide in their mothers. In particular, the daughters felt unable to go to their mothers for support or protection once their fathers had begun to make sexual advances to them. Some feared that their mothers would take action to expel the father from the house, but more commonly these daughters expected that their mothers would do nothing; in many cases the mothers tolerated a great deal of abuse themselves, and the daughters had learned not to expect any protection. Five of the women said they suspected that their mothers knew about the incest and tacitly condoned it. Two made attempts to bring up the subject but were put off by their mothers' denial or indifference.

Only two of the fifteen women actually told their mothers. Both had reason to regret it. Paula's mother reacted by committing her to an institution: "She was afraid I would become a lesbian or a whore." Sandra's mother initially took her husband to court. When she realized that a conviction would lead to his imprisonment, she reversed her testimony and publicly called her twelve-year-old daughter a "notorious liar and slut."

The message that these mothers transmitted over and over to their daughters was: your father first, you second. It is dangerous to fight back, for if I lose him I lose everything. For my own survival I must leave you to your own devices. I cannot defend you, and if necessary I will sacrifice you to your father.

At worst, the mother-daughter relations were marked by frank and open hostility. Some of the daughters stated they could remember no tenderness or caring in the relationship.

MARTHA: She's always picking on me. She's so fuckin' cold.

PAULA: She's an asshole. I really don't like my mom. I guess I am bitter. She's very selfish. She did a lousy job of bringing me up.

The most severe disruption in the mother-daughter relationship occurred in Rita's case. She remembers receiving severe beatings from her mother, and her father intervening to rescue her. Though the physical attacks were infrequent, Rita recalls her mother as implacably hostile and critical, and her father as by far the more nurturant parent.

Previous studies of incestuous families document the disturbance in the mother-daughter relationship as a constant finding.[24] In a study of eleven girls who were referred by courts to a child guidance center, Kaufman et al. reported that the girls uniformly saw their mothers as cruel, unjust and depriving, while the fathers were seen much more ambivalently: "These girls had long felt abandoned by the mother as a protective adult. This was their basic anxiety. . . . Though the original sexual experience with the father was at a genital level, the meaning of the sexual act was pregenital, and seemed to have the purpose of receiving some sort of parental interest."[25]

In contrast, almost all the victims expressed some warm feelings toward their fathers. Many described them in much more favorable terms than their mothers. Some examples:

ANNE-MARIE: A handsome devil.

THERESA: Good with kids. An honest, decent guy.

LENORE: He was my confidant.

RITA: My savior.

Although it may seem odd to have expressed such attitudes toward blatantly authoritarian fathers, there are explanations. These were men whose presentation to the outside world made them liked and often respected members of the community. The daughters responded to their fathers' social status and power and derived satisfaction from being their fathers' favorites. They were "daddy's special girls," and often they were special to no one else. Feelings of pity for the fathers were also common, especially where the fathers had lost social status. The daughters seemed much more willing to forgive their fathers' failings and weaknesses than to forgive their mothers, or themselves.

SANDRA: He was a sweet, decent man. My mother ruined him. I saw him lying in his bed in the hospital, and I kept thinking why don't they let him die. When he finally did, everyone cried at the funeral but me. I was glad he was dead. He had a miserable life. He had nothing. No one cared, not even me. I didn't help him much.

The daughters not only felt themselves abandoned by their mothers, but seemed to perceive their fathers as likewise deserted, and they felt the same pity for their fathers as they felt for themselves.

The victims rarely expressed anger toward their fathers, even about the incestuous act itself. Two of the three women who did express anger were women who had been repeatedly beaten as well as sexually abused by their fathers. Not surprisingly, they were angrier about the beatings than about the sexual act, which they viewed ambivalently. Most women expressed feelings of fear, disgust, and intense shame about the sexual contact and stated that they endured it because they felt they had no other choice. Several of the women stated that they learned to deal with the sexual approach by "tuning out" or pretending that it was not happening. Later, this response generalized to other relationships. Half of the women acknowledged, however, that they had felt some degree of pleasure in the sexual contact, a feeling which only increased their sense of guilt and confusion.

KITTY: I was in love with my father. He called me his special girlfriend.

LENORE: The whole issue is very complicated. I was very attracted to my father, and that just compounded the guilt.

PAULA: I was scared of him, but basically I liked him.

Though these women sometimes expressed a sense of disappointment and even contempt for their fathers, they did not feel as keenly the sense of betrayal as they felt toward their mothers. Having abandoned the hope of pleasing their mothers, they seemed relieved to have found some way of pleasing their fathers and gaining their attention.

Susan Brownmiller, in her study of rape as a paradigm of relations between men and women, refers briefly to father-daughter incest. Stressing the coercive aspect of the situation, she calls it "father-rape."[26] To label it thus is to understate the complexity of the relationship. The father's sexual approach is clearly an abuse of power and authority, and the daughter almost always understands it as such. But, unlike rape, it occurs in the context of a caring relationship. The victim feels overwhelmed by her father's superior power and unable to resist him; she may feel disgust, loathing, and shame. But at the same time she often feels that this is the only kind of love she can get, and prefers it to no love at all. The daughter is not raped, but seduced.

In fact, to describe what occurs as a rape is to minimize the harm to the child, for what is involved here is not simply an assault, it is a betrayal. A woman who has been raped can cope with the experience in the same way that she would react to any other intentionally cruel and harmful attack. She is not socially or psychologically dependent upon the rapist. She is free to hate him. But the daughter who has been molested is dependent on her father for protection and care. Her mother is not an ally. She has no recourse. She does not dare express, or even feel, the depths of her anger at being used. She must comply with her father's demands or risk losing the parental love that she needs. She is not an adult. She cannot walk out of the situation (though she may try to run away). She must endure it, and find in it what compensations she can.

Although the victims reported that they felt helpless and powerless against their fathers, the incestuous relationship did give them some semblance of power within the family. Many of the daughters effectively replaced their mothers and became their fathers' surrogate wives. They were also deputy mothers to the younger children and were generally given some authority over them. While they resented being exploited and robbed of the freedom ordinarily granted to dependent children, they did gain some feeling of value and importance from the role they were given. Many girls felt an enormous sense of responsibility for holding the family together. They also knew that, as keepers of the incest secret, they had an extraordinary power which could be used to destroy the family. Their sexual contact with their fathers conferred on them a sense of possessing a dangerous, secret power over the lives of others, power which they derived from no other source. In this situation, keeping up appearances and doing whatever was necessary to maintain the integrity of the family became a necessary, expiating act at the same time that it increased the daughters' sense of isolation and shame.

> **THERESA:** I was mortified. My father and mother had fights so loud that you could hear them yelling all over the neighborhood. I used to think that my father was really yelling at my mother because she wouldn't give him sex. I felt I had to make it up to him.

What is most striking to us about this family constellation, in which the daughter replaces the mother in her traditional role, is the underlying assumption about that role shared apparently by all the family members. Customarily, a mother and wife in our society is one who nurtures and takes care of children and husband. If, for whatever reasons, the mother is unable to fulfill her ordinary functions, it is apparently assumed that some other female must be found to do it. The eldest daughter is a frequent choice. The father does not assume the wife's maternal role when she is incapacitated. He feels that his first right is to continue to receive the services which his wife formerly provided, sometimes including sexual services. He feels only secondarily responsible for giving care to his children. This view of the father's prerogative to be served not only is shared by the fathers and daughters in these families, but is often encouraged by societal attitudes. Fathers who feel abandoned by their wives are not generally expected or taught to assume primary parenting responsibilities. We should not find it surprising, then, that fathers occasionally turn to their daughters for services (domestic and sexual) that they had formerly expected of their wives.

The Victims

The fifteen women who reported their incest experiences were all clients in psychotherapy. That is to say, all had admitted to themselves and at least one other person that they were suffering and needed help. Although we do not know whether they speak for the vast majority of victims, some of their complaints are so similar that we believe that they represent a pattern common to most women who have endured prolonged sexual abuse in childhood at the hands of parents.

One of the most frequent complaints of the victims entering therapy was a sense of being different, and distant, from ordinary people. The sense of isolation and inability to make contact was expressed in many different ways:

> **KITTY:** I'm dead inside.
>
> **LENORE:** I have a problem getting close to people. I back off.
>
> **LOIS:** I can't communicate with anyone.

Their therapists described difficulty in forming relationships with them, confirming their assessment of themselves. Therapists frequently made comments like "I don't really know whether I'm in touch with her," or "she's one of the people that's been the hardest for me to figure out." These women complained that most of their relationships were superficial and empty, or else extremely conflictual. They expressed fear that they were unable to love. The sense of an absence of feeling was most marked in sexual relationships, although most women were sexually responsive in the narrow sense of the word; that is, capable of having orgasms.

In some cases, the suppression of feeling was clearly a defense which had been employed in the incestuous relationship in childhood. The distance or isolation of affect seemed originally to be a device set up as protection against the feelings aroused by the molesting father. One woman reported that when she "shut down," did not move or speak, her father would leave her alone. Another remembered that she would tell herself over and over "this isn't really happening" during the sexual episode. Passive resistance and dissociation of feeling seemed to be among the few defenses available in an overwhelming situation. Later, this carried over into relations with others.

The sense of distance and isolation which these women experienced was uniformly painful, and they made repeated, often desperate efforts to overcome it. Frequently, the result was a pattern of many brief unsatisfactory sexual contacts. Those relationships which did become more intense and lasting were fraught with difficulty.

Five of the seven married women complained of marital conflict, either feeling abused by their husbands or indifferent toward them. Those who were single or divorced uniformly complained of problems in their relationships with men. Some expressed negative feelings toward men in general:

> **STEPHANIE:** When I ride the bus I look at all the men and think, "all they want to do is stick their pricks into little girls."

Most, however, overvalued men and kept searching for a relationship with an idealized protector and sexual teacher who would take care of them and tell them what to do. Half the women had affairs during adolescence with older or married men. In these relationships, the sense of specialness, power, and secrecy of the incestuous relationship was regained. The men were seen as heroes and saviors.

In many cases, these women became intensely involved with men who were cruel, abusive, or neglectful, and tolerated extremes of mistreatment. Anne-Marie remained married for twenty years to a psychotic husband who beat her, terrorized their children, and never supported the family. She felt she could not leave him because he would fall apart without her. "We were his kingdom," she said, "to bully and beat." She eventually sought police protection and separation only after it was clear that her life was in danger. Her masochistic behavior in this relationship was all the more striking, since other areas of her life were relatively intact. She was a warm and generous mother, a valued worker, and an active, respected member of her community. Lois was raped at age nineteen by a stranger whom she married a week later. After this marriage ended in divorce, she began to frequent bars where she would pick up men who beat her repeatedly. She expressed no anger toward these men. Three other women in this group of fifteen were also rape victims. Only one expressed anger toward her attackers; the others felt they "deserved it." Some of the women recognized and commented on their predilection for abusive men. As Sandra put it: "I'm better off with a bum. I can handle that situation."

Why did these women feel they deserved to be beaten, raped, neglected, and used? The answer lies in their image of themselves. It is only through understanding how they perceived themselves that we can make sense of their often highly destructive relations with others. Almost every one of these fifteen women described herself as a "witch," "bitch," or "whore." They saw themselves as socially "branded" or "marked," even when no social exposure of their sexual relations had occurred or was likely to occur. They experienced themselves as powerful and dangerous to men: their self-image had almost a magical quality. Kitty, for instance, called herself a "devil's child," while Sandra compared herself to the twelve-year-old villainess of a popular melodrama, *The Exorcist,* a girl who was possessed by the devil. Some felt they were invested with special seductive prowess and could captivate men simply by looking at them. These daughters seemed almost uniformly to believe that they had seduced their fathers and therefore could seduce any man.

At one level, this sense of malignant power can be understood to have arisen as a defense against the child's feelings of utter helplessness. In addition, however, this self-image had been reinforced by the long-standing conspiratorial relationship with the father, in which the child had been elevated to the mother's position and did indeed have the power to destroy the family by exposing the incestuous secret.

Moreover, most of the victims were aware that they had experienced some pleasure in the incestuous relationship and had joined with their fathers in a shared hatred of their mothers. This led to intense feelings of shame, degradation, and worthlessness. Because they had enjoyed their fathers' attention and their mothers' defeat, these women felt responsible for the incestuous situation. Almost uniformly, they distrusted their own desires and needs and did not feel entitled to care and respect. Any relationship that afforded some kind of pleasure seemed to increase the sense of guilt and shame. These women constantly sought to expiate their guilt and relieve their shame by serving and giving to others and by observing the strictest and most rigorous codes of religion and morality. Any lapse from a rigid code of behavior was felt as confirming evidence of their innate evilness. Some of the women embraced their negative identity with a kind of defiance and pride. As Sandra boasted: "There's *nothing* I haven't done!"

Those women who were mothers themselves seemed to be preoccupied with the fear that they would be bad mothers to their children, as they felt their mothers had been to them. Several sought treatment when they began to be aware of feelings of rage and resentment toward their children, especially their daughters. Any indulgence in pleasure seeking or attention to personal needs reinforced their sense that they were "whores" and unfit mothers. In some, the fear of exposure took the form of a constant worry that the authorities would intervene to take the children away. Other mothers worried that they would not be able to protect their daughters from a repetition of the incest situation. As one victim testified:

> I could a been the biggest bum. My father called me a "big whore" and my mother believed him. I could a got so disgusted that I could a run around with anyone I saw. I met my hus-

> band and told him about my father and my child. He stuck by me and we was married. I got to the church and I'm not so shy like I was. It always come back to me that this thing might get on the front pages and people might know about it. I'm getting over it since the time I joined the church.

Her husband testified:

> The wife is nervous and she can't sleep. She gets up yesterday night about two o'clock in the morning and starts fixing the curtains. She works that way till five, then she sleeps like a rock. She's cold to me but she tells me she likes me. She gets cold once in a while and she don't know why herself. She watches me like a hawk with those kids. She don't want me to be loving with them and to be too open about sex. It makes her think of her old man. I got to take it easy with her or she blows up.[27]

In our opinion, the testimony of these victims, and the observations of their therapists, is convincing evidence that the incest experience was harmful to them and left long-lasting scars. Many victims had severely impaired object relations with both men and women. The overvaluation of men led them into conflictual and often intensely masochistic relationships with men. The victims' devaluation of themselves and their mothers impaired development of supportive friendships with women. Many of the victims also had a well-formed negative identity as witch, bitch, or whore. In adult life they continued to make repeated ineffective attempts to expiate their intense feelings of guilt and shame.

Therapy for the Incest Victim and Her Family

Very little is known about how to help the incest victim. If the incestuous secret is discovered while the victim is still living with her parents, the most common social intervention is the destruction of the family. This outcome is usually terrifying even to an exploited child, and most victims will cooperate with their fathers in maintaining secrecy rather than see their fathers jailed or risk being sent away from home.

We know of only one treatment program specifically designed for the rehabilitation of the incestuous family.[28] This program, which operates out of the probation department of the Santa Clara County Court in California, involves all members of the incestuous family in both individual and family therapy and benefits from a close working alliance with Daughters United, a self-help support group for victims. The program directors acknowledge that the coercive power of the court is essential for obtaining the cooperation of the fathers. An early therapeutic goal in this program is a confrontation between the daughter and her mother and father, in which they admit to her that she has been the victim of "poor parenting." This is necessary in order to relieve the daughter from her feeling of responsibility for the incest. Mothers appear to be more willing than fathers to admit this to their daughters.

Though this program offers a promising model for the treatment of the discovered incestuous family, it does not touch the problem of undetected incest. The vast majority of incest victims reach adulthood still bearing their secrets. Some will eventually enter psychotherapy. How can the therapist respond appropriately to their needs?

We believe that the male therapist may have great difficulty in validating the victim's experience and responding empathically to her suffering. Consciously or not, the male therapist will tend to identify with the father's position and therefore will tend to deny or excuse his behavior and project blame onto the victim. Here is an example of a male therapist's judgmental perception of an incest victim:

> This woman had had a great love and respect for her father until puberty when he had made several sexual advances toward her. In analysis she talked at first only of her good feelings toward him because she had blocked out the sexual episodes. When they were finally brought back into consciousness, all the fury returned which she had experienced at the age of thirteen. She felt that her father was an impotent, dirty old man who had taken advantage of her trusting youthful innocence. From some of the details which she related of her relationship to her father, *it was obvious that she was not all that innocent.* [Our italics][29]

Not surprisingly, the client in this case became furious with her therapist, and therapy was unsuccessful.

If the male therapist identifies with the aggressor in the incest situation, it is also clear that the female therapist tends to identify with the victim and that this may limit her effectiveness. In a round-table discussion of experiences with incest victims, most of the contributing therapists acknowledged having shied away from a full and detailed exploration of the incestuous relationship. In some cases the therapist blatantly avoided the issue. In these cases, no trust was established in the relationship, and the client quickly discontinued therapy. In effect, the therapists had conveyed to these women that their secrets were indeed too terrible to share, thus reinforcing their already intense sense of isolation and shame.

Two possible explanations arise for the female therapist's flight. Traditional psychoanalytic theory might suggest that the therapist's own incestuous wishes and fantasies are too threatening for her to acknowledge. This might seem to be the most obvious reason for such a powerful countertransference phenomenon. The second reason, though less apparent, may be equally powerful: the female therapist confronting the incest victim reexperiences her own fear of her father and recognizes how easily she could have shared the victim's fate. We suspect that many women have been aware of, and frightened by, seductive behavior on the part of their own fathers. For every family in which incest is consummated there are undoubtedly hundreds with essentially similar, if less extreme, psychological dynamics. Thus the incest victim forces the female therapist to confront her own condition and to reexperience not only her infantile desires but also her (often realistic) childhood fears.

If the therapist overcomes this obstacle, and does not avoid addressing the issue with her client, another trap follows. As one therapist put it during the round-table discussion: "I get angry *for* her. How can she *not* be angry with her father?" Getting angry for a client is a notoriously unsuccessful intervention. Since the victim is more likely to feel rage toward the mother who abandoned her to her fate than toward her father, the therapeutic relationship must provide a place where the victim feels she can safely express her hostile feelings. Rage against the mother must be allowed to surface, for it is only when the client feels she can freely express her full range of feelings without driving the therapist away that she loses her sense of being malignantly "marked."

The feminist therapist may have particular difficulty facing the degree of estrangement between mother and daughter that occurs in these families. Committed as she is to building solidarity among women, she is bound to be distressed by the frequent histories of indifference, hostility, and cruelty in the mother-daughter relationship. She may find herself rushing to the defense of the mother, pointing out that the mother, herself, was a victim, and so on. This may be true, but not helpful. Rather than denying the situation or making excuses for anyone, the therapist must face the challenge that the incestuous family presents to all of us: How can we overcome the deep estrangement between mothers and daughters that frequently exists in our society, and how can we better provide for the security of both?

Beyond Therapy

For both social and psychological reasons, therapy alone seems to be an insufficient response to the situation of the incest victim. Because of its confidential nature, the therapy relationship does not lend itself to a full resolution of the issue of secrecy. The woman who feels herself to be the guardian of a terrible, almost magical secret may find considerable relief from her shame after sharing the secret with another person. However, the shared secrecy then recreates a situation similar to the original incestuous relationship. Instead of the victim alone against the world, there is the special dyad of the victim and her confidant. This, in fact, was a difficult issue for all the participants in our study, since the victims once again were the subject of special interest because of their sexual history.

The women's liberation movement has demonstrated repeatedly to the mental health profession that consciousness raising has often been more beneficial and empowering to women than psychotherapy. In particular, the public revelation of the many and ancient sexual secrets of women (orgasm, rape, abortion) may have contributed far more toward the liberation of women than the attempt to heal individual wounds through a restorative therapeutic relationship.

The same should be true for incest. The victims who feel like bitches, whores, and witches might feel greatly relieved if they felt less lonely, if their identities as the special guardians of a dreadful secret could be shed. Incest will begin to lose its devastating magic power when women begin to speak out about it publicly and realize how common it is.

We know that most cases do not come to the attention of therapists, and those that do, come years after the fact. Thus, as a social problem incest is clearly not amenable to a purely psychotherapeutic approach. Prevention, rather than treatment, seems to be indicated. On the basis of our study and the testimony of these victims, we favor all measures which strengthen and support the mother's role within the family, for it is clear that these daughters fall prey to their fathers' abuse when their mothers are too ill, weak, or downtrodden to protect them. We favor the strengthening of protective services for women and children, including adequate and dignified financial support for mothers, irrespective of their marital status; free, public, round-the-clock child care, and refuge facilities for women in crisis. We favor the vigorous enforcement (by female officials) of laws prohibiting the sexual abuse of children. Offenders should be isolated and reeducated. We see efforts to reintegrate fathers into the world of children as a positive development, but only on the condition that they learn more appropriate parental behavior. A seductive father is not much of an improvement over an abandoning or distant one.

As both Shulamith Firestone and Florence Rush have pointed out, the liberation of children is inseparable from our own.[30] In particular, as long as daughters are subject to seduction in childhood, no adult woman is free. Like prostitution and rape, we believe father-daughter incest will disappear only when male supremacy is ended.

NOTES

1. Claude Lévi-Strauss, *The Elementary Structures of Kinship* (Boston: Beacon Press, 1969), p. 481; Margaret Mead, "Incest," in *International Encyclopedia of the Social Sciences,* ed. David L. Sills (New York: Crowell, Collier & Macmillan, 1968).
2. Herbert Maisch, *Incest* (London: Andre Deutsch, 1973), p. 69.
3. Vincent De Francis, ed., *Sexual Abuse of Children* (Denver: Children's Division of the American Humane Association, 1967).
4. Alfred Kinsey, W. B. Pomeroy, C. E. Martin, and P. Gebhard, *Sexual Behavior in the Human Female* (Philadelphia: Saunders & Co., 1953), pp. 116–22.
5. S. Kirson Weinberg, *Incest Behavior* (New York: Citadel Press, 1955).
6. See n. 2 above.
7. De Francis.
8. Alfred C. Kinsey, W. B. Pomeroy, and Clyde Martin, *Sexual Behavior in the Human Male* (Philadelphia: Saunders & Co., 1948), pp. 167, 558.
9. Freud, *The Origins of Psychoanalysis: Letters to Wilhelm Fliess, Drafts and Notes: 1887–1902* (New York: Basic Books, 1954), p. 215.
10. Joseph Peters, "Letter to the Editor," *New York Times Book Review* (November 16, 1975).
11. L. Bender and A. Blau, "The Reaction of Children to Sexual Relations with Adults," *American Journal of Orthopsychiatry* 7 (1937): 500–18.
12. N. Lukianowitz, "Incest," *British Journal of Psychiatry* 120 (1972): 301–13.
13. Yokoguchi, "Children Not Severely Damaged by Incest with a Parent," *Journal of the American Academy of Child Psychiatry* 5 (1966): 111–24; J. B. Weiner, "Father-Daughter Incest," *Psychiatric Quarterly* 36 (1962): 1132–38.
14. P. Sloane and E. Karpinski, "Effects of Incest on the Participants," *American Journal of Orthopsychiatry* 12 (1942): 666–73.
15. I. Kaufman, A. Peck, and L. Tagiuri, "The Family Constellation and Overt Incestuous Relations between Father and Daughter," *American Journal of Orthopsychiatry* 24 (1954): 266–79.
16. J. Benward and J. Densen-Gerber, *Incest as a Causative Factor in Anti-social Behavior: An Exploratory Study* (New York: Odyssey Institute, 1975).
17. Weinberg.
18. Juliet Mitchell, *Psychoanalysis and Feminism* (New York: Pantheon Books, 1974).
19. Freud, *Three Essays on the Theory of Sexuality* (New York: Avon Books, 1962).
20. Freud, "Some Psychical Consequences of the Anatomical Distinction between the Sexes" (1925), "Female Sexuality" (1951), and "Femininity" (1933), all reprinted in *Women and Analysis,* ed. Jean Strouse (New York: Viking Press, 1974).
21. Phyllis Chesler, "Rape and Psychotherapy," in *Rape: The First Sourcebook for Women,* ed. Noreen Connell and Cassandra Wilson (New York: New American Library, 1974), p. 76.
22. Maisch, p. 140.
23. Kinsey et al. (n. 4 above), p. 121.
24. Maisch.
25. Kaufman et al., p. 270.

26. S. Brownmiller, *Against Our Will: Men, Women and Rape* (New York: Simon & Schuster, 1975), p. 281.

27. Weinberg, pp. 151–52.

28. H. Giarretto, "Humanistic Treatment of Father-Daughter Incest," in *Child Abuse and Neglect—the Family and the Community,* ed. R. E. Helfer and C. H. Kemp (Cambridge, Mass.: Ballinger Publishing Co., 1976).

29. R. Stein, *Incest and Human Love: The Betrayal of the Soul in Psychotherapy* (New York: Third Press, 1973), pp. 45–46.

30. Shulamith Firestone, *The Dialectic of Sex: The Case for Feminist Revolution* (New York: Bantam Books, 1970); Florence Rush, "The Sexual Abuse of Children: A Feminist Point of View," in Connell and Wilson.

Reflection

Afterword, 2000:
Understanding Incest Twenty Years Later

JUDITH LEWIS HERMAN

This book, like so many feminist writings, began with two women talking. Our simple acts of speaking and listening joined us to a world-wide liberation movement. In the "free space" we created in our intimate dialogues with our patients and with each other, we joined with numerous other women who were uncovering the secret crimes at the heart of patriarchal order.[1] When Lisa Hirschman and I began our study in the mid-1970s, incest was publicly invisible, yet the private confidences of numerous victims led us and a number of other feminist writers to suspect that sexual exploitation of women and children was endemic in our society.[2] Against the evidence of our patients' personal testimony, we encountered a suffocating array of denials, rationalizations, and excuses that passed for authoritative wisdom in literature, social science, medicine, and law. At the time it was generally held that sexual offenses were rare in reality but rampant in the overactive imaginations of women and children. The opposite turned out to be true.

In the past two decades, the original premises of our incest study have been amply confirmed. It is now widely understood that father-daughter incest is not an aberration but rather a common and predictable abuse of patriarchal power. It is also a means of perpetuating the power of fathers, one of the many private crimes (rape, sexual trafficking, domestic battery) by which male dominance and female subordination are enforced.[3] Perhaps those who grasp the importance of incest most fully are practical businessmen who profit from the sale of women's bodies. A pimp explains to a naive student what he looks for in a prostitute:

> Beauty, yes. Sexual expertise, somewhat. That can be taught easier than you think. What is important above all is obedience. And how do you get obedience? You get obedience if you get women who have had sex with their fathers, their uncles, their brothers—you know, someone they love and fear to lose so that they do not dare to defy.[4]

While conceding that incest is much more common than previously thought, some commentators have attempted to understand the problem apart from the context of male dominance. They point out, quite rightly, that not all perpetrators are men (only some 90 percent of them),[5] and not all victims are girls (boys are also sexually abused in significant numbers, mostly by older boys and men).[6] Nevertheless, a feminist analysis remains the only one capable of explaining how such widespread abuses visited mainly by one sex upon the other could be so long denied or condoned. Only a feminist analysis explains why incest perpetrators look like the ordinary men they are—indeed, why so many are men of power and respect. Only a feminist analysis explains why women have always been the most committed advocates for abused children and adult survivors. And only a feminist analysis explains why such bitter conflict arises any time a serious effort is made to hold incest perpetrators accountable for their crimes . . .

NOTES

1. Pamela Allen, *Free Space: A Perspective on the Small Group in Women's Liberation* (Washington, N.J.: Times Change Press, 1970).

2. Other feminist thinkers who investigated this issue at the same time were Florence Rush, *The Best Kept Secret: Sexual Abuse of Children* (Englewood Cliffs, N.J.: Prentice Hall, 1980); Louise Armstrong, *Kiss Daddy Goodnight: A Speak-Out on Incest* (New York: Hawthorne, 1978); Sandra Butler, *Conspiracy of Silence: The Trauma of Incest* (San Francisco: Glide, 1978); and Jean Goodwin, *Sexual Abuse, Incest Victims and Their Families* (Boston: John Wright, 1982).

3. Susan Brownmiller, *Against Our Will: Men, Women and Rape* (New York: Simon and Schuster, 1975); Catherine MacKinnon, *Feminism Unmodified: Discourses on Life and Law* (Cambridge, Mass.: Harvard University Press, 1987).

4. Richard Kluft, "On the Apparent Invisibility of Incest," in Richard Kluft, ed., *Incest-Related Syndromes of Adult Psychopathology* (Washington, D.C.: American Psychiatric Press, 1990), p. 25.

5. Diana Russell, *The Secret Trauma: Incest in the Lives of Girls and Women* (New York: Basic Books, 1986).

6. D. Finkelhor, G. Hotaling, I. A. Lewis, and C. Smith, "Sexual Abuse in a National Survey of Adult Men and Women: Prevalence, Characteristics, and Risk Factors," *Child Abuse and Neglect* (1990), 14:19–28.

CHAPTER

4 Sexually Victimized Children

DAVID FINKELHOR

This chapter presents thirteen theories about why children are sexually victimized. These theories are concerned with why offenders do it, why it happens to some particular children and in some particular families, and why it is apparently so common in our society. Altogether, however, they do not add up to an inspiring panorama of insight. Knowledge on this neglected subject is still in a primitive state, as is almost any topic related to sex.

Actually, a deeper flaw is the fact that we know more about sexual deviance than we do about sexual normality or ordinariness—to choose a less value-laden word—and this topic is a good case in point. Here we are inquiring how children come to have sexual experiences with adults when we hardly know how they come to have sexual experiences at all. Thus all theories about children's sexual victimization must be viewed against their true backdrop: a vast ignorance of the forces governing the development and expression of sexual behavior in general.

Theories about the Offender

Early theorizing on this subject was heavily moralistic and medical as the following view illustrates:

(1) Abuser as Degenerate

In this theory sexual abusers of children were seen as psychopathic, feeble-minded, physical and moral degenerates (Krafft-Ebing, 1935), but such preconceptions did not long withstand the light of evidence.

The early efforts to study sex offenders had a kind of heroic quality to them; long-suffering interviewers made meticulous studies of the dregs of humanity in dismal prisons as they tried to get beyond the myths of the sex fiend. Their research on this subject revealed that most of the stereotypes were false. Only a small portion of such sex offenders were psychotic, senile or mentally retarded (Cohen and Boucher, 1972; Glueck, 1954; Gebhard *et al.,* 1965). They painted a rather more human, sometimes even sympathetic, portrait of the child molester, one which in many cases made him sound more attractive than the run-of-the-mill criminal.

They were not primarily strange men who lured away their victims in parks, playgrounds, and alleyways. More often they were friends, neighbors, or relatives of the children they victimized. They were not brutal and sadistic, for the most part, but used their authority or charm to gain children's confidence, cooperation, or at least, passive assent. And unlike rapists, they did not try to have intercourse with their victims. Rather their penchant was for genital fondling, exhibition, and masturbation.

Since many of these researchers were psychoanalytically oriented, their theorizing focused on the developmental experiences of these offenders.

(2) Seductive Mothers

An offender's sexual interest in children resulted from a disturbance in his relationship to his parents. Many child molesters were viewed as men who had overly seductive mothers, whose overtures aroused their incest anxiety. The incest anxiety in turn spawned a fear of adult women and adult sexuality and a turning toward children, who did not present such a threat (Glueck, 1954).

Other theories followed the early Freudian model and focused on early childhood sexual trauma as the source of deviant behavior.

(3) Sexual Fixation

Sexual preoccupation with children resulted from an unusually pleasurable childhood sexual experience, so that the offender, like Lolita's notorious Humbert Humbert, becomes fixated at an early developmental stage or conditioned to respond to that early childhood stimulus (McGuire *et al.,* 1965; Nabokov, 1955). A negative sexual experience could have a similar effect by either deterring the individual from normal sexual maturation or driving him into a compulsive repetition of the original situation in an effort to change the outcome.

Imaginative as these psychoanalytic theories are, they have not received a great deal of empirical confirmation. Subsequent studies on larger samples have failed to find regular patterns. Only a minority of offenders show the childhood traumas and the warped parental relationships that the psychoanalytic approach would predict. Men who become sexually involved with children seem to be a much more heterogeneous group than was originally thought (Swanson, 1968). Researchers have more and more had to turn away from an overarching theory toward typologies that take account of the variety of personalities, situations, and behaviors.

The following five propositions are not theories in the sense previously cited. Rather they are empirical generalizations about sex offenders against children based on the most current research. For the most part, they explain some of the difficulty in establishing a theory of sexual victimization.

(4) Diversity of Sexual Offenders against Children

(4a) Only a minority of incarcerated child molesters (25 to 33 percent) have a primary and relatively permanent sexual interest in children, something that would be described as a personality characteristic (pedophilia). The rest became involved for what seem more transient reasons: an unusual opportunity, stress, the frustration of other sexual outlets, etc. (Gebhard *et al.* 1965; Groth, 1978).

(4b) A sexual involvement with children has very different motivational roots in different men. In some it is an act of sexual gratification, but for others it expresses a need for closeness or for aggression.

(4c) Sexual interest in children, particularly on an enduring basis, does seem to be connected to a fear of adults and adult sexuality. Children are often attractive to such men because they are naive, undemanding, and do not have adult physical characteristics (Hammer and Glueck, 1957).

(4d) The motivation for involvement with children depends a great deal on the age of the offender, the age of the child, and the activity involved. Adolescents molest children for different reasons than do adults. Men who are sexually interested in very young children differ from those interested in older ones. And the motivational roots of exhibitionism, for example, contrast strongly with those of incest (Gebhard *et al.,* 1965; Mohr *et al.,* 1964).

(4e) Alcohol shows a consistent connection with patterns of sexual abuse of children (Browning and Boatman, 1977; Gebhard *et al.,* 1965; Virkkunnen, 1974). Nonetheless, many social scientists doubt that this large number of sexual offenses means that alcohol causes or releases a sexual interest in children (or other deviant interests). Drinking may be more of a way in which the activity is excused or rationalized by the offender than a causative factor (Gebhard *et al.,* 1965; McCaghy, 1968).

Of course, even these generalizations must be taken with an appropriate dose of caution. What these men have in common may be more the fact that they have been caught than that they had sex with children. The vast majority of offenders against children, the undetected ones, may be of an entirely different breed.

Thus, although simple profiles of the typical sexual abusers have not been forthcoming from research on incarcerated offenders, the findings have at least influenced the direction of future efforts. It is acknowledged that they are not generally impulsive, raving, sex maniacs or psychopaths. This knowledge, combined with the frustration of efforts to account for their behavior psychologically, has led to a new focus for research—on the family situation where sexual abuse arises.

Theories about the Victim

Since it has been easier, on the whole, to talk to victims than to offenders, a great deal of theorizing has taken place about the children who are involved in child-adult sex. Many attempts have been made to relate its occurrence to something about the psychology of the victim.

From the time this question was first taken up, the idea that children might be the instigators, not the passive victims, of the offense has had a great deal of currency. For many years, the one myth researchers took the most relish in exploding was that children were helpless prey to adult offenders. It has been pointed out repeatedly in the literature that children do things that contribute to their victimization: they act suggestively, they go along with the offender's proposition, they allow the situation to continue, and they fail to report it to anyone who could take action to stop it. All these seem to indicate varying degrees of complicity in the offense (Ramer, 1973).

Freud, as we pointed out earlier, laid the groundwork for this orientation with his theory that every child in his or her fantasy life wishes for sex with his parents, and by extension, other adults and that this fantasy sometimes spills over into reality. Lauretta Bender, a famous American child psychiatrist and one of the earliest to research adult-child sexual encounters, found that all the victims she interviewed were unusually attractive children who made seductive overtures to the psychiatrists (Bender and Blau, 1937). The theory based on these kinds of observations usually is articulated as follows.

(5a) The Sexually Acting-Out Child

Some children act in ways that actively encourage adults to approach them sexually. These are children who have poor relationships with their parents, who are needy in other ways, and who have discovered that they can obtain attention and affection from an adult by arousing his sexual impulses (Burton, 1968).

A related theory which holds the child less fully responsible for the sex offense emphasizes the following:

(5b) The Sexually Defenseless Child

When approached by offenders, many children seem to collaborate in their victimization by failing to take self-protective actions. They accept the adult overtures, they agree to accompany the adult somewhere, they allow the situation to continue, and they do not take action to stop the molestation. Such children are believed to be disturbed, have sexual conflicts, few friends, or a passive outlook, all of which make them especially vulnerable (De Francis, 1969; Weiss *et al.,* 1955).

In the field known as "victimology," there is a tradition of theories like these that try to understand the ways in which victims contribute to their own victimization. The process is usually called "victim precipitation," and it highlights the fact that victims frequently contribute to their own murders—by striking a first blow or hurling an insult—or to their own robberies—by leaving doors unlocked and valuable possessions in plain sight.

What is unusual in the case of sexual abuse of children is the degree of importance that the victim precipitation analysis has assumed. The idea that murder victims bring on their own demise developed fairly late in the field and had a moderate effect on our understanding of homicide. In contrast, the idea that children are responsible for their own seduction has been at the center of almost all writing on sexual abuse since the topic was first broached.

Victim precipitation in sexual abuse is also unique because it is so poorly defined. In homicide cases, it has been given the very precise meaning that the victim was the one to strike the first blow (Curtis, 1976). In discussions of rape, it was defined as an actual offer of sexual intercourse that was later withdrawn. But in the case of sexual abuse, anything a child might do that does not conform to the standards of an "ideal" victim is liable to get the child called an accomplice.

Some critics have said this kind of preoccupation really reflects the fantasies the researchers have about the children and also the defense a male-dominated society erects to avoid recognizing a particularly seamy side of male sexuality (Rush, 1974). In addition, it also reflects the fact that researchers who have studied only the victim are likely to try to use what they know about his or her psychology to account for the experience. (In homicide cases, by contrast, victims are not usually available for study.) All these factors may account for an overemphasis on victim precipitation.

This theory has some important logical defects that should also be noted (Silverman, 1974). To an extent that has not been adequately recognized, the idea that victims contribute to their own victimization is a tautology. By the mere fact of acting and making choices, people have control over things that bring them to fateful junctures, an existential truth illustrated in Thornton Wilder's *Bridge of San Luis Rey.* It is too easy and incorrect to conclude from this truth that a victim had a desire or predisposition for the misfortune that befell him or her.

In addition, the whole notion of victim precipitation depends very much on whose point of view is taken. What may have seemed like a precipitating gesture from the point of view of the offender (or more likely the researcher)—such as rubbing up against someone—may not have been for the victim. Children most certainly do not share adult meanings of sexual gestures, but since researchers are also usually adults, they are more likely to identify with the offender's view. For some offenders, the mere fact of a child's physical beauty may be enough to precipitate sexual overtures. Is the victim responsible for this occurrence? Fortunately, in the last few years, largely as a result of consciousness raising by the women's movement on the subject of rape, investigators have become somewhat more circumspect about blaming the victim.

Theories about Family Context

Some of the earliest research discovered that much sexual abuse of children took place among family members, but it has been only recently that families, rather than family members, have been implicated in this problem. This new awareness required a willingness to talk to all the family members, instead of just the ones most handy. The discovery of family therapy as a method of clinical treatment, and also an increasing interest by sociologists in the problem, have also helped advance a family approach to sexual abuse, in contrast to the earlier psychodynamic approaches.

Family dynamics have been easiest to identify in the case of incest. Father-daughter incest has been the kind most theorized about, since it is the kind most frequently observed. Here the sexual abuse takes place in the heart of the nuclear family, and the group process is most readily analyzed. Thus we will review some theories about incestuous families and show how in some cases these theories can be generalized to include sexual abuse outside the family.

(6) Social Isolation

Incest occurs in families characterized by a high degree of social isolation (Bagley, 1969; Riemer, 1940; Weinberg, 1955). In the stereotype, such families come from backwoods Appalachia: they are poor and interbred. But similarly isolated families can be found in cities and suburbs too. The isolation appears to reflect and reinforce several forces that promote incest. These families shy away from social interaction and draw in upon themselves. As a natural part of this process, sexual attachments that would ordinarily develop with people outside the family occur in the family. The external outlets are not available, nor are they sought. Riemer (1940) shows how incest may develop in such families because they turn inward in response to family crises and life changes, whereas other families might turn to help from the outside.

Social isolation creates a climate in which deviance is freer to emerge. Also, such families are insulated from the scrutiny of public view, which must enforce the incest taboo in less isolated families, and without available models, incestuous behavior may come to be accepted as normal. It has been suggested that some of these isolated families are part of subcultures where incest is not regarded with the same kind of disapproval as in the culture at large. In fairly self-contained communities, the tolerance of incest can be transmitted from generation to generation, relatively unchanged.

(7) Role Confusion

Incest and other kinds of adult-child sex are forms of role confusion (Summit and Kryso, 1978; Zaphiris, 1978), and as such are eminently problems of sociopathology rather than psychopathology. In adult-child sex, adults place children in adult sexual roles. A father acts toward his daughter as he would toward his wife. Brothers and sisters treat each other as lovers rather than relatives. Ironically, this very sociological point of view on family pathology—that incest is a problem of role confusion in a family—has been elaborated most by psychiatrists, not sociologists (Minuchin, 1974).

In this theory, father-daughter incest is a kind of functional adaptation by a family to severe role strain (Henderson, 1972; Lustig *et al.,* 1966; Machotka *et al.,* 1966). Parents in these families usually have unhappy marriages, and sex between spouses is unpleasant or nonexistent (Molnar and Cameron, 1975). Fathers are often authoritarian and physically abusive within the family (Weiner, 1962) but incompetent as providers (Cormier *et al.,* 1962). Mothers, for their part, are either unwilling or unable to fulfill parental functions (Browning and Boatman, 1977). They are ill, still heavily under the sway of their own families, or uncomfortable with the responsibilities of motherhood. In addition to tension with their husbands, they have strained and alienated relationships with their daughters.

In this situation, incest is a possible outcome and sometimes even a solution to the family dilemma. Depressed, incapacitated, and subservient, many of these mothers are unable to provide any protection for their daughters. They are peripheral family members. In a situation where the father-daughter bond is the strongest emotional axis in the family, it eventually leads to sex. In cases where the mother is incapacitated, alcoholic, or absent, a daughter often assumes many of her housekeeping and childcaring responsibilities and displaces her sexually as a natural extension. Some mothers are even said to feel content at being relieved of these family and sexual obligations. What this all amounts to is a mother-daughter role reversal brought about by a strain and breakdown of the normal family relationships.

(8) The Milieu of Abandonment

According to still another theory, incest may occur in response to a pervasive kind of emotional climate, one dominated by the fear of abandonment. In such families where each member fears he or she may be abandoned by the others, sexuality may be the final resource used to stave off this trauma (Henderson, 1972; Kaufman *et al.,* 1954).

There are two themes that seem to characterize families in which this kind of crisis leads to incest. First, they have a record of abandonment that dominates family history. Second, the cast of characters seems to be constantly changing. Stepparents and foster children shuffle in and out of the family circle, and the family boundary seems to be diffuse and poorly maintained. Very frequently the fathers in such families have nomadic life styles and are away from the family for extended periods as a result of military service, job requirements or marital incompatibilities. Incest has often been noted to occur when the fathers return from such an extended absence. It is a desperate attempt to give some substance to tenuous family ties that can't seem to be sustained in any other way.

To explain why daughters tolerate and in some cases encourage incestuous relationships that extend over periods of months and years, one frequently cited factor is that daughters may be receiving a kind of attention and affection that was otherwise unavailable to them. Also daughters may harbor the perhaps accurate notion that without the incestuous relationship there would be no family at all (Lustig *et al.,* 1966). Of course, once the incest begins this fantasy becomes all the more real, since revelation and termination of the relationship are virtually certain to bring about the crisis of family dissolution that was feared all along, when authorities often move in to put the offender in jail or the victim in a foster home.

Sexual Victimization: The More General Case

The foregoing three theories have been formulated to explain father-daughter incest and not children's sexual victimization in general. One of the hypothesized mechanisms, mother-daughter role reversal, primarily applies specifically to the nuclear family. But the other theories, fear of abandonment and social isolation, can apply to sexual abuse in general.

Quite a bit of the reported sexual abuse takes place between members of the extended family: grandfathers, uncles, cousins, and other peripheral relatives. It is quite readily seen how both social isolation and its subculture, more tolerant of intrafamily sex, could explain these cases of sexual abuse outside the nuclear family. Fear of abandonment also can draw members of an extended family into a forbidden sexual relationship.

Other theories using family factors have emerged from the study of the more general case of sexual victimization both inside and outside the family.

(9) Marital Conflict

Marital conflict can make children vulnerable to sexual victimization by anybody, in two ways. First, it often subjects them to contradictory messages about sex, and the resulting sexual confusion hampers their ability to handle potential sexual abuse. Second, the conflict is hard on the child and leaves him or her insecure about where to turn for protection. When a child feels unprotected, he or she is more apt to become entangled in a sexual situation with an adult in which he or she feels helpless (Weiss *et al.,* 1955).

(10) Oversexualization

It has been suggested that some families are oversexualized, and children from these families are more vulnerable to sexual abuse, even outside the family (Litin *et al.,* 1956). Children in such families have inappropriate sexual models and an unusual kind of sexual socialization. Moreover, they are sexually stimulated by their own parents, perhaps not directly, but as a result of talk or exposure to unusual sexual behavior. These two factors make them vulnerable to sexual involvements with adults.

(11) Poor Supervision

Children are vulnerable to sexual abuse when they are poorly supervised (De Francis, 1969). This theory echoes ideas expressed in the two preceding theories, except that it is more general. Not just family conflict or oversexualization, but any situation resulting in neglect of a child can lead to vulnerability to sexual abuse.

Social and Cultural Sources

Sexual victimization of children is not universal. There are societies where it is not known to occur (Mead, 1968), and there are undoubtedly parts of our own society where it is less common. Unfortunately, we know little about the demography of sexual abuse. Although anthropology has taken a lively interest in why incest is almost universally tabooed, it has devoted little attention to the related question: why is the violation of the incest taboo more common in some societies than in others?

It is understandable that anthropology would have a difficult time addressing our question: what are the causes of sexual victimization? The concept itself is so culturally relative. In some societies sexual contact takes place on a regularly sanctioned basis between adults and children (Ford and Beach, 1951). It is not a deviant act and no victimization would be said to take place. For example, in some societies homosexual acts between men and boys play a part in tribal ritual. Among the Keraki of new Guinea, each prepubescent boy passes through an initiation in which he is introduced to anal intercourse by one of the tribe's older men (Ford and Beach, 1951). The same source cites several other such instances in other societies.

However, all societies prohibit most adult-child sexual contact, and the incest taboo, one form of this restriction, is virtually universal (Weinberg, 1955). Where adult-child sex is permitted, it is either in highly ritualized and structured circumstances or not considered sexual. What is important about sexual victimization in our own society is that this rather important taboo is violated fairly often. There are two major theories that account for the frequency of this violation from a social and cultural point of view.

(12) Male Supremacy

Sexual victimization may be as common as it is in our society because of its degree of male supremacy. It is one way in which men, the dominant status group, control women. To maintain control, men need a vehicle by which women can be punished, brought into line, and socialized to a subordinate status. Sexual victimization and the threat of it are useful in keeping women intimidated (Brownmiller, 1975). Inevitably the process starts in childhood with the victimization of girl children.

Whether or not it functions to maintain male dominance as Brownmiller argues, in a male-dominated society the sexual exploitation of women and children by men is certainly easier. Sex in any society is a valuable commodity, and a dominant group—such as men—will try to rig things to maximize their access to it. The cultural beliefs that underpin the male-dominated system contribute to making women and children sexually vulnerable. For example, to the extent that family members are regarded as possessions, men can take unusual and usually undetected liberties with them. The fact that the male sexual urge is viewed as overpowering and in need of satisfaction allows men to rationalize escapades of antisocial behavior, such as sexual abuse. In a system of severe sexual and generational inequality, women and children lack the resources to defend themselves against such sexual victimization.

The theory is fairly effective in explaining the sexual abuse of women by men and the preponderance of male offenders and girl victims. Children, however, are a subordinate group in almost every society, and probably have more power in our society than most. What the theory does less well at explaining is why, given their universal powerlessness, children are often sexually exploited in some societies and in others they are not.

(13) Social Fragmentation

Sexual abuse is common in this society, according to another theory, because of the increasing isolation of individuals and families. Although no one yet has formally articulated this theory to account for sexual abuse (but see Frederick Cuber of Odessey Institute quoted in Dudar, 1977), it can be used to explain many kinds of family and sexual pathology and is readily adaptable to sexual abuse as well.

We discussed earlier the theory that incest tends to occur among isolated families and in isolated subcultures. Some theorists have alleged that isolation is, in fact, the dominant feature of our society. The isolation encompasses not just families but also individuals and results from increased mobility and the disintegration of neighborhoods, communities, and kin networks (Lasch, 1977; Parsons, 1949; Slater, 1968).

As mentioned earlier, isolation facilitates sexual abuse in two ways. It reduces the intensity of general social supervision, so that all kinds of deviance can increase. Second, it deprives people of socially sanctioned forms of support and intimacy, so that they may turn to forms that are taboo. Sexual abuse is thus a symptom of pervasive loneliness.

Although both these theories leave certain aspects of the problem undiscussed, they highlight a need to analyze sexual victimization from the point of view of the organization of society as a whole, and not just as the outcome of the idiosyncrasies of certain individuals, families, and subgroups.

The Consequences to the Victims

There are still two more theories we need to review. These are theories not about causes but about consequences, and they have generated more furor than most of the previous theories combined.

Among those who study the problem, an intense dispute has raged for more than forty years over how serious a problem sexual abuse really is. On the one hand, there are those who argue that although generally unpleasant, the vast majority of sexual offenses against children are rather innocuous affairs best treated as one of the minor and transient hazards of childhood. Meanwhile, others point out the many case histories of children who have been permanently scarred by the experience, alleging that we have not yet begun to recognize the true toll of this widespread problem.

The first group tends to argue things as follows. The innocence of childhood, they say, is a form of natural protection against the long-term effects of sexual abuse. A great many ordinary things are frightening to children—a trip to the doctor, a ride on an airplane—but by the same token the pain passes quickly. The same is true of sexual abuse.

Moreover, children have only a dim sense of adult sexuality. What may seem like a horrible violation of social taboos from an adult perspective need not be so to a child. A sexual experience with an adult may be something unusual, vaguely unpleasant, even traumatic at the moment, but not a horror story. Most children's sexual experiences involve encounters with fondlers and exhibitionists, Kinsey pointed out, and "it is difficult to understand why a child, except for its cultural conditioning, should be disturbed at having its genitals touched, or disturbed at seeing the genitalia of other persons." (Kinsey, 1953, p. 121). Most of the women who reported such contacts in Kinsey's sample did not appear to suffer any long-term consequences (Gagnon, 1965). One other survey (Landis, 1956) and several other case studies (Bender and Grugett, 1952; Burton, 1968; Yorukoclu and Kemph, 1969) have also found children to be relatively unscathed.

On the other hand, there is no lack of reports of traumatic outcomes of such sexual experiences. Hospital emergency rooms, for example, are regularly visited by child victims of sex offenses, and the children seem to suffer many of the same severe consequences as do adult women who have been raped (Burgess and Holmstrom, 1974). There is confusion, crying, depression, and subsequently a sense of shame, guilt, and awareness of stigma. These emotions endure for some time.

It has been noted that child victims fare better to some extent than adult rape victims because they are less likely to have suffered massive physical coercion or threat (Peters, 1976), but not because they are so quick to forget. The fact that so many child victims fail to report their experiences to anyone, even parents, is powerful evidence that the experience is surrounded by conflict.

The picture from clinical records on adults who were former child victims also tends to support this view. Psychotherapists report an unusually large number of child sex victims among their clients (Herman and Hirschman, 1977; Swift, 1977), and note that women with such experiences are often suffering from depression (Henderson, 1972; Molnar and Cameron, 1975; Sloane and Karpinsky, 1942) and difficulty in relating to men (Herman and Hirschman, 1977).

Studies of specific deviant groups also reveal frequent experiences of sexual abuse in the histories of these people. A large proportion of female drug addicts (Benward and Densen-Gerber, 1975) and prostitutes (James and Meyerding, 1977) were found to have incest in their backgrounds. Adolescent runaways also commonly appear to be child sex victims (Weber, 1977). The trauma of these experiences does not easily fade away, say these observers. Sexual abuse victims are often doubly and triply victimized over an extended period of time, once by the offender and then again by parents, relatives, and the social agencies appointed to handle the problem. Parents often blame the child for getting into trouble. Finally, the police, social workers, and courts often subject the victims to brutal and insensitive interrogation, publicity, and exposure, which compounds the trauma (Burgess *et al.,* 1978; Schultz, 1975).

Many comments have been and will be made about this controversy before it is settled. Only three very elementary observations will be made here.

1. Obviously *some* people have been traumatized by early childhood sexual experiences (even this is conceded by the antialarmists), but the argument appears to be over whether such trauma is typical or occurs only in isolated cases. Actually, the real dispute is more of a political one: is this a social problem worthy, because of its serious harmful consequences, of a massive mobilization. It seems to me that even if only a small number of children are harmed by these experiences, it is still worthy of mobilization. So the real question to be answered is not whether or not children are harmed, but how are they harmed, in what instances, and how it can be avoided.

2. In favor of the antialarmists, it must be mentioned that the reports of trauma are subject to the clinical fallacy. Therapists, clinics, and drug treatment facilities are by definition dealing with traumatized individuals. It is not clear whether, for each person who seems to be badly affected by the childhood sexual experience, there are many others who were not affected.

Moreover, there is the additional difficulty of identifying the exact trauma-inducing factor. Many of the people reporting childhood sexual experiences also come from environments containing plenty of other trauma-inducing experiences (Geiser and Norberta, 1976). Are their current problems caused by the highly visible sexual experience or by some of the other environmental factors, the family disorganization, for example? These are strands of the puzzle that need to be disentangled.

3. In criticism of the antialarmists, however, it must be said that they have often demanded proof of unreasonably serious difficulties before accepting that any trauma occurred. If a person avoids mental hospitalization, manages to marry, and becomes a parent, antialarmist researchers have often concluded that no serious damage took place. This view seems overly optimistic. Even if the result were something so "comparatively" minor and subjective as an inability to feel comfortable in the presence of older men, it needs to be taken seriously as evidence of deleterious long-term effects.

REFERENCES

Bagley, C. Incest behavior and incest taboo. *Social Problems,* 1969, *16,* 505–519.

Bender, L., and Blau, A. The reaction of children to sexual relations with adults. *American Journal of Orthopsychiatry,* 1937, *7,* 500–518.

Bender, L., and Grugett, A. A follow up report on children who had atypical sexual experiences. *American Journal of Orthopsychiatry,* 1952, *22,* 825–837.

Benward, J., and Densen-Gerber, J. *Incest as a causative factor in anti-social behavior: an exploratory study.* Paper presented at the American Academy of Forensic Sciences, February 1975.

Browning, D. and Boatman, B. Incest: Children at risk. *American Journal of Psychiatry,* 1977, *134,* 69–72.

Brownmiller, S. *Against our will: Men, women and rape.* New York: Simon and Schuster, 1975.

Burgess, A. W., Groth, A. N., Holmstrom, L. L., and Sgroi, S. M. *Sexual assault of children and adolescents.* Lexington, Mass.: Lexington Books, 1978.

Burgess, A. W., and Holmstrom, L. L. *Rape: Victims of crisis.* Bowie, Md.: Robert Brady, 1974.

Burton, L. *Vulnerable children.* London: Routledge and Kegan Paul, 1968.

Cohen, M. L. and Boucher, R. Misunderstandings about sex criminals. *Sexual Behavior,* 1972, 57–62.

Cormier, B., Kennedy, M., and Sangowicz, J. Psychodynamics of father-daughter incest. *Canadian Psychiatric Association Journal,* 1962, *7,* 207–217.

Curtis, L. Present and future measures of victimization in forcible rape. In M. Walker and S. Brodsky (Eds.), *Sexual assault: The victim and the rapist.* Lexington, Mass.: D. C. Heath, 1976.

De Francis, V. *Protecting the child victim of sex crimes committed by adults.* Denver, Col.: American Humane Assn., 1969.

Dudar, H. America discovers pornography. *Ms.,* August 1977, p. 47.

Ford, C. S. and Beach, F. *Patterns of sexual behavior.* New York: Harper and Row, 1951.

Gagnon, J. Female child victims of sex offenses. *Social Problems,* 1965, *13,* 176–192.

Gebhard, P., Gagnon, J., Pomeroy, W., and Christenson, C. *Sex offenders: An analysis of types.* New York: Harper and Row, 1965.

Geiser, R. L. and Norberta, M. Sexual disturbance in young children. *American Journal of Maternal and Child Nursing,* 1976, *1,* 187–194.

Glueck, B. C., Jr. Psychodynamic patterns in sex offenders. *Psychiatric Quarterly,* 1954, *28,* 1–21.

Groth, N. Guidelines for assessment and management of the offender. In Burgess *et al.* (Eds.), *Sexual assault of children and adolescents.* Lexington, Mass.: Lexington Books, 1978.

Hammer, E. F., and Glueck, B. C., Jr. Psychodynamic patterns in sex offense: A four factor theory. *Psychiatric Quarterly,* 1957, *3,* 325–345.

Henderson, J. Incest: A synthesis of data. *Canadian Psychiatric Association Journal,* 1972, *17,* 299–313.

Herman J., and Hirschman, L. Father-daughter incest. *Signs,* 1977, *2,* 1–22.

James, J., and Meyerding, J. Early sexual experiences as a factor in prostitution. *Archives of Sexual Behavior,* 1977, *7* (1), 31–42.

Kaufman, I., Peck, A., and Tagiuri, C. K. The family constellation and overt incestuous relations between father and daughter. *American Journal of Orthopsychiatry,* 1954, *24,* 266–279.

Kinsey, A., *et al. Sexual behavior in the human female.* Philadelphia: Saunders, 1953.

Krafft-Ebing, R. von. *Psychopathia sexualis.* New York: Physicians and Surgeons Book Co., 1935.

Landis, J. Experiences of 500 children with adult sexual deviants. *Psychiatric Quarterly Supplement,* 1956, *30,* 91–109.

Lasch, C. *Haven in a heartless world.* New York: Basic Books, 1977.

Litin, E., Giffin, M., and Johnson, A. Parental influence in unusual sexual behavior in children. *Psychoanalytic Quarterly,* 1956, *25,* 37–55.

Lustig, N., Dresser, J. W., Spellman, S. W., and Murray, T. B. Incest: A family group survival pattern. *Archives of General Psychiatry,* 1966, *14,* 31–40.

McCaghy, C. Drinking and deviance disavowal: The case of child molesters. *Journal of Social Problems,* 1968, *16,* 43–49.

McGuire, R. J., Carlisle, J. M., and Young, B. G. Sexual deviations as conditioned behavior: A hypothesis. *Behavior Research and Therapy,* 1965, *2,* 185–190.

Mead, M. *Sex and temperament in primitive societies.* New York: Dell, 1968.

Minuchin, S. *Families and family therapy.* Cambridge, Mass.: Harvard, 1974.

Mohr, J. W., Turner, R. E., and Jerry, M. B. *Pedophilia and exhibitionism.* Toronto: University of Toronto, 1964.

Molnar, B., and Cameron, P. Incest syndromes: Observations in a General Hospital Psychiatric Unit. *Canadian Psychiatric Association Journal,* 1975, *20,* 1–24.

Nabokov, V. *Lolita.* New York: Putnam's Sons, 1955.

Parsons, T. Social structure of the family. In R. N. Anshen (Ed.), *The family: Its function and destiny.* New York: Harper, 1949.

Peters, J. J. Children who were victims of sexual assault and the psychology of offenders. *American Journal of Psychotherapy,* 1976, *30,* 398–412.

Ramer, L. *Your sexual bill of rights.* New York: Exposition Press, 1973.

Riemer, S. A research note on incest. *American Journal of Sociology,* 1940, *45,* 566.

Rush, F. The sexual abuse of children: A feminist point of view. In N. Connell and C. Wilson (Eds.), *Rape: The first sourcebook for women.* New York: NAL Plume, 1974.

Schultz, L. G. The child as sex victim: Socio-legal perspectives. In *Rape Victimology.* Springfield, Ill.: C. C. Thomas, 1975.

Silverman, R. Victim precipitation: An examination of the concept. In I. Drapkin and E. Viano (Eds.), *Victimology: A new focus,* Vol. I. Lexington, Mass.: Lexington Books, 1974.

Slater, P. *Pursuit of loneliness.* Boston: Beacon, 1968.

Sloane, P., and Karpinsky, F. Effects of incest on participants. *American Journal of Orthopsychiatry,* 1942, *12,* 666–673.

Summit, R., and Kryso, J. Sexual abuse of children: a clinical spectrum. *American Journal of Orthopsychiatry,* 1978, *48,* 237–251.

Swanson, D. W. Adult sexual abuse of children. *Diseases of the Nervous System,* 1968, *29,* 677–683.

Swift, C. Sexual victimization of children: An urban mental health center survey. *Victimology,* 1977, *2,* 322–327.

Virkkunen, M. Incest offenses and alcoholism. *Medicine, Science and Law,* April 1974, *14,* 124–128.

Weber, E. Sexual abuse begins at home. *Ms.,* April 1977, pp. 64–67.

Weinberg, S. K. *Incest behavior.* New York: Citadel, 1955.

Weiner, I. Father-daughter incest: A clinical report. *Psychiatric Quarterly,* 1962, *36,* 607.

Weiss, J., Rogers, E., Darwin, M., and Dutton, C. A study of girl sex victims. *Psychiatric Quarterly,* 1955, *29*(1), 1–27.

Yorukoclu, A., and Kemph, J. Children not severely damaged by incest. *Journal of the Academy of Child Psychiatry,* 1969, *8,* 606.

Zaphiris, A. *Assessment and treatment for sexually abused families.* Workshop presented at the meeting of the National Conference on Child Abuse and Neglect, April 1978.

Reflection

DAVID FINKELHOR

Sexually Victimized Children was written largely as a Ph.D. dissertation in sociology at the University of New Hampshire in 1978. Somewhat before that time, I learned about the topic of sexual abuse from writers like Florence Rush and Louise Armstrong, and also from local child welfare professionals whom I had encountered. This seemed to me to be an emerging social problem badly in need of social scientific research. In thinking about how to approach it, I was particularly influenced by the experience of Murray Straus, who was my dissertation adviser, and his former graduate student, Richard Gelles. Two things seemed clear at the time from their work, and from a number of other sociologists in the fields of both criminology and sexuality. One was that experiences that were generally considered as rare and deviant occurred at a much higher frequency among the population than most people imagined. Second was that sensitively designed survey research could motivate people to disclose stigmatized experiences that were generally considered too private to talk about. I wasn't yet as thoroughly convinced of this second conclusion as I later became, but it seemed as though college students at least might be a good place to start to find out. They were also handy, and didn't need a tremendous amount of research funding to study.

A lot of people have subsequently followed this model and used college student samples for studies of sexual abuse and other forms of intimate violence. I myself have not done any additional student studies, mostly out of concerns that these populations are not truly representative. I have instead turned my attention to general population surveys, an approach for which I think the efficacy of asking about sexual abuse and other forms and intimate violence has been clearly established.

My early work in *Sexually Victimized Children* was succeeded by a considerable volume of similar research looking at the long-term effects of retrospectively recalled sexual abuse and other forms of child maltreatment. These studies were very important at an earlier stage in trying to establish the potentially great developmental significance and importance of child maltreatment. However, I have come to the conclusion that for the most part this retrospective research is no longer so useful in the advancement of the field, which from my point of view has entered another stage.

The retrospective research model, from my point of view, is not adequate to disentangling the various complex sets of factors occurring before, in and around, and after abusive episodes, and thus has reached its limits in understanding how abuse affects development. Even more importantly, the retrospective research design doesn't allow us to focus enough on the things that can be changed to prevent abuse and modify its negative impact. So at the present time, my research focuses much more on studies of children themselves.

Another serious problem with the retrospective research, represented by my early studies, is that it portrays the experiences of victims in a different historical era, one that had not yet been touched by public awareness about family violence, women's victimization, and child maltreatment. I believe those changed historical circumstances have altered the experience of victims, and make it hard to generalize any longer from the older research, important as it has been.

CHAPTER

5 The Sexual Abuse of Afro-American and White-American Women in Childhood

GAIL WYATT

Introduction

There is empirical evidence to suggest that in America black women may be more frequently victims of sexual abuse than white women. This documentation of the sexual abuse of women and children has created a composite picture of a potential rape victim as a young, unmarried, black female of a lower socio-economic background who still attends school [1]. Black women have also been reported to be at risk for both rape and child sexual abuse across all age groups [2–7]. However, there is little verification regarding the accuracy of this composite picture for nonclinical populations.

Until recently, research regarding the sexual abuse of white women has had limited generalizability to larger populations because select samples [3, 7, 9, 10] or restrictive definitions of sexual abuse have been utilized [11]. One study has documented the prevalence of child sexual abuse in a community sample, but its generalizability to other ethnic groups is limited [12].

This study examined sexual abuse of a comparable and representative community sample of Afro-American and white-American women to provide empirical documentation regarding the experiences of child sexual abuse for both ethnic groups of women.

Literature

In the last 10 years, literature describing the experience of sexual abuse among women in childhood has increased [6–12]. Research with clinical samples has generated most of the findings related to black women [1–6]. However, these studies have a number of shortcomings that limit our understanding of the abuse experiences as distinct or similar to the experiences of other ethnic groups. They have included low income families exclusively [6, 9], utilized small unrepresentative samples [7, 11–13] or they have excluded ethnic minorities altogether [8]. Additionally, black women ranging in income, education and marital status have been overlooked in research on child sexual abuse.

Generally, black samples have been reported as having a higher prevalence of sexual abuse [1–5], although no ethnic differences have been noted in some of the circumstances around the incidents. Only two studies have not found a higher prevalence of sexual abuse in childhood for black women [14, 15]. However, generalizations to larger populations are again limited by the samples studied: drug abusers and college students, respectively.

Research on non-clinical samples has identified the increase in reports of child sexual abuse among white, mostly young, well-educated groups of women [10, 11]. Only within the last five years has a representative community sample ranging in demographic characteristics reported the prevalence of child sexual abuse [12]. Interestingly, Russell's finding that 54% of her sample reported at least one abuse experience before age 18 was higher than previous reports.

The increase in the prevalence of abuse can partly be accounted for by the types of behaviors included in the definition of abuse, the methodology utilized and in the randomness of the sample. However, although the ethnic minorities in Russell's sample are roughly representative of the percentages of ethnic minority residents in San Francisco, information regarding the demographic characteristics of each sample of ethnic minorities and their comparability to the white sample is not yet available [16].

The experience of sexual abuse in childhood needs to be examined for representative community samples ranging in demographic characteristics, in order for generalizations to be made to larger populations including both Afro-American and white women. This study examined the prevalence of child sexual abuse in a sample of Afro-American and white American women, reflecting the composition of the population of women 18–36 years residing in Los Angeles County. The prevalence of child sexual abuse and the circumstances under which it occurred for both ethnic groups will be discussed.

Method

The method of sampling involved a multi-stage stratified probability sample using quotas to recruit comparable samples of Afro-American and white American women ages 18 to 36 years. The age criteria was used to obtain subjects who were not minors and who could participate without parental consent. Secondly, the age range allowed for the examination of changes in prevalence rates: women 27–36 years who were born after World War II and women 17 to 26 years, born in the 1960s during the sexual revolution.

Los Angeles was selected as the location for the study because of the availability of samples of both desired ethnic groups with a wide range of demographic characteristics. The sampling procedure was based upon 20,000 computer readable addresses for the Los Angeles Metropolitan Area Survey (LAMAS), conducted semiannually by the UCLA Institute for Social Science Research [17]. The actual quotas used for the study were based upon the population of Afro-American women 18 to 36 years of age, ranging in education, marital status and the presence of children. For this study, women are asked to identify their own ethnic identity [18].

The subjects were obtained by random-digit dialing of telephone prefixes in Los Angeles County combined with four randomly generated numbers. The first prefixes were selected to represent specific areas in the County where potential subjects might be located and the final set of prefixes represented the remaining areas in the County. While 11,834 telephone numbers were generated, 6,562 were found to be unusable numbers. The remaining 5,272 eventuated to 1,348 households in which a woman resided. Of the women who met the demographic criteria, 709 women agreed to participate and 266 refused. There were 335 women who terminated telephone contact before information regarding their demographic characteristics could be obtained. Excluding those women, there was a 27% refusal rate. The estimated rate of refusal including those who terminated phone contact before their eligibility could be assessed, as well as those who could not be contacted (i.e., no answers) but who might have been eligible was 33%. However, if the 335 women who terminated contact were considered, the refusal rate would increase to 45%. Although the latter refusal rate is higher than desired, it should be noted that this is the only multiethnic community sample in research on sexuality or sexual abuse with comparable demographic characteristics of both ethnic groups. In order to meet the desired quotas of women by demographic characteristics described above, the first 248 women were interviewed: 126 Afro-American women and 122 white American women. Table 5.1 illustrates the comparability of their demographic characteristics. Considering the other control variables, it was not possible to match both samples on income level. However, the range extended from less than $5,000 to above $50,000 per year, with comparability between groups except at the very low income levels. Of those women reporting less than $5,000 per year, 80% were Afro-American and 20% were white women. However, the discrepancies between groups were also found in LA County statistics for income, by ethnicity.

The numbers of interviewed women in the quota categories were compared by the same demographic characteristics with 1980 census data for Afro-American women in Los Angeles County, using a chi-square test as a measure of agreement. The results, together with the randomness of the random-digit dialing method of selection, support the general representativeness of the sample based upon the quotas.

In order to allow for both within and across ethnic group comparisons, the quotas set for white women were selected to match those for Afro-American women. However, as a consequence, the sample of white women did not match the population distribution characteristics for white women in Los Angeles County as well as they did for their Afro-American peers. For example, as is evident in Table 5.1, in the younger group (18 to 26 years), women ranging in marital status were under- or overrepresented. In the older group (27 to 36 years) women ranging in education and the presence of children were under- or overrepresented. However, if weighted estimates were made, adjusting for the discrepancies, the relative efficiencies would be 97% for the 18–26-age group and 81% for the level of education for the 27–36-age group. Efficiencies for estimates adjusted for marital status would be 85% for younger women and 96% for older women. Thus, the moderate distortions can be adjusted

TABLE 5.1 Demographic Characteristics of Multi-Stage Stratified Probability Sample of Afro-American and White American Women ($N = 248$)

	Afro-American Women (126)		White American Women (122)	
	Number	*Percent*[a]	*Number*	*Percent*[a]
Age Range				
18–26	58	46	47	39
27–36	68	54	75	61
Education				
11th Grade or Less	19	15	20	16
High School Graduate	43	34	37	30
Partial College	47	37	43	35
College Graduate	10	8	10	8
Graduate Education	7	6	12	10
Children				
No Children	38	30	53	43
1 child or more	88	70	69	58
Marital Status				
Ever married	73	58	90	74
Never married	53	42	32	26
Area of Country Reared				
North	7	6	18	15
Midwest	14	11	17	14
South	29	23	4	3
West	75	60	82	68
Moved around too much	1	-0-	1	-0-

[a]Percentages may not total 100% due to rounding.

for with little loss of efficiency in estimating population averages based upon quotas for white women.

The Procedure

When subjects agreed to participate, they were interviewed by one of four highly trained and experienced women who matched the subject's ethnicity. The interviewers underwent an intensive three-month training program, including practice interviews, scoring a videotaped interview, conducting interviews with pilot subjects and establishing consistency in coding responses.

Subjects were interviewed at the location of their choice, and were reimbursed $20.00 for their time and up to $2.50 for babysitting or transportation costs. Interviews were usually conducted in two sessions and ranged in total from 3 to 8 hours. At the completion of the interview, referrals for mental health services were provided for those subjects who expressed an interest or need.

Definition of Sexual Abuse in Childhood

The definition of sexual abuse had several components:

Types of Behaviors. Sexual abuse required contact of a sexual nature, ranging from those involving non-body contact such as solicitations to engage in sexual behavior and exhibitionism, to those involving body contact such as fondling, intercourse and oral sex.

Age of Subject. Childhood sexual abuse experiences had to occur prior to age 18, the age at which legal adult status is achieved.

Age of the Perpetrator. An experience was defined as abuse if the perpetrator was 5 years older than the subject. If the age difference between a subject and the perpetrator was less than 5 years, only situations which were not wanted by the subject and which involved some degree of coercion were included (termed peer abuse). An example of such an experience was a rape of a 14-year-old female by a 16-year-old classmate.

Relationship of Perpetrator to Subject. Experiences could involve all types of perpetrators: family members, acquaintances or strangers.

Willingness of the Subject to Participate. Experiences were considered as abuse depending upon the perpetrator's age and the willingness of the victim to participate. If the victim was 12 or younger, experiences were included if the perpetrator was older, even if she willingly participated, the reason being that children do not understand what they are consenting to and are not really free to say no to an authority figure [18]. If the victim was 13 to 17 years old, experiences were considered abusive if the perpetrator was older and if the experiences were unwanted. If the perpetrator was an age peer, regardless of the age of the victim, the experiences had to be unwanted. Consensual, exploratory sexual behaviors between minors were not included in the definition of abuse. Such a multifaceted definition differed from Finkelhor's [11] in that the age range between the victim and perpetrator was not used as a criteria for the exclusion of incidents. While Russell [12] examined only attempted or completed rapes between victims 14 to 17 years and non-family perpetrators, this definition included a range of sexual behaviors with all perpetrators, regardless of their relationship to the victim. Finally, rather than to include only incidents involving the procurement of children under age 14 only for "lewd or lascivious acts," as is specified in the California Penal Code 11165-11174, incidents involving these acts for children under age 18 are also included.

The Interview Schedule

The Wyatt Sexual History Questionnaire is a 478-item structured interview including both open- and closed-ended questions. It was developed for use in research regarding the sexual socialization of women; information regarding sex education, a range of sexual behaviors, and the extent of sexual abuse was obtained. Before its use in research, it was initially pretested on two multi-ethnic groups (77 female volunteers and on 16 pilot subjects) for clarity of information requested. Questions were arranged chronologically from childhood to adulthood so that inconsistencies in the ages at which behaviors were engaged were apparent. In cases where inconsistencies were noted, immediate clarification from the subject was possible.

Reliability was established for certain portions of the questionnaire. Each interviewer rated the severity of each abuse history on a 10-point scale at the completion of an interview. Reliability was established on a weekly basis amongst the four interviewers, and inter-rater reliability averaged .90. When 10 audio-tapes were randomly selected to be examined for accuracy of interviewers' written transcriptions of the subjects' open-ended responses to questions, only two responses out of 4,780 items were noted to have been in error.

Several additional analyses were conducted to examine the reliability of the data. Since data was collected retrospectively, subjects were asked about their demographic characteristics during telephone recruitment and again during the interview between one to nine months later. Pearson correlations ranged from .82 to 1.0.

The reliability of information collected regarding both current and past demographic characteristics of the subjects and their parents was obtained for 119 women who were interviewed for this study and re-interviewed for another study [20] one month to two years later. Pearson correlations ranged from .65 to .98. The lowest correlation ($r = .65$) was the employment status of subjects which tended to change between interviews. Overall, subjects' responses to over time were consistent, strengthening the probability that the responses to other questions were consistent, as well.

Specific questions were developed for seven types of abuse most commonly reported in the literature [11]. An additional open-ended question was asked to elicit other types of abuse the subject may have experienced, including sexual abuse committed by an age peer (peer abuse) or other sexual behaviors such as oral sex, or participation in pornographic activities. A small number of incidents (12) involving other behaviors such as unwanted kisses and solicitations to engage in sexual behaviors, were volunteered by subjects in response to question # 8. The specific items used in the interview are presented below, along with the introductory statement read to the subjects:

> It is now generally realized that many women, while they were children or adolescents, have had a sexual experience with an adult or someone older than themselves. By sexual, I mean behaviors ranging from someone exposing themselves (their genitals) to you, to someone having intercourse with you. These experiences may have involved a relative, a friend of the family, or a stranger. Some experiences are very upsetting and painful while others are not, and some may have occurred without your consent.
>
> Now I'd like you to think back to your childhood and adolescence and remember if you had any sexual experiences with a relative, a family friend, or stranger. Describe each experience completely and separately.

1. During childhood and adolescence, did anyone ever expose themselves (their sexual organs) to you?
2. During childhood and adolescence, did anyone masturbate in front of you?

3. Did a relative, family friend or stranger ever touch or fondle your body, including your breasts or genitals, or attempt to arouse you sexually?
4. During childhood and adolescence, did anyone try to have you arouse them, or touch their body in a sexual way?
5. Did anyone rub their genitals against your body in a sexual way?
6. During childhood and adolescence, did anyone attempt to have intercourse with you?
7. Did anyone have intercourse with you?
8. Did you have any other sexual experiences involving a relative, family friend, or stranger?

If a woman said that she had experienced a particular form of abuse, the interviewer asked her a series of questions about each incident. The questions on abuse were placed towards the end of the interview. This allowed sufficient time for rapport to develop between subject and interviewer before inquiring about such a sensitive area. However, it was not unusual for subjects themselves to disclose abuse incidents in response to other questions earlier in the interview.

The chi-square test was used in two analyses per question: to examine differences between the two ethnic groups and the circumstances of the incidents by type of abuse (contact versus non-contact). While the chi-square statistic was useful for assessing statistical significance, the null distribution did not follow the chi-square distribution, since some tables were constructed on a per occurrence basis, with some women being represented more than once. Thus, a small simulation study assessed the effects of this departure from underlying assumptions. For each cross-classification variable, the subject's identification number was written in a random permutation order. The procedure was repeated 50 times and the resulting cross-tabulations were formed on a per occurrence basis. A chi-square was computed for each of the 50 tables per question. The statistical significance of the observed chi-square was estimated as p = exp(-log po/average log p), in which exp denotes the exponential function, po is the p value corresponding to the observed table and average log p is the average of logarithms of the p values from the randomized tables. In general, the simulation study showed that nonsignificant values remained nonsignificant, and significant p values cited are based on randomization tests.

Findings

Prevalence of Sexual Abuse

Of the sample of 248 subjects, 154 (62%) reported at least one incident of sexual abuse prior to age 18. Looking, at each ethnic group separately, 72 out of 126 Afro-American women (57%) and 82 out of 122 white women (67%) were abused. This slight ethnic difference in prevalence rates was not statistically significant, χ^2 $(2, n = 248) = 3.40, p > .05$. When all incidents of peer abuse were deleted, prevalence rates were only slightly lower—59% for the sample as a whole, 54% for Afro-American women and 65% for white women.

When incidents of solicitations and unwanted kissing were deleted as well, the rates remained at 54% for Afro-American women and dropped very slightly to 65% for white women.

In all, 305 incidents of childhood and adolescent sexual abuse were reported, 147 by Afro-American women and 158 by white women. While the total of incidents reported were quite comparable for Afro-American and white women, there was a slight, though nonsignificant ethnic difference in the number of abuse incidents per person. The percentage of abused women who reported more than one abuse incident was 52% among Afro-American women as compared to 48% among white women, $\chi^2(2, n = 153) = 1.19, p > .05$.

Since the range of sexual behaviors was so great, a further distinction was made by two categories. Incidents which involved body contact (from fondling to vaginal or oral intercourse) were termed contact abuse and those which did not (e.g., verbal propositions, exposure, and masturbation) were termed non-contact abuse. Utilizing this distinction, women in the sample were divided into three groups:

1. Non-abused. Women who reported no incidents of abuse prior to age 18;
2. Non-contact abuse. Women who reported only abuse that did not involve body contact prior to age 18; and
3. Contact abuse. Women who experienced some form of abuse that involved body contact prior to age 18. (Women who experienced both contact and non-contact abuse were included in this group.)

Among the Afro-American women, 43% were non-abused, 17% had experienced only non-contact abuse, and 40% had experienced contact abuse. Comparable figures for the white women were 33% non-abused, 16% non-contact abuse, and 51% with contact abuse. Aspects of victims' experiences will be also discussed by the categories contact and non-contact abuse.

To determine if there were generational differences in the prevalence of child sexual abuse, subjects were categorized into two age groups, 18 to 26 and 27 to 36. When their abuse histories were examined, a similar pattern was noted, but they failed to differ significantly for Afro-American, $\chi^2(2, n = 126) = 4.00, p > .05$, and white women, $\chi^2(2, n = 122) = 2.42, p > .05$.

For Afro-American women the rate for the younger age group was 31% for contact, 17% for non-contact and 52% for non-abuse. For the older age group the rate was 47% for contact, 8% for non-contact and 35% for non-abuse. For white women, the rate for the younger group was 53% for contact, 21% for non-contact and 26% for non-abuse. For the older group, the rate was 49% for contact, 13% for non-contact and 37% for non-abuse.

Since the prevalence of sexual abuse in childhood was not found to diminish significantly for women by age group, the next concern was whether women were being abused more (per person) by age group. When younger women (18–26 years) and older women (27–36 years) were examined by the number of abuse incidents they reported, no significant differences were noted, $\chi^2(2, n = 82) = .23, p > .05$. The trend was for women of both ethnic groups to have experienced slightly, but not significantly, less repeated sexual abuse (two or more incidents per person) in the younger group than in the older group.

The Type of Abuse Occurring before 18 Years of Age

The age at which subjects recalled childhood sexual abuse ranged from 2 years to 17 years. A frequency table of the types of abuse experienced in childhood and adolescence by non-body contact and contact abuse is presented in Tables 5.2 and 5.3. It should be noted that solicitations for sexual behavior and unwanted kissing constituted only 8% of non-contact incidents for Afro-American women and 9% of non-contact incidents for white American women (Table 5.2). On the other hand, experiences involving intercourse totalled 15% of the contact incidents for Afro-American women and 17% of contact incidents for their white peers (Table 5.3).

The Age at Which Abuse Occurred

The age at which victims were abused was divided into 5 groups: preschool, 2–5 years; early childhood, 6–8 years; pre-adolescence, 9–12 years; early adolescence, 13–15 years; and adolescence, 16–17 years. White women were found to have experienced significantly more abuse in the early childhood period (6 to 8 years), whereas Afro-American women reportedly experienced more abuse as pre-adolescents (9–12 years), $\chi^2(4, n = 305) = 13.18$, $p < .01$.

While there were no significant differences in the type of abuse reported involving contact or non-contact in childhood (0–12 years) or adolescence (13 and above) for Afro-American women, $\chi^2(1, n = 147) = .56$, $p > .05$, white women experienced significantly more abuse involving body contact before the age of 8, $\chi^2(4, n = 158) = 19.66$, $p < .001$.

TABLE 5.2 Types of Non-Contact Abuse by Ethnicity

	Afro-American Women (n = 67 incidents)		White American Women (n = 65 incidents)	
Type of Abuse	*N*	%	*N*	%
Exposure	34	51	31	48
Masturbation	26	39	28	43
Masturbation (peer)	1	1	0	0
Solicitations (peer)[b]	3	4	1	1
Solicitations[b]	1	1	5	8
Kiss[b]	2	3	0	0
Total	67	99[a]	65	100

[a]Percentages may not add to 100% due to rounding.

[b]Solicitations for sexual behavior and unwanted kissing were included with noncontact abuse because they were low in frequency and were less serious than other contact abuse behaviors. Additionally, persons reporting these incidences reported more serious abuse experiences, as well.

TABLE 5.3 Types of Contact Abuse by Ethnicity

	Afro-American Women (*n* = 80 incidents)		White American Women (*n* = 93 incidents)	
Type of Abuse	*N*	%	*N*	%
Fondling	32	40	35	38
Fondling (peer)	4	5	5	5
Fondling of Perpetrator	8	10	13	14
Mutual fondling (peer)	0	0	1	1
Rubbing genitals against body of Subject	5	6	5	5
Rubbing genitals (peer)	1	1	0	0
Attempted Intercourse	9	11	7	8
Attempted Intercourse (peer)	3	4	1	1
Intercourse	12	15	17	18
Intercourse (peer)	1	1	0	0
Attempted oral sex	0	0	1	1
Oral sex on Subject	2	3	3	3
Oral sex on Perpetrator	2	3	1	1
Mutual Oral Sex	1	1	2	2
Combination	0	0	2	2
Total	80	100	93	99[a]

[a]Percentages may not add to 100% due to rounding.

Where Sexual Abuse Occurred

The most common locations for childhood sexual abuse to occur for both ethnic groups were in the home of the child or perpetrator, on the street or in the neighborhood. Table 5.4 illustrates that a substantial number of incidents took place in cars. In a few reports of abuse, the location was not clearly recalled.

When responses to the location of child sexual abuse were examined by ethnicity, a chi-square test revealed that Afro-Americans appear to be slightly but not significantly at risk for child sexual abuse in locations in very close proximity to them (in their homes or neighborhoods). White women appear to be at risk for child sexual abuse at home but also in unexpected places, such as the perpetrator's home and in outdoor public places, $\chi^2(7, n = 305) = 7, p < .05$.

The location of childhood-sexual abuse was examined by type of abuse, and similar patterns were noted for both ethnic groups. Significantly more contact abuse (73%) versus non-contact abuse (27%) occurred in the homes of Afro-American women or in the perpetrator's home (39% contact abuse versus 11% non-contact incidents), $\chi^2(6, n = 147) = 44.75, p < .01$. Likewise 91% of abuse that occurred in the homes of white women and 75% of incidents occurring in the homes of the perpetrators involved contact abuse, com-

TABLE 5.4 Location of Abuse Incidents, by Ethnicity

	Incidents Reported by Afro-American Women[a]		Incidents Reported by White Women	
	N	%	*N*	%
Home of subject	48	33	32	20
Home of perpetrator	19	13	32	20
In the street	17	12	17	11
In the neighborhood	19	13	13	8
In a car	19	13	22	14
Public outdoors, i.e., playgrounds, beaches, parks and woods	6	4	20	13
Public indoors, i.e., schools, churches, libraries and shopping malls	10	6	14	9
Unclear responses	9	6	8	5
Total	147	100	158	100

[a] $\chi^2(7, n = 305) = 15.7$ $p > .05$

pared to the remaining 9% and 25% that were non-contact abuse incidents, respectively, $\chi^2(6, n = 158)$ 47, $p < .0001$.

Of the abuse occurring in the neighborhood, almost all (95%) involved non-contact abuse of Afro-American women. The remaining 5% involved contact abuse. Abuse occurring in neighborhoods of white women included 69% non-contact incidents, compared to 31% contact incidents. As expected, sexual abuse involving body contact appeared to occur indoors.

Number of Times Abuse Occurred with the Same Perpetrator

Three-fourths of the incidents reported by women of both ethnic groups (75% for Afro-American women and 76% for white American women) involved a single occurrence of abuse with a given perpetrator. For the remaining 25% of incidents, the responses of women who were abused before the age of 18 ranged from two times to so many occurrences that subjects could not recall the number. However, no significant differences between the two ethnic groups and the number of occurrences with the same perpetrator were found, $\chi^2(2, n = 304) = 1.64$, $p > .05$.

The Perpetrator

The sex, age, ethnicity and the relationship of the perpetrator to the subject are discussed as follows: Similar to other recent studies of the prevalence of sexual abuse before age 18 [11, 12], 97% of the incidents reported by Afro-American women and 100% of the incidents reported by their white peers involved abuse by male perpetrators. The four female perpetrators, including a cousin, a neighbor and a peer, abused Afro-American women.

The age of the perpetrators ranged from teenagers (who engaged in sexual activities without the consent of victims and used some form of coercion in the acts) to persons over 55 years of age. Regardless of the "myth of the dirty old man," the stereotype of the person most likely to abuse women, age was no factor in the childhood sexual abuse of these subjects. When 4 age groups were considered (19 or younger, 20 to 24, 25 to 55 and over 55), only 12 of the perpetrators were over 55 years of age. Sixty-one percent of perpetrators of abuse of both Afro-American and white women were in the 25 to 55 age group.

As in other studies [11, 15], 81% of women of both ethnic groups were abused by a perpetrator of their own ethnic group, $\chi^2(2, n = 303) = 169, 48, p < .001$. Additionally, a Fisher's Exact Test [21] revealed that black perpetrators involved Afro-American victims in significantly more contact abuse than non-contact incidents, $p < .0001$. When cross-ethnic group abuse did occur for Afro-American women, one-third (33%) of non-contact incidents were perpetrated by white and Hispanic males compared to 8% of contact abuse incidents. On the other hand, black, Hispanic, native American and Asian men were involved in 14% of non-contact and 22% of contact abuse incidents with white women. These perpetrators included a broader range of ethnic group membership, particularly for contact abuse incidents.

The relationship of the perpetrator to the victim (Table 5.5) is one of the most controversial and alarming areas of child sexual abuse research. The presence of a stepfather in the home has been identified as a risk factor for child sexual abuse of the most serious type [12]. Although Afro-American women reported more abuse incidents involving stepfathers, mother's boyfriends, foster fathers, male cousins and other relatives than did white women, this difference did not reach statistical significance, $\chi^2(3, n = 303) = 6.75, p > .05$. While the risk of stepfathers as perpetrators has been acknowledged in the literature [11, 12], the finding in this study regarding the slight increase in stepfathers and cousins as perpetrators of abuse of Afro-American women may be related to differences in the family constellation between the two ethnic groups [22]. For instance, a larger number (28 or 22%) of black women lived in families with stepfathers during childhood or adolescence, as compared to 16 or 13% of white women. Additionally, for the period of childhood or adolescence, four Afro-American women reported that male cousins lived in their home; white women reported only one such case. While it was not possible to determine whether these specific persons living in the home of the subject were the perpetrators of the incidents, this information suggests that there may have been slightly more opportunities for abuse to occur between stepfathers and male cousins and specifically, Afro-American female child victims.

When the relationship of the perpetrator to the victim by type of abuse was examined for white women, the proportion of contact abuse was 31% for strangers, 100% by fathers

TABLE 5.5 Relationship of Perpetrator to Subject, by Ethnicity

	Incidents Reported by Afro-American Women		Incidents Reported by White American Women	
Perpetrators	*N*	%	*N*	%
Strangers	55	37	81	51
Father	1	1	3	2
Stepfather/Mother's boyfriend/ Foster father	13	9	6	4
Uncle	10	7	9	6
Grandfather	1	1	0	0
Brother/Stepbrother	5	3	5	3
Male cousin	12	8	7	4
Authority figures, i.e., ministers, teachers, doctors	3	2	6	4
Persons known to subject, i.e., babysitters, neighbors, friends of family	47	32	41	26
Total	147	100	158	100

and stepfathers, 90% for other relatives and 85% for acquaintances, $\chi^2(3, n = 158) = 54.55$, $p < .0001$.

For Afro-American women, the proportion of contact abuse was 15% for strangers, 93% for fathers and stepfathers; 75% for other relatives and 76% for acquaintances, $\chi^2(3, n = 147) = 7.76$, $p < .0001$. Apparently abuse involving body contact was more often committed by a family member or someone known to a victim, regardless of ethnicity.

Methods Used to Involve Subjects in Abuse Incidents

The patterns of responses were almost identical for methods used to involve both ethnic groups in abuse incidents. About 25% of incidents each involved physical coercion or happened without any apparent warning. The latter category more often included perpetrators who appeared suddenly in front of victims, exhibiting their genitals or masturbating. Only about 10% of incidents involved the psychological coercion of the victims. The remaining 15% of incidents included situations that began as a game and resulted in abuse, and a few other methods.

When methods of involving subjects were examined in regard to contact and noncontact abuse, incidents involving psychological and physical coercion were used more in the contact abuse of both Afro-American women, $\chi^2(2, n = 144) = 54.38, p < .0001$, and on their white peers, $\chi^2(2, n = 156) = 17.88, p < .0001$. Of the incidents that occurred spontaneously, the proportion involving non-contact abuse was 91% among Afro-American women and 68% among white women. The remaining 9% and 32%, respectively, were contact abuse incidents.

Summary and Conclusions

This study examined the prevalence and circumstances of child sexual abuse in a multiethnic community sample of women 18 to 36 years of age, representing the composition of Los Angeles County by certain demographic characteristics. The prevalence of child abuse for this sample of 248 women was higher than any previously cited in comparable studies [11, 12]. The differences are most likely due to the scope of the definition, the range of the sample across demographic characteristics, and the fact that abuse was one of several topics covered well into an extensive structured interview. Even when less serious types of abuse and incidents committed by peers are deleted, the prevalence remains higher than previous reports. Several measures of reliability of this data demonstrated the subjects' accurate recall of personal information over time and provided some assurance regarding the accuracy of their recall of more sensitive abuse experiences.

Notwithstanding the prevalence of child sexual abuse of women since the mid 1940s, its occurrence apparently has not diminished significantly even in the last 20 years, although women born in the 1960s were a bit less likely to be repeatedly abused. Society's increased awareness of child abuse may have contributed to slightly less abuse experienced by women 18 to 26 years of age. However, with no significant dimunition in the prevalence of child sexual abuse and its repeated occurrence in females before age 18, there is still cause for great concern. Considering the prevalence of sexual abuse before 18 years of age for this sample of women, 1 in 2.5 Afro-American women experienced some form of abuse involving body contact as did 1 in 2 white American women. Based upon the results of this study, the profile of Afro-American women who are most at risk for child sexual abuse has been expanded upon from that developed in previous research [1]. Young Afro-American pre-teens are most likely to experience contact abuse in their homes, by mostly black male perpetrators, who may be nuclear or extended family members. Incidents involving non-contact abuse may occur in neighborhoods and be perpetrated by white men.

These findings also generated a profile for white women most at risk for sexual abuse in childhood. White women may be at risk during the early childhood and pre-school years by mostly white perpetrators, who may involve them in contact abuse incidents indoors and non-contact abuse incidents out-of-doors. Young white children are also more likely to experience contact abuse by men of other ethnic groups. Both ethnic groups of potential victims share the likelihood that physical or psychological coercion will be used in incidents involving body contact.

In light of these findings for women 18 to 36 years of age, sexual abuse in childhood appears to be of equal concern today for Afro-American and white women alike. However, while the circumstances under which these incidents occurred were similar, the age at which abuse occurred for Afro-American women was later in childhood than for white women. The relationship of the age of the victim and other effects of the abuse experience upon community samples needs to be explored further in research.

REFERENCES

1. Katz, S. and Mazur, M. A. *Understanding the Rape Victim: A Synthesis of Research Findings.* John Wiley and Sons, New York (1979).
2. Hinderland, M. J. and Davis, B. L. Forcible rape in the United States: A statistical profile. In: *Forcible Rape: The Crime, the Victim and the Offender,* D. Chappell, R. Geis and G. Geis (Eds.). Columbia University Press, New York (1977).
3. Miller, J., Moeller, D., Kaufman, A., Awasto, P., Pathak, D. and Christy, J. Recidivism among sexual assault victims. *American Journal of Psychiatry* 135:1103–1104 (1978).
4. National Crime Panel Survey Report. Criminal victimization surveys in the nation's five largest cities. U.S. Department of Justice, Law Enforcement Assistance Administration, National Criminal Justice Information and Statistics Service, U.S. Government Printing Office, Washington, DC (1975).
5. Amir, M. *Patterns of Forcible Rape.* University of Chicago Press, Chicago (1971).
6. Peters, J. J. Children who are victims of sexual assault and the psychology of offenders. *American Journal of Psychotherapy* 30:393–421 (1976).
7. Kercher, G. and McShane, M. The prevalence of child sexual abuse victimization in an adult sample of Texas residents. *Child Abuse & Neglect* 8:495–502 (1984).
8. Kinsey, A. C., Pomeroy, W. B., Martin, C. E. and Gebhard, P. H. *Sexual Behavior in the Human Female.* W. B. Saunders, Philadelphia (1953).
9. Defrancis, V. Protecting the child victim of sex crimes committed by adults. Final report. The American Humane Association, Children's Division, Denver (1969).
10. Fromuth, M. E. The long-term psychological impact of childhood sexual abuse. Unpublished doctoral dissertation, Auburn University, Auburn, AL (1983).
11. Finkelhor, D. *Sexually Victimized Children.* The Free Press, New York (1979).
12. Russell, D. E. H. The incidence and prevalence of intrafamilial and extrafamilial sexual abuse of female children. *Child Abuse & Neglect* 7:133–146 (1983).
13. Landis, J. T. Experiences of 500 children with adult sexual deviation. *Psychiatric Quarterly Supplement,* 30:91–109 (1956).
14. Benward, J. and Densen-Gerber, J. Incest as a causative factor in antisocial behavior: An exploratory study. *Contemporary Drug Problems* 4:323–340 (1975).
15. Sedney, M. A. and Brooks, B. Factors associated with childhood sexual abuse in a non-clinical population. In: *Psychotherapeutic Perspectives in the Treatment of Child Sexual Abuse,* A. G. Kaplan (Chair), symposium presented at the meeting of the American Psychological Association. Los Angeles (1981).
16. Russell, D. E. H. *The Secret Trauma.* Basic Books, New York (In press).
17. Bureau of the Census. Statistical abstracts of the United States. U.S. Department of Commerce, Washington, DC 20233 (1980).
18. Afro-American women were of African descent, whose parentage also included a variety of other ethnic and racial groups found in America. White women were of Caucasian descent, whose parentage

included women of Jewish heritage as well. Women in both ethnic groups spent at least 6 of the first 12 years of their childhood in the United States.

19. Finkelhor, D. *Child Sexual Abuse: New Theory and Research.* Free Press, New York (1984).
20. Peters, S. D. The relationship between childhood sexual victimization and adult depression among Afro-American and white women, unpublished doctoral dissertation, University of California at Los Angeles (1984).
21. Fisher, R. A. *Statistical Methods for Research Workers,* (12th ed.). E. Liver & Boyd Ltd., London (1954).
22. Billingsley, A. *Black Families in White America.* Prentice Hall, Englewood Cliffs (1968).

Reflection

CAROLYN M. WEST

As a Black feminist scholar, I have devoted my academic career to creating culturally sensitive research that addresses the complexity of violence in the lives of women, particularly women who are marginalized, such as women of color and lesbians. My recent book, *Violence in the Lives of Black Women: Battered, Black, and Blue* (2002a), is a collaborative effort to articulate a Black feminist approach that considers how living at the intersection of various forms of oppression, including racism, classism, sexism, and homophobia converges to shape Black women's experience with violence. A challenging task, indeed!

My objective was to build on previous research, while avoiding three common mistakes. Specifically, researchers have used a color blind approach, conducted inappropriate racial comparisons, and failed to investigate within-group differences (West, 2002b). In order to accomplish this goal, I turned to Gail Wyatt's (1985) article, "The Sexual Abuse of Afro-American and White-American Women in Childhood." In the not so distant past, researchers were reluctant to explore ethnic differences in sexual abuse. In fact, some investigators avoided the topic. Judith Herman (1981) explains why she excluded African American women in her study of incest survivors:

> We made the decision to restrict the interviewing to white women in order to avoid even the possibility that the information gathered might be used to fuel idle speculation about racial differences. . . . There is no question, however, that incest is a problem in black families, as it is in white families. (p. 67)

Although her efforts to avoid racial stereotyping were appreciated by some researchers, the failure to explore ethnic differences will not dispel racial myths about sexual abuse. These stereotypes exist, and will persist unless we conduct culturally appropriate research. The pervasiveness of sexual violence led other researchers to take a "color blind" approach by assuming that the prevalence and circumstances surrounding sexual abuse were similar across ethnic groups. Gail Wyatt's work is significant because she critically examined racial differences, rather than ignoring or minimizing them. This has encouraged me to continue the difficult, but rewarding, dialogue about ethnic differences in sexual abuse.

Alternatively, other researchers have considered violence to be a problem that plagues people of color, particularly African Americans. Certainly race, class, and gender inequalities contribute to elevated rates of violence in the lives of Black women. Consequently, many investigators have focused their research on incarcerated or impoverished Black women, who often suffer from mental illness and drug addiction. Although this represents the experience of an alarmingly high number of African American women, the majority of Black women are not impoverished or institutionalized. Unfortunately, many researchers have made racial comparisons without considering these socioeconomic and demographic differences. As a result, what appear to be race differences are actually social class differences. Sometimes this misinformation has been used to stereotype Black women as pathological and violent. Gail Wyatt (1985) wisely avoided these mistakes by using a representative community sample with comparable demographic characteristics of both ethnic groups. More recently she and her colleagues conducted a study that used a comparable methodology, which enabled them to investigate racial differences in child sexual abuse over a ten year period (Wyatt, Loeb, Solis, & Carmona, 1999).

Researchers also have mistakenly treated Black women as a monolithic group. In Wyatt's sample (1985) we see the demographic diversity among African American women. For example, they differ in level of education and marital status. This inspired me and other researchers to investigate within ethnic group differences. It is not enough to make racial comparison. We need to know more about the differences among Black women. For example, in a sample of Black survivors of child sexual abuse, which women are at greatest risk to be revictimized in adulthood? With this information, we can develop better intervention and prevention strategies (West, Williams, & Siegel, 2000).

I am frequently asked, "Why does your research focus on ethnic differences?" My response: "Violence in the lives of Black women is both very similar and at times vastly different from the violence experienced by their White counterparts." The challenge for researchers is to articulate the racial similarities without negating the experiences of Black women, while simultaneously highlighting racial differences without perpetuating racial stereotypes. Gail Wyatt's (1985) article achieves this balance which, in my opinion, is the most significant contribution she has made to the literature.

REFERENCES

Herman, J. (1981). *Father-daughter incest.* Cambridge: Harvard University Press.

West, C. M. (Ed.) (2002a). *Violence in the lives of Black women: Battered, Black, and Blue.* Binghamton, NY: The Haworth Press.

West, C. M. (2002b). Black battered women: New directions for research and Black feminist theory. In L. H. Collins, M. R. Dunlap, and J. C. Chrisler (Eds.). *Charting a new course for feminist psychology* (pp. 216–237). Westport, CT: Praeger.

West, C. M., Williams, L. M., & Siegel, J. A. (2000). Adult sexual revictimization among Black women sexually abused in childhood: A prospective examination of serious consequences of abuse. *Child Maltreatment,* 5, 49–57.

Wyatt, G. E. (1985). The sexual abuse of Afro-American and White-American women in childhood. *Child Abuse & Neglect, 9,* 507–519.

Wyatt, G. E., Loeb, T. B., Solis, B., & Carmona, J. V. (1999). The prevalence and circumstances of child sexual abuse: Changes across the decade. *Child Abuse & Neglect, 23,* 45–60.

CHAPTER

6 The Sexual Harassment of Working Women

CATHARINE MACKINNON

Most women wish to choose whether, when, where, and with whom to have sexual relationships, as one important part of exercising control over their lives. Sexual harassment denies this choice in the process of denying the opportunity to study or work without being subjected to sexual exactions. Objection to sexual harassment at work is not a neopuritan moral protest against signs of attraction, displays of affection, compliments, flirtation, or touching on the job. Instead, women

> are rattled and often angry about sex that is one-sided, unwelcome or comes with strings attached. When it's something a woman wants to turn off but can't (a co-worker or supervisor who refuses to stop) or when it's coming from someone with the economic power to hire or fire, help or hinder, reward or punish (an employer or client who mustn't be offended)—that's when [women] say it's a problem.[1]

Women who protest sexual harassment at work are resisting economically enforced sexual exploitation.

This chapter analyzes sexual harassment as women report experiencing it.[2] The analysis is necessarily preliminary and exploratory. These events have seldom been noticed, much less studied; they have almost never been studied as sexual harassment.[3] Although the available material is limited, it covers a considerably broader range of incidents than courts will (predictably) consider to be sex discrimination. Each incident or facet of the problem mentioned here will not have equal *legal* weight or go to the same legal issue; not every instance or aspect of undesired sexual attention on the job is necessarily part of the legal cause of action. Some dimensions of the problem seem to contra-indicate legal action or to require determinations that courts are ill suited to make. The broader contextual approach is taken to avoid prematurely making women's experience of sexual harassment into a case of sex discrimination, no more and no less. For it is, at times, both more and less.

I envision a two-way process of interaction between the relevant legal concepts and women's experience. The strictures of the concept of sex discrimination will ultimately constrain those aspects of women's oppression that will be legally recognized as discriminatory. At the same time, women's experiences, expressed in their own way, can push to expand that concept. Such an approach not only enriches the law. It begins to shape it so that what *really* happens to women, not some male vision of what happens to women, is at the core of the legal prohibition. Women's lived-through experience, in as whole and truthful a fashion as can be approximated at this point, should begin to provide the starting point and context out of which is constructed the narrower forms of abuse that will be made illegal on their behalf. Now that a few women have the tools to address the legal system on its own terms, the law can begin to address women's experience on women's own terms.[4]

Although the precise extent and contours of sexual harassment await further and more exacting investigation, preliminary research indicates that the problem is extremely widespread. Certainly it is more common than almost anyone thought. In the pioneering survey by Working Women United Institute,[5] out of a sample of 55 food service workers and 100 women who attended a meeting on sexual harassment, from five to seven of every ten women reported experiencing sexual harassment in some form at some time in their work lives. Ninety-two percent of the total sample thought it a serious problem. In a study of all women employed at the United Nations, 49 percent said that sexual pressure currently existed on their jobs.[6] During the first eight months of 1976, the Division of Human Rights of the State of New York received approximately 45 complaints from women alleging sexual harassment on the job.[7] Of 9,000 women who responded voluntarily to a questionnaire in *Redbook Magazine,* "How do you handle sex on the job?" nine out of ten reported experiences of sexual harassment. Of course, those who experience the problem may be most likely to respond. Nevertheless, before this survey, it would have been difficult to convince a person of ordinary skepticism that 8,100 American women existed who would report experiencing sexual harassment at work.

Using the *Redbook* questionnaire, a naval officer found 81 percent of a sample of women on a navy base and in a nearby town reported employment-related sexual harassment in some form.[8] These frequency figures must, of course, be cautiously regarded. But even extrapolating conservatively, given that nine out of ten American women work outside the home some time in their lives[9] and that in April 1974, 45 percent of American women sixteen and over, or 35 million women, were employed in the labor force,[10] it is clear that a lot of women are potentially affected. As the problem begins to appear structural rather than individual, *Redbook's* conclusion that "the problem is not epidemic; it is pandemic—an everyday, everywhere occurrence"[11] does not seem incredible.

One need not show that sexual harassment is commonplace in order to argue that it is severe for those afflicted, or even that it is sex discrimination. However, if one shows that sexual harassment in employment systematically occurs between the persons and under the conditions that an analysis of it as discrimination suggests—that is, as a function of sex as gender—one undercuts the view that it occurs because of some unique chemistry between particular (or aberrant) individuals. That sexual harassment does occur to a large and diverse population of women supports an analysis that it occurs *because* of their group characteristic, that is, sex. Such a showing supports an analysis of the abuse as structural, and as such, worth legal attention as sex discrimination, not just as unfairness between two individuals, which might better be approached through private law.

If the problem is so common, one might ask why it has not been commonly analyzed or protested. Lack of public information, social awareness, and formal data probably reflects less its exceptionality than its specific pathology. Sexual subjects are generally sensitive and considered private; women feel embarrassed, demeaned, and intimidated by these incidents.[12] They feel afraid, despairing, utterly alone, and complicit. This is not the sort of experience one discusses readily. Even more to the point, sexual advances are often accompanied by threats of retaliation if exposed. Revealing these pressures enough to protest them thus risks the very employment consequences which sanctioned the advances in the first place.

It is not surprising either that women would not complain of an experience for which there has been no name. Until 1976,[13] lacking a term to express it, sexual harassment was literally unspeakable, which made a generalized, shared, and social definition of it inaccessible. The unnamed should not be mistaken for the nonexistent. Silence often speaks of pain and degradation so thorough that the situation cannot be conceived as other than it is:

> When the conception of change is beyond the limits of the possible, there are no words to articulate discontent, so it is sometimes held not to exist. This mistaken belief arises because we can only grasp silence in the moment in which it is breaking. The sound of silence breaking makes us understand what we could not hear before. But the fact we could not hear does not prove that no pain existed.[14]

As Adrienne Rich has said of this kind of silence, "Do not confuse it/for any kind of absence."[15] Until very recently issues analogous to sexual harassment, such as abortion, rape, and wife beating existed at the level of an open secret in public consciousness, supporting the (equally untrue) inference that these events were infrequent as well as shameful, and branding the victim with the stigma of deviance. In light of these factors, more worth explaining is the emergence of women's ability to break the silence.

Victimization by the practice of sexual harassment, so far as is currently known, occurs across the lines of age, marital status, physical appearance, race, class, occupation, pay range, and any other factor that distinguishes women from each other.[16] Frequency and type of incident may vary with specific vulnerabilities of the woman, or qualities of the job, employer, situation, or workplace, to an extent so far undetermined. To this point, the common denominator is that the perpetrators tend to be men, the victims women. Most of the perpetrators are employment superiors, although some are co-workers or clients. Of the 155 women in the Working Women United Institute sample, 40 percent were harassed by a male superior, 22 percent by a co-worker, 29 percent by a client, customer, or person who had no direct working relationship with them; 1 percent (N = 1) were harassed by a subordinate and 8 percent by "other."[17]

As to age and marital status, *Redbook* finds the most common story is of a woman in her twenties fending off a boss in his sixties, someone she would never choose as a sexual partner. The majority of women who responded to the survey, in which 92 percent reported incidents of sexual harassment, were in their twenties or thirties, and married. Adultery seems no deterrent. However, many women were single or formerly married and ranged in age from their teens to their sixties. In the Working Women United Institute speak-out, one woman mentioned an incident that occurred when she was working as a child model at age ten; another reported an experience at age 55.[18] The women in that sample ranged in age from 19 to 61. On further investigation, sexual harassment as a system may be found to affect women differentially by age, although it damages women regardless of age. That is, many older women may be excluded from jobs because they are considered unattractive sex objects, in order that younger women can be hired to be so treated. But many women preface their reports of sexual harassment with evaluations of their appearance such as, "I am fat and forty, but . . . "[19]

Sexual harassment takes both verbal and physical forms. In the Working Women United Institute sample, approximately a third of those who reported sexual harassment reported physical forms, nearly two-thirds verbal forms.[20] Verbal sexual harassment can include anything from passing but persistent comments on a woman's body or body parts to the experience of an eighteen-year-old file clerk whose boss regularly called her in to his office "to tell me the intimate details of his marriage and to ask what I thought about different sexual positions."[21] Pornography is sometimes used.[22] Physical forms range from repeated collisions that leave the impression of "accident" to outright rape. One woman reported unmistakable sexual molestation which fell between these extremes: "My boss . . . runs his hand up my leg or blouse. He hugs me to him and then tells me that he is 'just naturally affectionate.' "[23]

There is some suggestion in the data that working class women encounter physical as well as verbal forms of sexual harassment more often than middle class and/or professional women, who more often encounter only the verbal forms.[24] However, women's class status in the strict sense is often ambiguous. Is a secretary for a fancy law firm in a different class from a secretary for a struggling, small business? Is a nurse married to a doctor "working class" or "middle class" on her job? Is a lesbian factory worker from an advantaged background with a rich ex-husband who refuses to help support the children because of her sexual preference "upper class"? In any case, most women who responded to the *Redbook* survey, like most employed women, were working at white collar jobs earning between $5,000 and $10,000 a year. Many more were blue collar, professional, or managerial workers earning less than $5,000 or more than $25,000 a year. They report harassment by men independent of the class of those men.

The Working Women United Institute sample, in which approximately 70 percent reported incidents of sexual harassment, presented a strikingly typical profile of women's employment history. Almost all of the women had done office work of some kind in their work life. A quarter had done sales, a quarter had been teachers, a third file clerks, 42 percent had been either secretaries or receptionists, and 29 percent had done factory work. Currently, fifty-five were food service workers with the remainder scattered among a variety of occupations. The average income was $101–$125 per week. This is very close to, or a little below, the usual weekly earnings of most working women.[25]

Race is an important variable in sexual harassment in several different senses. Black women's reports of sexual harassment by white male superiors reflect a sense of impunity that resounds of slavery and colonization. Maxine Munford, recently separated and with two children to support, claimed that on the first day at her new job she was asked by her employer "if she would make love to a white man, and if she would slap his face if he made a pass at her." She repeatedly refused such advances and was soon fired, the employer alleging she had inadequate knowledge and training for the job and lacked qualifications. His last statement before she left was: "If you would have intercourse with me seven days a week I might give you your job back."[26] Apparently, sexual harassment can be both a sexist way to express racism and a racist way to express sexism. However, black women also report sexual harassment by black men and white women complain of sexual harassment by black male superiors and co-workers. One complaint for slander and outrageous conduct accused the defendants of making statements including the following:

> warning customers about plaintiffs alleged desire to "get in his pants," pointing out that plaintiff had large breasts, stating "Anything over a handful is wasted," calling plaintiff "Momma Fuller" and "Big Momma," referring to her breasts, "Doesn't she have nice (or large) breasts?" "Watch out, she's very horny. She hasn't gotten any lately" "Have you ever seen a black man's penis?" "Do you know how large a black man's penis is?" "Have you ever slept with a black man?" "Do you want to stop the car and screw in the middle of the street?"[27]

One might consider whether white women more readily perceive themselves as *sexually* degraded, or anticipate a supportive response when they complain, when they are sexually harassed by a black man than by a white man. Alternatively, some white women confide that they have consciously resisted reporting severe sexual harassment by black men to authorities because they feel the response would be supportive for racist reasons. Although racism is deeply involved in sexual harassment, the element common to these incidents is that the perpetrators are male, the victims female. Few women are in a position to harass men sexually, since they do not control men's employment destinies at work,"[28] and female sexual initiative is culturally repressed in this society.[29]

As these experiences suggest, the specific injury of sexual harassment arises from the nexus between a sexual demand and the work-place. Anatomized, the situations can be seen to include a sexual incident or advance, some form of compliance or rejection, and some employment consequence. Sometimes these elements are telescoped, sometimes greatly attenuated, sometimes absent. All are variable: the type of incident or advance, the form of response, and the kind and degree of damage attributable to it.

The critical issues in assessing sexual harassment as a legal cause of action—the issues that need to be explored in light of women's experiences—center upon the definition of and the relationship among three events: the advance, the response, and the employment consequence. Critical questions arise in conceptualizing all three. Where is the line between a sexual advance and a friendly gesture? How actively must the issue be forced? If a woman complies, should the legal consequences be different than if she refuses? Given the attendant risks, how explicitly must a woman reject? Might quitting be treated the same as firing under certain circumstances? To get legal relief, must a job benefit be shown to be merited independent of a sexual bargain, or is the situation an injury in itself? When a perpetrator insists that a series of touchings were not meant to be sexual, but the victim experienced them as unambiguously sexual, assuming both are equally credible, whose interpretation controls when the victim's employment status is damaged? These issues will be explored here in the context of women's experiences. In addressing these questions, it is important to divide matters of persuasion from issues of fact, and both of these from issues which go to the core of the legal concept of the discrimination. The first distinguishes the good from the less good case; the second sets a standard of proof; the third draws a line between a legal claim and no claim at all.

Women's experiences of sexual harassment can be divided into two forms which merge at the edges and in the world. The first I term the *quid pro quo,* in which sexual compliance is exchanged, or proposed to be exchanged, for an employment opportunity. The second arises when sexual harassment is a persistent *condition of work.* This distinction highlights different facets of the problem as women live through it and suggests slightly different legal requirements. In both types, the sexual demand is often but an extension of a gender-defined work role. The victim is employed, hence treated, "as a woman." In the quid pro quo, the woman must comply sexually or forfeit an employment opportunity. The quid pro quo arises most powerfully within the context of horizontal segregation, in which women are employed in feminized jobs, such as office work, as a part of jobs vertically stratified by sex, with men holding the power to hire and fire women. In a job which is defined according to gender, noncompliance with all of the job's requirements, which may at the boss's whim come to include sexual tolerance or activity, operatively "disqualifies" a woman for the job. In sexual harassment as a condition of work, the exchange of sex for employment opportunities is less direct. The major question is whether the *advances themselves* constitute an injury in employment.

Quid Pro Quo

This category is defined by the more or less explicit exchange: the woman must comply sexually or forfeit an employment benefit. The exchange can be anything but subtle, although its expression can be euphemistic: "If I wasn't going to sleep with him, I wasn't going to get my promotion";[30] "I think he meant that I had a job if I played along";[31] "You've got to make love to get a day off or to get a good beat";[32] "[Her] foreman told her that if she wanted the job she would have to be 'nice' ";[33] "I was fired because I refused to give at the office."[34]

Assuming there has been an unwanted sexual advance, a resulting quid pro quo can take one of three possible shapes. In situation one, the woman declines the advance and forfeits an employment opportunity. If the connections are shown, this raises the clearest pattern: sexual advance, noncompliance, employment retaliation. In situation two, the woman complies and does not receive a job benefit. This is complex: was the job benefit denied independently of the sexual involvement? Is employment-coerced sex an injury in itself or does compliance mean consent? Should the woman in effect forfeit the job opportunity as relief *because* she complied sexually? In situation three, the woman complies and receives a job benefit. Does she have an injury to complain of? Do her competitors? In a fourth logical possibility, which does not require further discussion, the woman refuses to comply, receives completely fair treatment on the job, and is never harassed again (and is, no doubt, immensely relieved). In this one turn of events, there truly is "no harm in asking."[35] . . .

Condition of Work

In the quid pro quo, the coercion behind the advances is clarified by the reprisals that follow a refusal to comply. Less clear, and undoubtedly more pervasive, is the situation in which sexual harassment simply makes the work environment unbearable. Unwanted sexual advances, made simply because she has a woman's body, can be a daily part of a woman's work life. She may be constantly felt or pinched, visually undressed and stared at, surreptitiously kissed, commented upon, manipulated into being found alone, and generally taken advantage of at work—but never promised or denied anything explicitly connected with her job. These events occur both to "token women," whose visibility as women is pronounced and who often present a "challenge" to men,[36] and to women in traditional "women's jobs," who are defined as accessible to such incursions by the same standard that gives them the job at all. Never knowing if it will ever stop or if escalation is imminent, a woman can put up with it or leave. Most women hardly choose to be confronted by "the choice of putting up with being manhandled, or being out of work."[37] Most women are coerced into tolerance.

This feature of women's lives has sometimes surfaced in other people's lawsuits, although it has not been previously considered actionable in itself. One case from 1938 presents a zenith in women's vicarious relationship to the workplace. A long-time employee alleged (without success) that he was fired because his wife refused his superior's sexual advances.[38] In another case for reinstatement and back pay, in which the employer was accused of firing an employee because of his union activity, one comes upon the following account of the employee's conduct on the job:

> He regularly made lewd remarks and suggestions to the waitresses and customers. . . . He caused at least one waitress to quit her job when he told her she would have to have sexual relations with him or he would make life difficult for her. He made similar advances to another waitress. Once Nichols called a waitress over to where he was seated drinking with a customer and solicited her to engage in an act of prostitution with the customer.[39]

Sexual harassment is effective largely because women's employment status is depressed. The following account, a composite of several individual accounts, illustrates the interplay of women's feelings of inadequacy with an objective assessment of their options in the labor market. The employer has an eye for energetic, competent, chronically underemployed women in a captive labor market (such as spouses of university men). They are intimidated by the work world. For the first time in their lives, the job gives these women responsibilities, a real salary, a chance to be creative, and quick advancement for good performance. They are grateful; "thrilled." They love the work and feel recognized for their achievements and potential. They work hard and create a niche for themselves. They need the money. Then, beginning on off-times, perhaps when there are unusual work demands, the underlying sexual innuendo is made explicit. Or the man sends the woman on a business trip, shows up at the hotel room where he had booked her, and rapes her.

At this point, otherwise small things come together: all the other women who have precipitously left "such a good job"; the number of women on long, paid leaves that become terminal; the stereotypically attractive appearance of the women, including a ban on long pants at the office. To an individual woman, his demand that she be constantly emotionally available to him; increasingly using her "as a verbal carpet"; his jealousy of her friendships on the job; his casual, even concerned inquiry into her sex life; his lack of desire to meet her husband and his uncomfortableness (or transparent obsequiousness) when he drops in. It becomes clear that his personnel policy is based on his sexual feelings.

Given the woman's insecurity about her work competence, the job may begin to seem like make work to her, an excuse to keep her available so long as she is sexually compliant, or he thinks she might be. Or the job may continue to be very important to her. Surely she knows there are many women just like her who will take her place if she leaves. Should a woman have to leave a job she needs financially, qualifies for, or finds fulfilling because the employer can make his sexual needs part of it? Or should she have no recourse other than the hope he will stop, or never try again, or that she can stand it just for the chance to work there, or to work at all? Will it ever be different any place else? When workplace access, advancement, and tolerability (not to mention congeniality) depend upon such an employer's good will, women walk very thin lines between preserving their own sanity and self-respect and often severe material hardship and dislocation.

Two recent cases of women seeking unemployment compensation from jobs they left because of employer sexual harassment illustrate the problem, with variations, in somewhat more detail. In a California case, Nancy Fillhouers[40] left work because she could no longer tolerate the remarks of her employer, which were "slanderous, crude and vulgar," and because he had "tried to exploit her, thus making her job unbearably difficult from an emotional standpoint." In the language of the referee:

> She said he was constantly remarking concerning his wishes to have sexual contact with her, and that she reacted in such a way as to certainly inform him that such intentions were not welcome. When she would walk by him, he would occasionally pat her behind. He would make comments to his friends about her figure or legs whenever she wore a dress, implying that she was a loose woman and would do anything with anyone. The claimant asserted that the employer attempted to arrange a liaison with one of his friends for a price. On another occasion, she said one of his friends came to the office and made a comment about the weather being cold, and the employer said that the claimant could keep him warm.[41]

In a similar case in New York State, Carmita Wood[42] reported that she was forced to leave her job because of the physical and emotional repercussions of a superior's sexual advances. He constantly "incorporated palpably sexual gestures into his movements."[43] When speaking to her "he would lean against her, immobilizing her between his own body and the chair and the desk."[44] Sometimes he would "stand with his hands shaking in his pockets and rock against the back of a chair, as if he were stimulating his genitals."[45]

A similar barrage of indignities sustained by one woman in her job as a "photo finishing girl" at a camera store in Oregon provides a third example. Her complaint alleges that on many occasions her superiors and co-workers, in the presence of other employees and customers, "peer[ed] down plaintiff's blouse from the upper level and stairways above the main sales area of Mr. Pix Camera Store, assisted by binoculars or telephoto lenses." In addition to making frank propositions and references to the large size of her breasts and of their penises, the defendants described the woman as desiring them sexually. Specific statements included:

> 'Did you just have sex with your husband: What was it like?', 'Is that all you do is have sex with your husband?', 'Do you sleep naked with your husband' pointing out that women were 'better off in bed,' meant 'only for the bedroom or the kitchen,' that plaintiff and other women employees were 'only interested in sleeping with the male employees,' that the former photofinishing 'girl' 'was a good lay. We screwed her down in the basement. We all had sex with her.', 'Do you think your husband would let me take his pants off in front of my camera if I lined him up with a nude female model?', 'Tell your husband I want to do nudes of him. I must photograph him,' that plaintiff was unfit to perform her duties, that women, including plaintiff, were 'not fit for the photography business,' 'incompetent,' 'unable to work under pressure without bursting into tears,' 'couldn't take it,' 'often stayed home due to headaches,' 'can't be relied upon,' 'possess a lesser ability to photograph,' 'don't know which end of a camera is up,' 'get shows in galleries by sleeping with gallery directors,' 'We've never had a girl selling cameras here. It might be an interesting experiment.' 'We can't hire a woman who has a boyfriend or a husband and have them last any length of time because their partners become very jealous of all us good looking males.'[46]

The connections between sexual desirability and contempt for women, the denigration of women as workers, and exclusion of women from job opportunities have seldom been more vivid. All the careful admissions that women may be oversensitive cannot overwhelm the fact that such comments make women feel violated for good reason. Nor are these remarks aberrations. They make graphic and public the degradation women commonly experience as men's sexual playthings.

At no point in these cases was there an attempt to force the victim into more extensive sexual involvement. But the only reason sexual intercourse was not included was that the perpetrator did not so choose. Nor were the women told that if they did not submit to this molestation, they would be fired, although again this was the employer's choice. The victim's active cooperation with, or submission to, this behavior is relatively irrelevant to its occurrence. Short of physical assault, there is very little one can do to stop someone intent upon visual and verbal molestation, particularly if one has access to few forms of power in the relationship. These are hardly "arm's length" transactions, with the man as dependent upon an affirmative response as the woman is upon maintaining his good will. They are transactions which make his sexism a condition of her work.

Sexual harassment as a working condition often does not require a decisive yes or no to further involvement. The threat of loss of work explicit in the quid pro quo may be only implicit without being any less coercive. Since communicated resistance means that the woman ceases to fill the implicit job qualifications, women learn, with their socialization to perform wifelike tasks, ways to avoid the open refusals that anger men and produce repercussions. This requires "playing along," constant vigilance, skillful obsequiousness, and an ability to project the implication that there is a sexual dimension to, or sexual possibilities for, the relationship, while avoiding the explicit "how about it" that would force a refusal into the open.

A cocktail waitress, whose customer tips measure her success at this precarious game, reflects upon it.

> [A waitress] must learn to be sexually inviting at the same time that she is unavailable. This of course means that men will take out their lust vicariously through lewd and insinuating words, subtle propositions, gestures. She must manage to turn him off gently without insulting him, without appearing insulted. Indeed she must appear charmed by it, find a way to say no which also flatters him.[47]

Another waitress makes the economic connection explicitly:

> [Men think] they have a right to touch me, or proposition me because I'm a waitress. Why do women have to put up with this sort of thing anyway? You aren't in any position to say "get your crummy hands off me" because you need the tips. That's what a waitress job is all about.[48]

Still another corroborates:

> Within my first month as a waitress, it was made very clear to me that if you are friendly enough, you could have a better station, better hours, better everything. . . . If you're tricky enough, you just dangle everybody but it reaches a point where it's too much of a hassle and you quit and take something else. But when you have children, and no support payments, you can't keep quitting.[49]

While these women's responses do not constitute "compliance" in the fullest sense, in another sense nonrejection is all the compliance that is required.

Noncompliance is very problematic when sexual harassment is a working condition. Consider the opportunities for rejection, both immediate and long term, allowed by the situation depicted in the following woman's statement, prepared in an attempt to organize the women in her office:

> I, ______, do hereby testify that during the course of my employment with the [company] I have suffered repeated and persistent sexual harassment by Mr. X, [head] of the [company].
>
> Mr. X has directly expressed prurient interest in me on several occasions when he called me into his office as an employee, in his capacity as my superior, during normal work-

> ing hours. I have been made audience to sexually explicit language and imagery in Mr. X's office during normal working hours. I have been intimidated by his power over my job and future, his connections in [the local government], his reputation for vindictiveness, and the gun he carries, often visibly. In his office, Mr. X has initiated physical sexual contact with me which I did not want.
>
> I believe, and have been made to feel by Mr. X, that my well-being on the job and advancement as an employee of the [company], as well as my recommendations for future jobs, are directly contingent upon my compliance with Mr. X's sexual demands.
>
> It is my opinion that Mr. X's hiring procedures are directly influenced by his sexual interests and that most if not all women who work for the [company] undergo some form of sexual harassment.

Tolerance is the form of consent that sexual harassment as a working condition uniquely requires. The evidence of such cases after they *become* quid pro quo tends to confirm the implicit judgment by the woman who "goes along": it is important, beyond any anticipated delivery, to maintain the *appearance* of compliance with male sexual overtures, a posture of openness. In many cases, the men seem only to want to know they can have a date, to be able "accidentally" to touch a woman intimately at will, or, in a verbal analogue to exhibitionism, say sexy words in her presence, while acting as if something else entirely is happening. The telling aspect is that the decisively nontolerating woman must suddenly be eliminated. Her mere presence becomes offensive; to be reminded of her existence, unbearable. Desperate strategies are devised, including flat lies, distortions, and set-ups, to be rid of her immediately. Something fundamental to male identity feels involved in at least the appearance of female compliance, something that is deeply threatened by confrontation with a woman's real resistance, however subtly communicated. At the point of resistance the quid pro quo that was implicit all along in the working condition—the "tolerate it or leave" in her mind becomes "now that you don't tolerate it, you're leaving" from the boss—is forced into the open, and the two categories converge.

Before this point, the issues are considerably more difficult. The examples suggest that when sexual harassment occurs as a condition of work, it does not require compliance, exactly, on the woman's part. For consummation, nonrejection is not even required; rejection often has no effect. Since little or no active participation or cooperation is required of women in these sexual situations, how explicit should rejection have to be before she can protest the treatment? This is somewhat analogous to asking how ardently a woman must resist rape before she will be considered to have resisted, that is, not to have consented to it. In a case of sexual harassment, it would be paradoxical if, so long as a superior has the power to force sexual attentions by adopting forms of sexual expression that do not require compliance—for example, sitting naked in his office in her presence while giving dictation—a woman would be precluded from legal action or other complaint because she had not properly "refused." How is nontolerance to be conveyed? She can threaten or throw tantrums, but ultimately, what is she supposed to do besides leave work?

Should women be required to counterattack in order to force the man into explicit employment retaliation so she has something to complain about? The problem here is again analogous to a problem with the rape laws: a victim who resists is more likely to be killed, but unless she fights back, it is not rape, because she cannot prove coercion. With sexual harassment, rejection proves that the advance is unwanted but also is likely to call forth retaliation, thus forcing the victim to bring intensified injury upon herself in order to demonstrate that she is injured at all. Aside from the risks this poses to the woman, in a situation not her fault, to require a rejection amounts to saying that no series of sexual advances alone is sufficient to justify legal intervention until it is expressed in the quid pro quo form. In addition, it means that constant sexual molestation would not be injury enough to a woman or to her employment status until the employer retaliates against her *job* for a sexual refusal which she never had the chance to make short of leaving it. And this, in turn, means that so long as the sexual situation is constructed with enough coerciveness, subtlety, suddenness, or one-sidedness to negate the effectiveness of the woman's refusal, or so long as her refusals are simply ignored while her job is formally undisturbed, she is not considered to have been sexually harassed.

Impact of Sexual Harassment

Women's feelings about their experiences of sexual harassment are a significant part of its social impact. Like women who are raped, sexually harassed women feel humiliated, degraded, ashamed, embarrassed, and cheap, as well as angry. When asked whether the experience had any emotional or physical effect, 78 percent of the Working Women United Institute sample answered affirmatively. Here are some of their comments:

> As I remember all the sexual abuse and negative work experiences I am left feeling sick and helpless and upset instead of angry. . . . Reinforced feelings of no control—sense of doom . . . I have difficulty dropping the emotion barrier I work behind when I come home from work. My husband turns into just another man. . . . Kept me in a constant state of emotional agitation and frustration; I drank a lot. . . . Soured the essential delight in the work. . . . Stomachache, migraines, cried every night, no appetite.*[50]

In the Working Women United Institute study, 78 percent of the women reported feeling "angry," 48 percent "upset," 23 percent "frightened," 7 percent "indifferent," and an additional 27 percent mentioned feeling "alienated," "alone," "helpless," or other. They tend to feel the incident is their fault, that they must have done something, individually, to elicit or encourage the behavior, that it is "my problem."[51] Since they believe that no one else is subjected to it, they feel individually complicit as well as demeaned. Almost a quarter of the women in one survey reported feeling "guilty."

Judging from these responses, it does not seem as though women want to be sexually harassed at work. Nor do they, as a rule, find it flattering. As one explanation for women's apparent acquiescence, Sheila Rowbotham hypothesizes that (what amounts to) sexually

*Ellipses separate different persons' responses.

harassed women are "subtly flattered that their sex is recognized. This makes them feel that they are not quite on the cash nexus, that they matter to their employer in the same way that they matter to men in their personal lives."[52] While the parallel to home life lends plausibility to this analysis, only 10 percent of the women in the Working Women United Institute sample and 15 percent of the *Redbook* sample* reported feeling "flattered" by being on the sex nexus. Women do connect the harasser with other men in their lives, but with quite different results: "It made me think that the only reason other men don't do the same thing is that they don't have the power to." The view that women really want unwanted sex is similar to the equally self-serving view that women want to be raped. As Lynn Wehrli analyzes this:

> Since women seem to "go along" with sexual harassment, [the assumption is that] they must like it, and it is not really harassment at all. This constitutes little more than a simplistic denial of all we know about the ways in which socialization and economic dependence foster submissiveness and override free choice. . . . Those women who are able to speak out about sexual harassment use terms such as "humiliating," "intimidating," "frightening," "financially damaging," "embarrassing," "nerve-wracking," "awful," and "frustrating" to describe it. These words are hardly those used to describe a situation which one "likes."[53]

That women "go along" is partly a male perception and partly correct, a male-enforced reality. Women report being too intimidated to reject the advances unambivalently, regardless of how repulsed they feel. Women's most common response is to attempt to ignore the whole incident, letting the man's ego off the hook skillfully by *appearing* flattered in the hope he will be satisfied and stop. These responses may be interpreted as encouragement or even as provocation. One study found that 76 percent of ignored advances intensified.[54] Some women feel constrained to decline gently, but become frustrated when their subtle hints of lack of reciprocity are ignored. Even clear resistance is often interpreted as encouragement, which is frightening. As a matter of fact, any response or lack of response may be interpreted as encouragement. Ultimately women realize that they have their job only so long as they are pleasing to their male superior, so they try to be polite.[55]

Despite the feelings of guilt, self-loathing, and fear of others' responses, many women who have been sexually harassed do complain about it to someone—usually a woman friend, family member, or co-worker. About a quarter of them complain to the perpetrator himself.[56] Those who complain, as well as those who do not, express fears that their complaints will be ignored, will not be believed, that they instead will be blamed, that they will be considered "unprofessional," or "asking for it," or told that this problem is too petty or trivial for a grown woman to worry about, and that they are blowing it all out of proportion. Carmita Wood's immediate supervisor, to whom she had reported incidents with her other superior at length, when asked to recall if she mentioned them, stated: "I don't

*In both surveys, women could indicate as many feelings as they felt applied to them.

remember specifically, but it was my impression, it was mentioned among a lot of things that I considered trivia."[57]

Women also feel intimidated by possible repercussions of complaint, such as being considered a "troublemaker,"[58] or other men in their lives finding out about the incidents, men who typically believe they must have been asking for it. One article reports a man "recalling a woman purchasing clerk who had just received a 'really good raise' and then showed up at work 'all black and blue.' Her husband had 'slapped her around' because he thought the raise was a result of 'putting out.' "[59] Women students (and women junior faculty) fear the repercussions of complaint more than the academic and professional consequences of the harassment itself.[60]

Women's worst fears about the impact of complaint are amply justified. "Most male superiors treat it as a joke, at best it's not serious. . . . Even more frightening, the woman who speaks out against her tormentors runs the risk of suddenly being seen as a crazy, a weirdo, or even worse, a loose woman."[61] Company officials often laugh it off or consider the women now available to themselves as well. One factory worker reports: "I went to the personnel manager with a complaint that two men were propositioning me. He promised to take immediate action. When I got up to leave, he grabbed my breast and said, 'Be nice to me and I'll take care of you.' "[62] . . .

Women's confidence in their job performance is often totally shattered by these events. They are left wondering if the praise they received prior to the sexual incident was conditioned by the man's perception of the sexual potential in the relationship—or is it only that the later accusations of incompetence are conditioned by his perception of the lack of this possibility? Attempting to decline gracefully and preserve a facade of normalcy also has its costs: "We've all been so polite about it for so long to the point we are nauseated with ourselves."

Jokes are another form that the social control over women takes. Women who consider noncompliance dread the degradation of male humor. At Carmita Wood's hearing, when she was describing disabling pains in her neck and arm which vanished upon leaving the job, the referee said, "So you're saying, in effect, that [the professor] was a pain in the neck?" On being told the perpetrator's age, the referee remarked, "Young enough to be interested anyway."[63] As the brief for Ms. Wood put it, "Nowhere is the existence of a persistent sexual harassment . . . questioned, it is merely treated lightly."[64] Trivialization of sexual harassment has been a major means through which its invisibility has been enforced. Humor, which may reflect unconscious hostility, has been a major form of that trivialization. As Eleanor Zuckerman has noted, "Although it has become less acceptable openly to express prejudices against women, nevertheless, these feelings remain under the surface, often taking the form of humor, which makes the issues seem trivial and unimportant."[65]

Faced with the spectre of unemployment, discrimination in the job market, and a good possibility of repeated incidents elsewhere, women usually try to endure. But the costs of endurance can be very high, including physical as well as psychological damage:

> The anxiety and strain, the tension and nervous exhaustion that accompany this kind of harassment take a terrific toll on women workers. Nervous ticks of all kinds, aches and pains (which can be minor and irritating or can be devastatingly painful) often accompany the

> onset of sexual harassment. These pains and illnesses are the result of insoluble conflict, the inevitable backlash of the human body in response to intolerable stress which thousands of women must endure in order to survive.[66]

Without further investigation, the extent of the disruption of women's work lives and the pervasive impact upon their employment opportunities can only be imagined. One woman, after describing her own experiences with sexual harassment, concluded:

> Many women face daily humiliation simply because they have female bodies. The one other female union member at my plant can avoid contact with everyone but a few men in her department because she stays at her work bench all day and eats in a small rest room at one end of her department.[67]

For many women, work, a necessity for survival, requires self-quarantine to avoid constant assault on sexual integrity. Many women try to transfer away from the individual man, even at financial sacrifice. But once a woman has been sexually harassed, her options are very limited:

> If she objects, the chances are she will be harassed or get fired outright. If she submits, the chances are he'll get tired of her anyway. If she ignores it, she gets drawn into a cat-and-mouse game from which there is no exit except leaving the job.[68]

Women do find ways of fighting back short of, and beyond, leaving their jobs.[69] As has been noted, nonrejection coupled with noncompliance is a subtle but expensive form. One shuffles when one sees no alternative. Women have also begun to oppose sexual harassment in more direct, visible, and powerful ways. The striking fact that black women have brought a disproportionate number of the sexual harassment lawsuits to date points to some conditions that make resistance seem not only necessary but possible. Protest to the point of court action before a legal claim is known to be available requires a quality of inner resolve that is reckless and serene, a sense of "this I won't take" that is both desperate and principled. It also reflects an absolute lack of any other choice at a point at which others with equally few choices do nothing.

Black women's least advantaged position in the economy is consistent with their advanced position on the point of resistance. Of all women, they are most vulnerable to sexual harassment, both because of the image of black women as the most sexually accessible and because they are the most economically at risk. These conditions promote black women's resistance to sexual harassment and their identification of it for what it is. On the one hand, because they have the least to fall back on economically, black women have the most to lose by protest, which targets them as dissidents, hence undesirable workers. At the same time, since they are so totally insecure in the marketplace, they have the least stake in the system of sexual harassment as it is because they stand to lose everything by it. Since they cannot afford any economic risks, once they are subjected to even a threat of loss of means, they cannot afford *not* to risk everything to prevent it. In fact, they often must risk everything even to have a chance of getting by. Thus, since black women stand to lose the most from sexual harassment, by comparison they may see themselves as having the least to lose by a struggle against it. Compared with having one's children starving on welfare, for example, any battle for a wage of one's own with a chance of winning greater than zero looks attractive. In this respect, some black women have been able to grasp the essence of the situation, and with it the necessity of opposition, earlier and more firmly than other more advantaged women.

Other factors may contribute to black women's leadership on this issue. To the extent they are sensitive to the operation of racism on an individual level, they may be less mystified that the sexual attention they receive is "personal." Their heritage of systematic sexual harassment under slavery may make them less tolerant of this monetized form of the same thing. The stigmatization of all black women as prostitutes may sensitize them to the real commonality between sexual harassment and prostitution. Feeling closer to the brand of the harlot, black women may more decisively identify and reject the spectre of its reality, however packaged.

The instances of sexual harassment described present straightforward coercion: unwanted sex under the gun of a job or educational benefit. Courts can understand abuses in this form. It is important to remember that affirmatively desired instances of sexual relationships also exist which begin in the context of an employment or educational relationship. Although it is not always simple, courts regularly distinguish bona fide relationships from later attempts to read coercion back into them. Between the two, between the clear coercion and the clear mutuality, exists a murky area where power and caring converge. Here arise some of the most profound issues of sexual harassment, and those which courts are the least suited to resolve.

In education, the preceptive and initiating function of the teacher and the respect and openness of the student merge with the masculine role of sexual mastery and the feminine role of eager purity, especially where the life of the mind means everything. The same parallel between the relationship that one is supposed to be having and the conditions of sexual dominance and submission can be seen in the roles of secretary and boss. Rosabeth Kanter notes that the secretary comes to "feel for" the boss, "to care deeply about what happens to him and to do his feeling for him," giving the relationship a tone of emotional intensity.[70] Elsewhere, she sees that a large part of the secretary's job is to empathize with the boss's personal needs; she also observes that, since the secretary is part of the boss's private retinue, what happens to him determines what happens to her. Kanter does not consider that there may be a connection between the secretary's objective conditions and her feelings—sexual feelings included—about her boss.

Although the woman may, in fact, be and feel coerced in the sexual involvement in some instances of sexual harassment, she may not be entirely without regard for, or free from caring about, the perpetrator. Further investigation of what might be called "coerced caring," or, in the most complex cases, an "if this is sex, I must be in love" syndrome, is vital. It is becoming increasingly recognized that feelings of caring are not the only or even a direct cause of sexual desires in either sex.[71] In light of this, it cannot be assumed that if the woman cares about the man, the sex is not coerced. The difficulties of conceptualization and proof, however, are enormous. But since employed women are supposed to develop, and must demonstrate, regard for the man as a part of the job, and since women are taught to identify with men's feelings, men's evaluations of them, and with their sexual attractiveness to men, as a major component of their *own* identities and sense of worth,[72] it is often unclear and shifting whether the coercion or the caring is the weightier factor, or which "causes" which.

This is not the point at which the legal cause of action for sexual harassment unravels, but the point at which the less good legal case can be scrutinized for its social truths. The more general relationship in women between objective lack of choices and real feelings of love for men can be explored in this context. Plainly, the wooden dichotomy between "real love," which is supposed to be a matter of free choice, and coercion, which implies some form of the gun at the head, is revealed as inadequate to explain the social construction of women's sexuality and the conditions of its expression, including the economic ones. The initial attempts to establish sexual harassment as a cause of action should focus upon the clear cases, which exist in profusion. But the implications the less clear cases have for the tension between women's economic precariousness and dependency—which exists in the family as well as on the job—and the possibilities for freely chosen intimacy between unequals remain.

There is a unity in these apparently, and on the legal level actually, different cases. Taken as one, the sexual harassment of working women presents a closed system of social predation in which powerlessness builds powerlessness. Feelings are a material reality of it. Working women are defined, and survive by defining themselves, as sexually accessible and economically exploitable. Because they are economically vulnerable, they are sexually exposed; because they must be sexually accessible, they are always economically at risk. In this perspective, sexual harassment is less "epidemic" than endemic.

NOTES

1. Claire Safran, *Redbook Magazine* (November 1976), at 149 (hereinafter, *Redbook*). That respondents were self-selected is this study's most serious drawback. Its questions are perceptively designed to elicit impressionistic data. (The questionnaire was published in the January 1976 issue.) When the results are interpreted with these characteristics in mind, the study is highly valuable. Scholars who look down upon such popular journalistic forays into policy research (especially by "women's magazines") should ask themselves why *Redbook* noticed sexual harassment before they did.

2. Much of the information in this chapter is based upon discussions with ten women who shared their experiences of sexual harassment with me from five to twenty or more hours apiece. In addition, I have studied lengthy first person written accounts by five other women. Several women reported the situations and feelings of other women who were being sexually harassed by the same man they were discussing with me. Where permission has been sought and obtained, some of this material will be quoted or referenced throughout. Where quotations in this chapter are unattributed, or statements of fact (such as the racial characteristics of victims and perpetrators) or feelings (such as caring about the man involved) are not otherwise footnoted, they are derived from one or several women from my own research.

Finally, although the context was education rather than employment, much of my grasp of sexual harassment as an experience is owed to the extensive investigation conducted at Yale from 1976 to 1979 by the plaintiffs and the Yale Undergraduate Women's Caucus Grievance Committee in connection with *Alexander v. Yale,* 459 F. Supp. 1 (D. Conn. 1977). In this research, incidents involving at least half a dozen faculty members or administrators and a total of about fifty women were systematically uncovered and pursued, to the extent the victims were willing.

3. Sex on the job has not gone entirely unnoticed; it is only sexual harassment conceived as such that has been ignored. Two examples illustrate. One study entitled "Rape at Work" reports rapes of women on their jobs by hospital or prison inmates, students or clients; employers, superiors, or co-workers are not mentioned. Carroll M. Brodsky, "Rape at Work," in Marcia J. Walker and Stanley L. Brodsky, eds., *Sexual Assault, the Victim and the Rapist* (Lexington, Mass.: D. C. Heath & Company, 1976), at 35–52. This study is useful, however, for observing dynamics of on-the-job rape that are also true for sexual harassment, whether it includes rape or not. Rape at work was experienced as worse than at other places because it had been seen as a safe place, where the woman did not have to be constantly on guard (at 43–44). And the site of the assault is difficult to avoid (at 44). In another study of "occupations and sex," the examination is divided between jobs "where the occupation involves sex"—cab driving, vice squad duty, and gynecology—and jobs "where the occupation is sex"—stripteasing and prostitution. James M. Henslin, *Studies in the Sociology of Sex* (New York: Appleton-Century-Crofts, 1971). This defines as the universe for study the rarified extremes of the convergence of sexuality with work to the neglect of the common experience of thousands of women. See, however, Carroll M. Brodsky, *The Harassed Worker* (Lexington, Mass.: Heath, 1976), at 27–28 for a useful if brief discussion.

4. Recent attempts to understand women's experience from women's point of view have produced upheavals in standard conceptions in many academic disciplines. One clear example is in the field of history. See Gerda Lerner, *The Female Experience: An American Documentary* (Indianapolis: Bobbs-Merrill, 1977), especially the introduction; Joan Kelly-Gadol, "The Social Relation of the Sexes: Methodological Implications of Women's History," *Signs: Journal of Women in Culture and Society,* vol. 1, no. 4 (1976), at 809–824; Hilda Smith, Feminism and the Methodology of Women's History," in Berenice A. Carroll, ed., *Liberating Women's History* (Chicago: University of Illinois Press, 1976), at 369–384.

5. References to this survey come from three sources. One is my own interpretation of a simple collation of the marginals from the survey, generously provided by Working Women United Institute (hereinafter, WWUI). The total is 145 women, because 5 women both attended the speak-out and worked in Binghamton. Whenever possible, I will refer to the published article which reports some of the data and provides some analysis. Dierdre Silverman, "Sexual Harassment: Working Women's Dilemma," *Quest: A Feminist Quarterly,* vol. III, no. 3 (1976–1977), at 15–24 (hereinafter, Silverman). Finally, Lin Farley's testimony before the Commission on Human Rights of the City of New York, Hearings on Women in Blue-Collar, Service and Clerical Occupations, "Special Disadvantages of Women in Male Dominated Work Settings" (April 21, 1975) (mimeograph) refers to the same study.

6. United Nations Ad Hoc Group on Equal Rights for Women, Report on the Questionnaire xxxvi, Report on file at the New York University Law Review, reported in Note, 51 *New York U. L. Rev.* 148, 149, n. 6.

7. Letter of December 8, 1976, from Marie Shear, public information officer of the division, to Lynn Wehrli, copy in author's file.

8. Redbook, at 217, 219.

9. Nancy Seifer, "Absent from the Majority: Working Class Women in America" (New York: Institute of Human Relations, National Project on Ethnic America of the American Jewish Committee, 1973), at 11.

10. *1975 Handbook,* at 28.

11. *Redbook,* at 217. The only study I have found that sheds further light upon the statistical prevalence of sexual harassment of women is Diana E. H. Russell's 1978 pretest interviews of ninety-two women randomly selected from San Francisco households. The general purpose of the study was to investigate sexual assault and rape. Her question #46a was: "Some people have experienced unwanted sexual advances by someone who had authority over them such as a doctor, teacher, employer, minister, or therapist. Did you ever have any kind of unwanted sexual experience with someone who had authority over you?" Responses to this question were 16.9 percent yes, 83.1 percent no. From an examination of the rest of the marginals, it seems possible that these results are low. The more specific and detailed the questions became, the higher the affirmative responses tended to be. A woman who was sexually harassed by more than one authority figure would be counted only once. The percentage of affirmative responses to this question is about the same as to the question about sexual experiences with close relatives, but lower than to those about rape. Several questions were asked about rape. Perhaps more questions on authority figures would have increased the prevalence figures. Since the sampling was done by households, the incidence of sexual harassment might

not be as high as it would be in subsamples, for instance, of employed women only. Nevertheless, nearly one-fifth of *all women* is a lot of women. The most startling result of the pretest is that thirty-four respondents reported a total of sixty-five incidents of rape and attempted rape in the course of their lives, with a pair or group assault counted as one attack. This means that approximately one-third of all women have been raped, or experienced an attempted rape. The preliminary analysis of the full sample of 935 interviews will be available April 1, 1979. Information from Diana E. H. Russell, "The Prevalence of Rape and Sexual Assault," *Summary Progress Report,* March 31, 1978; Appendix IV: Edited Interview Schedule with Marginals. This research was sponsored by the National Institute of Mental Health and funded through the Center for the Prevention and Control of Rape.

12. *Redbook,* at 217; Silverman, at 18.

13. Working Women United Institute (now at 593 Park Ave., New York, N.Y. 10021) seems to have been the first to use these words as anything approaching a term of art, at first in connection with the case of Carmita Wood in October, 1975 (*infra,* note 61). The concept was also used and developed by the Alliance Against Sexual Coercion (P.O. Box 1, Cambridge, Mass. 02139), for example in their "Position Paper #1" (September 1976) and appears in Carroll Brodsky, *The Harassed Worker* (Lexington, Mass.: Heath, 1976), at 27–28.

14. Sheila Rowbotham. *Woman's Consciousness, Men's World* (London: Penguin, 1973), at 29–30.

15. Adrienne Rich, *The Dream of a Common Language, Poems 1974–1977* (New York: W. W. Norton & Co., 1978), "Cartographies of Silence," at 17.

16. This statement is supported by every study to date and by my own research. These dimensions of sexual harassment were further documented at a speak-out by Women Office Workers, 600 Lexington Avenue, New York, N.Y., in October 1975. Accounts of the event, and WOW's complaint to the Human Rights Commission, can be found in *Majority Report,* November 1–15, 1975; Paula Bernstein, "Sexual Harassment on the Job," *Harper's Bazaar* (August 1976); *New York Daily News,* April 22, 1976; *New York Post,* April 22, 1976.

17. WWUI.

18. Silverman, at 18.

19. The information from the *Redbook* study in this paragraph is at 217, 219.

20. WWUI.

21. *Redbook,* at 217.

22. The use of pornographic videotapes is reported in "2 Phone Executives Called Promiscuous—Witnesses Tell of Sex in Offices as Trial on Wrongful Death Nears End in Texas," *New York Times,* September 3, 1977. The legal action is for the wrongful death of the man who committed suicide on being accused of a fact pattern seeming to amount to sexual harassment of many women employees.

23. *Redbook,* at 149.

24. Silverman, at 18; *Redbook,* at 217, 219.

25. WWUI; in May 1974, the median weekly earning for women working full time was $124.00. *1975 Handbook,* at 126.

26. The quotations are Ms. Munford's allegations from the Joint Pre-Trial statement in her case, at 7 and 8, respectively. The decision in the case is *Munford v. James T. Barnes & Co.*, 441 F. Supp. 459 (E.D. Mich. 1977). In addition to Munford, the plaintiffs in *Alexander* (Price), *Barnes,* and *Miller* (see Map. 1, *supra,* note 5) are black women charging sexual harassment by white men. (Diane Williams is a black woman charging sexual harassment by a black man.)

27. First Amended Complaint for Outrageous Conduct and Slander; Law Action for Unpaid Wages; Demand for Jury Trial, Count IX, *Fuller v. Williames,* No. A7703–04001 (Ore. Cir. Ct. 1977).

28. See the discussion of vertical stratification in chap. 2.

29. See the discussion of sex roles and sexuality, in chap. 5.

30. Working Women United Institute, "Speak-Out on Sexual Harassment," Ithaca, N.Y., May 4, 1975 (typescript), at 15.

31. *Id.,* at 30.

32. Peggy A. Jackson, quoted in Jane Seaberry, "They Don't Swing to Sex in the Beat," *Washington Post,* October 13, 1975.

33. *Monge v. Beebe Rubber,* 316 A.2d 549, 560 (N.H. 1974).

34. *Redbook,* at 149.

35. See discussion in chap. 6, beginning p. 167, The reference is to the classic formulation by Herbert Magruder of the position that a man should not be liable in tort for emotional harm resulting from his sexual advances. Magruder, "Mental and Emotional Disturbance in the Law of Torts," 49 *Harv. L. Rev.* 1033, 1055 (1936).

36. See Rosabeth M. Kanter, *Men and Women of the Corporation* (New York: Basic Books, 1977), at 233–236. Gloria Steinem has suggested that "sexual harassment might be called the taming of the shrew syndrome." "Women Tell of Sexual Harassment," *New York Times,* October 25, 1977. This may be true of women who are perceived as powerful, but my investigations suggest that as many, if not more, women are sexually harassed whom the perpetrators perceive as powerless.

37. Brief for Appellants, at 17, *Corne v. Bausch & Lomb,* 562 F.2d 55 (9th Cir. 1977).

38. *Comerford v. International Harvester Co.,* 235 Ala. 376 (178 So. 894 1938). Discharge in revenge for what was termed "the superior's failure to alienate the affections of the employee's wife" was held to impose no employer liability under a contract of employment. Here, the contract expressly provided that the employee would not be terminated as long as his services were satisfactory. The supervisor had reported that the plaintiff's services were unsatisfactory in revenge for the employee's wife's refusal of the supervisor's sexual advances. The discharge, although found malicious and improper and based on a false report of unsatisfactory performance, was held within the employer's right under the contract. This is not atypical of judicial interpretation of employment contracts.

39. *NLRB v. Apico Inns of California,* 512 F.2d 1171, 1173 (9th Cir. 1975).

40. *In re Nancy J. Fillhouer,* No. SJ-5963, California Unemployment Insurance Appeals Board (May 12, 1975) (Referee), *rev'd,* Appeals Board Decision No. 7505225 (July 2, 1975).

41. This and prior statement are contained in the statement by the referee of allegations of claimant, Decision of the Referee, at 1.

42. *In re Carmita Wood,* App. No. 207, 958, New York State Department of Labor, Unemployment Insurance Division Appeal Board (October 6, 1975).

43. Brief for Claimant-Appellant, at 1.

44. *Id.,* at 2; Affidavit of Carmita Wood, at 3.

45. Affidavit of Carmita Wood, at 3.

46. *Fuller v. Williames,* No. A7703-04001 (Ore. Cir. Ct. 1977).

47. Shulamith Firestone, "On the Job Oppression of Working Women: A Collection of Articles" (Boston: New England Free Press, n.d.).

48. An unnamed woman quoted in Enid Nemy, New York Times News Service, *Newark Star-News,* August 24, 1975.

49. *Id.* (This is a different woman from that quoted in the foregoing quotation.)

50. Silverman, at 18, 19.

51. *Redbook,* at 149; WWUI; *all* my own cases.

52. Rowbotham, *supra,* note 14, at 90.

53. Lynn Wehrli, "Sexual Harassment at the Workplace: A Feminist Analysis and Strategy for Social Change" (M.A. thesis, Massachusetts Institute of Technology, December 1976).

54. Silverman, at 19.

55. All my cases and all the studies comment upon a need to be polite during the incident, or to exit politely.

56. WWUI; Silverman, at 19.

57. Statement by [Mr. X], Lab. of Nuclear Studies, Transcript at 37, *In re Carmita Wood,* Case No. 75–92437, New York State Department of Labor, Unemployment Insurance Division (Referee).

58. *Redbook,* at 219; all my own cases mentioned this fear as substantial, even paralyzing.

59. Bill Korbel, quoted in Lin Farley, "Sexual harassment," *New York Sunday News,* August 15, 1976, at 12.

60. One Yale graduate student observed: "A student making a major complaint would expose herself in a way that's more harmful than harassment. The complaint could have a much more profound effect on your future and the focus of your education than the instance of harassment." Quoted by Alice Dembner, "A Case of Sex Discrimination," *Yale Graduate-Professional,* vol. 7, no. 14 (March 6, 1978), at 7. See also "Sexual Harassment: A Hidden Issue" (Project on the Status and Education of Women, Association of American

Colleges, 1818 R. Street, N.W., Washington, D.C. 20009, June 1978), at 3; and Donna Benson, "The Sexualization of Student-Teacher Relationships" (unpublished paper: Berkeley, California, 1977).

61. Lin Farley, quoted by Enid Nemy, *supra,* note 49; see also Farley's testimony, *supra,* note 5.

62. *Redbook,* at 219.

63. Transcript of hearing, *In re Carmita Wood,* Case No. 75–92437, New York State Department of Labor, Unemployment Insurance Division, at 19, 37.

64. Brief for Claimant-Appellant, *In re Carmita Wood,* App. No. 207, 958, New York State Department of Labor, Unemployment Insurance Division Appeal Board (October 6, 1975), at 19.

65. Eleanor L. Zuckerman, "Masculinity and the Changing Woman," in Zuckerman, ed., *Women and Men: Roles, Attitudes and Power Relationships* (New York: Radcliffe Club of New York, ca. 1975), at 65.

66. Lin Farley, testimony, *supra,* note 5, at 6.

67. Transcript, Permanent Commission on the Status of Women, Public Hearing, New Haven, Connecticut, January 22, 1975.

68. Lin Farley, testimony, *supra,* note 5, at 3.

69. One example is provided in a recent news article which reported a strike by eight waitresses against sexual harassment by the management at a restaurant in Madison, Wisconsin: "Ellen Eberle, a waitress at Dos Banditos said that sexual harassment by the management was a constant problem. 'Pete says he never touches 'his girls' but it's not true. He's touched me a number of times and I didn't like it and I've told him so. It's perverted and it makes me sick. He's very blatant about it and he makes gross jokes.' " The strike was called after the owners and management refused to listen to the grievances; the waitresses went back to work after a settlement that they described as a "complete victory." *Off Our Backs,* vol. VIII, no. 5 (May 1978), at 10.

70. Kanter, *supra,* note 36, at 88.

71. See discussion at 156–58, *infra.*

72. For commentary on this point written by men, see Jack Litewka, "The Socialized Penis," and other articles in *For Men Against Sexism,* Jon Snodgrass, ed. (Albion, Cal.: Times Change Press, 1977), at 16–35.

Reflection

PHOEBE MORGAN

In 1979, the year that *The Sexual Harassment of Working Women* was published, I was fired. I had been the front office receptionist for a small business in a large town. I was the only employee with a college degree, the only woman on the payroll, and the lowest paid worker. As such, it was my job to keep the coffee fresh and hot. I was also the only employee who did not join our clients at the local topless bar for drinks each payday. As the president handed me two weeks' severance pay, he lamented that while he liked me a lot, he had to let me go for two reasons. First, ever since I had arrived the sexual horseplay had escalated; as a result both decorum and productivity had hit an all time low. Second, I was a bad receptionist—my lack of humor and negative attitude toward men made for a chilly front office. I was Monica Lewinsky's age, living on my own for the first time and my new car payment required half of the pay I had just lost. I was devastated.

Even though the term "sexual harassment" had been coined five years prior, I had never heard it and I had no idea the law was on my side. But for the first time since college the lessons of my only feminist professor rang true. Two years before my firing I had confessed to her that feminism seemed irrelevant to my very successful (and quite brief) life. Couldn't she see the revolution was over? She replied by patiently explaining: "a feminist is not born but made, and someday, life will make you a feminist." It had indeed.

Ten years after losing that job I read the first page of *The Sexual Harassment of Working Women.* Like Yale law professor Reva Siegal and Stanford law professor Janet Halley (Shalit 1998), the experience was so profound that I can still remember the minute details of that moment. I was completing my second year of graduate school, working as a research intern in the Governor's Office of Women's Services. I was on my lunch break, sitting in the back booth of the Arizona Capitol's cafeteria. I was in a hurry to complete the week's requirements for a course on "Feminism and Justice." The professor had prefaced the assignment by asking us to consider how MacKinnon's work makes Marxism stand on its head. The more I read, the less I cared about how Marxism stood. *The Sexual Harassment of Working Women* gave my trauma a name and bonded me to the millions of other women suffering similar fates (U.S. Merit Systems Protection Board, 1981). More importantly, it told me exactly how the law should prohibit it and how I could have used law to regain if not my job, then my lost wages and a little of my dignity. If only I had known.

The discovery of *The Sexual Harassment of Working Women* began my career in sexual harassment research. I continue to work in this area today and with each project, I consult *The Sexual Harassment of Working Women.* Like most novice researchers, I launched my career with a critique of MacKinnon's legal treatise. I sought to prove all the ways in which it was inadequate or plain wrong. Initially, I naively thought my road to a national reputation lay in joining the chorus of feminists and anti-feminists who blamed *The Sexual Harassment of Working Women* for the inability of sexual harassment law to realize the book's promise. Each critique has given me a new appreciation of the book's exceptional explanatory power. Even anti-feminist Wendy Shalit (1998) admits the book succeeds at least in articulating the irrefutable fact that most women remain unhappy about how men treat them. But, as MacKinnon's own criticisms of *The Sexual Harassment of Working Women* remind us, dismantling the master's house with his own tools is an inherently conservative project and simply being right is no guarantee against failure (1995; 1991).

Once this collection becomes print, *The Sexual Harassment of Working Women* will have been in print for a quarter of a century. In it, MacKinnon articulates with exceptional clarity how all women suffer from the sexual harassment of just one woman. Even today, the book accomplishes what subsequent scholars have attempted to do but failed: in everyday language, MacKinnon connects sexual violence with male domination, and then locates that nexus squarely in the workplace. She does so by drawing upon legal doctrine and case law. It has been twelve years since I first read *The Sexual Harassment of Working Women.* While I have grown well beyond the personal experience that resonated with the book, I have learned that *The Sexual Harassment of Working Women* is one of those rare books you grow into, not out of.

REFERENCES

Brawley, P. (1991). What exactly is sexual harassment? *People Weekly, 36*(16), 48–50.

MacKinnon, C. (1995) Sexual harassment: Its first decade in court. In B. Price and N. Sokoloff (Eds,.), *The Criminal Justice System and Women* (pp. 297–311). New York: McGraw Hill.

Shalit, W. (1998). Feminism Lives! *National Review, 50*(6), 36–39.

U.S. Merit Systems Protection Board. (1981). *Sexual Harassment in the Federal Government.* Washington, DC: Author.

CHAPTER

7 Rape in Marriage

DIANA E. H. RUSSELL

"I would never think of taking it by force—except from my wife. I don't think I could get it up in a rape situation. It so appalls me that I couldn't do it."

"I don't think I have ever wanted to rape a woman except maybe my wife and I am not sure why I would want to rape her at this point. . . . I don't even believe in rape in marriage."

—Male respondents, *The Hite Report on Male Sexuality,* Shere Hite, 1981

In recent years, growing attention has been paid to various types of violence in the family. Nonsexual child abuse, particularly the physical beating of children as well as their gross emotional neglect or maltreatment, was the first type of violence in the family to be generally acknowledged. This was followed by attention to nonsexual wife abuse—"wife-battering," as it has been termed—and more recently, to child *sexual* abuse, particularly incest. The increased attention has produced a number of books on all three issues, and in turn these books have helped foster concern about these problems.

This is the first book to be published in the English language on the violent sexual abuse of women by their husbands.[1] However, the recent recognition in some states that rape in marriage is legally possible, combined with the publicity surrounding a few controversial trials of husbands accused of raping their wives, indicates that the problem of rape in marriage is finally being recognized. It is the goal of this book to increase this recognition; to provide an understanding of why the problem of wife rape exists; to show how it is connected with other problems such as unwanted sex in marriage, wife beating, and even the torture and killing of wives; and to suggest solutions to these problems.

The study I undertook and will report on here, and which informs this book, is the only study of wife rape in the United States to be based on interviews with a random sample of women. *Fourteen percent (14%) of the 930 women interviewed who had ever been married had been raped by a husband or ex-husband.* To the extent that this finding may be generalized to the population at large,[2] it suggests that at least one woman out of every seven who has ever been married has been raped by a husband at least once, and sometimes many times over many years. In other words, we all know women who have been raped by husbands.

The fact that these women were located by a random sample is important, because the results of studies based on volunteers from nonrepresentative populations may not be generalized, since volunteers are likely to be different from non-volunteers. For a start, those willing to seek out a stranger to talk to about being raped are more likely to have an experience that fits the stereotyped notion of what rape is. In particular, they are more likely to have been raped by a stranger. That is why it would be totally invalid to generalize about rape victims from the sample of volunteers whose experiences are described in *The Politics of Rape.* The most uniquely valuable aspect of the data to be presented here is that they show neither a selection of the most extreme cases, nor of the least extreme cases, but reveal the full gamut of such experiences.

Wife rape has presumably been with us as long as the institution of marriage—at least in western culture.* Though no one has yet written a history of wife rape, Susan Brownmiller does address the issue in her brilliant and comprehensive history of rape in general, *Against Our Will.* According to Brownmiller: "The exemption from rape prosecutions granted to husbands who force their wives into acts of sexual union by physical means is as ancient as the original definition of criminal rape, which was synonymous with that quaint phrase of Biblical origin, 'unlawful carnal knowledge.' To our Biblical forefathers," she continues, "any carnal knowledge outside the marriage contract was 'unlawful.' And any carnal knowledge within the marriage contract was, by definition, 'lawful.' Thus, as the law evolved, the idea that a husband could be prosecuted for raping his wife was unthinkable, for the law was conceived to protect his interests, not those of his wife."[3]

As Brownmiller and other feminist writers (such as Florence Rush in *The Best Kept Secret Sexual Abuse of Children* and Lorenne Clarke and Debra Lewis in *Rape The Price of Coercive Sexuality*) have shown, the idea that females are the property of males is the key to understanding the history of extramarital rape and the laws pertaining to it. This has been so well presented, I take it as a premise without going through the argument. Many cases cited in this book will show that the notion of wives as property is equally fundamental to an understanding of wife rape. Not only are wives commonly viewed as the property of their husbands, but more specifically, they are seen as the *sexual* property of their husbands. As John Stuart Mill pointed out in *The Subjection of Women* published in 1869:

> [A] female slave has (in Christian countries) an admitted right, and is considered under a moral obligation, to refuse to her master the last familiarity. Not so the wife: however brutal a tyrant she may unfortunately be chained to—though she may know that he hates her,

*Margaret Mead has claimed that a society called the Arapesh in New Guinea knew nothing of rape except that it was the unpleasant custom of another nearby society. Certainly, given Mead's description of the loving, gentle, nurturant relationships between Arapesh men and women, as well as between the parents and their children, it would be surprising to learn that rape in marriage occurred there. Presumably a few other societies once existed like the Arapesh. *Sex and Temperament in Three Primitive Societies* (New York: Dell, 1935), p. 110.

> though it may be his daily pleasure to torture her, and though she may feel it impossible not to loathe him—he can claim from her and enforce the lowest degradation of a human being, that of being made the instrument of an animal function contrary to her inclinations.*

But the viewing of wives as their husbands' property is not inevitable; it is part of our patriarchal heritage. The phenomenon of wife rape must be seen in the context of the patriarchal family.

Patriarchy refers to "a form of social organization in which the father is recognized as the head of the family." Outside of the family it also refers to "government by men."[4] The key elements of the contemporary patriarchal family involve the husband-father as the primary breadwinner, and the wife-mother as having the primary responsibility for childrearing and housework. Whether or not the wife also has paid employment outside the home is significant, and often has some impact on the balance of power within the family, but it certainly does not equalize the power between husband and wife as long as the basic division of labor and responsibility within the family is unchanged. This conclusion is supported by the fact that in the Soviet Union and other socialist countries, where a much higher percentage of married women work outside the home than in western nations, and where women have more access to high status jobs, wives still have the primary responsibility for housework and child care.[5] The concept of "the double day" for working women, and the quip that in socialist countries women are free to do two jobs, one paid and one unpaid, reflect this situation. The same "double day" applies to working women in western nations.

The point is not that any differentiated division of labor results in inequality (though it often does), but rather that the particular division of labor characteristic of the patriarchal family leads to inequality. This division of labor has been more or less culturally universal, with a few exceptions;[6] the oppression of women as a class by men as a class has been equally universal. The typical division of labor in patriarchal societies places the husband in the position of economic power, and the wife in the position of economic as well as status dependency. Given that women only earn fifty-nine cents to every dollar earned by a man, this economic dependence is diminished when wives have jobs outside the home, but the economic power imbalance is still present in most two-parent American families. If there are children, this economic dependency becomes economic vulnerability for the woman; if either the husband or the wife decides to end the marriage, the wife-mother can find herself in a critical economic situation, particularly if the children are young, and particularly in countries like the United States that have very few and very poor childcare facilities. Many wives in this situation can be coerced by their vulnerability into living with objectionable or abusive husbands. And if their husbands become disaffected with the marriage, wives may be forced to placate and accommodate them in an attempt to prevent being abandoned.

Having the primary responsibility for the care of children who are dependent and vulnerable and who demand much time and emotion, leaves mothers unable to pursue their

*The so-called right of the female slave mentioned by Mill hardly served as an effective protection. The right of women to reject the sexual advances of men other than their husbands was and is also constantly violated.

own interests, unless they are willing to reject the notion that children are their responsibility. Rejecting this role sometimes requires a willingness to abandon the children. Most mothers cannot do this. Most mothers feel this responsibility far more strongly than most fathers feel their responsibility to support the family, as evidenced by the fact that very few husbands continue to pay child support when a marriage breaks up, while the vast majority of wives continue to take care of the children (unless their economic situation makes this quite impossible).

The primary problem, however, is not that husbands or ex-husbands are being irresponsible. The problem is that the division of labor in the patriarchal family both reflects and perpetuates the husband's power over the wife. This is the context within which wife rape and wife beating occur, and often continue. Wife rape and wife beating are two very serious and cruel forms of husbands' abuse of their power over their wives. They are both extreme acts of domination. Other forms of domination that are effected without violence can be as devastating—for example, extreme verbal cruelty, or inordinate possessiveness. The fundamental problem is not that husbands abuse their power, but that they have so much of it in the first place. Not everyone who has power in an unbalanced power situation abuses it, but in general, where there is power imbalance, there is abuse.

Wife Rape and Social Science Research

Wife rape was rarely mentioned in social science literature until very recently. Even feminist analyses of rape have given little attention to wife rape. One exception: feminist sociologist Pauline Bart reported in 1975 that in her analysis of 1,070 questionnaires completed by rape victims who responded to a request published in *Viva* magazine, only four of the women had been raped by their husbands (i.e., 0.4 percent). Bart attributed this low figure to the fact that wife rape is legal in most states in the United States, so victims of wife rape were as unlikely as the law to recognize themselves as rape victims.[7] This is no doubt true, but another factor is the tendency already referred to for women with rape experiences that seem to be atypical to be less inclined to volunteer. This includes completing a questionnaire.

The first article to appear in a scholarly journal on the subject of wife rape was Richard Gelles' "Power, Sex, and Violence: The Case of Marital Rape," published in 1977.[8] Although Gelles deserves credit for being one of the first to introduce the problem to the scholarly community, he makes some very questionable statements.* For example, he writes that "labeling sexual intercourse forced on a wife by a husband 'marital rape' implies a major value judgment by the labeler concerning appropriate interpersonal relations between family members."[9] Clearly, however, *not* labeling such an act marital rape implies a major value judgment, too. Gelles next raises the question: "If the victim herself is unlikely to view the behavior as 'rape,' how can we discuss the phenomenon 'marital

*In his first book *The Violent Home,* Gelles even maintained that "sex-related violence is one of the types of violence where husbands and wives are equally aggressive." (Beverly Hills, Calif.: Sage Publications), p. 84.

rape'?" But sociologists have never limited themselves to studying only phenomena where the participants or victims subscribe to the same phenomenological viewpoint as themselves. Incest victims, for example, may never have heard the word incest, but that does not mean sociologists cannot study incest. It may simply mean they should not use the word incest when talking to the victims.

In this article Gelles offers as "one reason why so little attention has been directed toward forced sexual intercourse in marriage" the notion that "this is not viewed as a problem by most wives."[10] My own view is that it has been the researchers rather than the wives who did not see forced sex in marriage as a problem.*

For all the shortcomings of this article, Gelles did emphasize that "the topic of marital rape is an important area of investigation for social scientists," and that "the head-in-the-sand approach to marital rape is no longer acceptable."[11]

In 1978, Edward Sagarin, a well-known sociologist and past president of the American Society of Criminology, wrote in answer to the question "Is it legally possible to 'rape' one's own wife?":

> The rationale for not including an assault on the wife as rape was that marriage gave the husband the right to sexual intercourse with his spouse; that it did not give the woman the same right may be regarded by many as grossly unfair, but there are many obvious biological and physiological impediments to forcible sexual relations demanded by a willing woman of an unwilling man.[12]

Sagarin implies here that the essential problem is the inequity of married women not being able to rape their husbands; this indicates a serious misunderstanding of the issue.†

In 1979, Nicholas Groth included some discussion of wife rape in his book *Men Who Rape,* which he expanded on in an article published in 1981.[13] Based on extensive research with incarcerated sexual offenders, Groth observed that: "Some offenders assault only their own wives, others rape only strangers, and some sexually assault both. However, based on our clinical experience with identified offenders, *it makes little difference whether the victim is wife or stranger, the dynamics of the offender are the same*"[14] (emphasis mine). Unfortunately, Groth's data base does not make such a generalization permissible: his data are particularly poor as a basis for discussing and analyzing husbands who rape their wives, since they were collected on over five hundred offenders, all of whom had been convicted of raping someone *other than* their wives—usually strangers. This is an exceedingly select group. Groth shows extraordinary naïvete when he optimistically states: "There is no way of determining whether the subjects we have worked with and studied constitute a random sample of all men who rape. They are representative, however, of those offenders who

*A similar phenomenon occurred in the area of child abuse. Researchers failed for years to ask women and children whether or not they had been sexually abused in their early years.

†Sagarin goes on to caution his readers as follows: "Some people are agitating for a change in legal definitions of rape so that a husband can be held accountable as a rapist. Although it would meet the canons of fairness, such a law would be virtually unenforceable and it is unlikely that a successful prosecution could be made." (Ibid.) Fortunately, Sagarin has already been proved wrong, as will be evident from the many cases of wife rape that have already been prosecuted.

directly or indirectly come to the attention of criminal justice and mental health agencies and with whom law enforcement officials and providers of social services are expected to deal in some effective manner."[15]

First, we can be sure that it is not a random sample, because Groth did not apply random sampling techniques. Second, identified sexual aggressors—as he sometimes refers to them—are a unique group who in no way represent the population of rapists at large. The psychological and social characteristics (e.g., race, social class) of rapists who are not apprehended are likely to be very different from their less fortunate brothers. Brownmiller is among those suggesting that it is only the most disturbed rapists who are convicted, though studies on this issue are inconsistent.[16] Third, reported cases are not representative of unreported cases: only a fraction of the reported cases of rape ever result in offenders who "come to the attention of criminal justice and mental health agencies." Hence, if reported rape is the tip of the iceberg, the rapist who becomes an offender known to the criminal justice system is the speck of dust on the tip of the iceberg.

I think Groth's study is very valuable. I object only because he generalizes from this highly select and unrepresentative group to men who rape in general. For example, Groth states: "Although there is a wide variety of individual differences among men who rape, there are certain general characteristics that men who are prone to rape appear to have in common."[17] He goes on at length to enumerate these supposedly common characteristics, for example:

> His overall mood state, then, is dysphoric, characterized by dull depression, underlying feelings of fear and uncertainty and an overwhelming sense of purposelessness. At the root of all this are deep-seated doubts about his adequacy and competency as a person. He lacks a sense of confidence in himself as a man in both sexual and nonsexual areas—a feeling that is often unacknowledged since he exhibits little capacity for self-awareness.[18]

Groth proceeds to describe 10 percent of these men as being in a psychotic state at the time of the offense, and maintains that 56 percent "were diagnosed as belonging to various types of personality disorders (inadequate, antisocial, passive-aggressive, borderline, and the like)."[19] This picture may well be appropriate for incarcerated rapists; however, it is hopelessly limited and inadequate for the many different types of men who rape women in a culture that has itself been described as a "rape culture."[20] An account of the results of psychological research that has been conducted in the last few years should bring this point home.

Sociologist Martha Burt has reported that over half of a representative sample of 598 residents of Minnesota believed in the following kinds of rape myths: "Any healthy woman can resist a rapist"; "In the majority of rapes, the victim was promiscuous or had a bad reputation"; "If a girl engages in necking or petting and she lets things get out of hand, it is her fault if her partner forces sex on her"; "One reason that women falsely report a rape is that they frequently have a need to call attention to themselves."[21]

Burt found that rapists also believe such myths and that they "use them to excuse or deny their behavior after the fact."[22] She concluded that these attitudes effectively support rape, and hence that it is appropriate to talk about this being a rape supportive culture. Burt's findings have been supported by other researchers who have used college students as their subjects.[23]

In the first of a series of experiments, psychologist Neil Malamuth and his colleagues Scott Haber and Seymore Feshbach asked a sample of fifty-three male students to read a five-hundred-word "rape story," an excerpt of which follows:

> Bill soon caught up with Susan and offered to escort her to her car. Susan politely refused him. Bill was enraged by the rejection. "Who the hell does this bitch think she is, turning me down," Bill thought to himself as he reached into his pocket and took out a Swiss army knife. With his left hand he placed the knife at her throat. "If you try to get away, I'll cut you," said Bill. Susan nodded her head, her eyes wild with terror.

"The story then depicted the rape. There was a description of sexual acts with the victim continuously portrayed as clearly opposing the assault."[24] As is customary in much psychological research, the students were not drawn by any random sampling process; they volunteered to participate in the research as part of a requirement of introductory psychology courses. After they had read the rape story they were asked whether they personally would be likely to act as the rapist did in the same circumstances. The same question was then repeated, this time with an assurance that they would not be punished. The results: "On a response scale ranging from 1 to 5 (with 1 denoting 'none at all' and 5 'very likely'), 17 percent of the men specified 2 or above when asked if they would emulate such behavior 'under the same circumstances.'[25] But a total of 51 percent responded that they might do it if they were assured that they would not be caught."[26]

This study has since been replicated, mostly with college students in various areas of North America including Los Angeles and Palo Alto in California, and Winnipeg in Canada. Malamuth writes that across these varied studies, an average of about 35 percent of the males surveyed indicated at least some likelihood of raping if they could get away with it, and an average of about 20 percent reported a higher likelihood of raping, also if they could be assured of no punishment.[27] In a study by John Briere and his colleagues which focused on male students' willingness to force sex on a woman as well as to rape, 60 percent of their sample indicated some likelihood of rape or force or both given the right circumstances.[28] They concluded that their findings "reinforce the contention of feminist writers that there exists within the general population many males with a propensity toward sexual violence."[29]

Although male college students are clearly not representative of the male population at large, many researchers in this field would argue that college students are less inclined to rape than non-college students.[30] In a study of high school students, Roseann Giarusso and her colleagues report that more than 50 percent of the high school males they interviewed believed it was acceptable ". . . for a guy to hold a girl down and force her to have sexual intercourse in instances such as when 'she gets him sexually excited' or 'she says she's going to have sex with him and then changes her mind.' "[31]

Groth's psychological portrait (an extract of which was cited above) is supposed to apply to "men who are prone to rape." But the accumulating research that reveals how widespread the proclivity to rape is in the male population argues strongly against Groth's notion that 66 percent of all rape-prone men have psychotic episodes or suffer from clinically diagnosable personality disorders.

Terminology

The term "wife rape" is preferred over "marital rape" or "spousal rape" because it is not gender neutral. The term "spousal rape" in particular seems to convey the notion that rape is something that wives do to husbands, if not as readily as husbands do it to wives, at least sufficiently often that a gender neutral term should be used. When the spousal rape legislation was being discussed in the Senate Committee in California, use of this phrase seemed to help foster the illusion that the protection of husbands was being sought, not just the protection of wives. It was repeatedly emphasized that this legislation would also allow a husband to charge his wife with rape. The legislators, it seems, were believed to be more likely to support legislation that on the surface at least, was not totally inimical to their interests as males. But since all other researchers appear to prefer the term marital rape, it will necessarily be used here from time to time, particularly when discussing their work. The term husband-rapist will sometimes be used for husbands who rape their wives.

The two terms most widely used to describe violence in marriage aside from rape are "wife beating" and "wife battering." Both are highly problematic. The term "battering," for example, conveys the notion of extreme violence, and is appropriate only when the violence *is* extreme. It is not a suitable phrase to describe a marriage in which a woman is slapped from time to time. It is equally inappropriate to use the word rape to apply to all degrees of sexual abuse and assault. One of the consequences of using words like battery or rape to apply to all degrees of violence or sexual abuse is that less drastic but nevertheless serious experiences can easily be neglected. Hence in this book, the term "battered" will be reserved for severe violence such as repeated beating, slugging, kicking, choking, use of weapons, and the like.

"Wife beating" is a term with less extreme connotations. However, not all violence in marriage can accurately be described as beating. For example, the use of weapons to coerce, hurt, or even kill, is not always accompanied by beating. Throwing an object at another person is usually violent and may be highly dangerous, but it is not a beating. Violent acts such as shoving someone against a wall, throwing her to the floor, twisting an arm behind her back, are not accurately described by the term beating. Even slapping or being struck once, as opposed to repeatedly, seems to be too "minor" to warrant the term.

However, introducing a new phrase such as "husband violence" results in other problems. It is often necessary to differentiate between rape and other violent behavior, but to use the term "husband violence" for everything aside from rape implies that rape itself is not violent. Hence, the reader should be aware that when the term "wife beating" is used, it may refer to a wide range of violent acts toward wives, not beating alone. . . .

Finally, a word about what to expect in the ensuing pages may be helpful. I have written this book with two major purposes in mind: first, that it provide heretofore unavailable information about wife rape, and place it in an appropriate context that will enlighten the general public, and provide both ammunition and inspiration to those who seek to change the conditions that have caused the problem, as well as to those who seek to help the victims of wife rape. The second major purpose is to have an impact on the scholars working in the areas of violence against women, marriage, heterosexual sexuality, rape, and the oppression of women in general. . . .

Because this is the first book on rape in marriage, I felt it was important to include materials from all sources, published and unpublished, scholarly and journalistic, that I could find on this subject. This book does not attempt to provide a well-rounded picture of marriage today, or in the past, but instead, focuses on an ugly form of violation that occurs in many more marriages than most people would like to believe. My hope is that this book will make it impossible for the crime of wife rape to remain in the closet any longer.

NOTES

1. A short monograph titled *Vergewaltigung in der Ehe (Rape in Marriage)* by Dierk Helmken was published by Kriminalistik Verlag in Germany in 1979.
2. The validity of so generalizing will be discussed in Chapter 5.
3. *Against Our Will: Men, Women and Rape* (New York: Simon and Schuster, 1975), p. 380.
4. *Webster's Dictionary.*
5. See Paul Hollander, *Soviet and American Society; A Comparison* (New York: Oxford University Press, 1973) and Gail Lapidus, *Women in Soviet Society: Equality, Development, and Social Change* (Berkeley: University of California Press, 1978).
6. For example, the Nayar of India, described by E. Kathleen Gough, "The Nayars and the Definition of Marriage," *Journal of the Royal Anthropological Institute of Great Britain and Ireland,* Vol. 89, Part 1 (1959); and the Kibbutzim of Israel, Mel Spiro's "Is the Family Universal?—The Israeli Case" in Norman Bell and Ezra Vogel (eds.), *A Modern Introduction to the Family* (New York: The Free Press, 1960).
7. "Rape Doesn't End With a Kiss," *Viva,* June 1975, p. 40.
8. *The Family Coordinator,* Vol. 26, October 1977. This discussion of the social scientific literature of wife rape is limited to published works. Research on rape in marriage is being pursued by Irene Frieze (a social psychologist at the University of Pittsburgh), David Finkelhor (a sociologist at the University of New Hampshire), and Julie Doron (a sociologist at Barnard College). Their unpublished work is referred to and cited where appropriate throughout this book.
9. Ibid., p. 339.
10. Ibid., p. 344.
11. Ibid., p. 346.
12. "Rape of One's Wife," *Medical Aspects of Human Sexuality,* Vol. 12, No. 2 (February 1978), p. 153.
13. "Marital Rape," *Medical Aspects of Human Sexuality,* Vol. 15, No. 3 (March 1981).
14. Ibid., p. 127.
15. *Men Who Rape: The Psychology of the Offender* (New York: Plenum Press, 1979), p. xiii.
16. For a recent summary of some of these studies, see Mary P. Koss, Kenneth E. Leonard, Dana A. Beezley, and Cheryl J. Oros, "An Empirical Investigation of the Social Control and Psychopathological Models of Rape" (Paper delivered at the Annual American Psychological Association Meetings, August 1981).
17. *Men Who Rape,* p. 106.
18. Ibid., p. 107.
19. Ibid., p. 109.
20. *Rape Culture* is the title of one of the best-known documentary films about rape. The notion that the United States has a rape-supportive culture has also been argued and substantiated by Martha R. Burt, "Cultural Myths and Supports for Rape," *Journal of Personality and Social Psychology,* Vol. 38 (1980); and

"Attitudes Supportive of Rape in American Culture," House Committee on Science and Technology, Subcommittee on Domestic and International Scientific Planning, Analysis and Cooperation, *Research into Violent Behavior: Sexual Assaults.* Hearing, 95th Congress, 2nd Session, January 10–12, 1978 (Washington, D.C.: U.S. Government Printing Office, 1978), pp. 277–322.

21. Burt, "Attitudes Supportive of Rape" (Hearings).

22. Ibid., p. 5.

23. James V. P. Check and Neil M. Malamuth, "Feminism and Rape in the 1980's: Recent Research Findings" (Unpublished paper, portions of which were presented at the Section on Women and Psychology, Canadian Psychological Association Meetings, Toronto, Canada, June 1981).

24. "Testing Hypotheses Regarding Rape: Exposure to Sexual Violence, Sex Differences, and the 'Normality' of Rapists," *Journal of Research in Personality,* Vol. 14, No. 1, 1980, p. 124.

25. Ibid., p. 130.

26. Ibid.

27. Neil M. Malamuth, "Rape Proclivity Among Males," *Journal of Social Issues,* Vol. 37, No. 4 (December 1981).

28. John Briere, Neil Malamuth, and Joe Ceniti, "Self-Assessed Rape Proclivity: Attitudinal and Sexual Correlates" (Paper presented at the American Psychological Association Meetings, Los Angeles, August 1981).

29. Ibid., p. 2.

30. According to police statistics, those arrested for rape are disproportionately Black (*Uniform Crime Reports* [annual]) and lower class; see also the results of a seventeen-city survey undertaken by the Government Commission on Violence: Donald Mulvihill, Mehin Tumin, and Lynn Curtis, *Crimes of Violence: A Staff Report,* submitted to the National Commission on the Causes and Prevention of Violence, Government Printing Office, Washington, D.C. (1969), Vol. 11; and Susan Brownmiller, *Against Our Will,* 1975.

31. "Adolescents' Cues and Signals: Sex and Assault" (Paper presented at the Annual Meeting of the Western Psychological Association, San Diego, California, April 1979).

Reflection

DIANA E. H. RUSSELL

In 1977, I received funding from the National Institute of Mental Health to do a large-scale probability sample survey of women residents in San Francisco to try to ascertain the prevalence of rape and other forms of sexual assault. Although I included a question in the interview schedule asking the 930 respondents if they had ever been the victim of wife rape (these were not the actual words used), I had no intention of writing a book on rape in marriage at that time.

While I was still analyzing the survey data, legislation making "spousal rape" a crime in California was proposed in 1978 by Assemblyman Floyd Mori, who had been working against strong opposition to achieve this legal reform since 1976. Given the paucity of information on wife rape, particularly information obtained from a scientifically sound survey, I was asked to speak in support of the legislation when it came before the all-male Senate Judiciary Committee in Sacramento. On accepting this invitation, I focused on analyzing my data on wife rape.

As it turned out, I and 17 others—mostly women—never testified to the Senate Judiciary Committee. There was a last-minute decision to permit only four men and one woman to testify. Based on the questions asked and the answers given by the five selected individuals, it seemed clear that their major function was to reassure the worried Senators that if the law were passed, very few wives would likely try to prosecute their husbands for spousal rape. This made me realize that it was fortunate that I was not permitted to testify that 14 percent of the women who had ever been married in my survey had been the victims of rape or attempted rape by a husband.

After Assemblyman Mori agreed to several last-minute compromises, the bill on marital rape was approved unanimously, becoming law on January 1, 1980. Although my contribution to a change in the California law on spousal rape ended up being insignificant, I became aware of the need to publicize my findings about wife rape—not only as a tool for those campaigning to change the law in other states, but also to bring public attention to the appalling reality that many men considered rape in marriage to be their prerogative if their wives refused their advances. To continue to see rape in marriage as a husband's privilege is not only an insult, a gross violation of women's right to control their own bodies, but a very profound indicator of the flagrant inequity that is built into the institution of marriage in the United States—as well as in most other countries at that time.

I hoped that publishing a book on wife rape would publicize this scandalous situation, as well as the widespread prevalence and the traumatic effects experienced by the victims of rape by their husbands. I knew that changing the law would not be enough to empower women to report their husbands' rapes and seek their prosecution for these crimes without an educational campaign to publicize the new law. I hoped that my book would prove useful to the campaigners in states where rape in marriage was still legal. I personally traveled to a few states to share my findings with women advocates for battered women, who were the primary ones working on this issue. Finally, *Rape in Marriage* was published by Macmillan Press in 1982—the first book in the world on this topic.

Although the movement to criminalize rape in marriage in all states continued over the years, I felt very dissatisfied and disappointed with what I perceived to be the failure of the rape crisis centers and the battered women's movement to deal with wife rape after the publication of *Rape in Marriage.* The obvious inference is that my book did not have much impact on these two key feminist movements. Besides rarely getting invitations to lecture about wife rape after *Rape in Marriage* was published, hard evidence for my perception was provided by a national survey of services for victims of wife rape undertaken by Lynn Thompson-Haas, the Executive Director of the Austin Rape Crisis Center at the time (her unpublished report was completed in 1987).

When a second edition of *Rape in Marriage* was published by Indiana University Press in 1990, I decided to use my new introduction to criticize the rape crisis centers and the battered women's movement for their continuing neglect of wife rape—the most frequent form of this crime. I summarized the methodology and findings of Thompson-Haas's study, including her conclusion that "many sexual assault programs see marital rape as a 'family violence problem,' and many programs for battered women see it as a 'sexual assault issue' " (p. xxv). Neither movement considers it their responsibility to deal with rape in marriage. Hence, it continues to be neglected by the very organizations that should be assisting and advocating for these traumatized victims. Tragically, I believe this is still the case. This is particularly reprehensible for the battered women's movement, most of whose clientele have been raped by their violent husbands. In addition, there are a large number of victims of wife rape who have never been physically battered. There is no sound reason for rape crisis centers not to assist and counsel these women.

Happily, the literature on wife rape has grown considerably since I published both editions of *Rape in Marriage.* Although I've been disappointed that my book did not have a greater impact on the feminist movement against violence against women and influential policy makers in this country, I know that I have good reason to be proud of the quality of my study and my book and that both were groundbreaking achievements. I am also very gratified to know that *Rape in Marriage* has helped many survivors of this heinous form of misogyny.

CHAPTER

8

The Scope of Rape

Incidence and Prevalence of Sexual Aggression and Victimization in a National Sample of Higher Education Students

MARY P. KOSS, CHRISTINE A. GIDYCZ, AND NADINE WISNIEWSKI

The Federal Bureau of Investigation (FBI) defines rape as "carnal knowledge of a female forcibly and against her consent" and reports that 87,340 such offenses occurred in 1985 (FBI, 1986). However, these figures greatly underestimate the true scope of rape because they are based only on instances reported to police. Government estimates suggest that for every rape reported, 3–10 rapes are committed but not reported (Law Enforcement Assistance Administration [LEAA], 1975). Likewise, it is difficult to obtain realistic estimates of the number of men who perpetrate rape because only a fraction of reported rapes eventually result in conviction (Clark & Lewis, 1977). Victimization studies, such as the annual National Crime Survey (NCS), are the major avenue through which the full extent of the crime is estimated (e.g., Bureau of Justice Statistics [BJS], 1984). In these studies, the residents of a standard sampling area are asked to indicate those crimes of which they or anyone else in their household have been victims during the previous 6 months. These rates are then compared with official crime statistics for the area and the rate of unreported crime is estimated. The authors of the NCS have observed on the basis of their research that "rape is clearly an infrequent crime" (Kalish, 1974, p. 12) and that it is "the rarest of NCS measured violent offenses" (BJS, 1984, p. 5).

The NCS (e.g., BJS, 1984) includes items such as, "Were you knifed, shot at, or attacked with some other weapon by anyone at all during the last six months?" The screen question to alert the interviewer to a possible rape is "Did someone try to attack you in some other way?" Affirmative responses are followed by questioning that uses the word "rape" repeatedly. Several features of this approach may lead to underreporting of rape, including the use of a screen question that requires the subject to infer the focus of inquiry, the use of questions about rape that are embedded in a context of violent crime, and the assumption that the word rape is used by victims of sexual assault to conceptualize their experiences.

When viewed from the vantage point of mental health research, criminal victimization data are also limited. Studies such as the NCS (e.g., BJS, 1984) adopt a typological approach to rape: a woman is either a rape victim during the past 6 months or she is not a victim. In clinical research, finer gradations of victimization and a longer time frame would be useful (e.g., Koss & Oros, 1982; Weis & Borges, 1973). Prevalence data that reflect the cumulative number of women who have been sexually victimized within a specified time period are more appropriate in mental health research because the aftereffects of sexual assault remain for a considerable period.

Recently, several estimates of the prevalence of sexual victimization have been reported. Kilpatrick and colleagues (Kilpatrick, Best, Veronen, Amick, Villeponteaux, & Ruff, 1985; Kilpatrick, Veronen, & Best, 1984) conducted a criminal victimization survey via telephone of 2,004 randomly selected female residents of Charleston County, South Carolina. In their sample, 14.5% of the women disclosed one or more attempted or completed sexual assault experiences, including 5% who had been victims of rape and 4% who had been victims of attempted rape. Of the women who had been raped, only 29% reported their assault to police. Russell (1984) found that 24% of a probability sample of 930 adult women in San Francisco described in a personal interview experiences that involved "forced intercourse or intercourse obtained by physical threat(s) or intercourse completed when the woman was drugged, unconscious, asleep, or otherwise totally helpless and unable to consent" (p. 35). Only 9.5% of these women reported their experience to the police.

Many studies of the prevalence of rape and lesser forms of sexual aggression have involved college students. There are scientific and pragmatic reasons to study this group. They are a high risk group for rape because they are in the same age range as the bulk of rape victims and offenders. The victimization rate for women peaks in the 16–19-year-old age group, and the second highest rate occurs in the 20–24-year-old age group. The victimization rates for these groups are approximately 4 times higher than the mean for all women (BJS, 1984). Also, 45% of all alleged rapists who are arrested are individuals under age 25 (FBI, 1986). Approximately 26% of all persons aged 18–24 are attending school (U.S. Bureau of the Census, 1980).

Kanin and his associates (Kanin, 1957; Kanin & Parcell, 1977; Kirkpatrick & Kanin, 1957) found that 20%–25% of college women reported forceful attempts at sexual intercourse by their dates in which the woman ended up screaming, fighting, crying, or pleading, and 26% of college men reported a forceful attempt to obtain sexual intercourse that caused observable distress in the woman. Rapaport and Burkhart (1984) reported that 15% of a sample of college men acknowledged that they had obtained sexual intercourse against their dates' will. Koss and colleagues (Koss, 1985; Koss, Leonard, Beezley, & Oros, 1985; Koss & Oros, 1982) administered the self-report Sexual Experiences Survey to a sample of 2,016 female and 1,846 male midwestern university students. They found that 13% of female college students revealed a victimization experience that involved sexual intercourse against their consent obtained through the use of actual force or the threat of harm, and 4.6% of male college students admitted perpetrating an act of sexual aggression that met legal definitions of rape.

To extend previous research to a national basis, the present study of students enrolled in higher education was undertaken. Although the rape laws in many states are sex neutral, women victims and male perpetrators were focused on in the present study because women represent virtually 100% of reported rape victims (LEAA, 1975). Furthermore, the FBI definition of rape that is used in victimization studies such as the NCS limits the crime of rape to female victims (BJS, 1984).

Method

The study involved administration of a self-report questionnaire to a national sample of 6,159 students enrolled in 32 institutions of higher education across the United States.

Sampling Plan

The sampling goal of the project was to represent the higher education student population in the United States in all its diversity—men, women, technical schools, community colleges, Ivy League schools, state universities, and so forth. No sample design was expected to result in a purely random or representative sample, however, because the subject matter is sufficiently controversial that some schools targeted by a systematic sampling plan were expected to refuse to participate.

Initial Decisions. Several initial decisions were made that governed subsequent decisions. First, the commitment to replicability and representativeness meant using as a sample frame all of the institutions of academic postsecondary education in the United States. Second, it was concluded that administration of the instrument had to be conducted by self-report and not in private interview. Serious problems with sample attrition and selective participation have been encountered in studies that have used a two-stage sample process where a mass screening is followed by a private interview (Ageton, 1983; Koss, Leonard, Beezley, & Oros, 1985). Third, administration of the questionnaire was to be conducted on-site and not by mail because the latter may have produced a strong self-selectivity bias. On-site administration in classrooms was considered to produce a more reliable representation of those asked to complete the questionnaire. These requirements dictated that the sample be selected in stages. The first stage was the selection of institutions and the second stage was the selection of classes within institutions.

Selection of Institutions. The United States Department of Education maintains records of the enrollment characteristics from the 3,269 institutions of higher education in the United States (Office of Civil Rights, 1980). The Office of Civil Rights provided a copy of their information for 1980 (the latest available) on data tape to the survey consultants, Clark/Jones, Incorporated of Columbus, Ohio. On the basis of these data, institutions across the nation were sorted by location into the ten Department of Education regions of the

United States (i.e., Alaska, Hawaii, New England, Mideast, Great Lakes, Plains States, Southeast, Southwest, Rocky Mountain, and West). Within each region, institutions were placed into homogeneous clusters according to five criteria: (a) location inside or outside of a standard metropolitan statistical area (SMSA) of certain sizes (i.e., SMSA greater than 1,000,000 people; SMSA less than 1,000,000 people; outside an SMSA); (b) enrollment above or below the national mean percentage enrollment of minority students; (c) control of the institution by private secular; private religious, or public authority; (d) type of institution, including university, other 4-year college, 2-year junior college, and technical/vocational; and (e) total enrollment within three levels (i.e., 1,000–2,499 students; 2,500–9,999 students; more than 10,000 students).

Two sampling rules were developed to select the schools to be recruited into the sample. First, the largest institution in each region was always included. Without this rule, it would have been possible to omit the "Big Ten" or other major schools from the sample entirely. Second, every *x*th cluster was sampled according to the proportion of total enrollment accounted for by the region. Replacements were sought from among other schools in the homogeneous cluster if the original target proved uncooperative. Several exceptions to the sampling rules were made for the sake of reasonableness and cost constraint. The following types of schools were eliminated from the sample: military schools, schools with enrollments of less than 1,000 students, schools not in the contiguous United States, and graduate schools with no undergraduate affiliation. The descriptive characteristics of the institutions of higher education in the United States, the number of institutions of each type that were proposed for the national sample, and the number of institutions of each type that participated in the survey are summarized in Table 8.1.

Institutional Recruitment. The process of obtaining institutional cooperation began by identifying the responsible individual in the central administration. Due to the nature of institutional decision making and to the controversial subject matter of the study, the amount of time required to obtain a sample was extensive; some schools required 15 months to arrive at a final decision. During that period, 93 schools were contacted and 32 participants were obtained. Nineteen of the institutions were first choices; the remaining 13 were solicited from among 60 replacements. Actual institutional participants cannot be listed because they were guaranteed anonymity. However, the characteristics of institutional participants summarized in Table 8.1 indicate that they reasonably approximated the sampling plan.

It might be argued that the resulting sample would be biased toward schools with a liberal administration. However, some schools with the most liberal reputations in the nation refused. The rationales given for nonparticipation by the 60 administrations that refused included religious objections (11); concerns about subject anonymity (2); concerns about sensationalization of the results (3); human subject concerns or human subject's disapproval (10); lack of interest (8); lack of administrative time (6); no research allowed in classes (6); doing their own survey (3); and no reasons (11).

Inevitably, the final sample was the result of an interplay of scientific selection and head-to-head negotiation but was within the limits of substitution rules requiring replacement within homogeneous clusters. The final sample of institutions was as replicable and

TABLE 8.1 Descriptive Characteristics of Higher Education Institutions

Sample Parameter	Institutions *N*	*In Sample Plan*	*In Actual Sample*
Location			
Not in SMSA	643	11	10
SMSA < 1,000,000	706	13	8
SMSA > 1,000,000	649	11	14
Region			
New England	140	3	2
Mideast	374	6	5
Great Lakes	334	5	7
Plains	172	3	3
Southeast	442	8	7
Southwest	183	5	4
Rocky Mountain	60	1	1
West	259	4	3
Minority tally			
Below mean	1451	25	23
Above mean	547	10	9
Governance			
Public	1307	23	23
Private	392	7	7
Religious	299	5	2
Type			
University	156	7	16
Other 4-year	1013	15	11
2-year	829	13	5
Size			
1,000–2,499	843	14	6
2,500–9,999	820	14	10
>9,999	335	7	16

Note: SMSA = standard metropolitan statistical area.

representative a sample of postsecondary institutions as it was possible to obtain within time and budgetary limitations and given the nature of the inquiry. Although sampling error cannot be measured precisely with a sample of this type, representativeness can be tested by reference to other data sources. These data will be presented in a later section.

Selection of Classes. A random selection process was used to choose target classes and alternates in the case of schedule conflicts or refusals. The only limitations on class selection were that classes under 30 students and large lecture sections were eliminated to ensure that one experimenter's time on campus was used efficiently while avoiding classes that were too large for one person to handle. The actual number of classes visited was a mean of 7 at smaller and medium-sized schools and a mean of 12 at major universities. Because their presence could be coercive on students, instructors were absent during the administration.

Administration Procedures. The questionnaire was administered in classroom settings by 1 of 8 postmaster's level psychologists, including 2 men and 6 women who used a prepared script and were trained by the first author in standard procedures to handle potential untoward effects of participation. The questionnaire was completely anonymous and was accompanied by a cover sheet that contained all the elements of informed consent. Students who did not wish to participate were asked to remain in their seats and do other work. This insured that persons who objected to participation would not be stigmatized. Only 91 persons (1.5%) indicated that they did not wish to participate. Students were debriefed by the experimenter according to a prepared script and received a printed statement that explained the purpose of the study and indicated where the experimenter would be available on campus for private conferences. The phone numbers of local agencies that had agreed to offer services to participants were also provided. The college counseling center of every campus visited was informed of the project and was invited to name a sexual assault specialist whose name would be listed on the debriefing sheet and to send observers to the questionnaire administrations.

Subjects

The final sample consisted of 6,159 persons, including 3,187 women and 2,972 men. The 3,187 women were characterized as follows: their mean age was 21.4 years; 85% were single, 11% married, and 4% divorced; 86% were White, 7% Black, 3% Hispanic, 3% Asian, and 1% Native American; and 39% were Catholic, 38% Protestant, 4% Jewish, and 20% other or none. The 2,972 men were characterized as follows: their mean age was 21.0 years; 91% were single, 9% married, and 1 % divorced; 86% were White, 6% Black, 3% Hispanic, 4% Asian, and 1% Native American; and 40% were Catholic, 34% Protestant, 5% Jewish, and 22% other or none.

Comparisons with National Enrollment Data. Because of the assumptions on which the sampling plan was based and the institutional hesitancy to participate, the sample was not absolutely representative. However, within the limitations of our assumptions, it was a close approximation of the higher education enrollment. A comparison of the characteristics of the present sample with the characteristics of the entire U.S. higher education enrollment is presented in Table 8.2. (No tests of significance were performed because even minute differences would be statistically significant given the large population size.)

Four variables were examined to determine the extent to which this sample was representative of U.S. higher education enrollment: institution location and region and subject ethnicity and income. Institution region was the only variable on which significant discrepancy was noted. The present sample overrepresented the proportion of students who were enrolled at institutions in the Northeast and Southwest and underrepresented students who

TABLE 8.2 Comparison of Sample and National Student Characteristics

Sample Parameter	Present Sample[a]	U.S. Higher Education Enrollment[b]
Location		
Not in SMSA	31.0	32.0
SMSA < 1,000,000	25.0	21.0
SMSA > 1,000,000	44.0	47.0
Ethnicity		
White	86.0	82.4
Black	6.4	9.6
Hispanic	3.3	4.4
Asian	3.3	2.7
Native American	0.6	0.7
Income (yearly)		
$0–$15,000	13.4	16.7
$15,000–$25,000	17.2	16.2
$25,000–$35,000	22.5	19.8
>$35,000	45.7	46.3
Region (no. institutions)		
New England	6.2	7.7
Mideast	15.6	19.4
Great Lakes	21.9	15.9
Plains	9.4	10.2
Southeast	21.9	22.7
Southwest	12.5	7.5
Rocky Mountain	3.1	2.8
West	9.4	12.1
Region (% enrollment)		
New England	12.7	6.3
Mideast	12.4	18.0
Great Lakes	17.6	18.3
Plains	9.4	7.4
Southeast	16.8	18.8
Southwest	20.6	9.8
Rocky Mountain	4.4	4.0
West	6.0	18.3

Note: All results, except where noted, are reported in percentages.

SMSA = standard metropolitan statistical area.

[a]Data collected from study survey for period from 1984–1985.

[b]Data for location and region reported in Office of Civil Rights (1980); data for ethnicity (1982) and income (1983) reported in U.S. Department of Commerce (1986).

were enrolled at institutions in the West. These discrepancies reflected irremediable difficulties in obtaining institutional access on the west coast. After 15 months, only 3 institutions had agreed to allow data collection. Therefore, it was decided to proceed without full representation from western schools.

The regional disproportion is unimportant in many respects because, without extensive sampling in the West, the individual participants in the sample were still reflective of national enrollment in ethnicity and family income. Nevertheless, for purposes of calculating prevalence data, weighing factors were used. The sample was weighted using the proportions of higher education enrollment in each of the federal regions. These data are found at the bottom of Table 8.2. Whereas 12.7% of the present sample were attending institutions in the Northeast, only 6.3% of the national enrollment was represented by that region. Hence, responses from students at these institutions were weighted to be equivalent to 6.3% of the present sample. Likewise, responses of the 20.6% of the sample that came from the Southeast were weighted to be equivalent to 9.8% of the sample. Finally, responses of the 6.0% of the subjects who were attending schools in the West were weighted to be equivalent to 18.3% of the present sample.

Measurement of Sexual Aggression or Victimization

Survey Instrument. All data were obtained via a self-report questionnaire titled, "National Survey of Inter-Gender Relationships." (This title was selected to be neutral and to avoid the word "sex" so that participants would not prejudge the content.) The questionnaire consisted of approximately 330 questions divided into seven sections. The data set is too extensive to be summarized in a single paper; therefore, only data on demography, incidence, and prevalence of sexual aggression and victimization after the age of 14 are reported here.

The data on the incidence and prevalence of sexual aggression were obtained through the use of the 10-item Sexual Experiences Survey (SES; Koss & Gidycz, 1985; Koss & Oros, 1982). This survey is a self-report instrument designed to reflect various degrees of sexual aggression and victimization. During actual administration, separate wordings were used for women and for men. However, for purposes of demonstration, the female wording is presented in the following sample item and the male wording is indicated in brackets: "Have you ever had [engaged in] sexual intercourse when you [the woman] didn't want to because a man [you] used some degree of physical force (twisting your [her] arm, holding you [her] down, etc.) to make you [her]?" The text of all 10 items (female wording) can be found in Table 8.3, which is discussed further in the results section.

Reliability and Validity Studies. Internal consistency reliabilities of .74 (for women) and .89 (for men) have been reported for the SES, and the test-retest agreement rate between administrations 1 week apart was 93% (Koss & Gidycz, 1985). However, many investigators have questioned the validity of self-reported sexual behavior. The accuracy and truthfulness of self-reports on the SES have been investigated (Koss & Gidycz, 1985). The Pearson correlation between a woman's level of victimization based on self-report and her level of victimization based on responses related to an interviewer several months later

TABLE 8.3 Frequencies and Prevalence of Individual Sexual Experiences Since Age 14

	Women (*N* = 3,187)			Men (*N* = 2,972)		
Sexual Behavior	%	*M*	*SD*	%	*M*	*SD*
1. Have you given in to sex play (fondling, kissing, or petting, but not intercourse) when you didn't want to because you were overwhelmed by a man's continual arguments and pressure?	44	3.2	1.5	19	2.9	1.5
2. Have you had sex play (fondling, kissing, or petting, but not intercourse) when you didn't want to because a man used his position of authority (boss, teacher, camp counselor, supervisor) to make you?	5	2.7	1.7	1	2.5	1.5
3. Have you had sex play (fondling, kissing, or petting, but not intercourse) when you didn't want to because a man threatened or used some degree of physical force (twisting your arm, holding you down, etc.) to make you?	13	2.1	1.5	2	2.3	1.5
4. Have you had a man attempt sexual intercourse (get on top of you, attempt to insert his penis) when you didn't want to by threatening or using some degree of force (twisting your arm, holding you down, etc.), but intercourse *did not* occur?	15	2.0	1.4	2	2.0	1.2
5. Have you had a man attempt sexual intercourse (get on top of you, attempt to insert his penis) when you didn't want to by giving you alcohol or drugs, but intercourse *did not* occur?	12	2.0	1.4	5	2.2	1.4
6. Have you given in to sexual intercourse when you didn't want to because you were overwhelmed by a man's continual arguments and pressure?	25	2.9	1.6	10	2.4	1.4
7. Have you had sexual intercourse when you didn't want to because a man used his position of authority (boss, teacher, camp counselor, supervisor) to make you?	2	2.5	1.7	1	2.0	1.4
8. Have you had sexual intercourse when you didn't want to because a man gave you alcohol or drugs?	8	2.2	1.5	4	2.5	1.5
9. Have you had sexual intercourse when you didn't want to because a man threatened or used some degree of physical force (twisting your arm, holding you down, etc.) to make you?	9	2.2	1.5	1	2.3	1.5
10. Have you had sex acts (anal or oral intercourse or penetration by objects other than the penis) when you didn't want to because a man threatened or used some degree of physical force (twisting your arm, holding you down, etc.) to make you?	6	2.2	1.6	1	2.5	1.5

Note: Sexual intercourse was defined as penetration of a woman's vagina, no matter how slight, by a man's penis. Ejaculation was not required.

was .73 ($p < .001$). More important, only 3% of the women (2 out of 68) who reported experiences that met legal definitions of rape were judged to have misinterpreted questions or to have given answers that appeared to be false. The Pearson correlation between a man's level of aggression as described on self-report and as given in the presence of an interviewer was .61 ($p < .001$).

A further validity study was conducted in conjunction with the present project. Male students were selected as subjects because previous work had raised more questions about the validity of their responses than about women's responses. The SES items were administered both by self-report and by a one-to-one interview on the same occasion and in one setting. The interviewer was a fully trained, licensed, and experienced male PhD clinical psychologist. Subjects were 15 male volunteers, identified by first name only, recruited through newspaper advertisements on the campus of a major university. All subjects were juniors or seniors (psychology majors were eliminated from consideration to reduce the possibility that the interviewer would know any of the subjects) and were paid $10 for participation. Their demographic characteristics were as follows: mean age was 21.3 years; 100% were single; 87% were White and 13% minority; 27% were Catholic, 27% Protestant, 27% none or other, and 20% Jewish; and 40% had family incomes greater than $35,000. These demographic characteristics closely paralleled those of the men in the national sample.

Participants gave their self-reports first and were then interviewed individually. The intent was to match the participants' verbal responses with their self-reports on the SES. The results indicated that 14 of the participants (93%) gave the same responses to SES items on self-report and in interview. The one inconsistency involved an individual who admitted a behavior on self-report that he later denied to the interviewer. On average, subjects rated their honesty at 95% and indicated that the reason for lack of full honesty was time pressure for getting through the questionnaire.

Scoring Procedure. Because some individuals had experienced several different forms of sexual aggression or victimization, summing the percentage of persons who reported each individual act would have given an inflated estimate of the total number of sexually aggressive or victimized persons. Therefore, respondents were classified according to the most severe sexual aggression or victimization they reported, including no sexual aggression or victimization, sexual contact, sexual coercion, attempted rape, and rape. The groups labeled "rape" (yes responses to Items 8, 9, or 10 and any lower numbered items) and "attempted rape" (yes responses to Items 4 or 5 but not to any higher numbered items) included individuals whose experiences met legal definitions of these crimes. The legal definition of rape in Ohio (as in many states) is "vaginal intercourse between male and female, and anal intercourse, fellatio, and cunnilingus between persons regardless of sex. Penetration, however slight, is sufficient to complete vaginal or anal intercourse . . . No person shall engage in sexual conduct with another person . . . when any of the following apply: (1) the offender purposely compels the other person to submit by force or threat of force, (2) for the purpose of preventing resistance the offender substantially impairs the other person's judgment or control by administering any drug or intoxicant to the other person" (Ohio Revised Code, 1980).

The group labeled "sexual coercion" (yes responses to Items 6 or 7 but not to any higher numbered items) included subjects who engaged in or experienced sexual intercourse subsequent to the use of menacing verbal pressure or the misuse of authority. No threats of force or direct physical force were used. The group labeled "sexual contact" (yes responses to Items 1, 2, or 3 but not to any higher numbered items) consisted of individuals who had engaged in or experienced sexual behavior such as fondling or kissing that did not involve attempted penetration subsequent to the use of menacing verbal pressure, misuse of authority, threats of harm, or actual physical force.

Results

The Prevalence of Sexual Aggression or Victimization

The unweighted response frequencies for each item of the SES are presented in Table 8.3. The frequencies of victimization ranged from 44% of women who reported unwanted sexual contact subsequent to coercion to 2% of women who reported unwanted sexual intercourse subsequent to misuse of his authority. The frequency with which men reported having perpetrated each form of sexual aggression ranged from 19% of men who indicated that they had obtained sexual contact through the use of coercion to 1% of men who indicated that they had obtained oral or anal penetration through the use of force. Those respondents who had engaged in or experienced sexually aggressive acts indicated that each act had occurred a mean of 2.0–3.2 times since age 14. The unweighted item response frequencies and the means and standard deviations for the number of times that a behavior was reported are contained in Table 8.3.

As mentioned previously, respondents were classified according to the highest degree of sexual victimization or aggression they reported, using the designated scoring procedures. Using weighted data to correct for regional disproportions, we found that 46.3% of women respondents revealed no experiences whatsoever with sexual victimization whereas 53.7% of women respondents revealed some form of sexual victimization. The most serious sexual victimization ever experienced was sexual contact for 14.4% of the women; sexual coercion for 11.9%; attempted rape for 12.1%; and rape for 15.4%. Weighted male data indicated that 74.8% of men had engaged in no form of sexual aggression, whereas 25.1% of men revealed involvement in some form of sexual aggression. The most extreme level of sexual aggression ever perpetrated was sexual contact for 10.2% of the men, sexual coercion for 7.2%; attempted rape for 3.3%; and rape for 4.4%. The weighted and unweighted prevalence rates for sexual aggression and victimization are found in Table 8.4. Examination of these figures reveals that the effect of weighting was minimal and tended to reduce slightly the prevalence of the most serious acts of sexual aggression.

The relation of prevalence rates to the institutional parameters used to design the sample was examined via chi-square analysis and analysis of variance (ANOVA). Due to the large sample size, differences with no real practical significance could reach statistical significance. Therefore, effect sizes were calculated using Cohen's (1977) method (*w* for chi-

TABLE 8.4 Weighted and Unweighted Prevalence Rate Percentages for Sexual Aggression and Victimization Since Age 14

	Women (N = 3,187)		**Men (N = 2,972)**	
Aggression or Victimization Level	*Weighted*	*Unweighted*	*Weighted*	*Unweighted*
No sexual aggression or victimization	46.3	45.6	74.8	75.6
Sexual contact	14.4	14.9	10.2	9.8
Sexual coercion	11.9	11.6	7.2	6.9
Attempted rape	12.1	12.1	3.3	3.2
Rape	15.4	15.8	4.4	4.6

squares and f for F ratios) to gauge the importance of any significant differences. Cohen's guidelines for interpretation of effect sizes state that a w or f of .10 indicates a small effect, a w of .30 or an f of .25 indicates a medium effect, and a w of .50 and an f of .40 indicates a large effect. The prevalence of sexual victimization did not differ according to the size of the city where the institution of higher education was located, $\chi^2(8, N = 2{,}728) = 5.55, p < .697, w = .05$; the size of the institution, $\chi^2(8, N = 2{,}728) = 6.35, p < .608, w = .05$; the type of institution, $\chi^2(8, N = 3{,}086) = 10.37, p < .240, w = .05$; or whether the minority enrollment of the institution was above or below the national mean, $\chi^2(4, N = 2{,}728) = 4.03, p < .401, w = .04$. However, rates of sexual victimization did vary by region, $\chi^2(28, N = 3{,}086) = 63.00, p < .001, w = 14$; and by the governance of the institution, $\chi^2(8, N = 3{,}086) = 22.93, p < .003, w = .09$. The rate at which women reported having been raped was twice as high in private colleges (14%) and major universities (17%) as it was at religiously affiliated institutions (7%). Victimization rates were also slightly higher in the Great Lakes and Plains States than in other regions.

The prevalence of sexual aggression also did not differ according to city size, $\chi^2(8, N = 2{,}641) = 6.41, p < .600, w = .05$; institution size, $\chi^2(8, N = 2{,}641) = 3.76, p < .878, w = .04$; minority enrollment, $c^2(4, N = 2{,}641) = 4.84, p < .303, w = .04$; governance, $\chi^2(8, N = 2{,}875) = 13.66, p < .091, w = .07$; and type of institution, $\chi^2(8, N = 2{,}875) = 3.99, p < .858, w = .04$. However, the percent of men who admitted perpetrating sexual aggression did vary according to the region of the country in which they attended school, $\chi^2(28, N = 2{,}875) = 56.25, p < .001, w = .14$. Men admitted rape twice as often in the Southeast (6%) as in the Plains States (3%) and three times as often as in the West (2%).

Finally, the relation between prevalence rates and individual demographic variables, including income, religion, and ethnicity, was also studied. The rate at which women reported experiences of sexual victimization did not vary according to subject's family income, $F(4, 3010) = .31, p < .871, f = .06$; or religion, $\chi^2(16, N = 3{,}077) = 17.86, p < .332, w = .08$. However, the prevalence rates of victimization did vary according to ethnicity, $\chi^2(16, N = 3{,}075) = 37.05, p < .002, w = .11$. For example, rape was reported by 16% of White women ($N = 2{,}655$), 10% of Black women ($N = 215$),12% of Hispanic women ($N = 106$), 7% of Asian women ($N = 79$), and 40% of Native American women ($N = 20$).

The number of men who admitted acts of sexual aggression did not vary according to subject's religion, $\chi^2(16, N = 2{,}856) = 20.98$, $p < .179$, $w = .09$; or family income, $F(3, 2821) = .08$, $p < .987$. However, the number of men who reported acts of sexual aggression did differ by ethnic group, $\chi^2(16, N = 2{,}861) = 55.55$, $p < .000$, $w = .14$. For example, rape was reported by 4% of White men ($N = 2{,}484$), 10% of Black men ($N = 162$), 7% of Hispanic men ($N = 93$), 2% of Asian men ($N = 106$), and 0% of Native American men ($N = 16$).

The Incidence of Sexual Aggression or Victimization

Incidence rates indicate how many new episodes occurred during a specified time period. In this study, respondents were asked to indicate how many times during the previous year (to improve recall, the question referred to the previous academic year from September to September, time boundaries that are meaningful to students) they had engaged in or experienced each item in the SES. Even when consideration was limited to the previous year, some subjects reported multiple episodes of sexual aggression or victimization. Therefore, the incidence of sexual aggression or victimization was calculated two ways. First, the number of people who reported one or more episodes during the year was determined. Second, the total number of sexually aggressive incidents that were reported by women and by men was calculated. For example, the responses to the three items that operationalize rape for the 12-month period preceding the survey indicated that intercourse by physical force was experienced by 63 women who reported 98 incidents; intercourse by intentional intoxication was experienced by 91 women who reported 159 incidents; and forcible oral or anal penetration was experienced by 53 women who reported 96 incidents. The responses to these individual items were totaled to obtain an incidence rate for rape of 353 rapes involving 207 different women during a 12-month period in a population of 3,187 women. Figures for the other levels of sexual victimization were 533 attempted rapes (323 victims), 837 episodes of sexual coercion (366 victims), and 2,024 episodes of unwanted sexual contact (886 victims). The incidence data for the individual items used to calculate these rates are found in Table 8.5.

Incidence rates for the sexual aggression admitted by men were also calculated. For example, the responses to the three items that operationalize rape for the 12-month period preceding the survey indicated that nonconsentual intercourse was obtained through force by 20 men who revealed 36 incidents, nonconsentual intercourse was obtained through intentional intoxication by 57 men who reported 103 incidents, and nonconsentual forcible oral or anal penetration of a woman was obtained by 19 men who reported 48 incidents. Totaled responses to these individual items for the 12 months preceding the survey yielded 187 rapes perpetrated by 96 different men. Incidence rates during the 12-month period for the other levels of sexual aggression were 167 attempted rapes (105 perpetrators), 854 episodes of unwanted sexual contact (374 perpetrators), and 311 episodes of sexual coercion (167 perpetrators). The incidence data for the individual items that were used to calculate these rates are presented in Table 8.5.

From the present data, victimization rates can be calculated. The number of women (who reported a sexual experience during the previous year that met legal definitions of rape and attempted rape) divided by 2 (to obtain a 6-month basis) and set to a base of 1,000

TABLE 8.5 One-Year Incidence Frequencies of Sexual Experiences

Sexual Experience	Women (*N* = 3,187)		Men (*N* = 2,972)	
	n	*Incidents*	*n*	*Incidents*
1. Sexual contact by verbal coercion	725	1716	321	732
2. Sexual contact by misuse of authority	50	97	23	55
3. Sexual contact by threat or force	111	211	30	67
4. Attempted intercourse by force	180	297	33	52
5. Attempted intercourse by alcohol or drugs	143	236	72	115
6. Intercourse by verbal coercion	353	816	156	291
7. Intercourse by misuse of authority	13	21	11	20
8. Intercourse by alcohol or drugs	91	159	57	103
9. Intercourse by threat or force	63	98	20	36
10. Oral or anal penetration by threat or force	53	96	19	48

(instead of the 3,187 women actually surveyed) yields a victimization rate of 83 per 1,000 women for the present population during a 6-month period. However, the FBI definition of rape (i.e., forcible actual or attempted vaginal intercourse with a woman against consent by force or threat of force) on which the NCS is based is narrower than the state laws (i.e., oral, anal, vaginal intercourse, or penetration by objects against consent through threat, force, or intentional incapacitation of the victim via drugs) on which the present study was based (BJS, 1984). Therefore, the victimization rate was also calculated in conformance with the FBI definition. Elimination of all incidents except those that involved actual or attempted vaginal sexual intercourse through force or threat of harm resulted in a victimization rate of 38 per 1,000 women during a 6-month period.

Perpetration rates were also determined using the male data. When all unwanted oral, anal, and vaginal intercourse attempts and completions were included in the calculations, a perpetration rate of 34 per 1,000 men was obtained. Use of the FBI definition resulted in a perpetration rate of 9 per 1,000 men during a 6-month period.

Discussion

In the present study, behaviorally specific items regarding rape and lesser forms of sexual aggression or victimization were presented in a noncrime context to an approximately representative national sample of higher education students. The result indicated that, since the age of 14, 27.5% of college women reported experiencing and 7.7% of college men reported perpetrating an act that met legal definitions of rape, which includes attempts. Because virtually none of these victims or perpetrators had been involved in the criminal justice system, their experiences would not be reflected in official crime statistics such as the *Uniform Crime Reports* (e.g., FBI, 1986).

A victimization rate for women of 38 per 1,000 was calculated, which represented the number of women per thousand who experienced a rape (that met the FBI definition) during the previous 6 months. A corresponding perpetration rate of 9 per 1,000 men was also reported, which represented the number of men per thousand who admitted an act during the previous 6 months that met the FBI definition of rape. This rape victimization rate is 10–15 times greater than rates that are based on the NCS (BJS, 1984), which are 3.9 per 1,000 16–19-year-old women and 2.5 per 1,000 20–24-year-old women. Even men's rates of admitting to raping are 2–3 times greater than NCS estimates of the risk of rape for women between the ages of 16–24. At least among students in higher education, it must be concluded that official surveys such as the NCS fail to describe the full extent of sexual victimization.

Of course, NCS rates are based on representative samples of all persons in the U.S. in the 16–24-year-old group, whereas the present sample represented only the 26% of persons aged 18–24 who attended higher education. Using other available data for guidance, one can speculate how the victimization rates among postsecondary students might compare with rates among nonstudents in the same age group. Persons over age 25 with at least some college training have a rape incidence of .7 per 1,000 compared with .4 per 1,000 for persons with some high school and .5 per 1,000 for persons with elementary education only (BJS, 1984). Crime rates by education are not calculated for persons under age 25. However, these data do not suggest a direct relation between educational attainment and rape victimization rates. On the other hand, rape victimization rates are clearly related to family income. The victimization rate is 3 per 1,000 for yearly incomes less than $3,000, 2 per 1,000 for yearly incomes of $3,000–$7,499, 1 per 1,000 for yearly incomes $10,000–$14,999, and .4–.5 per 1,000 for yearly incomes of $15,000 or more (BJS, 1984). The mean family income of the students in the national sample was in the $25,000–$35,000 range. Thus, nonstudents who are likely to come from poorer families than students enrolled in higher education might show even higher incidence rates than those found in the present sample. Only when empirical data become available on young persons not attending school, however, can the victimization rates reported in the NCS for persons aged 18–24 be fully critiqued.

The findings of the present study demonstrate that men do not admit enough sexual aggression to account for the number of victimizations reported by women. Specifically, 54% of college women claimed to be sexually victimized, but only 25% of college men admitted any degree of sexually aggressive behavior. The number of times that men admitted to perpetrating each aggressive act was virtually identical to the number of times women reported experiencing each act. Thus, the results of the present study failed to support notions that a few extremely sexually active men could account for the victimization of a sizable number of women. Clearly, some of the victimizations reported by college women occurred in earlier years and were not perpetrated by the men who were surveyed. In addition, some recent victimizations may have involved community members who were not attending higher education institutions. Future research must determine whether these explanations can account for the sizable difference in rates.

The data on validity reported in the present study suggest that those sexual experiences that are revealed are true, but it is possible that additional relevant sexual experiences are not being reported by men. This is not to imply that intentional withholding is taking place but rather to suggest that men may be perceiving and conceptualizing potentially relevant sexual experiences in a way that is not elicited by the present wording of the SES. Scully and Marolla (1982) studied incarcerated rapists who denied that the incident for which they were convicted was a rape. Many of these men, although they used physical force and injured their victims, saw their behavior as congruent with consentual sexual activity. It may be that some men fail to perceive accurately the degree of force and coerciveness that was involved in a particular sexual encounter or to interpret correctly a women's nonconsent and resistance. A promising line for future research would be to compare violence and resistance attributions among sexually aggressive and sexually nonaggressive men. If differences were found, the line of inquiry would lead to a new foci for rape prevention programs.

The results of the present study also have implications for clinical treatment and research. The extent of sexual victimization reported in the national survey suggests that clinicians should consider including questions about unwanted sexual activity in routine intake interviews of women clients and that they should more frequently consider sexual victimization among the possible etiological factors that could be linked to presenting symptoms. Of course, the present sample consisted of students and many psychotherapy seekers are adults. However, the *Diagnostic and Statistical Manual of Mental Disorders* (American Psychiatric Association, 1980) discussion of post-traumatic stress disorder, which victims of rape may experience, specifically states, "It is not unusual for the symptoms to emerge after a latency period of months or years following the trauma" (p. 237).

For researchers these results, along with the work of others, begin to describe the full extent of rape and to suggest how the total number of rapes are partialed into those reported to police (5%), those acknowledged as rape by the victim (27%), and those for which victim assistance services are sought (5%) versus those that are never revealed to anyone (42%). Much of the existing rape research is based on samples of acknowledged rape victims recruited through newspaper advertisements, reported rape victims obtained from police and court records, or victims who have sought services at emergency rooms and rape crisis centers. It must be recognized that victims recruited in these ways represent only a portion of the total group of victims. Hidden victims (Koss, 1985) who do not report rape, seek services, or even identify themselves as rape victims should also receive attention in future rape research.

Statistically significant regional and ethnic differences in the prevalence of sexual aggression or victimization were found. Unfortunately, the meaning of these results could not be fully interpreted on the basis of data analyzed in the present study because ethnicity and region were confounded (i.e., minority students were not distributed randomly across the regions of the country). However, effect sizes calculated on the variables of region and ethnicity indicated that their true impact on prevalence rates was small. In the future, the effect of ethnicity will have to be analyzed while controlling for region, and vice versa. Then other data available on the subjects, including personality characteristics, values, beliefs, and current behavior, can be analyzed to account for any remaining differences. Overall, prevalence rates for sexual victimization or aggression were robust and did not vary extensively from large to small schools, across types of institutions, or among urban areas, medium-sized cities, and rural areas. The ubiquity of sexual aggression and victimization supports Johnson's (1980) observation that, "It is difficult to believe that such widespread violence is the responsibility of a small lunatic fringe of psychopathic men. That sexual violence is so pervasive supports the view that the locus of violence against women rests squarely in the middle of what our culture defines as 'normal' interaction between men and women" (p. 146). Recently, the editors of the *Morbidity and Mortality Weekly Report,* issued by the Centers for Disease Control in Atlanta, noted that there is an "increasing awareness in the public health community that violence is a serious public health problem and that nonfatal interpersonal violence has far-reaching consequences in terms of morbidity and quality of life" (Centers for Disease Control, 1985, pp. 739). Future research must devote attention to the preconditions that foster sexual violence.

Within the rape epidemiology literature are studies that have differed in methodology and have reported varying prevalence rates for attempted and completed rape, including Russell's (1984) 44% rate, which was based on a sample of 930 adult women residents of San Francisco who were interviewed in their homes; Kilpatrick et al.'s (1985) 14.5% rate, which was based on a random digit dialing telephone survey of 2,004 adult women residents of Charleston County, South Carolina; and the 27.5% rate reported in the present study, which was based on the self-reports of a national sample of students in higher education. Each data collection method has advantages and disadvantages and cannot be fully evaluated without reference to the special requirements of the topic of inquiry, the target population, and practical and financial limitations. Future epidemiological research must determine how much variation in rates is due to the method of data collection or the screening question format and how much variation is due to sample differences. Currently, the most important conclusion suggested by this entire line of research is that rape is much more prevalent than previously believed.

REFERENCES

Ageton, S. S. (1983). *Sexual assault among adolescents.* Lexington, MA: Lexington Books.

American Psychiatric Association. (1980). *Diagnostic and statistical manual of mental disorders* (3rd ed.). Washington, DC: Author.

Bureau of Justice Statistics. (1984). *Criminal victimization in the United States, 1982* (Publication No. NCJ-92820). Washington, DC: U.S. Department of Justice.

Centers for Disease Control, U.S. Department of Health and Human Services. (1985, December 13). Adolescent sex offenders—Vermont, 1984. *Morbidity and Mortality Weekly Report, 34*(49), 738–741.

Clark, L., & Lewis, D. (1977). *Rape: The price of coercive sexuality.* Toronto, Ontario, Canada: The Women's Press.

Cohen, J. (1977). *Statistical power analysis for the behavioral sciences* (Rev ed.). New York: Academic Press.

Federal Bureau of Investigation. (1986). *Crime in the United States: Uniform crime reports.* Washington, DC: U.S. Department of Justice.

Johnson, A. G. (1980). On the prevalence of rape in the United States. *Signs: Journal of Women in Culture and Society, 6,* 136–146.

Kalish, C. B. (1974). *Crimes and victims: A report on the Dayton-San Jose pilot study of victimization.* Washington, DC: National Criminal Justice Information and Statistics Service.

Kanin, E. J. (1957). Male aggression in dating-courtship relations. *American Journal of Sociology, 63,* 197–204.

Kanin, E. J., & Parcell, S. R. (1977). Sexual aggression: A second look at the offended female. *Archives of Sexual Behavior, 6,* 67–76.

Kilpatrick, D. G., Best, C. L., Veronen, L. J., Amick, A. E., Villeponteaux, L. A., & Ruff, G. A. (1985). Mental health correlates of criminal victimization: A random community survey. *Journal of Consulting and Clinical Psychology, 53,* 866–873.

Kilpatrick, D. G., Veronen, L. J., & Best, C. L. (1984). Factors predicting psychological distress among rape victims. In C. R. Figley (Ed.), *Trauma and its wake: The study and treatment of postraumatic stress disorder* (pp. 113–141). New York: Brunner/Mazel.

Kirkpatrick, C., & Kanin, E. J. (1957). Male sexual aggression on a university campus. *American Sociological Review, 22,* 52–58.

Koss, M. P. (1985). The hidden rape victim: Personality, attitudinal, and situational characteristics. *Psychology of Women Quarterly, 9,* 193–212.

Koss, M. P., & Gidycz, C. A. (1985). Sexual Experiences Survey: Reliability and validity. *Journal of Consulting and Clinical Psychology, 53,* 422–423.

Koss, M. P., Leonard, K. E., Beezley, D. A., & Oros, C. J. (1985). Non-stranger sexual aggression: A discriminant analysis of the psychological characteristics of undetected offenders. *Sex Roles, 12,* 981–992.

Koss, M. P., & Oros, C. J. (1982). Sexual Experiences Survey: A research instrument investigating sexual aggression and victimization. *Journal of Consulting and Clinical Psychology, 50,* 455–457.

Law Enforcement Assistance Administration. (1975). *Criminal victimization surveys in 8 American cities* (Publication No. SD-NCS-C-5). Washington, DC: U.S. Government Printing Office.

Office of Civil Rights. (1980). *Fall enrollment and compliance report of institutions of higher education* (DHEW Publication No. NCES 76–135). Washington, DC: U.S. Department of Education.

Ohio Revised Code, Supp. 2907.01 A, 2907.02 (1980).

Rapaport, K., & Burkhart, B. R. (1984). Personality and attitudinal characteristics of sexually coercive college males. *Journal of Abnormal Psychology, 93,* 216–221.

Russell, D. E. H. (1984). *Sexual exploitation: Rape, child sexual abuse, and workplace harassment.* Beverly Hills, CA: Sage Publications.

Scully, D., & Marolla, J. (1982, September). Convicted rapists' construction of reality: The denial of rape. Paper presented at the American Sociological Association Convention, San Francisco, CA.

U.S. Bureau of the Census. (1980). *Current population reports 1980–1981* (Series P-20, No. 362). Washington, DC: U.S. Government Printing Office.

U.S. Department of Commerce. (1986). *Statistical abstracts of the United States: 1986* (106th ed.). Washington, DC: U.S. Government Printing Office.

Weis, K., & Borges, S. S. (1973). Victimology and rape: The case of the legitimate victim. *Issues in Criminology, 8,* 71–115.

Reflection

MARY P. KOSS

Look me up on the Internet and you'll see the extent to which this single paper appears to define my career. Most papers on incidence and prevalence have a short life because that kind of information is quickly replaced by a more recent source. I had no idea when writing this paper what its impact would be. The paper received recognition in the public media almost immediately, including coverage in the *New York Times, Newsweek,* all the major women's magazines, and a few talk shows. That was thrilling for me personally and it was gratifying that the work, combined with other events and contributions, seemed to be giving women the vocabulary to talk about date rape and to interest colleges and universities in doing prevention education. In 1990, I was called to testify before the U.S. Senate Committee on the Judiciary, which was holding hearings on the Violence Against Women Act. One of the titles in this act was specifically directed at campus rape and used statistics drawn from this paper to demonstrate the magnitude of the rape problem. And just recently, I learned that the charges made in this paper about underestimates in federal statistics had hit their mark when the National Institute of Justice released a second national study of college students that compared the type of questioning used here to the standard National Crime Victimization Survey items and reported that the former resulted in estimates of rape prevalence that were 11 times higher than what the federal survey was identifying (see Fisher, Cullen, & Turner, 2000).

Doing empirical research that influenced public policy is the fulfillment of every social scientist's dream, but in so doing, this paper became a target for those opposed to change. I have woken up to the *Sunday New York Times Magazine* to find these data identified as the source of "rape hype that betrays feminism," and had the discomfort of seeing them the subject of chapters in scholarly books as examples of fraud in social science, lying with statistics, and stealing feminism. I was at the time and continue to be especially grateful to case studies of the media treatment of my work done by Fairness and Accuracy in Reporting and by the Media Education Foundation in their video, *Date Rape Backlash: The Media and the Denial of Rape.*

The best response to backlash is to keep turning out the work, and there is certainly more work to be done. The Sexual Experiences Survey that is reported in this paper is the most widely used instrument for survey-based assessments of sexual assault victimization and perpetration. It is used for a variety of research goals, including estimation of incidence and prevalence, testing of theoretical models of victimization and perpetration, and conducting outcome studies. However, my colleagues and I believe that it could benefit from revision to ensure that the questions cover the full range of relevant experiences in terms that young adults from diverse backgrounds can easily comprehend and are consistent with existing state and federal statutes. We also believe that it is critical to conduct follow-up questions to the survey to verify that a revised Sexual Experiences Survey is categorizing sexual assault experiences accurately.

Starting with this paper and throughout my many years in this field, I seem to have an ability to pick research directions that push the envelope. My present work on applying restorative justice philosophy to healing victims and holding perpetrators accountable is not an exception. For someone who doesn't like criticism and prefers to be liked, it has been an interesting psychological journey and I must acknowledge the support I have received from friends, feminist colleagues, and the victims themselves.

REFERENCE

Fisher, B., Cullen, F. T., & Turner, M. G. (2000). *The Sexual Victimization of College Women.* Washington, D.C.: United States Department of Justice, National Institute of Justice and Bureau of Justice Statistics.

CHAPTER 9

Sexual Violence, the Unmentionable Sin

An Ethical and Pastoral Perspective

MARIE MARSHALL FORTUNE

Why would someone who has been raped or someone who has sexually abused another go to a minister for help? For some people, the Church is a primary reference point in their lives. When faced with a personal crisis they turn first to their minister. For them, the minister is a trusted and known resource; they assume that he/she will know what to do in this situation. For others, the minister may be the only resource. In a small town or rural area which does not have specialized community services (e.g., a Rape Crisis Line), the minister is the only "helper" available. Still others may seek out a minister because this crisis of sexual victimization is also a crisis of faith. The experience may have raised basic spiritual questions for which the victim or offender needs counsel.

Often ministers are avoided by individuals or families coping with the trauma of sexual violence. Many clergy say that they have never had someone involved in rape or sexual abuse come to them for assistance. Furthermore, they conclude that there is no one in their congregation who is a victim or offender. Given the large numbers of persons who have experienced sexual violence, this assumption is questionable. The more logical conclusion is that many people hesitate to go to their minister when faced with such an experience.

There are several reasons for this hesitation. Generally, any experience of sexual abuse or violence is stigmatizing for the victim. Although society's attitudes are slowly changing, many victims are still afraid to tell anyone about their abuse, because they fear disbelief, judgment, ostracism, and lack of support. Unfortunately, the Church has adopted an attitude, not unlike society's, which says that experiences of sexual abuse or violence are unmentionable and unacceptable in the Church. When the minister and congregation do not initiate discussion of sexual violence, the silence reinforces the stigmatization. Thus, for many the Church and the minister (as representative of the Church) are not viewed as potential resources in this situation.

Another reason for hesitation on the part of the victim or offender may be a perception that the minister lacks knowledge, sensitivity, and/or experience in dealing with sexual assault. A level of trust between pastor and parishioner which is adequate to other situations may not be adequate to this one. The victim or offender fears that the minister will not understand or know what to do. Or perhaps the minister will be so surprised and shocked, that the person seeking help ends up having to help the minister deal with his/her reaction.

Finally, female victims are often hesitant to go to their minister because their minister is male. Having a male minister may heighten the victim's fear that he will not understand or respond sensitively. A clergywoman is often preferred because the victim feels her chances of being understood are better.

The concerns that victims or offenders express about a minister's possible insensitivity are real and reasonable. When one is facing a personal crisis of this magnitude, it is not a good time to risk rejection or lack of understanding from one's minister. So for many people the silence continues. They do not seek help at all. A minister can open the door and let it be known that he/she is available to help with the problem of sexual violence by giving permission for the subject to be discussed in Church and by being prepared to help.

At the end of a four week seminar on sexual and domestic violence, a Lutheran pastor of a small congregation reported with some distress that in the past several weeks he had had a rape and two incest cases in his congregation. He could not understand why this "sudden outbreak" of sexual abuse in his congregation had occurred. The seminar coordinator explored this further with the group and discovered that the pastor, on the first Sunday after the first seminar session had announced from the pulpit that he was taking a seminar on sexual abuse and domestic violence which he was finding very helpful. In the weeks following that announcement, parishioners came forward for the first time with their concerns about sexual assault. Rather than "a sudden outbreak," each shared a past or chronic unresolved problem.

By making that announcement from the pulpit, the pastor in effect hung up a sign saying, "I am learning about these problems, I know that some of you are facing them, and I am available to help." It should have come as no surprise that people sought his assistance.

Giving permission to victims or offenders to seek help regarding sexual violence happens when the minister communicates that it is acceptable to talk about sexual violence in church and that he/she has the knowledge and expertise to help. This can be accomplished through a sermon, adult/youth/child educational presentations, fliers posted in the narthex advertising local resources like a Rape Crisis Line, use of denominational curricula dealing with the topic, etc.

Being Prepared to Help

It is unlikely that any minister is adequately prepared to respond to a victim or offender of sexual violence unless he/she has had some means to increase his/her knowledge and counseling skills in this area (special training, experience, materials, etc.) The topic remains unmentionable in most seminaries or ministry training programs. While most seminaries and training programs offer education in counseling and crisis intervention, this is not sufficient preparation to respond to sexual violence. Although sexual assault and abuse have some similarities with other life crises, they are, in many ways, unlike any other experience that a person will face. Some degree of specialized knowledge is necessary in order to respond effectively.

A minister must be comfortable with the issue of sexual violence in order to help the victim or offender. Talking with a victim or offender is often a very disquieting experience. The minister may be reminded of her/his own experience of violence or abuse as a victim or an offender. The important thing is that the minister be aware of those feelings and of their source in his/her experience. For example, if a minister has been a victim of sexual assault or abuse, she/he may be better prepared to empathize with a victim. Or, if the personal pain of the experience is still acute, it may have the opposite effect of blocking the minister's response. In this case, it is advisable that the minister refer the victim to another minister who is more able to respond.

The minister may be confronted with things which he/she does not want to hear, experiences which are horrendous and disturbing. The temptation is to minimize or not believe what is being said. Some of the stories may seem "unbelievable," i.e., things we would like to believe are not happening to people, but in fact are. For example, the daughter of the sunday school superintendent who ran away from home finally returns only to reveal to the minister that she ran away because her father was sexually abusing her. Such a situation has numerous ramifications and no simple solutions. While the gut reaction might be disbelief, horror, and minimization, none of these is helpful to a victim.

Developing a level of comfort can be accomplished by exploring one's experiences with, feelings about, and attitudes concerning sexual violence. Ministers (and other helpers) need to reflect on several questions: To what extent does the minister identify with the victim or with the offender? What personal experiences of the minister relate in some way, for example, when has the minister felt powerless, frightened, or alone? What beliefs about sexual violence does the minister have which are not based on fact, for example, the belief that some women ask to be raped or rapists are just sexually over-active? A minister can respond calmly and yet not minimize the situation by being knowledgeable about the subject of sexual violence, knowing what to do next, and not allowing feelings of anger, disgust, disbelief, or discomfort to dominate the response.

Reassurance and Support

Following a sexual assault, victims need to hear that they are acceptable and worthy persons, that they are not to blame for their assault, and that they will not be abandoned in this crisis. The minister's efforts to reassure and support a victim in these ways are much more meaningful if the congregation is also able to be supportive. Then the minister can communicate that the church as a whole is prepared to be with the victim through this experience.

One frequent question is whether a male minister can be of assistance to a female victim of sexual violence. The concern raised by this question is whether or not the maleness of the minister may be too great an obstacle to the victim's feeling comfortable and trusting with him. Following the assault, some victims find it very difficult to feel safe talking with any male helper be it police, medical personnel, or clergy. In such instances, the sensitive male minister can refer the victim to a qualified female minister or laywoman. For other victims, it can be reassuring to talk with a male they trust. In these cases, it is important that the minister avoid reacting in a patronizing or protective manner. A victim needs someone who can listen and be supportive rather than someone who wants to rescue her from the experience. When giving support, the male minister should avoid any action which might be perceived by the victim as physically or sexually threatening; thus, touching should be kept to a minimum.

A male clergy colleague told of his initial meeting with a 23 year-old woman rape victim. As they talked in his office, he got up from his chair, walked around behind her and put his hands on her shoulders to reassure her and offer her physical support. She froze and stopped talking with him. His action was frightening and threatening to her. The man who had raped her had approached her from behind. His action toward her, although well-intended, was entirely inappropriate and counterproductive. Reassurance and support may best be communicated in nonphysical ways.

Initial Assessment

During the initial meeting with a victim or offender, the minister needs to assess several areas in order to determine his/her appropriate role in the particular situation. If the assault occurred within the past 48 hours and if no other resources (rape crisis agency, police, medical personnel) have been contacted, then the minister should assume a crisis intervention role. The way that the minister will carry out the role will depend on what community resources are available for referral and on who the person is—victim or offender. If the assault or abuse is chronic (incestuous abuse) or has occurred earlier in the person's life, then the minister's response will be less crisis-oriented and more focused on assessing the current needs of the person seeking help and the impact of the sexual violence on that person's life.

If other crisis resources have been contacted and are being utilized, then the minister's attention will be directed towards areas not covered by those resources, particularly spiritual or religious concerns. In either case, the minister's role in assessing the situation is a critical one. This is especially true if the minister is the only person who has been told about the assault or abuse.

Working with Other Community Resources

Most urban and suburban communities now have sexual assault services available, either through a crisis line, a community mental health center, or a specialized service such as a rape crisis center. Services for sex offenders are not as common, but are sometimes available regionally. Persons providing these services are trained to respond to sexual violence whether it is a crisis or chronic problem. They are available as resources to ministers and congregations.

A Cooperative Style

Unfortunately, some ministers hesitate to utilize secular resources in response to a problem like sexual assault. A gulf seems to have developed over the years between mental health/social services and religious professionals, resulting from long-standing mistrust and skepticism. Social workers and counselors do not trust ministers to know what to do when faced with sexual assault or abuse, and ministers do not trust social workers and counselors to be sensitive to the spiritual needs of their parishioners. This attitude of mutual mistrust comes from experiences of poor communication, insensitivity, inappropriate treatment or counsel, etc., on both sides. The resulting lack of cooperation means that persons who need help are placed in a position of choosing either social services and counseling or pastoral support. In some communities, little effort has been made by either side to overcome this gulf and to begin to relate to each other as professional peers who have special training and skills much needed by the people they serve.

In other communities, both clergy and secular resources have sought to bridge the gap and there has been remarkable success in sharing resources and in developing a network of services. They work cooperatively in response to victims and offenders. For example, in one particular community, a group of ministers has been trained by the rape crisis center to deal with sexual assault. In turn the rape crisis center staff/volunteers have been trained by the ministers to respond sensitively to the religious concerns expressed by victims. Here, a mutual referral agreement exists where ministers refer victims for crisis counseling to the rape crisis center and the rape crisis center refers victims with religious questions to the ministers. In addition, ministers help with fund raising and community education and encourage lay participation in the center as volunteers.

Seldom does a minister have the training, time, and energy to adequately provide the immediate and long-term counseling which a victim or offender may need. A network develops when religious and secular professionals reach out to each other as peers, sharing information, providing training for each other, serving on boards of agencies, and offering to provide services when referred to by the other. Working together to meet the needs of victims and offenders begins to build the mutual trust that is needed for effective work.

Know Your Resources

Research conducted in 1977 in a large urban area indicated that seventy-six percent of parish ministers in that area did not know of a single resource (general or specialized) which they could call upon to assist victims or offenders of sexual violence. At that time, this city had the highest concentration of sexual assault services of any area in the region. Yet parish ministers were not utilizing these services because they did not even know what was available.[1]

It is often up to the minister to find out what services are available in his/her community. A minister should contact any agency which sounds like it addresses sexual assault and request copies of brochures to keep on hand. If possible, go and talk to an agency staff person in order to clarify what they do offer. Attend any training events offered by the agency. Know and use the resources in the community.

Making Referrals

When resources are available, it is preferable to refer a victim or offender to a specialized agency prepared to deal with sexual assault. The staff and volunteers of these agencies have the knowledge and experience to provide the needed counseling and advocacy. They know the medical and legal systems and can minimize the difficulties that a victim may face dealing with them.

In making a referral to an agency, it is preferable to refer to a specific person who is known and trusted by the minister. This is another reason to get to know an agency's staff and volunteers either through self-introduction or through participation in a conference or training workshop. Giving a victim or offender a name of someone at the agency reassures them that they will connect with an individual who can help.

A minister's wise use of referrals comes from an awareness of his/her limitations and from a clear understanding of what his/her role should be. Particularly from a parish minister's point of view, limited expertise, time and energy necessitate utilization of all available resources.

Pastoral Role

The minister, in a pastoral role, can offer a victim or offender a unique resource. His/her expertise in pastoral care, theology, and ethics can be invaluable to a religiously-affiliated person facing the aftermath of a sexual assault. The minister is the primary resource when a victim or offender faces questions such as: Why did God let this happen to me? Does God still love me? Can God forgive me for this? Through prayer, spiritual counsel and reflection, and Scripture study, the minister can assist a person with primary issues in her/his life.

When a minister makes a referral to a secular agency, this does not mean that the minister's responsibility ends. The pastoral and supportive role is often still needed by the person seeking help. A minister who tries to pass total responsibility on to another helper is said to be "dumping the client." Even if the religious concerns seem to be initially resolved, it is important to check in with a victim for the next six months to a year, reminding her/him of the continuing care and support of the church. For an offender, weekly contact may be necessary to insure that he remains in treatment and to assure him of the support of the church as he goes through that rehabilitation process.

Confidentiality

While all helping professionals have a responsibility to maintain confidentiality regarding interaction between them and their clients, clergy have an additional responsibility within the context of a pastoral and confessional role. There are a number of states which recognize the special nature of the clergy-penitent relationship and provide the legal privilege for clergy not to be forced to divulge information learned within a pastoral relationship.[2] In sexual assault situations this can sometimes create a bind for the minister. On the one hand, there is the minister's commitment not to repeat information shared in a counseling or confessional setting. On the the other hand, when information comes from an offender or relates to the sexual abuse of a child the minister has an ethical responsibility to do whatever is necessary to prevent any further assault or abuse from occurring. This may involve reporting information to a law enforcement agency.

In some states, clergy are required by law (along with teachers, social workers, doctors, counselors, etc.) to report any suspicion of child abuse (including child sexual abuse) to a law enforcement or child protection agency. In other states, clergy are exempt from this reporting requirement. Suspicion or confirmation that sexual abuse has occurred, coupled with the knowledge that unless the offender is stopped, he will offend again, press a minister to choose between conflicting ethical principles. Shall the pastor break confidentiality in order to protect a child or shall he/she safeguard confidentiality and place the child at further risk? In this case, concern for the welfare of potential or actual victims takes precedent. This is particularly true for child victims who are at high risk and often powerless to stop the abuse. Acting on this concern may then mean reporting an offender to the authorities. This action is also a function of concern for the welfare of the offender. His confession or indication that he is sexually offending may be a call for help. This help is only possible if he is held accountable for his acts and provided with appropriate treatment. For his sake as well as the sake of the victim, it is the pastor's responsibility to intervene to stop the offender's abusive behavior. Allowing him to continue to offend with our knowledge is unfair to him and only multiplies the legal difficulties he will face.

The church has addressed the question of confidentiality. Within the Anglican Communion the "Seal of Confession" is defined as follows:

> The absolute obligation not to reveal anything said by a penitent using the Sacrament of Penance. . . . The obligation arises from a tacit contract between penitent and confessor, from its necessity for maintenance of the use of the sacrament by the faithful, and from canon law. The obligation covers direct and indirect revelation, e.g., unguarded statements from which matters heard in confession could be deduced or recognized, and admits of no exception, no matter what urgent reasons of life or death, Church or state, may be advanced.[3]

The Roman Catholic provision is equally stringent. The United Methodist Book of Discipline is more straightforward but also strict: "Ministers of the United Methodist Church are charged to maintain all confidences inviolate, including confessional confidences."[4] Some denominations have addressed the issue with limited conditions.

> In keeping with the historic discipline and practice of the Lutheran Church and to be true to a sacred trust inherent in the nature of the pastoral office, no minister of The Lutheran Church in America shall divulge any confidential disclosure given to him in the course of his care of souls or otherwise in his professional capacity, except with the express permission of the person who has confided in him or *in order to prevent a crime* [emphasis added].[5]

This provision is very important in questioning the absolute nature of pastor-penitent privilege when communication is exchanged which indicates that there will be further sexual assault or abuse. It is important for the Church to face the conflict in ethical values which results from an awareness of sexual assault or abuse committed by a counselee or penitent.

When a minister feels an ethical mandate to report knowledge of sexual abuse or assault, it need not be done in such a way as to deceive the offender; it need not be done secretively. Rather the minister should inform the person at the time the information is shared that it needs to be reported to the appropriate authorities. The pastor can then ask the person's permission to notify police or a child protection service. Or the pastor can suggest to the person that it is in their own best interest to report it himself/herself (in the presence of the minister). These approaches hold the greatest potential for maintaining some level of trust between minister and offender. In this way an ongoing relationship between minister and offender may be maintained and effective intervention can be carried out to stop the abuse.

Working Alone: A Rural or Small Town Setting

Ministers serving in a rural area or small town may find that they are *the* primary resource for victims or offenders. In this case, they may be called upon to provide crisis counseling and support as well as advocacy with medical and legal systems. This can be a very demanding role. The minister needs to keep in mind his/her time and energy limitations and develop additional support resources within the congregation. Ideally, members of the congregation can assist, for example, by accompanying a victim to a medical appointment or prosecutor interview. The pastoral role of providing spiritual guidance and counsel is basically the same as for the urban/suburban minister. For the rural minister, this role may be more integrated into the overall assistance he/she provides for the victim, offender, and their families.

Often confidentiality arises as an additional complication in a rural or small town setting. Where everyone knows everyone else and news travels fast through informal networks of communication, it is difficult to keep anything confidential. Fears about having their experience become public knowledge may prevent victims from seeking help from clergy, police, or doctors in their own community. Ministers especially need to be sensitive to this fear so that a victim can be assured that confidences with her/him will be respected. A minister should specifically mention his/her awareness of the need for extra care in safeguarding the privacy of a victim and assure her/him that he/she will not share any information about the victim's situation without her/his permission. The minister should be careful not to share *any aspect* of a story which might identify the victim.

An additional responsibility which may arise for the rural minister in response to an incident of sexual violence is the need to minister to the community as a whole (if news of the incident becomes public). The community may react with some of the same characteristics as the victim: fear, panic, anger, grief, etc. The local minister(s) can provide factual information about sexual violence, help direct the community's anger in appropriate channels to minimize tendencies toward revenge, and generally assist the community in working through its feelings.

NOTES

1. This research was conducted by Denise Hormann for the Center for the Prevention of Sexual and Domestic Violence. Partial results were published in JSAC *Grapevine,* vol. 11, no. 3 (September 1979), pp. 1–2.

2. There is a great deal of controversy surrounding this provision, including the question of who is a clergyperson, what about clergy in churches which do not have a doctrine of sacramental confession, what about nonsacramental confidential communications, etc. For additional discussion of the legal issues involved, see Seward Reese, "Confidential Communications to the Clergy," *Ohio State Law Journal,* vol. 24 (1963), pp. 55–88.

3. *The Oxford Dictionary of the Christian Church* 1234 (London: 1957) as cited in Seward Reese, "Confidential Communications to Clergy," *Ohio State Law Journal,* vol. 24 (1963), p. 68.

4. *The Book of Discipline of the United Methodist Church* (Nashville, Tn.: United Methodist Publishing House, 1980), para. 440.4, p. 220.

5. The Minutes of the United Lutheran Church in America, the 22nd Biennial Convention, 1960, at 277, as quoted in Reese, p. 69.

Reflection

MARIE MARSHALL FORTUNE

I wrote *Sexual Violence: The Unmentionable Sin* while I was temporarily unemployed, the result of tenuous funding for non-profits working on violence against women in the early '80s. But I am thankful for the time I had to write. What I felt was needed then, and now, was a book directed to clergy about sexual violence. What I didn't anticipate then was that this book would also be of use to survivors who often struggle with religious concerns. *Sexual Violence* has remained in print for twenty years. I am in the process of revising and updating it. But the basic approach that I suggest for clergy in response to sexual violence remains the same now as then.

In addressing the "Role of the Minister," I wanted to challenge and encourage clergy to be prepared (i.e., to get trained) and to collaborate with secular community resources in order to be part of the team of support that a victim/survivor or perpetrator needs. It has always been my expectation that clergy serve an important role as a "generalist" in response to sexual or domestic violence. This means that they should be trained in the basics (identification and assessment) and how to make good referrals and work cooperatively with secular helpers. In addition, they should offer their expertise in the area of pastoral or religious concerns to support healing for victims and accountability for perpetrators. All of this presupposes a setting in which there are multiple resources. The problem is that in some rural areas, the local pastor may be the only resource. So he or she unfortunately may have to shoulder the whole responsibility for support and intervention.

The issues surrounding confidentiality and mandatory reporting continue to be challenges. The experience of child sexual abuse in the Roman Catholic Church points up the harm when there is confusion or avoidance of appropriate reporting. There is always the need for further training on confidentiality and pastoral response.

The fundamental approach for clergy (training, clarity of role, and collaboration) continues to be a needed and valuable aspect of the overall response to sexual violence in our society. My colleague, Judy Beals, summarized it well in an editorial discussing the crisis in the Roman Catholic Church:

> The turning point in every social justice movement occurs when the authentic leadership of survivors is met with the genuine commitments of our most powerful social institutions. The result, inevitably, is the strengthening of existing systems that work and the continual development of new innovations, protections, and partnerships that we have yet to even imagine. If there is any silver lining to the recent tragic events [Boston Diocese disclosure of child sexual abuse by priests], it is the opportunity to channel public outrage into lasting structures and commitments that will rid society of sexual violence. If we fail to do this, the shame is ours.

Those of us who work within religious institutions continue to challenge ourselves and our colleagues to take appropriate leadership to change our society's response to sexual violence.

CHAPTER

10 Female Sexual Slavery

KATHLEEN BARRY

There are small prostitution hotels in one part of the North African *quartier* of Paris known as *maisons d'abattage.* I was warned to stay out of this section of the 18th *arrondissement* of Paris because it is dangerous for women, at any time of day or night. But I did walk through the area. I needed to see the *maisons d'abattage.* It was early evening when another woman and I emerged from the Barbes-Rochecauart Metro station. We were jostled and pushed as we made our way through the crowded shopping section. Once we were on the quiet side streets no other women were to be seen. As we walked through the neighborhood streets of this North African section of Paris, we were suddenly struck by the sight of a crowd of about 300 men in a narrow street ahead. We stopped and gazed, assuming there must have been an automobile accident or a fight. The frantic, jostling crowd of men spanned the full width and half the length of the small street. As we approached the rue de la Charbonniere, just above the crowd of pushing and shoving men we saw a small "Hotel" sign.

We continued down the street and around the corner. We stopped again, stunned to see a small neighborhood police station with a smiling policeman standing in the doorway, while about 20 yards away from him, next door but in the same building, was another "Hotel" sign and another group of men, about 100 North Africans pushing, body-to-body, against the gates of the hotel. It was only 6:00 P.M. on Saturday of Easter weekend. The crowds of men were to grow larger as the evening progressed. Although closed prostitution houses are illegal in France, these hotels are not only tolerated but obviously supported by the police.

In each of these *maisons d'abattage* (literal translation: houses of slaughter), six or seven girls each serve 80 to 120 customers a night. On holidays their quota might go up to 150. After each man pays his 30 francs (approximately $6.00) at the door, he is given a towel and ushered into a room. A buzzer sounds after six minutes, and he must leave immediately as another man comes in. The girl never even gets out of bed.

The girls are told that they will get a certain percentage of the money if they meet their quota. From their earnings is deducted the cost of room and meals; after these deductions—with the hotel doing the bookkeeping—the girls always find they are indebted to the house. Giving a false sense of earning money, and subsequent indebtedness, are traditional strategies for keeping enslaved prostitutes from rebelling.

> In May 1975 a French doctor submitted a confidential report to UNESCO documenting the torture of prostitutes. The report, which was to became the basis of testimony at the International Women's Year Conference in Mexico City, was based on testimony of patients she had treated who had been held in the *maisons d'abattage.* It indicated that the women were "detained indoors without ever having the right to move outside unaccompanied, were subjected to cruel, inhuman, and degrading treatment. Torture was also used if it was needed to obtain their complete submission. This form of terrorism was aimed at making them totally subject to the wishes of those who benefited from it, either by financial profit or sexual satisfaction." The women were described as being of normal intelligence and in a state of depression and considerable anxiety. "They were passive and apathetic, unable to readjust to freedom."

This is not the kind of work a woman looks for when she considers becoming a prostitute. How do women get to places like Paris's *maison d'abattage?*

From my research, I found the women may be purchased, kidnapped, drawn in through syndicates or organized crime, or fraudulently recruited by fronting agencies which offer jobs, positions with dance companies, or marriage contracts that don't exist. Or they may be procured through seduction by being promised friendship and love. Conning a girl or young woman by feigning friendship or love is undoubtedly the easiest and most frequently employed tactic of slave procurers (and one that is also used for procuring young boys) and it is the most effective. Young women readily respond to male attention and affection and easily become dependent on it. Once a procurer has drawn a young woman in by his attention to her and she commits her affection to him it is relatively easy for him to transport her to a brothel. Sometimes she can quickly be turned out on the streets by simply being asked to; he tells her that if she really loves him she will do it for him. If that fails, if she resists his request, traditional seasoning tactics are employed—beating, rape, torture. Either way she gets hooked.

When a friend first suggested that I write a book on what I was describing to her as female sexual slavery, I resisted the idea. I had gone through the shock and horror of learning about it in the late 1960's when I discovered a few paternalistically written books documenting present-day practices. During that same period I found a biography of Josephine Butler, who single-handedly raised a national and then international movement against forced prostitution in the nineteenth century but who is now virtually unknown. I realized that Josephine Butler's current obscurity was directly connected to the invisibility of sex slavery today. And so I wrote a few short pieces on the subject and incorporated my limited information into the curriculum of the women's studies classes I taught.

But to write a book on the subject—to spend two or three years researching, studying female slavery—that was out of the question. I instinctively withdrew from the suggestion; I couldn't face that. But as the idea settled over the next few weeks, I realized that my reaction was typical of women's response: even with some knowledge of the facts, I was moving from fear to paralysis to hiding. It was then that I realized, both for myself personally and for all the rest of us, that the only way we can come out of hiding, break through our paralyzing defenses, is to know the full extent of sexual violence and domination of women. It is knowledge from which we have pulled back, as well as knowledge that has been withheld from us. In *knowing,* in facing directly, we can learn how to chart our course out of this oppression, by envisioning and creating a world which will preclude female sexual slavery. In knowing the extent of our oppression we will have to discover some of the ways to begin immediately breaking the deadly cycle of fear, denial-through-hiding, and slavery.

Far from being the project I feared facing, the research, study, and writing of this book have given me knowledge that forced me to think beyond the confinement of women's oppression. Understanding the scope and depth of female sexual slavery makes it intolerable to passively live with it any longer. I had to realistically visualize a world that would preclude this enslavement by projecting some ways out of it. Reading about sexual slavery makes hope and vision necessary.

To study female sexual slavery, I could start only with the slender file of material I had developed over the previous ten years. Very little information was readily available. History provided some clue to the practices that defined it. Definition and description would have to emerge from the information I would get in the field through observation, interviews, and travel.

Traditional methods employed by those who study social life were of little use. One cannot, for example, find a sample population of sexual slaves, survey them, and then generalize from the results. Nor is participant observation a possibility. And interviewing those held in slavery is impossible. I began to look for the women who have escaped. My approach was to find any evidence of sexual slavery wherever I could, and to try to fill out fragmentary facts from interviewing people associated with a particular case.

To determine the nature and extent of the slave trade *today,* I decided that except for the historical example of nineteenth century sex slavery, I would keep my research to reports of incidents that took place within the ten years prior to beginning my research (that is, since 1966). I would use earlier material as background to substantiate patterns I found. Shortly after I began, I realized that the sex slave trade is so clandestine a practice that what I would find would only be an indication of a much vaster problem. In addition, I soon realized that my assumption that traffic in women and children was different from street prostitution was invalid. From interviews and other research I learned that virtually the only distinction that can be made between traffic in women and street prostitution is that the former involves crossing international borders. The practices used to force women into prostitution are the same whether they are trafficked across international boundaries or from one part of a city to another. It is currently estimated that over 90 percent of street prostitutes are controlled by pimps. I found that street pimp strategies and goals do not differ significantly from those of international procurers. Female sexual slavery then refers to international traffic in women *and* forced street prostitution taken together.

As I received information about each case of sexual slavery, I would confirm the story by contacting people close to the case—lawyers, reporters, police, district attorneys, antislavery organizations, and the victims themselves whenever possible. I restricted interviews with victims to those who had either escaped or left prostitution. Interviewing these women presented a special problem as their life experiences had taught them that few if any people are willing to believe their victimization. Indeed, society has been unwilling to even name it as a form of victimization. As a result I conducted long open-ended interviews which provided an opportunity to sort out possible contradictions or exaggerations. And it provided an opportunity for confidence to be developed allowing the women to describe their experiences without need for embellishment. As a further check, I used here only portions of the interviews when I could be satisfied with their report or that I could verify against other evidence.

After days of tracking down people, getting interviews, observing trials, and filling out the details of a particular case, I would consistently find that the extreme incident that I was studying was in fact part of a pervasive practice usually existing clandestinely over many years. Not only did my investigations confirm a particular incident, but that incident in turn revealed larger practices. . . .

As a result of my investigations and research I came in contact with several organizations whose titles alone suggest the seriousness of the problem. The British-based Anti-Slavery Society, through its secretary, Colonel Patrick Montgomery, has for years been presenting cases of female slavery to the United Nations and any other organization likely to take action. Then there is the French group, *Équipes d'Action,* whose full title, "Action Teams Against the Traffic of Women and Children (and against slavery by drugs, trickery, or violence)," conveys the scope of the problem. Their documentation amply substantiates the traffic's pervasiveness. The French Police Department, I found, has a Central Office for the Repression of the Traffic in Persons. Also, as recently as 1974 INTERPOL, the international police organization, conducted an international survey on the traffic in women for prostitution. My discovery of these organizations and activities was further evidence of the broad scale of the practice.

Once I was convinced of the pervasiveness of the problem, the immediate question facing me was why and how female sexual slavery has remained invisible. First, there is direct suppression of the evidence by authorities. In addition, it is invisible as a problem to those who handle practices of female sexual slavery every day. When I would illustrate to an authority how a particular situation fit the most rudimentary definition of slavery, generally I found that they saw the abuse but accepted sexual exploitation and violence as normal for particular groups of women under specific conditions. I noted how, *after* women are enslaved in their homes or in prostitution, they are accepted as part of the group of women destined for that life. When I challenged authorities, I ran up against the "don't confuse me with the facts" attitude. Despite evidence of force and dehumanizing violence in many cases, they were incredulous that anyone would question prostitution or see it as other than a necessary service for a particular group of women to perform.

Yet other, more subtle effects have contributed to the invisibility of the slave trade. For example, most research on prostitution looks at female motivation rather than the objective conditions which bring many women into prostitution, shifting the causal assumptions from those who traffic women to the psychological states of the women themselves. To those who study the victims of the practice I have called female sexual slavery, these women are the exceptions for whom exceptional behavior is normal; to sociologists they are deviants, to psychologists they are sadomasochists. Their life and experiences are construed as normal for them while they are supposedly different from the rest of us. It is in this kind of contradiction that feminists have learned to look for larger truths about female experience. It is in female sexual slavery that I have found conditions which affect all women.

Because of these problems it was necessary for me to develop a perspective for analyzing both the documentation of female sexual slavery and the attitudes that define it as normal, which would reveal self-interest on the part of those who label it. That self-interest may range from the actual profit from the traffic in women to a general participation in the sexual power that accrues to men from female sexual slavery. As I studied the attitudes that accept female enslavement, I realized that a powerful ideology stems from it and permeates the social order. I have named that ideology cultural sadism. . . .

Not all thinking on prostitution accepts violence as normal for prostitutes. Prostitution is both an indication of an unjust social order and an institution that economically exploits women. But when economic power is defined as the causal variable, the sex dimensions of power usually remain unidentified and unchallenged. Consequently, economic analysis has often functioned to undermine the feminist critique of sexual domination that has gone on since the beginning of the women's movement. Feminist analysis of sexual power is often modified to make it fit into an economic analysis which defines economic exploitation as the primary instrument of female oppression. Under that system of thought, institutionalized sexual slavery, such as is found in prostitution, is understood in terms of economic exploitation which results in the lack of economic opportunities for women, the result of an unjust economic order. Undoubtedly economic exploitation is an important factor in the oppression of women, but here we must be concerned with whether or not economic analysis reveals the more fundamental sexual domination of women. As unjust as the economic order may be, this analysis spins off a set of beliefs which again contradict fact. Those beliefs assume:

1. That prostitution is an economic alternative for women who are the objects of discrimination in the larger inequitable job market—despite the fact that pimps are known to take all or almost all of the money earned by their prostitutes.

2. That only lower-class or poor women and girls turn to prostitution—despite the knowledge that most pimps recruit girls who are runaways, many of whom are from middle-class homes.

3. That only ethnic minority women are trapped in prostitution—despite the fact that many white women and girls are visible hooking on the streets, and despite the fact that pimps recruit women based on customer demand and easy availability.

4. That black men from the ghetto have no economic alternatives to pimping—despite the fact that a) most black men from the ghetto do not become pimps; b) that not all pimps are black or from the ghetto; and c) that exploitation, abuse, and enslavement cannot be justified by someone's economic conditions.

By appearing to critique the conditions which lead to prostitution these assumptions actually obscure recognition of sexual domination which is the first cause of sexual power.

The right-wing attacks against feminism and the witch-hunts against homosexuals have further clouded recognition of female sexual slavery. Public attention has been turned to child abuse, specifically male child abuse; there has been a wave of protest over child pornography and boy prostitution. Attention to procuring young children for pornography and prostitution has singled out one aspect of sexual slavery to the exclusion of all others. Documentation of the problem of boy prostitution has led investigators to assert that sexual abuse of boys is a larger and more serious problem than female adult or child prostitution. Therefore, some people are asserting an increase in the problem. But new awareness does not indicate increased incidence. It only reveals that the homosexual witch-hunts have created an audience for those exposés.

The political climate has created arbitrary and false distinctions and definitions. Child prostitution has always been a part of the sex slave trade. Separating the enslavement of children from that of women distorts the reality of the practices and conveys the impression that on some level it is tolerable to enslave women while child slavery is still reprehensible. Within that distinction lies the implication that one form of slavery is intolerable and worth attention while the other is not.

On the other hand, including male prostitution (teenage boys and adult men) with female prostitution assumes that they are the same phenomena and thereby obscures the fundamental sex-object role of women in masculinist society. The sex-power relationship between men and women makes male prostitution quite a different practice than female prostitution. The victimization and enslavement to which women are subject in male-dominated society find no equivalent in male experience.

Finally, sensationalism has made the traffic invisible. The tendency of writers on this subject to render already horrible events in the format of a lurid novel leaves the impression that the material is less than believable, that it is fiction. Not all slave markets are lustful events where whips crack over writhing, naked bodies. Often they are subdued business transactions. Sensationalism was the method that many turn-of-the-century workers used to bring attention to the traffic in women. The net result of their paternalistic, highly dramatized concern was to characterize the victims as such poor, sweet young things as to make the stories about them unbelievable. The very effort to dramatize and create attention casts suspicion on the veracity of the stories. The issue is not whether a child, teenager, or adult woman is a poor, innocent, sweet young thing. It is, rather, that no one should have the right to force anyone into slavery.

As my research progressed, I realized that the bias that makes forced prostitution invisible as a form of slavery comes from the tendency to focus on how a girl gets into it. If she is kidnapped, purchased, fraudulently contracted through an agency or organized crime, it is easy to recognize her victimization. But if she enters slavery having been procured through love and befriending tactics, then few, including herself, are willing to recognize her victimization. Seeing this problem led me to develop a working definition which became the criterion of my research, the basis on which I decided whether or not a particular incident was one of female sexual slavery. That definition focuses on the procuring strategies as well as the objective conditions of enslavement in which a woman is held, conditions from which she cannot escape and in which she is sexually exploited and abused. Once the objective conditions of sexual slavery are recognized and analyzed, the violence that victimizes women forced into prostitution cannot go by unnoticed. Consequently, instead of accepting women's self-acceptance of their slavery, we must question whether those circumstances are tolerable for any human being.

Sexual terrorism is a way of life for women even if we are not its direct victims. It has resulted in many women living with it while trying not to see or acknowledge it. This denial of reality creates a form of hiding. One woman, overcome at hearing about some practices of sexual slavery, suggested that I put them in the Appendix of this book to allow the reader to choose whether or not to look at them. Another friend wrote, "Be patient with me about your book; it really strikes a terror in me and a paralysis and I don't know when I'll be ready to read it."

Often in hearing about sexual slavery, some people hide in disbelief denying its reality. When we do recognize the terrorism, we may simply put it out of our minds, not wanting to acknowledge it. Or we sometimes hide by sitting in judgment on the victim. When faced with examples of how women are procured for slavery, there are those who will draw themselves up and instinctively distance themselves from the situation by passing uninformed, albeit ponderous, judgments on how a girl should have behaved if she really meant to prevent herself from being procured (or raped.) "I would have . . . " "She could have . . . " "Why didn't she . . . " instantly divide protagonist from listener. Those who hide by sitting in judgment are making the assumption not that the victim did wrong, but that she just didn't do everything she could to prevent it or to get away. The judgment is that it didn't have to happen, that the victim had control she didn't exercise.

Women are bullied into denying the existence of sexual violence; when we expose it, we are called crazy by those who have a quiet interest in its continuation and therefore in its secrecy. Or, we are confronted by kindhearted men who would never think of committing such acts themselves and therefore are incredulous that members of their sex could be thought of as carrying out such transgressions.

Hiding has helped keep female sexual slavery from being exposed. But worse than that, it has kept us from understanding the full extent of women's victimization, thereby denying us the opportunity to find our way out of it through political confrontation as well as through vision and hope. Vision of a society that does not enslave women involves first the pain of recognizing the worst of women's oppression. But with hope there is the opportunity to create a new political structure and social order. To have this vision means demanding and finding a world that will be free of sexual terrorism. Knowing the worst frees us to hope and strive for the best.

Reflection

KATHLEEN BARRY

In the late 1960s, radical feminism shaped the direction of the Women's Liberation Movement by insisting on 1) going to the root cause of issues of oppression, 2) uncovering the commonality of women's experiences of exploitation across class, race, and nationality, and 3) identifying the agents of oppression in economics, social/cultural practices, political systems and laws, and individuals (the personal is political). In that framework, by 1970, we took on rape, until then an unspoken crime against women, and made it a central issue of Women's Liberation.

In Detroit, our Women's Liberation group published the *Stop Rape Handbook,* breaking the silence with women's groups all over the country. That is when I began to notice short articles in the newspapers every now and then about slave rings that trafficked women into prostitution, astonished at the extent and depth of misogyny.

By 1975 I had a file sufficient, I thought, for an article. In going to the root of women's oppression, we recognized that the most extreme conditions, such as sexual slavery, could reflect on and reveal the expanse of the general problem of rape. For liberation to occur, to free ourselves from fear and the terror of sexual violence, we had to face and confront the worst conditions of oppression.

So there I was in 1975 with my file and an article in progress. I immediately became aware that we had no conceptual framework for understanding sexual slavery that was treated as an exceptional problem, sometimes connected to deviancy and sometimes to trafficking in drugs. As I began to see connections between rape, a systematic practice in sexual slavery, and childhood sexual abuse, better understood as incest assault in predisposing victims' vulnerability, and matched those with prevailing thinking—that women sort of "fell into prostitution"—the sociologist in me turned toward creating a typology that would locate sexual slavery in systems of domination and ideologies of women hating. After another file full of unusable attempts at a typology that would connect childhood sexual abuse with prostitution and trafficking, I gave up, realizing that neither my small file of cases nor an article were sufficient to uncover and disclose sexual slavery. The article turned into a book proposal, and I turned to three years of research.

I was on the streets with vice squads, in courtrooms at trials of pimps, and in one country after another tracking down cases of sexual slavery. I developed my methodology from what we had already learned about wife abuse: that women's descriptions of abuse vary enormously whether they are still in it or have gotten away. I decided to interview women who were out of prostitution and had been controlled by pimps.

As the data flowed in, I periodically returned to my typology file to try again to frame the problem, only to discover that it was a fundamental definition that was needed. In all of my research, one theme predominated over all others, that in order to leave prostitution women had to escape. That was when I understood that any condition a woman is in where she cannot leave voluntarily, and is sexually exploited and physically abused, is female sexual slavery.

Female Sexual Slavery, originally published in 1979 (Prentice Hall) and still in print since 1983 (New York University Press), was a focal point for action at the World Conference of Women in Copenhagen in 1980. Although the organizers were embarrassed by the subject and were grudgingly willing to let me do one workshop, I saw the effects of radical feminism in action once more as the overflow of women at the workshop led to many more sessions and an appeal to the governmental conference to call on nations to address this problem. Senator Barbara Mikulski, a U.S. delegate, introduced a resolution we developed that was ultimately adopted by the conference and led a new 1983 United Nations report on trafficking in women. By the late 1980s, tired of carrying this issue, radical feminists from several countries came together and we launched the Coalition Against Trafficking in Women, a United Nations NonGovernmental Organization in human rights consultative status. Soon trafficking in women became an international human rights issue. With the Coalition and support from UNESCO, we developed a new human rights law, the proposed Convention Against Sexual Exploitation.

The reaction that I had not anticipated to my book came from new pro-pornography and lesbian sado-masochism movements. Throughout the 1980s I was attacked in one newspaper after another that had originally hailed my work as a feminist breakthrough, for making women engaged in S & M feel uncomfortable with their choices. Eventually those antifeminist campaigns led to the most severe backlash, the denial of women's victimization in rape. Although I had critiqued feminism myself in *Female Sexual Slavery* for sometimes lapsing into what I called victimism, making a status out of being a victim, I too was accused of reducing women to victims—odd, I thought, considering what female sexual slavery does to women. I often lectured and was interviewed with Linda Marciano, who had been pornography's Linda Lovelace after she published her experience of sexual slavery in *Ordeal* (1979). At the same time, the pro-prostitution lobby that had escalated under Margo St. James and often with funding from pimps, turned to me and my work with rage.

Despite two decades of constant attack, I discovered something about women's condition and sexual exploitation I had missed in writing *Female Sexual Slavery:* the self-prostitution of women. Self-submission to exploitation is a condition that arises in every form of domination—colonialism, imperialism, slavery, racism. Women's liberation was not exempt. And that became the focus of my 1996 book, *Prostitution of Sexuality, the Global Exploitation of Women.*

Even in facing the worst conditions of women's oppression there can be moments of light. I have had the joy of seeing trafficking in women that was thought of as having disappeared by the end of the nineteenth century become the basis of a global activism and an important human rights issue not only to feminists, but for governments. The Convention Against Sexual Exploitation, a draft UN law that calls for arresting those who buy human beings for sexual use in prostitution, in sexual slavery, has been adopted by Sweden, Japan, and Vietnam. And that brought me to the other most important element of radical feminism, making those who exploit women accountable.

REFERENCES

Barry, K. (1996). *The prostitution of sexuality: The global exploitation of women.* New York: New York University Press.

Lovelace, L. (1981). *Ordeal.* New York: Berkeley Books.

PART TWO

Physical Violence against Women

To many readers, some of the excerpted works that comprise this section of the book may appear incompatible. Indeed, as several authors note in their reflections, their work has been criticized—even castigated—by others whom they considered allies, a reaction that obviously continues to perplex them. But despite the apparent incompatibilities, what these authors share is a willingness to ask really tough questions and to doggedly puzzle out answers. Their answers may not satisfy everyone, but they have served as a catalyst for a tremendous amount of subsequent research and, even more important, collective social action to address the problem of violence against women.

The first three works excerpted in this section set out to answer the questions "How much intimate violence occurs?" and "Is wife abuse an anomaly?" The authors went about answering these questions in different ways. As Del Martin points out in her reflection, she did not have the benefit of empirical studies, but through her compilation of anecdotes and piecing together the findings of various scattered reports, she developed a "guesstimate" that has since been supported by empirical research. Her goal, though, was not so much to generate a precise accounting of wife abuse incidents, but rather to demonstrate that wife abuse occurs far more often than the general public supposes and to motivate people to do something about it. Certainly, few readers would quarrel about whether Martin succeeded.

Rebecca and Russell Dobash used both quantitative and qualitative methods to document the incidence of wife abuse. They provided a historical context with which to frame the problem and, perhaps most importantly, emphasized the gender-specific nature of most marital violence. Their work continues to be cited as a prime example of the feminist perspective on wife abuse.

Murray Straus approached the questions from a slightly different angle. His goal was to obtain objective, reliable data on domestic violence from a large random sample of the U.S. population—a task that fellow social scientists at that time said couldn't be done. Undaunted, Straus developed the Conflict Tactics Scales (CTS), but we doubt that he anticipated the firestorm of controversy that instrument and his subsequent national survey findings would unleash. The CTS has been roundly criticized by some of the most prominent researchers of violence against women. Yet, it continues to be the most widely used instrument in this field—even by its critics—and Straus's article, excerpted here, is still one of the most frequently cited.

One of the most commonly asked questions about abused women is "Why do they stay?" Setting aside for the moment what has become our almost knee-jerk response (i.e., "That's the wrong question to ask; you should ask why men are violent toward women"), we may consider the next four excerpts in this section. In her careful reconstruction of the emergence of the Battered Women's Movement, Susan Schechter provided not only an answer to this question ("Because they have nowhere to go"), but also produced a valuable historical document that, as she noted in her reflection, can be used by future generations of activists. While emphasizing the courage and perseverance of "ordinary" women in responding to violence and abuse, Schechter also showed that the movement, even in its formative years, did not speak with one voice and was not effectively responsive to all groups of women. Although she wrote in her reflection that *Women and Male Violence* "was written with very little movement history under its belt," this is one of the reasons the book is so significant: It constitutes the foundation of the chronology of the movement on which so many others have, and will continue, to build.

In sharp contrast to Schechter, Lenore Walker turned to her field of psychology for an answer to the question of why battered women stay. In applying the theory of learned helplessness to battered women, Walker clearly was trying to prompt greater understanding of the women's plight and elicit more sympathy for them from social institutions, such as the courts, as well as the general public. Although some readers may dispute the claim in her reflection that the theory has been "highly successful in persuading juries to understand how battered women killed their abusive partners in self-defense," few will argue that Walker has not had a substantial impact on the field in terms of both research and practice.

Angela Browne's book, *When Battered Women Kill,* the next excerpt in this section, is often contrasted with Walker's. Like Walker, Browne interspersed battered women's personal stories with a review of empirical research, but instead of focusing on the individual psychology of battered women, Browne framed their narratives in a social structural context. She documented the women's repeated *active* attempts to get help and the lack of responsiveness of "help providers." And she powerfully conveyed the desperate fear of these women as they perceived their intimate partners as "out of control" and their lives and the lives of their children in imminent danger. Browne's analysis depicted battered women who kill not as helpless, but as women who had exhausted all other potential solutions and who, given the circumstances, responded to threat the way any "rational person" might respond. In doing so, she, too, provided the criminal justice system and juries with a framework for understanding how battered women, with no police record or history of violence, could kill their abusive partners in self-defense.

As the excerpt from Browne's book shows, many battered women say they stay in abusive relationships for the sake of their children. But as Stark and Flitcraft demonstrated in their excerpted article, battered women are typically demonized rather than valorized for this. Stark and Flitcraft's article has been a major catalyst in bringing together child welfare and battered women's advocates who, as Stark points out in his reflection, previously often saw one another as opponents. Stark and Flitcraft's findings—that domestic violence is a typical context for child abuse and that mothers' male intimate partners, not mothers themselves, are usually the child abusers—has had, as Stark also notes in his reflection, a major impact in the courts recently.

The final two excerpts in this section address the question, as one of the authors states it in her reflection, "What difference does difference make?" Barbara Hart, while giving credit to many others in her reflection, nonetheless bravely "named the violence" in lesbian relationships. Hart provided a springboard analysis of lesbian battering when all that existed were anecdotes and, worse, a strong reluctance to say anything public about the problem at all. Today, few textbooks on violence against women or domestic violence exclude lesbian, gay, bisexual, and transgendered partner violence and, even more telling, as colleagues quoted by Hart attest, *Lesbian Battering: An Examination* continues to motivate battered lesbians to speak out and to challenge service providers, researchers, students, and the public to broaden their understanding of intimate violence.

Kimberle Crenshaw's article, *Mapping the Margins,* excerpted here, put the concept of *intersectionality* in the vocabulary of researchers, practitioners, and advocates. Crenshaw showed how women of color were multiply jeopardized when they were abused by intimates: The dominant culture didn't really care—in fact, had never really cared—what happened to them, and members of communities of color worried more about what would happen to the abusers than what happened to the women they victimized. Crenshaw demonstrated that in terms of understanding and responding to violence against women, one size does not fit all. Inequalities of race and ethnicity, social class, sexual orientation, age, and other social locating variables require diverse perspectives and nuanced responses to address the problem. Crenshaw's work continues to be a wake-up call: to articulate, as she puts it in her reflection, "when and how difference matters" so we can "effectively work to include our difference within the broader struggle to end the violence that circumscribes our lives."

CHAPTER

11 Battered Wives

DEL MARTIN

Violent solutions to social problems have been incorporated into the mainstream culture of the United States. Violence is not the only reaction; nor is it the most common one. But, whether or not violent behavior is illegal, certain situations exist in which it is expected and almost inevitably occurs. One terrifying aspect of this fact of American life is that both the expectation and the incidence of violent behavior increase every year. . . .

Descriptions or enactments of violent acts intrude into the American home many times each day by way of newspapers and television. Surveys show that acts of aggression take place every three and one-half minutes on children's Saturday morning shows.[1] The Federal Communications Commission has made moves to regulate the sexual content of family prime-time programming, but claims it has no jurisdiction over other content. As long as portrayals of violence remain popular, advertisers will continue to sponsor violent programs. As the situation stands now, during the prime-time evening hours Americans have their choice of endless depictions of death on the operating table or death on the streets.

Advertisers' use of violence is getting more subtle and thus more insidious. For example, the December 1975 issue of *Vogue* carried a fashion layout in which a couple was shown alternately fighting and caressing each other. In one photograph the male model had just walloped the female model (his arm was raised in the follow-through) and her face was twisted in pain. The caption made no mention of the sado-masochistic theme of the photographs. It merely noted that the woman's jumpsuit could "really take the heat."[2] And, reported in the "No Comment" section of the July 1973 *Ms.* magazine was this ad for a bowling alley in Michigan: "Have some fun. Beat your wife tonight. Then celebrate with some good food and drink with your friends."

Because of the increase in the crime of rape (62 percent in the five-year period ending in 1973),[3] American women are often advised to "stay at home where they won't get hurt." But people who would impose such a curfew on women's freedom of movement might change their tune if they had access to local police reports on domestic violence, which suggest that women may be even less safe in their homes than they are in the streets.

The Incidence of Domestic Violence

Accurately determining the incidence of wife-beating per se is impossible at this time. Obvious sources of information are police reports, court rosters, and emergency hospital admittance files, but wife-abuse is not an official category on such records. Information on the subject gets buried in other, more general categories. Calls to the police for help in marital violence, for instance, are usually reported as "domestic disturbance calls," or DDs. If the police respond to these calls but decide that everything is under control, they may not file a report. If serious injury has been sustained by a wife, or if a wife has been killed by her husband, the incident is reported as assault and battery, aggravated assault, or homicide; wife-abuse is not necessarily specified. Sometimes written complaints registered by wives against their husbands are the only source of statistics available. But who is to say how many abused women do not register complaints?

Emergency rooms in hospitals are not reliable sources of statistics either. For a variety of reasons, women are often reluctant to tell the truth about how they sustained their injuries. Doctors often accept explanations such as "I ran into a door" or "I accidentally fell down the stairs." Even if they suspect that a woman's injuries are due to a beating, they seldom want to risk personal involvement by asking questions.

Statistical evidence on wife-battering must therefore be culled from the more general statistics available on domestic disturbance calls, complaints, hospital emergency rosters, and crime reports. Here follows a random sample of such information from some American cities:

- In Chicago, a police survey conducted between September 1965 and March 1966 demonstrated that 46.1 percent of all the major crimes except murder perpetrated against women took place at home.[4] The study also revealed that police response to domestic disturbance calls exceeded total response for murder, rape, aggravated assault, and other serious crimes.[5]
- A study in Oakland, California, in 1970 showed that police there responded to more than 16,000 family disturbance calls during a six-month period.[6]
- The 46,137 domestic disturbance calls received by Kansas City, Missouri, police represented 82 percent of all disturbance calls received by them in 1972.[7]
- In Detroit, 4,900 wife-assault complaints were filed in 1972.[8]
- In New York, 14,167 wife-abuse complaints were handled in Family Court throughout the state during the judicial year 1972–73.[9] "Legal experts think that wife-abuse is one of the most underreported crimes in the country—even more underreported than rape, which the FBI estimates is ten times more frequent than statistics indicate. A conservative estimate puts the number of battered wives nationwide at well over a million," states Karen Durbin.[10] Using the New York court statistics and the "ten times" formula to account for the cases that dropped by the wayside or were never reported, 141,670 wife-beatings could have occurred in New York State alone. If we can take this kind of guesswork a step further and consider that wife-battering is probably even more underreported than rape, and that there are fifty states in the Union, Durbin's estimate of "well over a million" could be conservative. . . .
- Trends in domestic violence are similar in city after city. But the problem is not just an urban one; it is to be found in rural areas as well. For example, the police chief in a small Washtenaw County (Michigan) town of 6,000 reports that family assault calls come in every day.[11] And another police official with extensive rural experience esti-

mates that police calls for "family fights" are exceeded only by calls relating to automobile accidents.[12]

The figures cited here were randomly selected from a variety of sources. No attempt has been made to adjust them with respect to population or to compare them and discern regional trends. The point here is that a great many domestic-violence cases come to the attention of the authorities. The raw numbers themselves make it obvious that domestic violence is a social problem, and a serious one. Just how serious is anyone's guess, since no one knows how many cases of domestic violence go unreported.

Still, the terms "domestic violence" or "domestic disturbance" are not synonymous with "wife-battering." But you don't need a degree in criminology to realize that the police are not called into a domestic situation unless the weaker person(s) involved need help or are perceived to need help by witnesses. If the involved parties could control and resolve a domestic disturbance, no doubt they would do so without inviting the police to interfere. It can be assumed that someone in most reported cases of domestic disturbance was being overpowered or, at the very least, frightened, or that neighbors or passersby thought that was the case.

Two other commonsense factors will help clarify the relationship between domestic-disturbance figures and wife-battering. First, many households are composed of conventional heterosexual marriages or relationships; and second, in most such relationships the woman is physically weaker than the man. We can assume that a good many of the domestic disturbance calls that do not involve juveniles concern women being intimidated, frightened, or assaulted by men to the point where someone decides that help is needed from the police. This assumption is borne out by statistics. Of the figures available on complaints, 82 percent in New York,[13] 75 percent in Washington, D.C.,[14] 85.4 percent in Detroit,[15] and 95 percent in Montgomery County, Maryland,[16] were filed by female victims.

By looking at another random sampling of police statistics, we can get an idea of just how serious a "domestic disturbance" can be:

- In 1971, Kansas City police found that one-third of the aggravated assaults reported were due to domestic disturbance.[17] Police had been called previously at least once in 90 percent of these cases and five or more times in over half of them.[18] Also during 1971, 40 percent of all homicides in Kansas City were cases of spouse killing spouse.[19] In almost 50 percent of these cases, police had been summoned five or more times within a two-year period before the murder occurred.[20]
- Almost one-third of all female homicide victims in California in 1971 were murdered by their husbands.[21]
- Nationwide in 1973, according to the FBI, one-fourth of all murders occurred within the family, and one-half of these were husband-wife killings. In assault cases wives are predominantly the victims, but in homicides husbands are the victims almost as often as wives (48 percent compared with 52 percent in 1973).[22] This phenomenon is partially explained by the fact that, according to a report made to a government commission on violence, women who commit murder are motivated by self-defense almost seven times as often as male offenders. . . .[23]

It is worthwhile mentioning here that divorce statistics are not a reliable gauge of the frequency of wife-abuse, since mention of marital violence can be negotiated out of the record before the trial or because the wife was unable to produce medical and police records to prove it occurred. However, a survey conducted by George Levinger of 600 applicants for divorce in the Cleveland area revealed that 37 percent of the wives suing for divorce cited "physical abuse" as one of their complaints.[24] And a Wayne County (Michigan) judge stated that approximately 16,000 divorces are initiated in the county annually, and in 80 percent of those coming before him, beating is alleged. Commenting on another aspect of the problem, this judge estimated that fifty to sixty hearings are held in the Third Judicial Circuit Court each month on wives' claims that their estranged husbands have violated injunctions restraining them from physically abusing the wives.[25]

Wife-Abuse: The Skeleton in the Closet

Common sense tells us that statistics relating to domestic violence reflect, to some extent, the incidence of wife-beating. "Wife-beating has been so prevalent that all of us must have been aware of its existence—if not in our own lives, at least in the lives of others, or when a wife-beating case that resulted in death was reported in the press," states Betsy Warrior.[26] But, although governmental agencies and social scientists have begun to concentrate on social violence in recent years, wife-battering has merited no special attention in those quarters. Nor has it aroused the shocked indignation it should have from the women's movement until very recently. The fact is, the issue has been buried so deeply that no real data exist on the incidence of wife-beating.

The news media have often treated wife-abuse as a bizarre and relatively rare phenomenon—as occasional fodder for sensationalistic reporting—but rarely as a social issue worthy of thorough investigation. *Time* magazine demonstrated the news media's head-in-the-sand attitude in 1974 when it ran an article on Erin Pizzey's Chiswick Center, but carried it only in the European edition. Apparently the *Time* editors thought that wife-battering would not interest Americans.

In *Violence and the Family,* Suzanne Steinmetz and Murray Straus surveyed various kinds of literature in an effort to discern trends in the treatment of wife-beating. In their review of four hundred items, they located little material on husband-wife violence other than murder, even in novels. They were particularly puzzled by the fact that anthropologists had not uncovered evidence of marital violence in their studies of other cultures. But Paul Bohannon suggested to one of their colleagues two possible reasons: (1) middle-class anthropologists share the middle-class horror of violence, and (2) people in cultures under anthropological investigation do not necessarily conduct their family quarrels in the presence of anthropologists; nor do they talk about the violent episodes that might characterize their private lives.[27]

Occasionally, psychiatrists admit to coming across cases of marital violence in their clinical practices, but therapy-prone professionals tend to treat such incidents as exceptions and to see them in terms of the individual's pathology. Psychological studies of family dynamics tend to overlook the physical conflicts between husband and wife; they usually concentrate on the causes of tension within families, not on the means by which it is expressed.

An example of how social scientists skirt the issue of wife-battering is in the otherwise well-researched book by Eleanor Emmons Maccoby and Carol Nagy Jacklin, *The Psychology of Sex Differences.* Commenting on an article on wife-beating that appeared in the *Manchester Guardian,* these writers state, "Although incidents of this kind exist as an ugly aspect of marital relations in an unknown number of cases . . . there can be little doubt that direct force is rare in modern marriages. Male behavior such as that described above would be considered pathological in any human (or animal!) society, and, if widespread, would endanger a species."[28]

The wishful thinking demonstrated in this passage—that "direct force is rare in modern marriages"—even in its mildest form has done its share to keep information on wife-beating from surfacing. The fact that such information is all but lost in the tangle of police statistics on domestic disturbances substantiates the suspicions of those who think—and would like to go on thinking—that wife-beating is not a significant problem and does not deserve attention. But Pizzey's experience at the Chiswick Center has proved these Pollyannas to be wrong. When she opened a refuge for women, many abused wives showed up. Their very existence raises the issue of wife-battering.

In *Scream Quietly or the Neighbors Will Hear,* Pizzey points out that people try to ignore violence inside the home and within the family. Many abused wives who came to Chiswick Center told Pizzey that their neighbors knew very well what was going on but went to great lengths to pretend ignorance. They would cross the street to avoid witnessing an incident of domestic violence. Some would even turn up the television to block out the shouts, screams, and sobs coming from next door.[29]

From one point of view, the battered wife in her secrecy conspires with the media, the police, the social scientists, the social reformers, and the social workers to keep the issue hushed up. We can picture a very thick door locked shut. On the inside is a woman trying hard not to cry out for help. On the other side are those who could and should be helping, but instead are going about their business as if she weren't there.

The Great American Family

The door behind which the battered wife is trapped is the door to the family home. The white-picket-fence stereotype of the American family home still persists from the days of Andy Hardy. The privacy of the home supposedly protects a comfortable space within which intimate and affectionate relationships among spouses, parents and children, and siblings become richer and deeper with each passing year. Loyalty, constancy, and protectiveness are demonstrated by the parents and learned by the children. If you modernize the picture by adding some self-deprecating humor gleaned from television's situation comedies, the image of the ideal American family will be complete.

In one sense, the family home is supposed to provide refuge from the stormy turbulence of the outside world. In another, it is a family factory, designed to perpetuate its own values and to produce two or three replicas of itself as the children in the family marry—whether or not they are ready for or suited for marriage. The nuclear family is the building block of American society, and the social, religious, educational, and economic institutions of society are designed to maintain, support, and strengthen family ties even if the people involved can't stand the sight of one another.

Until very recently, no acceptable alternatives to the family home existed in the United States. People who chose to live alone or to share their homes with non-relatives, those who chose to set up same-sex households, or who married but chose not to have children—all were seen as outcasts, failures, or deviants. This attitude is changing, albeit very slowly, possibly more as a result of overpopulation than of growing openmindedness and tolerance. But even now, the stereotype of the happy, harmonious family persists in American society. Compared with this ideal, most actual families composed of real people appear to be tragic failures, and in many cases they are.

In reality, the glowing image of the American family is a myth. The privacy that protects the family can also muffle the blows and stifle the yells of a violent home. People who would not otherwise consider striking anyone, sometimes act as if establishing a household together gives them the right to abuse each other. "From our interviews," Richard Gelles says in *The Violent Home,* "we are still convinced that in most cases a marriage license also functions as a hitting license."[30] In his research, which admittedly was limited to eighty subjects who were legally married, Gelles found that numerous incidents of violence between married partners were considered by them to be normal, routine, and generally acceptable.[31] He also found a high incidence of violence in his control group and only one instance in which violence had occurred before the couple married. Furthermore, in the case of two couples in his sample who dated, married, divorced, dated again, and remarried, violence occurred *only* when these couples were *legally* married. These findings indicate to Gelles the possibility that violence between a couple is considered acceptable within, but not outside of, marriage.[32]

Unmarried women who have been beaten by their mates undoubtedly would take exception to Gelles's interpretation. It may well be that the shared home, not the marriage vow, is the key element here. Some men may feel that they have the right to exercise power over the women they live with whether or not they are legally married to them.

Our patriarchal system allows a man the right of ownership to some degree over the property *and* people that comprise his household. A feminist friend learned this lesson in an incident in Oakland, California. She witnessed a street fight in which a husband was hitting his pregnant wife in the stomach (a recurring theme in stories of wife-abuse). She saw the fight as she was driving by, stopped her car, and jumped out to help the woman. When she tried to intervene, the male bystanders who stood idly by watching the spectacle shouted at her, "You can't do that! She's his wife!" and "You shouldn't interfere; it's none of your business." Although the wife had begged the gathered crowd to call the police, no one did so until my friend was struck by the furious husband. (I have heard of a similar incident where a man interfered and *he* was the one who was arrested and charged with assault!)

Sociologist Howard Erlanger of the University of Wisconsin found that 25 percent of his sample of American adults actually approved of husband-wife battles. What is more surprising was that the greater the educational level, the greater was the acceptance of marital violence. Approval ranged from 17 percent of grade-school graduates to 32 percent of college postgraduate students, with a slightly lower 30 percent for those who had completed just four years of college. The study also showed that, contrary to popular belief, low-income respondents were no more prone to nor more readily accepting of violence in the home than were middle- or upper-income respondents.[33]

The popular assumption by the middle class that marital violence occurs more frequently in the ghetto and among lower-class families reflects the inability of middle-class investigators to face the universality of the problem. Evidence of wife-beating exists wherever one cares to look for it. Fairfax County, Virginia, for instance, is a suburb of the District of Columbia and considered to be one of the wealthiest counties in the United States. Police there received 4,073 family disturbance calls in 1974. They estimated that thirty assault warrants are sought by Fairfax County wives each week.[34]

Morton Bard's study of New York's 30th Precinct, a West Harlem community of about 85,000 people, is another example. This socially stable residential community consists mostly of working-class Blacks, with a sprinkling of Latin Americans (8 percent) and whites (2 percent).[35] Bard found that the number of wife-abuse cases reported in the 30th Precinct was roughly the same as that reported in another study conducted in Norwalk, Connecticut—a white, upper-middle-class area with approximately the same population.[36]

A survey conducted for the National Commission on the Causes and Prevention of Violence by Louis Harris and Associates bears out Erlanger's conclusions that a great many people approve of husband-wife battles. The Harris poll in October 1968, consisting of 1,176 interviews with a representative national sample of American adults, showed that one-fifth approved of slapping one's spouse on "appropriate" occasions. In this survey, 16 percent of those with eight years of schooling or less approved, and 25 percent of college-educated people approved of a husband slapping his wife.[37]

Rodney Stark and James McEvoy III further analyzed the Harris data and found that 25 percent of the Blacks, 20 percent of the whites, 25 percent of the males, and 16 percent of the females interviewed "could approve of a husband's slapping his wife's face." The percentage points rose in all of these categories (from 1 to 3 percent) when the question was reversed and subjects were asked if they "could approve of a wife's slapping her husband's face." Analyzed by regions of the country, persons from the West rated highest and the South lowest in approval of either action. Those with an income of $5,000 or less were considerably less approving than those in other income brackets. Persons under thirty years old were most approving, and those sixty-five years or older were least approving of husband-wife slappings.[38]

A slap in the face could be construed as a fairly innocent gesture compared with a full-fledged beating. But a friend of mine told me this story. Three months after her mother and stepfather were married, they had an argument and he gave her a sound "slapping." A few months later he "slapped" her again; this time the woman wound up in the hospital with her jaws wired together. When she came home from the hospital, her husband was contrite and conciliatory. He did his best to please her so that she wouldn't leave him. The woman stayed, though she never really forgave her husband. They still had their fights, but he never laid a hand on her again. However, two years later, when the couple got into a particularly heated argument in the kitchen, he grabbed a knife and killed her.

Later, my daughter was slapped by a friend's violent husband when she responded to the wife's call for help. He just slapped her on the cheek, but with such force that her head snapped back and pain shot through her head to the top of her skull. He struck her twice in this heavy-handed manner. Her face was sore for several days, though there were no bruises; she also suffered the effects of a minor whiplash. "I didn't think he would hit *me.* He was my friend," she said. "And I certainly didn't realize that a man could exert so much force with his open hand. It was just a short slap. He didn't need to take a long swing."

In the Harris poll cited above, if the word had been "hit" instead of "slap" would the results of the poll have been the same? Would 25 percent of the males and 16 percent of the females interviewed approve of a husband hitting his wife in the face? The answer to that question is anybody's guess. But there is a good chance that the interviewees would have considered the question an invasion of privacy had the word been "hit" rather than "slap." I cite this possibility to underscore the subtlety of the problem and the difficulty of interpreting the significance of the data.

Even agreeing on a definition of "violence" may be a problem for some people. Police, for instance, seem to think that few domestic disturbances are really violent. They tend to define violence in terms of its effect. Unless blood is drawn and injuries are visible, they are apt to discount the report of violence and call the incident merely a "family spat." To me, any physical attack by one person upon another is a violent act and an instance of illegal aggression, even if no visible injury results. Still, Gelles noted that after the bruises had healed, some of his subjects called even the most severe beatings they received "nonviolent."[39]

However the terms are defined, though, sufficient evidence of serious injury and homicide exists to show that domestic violence is a critical problem. In *The Violent Home,* Gelles determined where and when violence is most likely to occur. The "typical location of family violence was the kitchen. The bedroom and the living room are the next most likely scenes of violence. Some respondents are unable to pinpoint exact locations because their battles begin in one room and progress through the house. The *only* room in the house where there was *no violence* was the bathroom.[40]

Alex D. Pokorny says that murder seldom occurs in public places. The usual site is the home, though the car is the setting in a fair number of cases.[41] Other studies of homicides show that the bedroom is the deadliest room in the house and that the victims there are usually female.[42] The next most likely place for family murders is the kitchen; in those cases the women are more frequently the offender.[43]

According to Gelles, couples get into violent fights most often after dinner, between 8 and 11:30 P.M. The second most frequent time is during dinner (5 to 8 P.M.), and the third is late evening to early morning.[44] The same time-table applies to those acts of violence that result in death.[45] Also, violence of either variety occurs most frequently on weekends.[46] Kansas City police cite Monday as another day of reckoning.[47]

The Children

If the American-family dream is a nightmare for spouses involved in domestic violence, it is even more so for their children. They suffer the consequences of their parents' battles simply because they exist. When violence becomes a pattern in the household it can take many forms. In her desperation, the battered wife may strike out at the children, scapegoating them as she has been scapegoated by a violent husband. And the man who beats his wife may also beat his children. In J. J. Gayford's survey of one hundred battered women in England, 37 percent of the women admitted taking their own frustrations out on the children, and 54 percent claimed their husbands committed acts of violence against the children.[48] The breaking point for many of these women came when the children were made into victims too. At that point many of the women resolved, or tried, to leave.[49]

Children who "merely" witness physical violence between their parents suffer emotional trauma. They react with shock, fear, and guilt. This fact was brought home to me when my eight-year-old grandson witnessed his friend's drunk father hit my daughter, who had rushed to the aid of the man's wife. The incident happened in front of the house. The husband jumped down from the roof to confront my daughter and grandson. Terrified, my grandson ran for the car and locked himself in. While he was in the car, be saw the man give his mother a couple of hard slaps. Later, when my daughter and the child arrived at my house, my grandson flung himself on the couch. He was emotionally devastated. He could only mumble, "It was horrible!" When he was able to talk about it, he blurted out that if his older sister had been there "she would have done something!" He had been scared; he hadn't known what to do and felt guilty about that. Not until we started discussing self-defense tactics did the little boy perk up. He wanted to form a plan of action so that he would know how to react in the future.

In Bard's study of the 30th Precinct in New York City, children were present in 41 percent of the domestic disturbance cases in which police intervened. "If this is typical, one can only speculate on the modeling effects of parental aggression on such children—not to speak of the effects of a variety of police behaviors on the perception of children in such situations," he said.[50] The behavior of police officers is bound to have a strong effect on children. If the police identify with the father and treat the incident lightly, they will be reinforcing the role models of violent male and female victim. But if police efficiently calm down the angry parents and effectively communicate the attitude that violent behavior is not to be excused or tolerated, the children will be receiving healthier signals. . . .

Hidden behind the stereotyped image of the nuclear family, then, we find not only isolated instances of domestic violence, but also the potential for ever-increasing patterns of violence as, in literally millions of homes around the world, the children of battling parents establish their own families. If the building block of American society, the modern nuclear family, is ever more frequently wracked by physical brutality, what hope can we have for society as a whole? Past president of the National Council on Family Relations Murray A. Straus declares, "I don't think we are going to understand violence in American society until we understand violence in the family. . . . The home is where violence primarily occurs."[51]

We must stop protecting our myths and lies, and stop teaching our children to strike out blindly with their fists. If there is battering to be done, let it be directed against that sacred front door to the family home.

NOTES

1. John Harris, "Networks Claim They've Been Toned Down but . . . ," *National Enquirer* (August 19, 1975), p. 14.
2. Beth Pombeiro (Knight News Service), "Decadence Is Back—in Vogue," *San Francisco Examiner* (December 7, 1975), pp. 1, 28, and *Vogue* (December 1975), p. 149.
3. Federal Bureau of Investigation, *Unified Crime Reports* (1973), p. 14.
4. Letty Cottin Pogrebin, "Do Women Make Men Violent?" *Ms.* (November 1974), p. 55.
5. Raymond Parnas, "The Police Response to Domestic Disturbances," *Wisconsin Law Review* (1967), p. 914, n. 2.
6. Raymond Parnas, "Police Discretion and Diversion of Incidents of Intra-Family Violence," *Law and Contemporary Problems,* Vol. 36, No. 4 (Autumn 1971), p. 54, n. 1.
7. Northeast Patrol Division Task Force, Kansas City Police Department, "Conflict Management: Analysis/Resolution." Taken from first draft, p. 58 (hereinafter called Kansas City Police report).
8. Commander James D. Bannon, from a speech delivered before a conference of the American Bar Association in Montreal, 1975.
9. J. C. Barden, "Wife Beaters: Few of Them Ever Appear Before a Court of Law," *The New York Times* (October 21, 1974), Sec. 2, p. 38. Figures reported as 17,277 family violence cases, of which the wife was plaintiff in 82 percent.
10. Karen Durbin, "Wife-Beating," *Ladies Home Journal* (June 1974), p. 64.
11. Sue Eisenberg and Patricia Micklow, "The Assaulted Wife: 'Catch 22' Revisited," unpublished (University of Michigan, Ann Arbor, 1974), p. 18. A version of this study was published by *Women's Rights Law Reporter* in 1976.
12. Morton Bard, *Training Police As Specialists in Family Crisis Intervention* (Washington: U.S. Government Printing Office, 1970), p. 1.
13. Barden, p. 38.
14. Yankowski, p. 3.
15. Eisenberg and Micklow, p. 16.
16. Montgomery County Council, Maryland, "A Report by the Task Force to Study a Haven for Physically Abused Persons" (1975). p. 17.
17. Kansas City Police report.
18. Ibid.
19. Ibid.
20. Ibid.
21. *California Homicides,* 1971.
22. Federal Bureau of Investigation, *Uniform Crime Reports,* 1973.
23. *Crimes of Violence,* a staff report to the National Commission on the Causes and Prevention of Violence (Washington, D.C.: U.S. Government Printing Office, 1969), p. 360.
24. George Levinger, "Source of Marital Dissatisfaction among Applicants for Divorce," *American Journal of Orthopsychiatry* (October 1966), pp. 804–06.
25. Eisenberg and Micklow, p. 18.
26. Betsy Warrior, *Working on Wife Abuse* (7th supplemented ed.) (Cambridge, MA: Author, 1976), p. 25.
27. Suzanne K. Steinmetz and Murray A. Straus, eds., *Violence in the Family* (New York: Dodd, Mead, 1975), p. v.
28. Eleanor Emmons Maccoby and Carol Nagy Jacklin, *The Psychology of Sex Differences* (Stanford: Stanford University Press, 1974), p. 264.

29. Erin Pizzey, "Scream Quietly or the Neighbors Will Hear," *Manchester Daily Express* (October 29, 1974), p. 11.

30. Gelles, p. 153.

31. Ibid., p. 58.

32. Ibid., p. 136.

33. Joyce Brothers, "A Quiz on Crime," *San Francisco Sunday Examiner and Chronicle* (June 22, 1975), Sunday Scene, p. 6.

34. Bill Peterson, "System Frustrates Battered Wives," *Washington Post* (November 2, 1974), p. 18.

35. Morton Bard, "The Study and Modification of Intra-Familial Violence," *The Control of Aggression and Violence: Cognitive and Psychological* (New York: Academic Press, 1971), p. 154.

36. Sally Johnson, "What About Battered Women?" *Majority Report* (February 8, 1975), p. 4.

37. Rodney Stark and James McEvoy III, "Middle-Class Violence," *Psychology Today* (November 1970), pp. 30–31.

38. Ibid., p. 32.

39. Gelles, p. 25.

40. Ibid., pp. 95–96.

41. Alex D. Pokorny, "Human Violence: A Comparison of Homicide, Aggravated Assault, Suicide, and Attempted Suicide," *Journal of Criminal Law, Criminology and Police Science* 56 (1965), pp. 488–97.

42. Marvin E. Wolfgang, *Patterns in Criminal Homicide* (New York: John Wiley, 1958), p. 125.

43. Ibid., p. 126.

44. Gelles, p. 100.

45. Wolfgang, p. 108.

46. Gelles, pp. 104-05. D. J. Pittman and W. Handy, "Patterns in Criminal Aggravated Assault," *Journal of Criminal Law, Criminology and Police Science* 55 (1964), pp. 463.

47. Kansas City Police report.

48. J. J. Gayford, "Wife Battering: A Preliminary Survey on 100 Cases," *British Medical Journal* (January 25, 1975), p. 196.

49. Ibid., p. 195.

50. Bard, "The Study and Modification of Intra-Familial Violence," p. 161.

51. Quoted in Kuhn, p. A-14.

Reflection

DEL MARTIN

The idea for the book *Battered Wives* came from Ruth Gottstein, publisher of Volcano Press. On a trip to London she met Erin Pizzey, author of *Scream Quietly or the Neighbors Will Hear,* who was conducting an aggressive campaign on behalf of battered wives in England. Ruth decided to visit Chiswick Women's Aid, the refuge Pizzey had founded as an escape hatch for abused women and their children.

When she returned home, Ruth told me, "This can't be just a British problem. It has to be going on here in the States, too." She then began a campaign of her own to get me to write the American version. That wasn't difficult. Ruth had published *Lesbian/Woman,* the book Phyllis Lyon, my partner in life and work, and I had co-authored. I had been wanting to write something to show that as a lesbian feminist I was not a single-issue advocate.

At the outset I was told I had to produce extensive and verifiable statistics on the incidence of violence against women. Excerpts from this chapter, Violence in the Home, concentrated on the results of my research. I concluded that incidence and incidents of violence in the home reached into the millions. My editor deleted my estimate on the grounds that I couldn't prove it. Since then, academia has confirmed my *virtual* estimate and admitted that lacking uniformity in the way data are accumulated makes it impossible to provide *actual* statistics.

In the course of my research I came to the realization that all the women's issues we had tackled in the National Organization for Women related to the plight of battered women. I saw a common thread in the life experiences of all women, no matter their background, whereby males in a dominant position assigned, defined, and confined them to inferior roles by intimidation, threats, and the use of force. The power dynamics in patriarchal society have historically depended on control of women's sexuality and sex-stereotyping that links maleness to dominance and violence (Sonkin et al., 1985).

My book, *Battered Wives,* has been credited as the catalyst for the Battered Women's Shelter Movement. I am told that 27 years since it was first published it is still being used as an educational tool by shelters and related agencies in the prevention of domestic violence and treatment of its victims.

That is flattering, but in writing a foreword for K. J. Wilson's (1997) book, *When Violence Begins at Home,* I discovered the sequel to *Battered Wives.* Wilson did a superb job in summarizing what we have learned and accomplished in 27 years.

In closing I would like to share some of my own observations. There is much truth in the adage, "Nothing is permanent save change." Although great strides have been made to provide recourse and safety to battered women, the systems we have developed are not fail proof. It is necessary to watchdog every agency in the system and see that protocol is enforced. Personnel changes, for instance, make education a never-ending process.

REFERENCES

Pizzy, E. (1974). *Scream quietly or the neighbors will hear.* London: If Books.

Sonkin, D. J., Martin, D., & Walker, L. E. A. (1985). (Eds.). *The Male Batterer: A Treatment Approach* (p. 4). New York: Springer.

Wilson, K. J. (1997). *When violence begins at home: A comprehensive guide to understanding and ending domestic abuse.* Alameda, CA: Hunter House.

CHAPTER

12 Wives

The "Appropriate" Victims of Marital Violence

REBECCA EMERSON DOBASH AND
RUSSELL P. DOBASH

It has only been a hundred years since men were denied the legal right to beat their wives in Britain and the United States. Prior to the late 19th century it was considered a necessary aspect of a husband's marital obligation to control and chastise his wife through the use of physical force. The legal prescriptions which once supported this practice no longer exist yet the behaviour continues unabated. Behaviour which was once legally condoned is now proscribed by law, yet cultural and normative prescriptions still support such practice and it is only mildly condemned, if at all, by law enforcement and judicial institutions (cf. LaFave, 1969; Field and Field, 1973; Bannon, 1975; Straus, 1976; Dobash and Dobash, 1977).

We will elucidate the historical processes which aid in the understanding and explanation of this form of violence and provide evidence from diverse sources to document the prevalence and predominance of violence directed at wives[1] in contemporary western societies. Our understanding will not, however, be increased by merely documenting the prior existence of wifebeating. What is required is a form of historical analysis which illustrates the interrelationship between this form of violence and other social processes and institutions. This will provide a better understanding of the social meaning of wife beating, of its acceptability throughout society and of the institutional mechanisms by which it was supported and maintained. Placing violence against women in this wider socio-historical context, leads to a more complete understanding of its manifestations in contemporary society. This methodology enables one to go beyond a myopic empiricism which focuses solely upon individuals or couples, and provides a framework for placing such couples in a wider social context from which more meaningful explanations can be drawn (cf. Weber, 1949; Lukács, 1971).

When this methodology is applied to the problem of violence against women in the home, it leads to the indisputable conclusion that wifebeating is not, in the strictest sense of the words, a 'deviant,' 'aberrant,' or 'pathological' act. Rather, it is a form of behavior which has existed for centuries as an acceptable, and, indeed, a desirable part of a patriarchical family system within a patriarchical society, and much of the ideology and many of the institutional arrangements which supported the patriarchy through the subordination, domination and control of women are still reflected in our culture and our social institutions. The following sketch of the historical roots of this violence and the reinterpretation and deciphering of a wide variety of contemporary research provides overwhelming evidence that it is women in their position as wives who become the 'appropriate' victims of violence in the home. Before proceeding, it is vital that we make explicit the type of violence we intend to explore. Although we do not discount the cruelty nor the coerciveness of psychological forms of violence, it is not our intention to consider this form of violence. Our intent is to focus explicitly upon violence which involves the use of physical force. However, to define the domain of inquiry in such gross and all inclusive terms as physical violence or physical force would be both imprecise and misleading. A lack of specificity concerning the term 'physical violence' leaves the reader uncertain about the nature of the phenomenon being studied and thus unclear about the generalizations being made. There is considerable variation in the social meaning and the physical consequences of the acts involving force which occur between husbands and wives. This includes periodic slapping or pushing and shoving, which rarely if ever escalates and is not intended to result in serious injury or intimidation; repeated punching and kicking which is intended to do injury and to severely intimidate the victim but not to kill them (although this sometimes happens); and violence with the intention to kill. These behaviours differ in terms of motivations, purposes and coerciveness and should not be seen as necessarily cumulative or progressive. In this paper, we are not concentrating upon the least serious category, slapping and shoving, but upon homicides and especially upon the more severe and systematic assaults involving kicking and punching intended to injure and seriously intimidate.

The Legacy of the Patriarchy

Reputedly, the first law of marriage was proclaimed by the Roman, Romulus, in 753 B.C. It proclaimed that married women were "to conform themselves entirely to the temper of their husbands and the husbands to rule their wives as necessary and inseparable possessions" (O'Faolain and Martines, 1973:53). There was no place in Roman society for detached persons, and a woman had no alternative except to marry and become a 'necessary and inseparable possession.' By marriage a woman 'came into the hand,' or under the control, of her husband. The man was the absolute patriarch who owned and controlled all properties and people within the family. A wife was obligated to obey her husband and he was given the legal right and the moral obligation to control and punish her for any 'misbehaviour,' including adultery, drinking wine, attending public games without his permission or appearing unveiled in public. The husband was given full powers to judge and censor his wife and there was a definite standard which protected the rights and authority of husbands and legitimized the subjugation of wives through force. This was most clearly put in a speech delivered by Cato the Censor during the fifth century B.C. Speaking about the appropriate response to marital infidelity, he said, "if you catch your wife in adultery, you could put her to death with impunity, she, on her part, would not dare to touch you with her finger; and it is not right that she should" (Hecker, 1910:23).

There were numerous Roman laws about adultery, infidelity and sexual jealousy; they all reflected a double standard and punishments for such offences were very severe. The reasons were not related to thwarted love, but to property. The husband's authority had to remain inviolate in order that there would be no question about the pedigree of the male children who were to inherit the family name and possessions. Any indication that a wife was not under the complete control of her husband was deemed sufficient grounds for beating her, even to excess. There was the case of a husband:

> who beat his wife to death because she had drunk some wine; and this murder, far from leading to his being denounced was not even blamed. People considered that her exemplary punishment had properly expiated her offence . . . for any woman who drinks wine immoderately closes her heart to every virtue and opens it to every vice. (O'Faolain and Martines, 1973:55)

There were many changes in the Roman family in the later stages of the Empire. The Punic Wars meant that men were absent for long periods and during that time women had taken on more responsibility, gained more independence, and some of them inherited property, were educated, and engaged in traditional male pursuits such as politics and philosophy. The severe sexual code was modified and, relative to the earlier period, women were greatly emancipated. Although a man could still beat his wife, greater limits and restrictions were placed upon him, and it was made illegal to beat a woman of the upper classes (O'Faolain and Martines, 1973).

The changes in the independence of women and the dilution of the absolute patriarch were looked upon with particular horror among the poorer sections of society. In terms of family structures and relations, an obscure, small sect known as the Christians was not struggling for revolutionary change but for the maintenance of the power and authority of the patriarch. Christianity embraced the hierarchical family structure and celebrated the subordination of wives to their husbands. Their scriptures were teaching:

> " . . . wives be in subjection to your own husbands." (Peter, 3:1)
> " . . . the head of the woman is the man." (I Corinthians, 11:3)
> "But I suffer not a woman to teach or to usurp authority of man, but to be in silence." (I Timothy, 3:12)
> (Women) "are commanded to be under obedience." (I Corinthians 14:34)

Wives were to obey and be in subjection but the Christian attitude was that this should not be achieved through force but through an adherence to a moral order which made obedience sacred. "The law of marriage (I Corinthians, 7) and the prescriptions for conjugal duties" (Ephesians, 5; Titus, 2:4–5) stated that love and obedience constituted the proper role for a wife. A husband was also expected to love his spouse, but in addition he was to rule his household well and to keep everyone in subjection (I Timothy, 3).[2]

Continuing from these very early periods, both the Church and the State supported the subordination of women in marriage and the husband's control over his wife; the Church through a moral order and the State through actively propagandizing for the authority of husbands and legitimizing their use of violence against their wives (cf. Dobash and Dobash, forthcoming). This can be seen in the writings of Martin Luther (1531), John Knox (1558), and Calvin (1560), each of whom reiterated ideas similar to those in the Homily on Marriage, which was ordered by the Crown to be read in Church every Sunday from 1562 onward (Stone, 1975:52), and in the very popular marriage manuals of the day; ideas like, "the extent of wives subjection doth stretch itself very far, even to all things" (Gouge, 1634:270–71).

The Laws of Chastisement

Accompanying these moral imperatives were the many laws of chastisement. During the Middle Ages women throughout Spain, Italy, France and England could be flogged through the city streets, exiled for years or killed if they committed adultery or numerous 'lesser' offenses. In France a man could beat his wife, "when she contradicts or abuses him, or when she refuses, like a decent woman, to obey his reasonable commands" (Coutumes de Beauvaisis in O'Faolain and Martines, 1973:188). Even the French code of chivalry specified that the husband of a scolding wife could knock her to the earth, strike her in the face with his fist and break her nose so that she would always be blemished and ashamed. Thus, "the wife ought to suffer and let the husband have the word, and be the master" (Trevelyan, 1966:260).

Under English Common Law a married woman lost all of her civil rights, had no separate legal status and became the chattel of her husband. The right of the husband to chastise his wife was considered a natural part of his responsibilities. In 1763, Blackstone wrote, "The husband also, by the old law might give his wife moderate correction. For, as he is to answer for her misbehaviours, the law thought it reasonable to entrust him with his power of restraining her by domestic chastisement. . . ." (Commentaries on the Laws of England in Hecker, 1910:124–125). This was considered to be a reasonable part of the marital relationship and was thought to be for the benefit of both husband and wife. Blackstone stated emphatically that, "the female sex was a great favourite of the Laws of England" (Hecker, 1910:127). As the old common law was changed to the new civil law, this 'favouritism' was continued in statutes which allowed the husband, "for some misdemeanors to give his wife a severe beating with whips and clubs; for others, only to apply moderate correction" (Hecker, 1910:125).

All of the legal systems of Europe, England and early America supported a husband's rights to beat his wife and so did the community norms. In 18th Century France, for example, it was considered appropriate for a husband to chastise his wife for reasons such as assertion of her independence, wanting to retain control of her property after marriage, adultery, or even suspected infidelity (Castan 1976), but the beatings were supposed to conform to the rules of legitimate punishment. The chastisement of wives, like that of children, was to be restricted to "blows, thumps, kicks or punches on the back . . . which did not leave any marks . . . " (Castan 1976:9). Men were to control their wives because, "The man who is not master of his wife is not worthy of being a man," but he should restrict his attacks to the tacit limits set by the community. During that time, as today, physical violence against wives provoked little disapprobation unless it was extremely severe. Only if the attack was public and went beyond the tacit limits set by the community was the husband likely to be rebuked or subject to moral sanctions. Upon observing a man severely attacking his wife a neighbour exclaimed, "Oh, that's a bit much. We all know that wives need beating but you must be reasonable all the same" (Castan 1976:9).

Rejection of the Laws of Chastisement

It was not until the eighteenth century that the husband's power of correction even began to be doubted, and a woman could gain security of peace from her spouse (Hecker, 1910:125: Blackstone, 1865:444: Eisenberg and Micklow, 1974:3; Dobash and Dobash, forthcoming). Yet, it was not until the nineteenth century that the struggle for reform began in Britain and America and laws against wife beating were actually passed.

The American colonies had, as would be expected, adopted much of English law and incorporated it into their own legal structure. The husband's right to chastise his wife had a curious legal history, since it was not formally written into law until 1824 when the Supreme Court of Mississippi was the first U.S. Court to acknowledge this right. The principles stated were the same as Blackstone's, and other States soon followed Mississippi's lead (Eisenberg and Micklow,1974:4–5). In 1864 a court in North Carolina ruled that the State should not interfere in cases of domestic chastisement unless 'permanent injury or excessive violence' was involved. They preferred to "leave the parties to themselves as the best mode of inducing them to make the matter up and live together as a man and wife should" (Eisenberg and Micklow, 1974:5). The neutral terminology of this ruling ignored the fact that leaving the 'parties to themselves' meant leaving the husband to beat his wife.

Within fifty years of the legal recognition of wife beating in Mississippi, it was made illegal in Alabama and Massachusetts. In 1871 it was declared that, "the privilege, ancient though it be, to beat her with a stick, to pull her hair, choke her, spit in her face or kick her about the floor, or to inflict upon her other indignities, is not now acknowledged by our law" (Eisenberg and Micklow, 1974:6). The rejection of this legal right was not complete in America until 1891 when in the case of Reg. v. Jackson the courts declared that, "the moral sense of the community revolts at the idea that the husband may inflict personal chastisement upon his wife, even for the most outrageous conduct" (Eisenberg and Micklow, 1974:5–6; Hecker, 1910:127). The courts had declared that this offense was morally revolting and that no nonviolent behaviour on the part of wives could be defined as warranting such abuse. The idea of provocation had clearly been rejected in judicial statements, and by 1910 all but eleven States allowed absolute divorce for cruelty (Hecker, 1910:175, 235).

At about this same time, there was a struggle to change the English laws (See Dobash, Wilson and Cavanagh, 1977; Manchester, 1976). Speeches were made in the House of

Commons to the effect that, "the country should treat its married women no worse than it treated its domestic animals" (Manchester, 1976:22). The Act for Better Prevention and Punishment of Aggravated Assaults upon Women and Children (1853) was passed but later repealed (Young, 1976:3), and it is not surprising that in 1856 the members of a Protestant sect in Whitehaven "defended the practice of wife-beating as an article of faith" (Young, 1976:3). The practice was still quite legal, but there was considerable confusion about the legal limits which were being placed upon it. In the History of the Rod (1860's) the Reverend Cooper writes:

> Authorities are not agreed as to what constituted a 'moderate castigation,' and the instrument wherewith it was to be inflicted . . . though a husband might not by law beat his spouse with a stick of a certain size, he might safely do so with a switch of a certain size or with his hand. Some men, not inclined to be severe, used to restrict the size of the thickness of the rod to the little finger. (Cooper, quoted in Young, 1976:4)

When the public and parliamentary debate became more heated, Disraeli set up a special Parliamentary Committee to investigate the frequency of this practice and to consider the adequacy of fines and imprisonment, and the possible introduction of flogging as a punishment for those who *brutally* assaulted their wives (Parliamentary Papers:1875). Fifty-two counties from England and Wales reported hundreds of cases of brutal assault against wives which occurred between 1870–1875. The comments of the constables revealed a high level of intolerance of *brutal* assaults against wives but a high level of acceptance of what they called *ordinary* assaults against them.

By 1878 women were allowed to use cruelty as a grounds for divorce, but the law and its implementation were merely oriented toward setting limits on assaults against wives and not toward making it truly illegal. In the late 1800's there were at least four cases of aggravated assaults against wives in litigation each day (Britten, 1953:24), and thousands of women were "perambulating punching-bags, who knew this and who only wanted to get through life with as few bruises as possible" (Pearsall, 1969:79). So little was done to bring about any meaningful change in the daily lives of women that by 1910 the Suffragettes made assaults on wives one of their platforms (McLaren, 1909:15–18). Women were no longer the legitimate victims of marital violence, but were they still the 'appropriate' victims?

Violence in the Family

In this century research reports have consistently indicated that it is in a marital setting that women are most likely to be involved in violence, and this is usually as victims not attackers. It is in the institution of the family that the patriarchal legacy persists through the continuation of the hierarchical relationship between men and women. Male authority is still, regardless of the so-called liberation of women, revered and protected by social institutions and reinforced and perpetuated through the socialization of children.

Research findings relating to interpersonal violence consistently establish the association between intimate relationships and homicides and assaults, but social scientists have been just as consistent in their failure to note the direction of these attacks. In order to establish the direction and recurring patterns of violence in the family it is necessary to tease out findings and implications from existing research reports, and when this task is carried out it clearly indicates that it is women in their position as wives who are the most likely victims of systematic and persistent violent attacks in the family.

Homicides

MacDonald's early research on homicide in several countries revealed that men were much more likely to commit murder than women (see also Moran, 1971) and when women were killed they were predominantly the victims of attacks by intimates. In England and Wales between 1885–1905, of the 487 murders committed by men nearly a quarter of their victims (127) were their wives, another substantial proportion (115) were mistresses or 'sweethearts' (MacDonald, 1911:96). Von Hentig's research on homicide in Germany provided consistent evidence of the relationship between marriage and violence directed at women. Of all the women killed by an intimate in Germany during 1931 61.5 percent were killed by their husbands. The closer the attachment between a man and a woman the greater the risk to the woman of violent attack, "... when a woman is killed, (look) for her relatives, mainly the husband and after that her paramour" (Von Hentig, 1948:392).

Wolfgang's research in Philadelphia provides additional support for this pattern in North America (1958). He substantiates the association between close, intimate relationships and violence that was discussed most explicitly by Simmel (1955). Using police records, Wolfgang found that primary relationships were involved in the majority of the murders he investigated. Again, female victims of murder were more likely to be killed by their spouse while male victims were more likely to be killed by someone outside the family (see also, Voss and Hepburn, 1968). Forty one percent of all female victims were killed by their husbands, only 10 percent of male victims were killed by their wives. The investigations of murder in England and Wales conducted by Gibson and Klein (1969) and by Gibson (1975) reveal that, for females, "Wives (including common-law wives) were usually ... the most frequent victims of murder" (1969:19).

Not only were female victims likely to be married to their attacker, they were also much more likely to have experienced very violent deaths. Defining severe violence as consisting of more than five acts of physical attack, Wolfgang concludes, "Husbands killed their wives violently in significantly greater proportion than did wives who killed their husbands" (1958:214). Voss and Hepburn (1968:504–505) found that females are much more likely to be beaten to death than are males. Women were also much more likely to be slain by a close friend or member of the family. Of the slayings involving non-whites 68.7 percent of the women were killed by a member of the family or close friend, and in the slayings involving whites, 78.9 percent of the women were murdered by friends or family members (Voss and Hepburn, 1968:505). Other reports also reveal that the home is a violent setting (cf. Bard, 1971; Steinmetz and Straus, 1973; Curtis, 1974; Martin, 1976), but researchers have often failed to note that this violence is not randomly distributed among family members but is disproportionately directed at females. The homicide statistics outlined above provide an explicit verification of the differential use of violence between males and females. However, some research reports do not indicate a great divergence between the number of homicides committed by men and women (cf. Pittman and Handy, 1964), but we would suggest that the explanations of the homicides committed by men and women are quite different. For example, Boudouris concludes that the high rates of homicides among non-white females in Detroit could be explained as a "... result of the women's act of self-preservation when attacked by a non-white male usually her spouse" (1971:671). Wolfgang's work also points to this pattern, that husbands who were victims of homicide were a great deal more likely to have attacked their wives prior to their demise than were wives who were victims (1958:217).

The major implications to be drawn from research relating to homicides between men and women is that men are much more likely to commit homicides than women, and female victims are usually married to their attacker. Women become a great deal more susceptible to physical attacks as the intensity of their relationship with men increases, and this pattern is even stronger when one examines research reports relating to assaults.

Assaults

Research conducted in England and Wales reveals that in 1950 and 1960 "domestic disputes" occurring in the home accounted for over 30 percent of all violent offences and 90 percent of these attacks were directed at wives by their husbands (McClintock, 1963:251). Boudouris (1971) discovered that over 52 percent of a sample of assault cases in Detroit involved family relations. Unfortunately, Boudouris' work provides very little indication of the direction of this violence. Gelles' recent work reveals that violence was much more likely to be used by husbands than wives, and that nearly a quarter of the husbands attacked their wives on a regular basis (1974:50–51).

The work of Chester and Streather (1972) though primarily concerned with the general pattern of divorce complaints in a county in Southern England uncovered a great deal about the direction of violence between adults in the family. They discovered that ninety percent of the 1500 divorce complaints examined involved reports of women complaining about violence from their husbands, and the vast majority of these women reported that they were subjected to "repeated violence" during the marriage (Chester and Streather, 1972:709). In contrast to the work of Chester and Streather who analyzed divorce petitions in Britain, O'Brien (1971) interviewed individuals seeking a divorce in the United States. Of the 150 individuals interviewed 28 spontaneously mentioned physical violence and this violence was primarily directed at women. Levinger's research on divorce revealed that physical abuse was one of the most commonly mentioned reasons for divorce and wives complained eleven times more frequently of violence than did husbands (1966:805). Indeed, we would be very surprised if this was not the case. Whitehurst, reporting patterns similar to those described by O'Brien and Levinger, indicates that physical force is a technique for maintaining and attempting to regain control in the family and males being "heavily socialized in instrumental and aggressive ways" (1971:683) are much more likely to utilize force than women (on this point also see Goode, 1971; Straus, 1976). A recent extrapolation from divorce research in England estimates that 70 percent "of wives who petition for divorce each year . . . suffer from serious brutality" (Elston, Fuller, and Murch, 1976:10).

The research relating to violence occurring within the home points in an unequivocal manner to the differential nature of this violence. Men are usually violent toward their wives (common-law or legal) and this violence is often of a persistent nature. As Lystad recently concluded after an exhaustive review of the literature in this area, "The occurrence of adult violence in the home usually involves males as aggressors toward females" (1975:332). Men are more likely to be taught to be aggressive and dominant, to be sensitive to affronts to their authority and attempt to preserve such authority and dominance through the use of force. They are more likely to be taught the skills related to physical force and to be inculcated with the willingness to use them in circumstances which "warrant" their use. One of these circumstances is systematically structured within the family in which women are to be subordinate to their husbands.

Social scientists have primarily conceptualized violence as a breakdown in social order in which either individuals or social structures are thought to be deviant or aberrant. We prefer to see violence used by men against women in the family as attempts to establish or maintain a patriarchal social order. Violence is used by men to chastise their wives for real or perceived transgressions of his authority and as attempts to reaffirm and maintain a hierarchical and moral order within the family. This conception of violence against wives is irrefutable in the light of the evidence sketched above and takes us beyond the sociological reductionism that permeates most of the work relating to interpersonal violence, research which is primarily oriented to determining the background characteristics of offenders and/or victims. We must go beyond the individuals or couples involved in violent marriages and episodes and seek explanations that are firmly embedded in a wider socio-historical context. We must also be less abstract about our conceptions of this form of violence. To conceive of violence in the family as 'marital violence,' 'family violence' or even 'spousal violence' ignores the obvious fact that several types of violence occur in the family; husbands attack wives, children are assaulted by fathers or mothers, children attack each other and attack their parents, and wives use force against husbands. Even this degree of delimitation may not be enough since violence may mean anything from a slap to severe beatings resulting in death. The point is, we must be more concrete about our conceptions of violence, partialling out various types and forms of violence, not assuming a necessary interrelatedness between these forms and types and seeking explanations and understanding of these concrete forms in the wider society, as well as within family interaction.

Patterns of Violence in Scotland

We employed this methodology in our study of violence against women in Scotland. The results of a systematic analysis of police and court records and of in-depth interviews with women who have been beaten by their husbands[3] reveals that the incidence of wife beating is quite high and that it is firmly associated with the domination, control and chastisement of women in their position as wives.

Police and Court Records

We analyzed 33,724 police charges which were processed through the courts of Edinburgh and one court district of Glasgow during 1974.[4] Because of the numerous problems inherent in the use of police and court reports (cf. Box, 1971), we employed a technique which allowed us to go beyond the official charge and overcome the problem of uncritically equating the official charge with the nature of the event. All cases, despite the official charge, were read in order to ascertain if any physical violence was involved. All of the cases involving violence were then scrutinized more thoroughly in order to determine various aspects of the event, the sex of the offender and victim, and the nature of their relationship. When this examination was completed we found that violence was involved in only 11 percent of the cases (41 percent were traffic offences, 48 percent were non-violent breaches of the peace, theft and miscellaneous). A closer examination of the 3,020 cases involving violence reveals some rather extraordinary patterns. The violent offences were divided by sex of offender and victim into those which occurred between family members and those occurring between unrelated individuals. Only two of these categories contained 64.9 percent of all of the violent offences. Violence between unrelated males constituted the largest category (38.7 percent) and the second most frequent offence was violence by husbands directed at their wives (26 percent).

Almost all of the violent offenders reported to the police were males (91.4 percent) while a mere 8.6 percent of the offenders were females. In 1283 cases (44.6 percent) the victims were females while males were victims in 1589 cases (55.3 percent). Though men and women are almost equally likely to be victims they are not equally likely to be aggressors. Men are disproportionately represented as offenders.

The distribution of the sex of the victims and offenders for all cases of violence occurring between family members . . . included all assaults on spouses, children, siblings and parents. These data reveal that violence occurring between family members almost always involved male offenders and female victims, a pattern which prevailed in almost 94 percent of the cases. In every type of relationship, marital, parental, or sibling, the assaults followed the same pattern; males attacking females. In only 2.6 percent of the cases was the female the offender, but she was the victim in nearly 95 percent of the cases. Rarely were males assaulted in the home and even then it was more likely to be at the hands of another male member of the household. The home is simply not a dangerous setting for men, but it is for women. Females, whether they be sisters, mothers, wives or daughters, are more likely to be subject to control through the use of physical force than are their male counterparts—and it is in their capacity as wives that the risk is the highest and the danger the greatest.

Husbands are only rarely assaulted by their wives (1.1 percent) whereas attacks on wives represent over 75 percent of all violence in the family setting. Women were very rarely assaulted by strangers on the streets, only 15 percent of the cases involving female victims occurred outside the family setting.

The data from our analysis of police and court records corroborates the findings of other research (cf. Levinger, 1966; McClintock, 1963; O'Brien, 1971; Chester and Streather, 1972; Lystad, 1975), which indicate that women are much more likely to be the victims of violence which occurs between spouses.

The data presented here represent only a proportion of all the violence which occurs in the family. In the case of women, the rate of underreporting is very high and reflects feelings of shame, fear of retribution, negative experiences with past reportings, and the lack of viable alternatives available to them. Methodologically this presents a problem to which there is no real solution since no sampling procedure or data collection technique, no matter how sophisticated, well developed or anonymous will glean information about the incidence of violence unless the respondent is willing to make public (even if only on an anonymous questionnaire) what they consider to be secret and unshareable. In fact, evidence from our interview sample revealed that even among women who eventually did make their troubles public, only two out of every 98 assaults were reported to the police (Dobash, Wilson and Cavanagh, 1977:22).

We may well imagine that there is an equally high rate of underreporting of violence between all family members. It is unlikely, however, given the overwhelming body of evidence presented herein, that the proportion and direction of the violence between husbands and wives would be significantly altered even if we had complete information. Evidence from the interviews with battered women enables us to go beyond the issues of reporting and distribution and to capture some of the dynamics of the relationship in which women are assaulted.

Interviews with Battered Wives

In-depth interviews were conducted with 109 women who had been systematically and violently beaten on numerous occasions by their husband or paramour. These interviews lasted from two to six hours and covered a wide variety of topics from the childhood of the man and woman through the early stages of courtship and family life. Both the violent and nonviolent aspects of their relationship were examined in terms of factors associated with the emergence of violence and its continuation.

The early stages of the couple's relationship were not unlike those of any couple going out together. Most of the couples saw each other quite frequently and went out to movies, dancing and pubs several times a week. Once the relationship became somewhat serious both the men and the women began to restrict their activities with their same sex friends in order to spend more time together. Although more women were likely to restrict their social lives completely to their partner (61 percent), there was nevertheless a large percentage of men (41 percent) who did the same. During this period most of the men were very attentive and the women felt loved and satisfied with the relationship.

As the relationship continued there was a growing sense of exclusivity and possession. As would be expected, this was especially true among the males who were less likely to give up the 'nights out with the boys' but were more likely to expect that their girlfriend would go out exclusively with them. The man's increasing possessiveness and periodic displays of sexual jealousy served as signs of commitment to the relationship. Although, in retrospect, many of the women saw these as early warning signs, the behaviour was not uncharacteristic for courting couples and did not cause concern at the time. Some of the men did hit their future wives prior to marriage. Those who did (23 percent), usually did so because of sexual jealousy, usually unfounded, or as a protest against the women's threats to terminate the relationship. An analysis of these few cases indicates that the men came to consider it their right to question their future wife's activities and object through the use of physical force.

For most couples, however, violence did not occur until after they were married, but it usually occurred very soon after marriage. Fifty-nine percent of the women had experienced violence by the end of their first year of marriage, and 92 percent within the first five years. After marriage, the authority relationships between men and women become more explicit. Husbands came to feel that their wives should meet their demands immediately and without question no matter how reasonable or unreasonable. The major sources of contention centered on what might be called 'wifely obligations' and the husband's authority. The obligations of a wife to care for her husband, to serve his needs and remain his exclusive sexual partner are all expectations which are supported to some degree by most social institutions and have very heavy moral overtones. In western society, a man feels that marriage gives him the right to expect domestic service and sexual exclusivity from his wife. The fulfillment of these behaviours is not only personally pleasant for him; it also becomes an outward sign of his 'rightful' possession of her, authority over her and ability to control her.

In our research, it was the real or perceived challenges to the man's possession, authority and control which most often resulted in the use of violence. A late meal, an unironed shirt, a conversation with any man no matter how old or young all served as 'justifications' for beatings. Many of the precipitating factors were exceedingly innocuous and would appear inexplicable without an understanding of the context of authority, subordination and control in which they occurred.

The historical and contemporary documents presented in this article elucidate the legal, religious and cultural legacies which have supported a marital hierarchy, subordinated women in marriage and legalized violence against them. The husband's right to control his wife by force extended far beyond slaps and shoves and into systematic beatings and brutalizing which sometimes resulted in death. Although domestic chastisement of wives is no longer legal, most of the ideologies and social arrangements which formed the underpinnings of this violence still exist and are inextricably intertwined in our present legal, religious, political and economic practices. Wives may no longer be the legitimate victims of marital violence, but in social terms they are still the 'appropriate' victims. Thus, it would be truly ironic if in the current climate, some magical twist of egalitarian terminology were to be used to deny centuries of oppression and to further repress contemporary women by obscuring the undeniable fact that spousal violence is to all extents and purposes wife beating.

NOTES

1. The term wives is used to refer to the social relationship between cohabitees and is not meant to imply legality.

2. Although Christian writings about women were not always in this oppressive vein, it is the writings of Paul, who had an especially negative view of women, that have had a profound effect upon the ideology of marriage in the Christian World.

3. A fuller description of the techniques used in interviewing and a discussion of the issues concerning the representativeness of the sample of respondents and the police data appear in Dobash and Dobash (forthcoming).

4. Edinburgh and Glasgow are cities of very different socio-economic complexions. Edinburgh is a city of approximately half a million people, the centre of the Scottish Civil Service, the cultural and historical capital of Scotland. Glasgow, a city of over one million people is a product of industrialism. As one of the birthplaces of the industrial revolution it suffers from the withering away of heavy industry. A city with a particularly working-class character, it has a high unemployment rate and poor housing that is only gradually being replaced. The particular district in which we examined police records was rather mixed in its socioeconomic composition, since it included a large working-class estate as well as the University and its accompanying middle-class residences.

REFERENCES

Bannon, James
1975 "Law Enforcement Problems with Intra-family Violence". Presented to the American Bar Association Convention (August 12).

Bard, Martin
1971 "The study and modification of intra-familial violence" in the Control of Aggression and Violence: Cognitive and Psychological. New York: Academic Press.

Bible
I Corinthians 7; 11:3; 14:34; Ephesians 5; I Peter 3:1; I Timothy 3; 2:12; Titus 2:4–5.

Blackstone, Sir William
1865 Commentaries on the Laws of England 444.

Boudouris, James
1971 "Homicide and the family." Journal of Marriage and the Family 33:667–676.

Box, Steven
1971 Deviance, Reality and Society. London: Holt.

Britten, Vera
1953 Lady into Woman. New York: Macmillan.

Calvin, John
1560 Institution de la Religion Cretienne. Geneva. Cited in O'Faolain and Martines L, Not in God's Image, Glasgow: Collins, 1973.

Castan, Nicole
1976 "Divers Aspects de la Constraints Maritale, d'apres les Documents Judiciaries du XVIII Siecle." Paper presented at the American Sociological Society Meeting.

Chester, R. and J. Streather
1972 "Cruelty in English divorce: some empirical findings." Journal of Marriage and the Family, 34(4):706–710.

Curtis, Lynn
1974 Criminal Violence: National Patterns and Behaviour. Lexington, Mass.: Lexington Books.

Dobash, R. Emerson and Russell P. Dobash
1977 "Love, Honour and Obey: Institutional Ideologies and the Struggle for Battered Women", Contemporary Crisis (Forthcoming).
Dobash, R. Emerson and Russell P. Dobash
n.d. Violence Against Women: A Case Against the Patriarchy. New York: Free Press (forthcoming).
Dobash, R. Emerson, Monica Wilson and Catherine Cavanagh
1977 Violence Against Wives: The Legislation of the 1960's and the Policies of Indifference. Paper Presented at the National Deviancy Conference meeting.
Eisenberg, Sue and Patricia Micklow
1974 The Assaulted Wife: Catch 22 Revisited. Unpublished Manuscript. University of Michigan Law School.
Elston, Elizabeth, Jane Fuller and Mervyn Murch
1976 Battered Wives: The Problems of Violence in Marriages Experienced by a Group of Petitioners in Undefined Divorce Cases. Unpublished paper. Department of Social Work, University of Bristol.
Field and Field
1973 "Marital violence and the criminal process: neither justice nor peace." Social Service Review 47, 2 (Jun):221–40.
Gelles, Richard J.
1974 The Violent Home: A Study of Physical Aggressions Between Husbands and Wives. Beverly Hills, Calif: Sage.
Gibson, Evelyn
1975 Homicide in England and Wales 1967–1971. Home Office Research Study No. 31. London: Her Majesty's Stationery Office.
Gibson, Evelyn and S. Klein
1969 Murder 1957 to 1968. A Home Office Statistical Division Report on Murder in England and Wales. London: Her Majesty's Stationery Office.
Goode, William J.
1971 "Force and violence in the family." Journal of Marriage and the Family 39:624–636.
Gouge, William
1634 Of Domesticall Duties, Eight Treatifes. Third Edition. London: George Miller.
Hecker, Eugene A.
1910 A Short History of Women's Rights: From the Days of Augustus to the Present Time. London: Putnam Sons.
Knox, John
1558 The First Blast of the Trumpet against the Monstrous Regiment of Women. London: Southgate.
La Fave, Wayne
1969 "Non Invocation of the Criminal Law by Police" in Donald R. Cressey and David A. Ward (eds), Delinquency, Crime and Social Process. New York: Harper.
Levinger, George
1966 "Source of marital dissatisfaction among applicants for divorce." American Journal of Orthopsychiatry (October) 804–06.
Lukács, Georg
1971 "What is Orthodox Marxism?" in History and Class Consciousness: Studies in Marxist Dialectics. Translated and edited by Rodney Livingstone. Merlin Press.
Luther, Martin
1531 Sermons, translated and edited by J W Doberstein in Luther's Works. (Philadelphia, 1959) cited in O'Faolain, J and Martines, L, Not in God's Image. Glasgow: Collins, 1973.

Lystad, Mary Honemann
1975 "Violence at home: a review of the literature." American Journal of Orthopsychiatry 45(5):328–345.
MacDonald, Arthur
1911 "Death penalty and homicide." American Journal of Sociology, 16:96–97.
Manchester, A. H.
1976 The Legal History of Marital Violence in England and Wales, 1750–1976. Unpublished paper. Faculty of Law, University of Birmingham, England.
Martin, Del
1976 Battered Wives. San Francisco: Glide Publications.
McClintock, F.
1963 Crimes of Violence. New York: St Martins Press.
McLaren, L.
1909 The Women's Charter of Rights and Liberties, London: Grosvenor.
Moran, Richard
1971 "Criminal Homicide: External Restraint and Subculture of Violence." Criminology 8, 7 (Feb):357–74.
O'Brien, John E.
1971 "Violence in divorce prone families." Journal of Marriage and the Family, 33:692–98.
O'Faolain, Julia and Lauco Martines
1974 Not in God's Image. Glasgow: Collins.
Parliamentary Papers
1875 Reports to the Secretary of State for the Home Department on the State of the Law relating to Brutal Assaults C.1138.
Pearsall, Ronald
1969 The Worm in the Bud. London: Weidenfeld and Nicholson.
Pitman, D. J. and W. Handy
1964 "Patterns in criminal aggravated assault." Journal of Criminal Law, Criminology and Police Science 56(4):462–67.
Simmel, Georg
1955 Conflict and the Web of Group Affiliations. New York: Free Press.
Steinmetz, Suzanne K. and Murray A. Straus
1973 "The family as cradle of violence." Society (Sept/Oct):54–56.
Stone, Lawrence
1975 "The rise of the nuclear family in early modern England" In Rosenberg, Charles E (ed), The Family in History. University of Pennsylvania Press.
Straus, Murray A.
1974 "Leveling, Civility, and Violence in the Family." Journal of Marriage and the Family 36 (February):13–29.
Straus, Murray A.
1976 "Sexual Inequality, Cultural Norms, and Wife Beating", in Emilio Viano (ed), Victims and Society. Washington DC: Visage Press. Also in Victimology: An International Journal 1(1976):54–70.
Trevelyan, G. M.
1948 History of England. London: Longmans.
Von Hentig, Hans
1948 The Criminal and His Victim. New Haven: Yale University Press.
Voss, Harwin L. and John R. Hepburn
1968 "Patterns in criminal homicide in Chicago." Journal of Criminal Law, Criminology and Police Science 59(4):499-508.
Wolfgang, Marvin
1958 Patterns in Criminal Homicide. Philadelphia: University of Pennsylvania Press.

Weber, Max
1949 The Methodology of the Social Sciences. New York: Free Press.
Whitehurst, Robert N.
1971 "Violence Potential in Extra-marital Sexual Responses." Journal of Marriage and the Family, 33, 4 (November):683–691.
Young, Jim
1978 Wife-Beating in Britain: A Socio-historical Analysis, 1850–1914. Paper presented at the Conference of the American Sociological Association.

Reflection

REBECCA EMERSON DOBASH AND RUSSELL P. DOBASH

We completed our Ph.D.'s in sociology at Washington State University in 1972 and immediately moved to Scotland to share a temporary post at the University of Stirling for a period of one year. Our intention was to have a one-year "adventure" before beginning academic careers in the United States. During that year, we taught at a new and exciting university, traveled extensively around Britain and Europe, and learned a bit about how to live in a different country. At the end of the year, we were both offered full-time posts and decided to stay a bit longer. During that year, the first refuges for "battered women" began to open in England and Scotland. The problem was only just beginning to receive public attention and we saw a tiny, four-line note about it in a national newspaper. This struck our interest because it crossed our respective areas of academic training in crime, criminal justice, and the community, as well as the family, social psychology, and gender. We believed that social science should contribute to a better understanding of social problems and thereby make a contribution to their solution. With this combination of training, orientations, and interest, as well as the belief that this was an important area to study, we began what has now become a lifelong investigation into violence against women.

In order to gain initial insight into the problem, we started by talking to the women who were beginning to open the first refuges for battered women in England and Scotland and the women who became some of the first residents. We searched the libraries for literature and found almost nothing except historical accounts of laws and attitudes about the acceptability of wife beating. It was clear to us that this was an important issue whose acceptance and neglect had resulted in little or no knowledge about the problem. As social scientists, we hoped we might use our training and skills to help rectify this through research and we approached the Scottish Office to fund a small, exploratory study that was followed by a larger study. Thus, we began our first empirical study of violence against women and the institutional responses to it. The research provided the foundation of our first book, *Violence Against Wives* (Free Press), and our initial journal articles and contained many of the ideas, issues, concerns, and lines of investigation that have continued to inform our research agenda as it has expanded and developed since then. While it is for others to say what impact this article may have had on subsequent thinking, ideas, and research, we can reflect on the material contained in "The 'Appropriate' Victim" that has continued to appear in the now voluminous literature on intimate partner violence and that has continued to inform our own research agenda as it has expanded since this publication.

In revisiting this publication and reflecting on its content, we see strong lines of continuity in our current research and themes that now regularly appear in the literature but that were relatively unfamiliar at the time. Our main goal was to provide an explanation of the contemporary problem of violence against women that was comprehensive and helped us better understand the development of the problem and current responses to it. In order to do this we used a wide range of sources and evidence across disciplines, time periods, and different cultures. We used a context specific approach that examined the violence in the various contexts in which it occurs and must be understood as including institutional, cultural, interactional, and interpersonal. Violence was characterized as purposeful behavior and we argued for a definition of violence that was restricted to physical force.

The historical analysis of "wife beating" helped us understand the conditions under which the violence was used, its continuity over time, its legal and social acceptance, and the roles of men and women, as they were constituted in the institution of the family. This legacy is fundamental to understanding why it is women, and not men, who are the "appropriate" victims of violence in intimate relationships. It illustrates the foundations of male power, control, and authority over women in intimate relationships and provides an understanding of the use of violence for the purposes of maintaining, enforcing, and exercising that power. Cross-cultural evidence illustrates these common threads in differing contexts.

Contemporary evidence about assault and homicide within the family was used to illustrate the prevalence and severity of this violence and its asymmetrical nature, that is, that men are more likely than women to perpetrate this form of violence. It also revealed that women are far more likely to be killed by a male partner or former partner than the reverse, and that men often engaged in "overkill" in the act of uxoricide (killing a wife). The evidence further indicated that when women do kill a male partner it often occurs in the context of the man's use of violence against her.

The Violence Against Women study discussed in the article was based on our own research, which included an analysis of over 33,000 arrest records held by the police in the two largest Scottish cities and in-depth interviews with 109 women. Evidence gathered from these records suggested that approximately 10 percent of all crime is violent crime, with two types constituting the vast majority: violence between adult males and men's violence against a female partner. Violence against women perpetrated by male partners constituted 26 percent of all violent crime reported to the police. When considering violence within the family, the records revealed that 76 percent was directed at women by their partners and only 1 percent involved women's violence directed at male partners. The results of the interviews with women were only briefly considered in the paper; they revealed that men's violence occurred in the context of their increasing possessiveness and attempts to control and punish their partners. Chronic sources of conflict within these relationships that led to violence included disputes regarding sexual jealousy and possessiveness, the domestic responsibilities of women, and women's attempts to leave the relationships.

The theoretical and methodology themes considered in "The 'Appropriate' Victim" continue to inform our recent and current work. For example, we have explored the development of innovative social and legal responses to violence against women (Dobash & Dobash, 1992; Dobash et al., 2000) and maintained a strong interest in the issue of asymmetry in intimate partner violence (Dobash et al., 1998; Dobash & Dobash, forthcoming). The context specific approach is always to the fore in our research and leads to a specific focus on the contexts, situations, and motives associated with violence (Dobash & Dobash, 1998). When this is coupled with the use of qualitative and quantitative forms of research, we think it provides a comprehensive evidentiary base from which to draw theoretical conclusions. Additionally, in recent years we have turned our attention to violent men, having just completed a national study on homicide that considers all forms of homicide and also includes an explicit focus on intimate partner homicide (Dobash et al., forthcoming).

REFERENCES

Dobash, R. E., & Dobash, R. P. (1992). *Women, violence and social change.* New York: Routledge.

Dobash, R. E., & Dobash, R. P. (Eds.). (1998). *Rethinking violence against women.* Thousand Oaks, CA: Sage.

Dobash, R. E., Dobash, R. P., Cavanagh, K., & Lewis, R. (2000). *Changing violent men.* Thousand Oaks, CA: Sage.

Dobash, R. E., Dobash, R. P., Cavanagh, K., & Lewis, R. (forthcoming). Not an ordinary killer—just an ordinary guy: When men murder an intimate woman partner. *Violence Against Women.*

Dobash, R. P., Dobash, R. E., Cavanagh, K., & Lewis, R. (1998). Separate and intersecting realities: A comparison of men's and women's accounts of violence against women. *Violence Against Women,* 4, 382–414.

Dobash, R. P., & Dobash, R. E. (forthcoming). Women's violence to men in intimate relationships: Definitions, concepts and evidence. *British Journal of Criminology.*

CHAPTER

13 Measuring Intrafamily Conflict and Violence

The Conflict Tactics (CT) Scales

MURRAY A. STRAUS

Conflict theorists present a convincing case showing that conflict is an inevitable part of all human association (Adams, 1965; Coser, 1956; Dahrendorf, 1959; Scanzoni, 1972; Simmel, 1955; Sprey, 1969). They further hold that without the changes brought about by conflict, a social unit—be it a nation, an academic department, or a family—runs a high risk of collapse. If conflict is suppressed, it can result in stagnation and failure to adapt to changed circumstances and/or erode the bond of group solidarity because of an accumulation of hostility.

Despite the above, most people fear conflict and try to avoid it. Professionals concerned with the family also tend to take an almost opposite view to that of conflict theorists. They treat conflict as something to be avoided. Sociologists and psychologists do research to find out why conflict occurs, implicitly to be able to provide information which will enable people to avoid conflict. Marriage counselors, with a few exceptions such as Bach and Wyden (1968) and Shostrom and Kavanaugh (1971), focus much of their efforts on helping families avoid conflict.

There are a number of factors involved in creating this hiatus between the truths revealed to us by sociological conflict theorists and those revealed by our daily experience and emotional reactions to conflict. However, since this paper is concerned with methods of measuring conflict rather than with the important theoretical questions raised by this hiatus, the available space permits only a discussion of one of the factors. This is the conceptual confusion which characterizes analyses of conflict.

Some Conceptual Distinctions

It is essential to distinguish between a series of closely related yet clearly different phenomena, all of which are called conflict. For purposes of this paper, even this list must be confined to only three of these: "conflict of interest," "conflict," and "hostility" (further conceptual distinctions are discussed in Foss, 1979; Gelles and Straus, 1978).

Conflict of Interest

When conflict theorists talk about the ubiquity of conflict, they are referring to what is here called "conflict of interest;" that is, to the fact that members of a social group, no matter how small and intimate, are each seeking to live out their lives in accordance with personal agenda which inevitably differ. These differences range in importance. Which TV show will be watched at eight? Should money be saved or spent on a vacation? Which is more important to control: inflation or unemployment? There is no way to avoid such conflicts without running the risks to which conflict theorists have alerted us. However, there is a tendency among those writing from a conflict theory perspective to imply that "the more conflict the better," or at least not to discuss the question of how much conflict is necessary or desirable.

The question of how much conflict is desirable is also beyond the scope of a methodological paper such as this. But I would like to suggest that it is an important question for empirical research, and to further suggest the hypothesis that there is a curvilinear relationship between the amount of conflict and group well-being. That is, the absence of conflict (in the sense of conflict of interest) is theoretically impossible and (as noted in the introductory paragraph) even if it could be brought about, would be fatal for group well-being. But at the same time, very high levels of conflict can create such a high level of stress and/or such rapid change that group welfare is adversely affected.

Conflict [Tactics]

The second phenomenon which must be distinguished if we are to have any hope of doing sound theoretical or empirical research on intrafamilial conflict is the method used to advance one's own interest; that is, the means or the tactics used to resolve conflict. Two families can have the same level of conflict over the types of interests mentioned in the previous section. But even though conflict in that sense is identical, the two may differ vastly—and with profound consequences—in respect to how they deal with these conflicts. One family might resolve the issue of which TV program to watch by rotation, another by a "first there" strategy, and another by a threat of force by the physically strongest. . . .

[I]n the context of the present paper . . . "conflict" will refer to "conflict tactics" in the sense of the overt actions used by persons in response to a conflict of interest.

Hostility

When, for whatever reason, members of a group have a feeling of dislike or antipathy for each other, this fact is also often referred to as conflict. But, paradoxically, as conflict theorists have pointed out, hostility is likely to be extremely high when the existence of conflict (in the sense of conflict of interest) is denied. This is because such a situation prevents the actors from achieving ends which are important to them. Hostility develops out of this frustration. Of course, hostility can arise from other sources as well. However, that only highlights the need to keep distinct the phenomena of conflict of interest, conflict, and hostility. Therefore, in this paper, hostility will be restricted to refer to the level of negative cathexis between members of the family groups.

It follows from the previous discussion that further theoretical work on conflict in the family requires as a minimum first step that we avoid the all too common confusion of "conflict of interest," "conflict," and "hostility." Similarly, clear empirical work on intrafamily factors also depends on having separate measures of these three variables. This paper is, therefore, devoted to describing a technique for measuring one of these: intrafamily conflict in the sense of the means used to resolve conflicts of interest.

The Conflict Tactics Scales (CTS)

There is an almost infinite variety of techniques which members of a family can employ in a conflict. In principle, only open-ended free response methods can tap all of these. But, in practice, the way people deal with conflict is so much a part of the unrealized, "taken for granted," ongoing pattern of life that much will be missed unless the respondent is specifically asked. Other omissions occur because certain tactics, such as the use of physical force—although extremely common—may be pushed out of memory because they are unacceptable presentations of the self. Consequently, for any but the most lengthy and in-depth interviews carried out by a highly sensitive investigator, structured methods are needed. This means that some choice of conflict tactics must inevitably be made because one cannot include every possible act in such an instrument.

In the case of the Conflict Tactics Scales (CTS) described in this paper, the choice of the tactics to be measured was based on the fact that the following three modes of dealing with conflict are particularly important for testing the "catharsis theory" of violence control (Straus, 1974):

1. The use of rational discussion, argument, and reasoning—an intellectual approach to the dispute, which for purposes of this instrument is called the "Reasoning" scale.
2. The use of verbal and nonverbal acts which symbolically hurt the other, or the use of threats to hurt the other, which, for purposes of this instrument, are included in the "Verbal Aggression" scale.[1]
3. The use of physical force against another person as a means of resolving the conflict, which is called the "Violence" scale (see Gelles and Straus, 1978, for a more extended definition of violence as used in this statement). . . .

As previously noted, the three tactics measured by the CT Scales are theoretically based, but still arbitrary, selections from a much larger (but as yet undefined) set. Even though Reasoning, Verbal Aggression, and Violence were chosen with a specific theoretical issue in mind, these three are so important that they are likely to be found useful in a wide range of investigations. But, of course, there will be research issues which require data on other conflict tactics. Even in such cases, the general strategy of measurement outlined in this paper might still be applicable.

Another aspect of the CT Scales which needs to be made clear is that this instrument does not provide information on the extent to which conflicts get resolved. In fact, as conflict theorists such as Dahrendorf (1959) and Sprey (1969) note, some conflicts are never resolved; they may be regulated, but they remain part of the system.

Factorial Design

The CT Scales were developed through the use of a model analogous to a 3 by 8 factorial design experiment (Straus, 1964:350–351). The three levels of the first factor are the conflict tactics: Reasoning, Verbal Aggression, and Violence. The 8-level factor corresponds to the nuclear family role structure: husband-to-wife, wife-to-husband, father-to-child, child-to-father, mother-to-child, child-to-mother, child-to-sibling, and sibling-to-child. There are therefore a total of 3 × 8 = 24 different CTS scores. In addition, one can combine the pairs of role scores to get four "role-relationship" scores; one each for the conjugal, father-child, mother-child and sibling relationships. Finally, all the role scores can be summed to obtain total family scores for Reasoning, Verbal Aggression, and Violence. However, not every investigation will need the full 3 by 8 matrix of questions. For example, a study focusing on the husband-wife relationship would only need to obtain data on the husband-to-wife and the wife-to-husband roles.

The Component Items

The CTS consists of a list of actions which a family member might take in a conflict with another member. The items start with those low in coerciveness (such as discussing the issue with the other) and become gradually more coercive and aggressive towards the end of the list (such as using slapping and hitting). The response categories ask for the number of times each action occurred during the past year, ranging from "Never" to "More than 20 times." . . .

The page measuring conflict in the conjugal role is shown in Appendix 1. . . .

Acceptability to Respondents

The husband-wife Verbal Aggression scales and, even more, the husband-wife Violence scales ask about highly sensitive and normatively deviant types of behavior. There is, therefore, a corresponding risk of high refusal rates, arousal of antagonism in respondents and self-defensively distorted responses. All of these can result in invalid data. The question of validity is discussed in a later section. However, before one can even consider validity, the data must be obtained. Experience with the CTS indicates low refusal and antagonism rates. For example, in the national survey, a "completion rate" only slightly lower than is currently typical of such mass surveys was obtained (65 percent as compared to the now typical 70–75 percent). Four factors seem to account for the acceptability of the CTS.

First, the instrument is presented in the context of disagreements and conflicts between members of the family and the ways in which such conflicts are resolved. Since almost everyone recognizes that families have conflicts and disagreements this serves as the first step in legitimizing response.

Second, as previously explained, the items start with conflict tactics which most respondents positively value, and then gradually increase in coerciveness and social disapproval. The respondent is, therefore, given a chance to first present the "correct" things which he or she has done to resolve the conflict. In the context of a society in which there is wide-spread approval of violence "if all else fails," this serves to legitimize reporting the use of violence.

A third factor is the sequence in which the data on behavior in different family roles is obtained. The CTS begins with the items concerning parent-to-child relationships. This sequence was deliberately selected because the use of physical force between family members is most legitimate in the parental role, especially if everything else has been tried. Next, the CTS items are presented for conflicts between children in the family. Since fighting between children is also widely considered as normal, respondents are again being asked about behavior which, although not liked, is also not threatening to their self-esteem. The fact that they are describing the behavior of someone other than themselves also makes this cycle of the CTS more acceptable.

A final factor which seems to account for the willingness of respondents to provide data on acts of physical violence between themselves and their spouse's is that, by the time the husband-wife cycle of items is reached, they are familiar with the questions which will be asked. Having responded to these questions previously, the strangeness of responding to a question about throwing things or hitting someone else has sharply diminished.

Although this practice effect seems, on the face of it, to be important, the evidence from the Bulcroft and Straus (1975) study shows that it is far from essential. In that study, mail questionnaire versions of only the spousal role section of the CTS were used. These were completed and returned by 72 percent of the parents of a sample of university students to whom questionnaires were sent.

Scoring

There are several methods of scoring the CTS:

1. The simplest method is to add the response category code values for the items making up each CT Scale. Thus, the Reasoning score for Form [N] can range from 0 to [18] because it consists of the sum of items a, b, [and] c, . . . each of which is scored 0 to [6]. . . . The scores for Verbal Aggression and Violence are obtained in a similar way. . . .

Analysis of Violence Scores

With the exception of the child-to-child violence score, the violence indexes produce extremely skewed distributions. Consequently, even "robust" statistics such as correlation often produce incorrect results. The most satisfactory procedure is to dichotomize the Violence indexes into violent and nonviolent categories, scored 0 and 1. This produces violence rates, which can be analyzed using nonparametric statistics. Logit correlation may be particularly useful. . . .

Summary and Conclusions

The importance of the Conflict Tactics Scales (CTS) stems from the assumption that conflict is an inevitable part of all human association, including that of the family. A key factor differentiating what the public and many professionals regard as "high conflict families" is not the existence of conflict *per se,* but rather, inadequate or unsatisfactory modes of managing and resolving the conflicts which are inherent in the family. Therefore, research and professional services concerned with intrafamily conflict requires techniques for measuring the way in which families attempt to deal with conflicts. The CTS is a step in this direction. The evidence presented in this paper shows that the technique can be used under a variety of conditions, including personal interview and mail surveys. The CT Scales have moderate to high reliabilities, and there is evidence of concurrent and construct validity. It is hoped that the availability of this technique will encourage empirical research on one of the most central, yet neglected, aspects of the family.

NOTE

1. The concept of "aggression" is beset by even more conceptual confusion than is conflict. Space does not permit the kind of explication given in Gelles and Straus (1978). However, it is necessary to at least state the way the concept is used here: an act carried out with the intention of, or perceived as having the intention of, hurting another person. The injury can be either symbolic, material, or physical.

REFERENCES

Adams, Bert N.
1965 "Coercion and consensus theories: Some unresolved issues." American Journal of Sociology 71 (May):714–716.

Bach, George R., and Peter Wyden
1968 The Intimate Enemy. New York: Avon Books (William Morrow and Co.).

Bulcroft, Richard, and Murray A. Straus
1975 "Validity of husband, wife, and child reports of intrafamily violence and power." University of New Hampshire, Family Violence Research Program, mimeographed paper V16.

Carroll, Joseph C.
1977 "The intergenerational transmission of family violence: The long term effects of aggressive behavior." Aggressive Behavior 3 (Fall):289–299.

Coser, Lewis A.
1956 The Functions of Social Conflict. New York:The Free Press.

Cronbach, Lee J.
1970 Essentials of Psychological Testing (3rd ed.). New York:Harper and Row.

Dahrendorf, Ralf
1959 Class and Class Conflict in Industrial Society. London:Routledge and Kegan Paul.

Foss, Joyce
1979 "The paradoxical nature of family relationships and conflict resolution." Chapter 8 in Murray A. Straus and Gerald T. Hotaling (Eds.), The Social Causes of Husband-Wife Violence. Minneapolis:University of Minnesota Press.

Gelles, Richard J.
1974 The Violent Home: A Study of Physical Aggression Between Husbands and Wives. Beverly Hills:Sage Publications.

Gelles, Richard J., and Murray A. Straus
"Determinants of violence in the family: Toward a theoretical integration." Pp. 549–581 in Wesley R. Burr, Reuben Hill, F. Ivan Nye, and Ira L. Reiss (Eds.). Contemporary Theories About the Family. New York:The Free Press.

Jorgensen, Stephen R.
1977 "Societal class heterogamy, status striving, and perception of marital conflict: A partial replication and revision of Pearlin's contingency hypothesis." Journal of Marriage and the Family 39 (November):653–689.

Mulligan, Martha
1977 "An investigation of factors associated with violent modes of conflict resolution in the family." Unpublished master's thesis, University of Rhode Island.

Scanzoni, John
1972 "Marital conflict as a positive force." Pp. 61–102 in John Scanzoni (Ed.), Sexual Bargaining. New Jersey:Prentice-Hall.

Shostrom, Everett L., and James Kavanaugh
1971 Between Man and Woman. Los Angeles:Nash Publishing Company.

Simmel, Georg
1955 Conflict and the Web of Group Affiliations. Glencoe, Illinois:The Free Press. (Originally published 1908.)

Sprey, Jetse
1969 "The family as a system in conflict." Journal of Marriage and the Family 31 (November):699–706.

Steinmetz, Suzanne K.
1977a "The use of force for resolving family conflict: The training ground for abuse." The Family Coordinator 26 (January): 19–26.
1977b The Cycle of Violence: Assertive, Aggressive, and Abusive Family Interaction. New York: Praeger.

Straus, Murray A.
1964 "Measuring families." Pp. 335–400 in Harold T. Christensen (Ed.), Handbook of Marriage and the Family. Chicago:Rand McNally.
1973 "A general systems theory approach to a theory of violence between family members." Social Science Information (June):105–125.
1974 "Leveling, civility and violence in the family." Journal of Marriage and the Family 36 (February):13–29, plus addendum 36 (August):442–445.

Straus, Murray A., Suzanne K. Steinmetz, and Richard J. Gelles
1980 Behind Closed Doors: Violence in the American Family. New York:Doubleday/Anchor.

APPENDIX 1 Husband–Wife Page of CTS Form N, as Used in 1976 National Survey

No matter how well a couple gets along, there are times when they disagree on major decisions, get annoyed about something the other person does, or just have spats or fights because they're in a bad mood or tired or for some other reason. They also use many different ways of trying to settle their differences. I'm going to read a list of some things that you and your (husband/partner) might have done when you had a dispute, and would first like you to tell me for each one how often you did it in the past year.

Hand Respondent Card A	Q. 78 Respondent—in Past Year								Q. 79 Husband/Partner—in Past Year								Q. 80 Ever Happened		
	Never	Once	Twice	3–5 Times	6–10 Times	11–20 Times	More than 20 Times	Don't Know	Never	Once	Twice	3–5 Times	6–10 Times	11–20 Times	More than 20 Times	Don't Know	Yes	No	Don't Know
a. Discussed the issue calmly	0	1	2	3	4	5	6	X	0	1	2	3	4	5	6	X	1	2	X
b. Got information to back up (your/his) side of things	0	1	2	3	4	5	6	X	0	1	2	3	4	5	6	X	1	2	X
c. Brought in or tried to bring in someone to help settle things	0	1	2	3	4	5	6	X	0	1	2	3	4	5	6	X	1	2	X
d. Insulted or swore at the other one	0	1	2	3	4	5	6	X	0	1	2	3	4	5	6	X	1	2	X
e. Sulked and/or refused to talk about it	0	1	2	3	4	5	6	X	0	1	2	3	4	5	6	X	1	2	X
f. Stomped out of the room or house (or yard)	0	1	2	3	4	5	6	X	0	1	2	3	4	5	6	X	1	2	X
g. Cried	0	1	2	3	4	5	6	X	0	1	2	3	4	5	6	X	1	2	X
h. Did or said something to spite the other one	0	1	2	3	4	5	6	X	0	1	2	3	4	5	6	X	1	2	X
i. Threatened to hit or throw something at the other one	0	1	2	3	4	5	6	X	0	1	2	3	4	5	6	X	1	2	X
j. Threw or smashed or hit or kicked something	0	1	2	3	4	5	6	X	0	1	2	3	4	5	6	X	1	2	X
k. Threw something at the other one	0	1	2	3	4	5	6	X	0	1	2	3	4	5	6	X	1	2	X
l. Pushed, grabbed, or shoved the other one	0	1	2	3	4	5	6	X	0	1	2	3	4	5	6	X	1	2	X
m. Slapped the other one	0	1	2	3	4	5	6	X	0	1	2	3	4	5	6	X	1	2	X
n. Kicked, bit, or hit with a fist	0	1	2	3	4	5	6	X	0	1	2	3	4	5	6	X	1	2	X
o. Hit or tried to hit with something	0	1	2	3	4	5	6	X	0	1	2	3	4	5	6	X	1	2	X
p. Beat up the other one	0	1	2	3	4	5	6	X	0	1	2	3	4	5	6	X	1	2	X
q. Threatened with a knife or gun	0	1	2	3	4	5	6	X	0	1	2	3	4	5	6	X	1	2	X
r. Used a knife or gun	0	1	2	3	4	5	6	X	0	1	2	3	4	5	6	X	1	2	X
s. Other (PROBE): ____________	0	1	2	3	4	5	6	X	0	1	2	3	4	5	6	X	1	2	X

79. And what about your (husband/partner)? Tell me how often he (ITEM) in the past year.

For each item circled either "Never" or "Don't Know" for BOTH respondent and partner, ask:

80. Did you or your (husband/partner) *ever* (ITEM)?

Reflection

MURRAY A. STRAUS

My work on the Conflict Tactics Scales (CTS) grew out of a mix of motivations that has been with me for a lifetime. First was a humanitarian concern, and in this case, a desire to contribute to reducing violence. The earliest manifestation was a 1953 article on suicide and homicide (Straus & Straus, 1953). The concern with reducing violence lay dormant until revulsion with the Vietnam war, the rising violent crime rates, and the feminist campaign against rape and wife-beating led me to study corporal punishment by parents (Straus, 1971), family violence in general (Straus, 1973), and violence against women (Straus, 1976).

The second influence was a predilection for research others regard as impractical or sometimes as "crazy." Before the publication of the CTS, few believed it would be possible to knock on the door of a random sample of households and be able to obtain data on violent acts between members of the household. One of my most respected colleagues explicitly cautioned me that the national survey on family violence I was planning would not work because "you can't get this kind of information in a survey."

The third influence was a commitment to the scientific method, including the belief that scales to measure key phenomena are crucial for scientific progress. That belief has been amply supported. At least 400 articles and ten books have been published reporting research findings based on the CTS. Currently, about six articles are published every *month.* In 1979, I had to caution readers that "there is no definitive evidence supporting the validity of the CT scales." Now the evidence of validity is overwhelming.

The contribution of the CTS to understanding family violence is greater than the sheer number of studies. It enabled studies of violence against women that would not have been possible without this instrument. For example, the CTS made it possible to estimate the prevalence of violence against women and physical abuse of children in representative samples of the general population, and to measure trends in violence against women (Straus & Gelles, 1986). These national surveys revealed that violence against women in marital, cohabiting, or dating relationships is several times higher than the rate of cases known to the police, to shelters for battered women, and much higher than the rate revealed by crime victimization surveys (Straus, 1999). Similarly, the rates of physical abuse of children revealed by the parent-child version of the CTS are ten times higher than the number of cases known to the child protective services of the 50 states.

Conflict Theory, Feminist Theory, and the CTS

As explained in the introduction to the article, the CTS is based on conflict theory. This theory assumes that conflict is inherent in all human groups, including the family. It is inherent because group members, while sharing many interests, also have different interests.

These range from specifics, such as what color to paint the bedroom, to the desire of those in power to stay in power and of those at the bottom to gain more control of their lives.

Conflict is also a key part of the feminist theory of family violence. However, the feminist version assumes male dominance in the family and the society, and the use of violence to maintain male dominance, is the source of violence (see Chapters 11 and 12 and Straus, 1976). By contrast, the version of conflict theory on which the CTS is based assumes that *any* inequality in the family, including dominance by a *female* partner, increases the probability of violence because the dominant partner may use violence to maintain his or her position, or the subordinate partner may use violence to try to achieve a more equitable relationship. Thus, a key feature of the CTS is that it measures violence by both partners in a relationship.

Unfortunately, the fact that the CTS measures violence by both partners is also the basis of the rejection of this instrument by leading feminist scholars, including some who have chapters in this book. The CTS was the bearer of the bad news that women perpetrate assaults on male partners at about the same rate as men attack female partners (Straus, 1997). Many feminists perceived these results as both implausible and as a threat to funding of services for battered women and have been bitter in their denunciation of the CTS.

The other main reason for critical analyses of the CTS is, ironically, that it is such a widely used test. This is a manifestation of the fact that the more widely used a test is, the more carefully it will be reviewed. If the CTS were rarely used, there would not be much point to scrutinizing it because the results would rarely be useful. The scrutiny of the CTS has revealed a number of limitations which I summarized in an article on "the Conflict Tactics Scales and Its Critics" (Straus, 1990). Many of these are corrected in the revised versions of the CTS (Straus, Hamby, Boney-McCoy, & Sugarman, 1996; Straus, Hamby, Finkelhor, Moore, & Runyan, 1998). However, the revised versions deliberately do not "correct" the most frequent criticism because it is erroneous. This is the fact that the CTS does not measure the causes, context, and meaning of the violent acts. This criticism is analogous to criticizing a test of reading ability for not identifying the reasons a child reads poorly (such as limited exposure to books at home or test anxiety) and for not measuring the harmful effects of reading difficulty (such as low self-esteem or dropping out of school). These are vital issues, but they must be investigated by using separate measures of those variables along with the reading test. Similarly, the CTS is intended to be used with measures of whatever cause, context, and consequence variables are relevant for the study or the clinical situation, such as measures of the balance of power and feelings of fear and intimidation.

REFERENCES

Straus, J. H., & Straus, M. A. (1953). Suicide, homicide, and Ceylonese social structure. *American Journal of Sociology, 58,* 461–469.

Straus, M. A. (1971). Some social antecedents of physical punishment: A linkage theory interpretation. *Journal of Marriage and the Family, 33*(4), 658–665.

Straus, M. A. (1973). A general systems theory approach to a theory of violence between family members. *Social Science Information, 12,* 105–125.

Straus, M. A. (1976). Sexual inequality, cultural norms, and wife-beating. In E. C. Viano (Ed.), *Victims and society* (pp. 543–559). Washington, DC: Visage Press.

Straus, M. A. (1990). The conflict tactics scales and its critics: An evaluation and new data on validity and reliability. In M. A. Straus & R. J. Gelles (Eds.), *Physical violence in American families: Risk factors and adaptations to violence in 8,145 families* (pp. 49–73). New Brunswick, NJ: Transaction Publications.

Straus, M. A. (1997). Physical assaults by women partners: A major social problem. In M. R. Walsh (Ed.), *Women, men and gender: Ongoing debates* (pp. 210–221). New Haven, CT: Yale University Press.

Straus, M. A. (1999). The controversy over domestic violence by women: A methodological, theoretical, and sociology of science analysis. In X. Arriaga & S. Oskamp (Eds.), *Violence in intimate relationships* (pp. 17–44). Thousand Oaks, CA: Sage.

Straus, M. A., & Gelles, R. J. (1986). Societal change and change in family violence from 1975 to 1985 as revealed by two national surveys. *Journal of Marriage and the Family, 48,* 465–479.

Straus, M. A., Hamby, S. L., Boney-McCoy, S., & Sugarman, D. B. (1996). The revised Conflict Tactics Scales (CTS2): Development and preliminary psychometric data. *Journal of Family Issues, 17*(3), 283–316.

Straus, M. A., Hamby, S. L., Finkelhor, D., Moore, D. W., & Runyan, D. (1998). Identification of child maltreatment with the parent-child Conflict Tactics Scales: Development and psychometric data for a national sample of American parents. *Child Abuse and Neglect, 22,* 249–270.

CHAPTER

14 Women and Male Violence

The Visions and Struggles of the Battered Women's Movement

SUSAN SCHECHTER

No Place To Go

> After you have participated in this conference . . . be ever mindful of the hundreds of women who may *never* see their children again because . . . after taking as much abuse as they could . . . they've protected themselves by killing their husbands and are now serving prison terms.
>
> And don't forget the countless women who have died at their own hands, rather than live in fear of death at the hands of their spouse.
>
> Also keep in mind the endless women going in and out of mental institutions because they just can't deal with the reality of having an abusive husband so they relinquish their rights to reality.
>
> Do you have any idea of how many battered women there are out there? Women who could live normal lives and be productive members of our society.
>
> Many of these women would leave in a minute if they had a place to go and the help they needed to get on their feet and live in peace.[1]

Although a former battered woman spoke these words in 1979, she captured the pain and rage that motivated hundreds of women to organize in the mid-1970s. Earlier in the decade, no one knew the staggering statistics that soon would emerge on wife abuse; there was no reliable data, even within police departments, on a crime labeled insignificant. Soon, however, documentation substantiated the claims of battered women and feminists. In 1979, extrapolating from a sample of Kentucky women, researchers estimated that 80,000 women in that state were victimized by their spouses during the preceding twelve months, 33,000 of them seriously.[2]

Although the programs for battered women that emerged in the 1970s articulated a multiplicity of philosophies, they shared one common belief: battered women faced a brutality from their husbands and an indifference from social institutions that compelled redress. This theme stimulated networks among thousands of women and programs throughout the United States, Canada, and Europe. Even in 1982, the experiences of battered women often shock a politically diverse movement back into recognizing the unity imposed by violence, social indifference about that violence, and the desperate lack of services.

The brutal institutional experiences battered women endured are recorded in several excellent books and thousands of pages of testimony that read like the following.

> A woman who had experienced 14 years of beatings from a husband . . . had gotten 1-year Family Court injunctions against his assaults seven times. Frequently, when the police responded they told her to file a violation petition, requesting the court to hold her husband in contempt. They did not arrest him until the night they found her dazed and dripping blood from a large head wound. Her husband had smashed her in the head repeatedly with a chair. He had inflicted several stab wounds with a screwdriver. . . . As the officers arrested the man for attempted murder, he protested, "But she's my wife."[3]

Unofficially, the police concurred, further isolating and stigmatizing the woman and lending support to her husband.

Courts generally ignored the problem, consigning it the status of a minor, family squabble. In Washington D.C., in 1966, prosecutors issued only 200 arrest warrants to the 7,500 women who requested them.[4] Although 50% of the problems in Chicago's Domestic Relations Court were family assaults, in those cases that received a hearing, "the most common disposition was an unsecured, unrecorded, blank, fake peace bond." Even when men pleaded guilty or were found guilty, the official court docket almost always read "discharged for want of prosecution."[5]

The extent of the harassment was shocking.

> One of my clients pressed criminal charges against her husband. The judge asked her if this was the first time she had been beaten up. After observing court proceedings that morning, she knew that if she answered "yes" like all the other women had, her husband would be released with virtually no penalty. So wisely she answered, "No, this is not the first time." The judge dismissed the case, responding, "Well, it sounds like you must enjoy getting beaten up if it has happened before. There's nothing I can do."[6]

Women were also harassed if they attempted to leave their husbands. In Chicago in the early 1970s, as in many cities, battered women who left were denied welfare. Still legally married, their husbands' income made them ineligible for assistance. Without welfare, however, women had no money to rent apartments or pay moving expenses. . . .

In most cities, fire and catastrophe victims, alcoholics, and battered women found themselves in the same shelters. Often full, these facilities had to turn women away. And those who found shelter were sometimes made to feel responsible for their families' problems and their husbands' violence. No specialized assistance was offered nor was violent behavior labeled unjust. In most shelters operated by religious or charitable organizations, women were left to untangle their "personal" problems within a social and political context that extolled family unity and legitimated male dominance.

Prior to the battered women's movement, a few isolated shelters were formed to house victims of alcohol-related violence. For example, in California in 1964, women from Al-Anon opened the first shelter for battered women, Haven House. Outraged that beaten women were sleeping in cars with their children, Al-Anon women rented a large house in Pasadena. Although the shelter was specifically for victims of alcohol-related violence, many battered women simply arrived, asking for and receiving help. Between 1964 and 1972, using peer support and self-help, Haven House sheltered over 1000 women and children, surviving on a shoestring budget and the determination of grassroots women who believed in "women helping women." In 1972, because of new, strict fire codes, Haven House had to close, reopening in 1974 with a much larger budget and staff.[7]

In most cases, however, battered women truly had nowhere to go. Shelters were almost nonexistent, and medical, social service, and law enforcement agencies rarely provided battered women with the kind of support they needed. Although not all institutional personnel treated battered women badly, a pattern of hostility existed, leading many women to conclude: "No one wants to get involved," or "I guess I'll have to be dead for them to stop his violence."

The First Positive Responses

In the 1970s, feminists, community activists, and former battered women increasingly responded in a new way, providing emotional support, refuge, and a new definition of "the problem."

Feminist women's centers, like Women's Center South in Pittsburgh, sometimes offered a safe place for women in crisis. This women's center, with a kitchen, a place to sleep, a reading room, and an information center, had someone in the house 24 hours a day.[8] In an 11 month period in 1975, "the center logged 191 women sheltered, 86 children, and 839 visitors arriving to talk, create, nap, plan, work, or just be themselves. Incoming phone calls climbed to an astronomical 4961."[9] Two other Pennsylvania shelters, Women Against Abuse in Philadelphia and the Domestic Violence Service Center in Wilkes-Barre also evolved from women's centers.

Former battered women or women who had seen violence in their families of origin were among the first to reach out. In Boston in 1976, "Chris Womendez and Cherie Jimenez opened up their five room apartment as a refuge for battered women. . . . At the time, they supported Transition House as well as themselves and two children on their welfare checks and small contributions from friends."[10] Cherie Jimenez's earlier stay at Interval House, a Toronto program primarily for battered women, influenced her decision to found the Boston shelter. "I had never seen a place like that before . . . I had never seen women helping each other out like that."[11] When asked whether they had considered themselves feminists, Chris Womendez responded, "Cherie was more than I was. I never thought much about it then. I identified myself as a lesbian more."[12]

Marta Segovia Ashley, whose mother was murdered by her stepfather, describes the earliest discussions among the six women, both feminists and violence victims, who founded San Francisco's La Casa de Las Madres.

> In sharing the violence in our lives, we began to see that we were equally oppressed. There would be no separation between staff and resident. . . .
>
> We did not want the social worker/white missionary establishment to run La Casa. We wrote into the original proposal that the residents would, hopefully by the end of the first year, become staff at La Casa and that we would work ourselves out of jobs.[13]

As a result of discussions during 1973 and 1974 in Harrisburg, Pennsylvania, battered women in Al-Anon organized a shelter. Their motivation was to help themselves and other women. In their view, battered women needed the support of their peers rather than professional help which often made them feel judged or disabled. The women did not see themselves as part of a feminist movement, although their first staff person did, and "a loving struggle developed between the feminists and the Al-Anon women." The feminist notion of "empowerment" and the analysis that blamed male domination for violence were foreign to Al-Anon women, but self-help and treating women as adults, important concepts for the women's liberation movement, were central to their philosophy.[14]

During late 1974, a multi-racial group of women in Boston's South End began meeting to plan a shelter for neighborhood women and their children. They were concerned about the complete lack of bilingual services for Latina women in crisis and the absence of any Latina controlled organization for women in the city of Boston. The founders of Casa Myrna Vazquez explain further.

> The origins of Casa Myrna Vazquez Inc. and the development of its philosophy and structure was not only influenced by the desire of these women to help other community women using a self-help approach (particularly Latina women and other women of color), but it was also closely tied to the fight being waged in the neighborhood to preserve the right of long-term residents to remain in the neighborhood and determine the quality of life there. At the time the South End was a neighborhood undergoing transition and change brought on by urban renewal and public and private interests and capital; people of color, poor people, new immigrants and the people speaking different languages were being rapidly displaced by the affluent. These people were fighting for the right to continue to live and own property in this neighborhood and exercise community control of their space. In keeping with this spirit, these neighborhood women wanted to create and maintain community-controlled services for women and their families to ensure that their work would remain a part of the people receiving the services.[15]

Casa Myrna Vazquez was to become one important model of help emanating from neighborhood based rather than feminist models of organizing.

In the early 1970s, as they listened or reassessed their own experiences, women did more than provide housing for battered women. In a social climate alive with feminist organizing and community self-help projects, these women also uncovered, inch by inch, the sexist ideology that declared nothing wrong with battering a woman unless the violence went too far. Until the 1970s, "mild" forms of chastisement were still considered necessary and even helpful to keep a woman in line. A little slap was a sign of love. Most Americans grew up with ideas like "real men keep their women under control;" "she needed to be brought to her senses;" or "women like men who dominate." These ideas are a shared and assumed part of the culture. Social workers, probation officers, judges, or police often eagerly recount knowing beaten women who enjoy the violence, offering as evidence, "You know. They always go back." Activists had to assert that such attitudes deny women options for escape and give men permission to beat. They declared it brutal and misleading to label behavior masochistic or enjoyable when a person has no perceived options.

Activists learned to challenge the ideology that preaches the subordination of women, extols the moral superiority of men, and logically assigns husbands the duty of chastising their wives. Another specifically American form of ideology asserts the belief in freedom. "Women are free to go; why don't they just leave?" This definition of freedom ignores the fact that many women have nowhere to go and no money to stay there once they arrive. A third form of ideology focuses on the battering of poor women and women of color and asserts that for them, violence is an accepted and expected way of life and therefore need not be considered a problem. This is a racist and class biased distortion of reality which invalidates the suffering of poor and third world women while it hides the violence directed against white, middle class women. As they learned to help battered women, activists had to fight these views within themselves and within the community.

Shelter Life

From the beginning, shelters for battered women have assumed a variety of forms. Perhaps 20% share space in YWCA residences or use institutional settings, like motels or abandoned orphanages. Most often, shelters are old houses with many bedrooms where battered women and their children can stay for a few days or a few months. Although the buildings are often run-down, shelter staff become expert at repairing almost anything, valiantly attempting to keep them homelike. Capacity is usually five to ten families although size varies. Many women bring two or more children. Together women residents divide house chores, cook, and clean. Women may rotate tasks; for example, each woman chooses one or two meals that she will prepare for the entire group during the week. In many settings, each woman and her children share one bedroom; in others, because of severe space shortages, families double up in one room. Each shelter has rules about safety, drugs, curfew, care of children, and attendance at house meetings to discuss problems and chores. Often, length of stay agreements are made with residents.

Simply getting used to the shelter is an overwhelming task. As one woman described it, "the shelter is a hard place. Women like it but they also don't want to be here. It's just not home. Some women love it and still others hate how overcrowded it feels." As this Puerto Rican advocate explains, "Puerto Rican women who come to the shelter are very scared. They don't want to leave their community and come to a new place. They may have language problems. They don't drive. They may never have paid bills or done a budget. They particularly dislike having to share rooms with other people, both black and white women. They have never lived this way before. They're not used to living collectively or sharing apartments like white women do."[16]

During a shelter stay, women often pass through several stages. At first they are frightened and nervous, both about the decisions they have made and about their new environment of fifteen or more strangers. For the first several days or weeks, women are constantly busy with court proceedings, welfare applications or job hunts, medical appointments, and the search for affordable housing so that the next endangered woman can take her place at the shelter. After the initial flurry of activities, women wait for apartments and court proceedings, and at this point may feel intense doubts, fear, and pain. Women struggle with ambivalence, self-blame, and guilt as they contemplate their relationship ending and attempt to make sense of what happened. . . . Many women describe the shelter's assumed but most significant advantages as time and safety to think, free from coercion and violent interruption.

Support from staff and other residents sustains women during moments of doubt. Although there is rapid turnover in residents, relationships among women form quickly, based on similar experiences, common living spaces, and the necessity of accomplishing major tasks. Support often comes through sharing food or coffee at the kitchen table. At a discussion with residents at Women's Survival Space in Brooklyn, one woman remarked, "Being here—you feel safe and that's *very* important. But you also don't feel alone. Group sessions help you relieve things that build up inside of you. It feels good inside." . . .

Receiving more than courage from one another, women transform their understanding of why they were beaten. They hear repeatedly that the beatings were not their fault, and some take the first step toward freedom by rejecting responsibility for male violence. "Liberation" describes the experience of watching one shelter resident after another nod her head in recognition of another woman's plight, confusion, and eventual rage.

Shelters are havens, but they are not utopias. The atmosphere within a house varies, depending on the current group of residents, staff morale, and shelter organization. One resident describes typical problems in her shelter.

> Cliques seem to form here and as a newcomer I'm pretty uncomfortable. The older residents boss the new ones around. The women seem to be bored, complaining about missing men and sex. I wish there were more support groups, more to do.[17]

Often, however, this tension dissipates when women share with one another in groups or at house meetings, forming close bonds at least temporarily.

Because American society is so racially segregated, a shelter may be one of the few places women live interracially. Battering, living in a shelter, and starting over with nothing are the common experiences among sheltered women; racial and ethnic lines are crossed through mutual aid. Because no one escapes the racism in this society, differences and tensions are common.

> The kitchen becomes a battleground of ethnic righteousness. Women wrinkle their noses in disgust at each others' food or out-right refuse to eat. The children sit watching and

> listening, learning well the lessons of prejudice. . . . The kitchen is where everything happens. Women support each other, there they cry with each other, there they prepare the food and eat. . . .
>
> Food is an issue that people can relate to easily. It's an emotional issue, and compounded with women from different races and class backgrounds can be a very explosive one.[18]

Coming from extremely isolated areas, some rural women confront different problems.

> Isolation is intensified when there are not neighbors to hear her scream, when she has no car and there are no buses that come within 15 or 20 miles of her house. She may have no phone. There may be four feet of snow. Furthermore, . . . tradition dictates that one does not bring family problems to anyone external, particularly in a small town where once one's business is known by a few, it is known by all.[19]

Just getting to the shelter may be an overwhelming task.

> Recently in Nebraska, a woman tried to walk to a shelter for battered women that she had heard about. It was 150 miles from her home. She had walked nearly half way with her small children on back roads when she came to a town that had a volunteer task force on domestic violence which arranged for transportation . . . [20]

Once at a shelter, rural women may have to adjust to using indoor plumbing or washing machines for the first time. They may be members of a white ethnic minority in the community that is scorned by some women at the shelter.

For rural women and urban women, for women of different races and ethnic groups, shelters offered a chance to escape an unbearable situation. They created an environment in which diverse women came together to live, rebuilding pained lives. Finding the best way to do this would not be easy; few models existed and financial resources were always limited.

Shelter Philosophy and Structure

As shelters formed, they began to develop their own philosophies and structures and deal with the troubling question of their relationship to the state. Focusing on two of the first shelters, Transition House in Boston and Women's Advocates in St. Paul, highlights early shelter activity and helps clarify the philosophical differences that would emerge in the battered women's movement as it expanded.

The founding of Women's Advocates and Transition House were real and symbolic victories in the struggle of women to free themselves from male violence and domination. Their stories suggest the richness, complexity, chaos, and energy of the early battered women's movement. Women's Advocates emerged from a consciousness raising group which, in 1971, set itself the goal, typical in the early women's liberation movement, "to do something."[21] This determination led the group to produce a divorce rights handbook and organize a legal information telephone service, staffed by volunteers and two VISTA workers assigned to Women's Advocates through a Legal Aid Office.

> . . . .what to do next. The need for emergency housing was the one urgent and recurring problem for which there was no referral. . . . The immediate need of so many women moved us toward turning our vision into a reality.[22]

They began by asking friends for pledges toward the down payment on a house and for operating expenses. By 1973, monthly pledges of $350 helped pay rent for a small apartment and the cost of a telephone and answering service. Calls for help exceeded room in the apartment, and advocates soon took battered women into their homes. After three months, Women's Advocates was evicted from its apartment because of neighbors' complaints about the children. Their office then temporarily moved into the home of one of their VISTA workers.

> Several women needing emergency housing stayed together at her home that summer while her family was on vacation, and we realized the importance of women being together in one house, sharing their experiences, and getting support from one another.[23]

They also learned a lesson about how women together can transform fear. Searching all over town for a woman whose kidneys he had damaged in a beating, a pimp threatened Women's Advocates. At that moment, "there was another woman with four children, a woman with one child, and a single woman in the house. We had a meeting about this man. I remember one volunteer argued for everyone leaving the house because of the potential danger. The whole group decided to hold their ground and take shifts, staying up all night in case he showed up. It was the first time I felt that kind of power."[24] In this summer experiment, staff and residents had participated equally. Advocates maintained friendships with the women they were sheltering; staff were not just helpers.[25] Staff had seen the strength of battered women, which gave them the courage to move ahead and open a house; they had also experienced the reality of sheltering when women stole from them or did not like one another. Having sheltered women for eighteen months, Women's Advocates moved into their first house idealistic but seasoned, aware of the satisfaction and dangers ahead.

Women's Advocates' philosophy had been hammered out early in practical debates about whether a hotline worker should tell a caller what to do. Battered women's rights to self-determination, including the decision to leave or stay with their husbands, were to be respected; if sexism robbed women of control over their lives, Women's Advocates would work on methods for returning it, even if no one quite knew how. Outside agencies also forced a clarification of values. When the first funding sources suggested that Women's Advocates change its name to something "less inflammatory," the collective refused to compromise on its basic philosophy.

> We have never called women needing help "clients" or "cases," and this has not prevented effective communication with the professional community. When we were told that only

> trained and certified professionals could run the house, we insisted that professional credentials not be included as job requirements. We asserted our belief that women in need of shelter were not sick or in need of treatment, emphasizing instead their need for safety, support, and help with practical problems.[26]

The importance of a collective, rather than a hierarchical, model of work was emphasized as the shelter founders drew the connection between theory and practice.

> We want women to be able to take control of their own lives, and to share in an environment which supports their doing just that. For many women and children, being at the shelter may be the first time they have been outside of the controlling authority of an abusive relationship. Each woman who lives and works in the shelter is encouraged to trust herself to make decisions which are best for her, and to participate in determining what is best for the shelter as well. Here, there is no boss who has the answers. It isn't easy, but together we are learning to trust in ourselves, and in each other, to determine what is best for us.[27]

At Women's Advocates, all major decisions are made by the collective, usually through consensus. Sometimes voting has also been necessary, but "a slim majority . . . never carries a decision. When the collective is split on an important issue, we set it aside, placing it on the agenda for the next meeting."[28]

One of the central issues for many shelters is whether the shelter belongs to staff or residents. Often this question surfaces in discussions of rules. When Women's Advocates opened in 1974, they had no house rules. Immediately, however, they found they had to set limits. The first rules centered around mandatory house meetings, signing up for jobs so that the house could function, and a "no drugs" policy. One founder commented, "on the first day we declared that there were no pets; on the second, no drugs; and on the third, no furniture storage."[29] Rules were made on the basis of experience, often negative ones, and sometimes the collective had to remind itself or be reminded by the residents that it had created too many restrictions.

For most shelters, a vexing consideration was what relationship to assume toward the government and funding agencies. *Women's Advocates, The Story of a Shelter,* an excellent description of the shelter's organizing activity and history, captures women's ambivalence toward the state.

> For the first two years the shelter was in operation, we made no active effort to affect legislation. Although we were acutely aware of the inadequacy of current laws available to battered women and the need for funding for shelters, we were less certain of the benefits of legislation than we were of its potential dangers. As the only shelter or program of any kind for battered women in our state, we were isolated and in a state of political infancy. Before approaching state politics, we needed to be stronger—to know clearly what we wanted, and to know how to go about getting it without losing what little ground we had gained.[30]

Cautiously, Women's Advocates later took foundation funding and one local mental health grant that allowed them to preserve their autonomy. They hired a small staff and depended heavily on volunteers. State funding was to come later with the passage of legislation.

Working in isolation, but relying on feminist insight, battered women's input, and common sense, Women's Advocates learned through experience how to best help battered women. In the process, the advocates also found themselves transformed. As one shelter founder explains:

> We discovered our politics in the process of discovering ourselves. When we saw how totally the traditional system failed to meet the needs of battered women, we rushed in to save them. What kept us from being a bunch of Lady Bountifuls was that everything learned from the women themselves, and our struggles with policy, direction, and with each other, was moving *us* off that continuum from victim to survivor. The personal was political. Personally, I didn't call myself a feminist when we started. It sort of snuck up and embraced me as I lived it.[31]

Members of the original Advocates collective had neither the extensive experience with violence themselves nor the theoretical commitment that motivated several women at Transition House, the first east coast shelter. In both cases, however, experience led them to the creation of shelters with similar ideologies and practices. Transition House was born in 1976 in the apartment of two former battered women. Believing women together could pool their resources to help others, Chris Womendez and Cherie Jimenez, with determination and no money, simply declared their home a shelter. Betsy Warrior and Lisa Leghorn joined their work as did other radical feminists. Since 1974, Leghorn and Warrior had talked about battering and women's slavery in the home as a core part of women's oppression.[32] These politics informed the philosophy of Transition House.

> We are concerned not only with providing physical and emotional refuge from domestic violence, as a short term goal. We are concerned, more basically, with helping each woman who comes through here to discover that she is not alone, that the craziness she's being forced to deal with isn't unique to her and her children, but that it's a political issue which touches all women directly and indirectly.

Using informal consciousness raising techniques, the women at Transition House emphasize the political nature of the work.

> In doing support and advocacy work for her, we are telling her that as sisters, her plight is our plight, and that the only way we can fight these battles and hope to win is by working together and supporting each other in every way possible. As soon as a woman comes into Transition House for the first time, we talk with her about her experiences, share our own experiences with her, play her tapes we made of other women who've come through the house talking about what they'd been forced to deal with and how they came out of it, and we give her articles and news clippings which address the problem of wife abuse as a political issue.

Transition House clarifies the desired, liberating outcome.

> First of all, she gains a political awareness by viewing her own suffering for the first time in a social and political framework. And secondly, she discovers that the most effective way to

> confront the entire social, political, and economic system whose expressed interests are to keep the family with all its trappings of male supremacy and male privilege intact at her expense is to join together with other women and address the issues in a political way.[33]

From the beginning, Transition House has emphasized women's opportunities to share with and support one another. The growth of all women who pass through the house, battered women and staff, is seen as important. . . . Transition House staffers understood that the process of giving to others makes women feel stronger. Resident strengthening resident, a primary goal of the shelter, was considered more potent than staff helping residents.[34]

Because Transition House did not want the experience of staff to be vastly different from that of residents, women declared hiring former victims a priority.[35] According to Lisa Leghorn, peer support, especially among battered women, worked better than other models because it gave hope, power, and validation to women. She explains the Transition House philosophy further.

> We were not providing social services. As staffers, we were not different from the women except that they were in crisis. We only gave people safety and information. We emphasized women have to make their own decisions. Support came sitting around the dining room table and while doing advocacy. Our advocacy model was a woman who went to welfare yesterday taking another woman today . . . If you caretake, you don't give a woman what she needs. Shelters where women went back to their husbands were often shelters where they had been taken care of as opposed to being helped to develop survival skills. This didn't prepare the woman for living on her own in an often hostile world.[36]

Initially, Transition House was crowded and chaotic. Speaking of the early days in the apartment, one staffer recalls, "we had beds everywhere and lofts and a closet stuffed with mattresses that we took out at night. . . . People that did stay were extremely battered and really needed it. They had absolutely no choice. . . ."[37] Under the circumstances, it was difficult for a work structure to evolve. When Transition House rented its first house, conditions improved and more structure was created. Paid staff were added. Three working committees were formed—maintenance, fundraising, and outreach—and a whole wave of unpaid staff was recruited from a Boston Women Support Women rally that focused on violence against women and drew 5000 participants.

Initially, rules came from the women staying in the house. Then new women would arrive, and, furious at old restrictions, change the rules. The short-term interests of women staying in the house for a few weeks and the long-term survival needs of the shelter were sometimes in conflict. Eventually, the power to make rules and decisions came to reside primarily with staffers through committee work and collective meetings; any resident willing to make a longer term commitment to the shelter was invited to be part of the decision making process and Board of Directors. However, rules could be changed by residents, except those that applied to the long-term needs of the house—like keeping the location confidential and maintaining safety precautions.[38] Rules were based on residents' experiences together. One staffer emphasized, "Transition House is for the women who live there and for the women who will come, and this dual focus has to be maintained."[39]

Women working at Transition House had to be tremendously flexible. Change happened continually in a house holding ten women and their children, most of whom stayed six weeks or less and were instantly replaced by new women and children. There was no "correct" approach to the work, and at times the chaos and problems were overwhelming, especially when women had to confront the fact that "not all women are just wonderful." As one staffer said, "women have had to learn survival skills and some of these are negative. They may hurt other people and one has to learn this. It's a tough issue."[40] Learning to live with intense anger was also difficult for many. Staff had to explain why hundreds of women experience so much brutality from men, why the institutions seemed indifferent, and why women were trapped by financial, housing and child care problems.

Despite the pain and exhaustion that shelter workers sometimes felt, they were politicized through battered women's experiences and strengthened by the courage so many displayed as they reclaimed their lives.

> Running a shelter is very taxing . . . It goes back to mutual sharing, being there for each other . . . The shelter is a big connecting point between classes. I've changed being there . . . We get involved, excited, and have great respect and love for women we never would have met otherwise.[41]

A founder of Women's Advocates echoes these sentiments.

> As an advocate you got depressed and discouraged from hearing all the pain. The number of women, the severity of their problems, what they faced when they left the shelter—it weighed me down. What kept me going was that the shelter allowed the women's power to emerge. Listening to them was so moving . . . The women's options often seem hopeless but their spirit rises above hopelessness and gives me hope.[42]

Through redefining a social "problem" into a social movement, women from Transition House and Women's Advocates helped other shelters begin and served as catalysts for state, regional, and national coalitions. Using the self-help methods, egalitarian philosophy, and collective organizational structures developed within the women's liberation movement, these two groups discovered and then articulated a grassroots, non-professional view of battered women's needs. Through their struggle to define a feminist "shelter," they gave birth to one more alternative, democratic women's institution. Although their efforts and ideology were not always replicated in other cities, Transition House and Women's Advocates became respected and often copied pioneers.

Organizing Through a Coalition

Although providing shelter for abused women is a top priority of the battered women's movement, groups in the movement have organized in other ways too. In some cities, women representing a variety of organizations met together and decided to form coalitions.

In Chicago, for example, in the spring of 1976, women of the Loop Center YWCA convened a meeting of women's organizations and individuals whom they knew to be concerned about the lack of services for battered women. Over thirty groups were represented at the initial meeting and expressed interest in combining resources for public education on the issues, support groups for the victims, and agency accountability for missing programs.[43]

Women who attended this and subsequent meetings decided to plan a fall conference to found the Chicago Abused Women's Coalition. To the surprise of the organizers, 300 women came to the October conference. The coalition, which defined opening a shelter as an essential goal, also identified other needs of the movement and worked simultaneously on many fronts. Several task forces—shelter, legal, agency accountability, counseling, and publicity—were established and became the core working groups of the coalition. They emphasized the need for creating services and making concrete change. Two elected delegates from each task force formed the steering committee of the coalition, and met together frequently.

The Chicago Abused Women's Coalition's efforts to work on a range of projects is typical of organizing in other locales as well. In many places, women start with a hotline or counseling project and slowly build local support for a shelter. In others, as a result of circumstances or choice, they never open a refuge but continue ceaseless support for battered women through their hotlines, crisis counseling, legal advocacy, public speaking, and transportation to shelters in other towns.

Initially, the Chicago coalition itself offered no services and had no paid staff. Member organizations, specifically the YWCA and Women in Crisis Can Act (WICCA), divided day, evening, and weekend hours to become a crisis hotline for the entire city and sometimes suburbs, answering hundreds of phone calls each month from women with nowhere to go. The Women's Services Department at Loop Center YWCA, with 2½ paid staff, answered all daytime calls from rape victims and battered women. WICCA operated as a collective with no paid staff and answered its phone on specified weekday evenings and weekend hours. . . .

Early work of the shelter task force revolved around defining a philosophy; what emerged was similar to the values articulated by Women's Advocates. Learning about shelters for homeless women in the community further clarified the direction in which the task force would move. . . .

Women on the shelter task force, all volunteers, worked tirelessly to raise money through pledges, legally incorporate, write grants, and find a building. For over a year, financial pledges from individual women were the only source of hope, but were never enough to open a shelter. Discouragement was constant. The city of Chicago did much to obstruct progress through unkept promises of funding. The task force eventually approached religious organizations that owned buildings, and one house was secured in 1978, after the Chicago coalition and other Illinois shelters received funding through state Title XX grants. Two years of persistent work finally achieved results.

In the meantime, the legal task force moved forward. The first Chicago Abused Women's Coalition newsletter, published in December 1976, defined four primary goals of the legal task force, all of which were accomplished over the next several years. The first goal was to mobilize around proposed state legislation that would provide temporary injunctive relief, protective orders, and custody and property determinations for women who had not filed for divorce; would allow women to sue their husbands for damages; would require police training and statistics gathering; and would declare spouse beating a specific crime. The three non-legislative goals included working with the police to develop new procedures in wife abuse cases, developing a court watch program that would document the problems within the States Attorney's office and Domestic Relations Court, and establishing a court advocacy program for victims.[44] Not only were these goals accomplished but the first Legal Center for Battered Women in the United States was funded by a grant to the Legal Assistance Foundation of Chicago. For two years, the Legal Center advocated for thousands of individual women, forced the Chicago police department to change its practices, and kept close watch over all local and state legislative and criminal justice systems developments. A legal center specifically geared toward meeting battered women's needs and changing legal practices had been defined as a necessity; its closing after two years due to lack of funds was a major loss to the battered women's movement.

Changing social attitudes and generating concrete assistance through educational efforts has been a primary organizing strategy of the battered women's movement. In its first two years, members of the Chicago Abused Women's Coalition spoke to hundreds of community groups, women's organizations, and professional agencies. Early coalition discussions served to clarify the analysis as well as the methods for conveying it. Almost every speaker shared battered women's stories, explained the significance of violence, detailed how victims are blamed and violence is sanctioned, dispelled common myths, and challenged her audience to help battered women and look at the broader social conditions that create abuse. Social attitudes toward battered women were painfully obvious through these efforts as audiences searched for "characteristics" of abusers and battered women. Professionals in particular hunted for pathology and a "battered woman syndrome," locating the cause of violence in women's personalities or their families of origin.

In addition to numerous speaking engagements, the Chicago Abused Women's Coalition, through a grant from the Illinois Humanities Council, co-sponsored three conferences in 1976 and 1977—one in the downtown business section of Chicago; another coordinated by Latinas as a Spanish-speaking conference with the first locally translated materials; and a third in the black community on Chicago's westside.

Community education efforts provided an alternative and a challenge to dominant views about violence against women. Although audiences revealed their prejudices, they were often deeply moved and supportive of coalition activity. The movement's ability to balance moral outrage about battering with a deep concern for its victims and a vision of a better world led many to join in the struggle. For example, hospitals and social service agencies began to increasingly ask the coalition to provide their staff with in-service education and training. Some institutions became highly supportive of coalition activity, writing endorsement letters for coalition grants and, in some cases, starting their own services for battered women. These outreach activities had their effect on battered women as well. They heard the messages: "You don't deserve to be beaten; it's not your fault; you are beaten because society sanctions his behavior, not because of anything you do wrong;

evidence suggests that no matter how many times you change your behavior to respond to his criticisms, you will probably be beaten again; through the years, violence grows more severe." Battered women reacted by reaching out for help and by involving themselves in the movement.

Activists in the Chicago Abused Women's Coalition developed skills as speakers, lobbyists, and planners. A core of fifteen feminists—lawyers, social workers, psychologists, and activists—fought for essential services. Ideological and political differences were muted until decisions had to be made about applying for government funding, cooperating with religious organizations, or working with men. At this point, after years of hard work, one of the most radical women left in principled and caring disagreement over the choice to work with religious organizations that oppress women. Repeated around the country, sometimes with far greater bitterness and divisiveness, are the stories of many hard working women who never saw the opening of the shelters they had envisioned.

To the Chicago women, shelter was only one step in a long-range, dimly articulated plan to stop violence. Battling with the bureaucracy and raising money for more than two years before a shelter opened, however, were trying. Working on the legal task force, doing community outreach—all took enormous time and energy. Although many women participated in the coalition on a sporadic basis, most of the work was done by a small group of approximately fifteen. In the rush to make concrete change, women stayed task oriented; no one stopped to see herself as an organizer for the coalition itself. In the constant push to respond to battered women and organizational emergencies, there was no time to build the organization's membership, a familiar story within the movement. When several key coalition members "burned out" or moved, the coalition and its newly opened shelter faced difficult days.

External Influences on the Movement

Even in its infancy, the battered women's movement had to contend with more than its own internal dynamics. It faced contradictory external reactions and pressures. The media, for example, was both help and hinderance. At first, the plight of battered women—like that of rape victims—made "good news stories." Women reporters, working cooperatively and thoughtfully with battered women's programs, often produced excellent and thorough articles, drawing attention to institutional hostility to abused women and the lack of services available to them. These stories brought more calls from battered women and supporters and also legitimated the need for services and institutional change. A message challenging hundreds of years of male domination reached many. This kind of coverage, combined with the movement's extensive outreach to women's organizations, sometimes led to concrete support from traditional women's clubs or women's auxiliaries who "adopted" shelters, furnishing rooms or coordinating fundraising benefits. Sometimes, however, publicity was counter-productive. Reporters produced sensationalized accounts which made battered women look foolish; worse, they sometimes revealed the addresses of shelters, thereby endangering staff and residents and forcing groups to move after they had spent years finding housing.

Government and community agencies could help direct important resources toward the movement, although, as in the case of the media, the movement's relationship to such groups was ambivalent. . . . Simply recounting the experiences of battered women sometimes brought the desperately needed first grants; in other cases, funders changed their original negative responses after they visited shelters.[45] One or two key people, some of them feminists, within welfare departments, community or county planning boards, or United Way agencies, made the issue theirs, pushing others to support programs that had no legitimacy, credibility, or fiscal strength. . . . Women from around the country tell of anonymous donors or key progressive legislators, male and female, who made a real difference in the early years.

Often, however, outside agencies' impact on the movement has been more negative than positive. Bureaucracies, especially local welfare and legal ones, constantly harassed battered women and their advocates. . . . Zoning boards and county governments wrought misery upon programs searching for affordable property that met the criteria for shelter. The Pittsburgh shelter experienced a series of disasters with zoning boards and realtors denying them access to one house after another. County governments and fire departments withheld funds or licensing approval for a series of nitpicking reasons. Sometimes community members packed public hearings, insisting that they did not want violent husbands in their neighborhood, and successfully blocked a shelter's opening.

As in the anti-rape movement, once the issue of battering gained legitimacy and funding was made available, more established organizations took over the issue that grassroots women had worked so hard to raise. . . . Competition over limited dollars allowed conservative private and governmental bodies to direct funds toward traditional, non-feminist agencies.

Generalizing about agency and governmental responses to the battered women's movement is difficult. In some locations, agencies like the United Way, offering funds or legitimacy, or the YWCA, giving its space or staff time, were extremely helpful; in others, similar agencies turned their backs or actively set up barriers to prevent grassroots groups from encroaching on their "turf." Battered women and their advocates had pointed out that established agencies were not meeting their needs; some of these agencies moved to redress the complaint while others reacted with discomfort and fought back with intense pettiness that caused long delays in shelter openings. Issues of power, control, and funding were often at stake, and newcomers, especially those with anti-professional or non-professional biases, were not necessarily welcome.

The Early Sustenance of the Movement

Battered women's shelters have, from the beginning, operated under extremely difficult conditions and been subject to many conflicting demands. Living and working in a shelter implies crises for all involved. In addition to dealing with the overwhelming problems of shelter residents, staff had to face daily pressures. Since there was never enough money, women had to learn quickly how to write grant proposals, lobby, generate publicity, speak on radio and television, apply for loans and mortgages. They also had to learn how to organize staff and develop work procedures. At the same time that shelter work and its accomplishments were exhilarating, the strains were wearing. In the early years especially, worker "burnout" was common, and some staff literally destroyed their health or personal lives.

In a few places, women encountered yet one more pressure. While community groups or individuals might sympathize publicly with battered women, "feminism" did not necessarily evoke similar reactions. Feminists were sometimes accused of hating men, and of being lesbians who were out to seduce battered women. The real purpose of these accusations—to divide collective efforts, undermine women's activism, and scare battered women away from the shelter—was often obvious. Although most women ignored the attacks and used their anger to continue organizing, some were diverted by this tactic. Bigotry and anti-feminist sentiment caused a few lesbians and heterosexual feminists to suffer through ugly, discrediting power struggles and ultimately lose their jobs.

In the midst of uncertainty, women turned to one another for multiple forms of sustenance. Women uniting, working cooperatively against huge odds, caring about one another and struggling together successfully carried small, isolated programs through the worst days. For many, a feminist analysis of wife abuse that placed the roots of male violence in domination could not be separated from a feminist process that actively struggled against recreating hierarchies and domination among women. . . .

Close friendship networks developed in early battered women's groups. As one shelter worker explained, "The work becomes all-consuming. You live and breathe together the battered women's movement—the horrible things that happen to women, power struggles with other agencies. I think this is why so many women in the movement become such close friends. The movement is your life."[46]

When asked how their programs started or how their work progressed, early movement organizers instead described each group member's unique skills and personality. With both positive and negative outcomes, the personalities involved were as important as the strategies chosen, and in assessing the movement, women organizers consistently interwove these two topics, insisting upon their inseparability. The energy needed to maintain impoverished shelters often was generated by close, caring relationships which sustained women through demeaning encounters with the police and daily demands from battered women in need of non-existent housing, jobs, and protection.

In feminist shelters, women created a new morality which was in sharp contrast to the ethos within competitive, male dominated organizations and the "heartless" bureaucracies around them. They developed their own organizational forms, celebratory events, music, and measures of success. As a reaction to isolation and as an affirmation of women, activists tried to form a sustaining sisterhood, a community with new cultural norms.

Feminist process, however, with its somewhat unspecified standard of conduct, could be problematic. Early groups, often politically and racially homogeneous and driven to accomplish a task, sometimes experienced or expressed few conflicts. Although differences tended to remain hidden for some time, when they emerged they often did so with great force and venom. Participants in the early movement, overworked and under severe strain, were ill prepared to deal with such problems. The close bonding among women which sustained the movement also made political and personal conflict extremely painful and hard to resolve. Power struggles, difficult in any organization, took trusting feminists by surprise and left them paralyzed or unwilling to resort to tactics that were politically abhorrent to them. Some dedicated women were driven out of the movement by "trashing"—vicious attacks on a woman's character and political motivations. In a few places, shelters or groups came precariously close to dissolving, and important work was sometimes left unfinished.

Despite difficult times, most women in the movement were sustained by their relationships with others, by the knowledge that their work was essential, and by the ways in which they worked. Many speak of personal transformation and growth. . . .

Individual growth also signified taking personal risks. Many women recount that friends avoided them when they joined the movement. Others rejected long time friends because they found them too "petty;" it is hard to work with battered women all day and then hear friends brutally criticize welfare recipients. Still other women left their marriages when husbands could not tolerate their wives' personal success or autonomy. Children sometimes resented mothers who were not always available for them. Some women lost much, but most insist that their self-respect has been a far greater gain.

For women in the movement, participating in something far larger than oneself was exhilarating. Depressing moments were overshadowed by a sense that one was helping to change the world. Each battered woman who moved from depression into anger and pride sustained that belief. Every phone call or scribbled note that said, "thanks for being there," or every woman who said, "you're the first person that I've ever told this story to, so please don't laugh at me," brought sustenance. Watching shelter residents strengthen one another and come back to join the movement reminded all that the world was different.

Being part of a larger national and international movement also energized activists. Initially, informal networks—women traveling from one city to another—conveyed information, strategies, and support. . . .

Personal contacts were but one way that women in the movement were linked nationally and internationally. The British battered women's movement, which began approximately four years before the U.S. movement, was known through Erin Pizzey's path-breaking *Scream Quietly or the Neighbors Will Hear* (1974). In the U.S., women found their work legitimated in the journal of the Feminist Alliance Against Rape (FAAR) and later in the first newsletter of the battered women's movement, the *National Communications Network (NCN)*. Even before a movement was publicly recognized, activists like Betsy Warrior and Lisa Leghorn wrote and distributed pioneering literature on battered women.[47] In 1976, the first edition of Warrior's invaluable directory of individuals and groups helping battered women, *Working on Wife Abuse,* was published. That same year, Del Martin's *Battered Wives* became a major source of information and validation for the movement. It legitimated the view, already put forward by local feminist shelters, that violence against women was caused by sexism. This analysis, no longer the "ravings" of a few individuals or groups, was the framework adopted by thousands.

Finally, women were sustained through their commitment to end male violence and female subordination. Helping battered women was, for many, part of a broader struggle for women's liberation. . . .

For women to have real alternatives to abusive relationships and for men to stop their violence, major social transformation would be necessary. The battered women's movement forged an analysis and a practice that would be an essential part of that struggle. The very existence of the movement announced that the world was different and that women together would not rest until changes were made.

NOTES

1. Diane Brown, "Out On My Own—Still Being Victimized," unpublished speech, Confronting Woman Abuse: A Working Conference for the Midwest, Chicago, 23–24 April 1979.
2. Mark A. Schulman, *A Survey of Spousal Violence Against Women in Kentucky,* U.S. Department of Justice, Law Enforcement Assistance Administration, Study No. 792701, July 1979, p. 1.
3. Marjory D. Fields, "Wife Beating: Government Intervention Policies and Practices," U.S. Commission on Civil Rights, *Battered Women: Issues of Public Policy,* a consultation, Washington, D.C., 30–31 January 1978, p. 235.
4. *Ibid.,* p. 249.
5. *Ibid.,* p. 257.
6. Candace Wayne, personal communication.
7. Telephone interview with Ruth Slaughter.
8. Women's Center-South, undated leaflet.
9. Suzanne Rini-McClintock, "Pittsburgh's Only Shelter For Women In Crisis May Soon Loose (sic) The Roof Over Its Head," *Pittsburgh New Sun,* 6 May 1976, p. 5.
10. Carol Ford, "Lifeline to Battered Women," *Sojourner,* September 1980.
11. *Ibid.*
12. *Ibid.*
13. Presentation of Marta Segovia-Ashley, read by Shelly Fernández, "Shelters: Short-Term Needs," U.S. Commission on Civil Rights, *Battered Women: Issues of Public Policy,* pp. 101–102.
14. Author's interview with Susan Kelly-Dreiss.
15. Curdina Hill, personal communication.
16. Author's interview with Nydia Diáz.
17. Anonymous interview.
18. Curdina Hill and Renae Scott, "Culture in the Kitchen," *Aegis,* November–December 1978, p. 39.
19. Joani Kamman, "Cost Factors in Providing Battered Women's Services in a Rural Community," NELCWIT, 23 January 1980, p. 2.
20. Shirley J. Kuhle, "Foreword" in Bobby Lacy, *Domestic Violence Services in Rural Communities,* Nebraska Task Force on Domestic Violence, undated, p. 3.
21. *Women's Advocates: The Story of a Shelter* (St. Paul: Women's Advocates, 1980), p. 3.
22. *Ibid.,* p. 4.
23. *Ibid.,* pp. 5–6.
24. Sharon Vaughan, personal communication.
25. *Ibid.*
26. *Women's Advocates: The Story of a Shelter,* p. 90.
27. *Ibid.,* p. 58.
28. *Ibid.,* p. 54.
29. Author's interview with Sharon Vaughan.
30. *Women's Advocates: The Story of a Shelter,* p. 75.
31. Author's interview with Sharon Vaughan.
32. See Betsy Warrior and Lisa Leghorn, *The Houseworker's Handbook,* a pamphlet about the social, political, and economic dimensions of women's role as houseworker.
33. Materials from the files of Transition House, undated.
34. *Ibid.*
35. Author's interview with Lisa Leghorn.
36. *Ibid.*
37. Carol Ford, "Lifeline to Battered Women," *Sojourner,* September 1980.

38. Author's interview with Lisa Leghorn.
39. Author's interview with Rachel Burger.
40. *Ibid.*
41. *Ibid.*
42. Author's interview with Sharon Vaughan.
43. Materials distributed at Battered Lives: A Conference Sponsored by the Abused Women's Coalition, 9 October 1976.
44. Chicago Abused Women's Coalition *Newsletter,* Vol, 1, no. 1, December 1976.
45. Author's interview with Sharon Vaughan.
46. Anonymous interview.
47. Author's interview with Lisa Leghorn.

Reflection

SUSAN SCHECHTER

As I browse through the pages of *Women and Male Violence* more than twenty years after its publication, my attention drifts to the books beside it on my desk, Michael Cunningham's *The Hours* and Virginia Woolf's *Mrs. Dalloway,* the current rage of my women's reading group and probably thousands of others. Although *Mrs. Dalloway,* and its retelling in *The Hours,* is the almost perfect read for my middle age, thirty years ago it was another of Woolf's books—and the setting in which I found it—that rocked my youth and laid down a path to *Women and Male Violence.*

In the early 1970s, during my very first class in the Chicago Women's Liberation Union School, Woolf's *A Room of One's Own* was a revelation about the limitations and creative possibilities in women's lives. But reading it was only one of many revelatory moments in courses on everything from literature to car repair to socialist feminist theory. It was in the Union that women began organizing previously unimaginable projects such as Jane, the underground abortion service in Chicago, and drafted hundreds of statements about reproductive freedom and women's health. Women affiliated with the Liberation Union went on to work within groups such as Women Employed, Chicago Women Against Rape, and, in my case, the Chicago Abused Women's Coalition. Without the Women's Liberation Union and the larger feminist movement surrounding it, *Women and Male Violence* would not exist.

In the late 1970s I gave my first speeches about violence against women, cutting and pasting from the only good source available, Del Martin's recently published *Battered Wives.* I worked with other feminists in the Abused Women's Coalition to organize the first shelter in Chicago. The group found excitement in almost everything: in working collectively, starting new organizations, laying bare previously hidden aspects of women's oppression, and helping women and their children to safety.

In deciding to write *Women and Male Violence,* I hoped to tell a story about feminist, grassroots organizing and about the hard work required to build organizations, change law and social policy, and at the same time sustain a social movement. I wanted to brag about and document the accomplishments but also describe the hard, complicated work almost invisible underneath our new buildings and laws. It felt urgent to preserve this untouted knowledge that I could find nowhere else. I also wanted to extend a feminist exploration of theories about violence against women and open up debates about strategies, tactics, and future political directions. Even in 1980, I feared that the larger feminist spirit that guided the effort might slip away. Through the book, I hoped to create a text, a living feminist reference point for the next generation. During the 1980s and even sometimes today, I still hear that I succeeded.

As I interviewed activists around the country and read innumerable documents, digging through meeting minutes and the narrative fragments of how women organized shelters and statewide and national organizations, I also heard disturbing claims about the origins of the work. I documented one of these claims in the original Introduction to *Women and Male Violence.* In 1981, the president of the National Association of Social Workers (an organization to which I belong) stated, "The battered woman is not new. Rather, it is society's awareness of this problem that is new." While Nancy Humphrey, the president of NASW, was not completely wrong, as I claimed at the time, she missed the point that became one of my reasons for writing *Women and Male Violence.* As I stated then,

> "Society" did not recognize battered women; feminists and grassroots activists did. Nowhere in her Introduction is this fact acknowledged, so, unwittingly her statement rewrites the history of the battered women's movement.

Because I was determined that this history not be lost, *Women and Male Violence* was finished quickly. Looking back, I realize that the book was written with very little movement history under its belt. It roughly covers the time period between 1975 and 1981, the first six heady years. The ensuing decades have introduced hundreds of new projects and taught many of us about our blind spots—for example, about our inability to respond to the needs of children and families living with poverty, multiple experiences of violence, and racism.

Someday soon I would love to hand over the files in my basement, filled with notes and minutes from the 1970s and '80s, to the next generation of activists and writers interested in the history of the battered women's movement. It deserves at least several more tellings. Personally it is a history filled with great satisfaction and sometimes heartache. As I work within the movement today, I am still amazed at what has been accomplished, surprised and disappointed by what we failed to foresee, and awed by the passion, pain, and renewal in the work of liberating women from tyranny and violence. Luckily for me, revelations continue. May they also continue for those who come next!

CHAPTER

15 The Battered Woman

LENORE E. WALKER

Introduction

While social scientists have long been concerned with the nature of violence among different societies, violence among family members has not attracted much attention, despite the fact that most people live in some kind of family structure. The family has been viewed traditionally as an oasis of calm in an otherwise violent world. In recent years, however, it has become increasingly apparent that the family, especially the nuclear family, is not at all the expected tranquil refuge. On the contrary, it is frequently a fertile ground for often lethal aggression.

Prior research on family violence has tended to be clinically oriented and to focus on the pathology of the individuals involved, primarily the intrapsychic conflicts of the man and the woman. The research I have been conducting since 1975 suggests this approach is inadequate for understanding the battered woman problem. Sociologists Straus, Steinmetz, and Gelles found that at least 28 percent of all family members experience violence in their marriages. When the incidence rate reaches this level, we are dealing not with a problem of individual psychology but with a serious social disorder. A combination of sociological and psychological variables better explains the battered woman syndrome.

The sociological variables have been well documented by others. Del Martin, in her book *Battered Wives,* presents detailed evidence on how a sexist society facilitates, if not actually encourages, the beating of women. Her research indicates, as does mine, that these women do not remain in the relationship because they basically like being beaten. They have difficulty leaving because of complex psychosocial reasons. Many stay because of economic, legal, and social dependence. Others are afraid to leave because they have no safe place to go. Police, courts, hospitals, and social service agencies do not offer them adequate protection. Psychologists tend to counsel them to keep the family together at any cost, which often turns out to be their mental health and sometimes their lives. Both the batterer and the battered woman fear they cannot survive alone, and so continue to maintain a bizarre symbiotic relationship from which they cannot extricate themselves.

In this chapter, a psychological rationale will be developed to explain why the battered woman becomes a victim in the first place and how the process of victimization is perpetuated to the point of psychological paralysis. This psychological rationale is in the social-learning theory called "learned helplessness."

Does a man's superior physical strength, and society's message that a woman belongs to a man like property, influence a woman's self-perception? Have women learned to believe that they are powerless against men as the learned helplessness theory suggests?

Through research on animals, and more recently with humans, psychologists are attempting to understand how people's perception of their control over events in their lives contributes to the way they think and feel about themselves and their ability to act. A brief examination of some principles of learning theory provides a framework for understanding how the battered woman thinks and feels about herself and her situation.

Response-Outcome

Most plants and animals have little voluntary control over what happens to them in their environment. Much of the time they merely react to events that happen. For example, if you place a plant on a windowsill, its leaves and stem will grow toward the light. The way in which it grows has nothing to do with whether or not the plant can change the direction from which the light comes; thus its movements do not change the relationship between the response and the outcome. Growing toward the light is not a voluntary response; the plant will grow that way regardless. Such behavior cannot be changed or modified. However, since human beings are not plants, we make many voluntary responses which can be changed or modified, depending upon the outcome. If a voluntary response makes a difference in what happens, or operates on the environment in a successful way, we will tend to repeat that voluntary response. This is the principle of reinforcement. If we expect that a response we make is going to produce a certain outcome, and our expectations are met when we make that response, we then feel that we have had control over that situation. To check whether or not we have actually had some control over a particular situation, we choose to make the same response the next time, and if that outcome happens again, we verify our ability to control it. We can then choose *not* to make the response and the outcome does *not* happen. Human beings thus can decide whether or not to make that voluntary response again, depending upon whether or not they want their expectations met. This gives us a certain amount of power or control over our lives. If, on the other hand, we expect certain things to occur when we make a certain response, and they do not, we will often look for explanations as to *why* such expectations did not take place. If we cannot find any logical explanations, after a time we assume we have no control over the outcome. In this way, we learn what kinds of things in our environment we can control and what kinds of things are beyond our control.

Loss of Voluntary Control

Laboratory experiments have shown that if an organism experiences situations which cannot be controlled, then the motivation to try to respond to such events when they are repeated will be impaired. Even if later on the organism is able to make appropriate responses which do control events, the organism will have trouble believing that the responses are under its control and that they really do work. Furthermore, the organism will have difficulty in learning how to repeat those responses. This results in an apparent disturbance in the organism's emotional and physical well-being. Both depression and anxiety seem to be the characteristics of such an organism's behavior.

Learned Helplessness

The area of research concerned with early-response reinforcement and subsequent passive behavior is called learned helplessness. Experimental psychologist Martin Seligman hypothesized that dogs subjected to noncontingent negative reinforcement could learn that their voluntary behavior had no effect on controlling what happened to them. If such an aversive stimulus was repeated, the dog's motivation to respond would be lessened.

Seligman and his researchers placed dogs in cages and administered electrical shocks at random and varied intervals. These dogs quickly learned that no matter what response they made, they could not control the shock. At first, the dogs attempted to escape through various voluntary movements. When nothing they did stopped the shocks, the dogs ceased any further voluntary activity and became compliant, passive, and submissive. When the researchers attempted to change this procedure and teach the dogs that they could escape by crossing to the other side of the cage, the dogs still would not respond. In fact, even when the door was left open and the dogs were shown the way out, they remained passive, refused to leave, and did not avoid the shock. It took repeated dragging of the dogs to the exit to teach them how to respond voluntarily again. The earlier in life that the dogs received such treatment, the longer it took to overcome the effects of this so-called learned helplessness. However, once they did learn that they could make the voluntary response, their helplessness disappeared.

Similar experiments have been performed on other species, including cats, fish, rodents, birds, and primates and humans, with the same kind of results. Some animals learned to be helpless at a faster rate and became more helpless across a greater number of situations. For some, the learning was discriminate and only occurred in one situation. For others, the sense of powerlessness generalized to all behavior. . . .

The learned helplessness theory has three basic components: information about what will happen; thinking or cognitive representation about what will happen (learning, expectation, belief, perception); and behavior toward what does happen. It is the second or cognitive representation component where the faulty expectation that response and outcome are independent occurs. This is the point at which cognitive, motivational, and emotional disturbances originate. It is important to realize that the expectation may or may not be accurate. Thus, if the person does have control over response-outcome variables but believes she/he doesn't, the person responds with the learned helplessness phenomenon. If such a person believes that she/he does have control over a response-outcome contingency, even if she/he doesn't, the behavior is not affected. Therefore, the actual nature of controllability is not as important as the belief, expectation, or cognitive set. Some people will persevere longer than others in attempting to exert control; however, they will give up when they really believe the situation is hopeless. . . .

Once we believe we cannot control what happens to us, it is difficult to believe we can ever influence it, even if later we experience a favorable outcome. This concept is important for understanding why battered women do not attempt to free themselves from a battering relationship. Once the women are operating from a belief of helplessness, the perception becomes reality and they become passive, submissive, "helpless." They allow things that appear to them to be out of their control actually to get out of their control. When one listens to descriptions of battering incidents from battered women, it often seems as if these women were not actually as helpless as they perceived themselves to be. However, their behavior was determined by their negative cognitive set, or their perceptions of what they could or could not do, not by what actually existed. . . .

In addition to the way they perceive or think about what happens, people also differ in how they explain normal occurrences. Different people have different predispositions to believing in the causations of events. For example, some people believe that most of the events that occur in their life are caused by factors outside themselves. We call these people "externalizers." Deeply religious people fall into this category, as do people who believe in strictly following rigid rules and regulations. People who believe that they have a lot of influence over what happens in their life are called "internalizers." It has been found that externalizers tend to become victims of learned helplessness more easily than internalizers. Research remains to be done to discover whether battered women can be classified as externalizers. . . .

Feelings of helplessness among humans tend to spread from one specific aversive situation to another. A battered woman therefore does not have to learn that she cannot escape one man's battering, but rather that she cannot escape men's overall coercion.

Helplessness also has a debilitating effect on human problem solving. Experiments with college students show that while the damage is not irreversible, it does alter one's motivation to initiate problem-solving actions. Thus, learning ability is hampered and the repertoire of responses from which people can choose is narrowed. In this way, battered women become blind to their options. People who feel helpless really believe that they have no influence over the success or failure of events that concern them. Women who have learned to expect battering as a way of life have learned that they cannot influence its occurrence. . . .

The time sequence experienced by battering victims seems to be parallel to the time sequence experienced by victims of a major traumatic disaster. It has been shown that many people who experience a disaster immediately volunteer their time and energy in order to attempt to combat their feelings of helplessness. Some become Red Cross helpers over a large area; others become volunteers in the immediate vicinity. The feeling of being able to do something generally helps the volunteer as much as it helps the victim. This phenomenon is also seen in self-help groups such as Alcoholics Anonymous and Reach for Recovery. The general reaction to major traumas such as hurricanes, earthquakes, airplane crashes, or catastrophic fires is a feeling of powerlessness. However, unless such trauma is repeated, these feelings will usually dissipate over time. On the other hand, if there are repeated traumas within a short period of time, then people become immune, passive, and convinced that they cannot do anything to help themselves. Witness the results in concentration camps. A chronic feeling of powerlessness takes over which does not dissipate. The response of victims of repeated disasters is similar to battered women's perception of powerlessness. It is also probable that helplessness is learned on a relative continuum. There may be different levels of learned helplessness that a woman learns from an interaction of traditional female-role standards and individual personality development. The male-female dyadic relationship may be a specific area affected by this interactive developmental process. Battered women seem to be most afflicted with feelings of helplessness in their relationships with men. Women with responsible jobs and careers resort to traditional female-role stereotyped behavior with their men, even though such behavior is not present in other areas of their lives.

Thus, in applying the learned helplessness concept to battered women, the process of how the battered woman becomes victimized grows clearer. Repeated batterings, like electrical shocks, diminish the woman's motivation to respond. She becomes passive. Secondly, her cognitive ability to perceive success is changed. She does not believe her response will result in a favorable outcome, whether or not it might. Next, having generalized her helplessness, the battered woman does not believe anything she does will alter any outcome, not just the specific situation that has occurred. She says, "No matter what I do, I have no influence." She cannot think of alternatives. She says, "I am incapable and too stupid to learn how to change things." Finally, her sense of emotional well-being becomes precarious. She is more prone to depression and anxiety.

Are battered women "clinically" depressed? Many of the new cognitive theories in psychology define clinical depression as a state in which a person holds an exaggerated belief that whatever he or she does, it will not be good enough. Such people also believe that their inadequacies preclude them from controlling their lives effectively. A person who believes that she is helpless to control a situation also may believe that she is not capable enough to do so. The small number of women I have interviewed do not provide the basis for any scientific conclusions about depression; however, it does appear that much of their behavior is designed to ward off depression. For example, many of them attempted to exert a degree of control over their batterings. Although they accepted the batterings as inevitable, they tried to control the time and place. This small measure of control seemed to be an effort not to feel totally helpless. For example, when a woman begins to nag at a man after she knows he has had a hard day at work, she can justify her belief that she really deserved the battering she anticipated all along because she started it. Although she appears to be masochistically setting up her own victimization, such behavior may well be a desperate attempt to exercise some control over her life.

Another point we observed relative to depression concerned anxiety levels of battered women. When these women discussed living under the threat and fear of battering, there was less anxiety than we expected. In fact, in many cases it seemed that living with the batterer produced less anxiety than living apart from him. Why? She often feels that she has the hope of some control if she is with him. Another explanation is that a fear response motivates a search for alternate ways of responding that will avoid or control the threat. Anxiety is, in essence, a call to danger. Physiologically the autonomic nervous system sends out hormones that are designed to cope with the immediate stress. Once this stress is under control, anxiety returns to a normal level. Or higher levels of hormones are constantly emitted in order to live under such pervasive stress. This reaction will also occur when certain threats are considered uncontrollable. What also happens in this situation is that anxiety does not return to a normal level; rather, it decreases and depression takes over.

How Battered Women Become Victimized

There seems to be little doubt that feelings of powerlessness by both men and women contribute to the cause and maintenance of violent behavior. However, although many men do indeed feel powerless in relation to their control over their lives, it is my contention that the very fact of being a woman, more specifically a married woman, automatically creates a situation of powerlessness. This is one of the detrimental effects of sex-role stereotyping.

Women are systematically taught that their personal worth, survival, and autonomy do not depend on effective and creative responses to life situations, but rather on their physical beauty and appeal to men. They learn that they have no direct control over the circumstances of their lives. Early in their lives, little girls learn from their parents and society that they are to be more passive than boys. Having systematically trained to be second best, women begin marriage with a psychological disadvantage. Marriage in our patriarchal society does not offer equal power to men and women. The notion that marriage laws protect women is questionable when statistics reveal the mental health problems and criminal behavior married women suffer from. On the contrary, the law seems to perpetuate the historical notion of male supremacy. In most states a husband cannot be found guilty of raping his wife. The husband still has the legal right to decide where the family will live, restricting the woman's freedom of movement. Power in marriage also is related to economic and social status. Since men more often than women hold higher-paying jobs with more status, their occupational prestige gives them decision-making powers they can use to engage in physical and psychological one-up*man*ship. Finally, most men are also superior in physical strength, another source of masculine power and confidence.

Cultural conditions, marriage laws, economic realities, physical inferiority—all these teach women that they have no direct control over the circumstances of their lives. Although they are not subjected to electrical shocks as the dogs in the experiments were, they are subjected to both parental and institutional conditioning that restricts their alternatives and shelters them from the consequences of any disapproved alternatives. Perhaps battered women, like the dogs who learn that their behavior is unrelated to their subsequent welfare, have lost their ability to respond effectively.

Consequences of Learned Helplessness

One result of learned helplessness can be depression, as discussed previously. Another result seems to be a change in the battered woman's perception of the consequences of violence. Living constantly with fear seems to produce an imperviousness to the seriousness of violence and death.

There is an unusually high incidence of guns, knives, and other weaponry reported in the battering attacks. I am constantly amazed that more people are not accidentally killed during these incidents. The women interviewed declared that they did not fear death, although they also did not really believe they would die, either. Those women interviewed who murdered their husbands all stated they had no idea they had killed them until the police informed them. One woman fought furiously with police when they took her to the homicide precinct for booking. She felt her husband would recover from the severe bullet wounds that had been inflicted. Several men reported surprise that their rage had inflicted any pain or injuries to the women. Both the men and the women involved in this violence repeatedly reassured other people that they wouldn't really hurt each other. As we begin to see more battered women, we also realize the high probability that as the violence escalates, they will eventually be killed by or kill their men.

Stopping Learned Helplessness

If battering behavior is maintained by perceptions of helplessness, can this syndrome be stopped? Turning back to the animal studies, we see that the dogs could only be taught to overcome their passivity by being dragged repeatedly out of the punishing situation and shown how to avoid the shock. Just as the dogs have helped us understand why battered women do not leave their violent situations voluntarily, perhaps they can also suggest ways the women can reverse being battered. A first step would seem to be to persuade the battered woman to leave the battering relationship or persuade the batterer to leave. This "dragging" may require help from outside, such as the dogs received from the researchers. The safe houses for battered women are very effective here. Secondly, battered women need to be taught to change their failure expectancy to reverse a negative cognitive set. They need to understand what success is, to raise their motivation and aspiration levels, to be able to initiate new and more effective responses, so they can learn to control their own lives. Self-esteem and feelings of competence are extremely important in protecting against feelings of helplessness and depression. Women must be able to believe that their behavior will affect what happens to them. Counseling or psychotherapy can teach women to control their own lives and to be able to erase that kind of victim potential.

Battering behavior must cease. We cannot afford the toll it takes in our society. A thorough study of some of the particulars occurring in battering relationships may lead us to effective methods to reverse this tragic process. By examining some of the techniques the batterers use, how they victimize women and cause further psychological destruction, I hope to improve the understanding of the nature of battering.

Reflection

LENORE E. WALKER

When I first began my study of the psychological impact of domestic violence on the battered woman, it was the mid 1970s and the feminist movement had a negative reaction to anything that came with a clinical psychology label. I was fascinated with the fact that the hundreds of women I interviewed had such great difficulty in believing in their own ability to escape from the battering relationship, yet they had incredible coping skills to stay alive and minimize the harm they and their families experienced. The standard clinical psychology diagnoses or theories, including the ever-popular "masochism" or even "low self-esteem," could not account for the complexity of battered women's lives, nor could it explain the impact of the dual nature of the batterer who was sometimes very loving and other times extraordinarily mean and abusive. A social psychology theory that also accounted for personal behavior adding motivational factors seemed to be a more comprehensive approach.

I chose Seligman's theory of learned helplessness to study for several reasons: first, it is an economical explanation of the loss of escape skills with simultaneous development of extraordinary coping strategies to stay alive. After all, Seligman and his colleagues' dogs found the safest place in the cage to stay where they would experience the least pain from shock that was administered even if they couldn't stop it or leave the cage. Second, the feminist theory that accounted for gender differences in the experience of motivation once the link between cause and effect was broken was neatly accounted for in the social-learning theory that looked at attribution from personal efficacy and from luck or situational factors. Women's socialization was thought to interfere with women's ability to believe in their own competence in certain areas. Third, the theory accounted for the impact of the duality of the batterer's behavior. His Dr. Jeckyll–Mr. Hyde performance was analogous to the random and variable aversive stimulation in the animal and college student laboratory experiments. The women could learn the contingencies, the batterer's behavior would no longer be experienced as random and variable, and the psychological impact of the abuse would be lessened. Fourth, the theory accounted for reversibility. The dogs had to be shown over and over again how to escape, but they could relearn their original skills. So too for battered women. With participation in groups or individual therapy, battered women could relearn how to protect themselves and their children, even if it meant leaving the relationship.

I was delighted to find that the research supported the theoretical formulations applying learned helplessness theories to the experience of battered women. Here was a non-pathologizing theoretical explanation with good scientific grounding that could explain why battered women behaved in ways that puzzled friends, family, and service providers. Imagine my surprise when I found the theory misunderstood because of its name—learned helplessness—which was said to imply that the women were helpless and not able to do any of the courageous strategies that were so evident in the research. I was frustrated with the inability to explain the theory adequately to get beyond a decidedly erroneous image that the title gives it. The theory was highly successful in persuading juries to understand how battered women killed their abusive partners in self-defense and it was helpful in designing intervention strategies to help them become empowered and find safety. But, even psychology colleagues misunderstood its scientific underpinnings because of the title. Although Seligman himself has changed the title to "learned optimism," emphasizing the motivational piece that makes it more positive psychology, the misunderstanding and misapplication of the theoretical premises still remain rampant in the battered women's community. Nevertheless, twenty-five years later, I still believe that the scientific understanding of the psychological impact on battered women is well accounted for by this theory and my only regret is that I was unable to explain it better so it would have had wider acceptance to help battered women find safety and heal from their experiences.

CHAPTER

16 When Battered Women Kill

ANGELA BROWNE

A woman calls the police emergency number begging for help. She says she just shot her husband. Officers arriving at the scene note that she is bruised and there is evidence of an altercation. While ambulance attendants work on the dying man, police locate the weapon and test the woman's hands for traces of gunpowder. Then they wrap her hands in plastic and lead her to a squad car, wending their way past neighbors gathered on the sidewalk. The woman is taken to jail, where she is interrogated. She attempts to reply to the officers' questions, although her responses are disoriented and confused and she will later remember little of what she said. At some point she is informed that her husband is dead. She is asked to strip to the waist, so pictures can be taken of her injuries, and is booked on suspicion of murder. Later, testimony reveals that she had been beaten and sexually assaulted by her mate on numerous occasions, and that he threatened to kill her shortly before the shooting took place. The woman has no prior criminal record; she has a family, and has held a steady job.

Neighbors are shocked by the killing; such things don't happen in their part of town. Relatives are grieved and defensive. They struggle with what to say when questioned; what to say in court, when the private lives of their family become front-page news. The man's family, who knew the most about his abusiveness, are in the worst position: Will they aid in this woman's defense, when she has just killed their son and brother? Could they have prevented it? Was his drinking to blame? Or was it her fault, for staying with him? They knew he sometimes hit her, but no one ever dreamed she would kill him.

What leads a woman who has occupied the role of victim, and who usually has no history of violent or illegal behavior, to use deadly force against her mate? What factors—in her perceptions, in the relationship, and in our society—precipitate the woman's committing a homicide? Why would a woman remain with a man who assaults her or threatens to take her life? And why are men the primary perpetrators of severe violence against their partners? What evokes this response in some men? . . .

Homicide Between Partners

Nearly one-fourth of the nation's homicide victims in 1984 were related to their assailants; 4,408 murders in that one year were committed by family members.[1] The rate of homicide among families in the United States is quite high when compared to that of many other countries; it is higher, for instance, than the rate for *all* homicides in countries such as England, Denmark, and Germany. Of homicides occurring within the family, by far the largest category is that of a spouse killing a spouse. Nearly half (48 percent) of intrafamilial homicides in 1984, or the deaths of over 2,000 people, were between partners. Of these, the majority of the victims were women: Two-thirds (1,310) were wives killed by husbands, and one-third (806) were husbands killed by wives.

Women don't usually kill other people; they perpetrate less than 15 percent of the homicides in the United States.[2] When women do kill, it is often in their own defense. A report by a government commission on violence estimated that homicides committed by women were seven times as likely to be in self-defense as homicides committed by men.[3] In his study of criminal homicide, Wolfgang (1967) noted that 60 percent of the husbands who were killed by their wives "precipitated" their own deaths (i.e., were the first to use physical force, strike blows, or threaten with a weapon), whereas victim precipitation was involved in only 9 percent (5 of 53) of the deaths of wives. A review of police records on spousal homicides in Canada also found that almost all of the wives who had killed their mates had previously been beaten by them.[4] In such cases, it's the abusive mate who becomes the final victim. . . .

In the majority of homicide cases between partners, there were many "cries for help" prior to the lethal incident. A review of homicide records in Detroit and Kansas City revealed that, in 85 percent to 90 percent of the cases, police had been called to the home at least once during the two years before the incident, and in half (54 percent) of the cases, they had been called five or more times.[5] . . . Given their lesser physical strength and a history of physical jeopardy at the hands of the man, when abused women do strike back they typically use a weapon or an object as an equalizer.[6] However, Wolfgang (1958) found that beating, not the use of a weapon, was the usual method when a man killed a woman (p. 162). Women employed fewer acts of violence during the homicide incident as well; men were likely to employ five or more acts of severe violence in the killing of their partners.

Women charged in the death of a mate have the least extensive criminal records of any female offenders. However, they often face harsher penalties than men who kill their mates. FBI statistics indicate that fewer men are charged with first- or second-degree murder for killing a woman they have known than are women who kill a man they have known. And women convicted of these murders are frequently sentenced to longer prison terms than are men.[7]. . .

Each of the women in the present study had a documented history of physical abuse by the man she slayed. In many cases, the files contained police photographs of the woman's injuries at the time of her arrest and, in some instances, the woman was transported to a hospital for X-rays or treatment before being taken to jail. All of these women reported that the abuser had threatened them, and almost all had attempted to escape and had sought outside intervention against the violence. Yet of the 36 women whose husbands died, all but nine were charged with first-degree murder. None was charged with manslaughter. Their stories are unusual and little-known. But given the incidence of homicide between partners and the frequency with which a history of abuse is a factor, they cannot be called unique. Knowing the dynamics behind that final brief incident demonstrates how physical assault can gradually take over a relationship, and how women who find themselves trapped in a potentially deadly situation can become—suddenly—widows by their own hand.

Studying Women Who Kill

Results of the homicide study are based on interviews with 42 women who were charged with a crime in the death or serious injury of their mates.[8] The women came from 15 states; seven of them were incarcerated awaiting trial at the time of the interview. Initial contact was made with the women when their attorneys requested an evaluation based on evidence that the woman had been physically abused by her partner prior to the homicide incident. Thirty-three of the women were charged with murder, three with conspiracy to commit murder, and six with attempted murder. (In reporting the findings, no distinction is made between cases involving attempted murder and the homicide cases, since the same dynamics applied to both types of events.) Of the women who went to trial after the interview, twenty (about half) received jail terms, 12 received probation or a suspended sentence, and nine were acquitted. In one case, the District Attorney's office determined that the killing was justified on the grounds of self-defense and dropped the charges. Jail sentences generally ranged from six months to 25 years; one woman was sentenced to 50 years.

The purpose of the study was to understand more about the relationships of abused women who kill their husbands, and to identify the dynamics that lead up to the commission of a homicide. Thus, the inquiry focused on the women's actions—e.g., the killing of a mate—in the context of their position as victims, and investigated the impact that violence and threat from a romantic partner, as well as other situational and societal variables, had on their perception of danger and of alternatives. In an effort to understand more about battered women who kill, and to identify the factors that characterize their relationships with their abusers, reports from women in the homicide group were later compared to those of 205 women who had been in abusive relationships but did not take lethal action against their partners.[9]

Women in the comparison group came from a six-state region, and from both urban and rural areas. They were recruited through public-service announcements, newspaper ads, and posted notices, as well as through referrals from physicians, emergency-room personnel, and battered-women's shelters. The women in the comparison group were self-identified and self-referred (i.e., called up and said they had been battered), and were considered eligible to participate in the study if they reported being physically abused at least twice by a man with whom they had had an ongoing intimate relationship or to whom they had been married.[10] Since nearly all the women in the homicide group were living with their mates at the time of the lethal incident or were only recently out of the relationship, women in the comparison group were limited to those either still with the abusive partner or out of the relationship less than one year. . . .

The Killing of the Abuser

Molly's story illustrates a typical scenario in the escalation toward a lethal incident for women in the homicide group. By the end of their relationships, these women perceived their partners' behavior as totally out of control: In most cases, the men were intoxicated or using drugs nearly every day, their violence was more frequent and the severity of the violence more extreme, and their awareness of or contrition for their actions seemed almost non-existent. Not only had their aggression toward and threats to kill their mates escalated, it frequently generalized to others as well, placing other intimates, particularly children, in danger. Women who had observed the patterns of these men's violence for years now judged the abusers as beyond the point where they would be able to stop short of murder. It seemed only a matter of time before someone would be seriously hurt or killed. Considering their history as the men's primary target, women in the homicide group expected that they were the ones most likely to die.

Most of the women in the homicide group reached a point at which they lost all hope of improvement or relief. For some women, like Karen Simon or Irene Miller, this was when they were forced to return to the man after the last failed escape attempt. For others, like Molly Johnson, hope was lost with the onset of renewed violence after a period of surcease that suggested the possibility of freedom.

Another component of the buildup toward a lethal incident was the focus of dying. For women like Molly, it was an absolute conviction that death was inevitable within a certain timeframe; usually, this conviction was based on specific threats by the men. Others, like Karen Simon, began to look toward death as the only solution to the escalation of violence and their inability to escape the abuser, and either considered taking their own lives or assumed that their partner would soon do it for them. In every case, women in the homicide group believed that they (or a child) would be the victim if someone were to die. Recalling the man's dominance and their perception of his power as an aggressor, none of the women thought the abuser would be the final victim.

Typically, the killing of the abuser was unplanned and occurred in the midst of an attack against the woman, during the warning phase when it became apparent that an attack was about to begin, or during an escape attempt by the woman. In some cases, the woman waited until the man was sleeping or otherwise inattentive after an assault, sure that the attack would resume in a relatively short while. These delayed homicides were often related to an explicit threat by the abuser to "get" the woman or a child within a specific time; women killed the abuser to avert the threatened outcome.

Protection of a Child

Molly's case is an example of a woman killing to protect the life of a child. Although Molly was carrying a gun during much of the final incident, she didn't shoot at Jim—even when he was firing at her—until after she saw his hands around Kevin's neck and had warned him twice to move away. Similarly, Bella Harris endured severe abuse from her husband Isaac for 20 years, and killed him only when he told her he was going to shoot their oldest daughter when she came home. Bella remembered the time she had gone to the movies and Isaac threatened the same thing; he would have killed Bella that night, if someone hadn't intervened. When Isaac fell asleep, Bella and her younger daughter shot him and then set the house on fire. (This was the only completed homicide in which arson was involved, although, in this case, arson was not the cause of death.)

Wanda Bowles was also attempting to protect a child. After a particularly severe beating of her daughter Christie, Wanda could not shake the image of Randy's fist going toward Christie's face, the way his features were contorted with rage, his intention to do harm. Wanda's concentration narrowed to one thing: He must not ever hurt Christie again. Finally, she called her brother and asked, "How much does it cost to put a contract out on someone?" She felt she had tried everything else: She had talked to Randy about his drinking, but it did no good; talked to him about getting help, but he only laughed at her; tried to get away from him, but he always found them and threatened to kill them both. By the next day, Wanda had abandoned her idea and was getting information on safe houses, but that night her brother killed Randy, with the help of another man. (Wanda was unusual in even considering this plan of action. Only three women in the homicide group were charged with conspiracy to commit murder.)

Homicides during an Assaultive Incident

More typically, the abuser was killed during an assaultive incident in which the woman was the victim.

> Maggie and Duke Ortega had just returned home from a party at which Duke had been drinking heavily. Maggie knew Duke was in a bad mood, but they hadn't been arguing. She went into the bedroom to change clothes and when she came out, Duke was there. Without warning, he hit her in the head with his fist. Her neck snapped back against the door jamb and her glasses flew off (she has very poor vision). Maggie tried to run to the kitchen door, but Duke knocked her into a chair by the stove and began hitting her. He had that look on his face again; "like another person, not like Duke; not like anyone who recognized me." Maggie kept thinking that if she could just get outside it would be alright. It was a weekend and people were home in the apartments around them. Someone would protect her.
>
> Duke was towering over Maggie, choking her, digging in his thumbs. She reached over and pulled out a drawer by the sink to swing at him, hoping to divert his attention so she could run. But the drawer was heavy, full of utensils, and it fell to the

floor, scattering the contents across the room and under the chair where Maggie was sitting. Duke was on top of her now, pounding and screaming. Maggie reached down and picked up the first thing she touched and struck him with it. Duke backed off and Maggie stood up. Then she saw the knife handle in his neck and realized what she'd done. She pulled the knife out, and tried to stop the bleeding. She helped him sit down on the floor, propped up against the cabinets, and ran next door to call the ambulance and the police. Then she ran back and got some ice to put on his neck, telling him everything was going to be alright. Duke started leaning toward the floor and she laid him down, holding him in her arms until the police arrived.

Later, Maggie said, "It happened so fast. I didn't know why I was getting hit. I didn't know what I hit him with. When the police came, they took me away: They wouldn't even let me stay with him, and he was still alive." The detectives questioned her and had her strip to the waist so that pictures could be taken of her injuries. A couple of hours later, they told her that Duke was dead. Maggie doesn't remember much after that.

Often, homicides occurring during battering incidents were committed with the abuser's weapon. Sometimes, the men dared the women to kill them; it is difficult to know whether this was out of their own suicidal tendencies, or whether they simply believed the women would never carry out such an act. In the case of Karen and Hal Simon, Hal's final behaviors almost appeared as though he wanted to die.

Hal was angry with Karen again, and told her to go get the gun. She brought it to him; she knew if she disobeyed, the assault would be worse. He was yelling at her about nagging him, saying, "I've heard this shit and heard this shit, and I've had it. I'm going to fix you up right now." He shoved her down into a chair by the couch, pushing the gun up under her chin, then took the butt of the gun and began hitting her in the abdomen. Karen could smell food burning in the kitchen and told him she needed to go and turn off the stove, hoping he would change moods while she was away. But Hal said, "You're not going anywhere." He began pressing the gun against her head, clicking the hammer, talking about killing her. Suddenly, Karen was just tired of being threatened this way and never knowing if she was going to live or die. So she said to Hal, "Are we going to continue doing this? Every time I turn around, you're threatening to kill me, making me get the gun, saying you're going to blow me away. Why don't we get it over with? Why don't you just go ahead now and shoot me?"

Hal stared at her and then retorted, "You have so goddam much guts. . . . You kill me." He threw the shotgun at her, and laid down in a curled position on the floor in front of the couch with his back toward her. Karen thinks she intended to go and put the gun away, and turn off the stove. The next thing she remembers, she was standing in the kitchen and realized that Hal was shot. She went back to check on him, and then ran next door to call for help. The neighbors returned to the house and stayed with her until the police arrived. The police description of Karen at the scene notes that she was terrified and disoriented, and that they found it "very unusual to see somebody who wants to go back and just hold the deceased."

When Assault Was Imminent

Other homicides occurred during the warning phase, when it appeared that an assault was imminent. Sharon Bikson's killing of her husband Roy is one such case.

> Although Sharon tried to hide from him, Roy found her latest apartment and broke in several times. Sharon would come home at night and find the lock just hanging out of the door and be too afraid to go in. Roy attacked and severely injured her at work, and kidnapped and threatened her infant son. He spent much of his time threatening Sharon, and she never got over the fear that he would jump out at her from somewhere and finally kill her. She was just trying to get through their custody hearing, so that she and the children could go away. On one occasion, Roy came by her apartment and kicked in the door, but he left when Sharon ran toward the phone. The gun she purchased was stolen; Sharon wondered if Roy took it, since he was the one breaking in. She bought another handgun and hid it behind a cupboard. The fear and the tension were constant.
>
> One afternoon, Roy called Sharon just to let her know he'd found her new phone number. He was verbally abusive, threatening and calling her names until Sharon finally hung up. When the phone rang again, she didn't answer. She considered calling the police, but knew they wouldn't come out just for a phone call. They usually didn't come at all until after something had happened. Sharon tried to brace the door, just in case. It wouldn't lock properly, since the last time Roy had broken in, but she placed a chair under the door handle and wedged another chair between that and the wall. A few minutes later, she heard Roy outside, cursing and shouting. Sharon's children were with her, playing in the bedroom, and she thought he could probably hear their voices. She was afraid of what he would do to her for hanging up, and worried that he might take one of the children.
>
> Roy started to force the door open. Sharon was attempting to drag a dresser in from the other room when the doorknob came off and the chair fell over. Roy pushed his way into the room, shouting, "Get the gun, you bitch, 'cause I'm going to kill you and the bastard." (She thinks he meant the baby.)
>
> Sharon was so scared she couldn't think. She ran to the kitchen and got the handgun, struggling with the zipper on the case, afraid if Roy got to her and got his hands on the gun, he would kill her for sure. Roy was coming through the living room and Sharon met him there, pleading, "Don't come up on me, Roy. Don't come up on me now." He saw the gun in her hand, but still came toward her—arms out, yelling, "Shoot me. Shoot me, bitch!" Sharon fired once. Roy still moved toward her. She shot again. He gasped, and Sharon could see the stain on his chest. She warned him, "Please, don't come up on me," and he replied, "I won't. I won't."

Roy walked out of the apartment and told a neighbor he'd been shot and to call an ambulance. Then he came back in and sat down in the chair Sharon had used to brace the door. Sharon put the gun up then, and called an ambulance too. Roy was groaning, struggling to get a breath. Sharon stayed at a distance, watching him. She wanted to believe he was going to be alright, but she saw his last breath and knew. Then she heard the police loudspeaker, telling her to come out with her hands up, and was terrified again, thinking they would shoot her as she walked out the door. She raised her arms up over her head and stepped past Roy's body into the hall.

Weapons of Homicide

Guns were used in 81 percent of the homicide or attempted murder cases; knives were used in 7 percent; autos were involved in 7 percent (or 3 cases), and other methods were used in the remaining 5 percent of cases. In many of the homicides involving firearms, the men were killed with the same guns they had used earlier against the women: Even when several guns were available, the weapons they had been threatened with were the ones the women reached for in their moment of panic.

During a last desperate escape attempt, Irene Miller attempted to hold off Mark until help could arrive by threatening him with a .22. This was the gun that Mark had threatened to kill *her* with when he thought she was having an affair. All Irene knew about this gun was that Mark said it was old and not very powerful.

Janet VanHorn shot Rick with the .357 Magnum he had formerly made her hold to his head; she had hidden all the guns together, convinced he was planning to shoot her, and when she heard him coming up the stairs after her, this was the gun she picked up. Similarly, Bella Harris shot Isaac with the rifle he kept by the bed and had threatened to use on her—the one she sometimes woke up to find him pointing at her in the morning.

Women's Reactions to the Deaths of Their Mates

For some women in the homicide group, their fear of their partners—and their perceptions of the abusers as much stronger than they were and able to retaliate against them—dominated their immediate reactions after the killing. A few women were unable to realize that they were safe, even after their abusers were dead, and took further protective measures against the retaliation they expected to follow an aggressive attack. One woman locked her husband's body in the closet after she shot him: As long as she could see him, she was afraid he was going to reach out and grab her. Another hid outside in the shrubbery until the police arrived, and kept warning them as they entered the house to be careful; her husband was angry and might attack them. Even after Wanda Bowles was told by her brother that Randy was dead, she stayed up all night, watching for his return; expecting that he would be beaten up and angry, and that she and her daughter would be in danger. It was only the next afternoon, when the police came and showed her pictures of Randy's body lying in a field, that Wanda finally realized Randy was gone and broke down completely.

Most women reacted to the wounding or killing of their mates with sorrow and horror. Almost all of them called an ambulance and the police for assistance, and some attempted to give medical aid until other help arrived. Reports by officers at the scene frequently noted the women's attempts to reassure and comfort the men, and their requests to be allowed to remain with them, or to go back and spend time with their bodies, before they were transported to jail.

At the time of the homicide evaluations, their grief was still intense. In talking about the death of Hal Simon, Karen Simon began to cry, exclaiming, "I didn't want him dead! I thought it would be me. I didn't want him to have to die!" Janet VanHorn, disoriented and hospitalized, spent the first week after Rick's death asking for him and begging someone to bring him to her. Her attorney's first task was to try and convince Janet that Rick was dead. Susan Jefferson, although she had left Don several times and was separating from him at the time of the incident, still seemed bewildered by the loss six months later, saying, "Now I'm in this strange world where it's so still and I'm all alone. Now it will never be okay." Even Sharon Bikson, after all of Roy's harassment and violence and her struggles to escape him, later said, "You know, I never stopped loving him. I was willing to go through hell to get away from him, but I never stopped loving him." The anguish of many of the women over the deaths of their abusers was captured in a statement by one of them, who told me, "He had gotten so wild, and so reckless. I was afraid he was going to die somehow. But why by my hand? Why did it have to be by *my* hand?"

Bella Harris gave one of the most complete descriptions of the aftermath of a homicide, in recounting the sensations and behaviors that followed the killing of her husband Isaac.

> After Bella and her daughter set fire to the house, they walked down the hill to the community hospital and told them that Bella was ill; she was so cold and thirsty, and she felt like she couldn't breathe. Bella remembers a nurse saying, "Mrs. Harris, I just heard on the radio that your house is on fire." Bella thinks she said, "How could that happen?" She wondered how the fire could have started. It was like she was in a daze; she didn't really think she did it. Then someone told her that Isaac had been in the house, and that he was dead. She thinks she cried then, but all she really remembers is how strange she felt: All these people talking to her, the police there; she could see them all talking, but she couldn't hear anything. She doesn't think she answered at all. She says, "It was like I was a long way from home, and trying to find my way back."
>
> Bella remembers that she could not get herself together. She spent too much money on the funeral, and although people tried to talk to her about it, it just didn't seem to matter. She was charged with first degree murder and two counts of arson, and she and her daughter were jailed pending trial, but that hardly seemed real either. She kept trying to understand who had set the fire, who had killed Isaac, why Isaac was dead. Finally, one night, it all came back to her. Bella says, "I could just *see* it, then—see the fire, see shooting him, see myself walking away." It was like a huge weight came down on her head. Bella sat down and tried to understand it, but the pressure on her head was too great. So she wrapped her sweater up into a ball and laid

down on it, pressing her head against its firmness until she went to sleep. In jail, Bella says, that's what you do when things hurt.

There is much we do not know about these incidents. In a phenomenon as unknown—and as complex—as the occurrence of homicide between partners, the context of the situation, as well as the myriad personal and relational dynamics leading up to the incident itself, are vital in understanding the event; yet these nuances cannot be captured by relying solely on a questionnaire or structured interview format. In the current study, women were asked to describe the homicide and the factors leading up to it in their own words, and therefore much of the data on the homicides is qualitative in nature. Yet patterns or similarities can be derived from these accounts. Such factors as a final loss of hope, or the men's seeming to dare the women to kill them during the final incidents, were frequently reported. A darkening of their surroundings, or an effect of tunnel vision, was also reported by several of the women as occurring just prior to the lethal incident. For example, Wanda Bowles told of feeling as though she had "blinders" on, after Randy's final battering of Christie. Although it was only afternoon, she went around the house turning on all the lights, in an effort to dispel the darkness around her. Observations such as this are not easily reducible to categories or lists, yet such findings suggest new dimensions for future study.

Comparison of the Women's Reports with Other Studies of Homicide

Although in the current study we have only the women's reports of the abusers' behavior and the circumstances preceding the homicide event, these findings are supported by other, more localized, studies on homicide. For example, in a study of men and women in Florida who were charged with killing a spouse, Bernard, Vera, Vera, and Newman note that men who had killed their wives tended to be less educated than the female defendants, and were more likely to have a previous arrest record as well as a history of alcohol abuse. Women defendants were more likely to have a history of suicide attempts.[11]

Like women in the homicide group, women in the Bernard et al. study reported the primary problem in their relationships as verbal and physical violence by their mates, as well as substance abuse by their spouses: 73 percent reported having been battered by their partners; 73 percent also reported alcohol abuse by their husbands. Forty-six percent of the women reported a history of separation from the spouse victims, although only 9 percent of the women were living separately from their partners at the time the homicide occurred.

In contrast, of men who had killed their partners, 61 percent reported a major problem in their relationships as their suspicion of infidelities on the part of their wives, and 52 percent reported "desertion" by their wives. Fifty-seven percent of the men were in fact living separately from their wives at the time they killed them; further evidence that separation from a partner does not necessarily end the risk of violence, and may increase the risk of lethal violence in some cases. Fifty-seven percent of the men also reported that they had a problem with alcohol abuse.

Factors Precipitating Spousal Homicide

The Barnard study, in looking at both male and female perpetrators of homicide, found different factors to be operational in the killing of wives by husbands and husbands by wives. For men, the precipitating event was usually some form of perceived rejection by the partner. The most frequent type of male homicide was what Barnard et al. call "sex-role threat homicide." They note that "a walkout, a demand, a threat of separation were taken by the men to represent intolerable desertion, rejection, and abandonment."[12] In killing the women, men in this group believed they were reacting to a previous offense against them (e.g., leaving) by their wives. Barnard et al. note that "the theme most often expressed by [the men] as the precipitating event for the homicide was their inability to accept what they perceived to be a rejection of them or of their role of dominance over their eventual victims." Barnard and his colleagues see the men's "unspoken sense of dependency" on their wives as the key to this type of homicide; as well as the sex role stereotypes that encourage men to believe they have the right to control their wives' whereabouts and activities, and that lead them to express the pain of separation or rejection in aggressive, rather than more sensitive, ways.

In contrast, for females, the triggering event to the killing of their mates was usually a verbal or physical attack or threat by the partner. Following Marvin Wolfgang's earlier work, Barnard et al. term these "victim-precipitated homicides." They note that over 70 percent of the women charged with the deaths of their husbands had previously been beaten by them, and cite the physical abuse of wives as the major factor in the precipitation of lethal actions by wives against husbands.

As mentioned earlier, this conclusion is well-supported by more general studies of homicide. Wolfgang, in his foundational study of homicides in Philadelphia, reported that over 25 percent of the male victims of a partner's violence "provoked" their own deaths by being the first to use physical force, strike blows, or threaten with a weapon; compared to only 5 percent of the wife victims.[13] (This was based on "provocation recognized by the courts," and would not necessarily reflect the number of wives who had actually experienced physical abuse or threat from their spouse victims.) William Willbanks, in a recent study of male and female homicide offenders in Dade County, Florida, also found cases involving women perpetrators much more likely to have circumstances that made their homicides justifiable in self-defense.[14] Similarly, Peter Chimbos, in a study of spousal homicides in Canada, noted that the lethal act was usually the end point in an ongoing series of conflicts or threats.[15] Fifty-three percent of the respondents reported prior threats to kill on the part of the victim or offender, and 70 percent reported prior physical violence in the relationship. All of the women in the study had experienced beatings by their partners prior to the homicides.

Studies focusing solely on women perpetrators report similar observations. In a pretrial study of women charged with homicide in Missouri, Daniel and Harris note that 75 percent of women charged with the death of their husbands had been physically abused by them prior to the homicide. They observe that "these victims pose substantial threat to the lives of the perpetrators," and, like Bernard et al., conclude that "wife beating constitutes a major contributing factor in interspousal murder."[16] Jane Totman, studying women serving time in a California prison for the killing of their partners, found that the usual homicide situation tended to be triggered by an immediate crisis that followed a long-term problem or struggle with the victim. Of these women, 93 percent reported being physically abused by their partners, and 67 percent said that the homicide was in defense of themselves or a child. As with findings in the current study, Totman reports a major contributing factor to these homicide events was a perceived lack of viable alternatives to an "overwhelming and entrapping life situation" on the part of the women.[17] Women tried a series of alternatives prior to the occurrence of the lethal incident. Nearly one-third had left home. Many others said they wanted to leave, but were afraid to because of their partners' threatened retaliation. One had attempted suicide as a way out. Totman observes that, as these alternatives failed, the "situation seemed to become even more limited in its possibilities for modification . . . more than ever a 'trap' from which there was no escape."[18]

The importance of the perception of entrapment, based on specific studies of abused or threatened women who have killed their partners, is supported as well by a larger body of theory about the genesis of crime. For example, Seymour Halleck, writing about the perpetration of criminal behavior in general, asserted that "helplessness" or the "feeling of being oppressed and not being able to do anything about it. . . . plays an important role in the genesis of criminal action"; and further contends that "criminal behavior becomes more likely . . . when alternative adaptions are actively restricted by other people."[19]

For women in the homicide group, the escalation of violence and threats, combined with this perception of entrapment and the impact of failed alternatives, culminated in eventual lethal action against their abusers. The following case provides a summary of the dynamics found to be crucial in the progression of intimate relationships toward homicides perpetrated by physically abused women.

NOTES

1. Crime in the United States, 1984; Straus, 1985.
2. Uniform Crime Reports, 1983.
3. *Crimes of Violence,* 1969. See also Bourdouris, 1971; Fields & Kirchner, 1978; Stephens, 1977.
4. Chimbos, 1978.
5. Police Foundation, 1976; Sherman & Berk, 1984.
6. Fiora-Gormally, 1978; Fromson, 1977; Lewin, 1979; Martin, 1976; Wolfe, 1979.
7. Schneider & Jordan, 1981.
8. This work was performed as part of a consulting team at Walker & Associates in Denver, Colorado.
9. A subsample of 403 battered women interviewed during a National Institute of Mental Health-supported study, NIMH grant ROIMH30147, L. E. Walker, Principal Investigator.
10. Volunteer subjects for research often differ from non-volunteers. For example, in an investigation of types of battered women, Washburn & Frieze (1980) found that abused women who responded to posted notices differed from those referred by shelters on several measures: They were more likely to work full time, had more education and somewhat higher income, and had experienced somewhat less violence than women in the shelter group. (Even then, nearly 50 percent had sustained severe or permanent injuries.) In the present study, 18 percent of women in the comparison group were referred by a battered women's shelter to the research project, whereas the rest were predominantly self-referred. With 38 of 205 women being referred from a shelter, the present sample may somewhat underrepresent levels of violence experienced by women who utilize shelter facilities. Extremely low levels of violence may also be missing from this sam-

ple; volunteers do not typically include women experiencing very minor assaults in their relationships who do not think of themselves as battered. However, although a random-sample procedure is desirable for generalizability, survey methods would have been inadequate to obtain a comprehensive history of the *context* surrounding violent episodes and the unfolding of patterns of violence over time, due to time and cost restraints implicit in survey methodology. Intensive interviewing of identified populations—the basis of this study—is the first step in approaching a detailed description of little-known events and in generating relevant hypotheses for future research.

11. Bernard, Vera, Vera, & Newman, 1982. All the respondents in this study were interviewed as a part of psychiatric evaluations required by the courts, either to determine their competencey to stand trial or their legal sanity at the time of the alleged crime; obviously a very non-random sample. However, all but one male defendant were judged competent to stand trial at the time they were evaluated.

12. See also Tanay's (1976) chapter, "Until Death Do Us Part," on homicide precipitated by the threat of abandonment, and Simon's (1978) conclusion that the separation or the threat of separation is usually the trigger for this type of homicide.

13. Wolfgang, 1958, p. 252.

14. Willbanks, 1983. Willbanks studied all homicides perpetrated by females in Dade County, Florida, for the year of 1980, and compared these cases to homicide perpetrated by male offenders in that same jurisdiction. Study of these respondents began at the arrest level and followed the subjects from arrest through disposition of their cases, using data obtained from police records.

15. Chimbos, 1978. This study was conducted post-adjudication with individuals convicted of a crime in the killing of their spouses. Most respondents were serving time in a penal institution at the time of the interview, or had served time prior to the interview.

16. Daniel & Harris, 1982. Again, women in this study were those who had been referred to a State Hospital for psychiatric evaluation. Women charged with homicide were compared to a group of other female offenders admitted for evaluation in relation to other crimes. This sample would exclude women charged with homicide but not referred for psychiatric evaluation, and women for whom homicide charges were dropped due to mitigating circumstances.

17. Totman, 1978, p. 105.

18. Totman, 1978, p. 92.

19. See Halleck's section on "Oppression and Limitation of Adaptational Alternatives," 1967, pp. 67–72.

Reflection

ANGELA BROWNE

To write this reflection, I've come back to a cottage just down the road from the house at Sea Road where *When Battered Women Kill* was written so many years ago. The Atlantic Ocean stretches before me in the early sun; Star Island and the lighthouse lie directly in my view, five miles offshore.

I wrote *When Battered Women Kill* on the second floor of an old house two miles to the south, in a bow window overlooking the sea. My strongest memory is of writing the vignettes from the women's life histories. Integrating the literature into the book was easy; writing the narratives, however, was not. After conducting the original interviews, the women and their stories were etched into my heart. As I wrote I could see their faces, their hands; hear their voices, their inflections, the labored pauses during the most difficult accounts. My hands would still be writing when I realized my throat had closed from the pain of the content. At those times I would leave the writing, walk down the stairs, out the back door, across the long lawn, and over the rocks to the beach. There I would walk and walk, in any weather, silent, sometimes in tears, until it somehow seemed bearable again and I could start over. And this pain was just in bearing *witness* to their lives. I was amazed at their perseverance, heart, and courage in living those lives. The point of writing *When Battered Women Kill* was to be a channel for these women's stories, and to be an effective enough channel that others would respond with change and understanding.

I was raised in a safe family: no virtue of mine, it was where I first opened my eyes. There must have been violence in some of the homes around me in my small town of 7,000 during my years there, but no one spoke of it. I was grown, married, in college, and still living in safety before I learned that others lived in fear. That learning changed my life. In conducting 8-hour interviews with women with abusive partners, and 10- or 12-hour interviews with women charged with the death of violent mates, I heard accounts of attacks and atrocities I had previously associated only with hostage situations or prisoners of war. A newly dedicated student (I had dropped out of college the first time), I went straight to the law library for case law and was amazed to find that individuals faced with such intimidation and threat virtually had no legal recourse or protections. (This was in 1980.)

I was convinced that the majority of people in the United States were caring human beings who, if they understood the prevalence and severity of the violence within homes, would find it unacceptable and pave the way for change. I still believe that view was substantiated as the first wave of activists, survivors, and researchers communicated the urgency of these realities in multiple public venues. The rapidity with which laws and policies changed in the nation and then more broadly in democratic countries was historically noteworthy. I felt that if I died the year the book was published, being a part of that effort and shoulder to shoulder with those people would have been enough.

Now, at the beginning of the 2000s, I still celebrate those years and the critical changes that were accomplished. But now there is new—and quite urgent—work to be done. Although violence at home has theoretically become unacceptable, punitive measures are sometimes applied to assaulted women or to their children; protection and redress are ignored. Practical resources that would enable endangered women and children to leave or to escape their assailants continue to disappear, as budget cuts remove almost all community level opportunities for adequate income, health services, work, and safe housing for those with limited financial means.

Most frightening, for me, is the change in the valuing of women, men, and children who struggle. I see no evidence that the larger society or most of its leaders value women, men, or children living in poverty, those with disabilities, or those with mental illness at all—regardless of their suffering or the glaring inequities that cause and exacerbate this suffering. Indeed, budget cuts in the early 2000s seem to run in quite the opposite direction. We live now by an "extreme end" paradigm as a nation: ignoring basic needs and supports until dramatically negative outcomes occur, and then reacting with extreme, expensive, and often punitive measures. Responses that formerly were considered a last resort (emergency or acute care, long prison sentences, incarceration of many citizens) are now often the only response.

What our efforts in the late seventies and early eighties taught me is that individuals, separately and collectively—operating in their own unique ways, but for the same goal—can make a difference, in a nation and a world. It is now time for a collaborative and unstoppable movement as large as the one documented in this book to address these new and pervasive dangers.

RELATED READINGS

Browne, A. & Bassuk, S. S. (1997). Intimate violence in the lives of homeless and poor housed women: Prevalence and patterns in an ethnically diverse sample. *American Journal of Orthopsychiatry,* 67, 261–278.

Browne, A. & Lichter, E. (2001). Imprisonment in the United States. *Encyclopedia of women and gender,* Volume A–K (pp. 611–623). London: Academic Press.

Browne, A., Miller, B. A. & Maguin E. (1999). Prevalence and severity of lifetime physical and sexual victimization among incarcerated women. *International Journal of Law & Psychiatry,* 22, 301–322.

Browne, A., Williams, K. R. & Dutton, D. G. (1999). Homicide between intimate partners: A 20-year review. In M. D. Smith & M. A. Zahn (Eds.), *Homicide: A sourcebook of social research* (pp. 149–164). Thousand Oaks, CA: Sage.

CHAPTER

17 Women and Children at Risk

A Feminist Perspective on Child Abuse

EVAN STARK AND ANNE H. FLITCRAFT

Viewing child abuse through the prism of woman battering reveals that both problems originate in conflicts over gender identity and male authority. Data indicate that men, not women, typically commit serious child abuse. A study of the mothers of child abuse victims shows that battering is the most common context for child abuse, that the battering male is the typical child abuser, that the battered mothers have no distinctive pathology in their backgrounds, and that clinicians respond punitively to the battered mothers. The child abuse establishment assigns responsibility for abuse to mothers regardless of who assaults the child, and responds punitively to women, withholding vital resources and often removing the child to foster care, if women are battered or otherwise fail to meet expectations of "good mothering." The combination of male control, misleading psychological knowledge about women's propensity for "bonding," and sanctions used to enforce gender stereotypes of motherhood combine to increase the entrapment and inequality from which battering and child abuse originate, a process termed "patriarchal mothering." The best way to prevent child abuse is through "female empowerment."

Introduction

In this article we examine the link between woman battering and child abuse from a feminist perspective. Viewing child abuse through the prism of woman battering reveals that both problems originate in conflicts over gender identity and male authority. Male authority is directly expressed in violent control over women and children. But just as important are the construction and use of clinical knowledge that distorts how women are perceived and subordinates their needs.

While a feminist approach to woman battering has gained some currency in mainstream thinking, feminists have had comparatively little impact on how child abuse is understood or managed. In part, this is because the view is widely shared that child abuse results from some combination of maternal pathology/inadequacy and "environmental stress." Where child abuse occurs against a background of "family violence," the presumption is that the violence is transmitted intergenerationally. A man who was beaten as a child now beats his wife. Then, unable to cope, she uses the child as scapegoat. Politics—including the politics of family life—play no role in this analysis.

In marked contrast to this emphasis, Gertrude Williams (1) suggests that sexism and pronatalism have taught these women that motherhood is the only fulfilling activity. Breines and Gordon (2) note a number of other gender-related issues, including the fact that women are primary parents, the lack of well-paid work alternatives to mothering, and the inadequacy of sex education (as well as contraceptive methods) leading to a large number of unwanted pregnancies.

Neither the conventional wisdom nor the nascent feminist analysis resolves these key questions:

1. Are men or women primarily responsible for child abuse?
2. What is the typical context for child abuse? Part of the answer to this question involves the link to battering and part lies in establishing whether the behavior of the abusing parent, regardless of gender, reflects some combination of pathology and stress (the dominant view) or a political struggle for control.
3. How do child protective services respond to battered women whose children are abused? The issue here is how women are "known" in clinical settings as well as how they are treated.
4. How do clinical interventions affect the dynamics in abusive relationships?
5. How can the current approach be improved?

The data examined in the first part of this article bear on the first three questions. We then sketch a theoretical framework that may account for the evidence and explain the effects of current interventions, and conclude with an examination of current and proposed policy in child abuse.

The Argument

Interestingly, even work that considers gender accepts the claim that child abuse is primarily a female crime. To the contrary, we argue, surveys and hospital and medical examiner's records indicate that men may be the typical child abusers, particularly when serious injury is involved (3–6). Similarly unfounded is the belief that battered mothers or mothers of abused children are "sick." In fact, while a significant minority have multi-problem backgrounds, the typical context for child abuse is a battering relationship for which the woman bears little responsibility. Widespread beliefs that women are responsible for child abuse and that child abuse results from environmental stress or family pathology justify interventions—such as therapy for mothers—that exacerbate the gender inequities from which battering and child abuse stem in the first place. Holding women responsible for child abuse and targeting their inadequacies as parents as the cause can deepen a woman's resentment toward her child and constrain her to behave in gender-stereotyped ways that seriously increase her risk in a battering relationship.

The problem goes beyond faulty assumptions and misguided policies and treatment strategies. In fact, law, social service practice, and psychological theory hold women "responsible" for child abuse even when a male assailant is clearly identified and is also battering the mother. This singular emphasis on women and their traditional roles converges with battering in the home. One result is that women experience gender identity as a vehicle for male domination, what we term "patriarchal monitoring," and their consequent resentment can often become violent.

Child Abuse: Gender Politics or Female Pathology?

Mothers or Fathers?

A classic vignette of the physically abused child has been that of an undernourished infant with multiple musculoskeletal trauma inflicted at different times by his or her depressed mother. Child abuse has been variously traced to maternal violence or neglect in the family of origin (7), current psychological dynamics such as role reversal (8), a lack of parenting skills (9), poverty or other environmental deprivations (6), the absence of needed institutional supports (10), or some combination of provocation, psychological predisposition, and environmental "trigger" events (11). But whether female psychology or a malfunctioning family system is emphasized, whether "destructive, disturbed mothers" are perceived or merely "sad, deprived, needy human beings," the fact that abuse results from a breakdown in appropriate mother-child bonding is taken as self-evident. The normative character of female domesticity and mothering is an unquestioned presumption in child psychology, pediatric medicine, and children's services. Thus the social consequences of adapting these images in problem solving remain unexamined.

But are most child abusers women? Representative sample surveys indicate that fathers may be as likely as or more likely than mothers to abuse children. Gil (6) estimates that 40 percent of the children in a national survey were abused by fathers, and an American Humane Society survey concluded that males were the assailants in 55 percent of reported cases of child abuse (3). Smaller surveys have produced somewhat different results, estimates of abuse by fathers running as low as 25 percent (12). Even this is remarkable given the division of child-care responsibilities and the proportion of children raised by single women.

While the percentage of abusing males is disputed, there is little doubt that, if a man is present, he is many times more likely to abuse the child than is the mother. For example, national survey data indicate that men were responsible for two-thirds of reported incidents in which men were present (6), probably an under-estimate of male responsibility. Surveys measure single acts without taking their consequences into account and cannot distinguish documented from alleged abuse or identify abuse resulting in severe injury or death. Of equal importance, punitive welfare regulations and fear of violence lead many women to conceal relationships with men.

A recent study of hospital and medical examiner's records indicates that men, not women, are primarily responsible for serious child abuse. In comparing the records of child abuse cases for two time periods, 1971–73 and 1981–83, Bergman, Larsen and Mueller (4) report that while the incidence of hospitalized cases has not changed, the proportion of severe injuries has increased dramatically. Also increasing is the proportion of known male perpetrators reported, rising from 38 percent to 49 percent for all cases, and from 30 percent to 64 percent for the severe cases. Meanwhile, for all cases the proportion of female perpetrators has decreased from 32 percent to 20 percent, and for severe cases from 20 percent to 6 percent. Fully 80 percent of the fatal cases in the most recent group are attributed to men, and 20 percent are "unknown." None are attributed to women. Finally, if a male perpetrator is identified, there is a 70 percent chance that the child's injury is severe, up from 25 percent a decade earlier. The authors (4) wisely suggest that the apparent increase in severe abuse by men—and a corresponding decline in cases categorized as "unknown"—reflects a growing willingness to report "male friends," not an actual shift in violence.

Battering and Male Control

Earlier work shows that child abuse occurs disproportionately in battering relationships, although it may be a relatively rare event overall (13–16). But how central is battering in child abuse? Is it merely one of many background factors? Or does its frequency as an etiological factor point to a common cause? And, in the latter case, is this cause inherited violence or current deficits? Or is female independence the root issue, as feminist theory suggests, whether it is the batterer or the abused woman who assaults the child?

Evidence is strong that male control over women, not female pathology, environmental "stress," or family history, leads to battering (17). Battered women experience a disproportionate risk of mental illness, alcoholism, and other problems only *after* the onset of abuse and frustrated help-seeking (16, 18), indicating that violence breeds psychopathology, not the reverse. Differences in battering by social class, race, and employment status are small (17). By contrast, "fights" typically center on gender issues (such as sex, housework, child care, and women's right to money and wage work) (19); rates of male violence against women who are single, separated, or divorced are actually higher than against married women (17); and the nature and pattern of assaultive injury strongly suggest the violence is directed at a woman's gender identity (including her sexual identity) and is neither impulsive nor random (13, 18, 20).

Have batterers "learned" their behavior from their own abuse as children? Although this belief is widely shared, its empirical support comes mainly from second-hand or anecdotal reports, psychiatric studies of unrepresentative or deviant populations (such as presidential assassins), and vague notions of childhood abuse. Thus a leading psychiatric authority on intergenerational transmission defines "abuse" and "neglect" as a "lack of empathetic mothering" (7) or "a variety of less than ideal responses of the caretaker (usually the mother) to the infant," which leads to "a lack of confidence or trust" in the child as an adult (21). The single random survey tracing abuse in the family-of-origin to current male violence finds "a clear trend for violence in childhood to produce violence in adult life" (22). But the actual data show the reverse. While boys experiencing violence as children are disproportionately violent as adults, 90 percent of all children from violent homes and even 80 percent from homes described as "most violent" do not abuse their wives. Conversely, a current batterer is more than twice as likely to have had a "nonviolent" than a violent childhood (7, p. 3) and seven times more likely to have had a nonviolent than a "most violent" childhood. Reviewing studies in this genre, Kaufman and Zigler (23) conclude that no more that 30 percent of those who experienced or witnessed violence as children are currently abusive, an estimate we believe is too high.

Medicine and Battering

Violence is only one dimension of the male control that entraps women in battering relationships. The other dimension is the response when abused women seek help. Although woman abuse is second only to male–male assault as a source of serious injury to adults (and is a major cause of death among younger black females), clinicians rarely identify the problem, minimize its significance, inappropriately medicate and label abused women, provide them with perfunctory or punitive care, refer them for secondary psychosocial problems but not for protection from violence, and emphasize family maintenance and compliance with traditional role expectations rather than personal safety (13–16, 24). Battering—the ongoing entrapment of women—is broken down into its medical symptoms (e.g., injuries, complaints, and psychosocial reactions to stress) and then the symptoms are reinterpreted so that the violence appears to result from rather than cause a woman's multiple problems. Within the health care system, women are increasingly isolated by inappropriate medication (such as tranquilizers), labels, psychiatric maintenance, and punitive interventions. And this process supports their being locked ever more tightly into relationships in which ongoing abuse is virtually inevitable.

In effect, clinical interventions manage the efforts of battered women to resist and escape domination, not domination itself. The political dimensions of battering are concealed behind a picture of "chaotic" families that need help "coping." "Restored functioning" is typically equated with getting the woman to better manage family conflict, usually by suppressing her own need for autonomy and development and by resuming traditional domestic responsibilities. As battering progresses through a range of increasingly severe psychosocial problems, abused women may come to know themselves as they are known. Thus, like their clinicians and their assailants, battered women in psychiatric facilities deny their problem, minimize its importance, or blame themselves (25).

Child Abuse: Responsible Mothers and Invisible Men

Can child abuse be understood as an extension of this entrapment process, as a problem rooted in the politics of gender inequality, occasioned by male violence and aggravated by the institutional response?

In contrast to battering, where sexist interpretations and practices confront a grassroots political movement, in the child abuse field, stereotypic and patronizing imagery of women goes unchallenged. One result is that men are invisible. Another is that "mothers" are held responsible for child abuse, even when the mother and child are being battered by an identifiable man.

Despite the evidence that men are a significant subset of abusive parents, there are few articles in the child abuse literature specifically on men. In a recent literature review, for instance, Martin (26) could identify only two individual case reports about men. Even in the minority of studies that consider both parents, women are the only source of direct information, no attempt is made to control for gender or to differentiate parental behavior and/or motivation by sex, and "abusing parent" is often a euphemism for mother.

Men are equally invisible in programs for abusing parents. Starting with images of appropriate gender behavior such as mother-child bonding, interventions proceed as if noncompliance with these norms reflects a character deficit that puts mother and child at risk. Varying combinations of parent education, counseling, peer pressure, and sanctions are used to instill appropriate maternal behavior, presumably so that the mother will adequately care for and protect the developing child.

Broad moral conceptions of women's "responsibility" for violence are incorporated in state regulations that define the mother's battering as a failure of her protective function. In New York State, for instance, an abusing parent includes one who "allows to be created a substantial risk of physical injury to the child," and this is frequently interpreted to mean allowing a child to witness violence against the mother. In Connecticut as well as many other states, women are interviewed by child protective services in determining foster placements, but not men, a practice undoubtedly linked to high rates of child abuse in foster homes.

Two decades of experience and thousands of monographs and programs offer no convincing evidence that child abuse has been reduced, let alone prevented, by this broad approach to mothering. But if child abuse is primarily a male crime and is rooted in subordinating women in gender-stereotyped roles, then the current emphasis on mothering may actually aggravate the problem it is designed to solve.

If violence is evoked by struggles around traditional sex roles, the practical result of re-enforcing these roles may be to restrict a woman's perceived options, increase her vulnerability to violence, decrease her capacity to protect her children from violence, exacerbate her own frustration and anger, and increase the probability that she will be destructive to self and others, including her children. This is what feminist theory leads us to expect. In this case, the best way to prevent child abuse is to protect women's physical integrity and support their empowerment. At a minimum, this implies close collaboration between child protective services and community-based shelters and a shift in child protection away from parenting education, therapy, and the removal of children. The question of whether the child-protection establishment would be receptive to this approach is examined later ("Conclusions").

Battering and Child Abuse: A Study

The disproportionate association of child abuse with battering is well established. Our earlier work (14, 17) indicates that battered women in a medical population are six times more likely than nonbattered women to have a report of child abuse (or "fear of child abuse") listed on their medical records (6 percent versus 1 percent). In their national survey of domestic violence, meanwhile, Straus and associates (22) found that abused women were 150 percent more likely to use severe violence with their children than were nonabused women. And after questioning women in a British shelter, Gayford (27) reported that 54 percent of abusive husbands and 37 percent of abused wives had also abused their children. From the vantage of its effect on children, exposure to parental violence may itself be counted as a form of "abuse."[1] Hilberman and Munson (13) report that one-third of 209 children exposed to marital violence exhibited somatic, psychological, and behavioral dysfunctions. Meanwhile, in his local medical practice, Levine (29) found that difficulty coping with children was a common presentation of woman battering. He suggests that the child's reaction depends on how violence is experienced. If the batterer's relation to the children is nonviolent, their response is limited to psychiatric problems. But in instances where children attempt to intervene and are, in turn, used as scapegoats and beaten by the batterer, they become more aggressive in their other relations.

It is possible that although children are at risk for abuse in battering relationships, battering is a relatively minor etiological factor in child abuse. This study identifies the importance of battering in the etiology of child abuse, examines whether the identity of the assailant and the parent held responsible are the same, assesses the role of disposition, and asks whether battered mothers have a distinctive psychiatric profile.

Study Population

At Yale–New Haven Hospital, the medical records of children suspected of being abused or neglected are specially marked or "darted" and the children are referred for investigation and disposition to a special hospital "Dart Committee." The *study population* includes the mothers of all children referred to the hospital Dart Committee for suspicion of abuse and/or neglect between July 1977 and June 1978, 116 mothers in all. Dart Committee reports on children were matched to the medical records of their mothers, and the mothers were then classified as battered or nonbattered based on their adult trauma history and the risk classification described below. The analysis of medical records was supplemented by data from family background notes in Dart Committee reports.

Methodology

The trauma screen employed in the study was designed to identify abuse in a population that had not been explicitly identified as battered and to generate sufficiently large groups of abused and nonabused women to permit statistical analysis and comparison. Each adult hospital visit prompted by trauma after the age of 16 was reviewed, and women were assigned to a "battering risk group" according to the following criteria:

- *Positive:* At least one episode in the woman's trauma history was attributed to assault by a male family member or male intimate.
- *Probable:* At least one episode in the trauma history was an assault (kicked, beaten, stabbed, etc.) but no personal etiology was indicated. (Note that muggings and anonymous assaults were *not* included in category.)

- *Suggestive:* At least one episode in the trauma history was not well explained by the recorded alleged etiology.
- *Negative:* All episodes in the trauma history were well explained by the recorded injury, including those sustained in muggings, anonymous assaults, etc.

Data were gathered on (*a*) the significance of battering in families experiencing child abuse, (*b*) the identity of perpetrators, (*c*) whether mothers who are battered come disproportionately from problem homes (as some research suggests), and (*d*) whether current dispositions respond appropriately to the family situation. . . .

Findings

Prevalence and frequency of battering. Of the 116 women, 52 (45 percent) had a trauma history that indicated battering and another 6 (5 percent) had a history of "marital conflict," though it was impossible to tell from their trauma history or other medical information whether they had been abused. Twenty-nine women (25 percent) presented "positive" episodes, an additional 18 (16 percent) were "probables," and five (4 percent) were "suggestive." Fifty-eight women (50 percent) had no documented trauma history indicating abuse and no record of "marital conflict." This frequency of at-risk women (45 percent) is 2.4 times greater than the frequency of battering among women presenting injuries to the surgical service (19 percent) and twice as great as the frequency of battering in the prenatal clinic (21 percent), making this the highest at-risk population yet identified.

The 52 abused women presented a total of 217 injury episodes during their adult histories, for a mean of 4.2 trauma presentations per woman. Women in the positive group averaged 4.9 episodes each, while those in the probable and suggestive groups each averaged 3.4 episodes. By contrast, women in the negative group averaged only 1.1 injury episodes, as one would expect in a "normal" population. Interestingly, the 1.8 trauma episodes averaged by the six mothers with a history of "marital conflict" fell somewhere between the suggestive and negative groups. Conceivably this group constitutes a battering risk category outside the purview of an identification method based solely on the trauma history. At any rate, for battered mothers as for battered women generally, abusive assault is an ongoing process, not an isolated incident.

Family History

A frequent claim is that the link between battering and child abuse reflects a multi-problem family history that includes violence or other serious problems. This was explored by drawing information on alcoholism, violence, "chaos" or "disorganization," suicide attempts, and incest, common indicators of a high-risk family history, from social services notes in the medical record and from Dart Committee files. To strengthen the conservative bias, women with a history of "marital conflict" were included with "negatives."

A significant subpopulation of these 116 mothers came from high-risk families of origin. It is evident, however, that abused mothers do not typically come from multi-problem backgrounds, are far less likely to come from a background that includes incest and/or alcoholism, and, perhaps most important, are no more likely to have a family background that includes violence. In sum, battered mothers of abused children cannot be distinguished by a background of family disorganization and, if anything, are even less likely than non-battered mothers in this group to have such a background.

Reason for "Dart"

Most children are "darted" because a clinician believes that they are "at risk" of abuse, neglected, or injured under "suspicious circumstances," or because the mother needs "support" to help her cope. Only a minority are darted because of documented physical abuse. However, children whose mothers have a positive history of being battered are twice as likely as the children of nonbattered mothers to be darted for actual abuse. Interestingly, they are also more likely to be darted because "mother needs support." At best, this represents a tacit recognition of the battered mother's predicament since in almost no instance is "abuse" or "battering" actually noted. . . .

The mothers in this study were selected because their children were darted in 1977–78. Thus it is not surprising that virtually all their trauma visits preceded the child's referral. The fact that battering is the context within which child abuse develops for these women cannot be generalized to other populations of women. Conceivably, mothers currently classified as nonbattered will be abused in the future. However, since a longer history of assault is associated with "positive" women whose children are also most likely to be physically abused, child abuse seems to appear after a pattern of battering is established, an issue taken up in the Discussion.

Identity of the Abuser

Dart Committee reports give the identity of the parent allegedly responsible for abusing the child. For families in which the mother is battered, the father or father substitute is more than three times more likely to be the child's abuser than in families of nonbattered mothers. Approximately 50 percent of darted children of at-risk women are abused by the male batterer, 35 percent are abused by the mother who is also being battered, and the rest are abused by others or by "both."

Removal of the Child

Of children darted for all reasons, almost one-third are removed from homes where mothers are being battered. This is significantly higher than the percentage of children removed for all reasons from families with nonbattered mothers. Does this simply reflect the greater likelihood, documented above, that children of battered mothers will be physically abused? To control for this possibility, we compared the disposition only for cases in which the children have been allegedly neglected or in which mothers needed support. Here too, if the mother was battered, the child was far more likely to be removed from her home than if she was not. Whatever the rationale for disproportionately removing children from battered mothers, the effect is obviously punitive.

Discussion

The findings support an analysis of child abuse as a component of female subordination. Even a highly conservative definition of battering requiring that at least one abusive injury be serious enough for hospital treatment reveals that 45 percent of these young mothers are battered and another 5 percent are experiencing "marital conflict." The documented prevalence of battering in this population is greater than in any other group yet identified, including emergency surgical patients, female alcoholics, drug abusers, women who attempt suicide, rape victims, mental patients, women filing for divorce, or women using emergency psychiatric or obstetrical services (15, 17). These women have already presented an average of four injury episodes to the hospital, only slightly fewer than the far older emergency room sample, corroborating our suspicion that child abuse in these relationships represents the extension of ongoing violence and is an intermediary point in an unfolding history of battering. Not only are the children of battered mothers significantly more likely to be physically abused than neglected, for instance, but the batterer also appears to be the typical source of child abuse, not a mother "overwhelmed with problems." The data shed little light on the dynamics of child abuse in battering homes. Again, however, the battering clearly predates the child abuse and, even when the battered mother is the abusive parent, she is less likely to have had a violent or "disorganized" family-of-origin, both facts suggesting that "transmission" involves the extension of the same unresolved conflict that elicits battering. The mothers divide into women with a problematic family history whose children are suspected of "neglect," and battered women whose background appears comparatively nonproblematic. In either case, the popular stereotype of the mother "predisposed by her history" to be battered and to abuse her child is a convenient fiction with little relation to documented cases.

To those familiar with the literature on child abuse, the clinical response to families in which mothers are battered will come as no surprise. As is the literature, the records of battered mothers are silent about physical abuse and the children's records rarely mention the man's violence. Instead, the mother's failure to fulfill her feminine role is emphasized ("mother needs support coping"). Here too, as in the clinical response to battering or in the literature on child abuse, women are held responsible when things go wrong. Even when we control for danger to the child, battered mothers are more likely to lose their children than nonbattered mothers.

Behind the ultimate threat—that a woman will lose her child—providers require periodic displays of nurturance and homemaker efficiency as prerequisites for basic family supports. In many cases, the mother does not report the abusing male and the caseworker lists the source of violence as "unknown" or "other." This may be because the woman defines the worker as her adversary, is afraid of the batterer's retaliation, or fears the withdrawal of welfare benefits if her relation with an unrelated man is discovered.

Ironically, since there are no therapeutic modalities to deal with men, foster placement—a punitive intervention as far as the mother is concerned—is more likely when a man is battering the mother and child. Not only are the mothers who pose least danger to their children most likely to lose them, but they may also lose access to whatever meager resources resulted from agency concern. With foster placement, the therapeutic focus shifts from the natural parents onto the child and his or her new milieu, while the underlying problems—including any violence toward the mother—are ignored (30).

In summary, and contrary to the prevalent view in the field, men are primarily responsible for child abuse, *not women*; battering is the typical context for child abuse, *not maternal deficits*; battered mothers whose children are abused are not distinguished by a family background of violence or psychopathology; and the response of the child abuse system—including neglect of the violence, support for mothering, and removal of the child to foster care—are ineffective at best and punitive at worst. In the next section, we place these findings in a feminist framework and link them to the dynamics in violent relationships.

A Feminist Approach to Battering and Child Abuse

Feminists approach the family as a system characterized by inequity, conflict, and contradiction. As a structure of male domination, it shapes intersubjective life into rigid gender identities to which real needs are subordinated (31). At the same time, the family must also provide the interpersonal and emotional support needed for subjective differentiation, autonomy, and independence (32, 33). The link of battering to child abuse can be defined by this dilemma. Autonomy is not attainable within rigid gender roles. Thus it is both inevitable that women will struggle to expand their options, including the option to engage openly in conflict, and appropriate for them to do so (34). Nevertheless, many men respond to these struggles violently, often seeking to subjugate children as well as their mothers.[2]

Women's growing independence and the withering of ideological supports for power based on gender make violence ever more central to male privilege in the home. One consequence is that women's health utilization is increasingly emblematic of their larger political situation. How medical and social services receive the myriad consequences of violence, including child abuse, is therefore crucial to women's political fate as well as their health.

Ideologically, battering and child abuse are connected by the presumption that women's responsibilities as wives and mothers supercede their personal needs and social rights, including their need for independence and physical safety. By normalizing these responsibilities through theories of women's character and mother-child bonding, psychology provides the health and social services with a rationale for making the delivery of vital resources contingent on women's acceptance of this ideology. By subsuming a woman's personal development to the stability of her family and the well-being of her children, both family stability and children's welfare are jeopardized.

The Knowledge of Mothers

Until recently, the child protection bureaucracy, including pediatrics, has dominated the field from which data on child abuse are produced. As a result, the knowledge base and practice of child protection form two dimensions of a single moral paradigm in which women's presumed propensity for nurturance and mothering is sacrosanct. It follows that women are and should be held responsible for abuse whether or not they actually assault (or neglect) their children.

The psychological knowledge of women as mothers has been largely developed through observational and interpretative studies that remove parenting from its political context. The structure, substance, and intensity of women's involvement with their children is obviously affected by pronatalist ideology, the absence of adequate daycare or health benefits, punitive welfare policies, and job, housing, and wage constraints. Not surprisingly, housewives subjected to these constraints exhibit high rates of situational depression (35), and behind housewife depression lie "high levels of anger and conflict towards husbands and children in families" (36). But on the videotapes of middle-class parent-child interaction used to support theories of mother-child bonding, these environmental factors are invisible (37). With the social and historical content of women's lives omitted, the intersubjective takes on an illusory comprehensiveness. Divorced from the factors that isolate mother with child, their reliance on one another appears to derive from inner principles (rather than external necessities), hence the conclusion: women have an innate propensity for "bonding." In this way, women's work as mothers is normalized and therapeutic management is justified for those who refuse or fail to perform this work.

The methodological short-sightedness that dominates research in maternal and child health may seem relatively benign. But the administration of the resulting "knowledge" is not. The normalization of mothering and the extension of patterns presumed to typify middle-class (i.e., "healthy") families to assessments of behavior among working-class, minority, or poor women is the ground on which pediatrics, social, and protective services shift child abuse from the realm of politics to pathology and "re-cognize" the violent suppression of women and children as a deficit in women's ability to parent. Thus, pediatric texts, popular advice literature, and psychological research "blame mother" when things go wrong (38–41). Child abuse is alternately interpreted as a failure or an exaggeration of the maternal function, a lack of parenting skills, or an inappropriate dependence on or resentment of a vulnerable other. If a man harms the child, this is because the mother is not present when the child returns from school, because adults other than the mother care for the child when ill, or because working mothers make unsatisfactory care arrangements (42, 43). . . .

Interestingly, holding women responsible for male violence (both against themselves and their children) reinforces the batterer's common tendency to deny or externalize responsibility for the assault.

Patriarchal Mothering: The Practice

The knowledge of mother-child bonding, of mother's responsibility for abuse, and of how violence evolves across generations of pathology is taken as self-evident by child rescue workers and is unreflectively incorporated into child protection. The administrative practices that follow include parent aides, homemaker services, "hot lines," Parents Anonymous, hospital-based outpatient therapy classes, comprehensive crisis intervention, shelter programs, and, if these fail, foster placement and/or legal prosecution. In each case, the governing assumption is that the parenting role needs "support" and that the "family unit" has dissolved into a structure of pathology that must somehow be managed by institutional and/or state intervention if its protective functions are to be restored.

The identification of responsibility for child abuse with rigid notions of women's role behavior engenders both conflict between agency representatives and women perceived as deviant mothers and growing resentment among women toward their children. Mothers are defined as people without needs of their own, who do or do not live up to their child's expectations and needs as service providers view them. When women's behavior differs from the projected expectations, service providers become frustrated and seek rationales to "help women shape up." One such rationale is provided by "retrospective reinterpretation." Deviance from perceived gender norms is transformed into disease by locating characteristics of abnormality in a woman's environment or history. Once so identified, a woman becomes a so-called "customer" of social services and each subsequent deviant act, no matter how common among women in similar situations, occasions ever more rigid case management, usually through some combination of "support" and therapy. Although peer treatment is widely touted as an alternative to traditional medical therapies, peer groups similarly interpret conflicts in social identity as an illness. Thus Parents Anonymous insists that child abuse stems from a problem that is "within us as a parent," that the woman is "a destructive, disturbed mother." Not surprisingly, women offered therapy and support parenting instead of protection and food stamps transfer some of their anger toward their caseworkers and some to their children (44).

The Battered Mother's Dilemma

Battered women cannot fully protect their children from the assailant. To protect themselves from child services, however, they pretend they can. In encounters with the caseworker, both sides know that the woman's behavior is a charade. Homemaking can hardly be "normal" when daily life is punctuated by male violence. "Home-visits" thus become exercises in mutual impression management. If the source of the trouble is obvious (e.g., the woman answers the door with a black eye) or the woman threatens to reveal it, the caseworker reminds her directly or by implication that a failure in maternal responsibilities could easily lead to the child's removal.

This situation creates a profound dilemma. The woman cannot protect her child unless she is protected. But if she asks for protection for herself, her child may be removed. In the matrix of power in which the woman finds herself, one way to seek aid is by drawing attention to her problems with her child whether or not these are particularly significant. As a result, she may project an image of herself as "unable to cope," hoping that, by accommodating the preconceptions of child protection, she will be given the supports she needs to protect herself. This is a dangerous game.

Another facet of the battered mother's dilemma is whether to expose the assailant's behavior and lose her child or conceal it and risk further child abuse. Here, being a good mother (having her child removed to safety) means admitting to being "bad" (i.e., to being battered). The effects of exposure are often tragic. Apart from the risk to children in foster care, the effects of foster placement on a battering relationship can include a depressive reaction; self-blame and a reduction in a woman's survival defenses; the internalization of anger formerly directed at the child scapegoat and attempted suicide; an escalation in abuse since the batterer has also lost a scapegoat; and pregnancy to prove readiness for a new child and to compensate for depression.

Patriarchal Mothering: The Lived Experience

But the dilemma goes deeper still. If women's situations were simply paradigmatic of "the weak and the governed," to borrow Elizabeth Janeway's phrase, then the complex system constructed to manage their behavior would be largely superfluous. Women confront male domination as active subjects, legally free and independent, struggling to shape reality to their needs. The women who are videotaped are not mere pawns, therefore, but their initiative has been displaced so that they must fulfill their gender identities through their relation to their children. As Foucault, Lacan, and the French feminists have shown, sexism in liberal societies rests less on open bias than in privileging certain definitions of feminine behavior within which women must both find themselves and survive. As the limited meanings through which women and children understand their experience are internalized, women may come to know themselves as men would have them known, i.e., in this case, to become locked into the knowledge of themselves as mothers.

In the laboratory, mother-infant bonding is observed devoid of its political context. As woman abuse evolves into "battering," women may experience the same diminished sense of themselves in relation to the social as is projected by the psychological paradigm. Just as they experience the mothering role as alien, it also feels as if it is all there is. Administrative transactions foster and aggravate role closure by simultaneously encouraging women to view the world through the prism of motherhood and to ask whether a "good mother" would have an abusing partner. This becomes a double bind when structural constraints leave a woman no alternative but to define herself through mothering. Forced to choose between liking herself as abused or deciding she is "bad," she develops a peculiar myopia to the political reality of her predicament, denying her own battering and living in a kind of fool's paradise of power "over" her children while at the same time feeling completely powerless or "overwhelmed." Child-abusing women themselves "yearn for good mothering" (7); they suffer low self-esteem because of a felt incongruence between how they view themselves and how they would like to be (45) and turn to their children for company and nurturance ("role reversal") (7, 11). Researchers trace these characteristics to a "breakdown in the maternal affection system" (7). However, at least in homes where women are also being assaulted, quite the contrary process is at work. Here women strive for selfhood ("how they would like to be") and nurturance ("good mothering") within the constraints of the mothering role, in part because children are the only source of nurturance in violent homes and in part because, as they define their options within a world bounded by a male *telos,* battered women lose access to the strains of resistance and initiative through which to establish themselves as something other than "his."

Thus, the matrix of power in which she is situated finds a parallel in a narrowing of the cognitive frame through which the battered mother perceives the world. Where she formerly sought control and autonomy to supplement nurturance and dependence, "mothering" must now mediate the impulse to power through the practice of nurturance and dependence, a process central to what we term patriarchal mothering. In any case, it is her restriction to mothering, not its abandonment, that may lead the battered woman to violence against her child.

There is an additional pathway by which the administrative response to woman and child abuse links the knowledge of women as mothers to their child abuse. We have seen that prevalent interventions to stop child abuse, like the response to battering, are inattentive to the woman's needs, holding her responsible for the child's predicament and making her rights as a parent contingent on her surpressing her own urge to self-development and survival. The autonomy she seeks to escape her assailant—getting a job, going to night school, moving in with friends—may provide the grounds for a judgment of "neglect" or removing her child to foster care. But if she stays at home, she and her child become more vulnerable to the batterer and her resentment at blocked opportunities builds. Whereas one reconciliation of this double bind is to deny her abuse, another is to hold the child responsible for the man's violence. By using the child as scapegoat, she momentarily reconciles the dilemma in which loving the child, being a "good mother," means putting herself at risk. But if the child is "bad," then its removal and her independence can be effected simultaneously with a minimum of internal conflict. Here too, child abuse is a "survival" strategy evoked by entrapment.

Child Protective Services and the Prospects for Reform

Policy Reform: Past Experience

How has the child protective establishment responded to the "news" about battering? The evidence is disheartening.

Internal pressure to acknowledge battering has been building in the child abuse field for almost a decade. For instance, while the American Humane Society championed the involuntary service approach to mothers throughout the 1950s and 1960s (46), by 1977–78, 20 percent of its child abuse reports from the field were accompanied by descriptions of wife abuse (3). Meanwhile, the team approach in hospital settings focused on the mother's "stressful environment."

Outside the child abuse field, the challenge to child rescue is framed within legislation and funding decisions that prioritize "spouse abuse" or "family violence." Child rescue lacks an activist base and, as a result, child savers tread a thin line between the narrow definition of child abuse needed to access political agendas and the broad concern with equity needed to placate the wider social welfare community (46). Moreover, shrinking social service resources exacerbate the contradictions between reformist rhetoric ("supporting families in trouble") and a narrowly protectionist practice (foster placement), engendering distrust within the larger liberal community.

The response to these pressures has been to deny their legitimacy and, more recently, to accommodate battering by rationalizing and broadening the punitive conception of mothering. When the Battered Women's Movement was still embryonic, the child protective establishment rejected battering as an issue simply to retain the economic status quo. As one prominent child policy maker asked (47, p. 8):

> Can we assume that new funding on a relatively large scale will be forthcoming? If not, we should [ask] . . . who will [be] winners and who losers, since it will be necessary to redistribute a limited pie. That redistribution will obviously be at the perceived expense of child abuse and neglect agencies.

But a broader jurisdictional appeal was needed for the welfare community (47, p. 8):

> We should ask whether the conceptual joining of these problems is likely to affect . . . the approach to families in which violence occurs. . . . At a time when a concerted effort is underway to move away from a punitive approach to parents who maltreat their children [there is a prevalent view] that violence against spouses is essentially a police problem. . . . Will joining the two issues result in an attitudinal and institutional retrogression to a reliance on punishment?

As the child protectionists feared, a shift in funds and media interest away from child rescue accompanied the growing recognition of battering. However, alongside the Battered Women's Movement emerged a new stratum of professionals and researchers specializing in "family violence" but fully willing to accommodate the child protectionists within a broader conceptual scheme in which the emphasis on child rescue is retained and supplemented by a more catholic perspective on "environmental" factors. In this schema, for instance, the link of battering to child abuse proves the importance of a primal injury to children (including child sexual abuse) and lends support to the claim that the family (termed a "cradle of violence") requires the same sort of social service policing as crime on the street (22). Again, "policing the family" becomes a euphemism for managing mothers. Indeed, having learned of the dangers to children when women are battered, child protective services in many states are seeking power to remove the battered woman's child if she fails to get a protective order against her assailant.

Proposals for Reform

Proposals for reforming child protective services run the gamut. Neoconservatives argue that to protect privacy, interventions should be limited to cases of documented physical abuse (48). By contrast, left-liberal child savers insist that the stigma of child abuse be eliminated altogether and that, instead, an "ecological definition" (which includes the child's "moral and social environment") be used to determine children at risk. Newberger (49), for example, normally a staunch critic of the punitive biases implicit in the helping response, proposes that we consider a variety of potential harms to the child—including poisoning, accidents, and the deprivation of medical care—"in the matrix of his developmental process, the family, neighborhood and helping environment."

Neoconservative proposals to limit interventions to the minority of cases in which physical abuse is documented offer a viable framework for a sharply curtailed protective establishment, on balance an attractive prospect. The neoconservatives view family intervention as a latent or aberrant function of vague laws and overzealous administrators (to be replaced by clear laws and hard-headed bureaucrats). But they fail to conceptualize this pattern in political terms, and hence never confront the possibility that managing mothers is the intended rather than the accidental consequence of child protection. In this case, restrictive policies may narrow the range of women who are controlled, but will still not protect children.

Liberal policy proposals shift attention from explicit violence to "the security of the environment" in which the child is raised. The environment rather than the woman is blamed and the woman is offered counseling and support. Although removing the stigma of abuse, it naively approaches clinical management as otherwise unproblematic, while extending the jurisdiction of treatment for the woman to a range of ills—such as the lack of medical coverage or a landlord's code violations—which she has even less control over than the batterer's violence. In practice, the ecological definition revives the old association of abuse with poverty. Thus investigators in Massachusetts are instructed that "An example of a home which poses a low risk to a child is one which is clean, with no apparent safety hazards such as exposed wiring or rodent infestation, and structurally sound" (cited in reference 49, p. 16). Like other models of multiple causation, the ecological picture can become so intricate that in trying to grasp the complexity of the relations between the physical, social, and interpersonal environments, we lose sight of the one event about which something immediate can be done: the political subordination of women and children in the home. More pointedly, in justifying access to nonabusing mothers (the majority of the current caseload) by a system whose means are almost exclusively punitive, the probability of removing children from battering or impoverished relationships would be dramatically increased.

Conclusions

From Entrapment to Empowerment

For many abused women, when assault combines with a history of frustrated, even punitive, help-seeking, the result is entrapment in a syndrome of escalating pathology. Isolated within the relationship and blocked from without from pursuing alternatives to it, the battered woman's self-development proceeds within an ever narrower realm, including the constricted realm of the mother-child relationship, and resentment and anger mount alongside the suppressed need for independence and autonomy. Multiple suicide attempts, homicidal rage, and violence against vulnerable others, including children, may result.

A similar process of entrapment is the typical context for child abuse. Men are the typical child abusers and, in almost half of all child abuse cases, are battering the woman as well. But whichever parent abuses the child in a battering relationship, the woman confronts a continuum of control extending from the violence at home through labeling and punitive clinical interventions at the hospital to sanctions and "support for mothering" from protective services. Even when the battered woman sacrifices the child (hoping the batterer will hit the child instead of her) or beats the child herself, the real source of her rage is entrapment in an enforced association of rigid gender roles and personal identity.

The imposition of "parenting skills" replaces the positive valence of motherhood with formal obedience and mounting rage. The obligations of mothering reappear as rules imposed by an alien force, depriving the woman of the very "responsibility" and sense of control over her environment that protective services claim to instill. Anger emerges as a defense against helplessness, and child abuse as a desperate way to exert control in the context of little or no control. But though rage is a "political emotion," to paraphrase Teresa Bernandez (34), it is often expressed symptomatically: resistance to mind control may evoke dissociation; resistance to isolation, imaginary companions, and resistance to guilt and shame, a "false self" that performs chores obediently, even cheerfully (50). Or, rage may find direct expression in killing the assailant.

If battering is the major context for child abuse and female independence is the basic issue for both, female empowerment is the best means to prevent child abuse. Empowerment primarily includes three components: (*a*) advocacy (to protect and expand women's entitlements); (*b*) collective support (to overcome estrangement and provide the political base for change); and (*c*) control. At a minimum, enhancing control implies that the battered mother can select the option she feels best suits her situation, even when she has abused the child.[3] A woman may choose to remain in a violent relationship of course; but in general, empowerment is impossible while the woman and child are accessible to the batterer.

These principles are anathema to a child welfare establishment that sees itself as advocating for children, but not their mothers; views politics as beyond the scope of treatment and protection; defines the mother as an "involuntary" client; and relies on a therapeutic or humanistic approach wholly lacking the means to limit, let alone prevent, male violence. By contrast, safety and empowerment guide the shelter movement's response to battering and are gradually being extended to an understanding of children. Many shelters now employ "child advocates," some run groups for mothers and children (51, 52), and virtually all have "no violence" rules as a precondition for residence. In Connecticut, meanwhile, the Division of Children and Youth Services has subcontracted to battered women's shelters for services to families in which mother and child are abused. Still, however central shelters may become in dealing with "family violence," the problem of providing for the long-term security and autonomy of women and children is far too vast to be solved by even so vital a community-based service as this.

Cooperative arrangements between shelters and the child welfare establishment can succeed only if there is mutual recognition that the autonomous women's movement—and the institutional alternatives it creates for battered women—is the safest place for children.

In its emphasis on equity and its political analysis of social ills, its community base, its willingness to take responsibility for problems few want to tackle, the excitement it communicates, and its capacity to dramatize issues and to mobilize constituencies, the Battered Women's Movement in particular can win over large segments of the social welfare audience from the child savers.

Acknowledging that child abuse originates in the politics of gender in no way diminishes personal responsibility for violence. To the contrary, as women are released from rigid role stereotypes and become more comfortable with their social power, they will be better able to accept real responsibility for the range of unresolved, ambivalent, and angry feelings all mothers share.

As the evidence of the common roots of battering and child abuse was first becoming clear, the Region II Director of the National Center on Child Abuse and Neglect issued this warning (47, p. 9):

> Perhaps the dynamics of child abuse, wife abuse and husband beating and rape are interrelated in ways that lend themselves to a common form of intervention. Are we prepared to follow the implications of this linkage? . . . We are unlikely to end with the intrafamilial dynamics of violence. . . . The discussion will almost certainly be extended to a systematic examination of the social causation of all forms of family violence.

It is to be hoped that this fear will prove prophetic.

NOTES

1. *But* Rosenbaum and O'Leary (28) found no differences for male children among violent, discordant, and satisfactorily married couples on the Behavior Problem Checklist. Interestingly, while they found no more behavioral problems in abused children than in those who had not been abused, 70 percent of the children whose mothers had been victims of spouse abuse were above the mean for a normative sample, suggesting that the psychological consequences of spouse abuse may be more serious for children than those of child abuse.
2. Baker-Miller writes "inequality generates hidden conflict around elements that the inequality itself has set in motion" (31, p. 14). The relevant point is that in the context of gender inequality, every "fight" concerns both the issue at hand and the larger—and usually unspoken—issue of inequality or "who will decide who will decide." In many battering relationships, once violence ensues, this larger political dimension grows in importance in direct proportion to its suppression, so that both sides attribute an importance to disagreements that appears inappropriate to outsiders. One goal of feminist intervention is to bring this hidden political dimension to the fore, to support the woman's (and incidentally the batterer's) perception that "the issue is not the issue."
3. Extraordinarily complex ethical and liability issues are involved in a decision to support a battered woman, even when she has previously put the child at risk or may do so, in a shelter environment, e.g., during the process of empowerment. Even in the worst case, however, this is preferable to the present practice of sacrificing the battered mother to rescue the child, (often to a worse fate), and so restricting the mother's options that further child abuse and battering are virtually ensured.

REFERENCES

1. Williams, G. Toward the eradication of child abuse and neglect at home. In *Traumatic Abuse and the Neglect of Children at Home,* edited by G. Williams and J. Money, pp. 588–605. Johns Hopkins University Press, Baltimore, 1980.
2. Breines, W., and Gordon, L. The new scholarship on family violence. *Signs: Journal of Women and Culture in Society* 8(3):490–531, 1983.
3. American Humane Society. *National Analysis of Official Child Neglect and Abuse Reporting.* AHS, Denver, 1978.
4. Bergman, A., Larsen, R. M., and Mueller, B. Changing spectrum of serious child abuse. *Pediatrics* 77(1): 113–116, 1986.
5. Stark, E., and Flitcraft, A. Woman-battering, child abuse and social heredity: What is the relationship? In *Marital Violence,* edited by N. K. Johnson, pp. 147–171. *Sociological Review Monograph.* No. 31. Routledge and Kegan Paul, London, 1985.
6. Gil, D. *Violence Against Children: Physical Child Abuse in the United States.* Harvard University Press, Cambridge, Mass., 1973.
7. Steele, B., and Pollack, C. A psychiatric study of parents who abuse infants and small children. In *The Battered Child,* edited by R. Helfer and C. Henry Kempe, pp. 103–147. University of Chicago Press, Chicago, 1976.
8. Kempe, R., and Kempe, C. H. Assessing family pathology. In *Child Abuse and Neglect: The Family and the Community,* edited by R. Helfer and C. H. Kempe. Ballinger, Cambridge, Mass., 1976.
9. Newberger, C. B., and Newberger, E. The etiology of child abuse. In *Child Abuse: A Medical Reference,* edited by N. F. Ellerstein, pp. 11–20. John Wiley and Sons. New York, 1981.
10. Newberger, E., and Bourne, R. E. The medicalization and legalization of child abuse. *Am. J. Orthopsychiatry* 48(4): 593–606, 1978.
11. Helfer, R. F. Basic issues concerning prediction. In *Child Abuse and Neglect: The Family and the Community,* edited by R. E. Helfer and C. H. Kempe. Ballinger, Cambridge, Mass., 1976.
12. Baher, E., et al. *At Risk: An Account of the Work of the Battered Child Research Department,* National Society for Prevention of Cruelty to Children. Routledge and Kegan Paul, Boston, 1976.
13. Hilberman, E., and Munson, K. Sixty battered women. *Victimology: An International Journal* 2(3–4): 460–470, 1977/78.
14. Stark, E., and Flitcraft, A. Personal power and institutional victimization: Treating the dual trauma of woman battering. In *Post-Traumatic Therapy,* edited by F. Ochberg. Bruner and Mazel, New York, 1987.
15. Stark, E. The Battering Syndrome: Social Knowledge, Social Therapy and the Abuse of Women, Doctoral dissertation, Department of Sociology, State University of New York, Binghamton, 1984.
16. Stark, E., Flitcraft, A., and Frazier, W. Medicine and patriarchal violence: The social construction of a "private" event. *Int. J. Health Serv.* 9(3): 461–493, 1979.
17. Stark, E., and Flitcraft, A. Violence among intimates: An epidemiological review, In *Handbook of Family Violence,* edited by V. N. Hasselt et al. Plenum Press, New York, 1987.
18. Stark, E., et al. *Wife Abuse in the Medical Setting: An Introduction for Health Personnel,* Monograph No. 7. Washington, D.C., Office of Domestic Violence, 1981.
19. Dobash, R. E., and Dobash, R. *Violence Against Wives.* Free Press, New York, 1979.
20. Rosenberg, M., Stark, E., and Zahn, M. A. Interpersonal violence: Homicide and spouse abuse. In *Maxcy-Rosenau: Public Health and Preventive Medicine,* Ed. 12, edited by J. M. Last, pp. 1399–1426. Appleton-Century-Crofts, New York, 1985.
21. Steele, B. F. Violence within the family. In *Child Abuse and Neglect: The Family and the Community,* edited by R. E. Helfer and C. H. Kempe. Ballinger, Cambridge, Mass., 1976.
22. Straus, M., Gelles, R., and Steinmetz, S. K. *Behind Closed Doors: A Survey of Family Violence in America.* Doubleday, New York, 1980.
23. Kaufman, J., and Zigler, E. Do abused children become abusive parents? *Am. J. Orthopsychiatry* 57(2): 186–193, 1987.

24. Kurz, D., and Stark, E. Health education and feminist strategy: The cases of woman abuse. In *Feminist Perspectives on Wife Abuse,* edited by M. Bograd and K. Yllo. Sage, Beverly Hills, Calif., 1987.
25. Carmen, E. H., Rieker, P. P., and Mills, T. Victims of violence and psychiatric illness. In *The Gender Gap in Psychotherapy, Social Realities and Psychological Processes,* edited by P. P. Rieker and E. H. Carmen, pp. 199–213. Plenum Press, New York, 1984.
26. Martin, J. Maternal and paternal abuse of children: Theoretical and research perspectives. In *The Dark Side of Families: Current Family Violence Research,* edited by D. Finkelhor et al., pp. 293–305. Sage, Beverly Hills, Calif., 1983.
27. Gayford, J. J. Wife battering: A preliminary survey of 100 cases. *Br. Med. J.* 25:194–197, 1975.
28. Rosenbaum, A., and O'Leary, D. Children: The unintended victims of marital violence. *Am. J. Orthopsychiatry* 51(4): 692–699, 1981.
29. Levine, M. Interparental violence and its effect on the children: A study of 50 families in practice. *Med. Sci. Law* 15(3): 172–183, 1975.
30. Green, A. Societal neglect and child abusing parents. *Victimology: An International Journal* 11(2): 285–293, 1977.
31. Baker-Miller, J. *Toward a New Psychology of Women.* Beacon Press, Boston, 1976.
32. Chodorow, N. J. Gender, relation and difference in psychoanalytic perspective. In *The Future of Difference,* edited by H. Eisenstein and A. Jardine, pp. 3–20. Rutgers University Press, New Brunswick, N.J., 1985.
33. Flax, J. Mother-daughter relationships: Psychodynamics, politics and philosophy. In *The Future of Difference,* edited by H. Eisenstein and A. Jardine, pp. 20–41. Rutgers University Press, New Brunswick, N.J., 1985.
34. Bernardez, T. Women and Anger, Cultural Prohibitions and the Feminine Ideal. Paper presented at Learning from Women: Theory and Practice, Boston, April 1987.
35. Brown, G. W., and Harris, T. *Social Origins of Depression—A Study of Psychiatric Disorder in Women.* Tavistock, London, 1978.
36. Weissman, M. The depressed mother and her rebellious adolescent. In *Children of Depressed Parents: Risk, Identification and Intervention,* edited by H. Morrison. Grune and Stratton, New York, 1983.
37. Henriques, J., et al. *Changing the Subject: Psychology, Social Regulation and Subjectivity.* Methuen, London, 1984.
38. Howell, M. C. Pediatricians and mothers. In *The Cultural Crisis of Modern Medicine,* edited by J. Ehrenreich. Monthly Review Press, New York, 1979.
39. Ehrenreich, B., and English, D. *For Her Own Good.* Anchor Books, New York, 1979.
40. Caplan, P., and Hall-McCorguodale, I. The scapegoating of mothers: A call for change. *Am. J. Orthopsychiatry* 55(4): 610–613, 1985.
41. Caplan, P. Mother blaming in major clinical journals. *Am. J. Orthopsychiatry* 55(5):345–353, 1985.
42. Garbarino, J., and Sherman, D. High risk neighborhoods and high risk families: The human ecology of child maltreatment. *Child Dev.* 51(1), 1980.
43. Robertson, B. A., and Juritz, J. M. Characteristics of the families of abused children. *Child Abuse and Neglect* 3: 861, 1979.
44. Kott-Washburne, C. A feminist analysis of child abuse and neglect. In *The Dark Side of Families,* edited by D. Finkelhor et al., pp. 289–293. Sage, Beverly Hills, Calif., 1984.
45. Rosen, B. Self-concept disturbance among mothers who abuse their children. *Psychol. Rep.* 43: 323–326, 1978.
46. Nelson, B. *Making an Issue of Child Abuse: Political Agenda Setting for Social Problems.* University of Chicago Press, Chicago, 1984.
47. National Center on Child Abuse and Neglect. *Child Abuse and Family Violence.* U.S. Children's Bureau, Washington, D.C., 1978.
48. Besharov, D. J. Right versus rights: The dilemma of child protection. *Public Welfare* 43(2): 19–46,1985.
49. Newberger, E. Child abuse. In *Source Book: Surgeon General's Workshop, Violence and Public Health.* Leesberg, Va., 1985.

50. Herman, J. Sexual Violence. Paper presented at Learning from Women: Theory and Practice, Boston, April 1987.

51. Rhodes, R. M., and Zelman, A. B. An ongoing multifamily group in a women's shelter. *Am. J. Orthopsychiatry* 56(1): 120–131, 1986.

52. Alessi, J. J., and Hearn, K. Group treatment of children in shelters for battered women. In *Battered Women and Their Families: Intervention Strategies and Treatment Programs,* edited by A. R. Roberts. Springer, New York, 1978.

Reflection

EVAN STARK

In 1974, shortly before we opened the New Haven shelter, a well-intentioned volunteer took the nine-year-old daughter of a battered woman who was staying at our house to Yale's Child Study Center for evaluation. The mother and daughter had been living in their car. When the girl explained that "Daddy was looking for us with a gun" and that they'd been eating mainly cornflakes, the psychiatrist was horrified. Concluding the girl was "inappropriately precocious," he reported the mother for neglect. Only tough negotiations kept the girl from being placed.

Six years later, we drew the child abuse sample, one of the first attempts to nail down the importance of battering for child protection, as part of the NIMH funded "Yale Trauma Studies" on the consequences of battering for women's health. The argument was cast in its present form after we co-chaired a prevention subgroup at the U.S. Surgeon General's Special Workshop on Violence and Public Health in 1985. The leading child welfare organizations in attendance refused to acknowledge evidence that battering was a critical context for child maltreatment because they feared it would open a political "Pandora's box" that could jeopardize their funding. The major obstacle to progress on this front was not ignorance, but a paradigm that saw women only as mothers and held mothers accountable when children were harmed, regardless of whether they too were being coerced or controlled. While the clinical approach pioneered by Kempe highlighted individual risk factors and therapeutic management, so-called "humanists" in the child welfare field focused on environmental deprivation as the cause of abuse. But, they too focused on "mothers" and considered CPS intervention a benign alternative to criminal justice involvement, which we demanded to protect adult victims. The larger women's movement avoided child abuse because it also bought into the myth that women were responsible for child maltreatment.

Much has changed since this article appeared. Research on how domestic violence harms children is now a major subspecialty. Although this body of work has been deservedly criticized for its methodological shortcomings, it leaves no doubt about two of our key findings, that domestic violence is a major context for child abuse and that abusive males are largely responsible for child maltreatment in these cases, not mothers. Our focus on the refusal of CPS to acknowledge domestic violence is also dated. In large part due to pressure from and training by domestic violence advocates, CPS services throughout the U.S. routinely intervene in domestic violence cases and often collaborate with local domestic violence services.

Despite these changes, our "feminist perspective" remains relevant because of a third development in the child welfare field—a growing body of case law supporting sanctions against non-offending parents in domestic violence cases. No longer is the overlap of domestic violence and child maltreatment questioned. Unfortunately, however, in presenting this information to CPS, advocates and researchers have frequently exaggerated the likely harms to children (e.g., confusing statistical significance with prevalence) or presented the evidence as if the dynamics that linked battering to child maltreatment were straightforward. When child welfare agencies, family courts, and policy makers have interpreted this "information" through the prism of their prevailing gender bias and their public mandate for child protection, many have concluded that "exposure" to domestic violence is tantamount to abuse or neglect, expanding the sorts of punitive responses to battered mothers we found at Yale. So dramatic is this trend that in June, 2000, Sharwlene Nicholson and other battered mothers brought a class action lawsuit to prevent the Administration of Children's Services (ACS) in New York City from charging women with neglect and removing their children solely because of the mother's abuse by her partner. In March, 2002, after months of testimony, federal judge Jack Weinstein ruled in the mothers' favor, enjoined ACS from its unconstitutional practices, and appointed a panel on which I am the plaintiff's representative to monitor the agency's compliance.

Domestic violence and child welfare experts testified on both sides of the Nicholson case, illustrating that confusion still plagues our field about how to frame the connection between domestic violence and child abuse without re-victimizing battered women. Post-Nicholson, it is necessary to qualify any representation of this connection by showing which specific harms can be traced to "exposure," linking specific harms to specific abusive dynamics, clearly delineating who is responsible for these harms, and building the enormous resilience exhibited by battered mothers and their children into intervention decisions. We touch only some of these issues. What our article *does* do is suggest that a path through the current dilemma starts with the recognition that the "fact" of child maltreatment is as likely to be the byproduct of the politics of sexual inequality as of individual pathology. When child welfare theory and practice rely on outdated gender stereotypes to analyze and respond to abusive dynamics, they perpetuate this inequality, contributing to "the battered mother's dilemma" and so heighten the risk to children. Unless this approach is abandoned by expanding public accountability for the safety and independence of *all* victims, CPS will not respond appropriately to battered women, no matter how much training is provided or by whom. It seems no less necessary today than when we wrote "Women and Children at Risk" to clear the deck of outdated sexist stereotypes by subjecting the tenets caretakers apply to women and children to the same critical scrutiny as child abuse itself. Support for this approach comes from the little noticed finding of our study that, since battered mothers typically enter the CPS caseload because of what has been done *to* rather than *by* them, their capacities as parents or partners are far less likely to be compromised than are those of the multi-problem mothers typically identified with "neglect." Recognizing this should make it easier for caseworkers to ally with battered mothers in dismantling the structures of male domination in personal life that currently obstruct the well-being of women and their children.

CHAPTER

18 Lesbian Battering

An Examination

BARBARA HART

Definition of Lesbian Battering

Lesbian battering is that pattern of violent and coercive behaviors whereby a lesbian seeks to control the thoughts, beliefs or conduct of her intimate partner or to punish the intimate for resisting the perpetrator's control over her.

Individual acts of physical violence, by this definition, do not constitute lesbian battering. Physical violence is not battering unless it results in the enhanced control of the batterer over the recipient. If the assaulted partner becomes fearful of the violator, if she modifies her behavior in response to the assault or to avoid future abuse, or if the victim intentionally maintains a particular consciousness or behavioral repertoire to avoid violence, despite her preference not to do so, she is battered.

The physical violence utilized by lesbian batterers may include personal assaults, sexual abuse, property destruction, violence directed at friends, family or pets or threats thereof. Physical violence may involve the use of weapons. It is invariably coupled with nonphysical abuse, including homophobic attacks on the victim, economic exploitation and psychological abuse.[1]

A lesbian who finds herself controlled by her partner because of fear of violence may be battered even if she has not been physically assaulted. If her intimate has threatened her with physical violence or if her partner is aware that merely menacing gestures intimidate her because of a past history as a primary or secondary[2] victim of violence, the lesbian is battered who is controlled or lives in fear of her lover because of these threats or gestures.

In determining whether lesbian violence is lesbian battering, the number of assaults may not be telling. The frequency of the acts of violence may not be conclusive. The severity of the violence may also not be determinative.

Lesbian battering is the pattern of intimidation, coercion, terrorism or violence, the sum of all past acts of violence and the promises of future violence, that achieves enhanced power and control for the perpetrator over her partner.

Why Do Lesbians Batter?

Like male batterers, lesbians who batter seek to achieve, maintain and demonstrate power over their partners in order to maximize the ready accomplishment of their own needs and desires. Lesbians batter their lovers because violence is often an effective method to gain power and control over intimates.

Lesbians, like their non-lesbian counterparts, are socialized in a culture where the family unit is designed to control and order the private relationships between members of the family. Men are assigned the ultimate power and authority in family relationships. This is true despite the fact that there is nothing inherent in the male gender which would render them the appropriate wielders of power. Rather, this attribution of "legitimate" power is given to men based on a system of beliefs and values that approves and supports men's power and control over women—*sexism.*

Roles in the family are defined based on this unequal power. A hierarchy of privilege, power and ultimate authority is established, with each family member being assigned a slot.

Family members constitute a discrete unit, separated somewhat from persons outside of the family. Individuals are treated like the property of the unit. Family members feel a strong connection of ownership to each other and expect a greater degree of loyalty and trust from each other than from outsiders. Intimate partners in family units believe that they are entitled to certain services from each other. They also feel that they have the right to exercise some degree of control over other family members.

Distribution of the limited resources of the family—energy, creativity, time and economic assets, to name a few—are determined by those most powerful in the hierarchy. Where there is a difference among family members in preferred utilization of the resources, those in power are able to choose among the several options. Critical and mundane decisions about the life of the family are also made by those persons, or the individual, holding the principal power.

Further, in this culture where many forms of violence are permissible—where violence often is not a crime, where there are few severe consequences for violence, such as incarceration, economic penalties, embarrassment or community ostracism—individuals may choose to use violence to enhance their control over other family members. Since violence is a tolerated tactic of control and is condoned within broad limits, particularly within the family, battering of intimate partners is widely practiced.

Lesbians, like non-lesbians, often desire control over the resources and decisions in family life that power brings and that violence can assure when control is resisted. The same elements of hierarchy of power, ownership, entitlement and control exist in lesbian family relationships. Largely this is true because lesbians have also learned that violence works in achieving partner compliance. Further, lesbian communities have not developed a system of norms and values opposing power abuse and violence in our relationships.

Which Lesbian Will Batter?

Perhaps the partner who is physically stronger and perhaps not.

We know that part of the effectiveness of men's violence as a tactic of control is that their size and physical strength, compared to women, is such that men's violence has the potential to inflict serious bodily harm on women. Non-lesbian women will often acquiesce in the demands of the violent partners because of the knowledge that noncompliance may be followed by violent attacks that could result in injury.

But just as men choose to batter and also choose to not batter because they are physically strong, so also with lesbians.

The lesbian who is big, strong, an experienced fighter, or trained in the martial arts may represent a greater threat or danger to her partner than a woman of similar physical prowess. As well, a sharp difference in physical power may give the violence clout or persuasive power that would be absent if the partner were more physically equal.

Thus, one lesbian might choose not to be violent because she concludes that it would not work by virtue of her lack of physical power relative to her partner. Another could choose to be violent because she concludes violence will intimidate her partner and because she believes she can handle any violent response safely. Another lesbian with years of street or bar fighting experience might choose not to use violence to control her partner because she believes that it would be unfair and morally wrong. Yet another lesbian might choose to use violence to control by employing a weapon to eliminate her comparative weakness and to overcome the physical power possessed by her partner.

Thus, even though superior strength can render violence a more effective tactic of control, many choose not to use it.

Perhaps the partner who has more personal power and perhaps not.

Men who batter usually possess more personal power in their lives than the women they victimize. Personal power is based on education, income and economic security, employment skills and marketability, class, age, religious experience, physical power, health, social skills and networks, etc. Each partner possesses a particular amount of every attribute of power. Some attributes, like income or employment skills, may be more significant measures of personal power than others in any particular relationship.

But men do not batter because they have more personal power than their partners. Nor do they batter because they happen to have less. Violence is not a necessary outgrowth of differential power.

Men batter because violence will usually give them immediate and total control over their partners, because it maximizes the power they have over the events of their family lives, because it feels strong and powerful to terrify the recipient of violence, and because there are relatively minor adverse consequences afterwards.

So also do lesbians batter. But not all powerful lesbians batter and not all batterers are powerful. Lesbians may choose to batter if they believe it will achieve the change or compliance desired of their partners, if they believe that coercive power is tolerably utilized in relationships, and if they conclude it is safe to batter.

Many lesbians who batter, regardless of their portion of personal power, demonstrate strong powers of coercion and intimidation, such that members of the couple's friendship network or their immediate lesbian community may defer to or pacify the batterer to avoid confrontation or humiliation.

Perhaps the partner who experienced violence as a child and perhaps not.

Many female children are physically or sexually abused by family members or friends as children. As victims of violence, young women certainly learn the power that violence grants. Violence can terrorize, immobilize and render fearful the most competent and extroverted, as well as the weak and powerless. Children, whether or not they are victims, observers or perpetrators, learn early that violence eliminates the recipient's control over her own life. Children learn the perverse pleasure they may derive from dominating others. Children learn that there may be few adverse consequences to violence. Children learn that parents or adults who espouse nonviolent, nonabusive philosophies may also batter and that adults sometimes behave very differently from the values they claim. Children who grow up in families where there is no model for negotiating over scarce family resources or for strategizing for maximizing the need and wish fulfillment of each family member, may lack ethical concepts of sharing and fairness and skills for problem-solving.

Surely, many girl children also learn that violence is not appropriate female behavior. Additionally, girl children who grow up as victims of violence often strongly reject violence as a tactic of control. This is particularly true for women who perceive the childhood violence as unjust and unnecessary.

Unfortunately, there is not any research data that answers the question of how many lesbians who were violated as children choose to be violators as adults. The fact that a woman was abused as a child is not a reliable indicator that she will batter her partner.

Perhaps the lesbian who is acutely homophobic and perhaps not.

All lesbians feel vulnerable and endangered to some extent because of the reality of the virulent prejudice and coercive, punitive power that has been brought to bear against us. To the lesbian who greatly fears exposure or self-hatred, an understanding of the risks of exposure may create a chronic emotional crisis where self-protection and self-validation consume exhausting amounts of energy.

The fragility of the control that lesbians can exercise to prevent exposure may leave the woman who feels highly at risk always in a state of at least mild anxiety. She may also be enraged that she cannot assure that her best efforts at invisibility will protect her. As a consequence, she may feel powerless—a pawn who can be hurt terribly at the whim or indiscretion of others.

Because of her vulnerability, the acutely fearful lesbian may expend endless energy to lead a duplicitous life—to act in the dominant culture as a non-lesbian and to live within herself as a lesbian. This expenditure of energy is enormous and continuous. It robs her of her best creativity and strength. It diminishes her. Often she may hate the system that oppresses her but also hate herself for being so vulnerable.

But this does not precipitate violence or abuse of her partner. Although the lesbian experiencing homophobia or internalized homophobia copes with inordinate stress and rage, these do not override her capacity to choose to be violent. Nor does the fact that she lives in terror due to injustice determine her decision to act justly or unjustly toward others.[3]

Perhaps the lesbian who holds contempt for women or who identifies with men and perhaps not.

Misogyny is the hatred of women. A misogynist attitude is one that devalues, discredits or disparages women. Young women are taught in this culture not to trust or respect women, to believe that women are less competent than men. The media, purveyors of cultural norms and values, constantly reinforce this inferiority of women. It is, therefore, not surprising that women harbor contempt and hatred for women. Women who have worked diligently to be rid of self-hatred will never totally succeed in that endeavor in a society where women-hating is endemic.

Lesbians who have been battered often report that a seemingly integral part of the pattern of violence inflicted upon them is derogatory, women-hating tirades by the batterer.

Does the lesbian who uses women-hating verbal attacks as a tactic of control hate herself as a woman or does she hate other women, distinguishing herself somehow from them, or does she permit herself to ventilate women-hating attitudes because she knows this type of assault will be a particularly effective tactic of control over the woman she is abusing?

It has been suggested that lesbians who batter do so because they are identifying with men, the powerful gender.

The process of identification with men is rarely a denial of the lesbian batterer's womanhood. It is not usually conscious self-hatred of herself as a woman. It may involve devaluing her partner based on her "lesser worth" because she is a woman. Sexually pejorative salvos may be used because they are most shameful and debilitating—most powerful. Identification may include an assessment that the lesbian batterer has the physical and personal power to batter successfully without adverse consequences—akin to men. It may entail a strong sense of ownership of the partner which brings with it the right to use her at will.

But identification with men or hatred of women does not compel violence, although it may allow the lesbian batterer to conclude that violence as a tactic of control will be successful or to feel justified in her actions.

Perhaps the lesbian who perceives herself to be victimized by the world and misused or controlled by her victim and perhaps not.

Most men who batter are said to feel controlled by people and circumstances other than themselves. That luck rules supreme and theirs is rotten. That disaster is more likely to befall them than other people.

Not only do male batterers describe themselves as the accidental or intentional victims of others' neglect or injury, they also see themselves as "henpecked"—controlled by their partners.

Lesbian batterers also express feelings of powerlessness and helplessness in their relationships and assert they are controlled and victimized by their partners. Lesbian assailants invariably utilize every disagreement by the partner, every failure to meet the batterer's needs, every independent/self-caring action by the partner as a violation or external control imposed by the victim.

Clearly, some lesbians who choose to batter are unjustly treated by persons and institutions. Some lesbians who batter are not in relationships with women who try to meet every expectation of the assailant. Many lesbians who batter are met with genuine adversity and hardship.

But there is no evidence to suggest that the lives of batterers are actually less rich or more fraught with injustice than lesbians who do not choose to batter. Furthermore, there is strong evidence from battered lesbians that they have persistently worked very hard to fulfill their partner's expectations and to nurture them through difficult times.

And many lesbians who meet with very trying circumstances and who are treated unkindly by their partners do not batter.

Perhaps the lesbian who has anger control or communications problems and perhaps not.

Many lesbian batterers speak of the inordinate anger that is generated by their partners. They acknowledge that identical behavior by another person would not propel them into the rage they feel toward their partners. Lesbian batterers describe themselves as angrier than other women; struggling hard to have some respite from the anger that is aroused by the partner. Sometimes the anger seems to come out of nowhere and sometimes it feels justified. There is no consistency about whether any particular attitude or behavior manifested by a battered lesbian will trigger the anger.

Batterers are not aware of the reasons behind the "triggering." They are often oblivious to the attitudes, beliefs and values that are the underpinning of the "triggering mechanism" that permit anger to explode sometimes even before they are aware the partner is resisting control or acting independently of the batterer's wishes. Lesbians who batter, like male batterers, strongly believe that once anger emerges, it becomes uncontrollable, and that violence subsequently erupts—the batterer having no control over either.

Battered lesbians report that batterers often appear to be looking for something about which to become angry to provide rationalization for battering. They also find that the batterer many times becomes angry only after she assaults to control and assault does not produce the desired compliance.

Whether anger is present or not, it does not eliminate the batterer's capacity to choose violence as a tactic of control. That choice is fully hers.

Battered lesbians are often told by partners who have sought help from therapists not informed about battering that she batters because she is not adequately able to communicate her needs and feelings, nor able to express herself. She somehow short-circuits and becomes violent, with violence being a reflection of frustration, not a tactic of control.

Underlying this claim is a misconception that better communication would produce a better understanding of needs and feelings which would, in turn, result in the partner working harder to accommodate the batterer and violence being thereby averted. This assumes that the batterer is a person whose needs are not well understood and that the battered lesbian has a responsibility to go the additional distance to respond positively to the batterer's needs.

Both assumptions are often false. Many batterers are excellent communicators. Batterers who have worked in therapy to increase their communication skills, without first achieving the termination of violence or threats of violence, become more skillful, sophisticated controllers of their partners—better terrorists.

Many lesbians who are not articulate or do not have a clear sense of their feelings and needs are not violent. Most lesbians striving to improve communication skills and to better identify and actualize their needs and feelings have never considered violence as appropriate activity in relationships.

There is no profile of a lesbian batterer—no personal attributes or circumstances which permit reliable prediction or identification of the lesbian who will batter her intimate partner.

For a lesbian to choose to batter her partner, she must conclude that:

- She is entitled to control her partner and that it is her partner's obligation to acquiesce in this practice.
- Violence is permissible. (She can live with herself and conclude that she is an ethical/moral person even if she chooses violence against her partner.)
- Violence will produce the desired effect or minimize a more negative occurrence.
- Violence will not unduly endanger her. (She will neither sustain physical harm nor suffer legal, economic, or personal consequences that will outweigh the benefit achieved through the violence.)

Isn't Lesbian Violence More Often Fighting Than Battering?

The notion that physical violence between lesbians is usually fighting in which both partners engage is false and gravely endangering to battered lesbians.

Certainly there may be lesbians who fight with their partners or relationships in which both partners assault each other. Many may prefer to think of the violence in lesbian relationships as trivial, nuisance behavior of little consequence. Perhaps it is because lesbian partners are often of similar strength and size, therefore seemingly incapable of inflicting any serious physical harm on the other, or because as women we have been taught that violence is not appropriate and have not learned to fight.

Battering occurs within all lesbian communities regardless of class, race, age and lifestyle. It is critical that lesbians not conspire in any effort that would trivialize the great danger and destruction in lesbian battering.

The definition of lesbian battering in this paper recognizes that there are lesbian relationships in which both partners (or in the case of nonmonogamous relationships, all lovers) participate in violent conduct toward each other. Even where this violence is repeated and a pattern evolves between the intimates, this violence is not battering unless the effect of the violent conduct is to render the perpetrator more powerful and controlling in relation to the recipient. This is not to say that the author is approving lesbian violence while concluding that lesbian battering is immoral, illegal, and damaging in contrast to the peaceful, egalitarian relationships valued by feminists. The author believes that lesbian violence or fighting is, similarly, damaging and endangering.

It is also not to say that battered lesbians have never been violent toward the women who have battered them. Many have. But the violence is largely self-defense and sometimes is rage at past violations.

Battered lesbians do not characterize the violence that occurs in their relationships as arising out of fighting that was safe ventilation, contests of strength or consensual. Battered lesbians describe the patterns of violence as terrorism and control as outlined briefly in the beginning of this paper.

A lesbian who has been battered often believes, as apparently do some therapists and advocates, that her experiences of violence at the hands of her partner were "mutual" since she may have knocked her partner down to escape from a room in which she was being confined or she may have violently ejected the batterer from her apartment after the batterer broke in or she may have picked up a baseball bat and threatened to assault the batterer if she approached one step closer or she may have in a rage beaten the woman who had been battering her.

A significant number of battered lesbians, when first seeking assistance from friends or from battered women's advocates, question whether they really were battered if they have acted violently even once toward the batterer. It is as if they have concluded that absent any violence they can with clarity identify themselves as victims of the abuser, but once they have been violent, especially if it has worked in the immediate situation to stop the batterer, they are compelled to see themselves as equally culpable—as batterers—and as obligated to fight back every time or otherwise to accept the ultimate responsibility for the battering.[4]

For many, the batterer has instigated and reinforced this blaming of the victim—this reversal of reality. Sometimes the batterer will threaten to report acts of violence by the battered lesbian to the police, pointing out that if the battered lesbian has acted violently to such an extent that she could be criminally liable, then she surely is not battered and has engaged in mutual violence. Sometimes the batterer points out that the battered lesbian has hit her in public, so that no one will believe that she is tyrannized in private.

Invariably batterers blame battered women for the violence they inflict—alleging that if only the battered lesbian had not provoked her, the batterer would not have been violent; that the batterer is really under the control of the victim, helpless in the face of her behavior, and compelled to violence.

Batterers always see themselves as the victims of the battered woman. This perceived victimization is repeatedly shared with the battered lesbian.

Most battered lesbians are ashamed of the violence they have inflicted on the batterer. Since all battered lesbians have engaged in extensive efforts to protect the batterer from exposure as a terrorist and from the consequences of her violence, battered lesbians may continue "taking care of" the batterer by blaming herself, maximizing her violence and minimizing that of the batterer.

Many battered lesbians are women of substantial physical prowess and power; women who are objectively very much more powerful than their assailants. They are women who choose not to use this power to control the perpetrator or would do so only to protect themselves or stop the batterer. It is particularly hard for these women to acknowledge to themselves and to others that they have been battered. The powerful lesbian may not live in fear of the violence of her partner. She may, rather, live in dread of the violent episodes and in anxiety about control confrontations. Even though not fearful, she alters her life to accommodate the batterer and worries that her efforts will not suffice to avoid abuse. She may not fear the batterer's usual violence, but may fear that escalation in violent behavior could include suicide or assault on third parties.

Therefore, because a battered lesbian may have used violence against her batterer and because the batterer is convinced that the victim is responsible for the batterer's abuse, it is not surprising that many battered lesbians are confused when first contacting battered women's advocates to break free of the violence and to establish lives outside of the control of the perpetrator. It is not surprising that they may view themselves as both a batterer and a victim.[5]

Although it is critical that a woman who seeks assistance be afforded an opportunity to look carefully at the violence in her relationship to assess whether she is battered, it is imperative that she receive any emergency shelter and support services she requires and that she not be denied safe shelter during assessment. The availability of services must not be conditioned on the clarity of the caller.

This analysis of lesbian battering assumes that it is a rarity that a woman who is a victim of lesbian battering becomes a batterer later on in the relationship with the same person who battered her, nor is she likely to become a batterer in subsequent relationships.

The patterns of control and terrorism precipitated by battering are not easily undone. There would have to be an incredible shift in the power of the partner so that the battered lesbian acquires the power to use violence as a tactic to control and terrorize her mate. This might happen where the batterer becomes physically or mentally disabled and consequently loses the power behind the implied threat of violence.

Merely a realignment in economic security between the couple is not likely to shift power enough to make violence an effective tactical tool for the victim in controlling the batterer. Neither is the victim predisposed to use violence as a tactic of control where the power is shifted. Furthermore, it becomes even less likely that the power and the availability of violence as an effective tactic of control will continue to shift back and forth between the partners as the imbalance of power shifts.

As [with] the battered women's movement, we should not reject the lessons learned about battering in non-lesbian relationships when attempting to understand battering in lesbians' relationships.

We know that some non-lesbian women who are battered by men are violent. The fact of their violence does not compel us to reach a conclusion that they are not battered. This does not mean that we as a movement have encouraged the violence of battered women. We have, however, supported and defended a woman's right to act violently to protect herself, particularly where violence directed at her is life endangering. When men have said to us that the victims of their violence have been violent, we have not concluded then that violence was mutual or that the woman had not been battered.

Future Work for Lesbians and the Battered Women's Movement

We have much yet to learn about lesbian battering. This paper, and perhaps much of this book, are only the beginning of our understanding about battering in lesbian relationships. Many questions remain unanswered. Much preliminary knowledge may require refinement, but as lesbians and as the battered women's movement, we must devote greater efforts and resources in order to assure that safe shelters and advocacy are available to every battered lesbian in programs that are antihomophobic and lesbian-empowering.

To learn how we may be helpful to the victims of lesbian battering and to effectively strategize to end violence in lesbian relationships, we must listen to battered lesbians. Just as we came to understand men's violence against women by listening to rape survivors and battered women, we must believe that our best and most reliable source of knowledge about lesbian battering is that which battered lesbians can share with us.

List of Violent and Coercive Behaviors Utilized in Lesbian Battering

Physical

Assaults with weapons—guns, knives, whips, tire irons, cars, tent poles, high-heeled shoes, chair legs, broken bottles, pillows, cigarettes, poison.

Assaults with the batterer's own body—biting; scratching; kicking; punching; stomping; slapping; throwing down stairs; smashing eye glasses on the face of the victim; locking the victim in a closet or utilizing other confinement; tickling until loss of breath or panic.

Sleep interference; deprivation of heat or food.

Sexual

Rape; sex on demand; sexual withholding; weapons utilized or threatened sexually; forced sex with others; involuntary prostitution; coercing monogamy or non-monogamy; denying reproductive freedom; physical assaults during sexual encounters; sexually degrading language.

Property

Arson; slashing of car tires, clothing, and furniture; pet abuse or destruction; stealing and destruction of property; breaking and entering; pulling out telephones; breaking household items.

Threats

Threats to commit physical, sexual or property destruction; threats of violence against significant third parties; stalking, harassment.

Economic Control

Control over income and assets of partner; property destruction; interfering with employment or education; economic fraud; purchase of valuable assets in the name of the batterer only; using credit cards without the partner's permission; not working and requiring the victim to support the batterer.

Psychological or Emotional Abuse

Humiliation, degradation; lying; isolation; selection of entertainment/friends/religious experience; telling the partner that she is crazy, dumb, ugly; withholding critical information; selecting the food the partner eats; bursts of fury; pouting or withdrawal; mind manipulation.

Homophobic Control

Threatening to tell family, friends, employer, police, church community, etc. that the victim is a lesbian if she does (or doesn't) . . . ; telling the victim she deserves all that she gets because she is a lesbian; assuring her that no one would believe she has been violated because lesbians are not violent; reminding her that she has no options because the homophobic world will not help her.

NOTES

1. Please see a list of violent and coercive behaviors at the end of this article. These acts of abuse are illustrative of behaviors reported by battered lesbians to the author over the course of the last ten years.

2. A secondary victim is one who witnesses either the violence inflicted on another or the effects of such violence.

3. It is often believed that oppressed people will explode with equally violent oppressive actions toward their oppressors when the opportunity and risks permit, displacing their rage at convenient and safe targets. This belief embodies the fear of the oppressors that retaliation in kind will occur if control of the oppressed is relaxed, justifying continued oppression. It does not accurately describe the response of the oppressed.

4. There is no statistical data to demonstrate the proportion of battered lesbians who have acted violently to stop battering—who have fought back. However, many battered lesbians who have acknowledged violence in defense of themselves or others have suggested that immediately after separation from the abuser, they were confused about whether they had been batterers, as well as victims. Their understanding of violence and battering in the relationship had become tailored to the belief system of the batterer, and it took careful reflection on issues of control and power for clarity to emerge. Often this process took several months. Where the battered lesbian did not have the opportunity to think through her experience with a person knowledgeable about violence in intimate relationships, the recipient of battering sometimes found that the sorting-out and clarification process took longer.

5. What is tricky about this is that lesbian batterers see themselves as victims also. Meticulous interviewing should occur before conclusions are drawn about the admissions made by a lesbian that she is both a batterer and a victim.

Reflection

BARBARA HART

There comes a time. A time when the secrets that undergird oppression must be revealed. A time to risk the antipathy of those among the oppressed people who believe that disclosure will compromise the gains achieved and invite an escalation of injustice. A time to name the oppression despite the resistance of theorists who assert that the wrongs identified do not fit within the parameters of accepted theory. A time to name the oppression even if in naming it, a fiercely held dream of utopian lifestyle is called into question.

There were intense pressures to remain silent.

Naming "lesbian battering," exploring its behaviors and constructing theory about this violent and coercive conduct, raised huge challenges for a lesbian community that was working against discrimination to create justice for lesbian and gay people and to celebrate same-sex relationships and community.

Simultaneously, homophobia in the battered women's movement in the early '80s was emerging. Many advocates feared that acknowledgement of the leadership and dedication of lesbians in the work to end violence against women would undermine strides made in establishing solid funding for shelters, in coordinating the work of community agencies, and in achieving legislative reform. Some state coalitions were contemplating withdrawal from the National Coalition Against Domestic Violence, hoping thereby to distance their organizations from accusations of being "man-hating" or lesbian.

Furthermore, feminist analysis conceived of woman abuse as an outgrowth and essential underpinning of patriarchy. Men's violence against their women partners was supported by sexism in the culture. Tolerance of men's coercive controls and violence was embedded in Western religious and cultural mores.

Those lesbians who talked about violence by lesbians against their partners too often concluded that it was a class-based phenomenon—that only poor and working class lesbians were violent. Beyond this, many lesbians figured that the violence was being inflicted by women who were "male-identified."

This was the political and personal context of my life. Yet, I recognized that the above perspectives of society, the battered women's movement, and the lesbian-feminist community did not fit with my experience.

In late 1982, Suzanne Pharr, then co-chair of the Lesbian Task Force of NCADV, and I began talking about the invisibility of lesbian battering and the social bankruptcy of a movement that denied this reality either from disbelief or in order to promote shelter, services, and advocacy for heterosexual battered women. We decided to convene a meeting of workers in the shelter movement. We faltered and did not then name the violence "lesbian battering." Instead, we put out a one-page call for people to gather to discuss "violence in the lesbian community." More than 100 women responded. We met in Washington, D.C., in September, 1983. The gathering had no firm agenda and no budget. Suzanne and I agreed, with significant trepidation, to facilitate conversation.

The conference was the first in the country to explore lesbian battering, to listen to the voices of battered lesbians, and to forge an analysis about lesbian battering. Space does not permit a report on the process and conversations of the meeting. The most significant product of that gathering was the "Letter to the Lesbian Nation," which offered the first analysis of lesbian battering, stated our unequivocal opposition to it, and suggested responses.

Thereafter, the Lesbian Task Force decided to craft an anthology to create public discourse on lesbian battering. I was invited to write an article. "Lesbian Battering: An Examination" was my contribution to this ground-breaking collection. *Naming the Violence: Speaking Out on Lesbian Battering*, remains the definitive work on lesbian domestic violence.

In preparing to write this reflective piece to accompany "Lesbian Battering" in *Classic Papers on Violence Against Women*, not only did I re-read the article (which I still like, although it is, not surprisingly, too wordy and a tad redundant), I also asked activists and advocates in the battered women's movement and leaders in the LGBT field to offer feedback about the impact of *Naming the Violence* and "Lesbian Battering" on their work and lives.

Some responses were very personal:

> Up until that time, my friend and I had never spoken of the violence in our relationships; never knew what the other was going through, and never had . . . until *Naming the Violence* . . . offered the language with which to discuss it. Years later, we both ended up working in the domestic violence field, both of us concentrating our efforts on ending same-sex domestic violence. I've bought numerous copies of *Naming the Violence* and have witnessed firsthand, the light that snaps on when one knows there is a name for what they've withstood; and that they are not alone.
>
> You got people to start talking and thinking about lesbian battering, as well as addressing the myths.

Others talked about these writings as a resource for education of young professionals.

> I always teach this piece in the Domestic Abuse law class I teach. At the time we get to it, we have been struggling through the "why does battering happen," and most particularly the feminist analysis of "men do it because they can, because societal sexism backs them up, etc." vs. the various psychological/social reasons. When we read your piece, it really helps crystallize the abuse of power dimensions of the dynamics, as well as the universality of the effects and sub-causes, e.g. isolation.

Others noted that the writings were an impetus for making lesbian battering visible and the precursor to legislative reform.

> Many state protection order statutes did not include same sex relationships. When statutes were amended dating relationships were added to statutes. Same sex partners are now offered the same protections as heterosexual partners.

Some noted that in the '90s there appeared to be a hiatus in activity. However, they are encouraged that new vision and energy is now focused on enriching services, advocacy, theory-building, and movement growth. They note that "Lesbian Battering" and *Naming the Violence* still offer a theoretical and experiential foundation for the work to end partner battering by LGBT people.

For example, the 2002 Report of the National Coalition of Anti-Violence Programs offers preliminary research on the prevalence of LGBT battering, enumerates the legal remedies available to survivors, and lists many organizations providing services and advocacy to LGBT survivors and perpetrators. The National Coalition Against Domestic Violence continues to offer leadership on intervention and organizing against LGBT battering.

Naming the Violence gave birth to a vital justice movement.

CHAPTER

19 Mapping the Margins

Intersectionality, Identity Politics, and Violence against Women of Color

KIMBERLE CRENSHAW

Introduction

Over the last two decades, women have organized against the almost routine violence that shapes their lives.[1] Drawing from the strength of shared experience, women have recognized that the political demands of millions speak more powerfully than the pleas of a few isolated voices. This politicization in turn has transformed the way we understand violence against women. For example, battering and rape, once seen as private (family matters) and aberrational (errant sexual aggression), are now largely recognized as part of a broad-scale system of domination that affects women as a class.[2] This process of recognizing as social and systemic what was formerly perceived as isolated and individual has also characterized the identity politics of African Americans, other people of color, and gays and lesbians, among others. For all these groups, identity-based politics has been a source of strength, community, and intellectual development.

The embrace of identity politics, however, has been in tension with dominant conceptions of social justice. Race, gender, and other identity categories are most often treated in mainstream liberal discourse as vestiges of bias or domination—that is, as intrinsically negative frameworks in which social power works to exclude or marginalize those who are different. According to this understanding, our liberatory objective should be to empty such categories of any social significance. Yet implicit in certain strands of feminist and racial liberation movements, for example, is the view that the social power in delineating difference need not be the power of domination; it can instead be the source of social empowerment and reconstruction.

The problem with identity politics is not that it fails to transcend difference, as some critics charge, but rather the opposite—that it frequently conflates or ignores intragroup differences. In the context of violence against women, this elision of difference in identity politics is problematic, fundamentally because the violence that many women experience is often shaped by other dimensions of their identities, such as race and class. Moreover, ignoring difference within groups contributes to tension among groups, another problem of identity politics that bears on efforts to politicize violence against women. Feminist efforts to politicize experiences of women and antiracist efforts to politicize experiences of people of color have frequently proceeded as though the issues and experiences they each detail occur on mutually exclusive terrains. Although racism and sexism readily intersect in the lives of real people, they seldom do in feminist and antiracist practices. And so, when the practices expound identity as woman or person of color as an either/or proposition, they relegate the identity of women of color to a location that resists telling.

My objective in this article is to advance the telling of that location by exploring the race and gender dimensions of violence against women of color.[3] Contemporary feminist and antiracist discourses have failed to consider intersectional identities such as women of color.[4] Focusing on two dimensions of male violence against women—battering and rape—I consider how the experiences of women of color are frequently the product of intersecting patterns of racism and sexism,[5] and how these experiences tend not to be represented within the discourses of either feminism or antiracism. Because of their intersectional identity as both women and of color within discourses that are shaped to respond to one or the other, women of color are marginalized within both.

In an earlier article, I used the concept of intersectionality to denote the various ways in which race and gender interact to shape the multiple dimensions of Black[6] women's employment experiences.[7] My objective there was to illustrate that many of the experiences Black women face are not subsumed within the traditional boundaries of race or gender discrimination as these boundaries are currently understood, and that the intersection of racism and sexism factors into Black women's lives in ways that cannot be captured wholly by looking at the race or gender dimensions of those experiences separately. I build on those observations here by exploring the various ways in which race and gender intersect in shaping structural, political, and representational aspects of violence against women of color.[8]

I should say at the outset that intersectionality is not being offered here as some new, totalizing theory of identity. Nor do I mean to suggest that violence against women of color can be explained only through the specific frameworks of race and gender considered here.[9] Indeed, factors I address only in part or not at all, such as class or sexuality, are often as critical in shaping the experiences of women of color. My focus on the intersections of race and gender only highlights the need to account for multiple grounds of identity when considering how the social world is constructed.[10]

Structural Intersectionality

Structural Intersectionality and Battering

I observed the dynamics of structural intersectionality during a brief field study of battered women's shelters located in minority communities in Los Angeles.[11] In most cases, the physical assault that leads women to these shelters is merely the most immediate manifestation of the subordination they experience. Many women who seek protection are unemployed or underemployed, and a good number of them are poor. Shelters serving these women cannot afford to address only the violence inflicted by the batterer; they must also confront the other multilayered and routinized forms of domination that often converge in these women's lives, hindering their ability to create alternatives to the abusive relationships that brought them to shelters in the first place. Many women of color, for example, are burdened by poverty, child care responsibilities, and the lack of job skills.[12] These burdens, largely the consequence of gender and class oppression, are then compounded by the racially discriminatory employment and housing practices women of color often face,[13] as well as by the disproportionately high unemployment among people of color that makes battered women of color less able to depend on the support of friends and relatives for temporary shelter.[14]

Where systems of race, gender, and class domination converge, as they do in the experiences of battered women of color, intervention strategies based solely on the experiences of women who do not share the same class or race backgrounds will be of limited help to women who because of race and class face different obstacles.[15] Such was the case in 1990 when Congress amended the marriage fraud provisions of the Immigration and Nationality Act to protect immigrant women who were battered or exposed to extreme cruelty by the United States citizens or permanent residents these women immigrated to the United States to marry. Under the marriage fraud provisions of the Act, a person who immigrated to the United States to marry a United States citizen or permanent resident had to remain "properly" married for two years before even applying for permanent resident status,[16] at which time applications for the immigrant's permanent status were required of both spouses.[17] Predictably, under these circumstances, many immigrant women were reluctant to leave even the most abusive of partners for fear of being deported.[18] When faced with the choice between protection from their batterers and protection against deportation, many immigrant women chose the latter.[19] Reports of the tragic consequences of this double subordination put pressure on Congress to include in the Immigration Act of 1990 a provision amending the marriage fraud rules to allow for an explicit waiver for hardship caused by domestic violence.[20] Yet many immigrant women, particularly immigrant women of color, have remained vulnerable to battering because they are unable to meet the conditions established for a waiver. The evidence required to support a waiver "can include, but is not limited to, reports and affidavits from police, medical personnel, psychologists, school officials, and social service agencies."[21] For many immigrant women, limited access to these resources can make it difficult for them to obtain the evidence needed for a waiver. And cultural barriers often further discourage immigrant women from reporting or escaping battering situations. Tina Shum, a family counselor at a social service agency, points out that "[t]his law sounds so easy to apply, but there are cultural complications in the Asian community that make even these requirements difficult. . . . Just to find the opportunity and courage to call us is an accomplishment for many."[22] The typical immigrant spouse, she suggests, may live "[i]n an extended family where several generations live together, there may be no privacy on the telephone, no opportunity to leave the house and no understanding of public phones."[23] As a consequence, many immigrant women are wholly dependent on their husbands as their link to the world outside their homes.[24]

Immigrant women are also vulnerable to spousal violence because so many of them depend on their husbands for information regarding their legal status.[25] Many women who are now permanent residents continue to suffer abuse under threats of deportation by their husbands. Even if the threats are unfounded, women who have no independent access to information will still be intimidated by such threats.[26] And even though the domestic violence waiver focuses on immigrant women whose husbands are United States citizens or permanent residents, there are countless women married to undocumented workers (or who are themselves undocumented) who suffer in silence for fear that the security of their entire families will be jeopardized should they seek help or otherwise call attention to themselves.[27]

Language barriers present another structural problem that often limits opportunities of non-English-speaking women to take advantage of existing support services.[28] Such barriers not only limit access to information about shelters, but also limit access to the security shelters provide. Some shelters turn non-English-speaking women away for lack of bilingual personnel and resources.[29]

These examples illustrate how patterns of subordination intersect in women's experience of domestic violence. Intersectional subordination need not be intentionally produced; in fact, it is frequently the consequence of the imposition of one burden that interacts with preexisting vulnerabilities to create yet another dimension of disempowerment. In the case of the marriage fraud provisions of the Immigration and Nationality Act, the imposition of a policy specifically designed to burden one class—immigrant spouses seeking permanent resident status—exacerbated the disempowerment of those already subordinated by other structures of domination. By failing to take into account the vulnerability of immigrant spouses to domestic violence, Congress positioned these women to absorb the simultaneous impact of its anti-immigration policy and their spouses' abuse.

The enactment of the domestic violence waiver of the marriage fraud provisions similarly illustrates how modest attempts to respond to certain problems can be ineffective when the intersectional location of women of color is not considered in fashioning the remedy. Cultural identity and class affect the likelihood that a battered spouse could take advantage of the waiver. Although the waiver is formally available to all women, the terms of the waiver make it inaccessible to some. Immigrant women who are socially, culturally, or economically privileged are more likely to be able to marshall the resources needed to satisfy the waiver requirements. Those immigrant women least able to take advantage of the waiver—women who are socially or economically the most marginal—are the ones most likely to be women of color.

Structural Intersectionality and Rape

Women of color are differently situated in the economic, social, and political worlds. When reform efforts undertaken on behalf of women neglect this fact, women of color are less likely to have their needs met than women who are racially privileged. For example, counselors who provide rape crisis services to women of color report that a significant proportion of the resources allocated to them must be spent handling problems other than rape itself. Meeting these needs often places these counselors at odds with their funding agencies, which allocate funds according to standards of need that are largely white and middle-class.[30] These uniform standards of need ignore the fact that different needs often demand different priorities in terms of resource allocation, and consequently, these standards hinder the ability of counselors to address the needs of nonwhite and poor women.[31] A case in point: women of color occupy positions both physically and culturally marginalized within dominant society, and so information must be targeted directly to them in order to reach them.[32] Accordingly, rape crisis centers must earmark more resources for basic information dissemination in communities of color than in white ones.

Increased costs are but one consequence of serving people who cannot be reached by mainstream channels of information. As noted earlier, counselors in minority communities report spending hours locating resources and contacts to meet the housing and other immediate needs of women who have been assaulted. Yet this work is only considered "information and referral" by funding agencies and as such, is typically underfunded, notwithstanding the magnitude of need for these services in minority communities.[33] The problem is compounded by expectations that rape crisis centers will use a significant portion of resources allocated to them on counselors to accompany victims to court,[34] even though women of color are less likely to have their cases pursued in the criminal justice system.[35] The resources expected to be set aside for court services are misdirected in these communities.

The fact that minority women suffer from the effects of multiple subordination, coupled with institutional expectations based on inappropriate nonintersectional contexts, shapes and ultimately limits the opportunities for meaningful intervention on their behalf. Recognizing the failure to consider intersectional dynamics may go far toward explaining the high levels of failure, frustration, and burn-out experienced by counselors who attempt to meet the needs of minority women victims.

Political Intersectionality

The concept of political intersectionality highlights the fact that women of color are situated within at least two subordinated groups that frequently pursue conflicting political agendas. The need to split one's political energies between two sometimes opposing groups is a dimension of intersectional disempowerment that men of color and white women seldom confront. Indeed, their specific raced and gendered experiences, although intersectional, often define as well as confine the interests of the entire group. For example, racism as experienced by people of color who are of a particular gender—male—tends to determine the parameters of antiracist strategies, just as sexism as experienced by women who are of a particular race—white—tends to ground the women's movement. The problem is not simply that both discourses fail women of color by not acknowledging the "additional" issue of race or of patriarchy but that the discourses are often inadequate even to the discrete tasks of articulating the full dimensions of racism and sexism. Because women of color experience racism in ways not always the same as those experienced by men of color and sexism in ways not always parallel to experiences of white women, antiracism and feminism are limited, even on their own terms.

Among the most troubling political consequences of the failure of antiracist and feminist discourses to address the intersections of race and gender is the fact that, to the extent they can forward the interest of "people of color" and "women," respectively, one analysis often implicitly denies the validity of the other. The failure of feminism to interrogate race means that the resistance strategies of feminism will often replicate and reinforce the subordination of people of color, and the failure of antiracism to interrogate patriarchy means that antiracism will frequently reproduce the subordination of women. These mutual elisions present a particularly difficult political dilemma for women of color. Adopting either analysis constitutes a denial of a fundamental dimension of our subordination and precludes the development of a political discourse that more fully empowers women of color.

The Politicization of Domestic Violence

That the political interests of women of color are obscured and sometimes jeopardized by political strategies that ignore or suppress intersectional issues is illustrated by my experiences in gathering information for this article. I attempted to review Los Angeles Police Department statistics reflecting the rate of domestic violence interventions by precinct because such statistics can provide a rough picture of arrests by racial group, given the degree of racial segregation in Los Angeles.[36] L.A.P.D., however, would not release the statistics. A representative explained that one reason the statistics were not released was that domestic violence activists both within and outside the Department feared that statistics reflecting the extent of domestic violence in minority communities might be selectively interpreted and publicized so as to undermine long-term efforts to force the Department to address domestic violence as a serious problem. I was told that activists were worried that the statistics might permit opponents to dismiss domestic violence as a minority problem and, therefore, not deserving of aggressive action.

The informant also claimed that representatives from various minority communities opposed the release of these statistics. They were concerned, apparently, that the data would unfairly represent Black and Brown communities as unusually violent, potentially reinforcing stereotypes that might be used in attempts to justify oppressive police tactics and other discriminatory practices. These misgivings are based on the familiar and not unfounded premise that certain minority groups—especially Black men—have already been stereotyped as uncontrollably violent. Some worry that attempts to make domestic violence an object of political action may only serve to confirm such stereotypes and undermine efforts to combat negative beliefs about the Black community.

This account sharply illustrates how women of color can be erased by the strategic silences of antiracism and feminism. The political priorities of both were defined in ways that suppressed information that could have facilitated attempts to confront the problem of domestic violence in communities of color.

Domestic Violence and Antiracist Politics. Within communities of color, efforts to stem the politicization of domestic violence are often grounded in attempts to maintain the integrity of the community. The articulation of this perspective takes different forms. Some critics allege that feminism has no place within communities of color, that the issues are internally divisive, and that they represent the migration of white women's concerns into a context in which they are not only irrelevant but also harmful. At its most extreme, this rhetoric denies that gender violence is a problem in the community and characterizes any effort to politicize gender subordination as itself a community problem. This is the position taken by Shahrazad Ali in her controversial book, *The Blackman's Guide to Understanding the Blackwoman.*[37] In this stridently antifeminist tract, Ali draws a positive correlation between domestic violence and the liberation of African Americans. Ali blames the deteriorating conditions within the Black community on the insubordination of Black women and on the failure of Black men to control them.[38] Ali goes so far as to advise Black men to physically chastise Black women when they are "disrespectful."[39] While she cautions that Black men must use moderation in disciplining "their" women, she argues that Black men must sometimes resort to physical force to reestablish the authority over Black women that racism has disrupted.[40]

Ali's premise is that patriarchy is beneficial for the Black community,[41] and that it must be strengthened through coercive means if necessary.[42] Yet the violence that accompanies this will to control is devastating, not only for the Black women who are victimized, but also for the entire Black community.[43] The recourse to violence to resolve conflicts establishes a dangerous pattern for children raised in such environments and contributes to many other pressing problems.[44] It has been estimated that nearly forty percent of all homeless women and children have fled violence in the home,[45] and an estimated sixty-three percent of young men between the ages of eleven and twenty who are imprisoned for homicide have killed their mothers' batterers.[46] And yet, while gang violence, homicide, and other forms of Black-on-Black crime have increasingly been discussed within African-American politics, patriarchal ideas about gender and power preclude the recognition of domestic violence as yet another compelling incidence of Black-on-Black crime.

Efforts such as Ali's to justify violence against women in the name of Black liberation are indeed extreme.[47] The more common problem is that the political or cultural interests of the community are interpreted in a way that precludes full public recognition of the problem of domestic violence. While it would be misleading to suggest that white Americans have come to terms with the degree of violence in their own homes, it is nonetheless the case that race adds yet another dimension to why the problem of domestic violence is suppressed within nonwhite communities. People of color often must weigh their interests in avoiding issues that might reinforce distorted public perceptions against the need to acknowledge and address intracommunity problems. Yet the cost of suppression is seldom recognized in part because the failure to discuss the issue shapes perceptions of how serious the problem is in the first place.

The controversy over Alice Walker's novel *The Color Purple* can be understood as an intracommunity debate about the political costs of exposing gender violence within the Black community.[48] Some critics chastised Walker for portraying Black men as violent brutes.[49] One critic lambasted Walker's portrayal of Celie, the emotionally and physically abused protagonist who finally triumphs in the end. Walker, the critic contended, had created in Celie a Black woman whom she couldn't imagine existing in any Black community she knew or could conceive of.[50]

The claim that Celie was somehow an unauthentic character might be read as a consequence of silencing discussion of intracommunity violence. Celie may be unlike any Black woman we know because the real terror experienced daily by minority women is routinely concealed in a misguided (though perhaps understandable) attempt to forestall racial stereotyping. Of course, it is true that representations of Black violence—whether statistical or fictional—are often written into a larger script that consistently portrays Black and other minority communities as pathologically violent. The problem, however, is not so much the portrayal of violence itself as it is the absence of other narratives and images portraying a fuller range of Black experience. Suppression of some of these issues in the name of antiracism imposes real costs. Where information about violence in minority communities is not available, domestic violence is unlikely to be addressed as a serious issue.

The political imperatives of a narrowly focused antiracist strategy support other practices that isolate women of color. For example, activists who have attempted to provide support services to Asian- and African-American women report intense resistance from those communities.[51] At other times, cultural and social factors contribute to suppression. Nilda Rimonte, director of Everywoman's Shelter in Los Angeles, points out that in the Asian community, saving the honor of the family from shame is a priority.[52] Unfortunately, this priority tends to be interpreted as obliging women not to scream rather than obliging men not to hit.

Race and culture contribute to the suppression of domestic violence in other ways as well. Women of color are often reluctant to call the police, a hesitancy likely due to a general unwillingness among people of color to subject their private lives to the scrutiny and control of a police force that is frequently hostile. There is also a more generalized community ethic against public intervention, the product of a desire to create a private world free from the diverse assaults on the public lives of racially subordinated people. The home is not simply a man's castle in the patriarchal sense, but may also function as a safe haven from the indignities of life in a racist society. However, but for this "safe haven" in many cases, women of color victimized by violence might otherwise seek help.

There is also a general tendency within antiracist discourse to regard the problem of violence against women of color as just another manifestation of racism. In this sense, the relevance of gender domination within the community is reconfigured as a consequence of discrimination against men. Of course, it is probably true that racism contributes to the cycle of violence, given the stress that men of color experience in dominant society. It is therefore more than reasonable to explore the links between racism and domestic violence. But the chain of violence is more complex and extends beyond this single link. Racism is linked to patriarchy to the extent that racism denies men of color the power and privilege that dominant men enjoy. When violence is understood as an acting-out of being denied male power in other spheres, it seems counterproductive to embrace constructs that implicitly link the solution to domestic violence to the acquisition of greater male power. The more promising political imperative is to challenge the legitimacy of such power expectations by exposing their dysfunctional and debilitating effect on families and communities of color. Moreover, while understanding links between racism and domestic violence is an important component of any effective intervention strategy, it is also clear that women of color need not await the ultimate triumph over racism before they can expect to live violence-free lives.

Race and the Domestic Violence Lobby. Not only do race-based priorities function to obscure the problem of violence suffered by women of color; feminist concerns often suppress minority experiences as well. Strategies for increasing awareness of domestic violence within the white community tend to begin by citing the commonly shared assumption that battering is a minority problem. The strategy then focuses on demolishing this strawman, stressing that spousal abuse also occurs in the white community. Countless first-person stories begin with a statement like, "I was not supposed to be a battered wife." That battering occurs in families of all races and all classes seems to be an ever-present theme of anti-abuse campaigns.[53] First-person anecdotes and studies, for example, consistently assert that battering cuts across racial, ethnic, economic, educational, and religious lines.[54] Such disclaimers seem relevant only in the presence of an initial, widely held belief that domestic violence occurs primarily in minority or poor families. Indeed some authorities explicitly renounce the "stereotypical myths" about battered women.[55] A few commentators have even transformed the message that battering is not exclusively a problem of the poor or minority communities into a claim that it equally affects all races and classes.[56] Yet these comments seem less concerned with exploring domestic abuse within "stereotyped" communities than with removing the stereotype as an obstacle to exposing battering within white middle- and upper-class communities.[57]

Efforts to politicize the issue of violence against women challenge beliefs that violence occurs only in homes of "others." While it is unlikely that advocates and others who adopt this rhetorical strategy intend to exclude or ignore the needs of poor and colored women, the underlying premise of this seemingly universalistic appeal is to keep the sensibilities of dominant social groups focused on the experiences of those groups. . . .

This strategy permits white women victims to come into focus, but does little to disrupt the patterns of neglect that permitted the problem to continue as long as it was imagined to be a minority problem. The experience of violence by minority women is ignored, except to the extent it gains white support for domestic violence programs in the white community.

Race and Domestic Violence Support Services. Women working in the field of domestic violence have sometimes reproduced the subordination and marginalization of women of color by adopting policies, priorities, or strategies of empowerment that either elide or wholly disregard the particular intersectional needs of women of color. While gender, race, and class intersect to create the particular context in which women of color experience violence, certain choices made by "allies" can reproduce intersectional subordination within the very resistance strategies designed to respond to the problem.

This problem is starkly illustrated by the inaccessibility of domestic violence support services to many non-English-speaking women. In a letter written to the deputy commissioner of the New York State Department of Social Services, Diana Campos, Director of

Human Services for Programas de Ocupaciones y Desarrollo Economico Real, Inc. (PODER), detailed the case of a Latina in crisis who was repeatedly denied accommodation at a shelter because she could not prove that she was English-proficient. The woman had fled her home with her teenaged son, believing her husband's threats to kill them both. She called the domestic violence hotline administered by PODER seeking shelter for herself and her son. Because most shelters would not accommodate the woman with her son, they were forced to live on the streets for two days. The hotline counselor was finally able to find an agency that would take both the mother and the son, but when the counselor told the intake coordinator at the shelter that the woman spoke limited English, the coordinator told her that they could not take anyone who was not English-proficient. When the woman in crisis called back and was told of the shelter's "rule," she replied that she could understand English if spoken to her slowly. As Campos explains, Mildred, the hotline counselor, told Wendy, the intake coordinator, that the woman said that she could communicate a little in English. Wendy told Mildred that they could not provide services to this woman because they have house rules that the woman must agree to follow. Mildred asked her, "What if the woman agrees to follow your rules? Will you still not take her?" Wendy responded that all of the women at the shelter are required to attend [a] support group and they would not be able to have her in the group if she could not communicate. Mildred mentioned the severity of this woman's case. She told Wendy that the woman had been wandering the streets at night while her husband is home, and she had been mugged twice. She also reiterated the fact that this woman was in danger of being killed by either her husband or a mugger. Mildred expressed that the woman's safety was a priority at this point, and that once in a safe place, receiving counseling in a support group could be dealt with.[58]

The intake coordinator restated the shelter's policy of taking only English-speaking women, and stated further that the woman would have to call the shelter herself for screening. If the woman could communicate with them in English, she might be accepted. When the woman called the PODER hotline later that day, she was in such a state of fear that the hotline counselor who had been working with her had difficulty understanding her in Spanish.[59] Campos directly intervened at this point, calling the executive director of the shelter. A counselor called back from the shelter. As Campos reports,

> Marie [the counselor] told me that they did not want to take the woman in the shelter because they felt that the woman would feel isolated. I explained that the son agreed to translate for his mother during the intake process. Furthermore, that we would assist them in locating a Spanish-speaking battered women's advocate to assist in counseling her. Marie stated that utilizing the son was not an acceptable means of communication for them, since it further victimized the victim. In addition, she stated that they had similar experiences with women who were non-English-speaking, and that the women eventually just left because they were not able to communicate with anyone. I expressed my extreme concern for her safety and reiterated that we would assist them in providing her with the necessary services until we could get her placed someplace where they had bilingual staff.[60]

After several more calls, the shelter finally agreed to take the woman. The woman called once more during the negotiation; however, after a plan was in place, the woman never called back. Said Campos, "After so many calls, we are now left to wonder if she is alive and well, and if she will ever have enough faith in our ability to help her to call us again the next time she is in crisis."[61]

Despite this woman's desperate need, she was unable to receive the protection afforded English-speaking women, due to the shelter's rigid commitment to exclusionary policies. Perhaps even more troubling than the shelter's lack of bilingual resources was its refusal to allow a friend or relative to translate for the woman. This story illustrates the absurdity of a feminist approach that would make the ability to attend a support group without a translator a more significant consideration in the distribution of resources than the risk of physical harm on the street. The point is not that the shelter's image of empowerment is empty, but rather that it was imposed without regard to the disempowering consequences for women who didn't match the kind of client the shelter's administrators imagined. And thus they failed to accomplish the basic priority of the shelter movement—to get the woman out of danger.

Here the woman in crisis was made to bear the burden of the shelter's refusal to anticipate and provide for the needs of non-English-speaking women. Said Campos, "It is unfair to impose more stress on victims by placing them in the position of having to demonstrate their proficiency in English in order to receive services that are readily available to other battered women."[62] . . .

The struggle over which differences matter and which do not is neither an abstract nor an insignificant debate among women. Indeed, these conflicts are about more than difference as such; they raise critical issues of power. The problem is not simply that women who dominate the antiviolence movement are different from women of color but that they frequently have power to determine, either through material or rhetorical resources, whether the intersectional differences of women of color will be incorporated at all into the basic formulation of policy. Thus, the struggle over incorporating these differences is not a petty or superficial conflict about who gets to sit at the head of the table. In the context of violence, it is sometimes a deadly serious matter of who will survive—and who will not.[63]

Political Intersectionalities in Rape

In the previous sections, I have used intersectionality to describe or frame various relationships between race and gender. I have used intersectionality as a way to articulate the interaction of racism and patriarchy generally. I have also used intersectionality to describe the location of women of color both within overlapping systems of subordination and at the margins of feminism and antiracism. When race and gender factors are examined in the context of rape, intersectionality can be used to map the ways in which racism and patriarchy have shaped conceptualizations of rape, to describe the unique vulnerability of women of color to these converging systems of domination, and to track the marginalization of women of color within antiracist and antirape discourses.[64]

Racism and Sexism in Dominant Conceptualizations of Rape. Generations of critics and activists have criticized dominant conceptualizations of rape as racist and sexist. These efforts have been important in revealing the way in which representations of rape both reflect and reproduce race and gender hierarchies in American society.[65] Black women, as both women and people of color, are situated within both groups, each of which has benefitted from challenges to sexism and racism, respectively, and yet the particular dynamics of gender and race relating to the rape of Black women have received scant attention. Although antiracist and antisexist assaults on rape have been politically useful to Black women, at some level, the monofocal antiracist and feminist critiques have also produced a political discourse that disserves Black women.

Historically, the dominant conceptualization of rape as quintessentially Black offender/white victim has left Black men subject to legal and extralegal violence. The use of rape to legitimize efforts to control and discipline the Black community is well established, and the casting of all Black men as potential threats to the sanctity of white womanhood was a familiar construct that antiracists confronted and attempted to dispel over a century ago.

Feminists have attacked other dominant, essentially patriarchal, conceptions of rape, particularly as represented through law. The early emphasis of rape law on the property-like aspect of women's chastity resulted in less solicitude for rape victims whose chastity had been in some way devalued. Some of the most insidious assumptions were written into the law, including the early common-law notion that a woman alleging rape must be able to show that she resisted to the utmost in order to prove that she was raped, rather than seduced. Women themselves were put on trial, as judge and jury scrutinized their lives to determine whether they were innocent victims or women who essentially got what they were asking for. Legal rules thus functioned to legitimize a good woman/bad woman dichotomy in which women who lead sexually autonomous lives were usually least likely to be vindicated if they were raped.

Today, long after the most egregious discriminatory laws have been eradicated, constructions of rape in popular discourse and in criminal law continue to manifest vestiges of these racist and sexist themes. As Valerie Smith notes, "a variety of cultural narratives that historically have linked sexual violence with racial oppression continue to determine the nature of public response to [interracial rapes]."[66] Smith reviews the well-publicized case of a jogger who was raped in New York's Central Park[67] to expose how the public discourse on the assault "made the story of sexual victimization inseparable from the rhetoric of racism."[68] Smith contends that in dehumanizing the rapists as "savages," "wolves," and "beasts," the press "shaped the discourse around the event in ways that inflamed pervasive fears about black men."[69] . . .

Other media spectacles suggest that traditional gender-based stereotypes that are oppressive to women continue to figure in the popular construction of rape. In Florida, for example, a controversy was sparked by a jury's acquittal of a man accused of a brutal rape because, in the jurors' view, the woman's attire suggested that she was asking for sex.[70] Even the press coverage of William Kennedy Smith's rape trial involved a considerable degree of speculation regarding the sexual history of his accuser.[71]

The racism and sexism written into the social construction of rape are merely contemporary manifestations of rape narratives emanating from a historical period when race and sex hierarchies were more explicitly policed. Yet another is the devaluation of Black women and the marginalization of their sexual victimizations. This was dramatically shown in the special attention given to the rape of the Central Park jogger during a week in which twenty-eight other cases of first-degree rape or attempted rape were reported in New York.[72] Many of these rapes were as horrific as the rape in Central Park, yet all were virtually ignored by the media. Some were gang rapes,[73] and in a case that prosecutors described as was "one of the most brutal in recent years," a woman was raped, sodomized and thrown fifty feet off the top of a four-story building in Brooklyn. Witnesses testified that the victim "screamed as she plunged down the air shaft. . . . She suffered fractures of both ankles and legs, her pelvis was shattered and she suffered extensive internal injuries."[74] This rape survivor, like most of the other forgotten victims that week, was a woman of color.

In short during the period when the Central Park jogger dominated the headlines, many equally horrifying rapes occurred. None, however, elicited the public expressions of horror and outrage that attended the Central Park rape.[75] To account for these different responses, Professor Smith suggests a sexual hierarchy in operation that holds certain female bodies in higher regard than others.[76] Statistics from prosecution of rape cases suggest that this hierarchy is at least one significant, albeit often overlooked factor in evaluating attitudes toward rape.[77] A study of rape dispositions in Dallas, for example, showed that the average prison term for a man convicted of raping a Black woman was two years,[78] as compared to five years for the rape of a Latina and ten years for the rape of an Anglo woman.[79] A related issue is the fact that African-American victims of rape are the least likely to be believed.[80] The Dallas study and others like it also point to a more subtle problem: neither the antirape nor the antiracist political agenda has focused on the Black rape victim. This inattention stems from the way the problem of rape is conceptualized within antiracist and antirape reform discourses. Although the rhetoric of both agendas formally includes Black women, racism is generally not problematized in feminism, and sexism, not problematized in antiracist discourses. Consequently, the plight of Black women is relegated to a secondary importance: The primary beneficiaries of policies supported by feminists and others concerned about rape tend to be white women; the primary beneficiaries of the Black community's concern over racism and rape, Black men. Ultimately, the reformist and rhetorical strategies that have grown out of antiracist and feminist rape reform movements have been ineffective in politicizing the treatment of Black women.

Race and the Antirape Lobby. Feminist critiques of rape have focused on the way rape law has reflected dominant rules and expectations that tightly regulate the sexuality of women. In the context of the rape trial, the formal definition of rape as well as the evidentiary rules applicable in a rape trial discriminate against women by measuring the rape victim against a narrow norm of acceptable sexual conduct for women. Deviation from that norm tends to turn women into illegitimate rape victims, leading to rejection of their claims. . . .

This type of feminist critique of rape law has informed many of the fundamental reform measures enacted in antirape legislation, including increased penalties for convicted rapists[81] and changes in evidentiary rules to preclude attacks on the woman's moral character.[82] These reforms limit the tactics attorneys might use to tarnish the image of the rape victim, but they operate within preexisting social constructs that distinguish victims from nonvictims on the basis of their sexual character. And so these reforms, while beneficial, do not challenge the background cultural narratives that undermine the credibility of Black women.

Because Black women face subordination based on both race and gender, reforms of rape law and judicial procedures that are premised on narrow conceptions of gender subordination may not address the devaluation of Black women. Much of the problem results from the way certain gender expectations for women intersect with certain sexualized notions of race, notions that are deeply entrenched in American culture. Sexualized images of African Americans go all the way back to Europeans' first engagement with Africans. Blacks have long been portrayed as more sexual, more earthy, more gratification-oriented. These sexualized images of race intersect with norms of women's sexuality, norms that are used to distinguish good women from bad, the madonnas from the whores. Thus Black women are essentially prepackaged as bad women within cultural narratives about good women who can be raped and bad women who cannot. The discrediting of Black women's claims is the consequence of a complex intersection of a gendered sexual system, one that constructs rules appropriate for good and bad women, and a race code that provides images defining the allegedly essential nature of Black women. If these sexual images form even part of the cultural imagery of Black women, then the very representation of a Black female body at least suggests certain narratives that may make Black women's rape either less believable or less important. These narratives may explain why rapes of Black women are less likely to result in convictions and long prison terms than rapes of white women.[83]

Rape law reform measures that do not in some way engage and challenge the narratives that are read onto Black women's bodies are unlikely to affect the way cultural beliefs oppress Black women in rape trials. While the degree to which legal reform can directly challenge cultural beliefs that shape rape trials is limited,[84] the very effort to mobilize political resources toward addressing the sexual oppression of Black women can be an important first step in drawing greater attention to the problem. One obstacle to such an effort has been the failure of most antirape activists to analyze specifically the consequences of racism in the context of rape. In the absence of a direct attempt to address the racial dimensions of rape, Black women are simply presumed to be represented in and benefitted by prevailing feminist critiques.

Antiracism and Rape. Antiracist critiques of rape law focus on how the law operates primarily to condemn rapes of white women by Black men.[85] While the heightened concern with protecting white women against Black men has been primarily criticized as a form of discrimination against Black men,[86] it just as surely reflects devaluation of Black women.[87] This disregard for Black women results from an exclusive focus on the consequences of the problem for Black men.[88] Of course, rape accusations historically have provided a justification for white terrorism against the Black community, generating a legitimating power of such strength that it created a veil virtually impenetrable to appeals based on either humanity or fact.[89] Ironically, while the fear of the Black rapist was exploited to legitimate the practice of lynching, rape was not even alleged in most cases.[90] The well-developed fear of Black sexuality served primarily to increase white tolerance for racial terrorism as a prophylactic measure to keep Blacks under control.[91] Within the African-American community, cases involving race-based accusations against Black men have stood as hallmarks of racial injustice. The prosecution of the Scottsboro boys[92] and the Emmett Till[93] tragedy, for example, triggered African-American resistance to the rigid social codes of white supremacy.[94] To the extent rape of Black women is thought to dramatize racism, it is usually cast as an assault on Black manhood, demonstrating his inability to protect Black women. The direct assault on Black womanhood is less frequently seen as an assault on the Black community.[95]

The sexual politics that this limited reading of racism and rape engenders continues to play out today, as illustrated by the Mike Tyson rape trial. The use of antiracist rhetoric to mobilize support for Tyson represented an ongoing practice of viewing with considerable suspicion rape accusations against Black men and interpreting sexual racism through a male-centered frame. The historical experience of Black men has so completely occupied the dominant conceptions of racism and rape that there is little room to squeeze in the experiences of Black women. Consequently, racial solidarity was continually raised as a rallying point on behalf of Tyson, but never on behalf of Desiree Washington, Tyson's Black accuser. Leaders ranging from Benjamin Books to Louis Farrakhan expressed their support for Tyson,[96] yet no established Black leader voiced any concern for Washington. The fact that Black men have often been falsely accused of raping white women underlies the antiracist defense of Black men accused of rape even when the accuser herself is a Black woman.

As a result of this continual emphasis on Black male sexuality as the core issue in antiracist critiques of rape, Black women who raise claims of rape against Black men are not only disregarded but also sometimes vilified within the African-American community. One can only imagine the alienation experienced by a Black rape survivor such as Desiree Washington when the accused rapist is embraced and defended as a victim of racism while she is, at best, disregarded, and at worst, ostracized and ridiculed. In contrast, Tyson was the beneficiary of the longstanding practice of using antiracist rhetoric to deflect the injury suffered by Black women victimized by Black men. Some defended the support given to Tyson on the ground that all African Americans can readily imagine their sons, fathers, brothers, or uncles being wrongly accused of rape. Yet daughters, mothers, sisters, and aunts also deserve at least a similar concern, since statistics show that Black women are more likely to be raped than Black men are to be falsely accused of it. Given the magnitude of Black women's vulnerability to sexual violence, it is not unreasonable to expect as much concern for Black women who are raped as is expressed for the men who are accused of raping them. . . .

Conclusion

This article has presented intersectionality as a way of framing the various interactions of race and gender in the context of violence against women of color. Yet intersectionality might be more broadly useful as a way of mediating the tension between assertions of multiple identity and the ongoing necessity of group politics. It is helpful in this regard to distinguish intersectionality from the closely related perspective of antiessentialism, from which women of color have critically engaged white feminism for the absence of women of color on the one hand, and for speaking for women of color on the other. One rendition of this antiessentialist critique—that feminism essentializes the category woman—owes a great deal to the postmodernist idea that categories we consider natural or merely representational are actually socially constructed in a linguistic economy of difference.[97] While the descriptive project of postmodernism of questioning the ways in which meaning is socially constructed is generally sound, this critique sometimes misreads the meaning of social construction and distorts its political relevance.

One version of antiessentialism, embodying what might be called the vulgarized social construction thesis, is that since all categories are socially constructed, there is no such thing as, say, Blacks or women, and thus it makes no sense to continue reproducing those categories by organizing around them.[98] . . .

But to say that a category such as race or gender is socially constructed is not to say that that category has no significance in our world. On the contrary, a large and continuing project for subordinated people—and indeed, one of the projects for which postmodern theories have been very helpful—is thinking about the way power has clustered around certain categories and is exercised against others. This project attempts to unveil the processes of subordination and the various ways those processes are experienced by people who are subordinated and people who are privileged by them. It is, then, a project that presumes that categories have meaning and consequences. And this project's most pressing problem, in many if not most cases, is not the existence of the categories, but rather the particular values attached to them and the way those values foster and create social hierarchies.

This is not to deny that the process of categorization is itself an exercise of power, but the story is much more complicated and nuanced than that. First, the process of categorizing—or, in identity terms, naming—is not unilateral. Subordinated people can and do participate, sometimes even subverting the naming process in empowering ways. One need only think about the historical subversion of the category "Black" or the current transformation of "queer" to understand that categorization is not a one-way street. Clearly, there is unequal power, but there is nonetheless some degree of agency that people can and do exert in the politics of naming. And it is important to note that identity continues to be a site of resistance for members of different subordinated groups. We all can recognize the distinction between the claims "I am Black" and the claim "I am a person who happens to be Black." "I am Black" takes the socially imposed identity and empowers it as an anchor of subjectivity. "I am Black" becomes not simply a statement of resistance but also a positive discourse of self-identification, intimately linked to celebratory statements like the Black nationalist "Black is beautiful." "I am a person who happens to be Black," on the other hand, achieves self-identification by straining for a certain universality (in effect, "I am first a person") and for a concommitant dismissal of the imposed category ("Black") as contingent, circumstantial, nondeterminant. There is truth in both characterizations, of course, but they function quite differently depending on the political context. At this point in history, a strong case can be made that the most critical resistance strategy for disempowered groups is to occupy and defend a politics of social location rather than to vacate and destroy it.

Vulgar constructionism thus distorts the possibilities for meaningful identity politics by conflating at least two separate but closely linked manifestations of power. One is the power exercised simply through the process of categorization; the other, the power to cause that categorization to have social and material consequences. While the former power facilitates the latter, the political implications of challenging one over the other matter greatly. . . .

With particular regard to problems confronting women of color, when identity politics fail us, as they frequently do, it is not primarily because those politics take as natural certain categories that are socially constructed but rather because the descriptive content of those categories and the narratives on which they are based have privileged some experiences and excluded others. . . .

If, as this analysis asserts, history and context determine the utility of identity politics, how then do we understand identity politics today, especially in light of our recognition of multiple dimensions of identity? More specifically, what does it mean to argue that gender identities have been obscured in antiracist discourses, just as race identities have been obscured in feminist discourses? Does that mean we cannot talk about identity? Or instead, that any discourse about identity has to acknowledge how our identities are constructed through the intersection of multiple dimensions? A beginning response to these questions requires that we first recognize that the organized identity groups in which we find ourselves are in fact coalitions, or at least potential coalitions waiting to be formed.

In the context of antiracism, recognizing the ways in which the intersectional experiences of women of color are marginalized in prevailing conceptions of identity politics does not require that we give up attempts to organize as communities of color. Rather, intersectionality provides a basis for reconceptualizing race as a coalition between men and women of color. For example, in the area of rape, intersectionality provides a way of explaining why women of color have to abandon the general argument that the interests of the community require the suppression of any confrontation around intraracial rape. Intersectionality may provide the means for dealing with other marginalizations as well. For example, race can also be a coalition of straight and gay people of color, and thus serve as a basis for critique of churches and other cultural institutions that reproduce heterosexism.

With identity thus reconceptualized, it may be easier to understand the need for and to summon the courage to challenge groups that are after all, in one sense, "home" to us, in the name of the parts of us that are not made at home. This takes a great deal of energy and arouses intense anxiety. The most one could expect is that we will dare to speak against internal exclusions and marginalizations, that we might call attention to how the identity of "the group" has been centered on the intersectional identities of a few. Recognizing that identity politics takes place at the site where categories intersect thus seems more fruitful than challenging the possibility of talking about categories at all. Through an awareness of intersectionality, we can better acknowledge and ground the differences among us and negotiate the means by which these differences will find expression in constructing group politics.

NOTES

1. Feminist academics and activists have played a central role in forwarding an ideological and institutional challenge to the practices that condone and perpetuate violence against women. See generally Susan

Brownmiller, *Against Our Will: Men, Women and Rape* (1975); Lorenne M. G. Clark & Debra J. Lewis, *Rape: The Price of Coercive Sexuality* (1977); R. Emerson Dobash & Russell Dobash, *Violence against Wives: A Case against the Patriarchy* (1979); Nancy Gager & Cathleen Schurr, *Sexual Assault: Confronting Rape in America* (1976); Diana E. H. Russell, *The Politics of Rape: The Victim's Perspective* (1974); Elizabeth Anne Stanko, *Intimate Intrusions: Women's Experience of Male Violence* (1985); Lenore E. Walker, *Terrifying Love: Why Battered Women Kill and How Society Responds* (1989); Lenore E. Walker, *The Battered Woman Syndrome* (1984); Lenore E. Walker, *The Battered Woman* (1979).

2. See, e.g., Susan Schechter, *Women and Male Violence: The Visions and Struggles of the Battered Women's Movement* (1982) (arguing that battering is a means of maintaining women's subordinate position); S. Brownmiller, supra note 1 (arguing that rape is a patriarchal practice that subordinates women to men); Elizabeth Schneider, The Violence of Privacy, 23 *Conn. L. Rev.* 973, 974 (1991) (discussing how "concepts of privacy permit, encourage and reinforce violence against women"); Susan Estrich, Rape, 95 *Yale L.J.* 1087 (1986) (analyzing rape law as one illustration of sexism in criminal law); see also Catharine A. Mackinnon, *Sexual Harassment of Working Women: A Case of Sex Discrimination* 143–213 (1979) (arguing that sexual harassment should be redefined as sexual discrimination actionable under Title VII, rather than viewed as misplaced sexuality in the workplace).

3. This article arises out of and is inspired by two emerging scholarly discourses. The first is critical race theory. For a cross-section of what is now a substantial body of literature, see Patricia J. Williams, *The Alchemy of Race and Rights* (1991); Robin D. Barnes, Race Consciousness: The Thematic Content of Racial Distinctiveness in Critical Race Scholarship, 103 *Harv. L. Rev.* 1864 (1990); John O. Calmore, Critical Race Theory, Archie Shepp, and Fire Music: Securing an Authentic Intellectual Life in a Multicultural World, 65 *S. Cal. L. Rev.* 2129 (1992); Anthony E. Cook, Beyond Critical Legal Studies: The Reconstructive Theology of Dr. Martin Luther King, 103 *Harv. L. Rev.* 985 (1990); Kimberle Williams Crenshaw, Race, Reform and Retrenchment: Transformation and Legitimation in Antidiscrimination Law, 101 *Harv. L. Rev.* 1331 (1988); Richard Delgado, When a Story is Just a Story: Does Voice Really Matter?, 76 *Va. L. Rev.* 95 (1990); Neil Gotanda, A Critique of "Our Constitution is Colorblind," 44 *Stan. L. Rev.* 1 (1991); Mari J. Matsuda, Public Response to Racist Speech: Considering the Victim's Story, 87 *Mich. L. Rev.* 2320 (1989); Charles R. Lawrence III, The Id, the Ego, and Equal Protection: Reckoning with Unconscious Racism, 39 *Stan. L. Rev.* 317 (1987); Gerald Torres, Critical Race Theory: The Decline of the Universalist Ideal and the Hope of Plural Justice—Some Observations and Questions of an Emerging Phenomenon, 75 *Minn. L. Rev.* 993 (1991). For a useful overview of critical race theory, see Calmore, supra, at 2160–2168.

A second, less formally linked body of legal scholarship investigates the connections between race and gender. See, e.g., Regina Austin, Sapphire Bound!, 1989 *Wis. L. Rev.* 539; Crenshaw, supra; Angela P. Harris, Race and Essentialism in Feminist Legal Theory, 42 *Stan. L. Rev.* 581 (1990); Marlee Kline, Race, Racism and Feminist Legal Theory, 12 *Harv. Women's L.J.* 115 (1989); Dorothy E. Roberts, Punishing Drug Addicts Who Have Babies: Women of Color, Equality and the Right of Privacy, 104 *Harv. L. Rev.* 1419 (1991); Cathy Scarborough, Conceptualizing Black Women's Employment Experiences, 98 *Yale L.J.* 1457 (1989) (student author); Peggie R. Smith, Separate Identities: Black Women, Work and Title VII, 14 *Harv. Women's L.J.* 21 (1991); Judy Scales-Trent, Black Women and the Constitution: Finding Our Place, Asserting Our Rights, 24 *Harv. C.R.-C.L. L. REV.* 9 (1989); Judith A. Winston, Mirror, Mirror on the Wall: Title VII, Section 1981, and the Intersection of Race and Gender in the Civil Rights Act of 1990, 79 *Cal. L. Rev.* 775 (1991). This work in turn has been informed by a broader literature examining the interactions of race and gender in other contexts. See, e.g., Patricia Hill Collins, *Black Feminist Thought: Knowledge, Consciousness, and the Politics of Empowerment* (1990); Angela Davis, *Women, Race and Class* (1981); bell hooks, *Ain't I a Woman? Black Women and Feminism* (1981); Elizabeth V. Spelman, *Inessential Woman: Problems of Exclusion in Feminist Thought* (1988); Frances Beale, Double Jeopardy: To Be Black and Female, in *The Black Woman* 90 (Toni Cade ed. 1970); Kink-Kok Cheung, The Woman Warrior versus The Chinaman Pacific: Must a Chinese American Critic Choose between Feminism and Heroism?, in *Conflicts in Feminism* 234 (Marianne Hirsch & Evelyn Fox Keller eds. 1990); Deborah H. King, Multiple Jeopardy, Multiple Consciousness: The Context of a Black Feminist Ideology, 14 *Signs* 42 (1988); Diane K. Lewis, A Response to Inequality: Black Women, Racism and Sexism, 3 *Signs* 339 (1977); Deborah E. McDowell, New Directions for Black Feminist Criticism, in *The New Feminist Criticism: Essays on Women, Literature and Theory* 186 (Elaine Showalter ed. 1985); Valerie Smith, Black Feminist Theory and the Representation of the "Other," in *Changing Our Own Words: Essays on Criticism, Theory and Writing by Black Women* 38 (Cheryl A. Wall ed. 1989).

4. Although the objective of this article is to describe the intersectional location of women of color and their marginalization within dominant resistance discourses, I do not mean to imply that the disempowerment of women of color is singularly or even primarily caused by feminist and antiracist theorists or activists. Indeed, I hope to dispel any such simplistic interpretations by capturing, at least in part, the way that prevailing structures of domination shape various discourses of resistance. As I have noted elsewhere, "People can only demand change in ways that reflect the logic of the institutions they are challenging. Demands for change that do not reflect . . . dominant ideology . . . will probably be ineffective." Crenshaw, supra note 3, at 1367. Although there are significant political and conceptual obstacles to moving against structures of domination with an intersectional sensibility, my point is that the effort to do so should be a central theoretical and political objective of both antiracism and feminism.

5. Although this article deals with violent assault perpetrated by men against women, women are also subject to violent assault by women. Violence among lesbians is a hidden but significant problem. One expert reported that in a study of 90 lesbian couples, roughly 46% of lesbians have been physically abused by their partners. Jane Garcia, The Cost of Escaping Domestic Violence: Fear of Treatment in a Largely Homophobic Society May Keep Lesbian Abuse Victims from Calling for Help, L.A. Times, May 6, 1991, at 2; see also *Naming the Violence: Speaking Out About Lesbian Battering* (Kerry Lobel ed. 1986); Ruthann Robson, Lavender Bruises: Intralesbian Violence, Law and Lesbian Legal Theory, 20 *Goldengate U.L. Rev.* 567 (1990). There are clear parallels between violence against women in the lesbian community and violence against women in communities of color. Lesbian violence is often shrouded in secrecy for similar reasons that have suppressed the exposure of heterosexual violence in communities of color—fear of embarrassing other members of the community, which is already stereotyped as deviant, and fear of being ostracized from the community. Despite these similarities, there are nonetheless distinctions between male abuse of women and female abuse of women that in the context of patriarchy, racism and homophobia, warrants more focused analysis than is possible here.

6. I use "Black" and "African American" interchangeably throughout this article. I capitalize "Black" because "Blacks, like Asians, Latinos, and other 'minorities,' constitute a specific cultural group and, as such, require denotation as a proper noun." Crenshaw, supra note 3, at 1332 n.2 (citing Catharine MacKinnon, Feminism, Marxism, Method, and the State: An Agenda for Theory, 7 *Signs* 515, 516 (1982)). By the same token, I do not capitalize "white," which is not a proper noun, since whites do not constitute a specific cultural group. For the same reason I do not capitalize "women of color."

7. Kimberle Crenshaw, Demarginalizing the Intersection of Race and Sex, 1989 *U. Chi. Legal* F. 139.

8. I explicitly adopt a Black feminist stance in this survey of violence against women of color. I do this cognizant of several tensions that such a position entails. The most significant one stems from the criticism that while feminism purports to speak for women of color through its invocation of the term "woman," the feminist perspective excludes women of color because it is based upon the experiences and interests of a certain subset of women. On the other hand, when white feminists attempt to include other women, they often add our experiences into an otherwise unaltered framework. It is important to name the perspective from which one constructs her analysis; and for me, that is as a Black feminist. Moreover, it is important to acknowledge that the materials that I incorporate in my analysis are drawn heavily from research on Black women. On the other hand, I see my own work as part of a broader collective effort among feminists of color to expand feminism to include analyses of race and other factors such as class, sexuality, and age. I have attempted therefore to offer my sense of the tentative connections between my analysis of the intersectional experiences of Black women and the intersectional experiences of other women of color. I stress that this analysis is not intended to include falsely nor to exclude unnecessarily other women of color.

9. I consider intersectionality a provisional concept linking contemporary politics with postmodern theory. In mapping the intersections of race and gender, the concept does engage dominant assumptions that race and gender are essentially separate categories. By tracing the categories to their intersections, I hope to suggest a methodology that will ultimately disrupt the tendencies to see race and gender as exclusive or separable. While the primary intersections that I explore here are between race and gender, the concept can and should be expanded by factoring in issues such as class, sexual orientation, age, and color.

10. Professor Mari Matsuda calls this inquiry "asking the other question." Mari J. Matsuda, Beside My Sister, Facing the Enemy: Legal Theory Out of Coalition, 43 *Stan. L. Rev.* 1183 (1991). For example, we should look at an issue or condition traditionally regarded as a gender issue and ask, "Where's the racism in this?"

11. During my research in Los Angeles, California, I visited Jenessee Battered Women's Shelter, the only shelter in the Western states primarily serving Black women, and Everywoman's Shelter, which primarily serves Asian women. I also visited Estelle Chueng at the Asian Pacific Law Foundation, and I spoke with a representative of La Casa, a shelter in the predominantly Latino community of East L.A.

12. One researcher has noted, in reference to a survey taken of battered women's shelters, that "many Caucasian women were probably excluded from the sample, since they are more likely to have available resources that enable them to avoid going to a shelter. Many shelters admit only women with few or no resources or alternatives." Mildred Daley Pagelow, *Woman-Battering: Victims and Their Experiences* 97 (1981). On the other hand, many middle- and upper-class women are financially dependent upon their husbands and thus experience a diminution in their standard of living when they leave their husbands.

13. Together they make securing even the most basic necessities beyond the reach of many. Indeed one shelter provider reported that nearly 85 percent of her clients returned to the battering relationships, largely because of difficulties in finding employment and housing. African Americans are more segregated than any other racial group, and this segregation exists across class lines. Recent studies in Washington, D.C., and its suburbs show that 64% of Blacks trying to rent apartments in white neighborhoods encountered discrimination. Tracy Thompson, Study Finds 'Persistent' Racial Bias in Area's Rental Housing, *Wash. Post,* Jan. 31, 1991, at D1. Had these studies factored gender and family status into the equation, the statistics might have been worse.

14. More specifically, African Americans suffer from high unemployment rates, low incomes, and high poverty rates. According to Dr. David Swinton, Dean of the School of Business at Jackson State University in Mississippi, African Americans "receive three-fifths as much income per person as whites and are three times as likely to have annual incomes below the Federally defined poverty level of $12,675 for a family of four." Urban League Urges Action, *N.Y. Times,* Jan. 9, 1991, at A14. In fact, recent statistics indicate that racial economic inequality is "higher as we begin the 1990s than at any other time in the last 20 years." David Swinton, The Economic Status of African Americans: "Permanent" Poverty and Inequality, in *The State of Black America* 1991, at 25 (1991).

The economic situation of minority women is, expectedly, worse than that of their male counterparts. Black women, who earn a median of $7,875 a year, make considerably less than Black men, who earn a median income of $12,609 a year, and white women, who earn a median income of $9,812 a year. Id. at 32 (Table 3). Additionally, the percentage of Black female-headed families living in poverty (46.5%) is almost twice that of white female-headed families (25.4%). Id. at 43 (Table 8). Latino households also earn considerably less than white households. In 1988, the median income of Latino households was $20,359 and for white households, $28,340—a difference of almost $8,000. *Hispanic Americans: A Statistical Sourcebook* 149 (1991). Analyzing by origin, in 1988, Puerto Rican households were the worst off, with 34.1% earning below $10,000 a year and a median income for all Puerto Rican households of $15,447 per year. Id. at 155. 1989 statistics for Latino men and women show that women earned an average of $7,000 less than men. Id. at 169.

15. See text accompanying notes 61–66 (discussing shelter's refusal to house a Spanish-speaking woman in crisis even though her son could interpret for her because it would contribute to her disempowerment). Racial differences marked an interesting contrast between Jenessee's policies and those of other shelters situated outside the Black community. Unlike some other shelters in Los Angeles, Jenessee welcomed the assistance of men. According to the Director, the shelter's policy was premised on a belief that given African Americans' need to maintain healthy relations to pursue a common struggle against racism, anti-violence programs within the African American community cannot afford to be antagonistic to men. For a discussion of the different needs of Black women who are battered, see Beth Richie, Battered Black Women: A Challenge for the Black Community, *Black Scholar,* Mar./Apr. 1985, at 40.

16. 8 U.S.C. ß 1186a (1988). The Marriage Fraud Amendments provide that an alien spouse "shall be considered, at the time of obtaining the status of an alien lawfully admitted for permanent residence, to have obtained such status on a conditional basis subject to the provisions of this section." ß 1186a(a)(1). An alien

spouse with permanent resident status under this conditional basis may have her status terminated if the Attorney General finds that the marriage was "improper," ß 1186a(b)(1), or if she fails to file a petition or fails to appear at the personal interview. ß 1186a(c)(2)(A).

17. The Marriage Fraud Amendments provided that for the conditional resident status to be removed, "the alien spouse and the petitioning spouse (if not deceased) jointly must submit to the Attorney General . . . a petition which requests the removal of such conditional basis and which states, under penalty of perjury, the facts and information." ß 1186a(b)(1)(A). The Amendments provided for a waiver, at the Attorney General's discretion, if the alien spouse was able to demonstrate that deportation would result in extreme hardship, or that the qualifying marriage was terminated for good cause. ß 1186a(c)(4). However, the terms of this hardship waiver have not adequately protected battered spouses. For example, the requirement that the marriage be terminated for good cause may be difficult to satisfy in states with no-fault divorces. Eileen P. Lynsky, Immigration Marriage Fraud Amendments of 1986: Till Congress Do Us Part, 41 *U. Miami L. Rev.* 1087, 1095 n.47 (1987) (student author) (citing Jerome B. Ingber & R. Leo Prischet, The Marriage Fraud Amendments, in *The New Simpson-Rodino Immigration Law of 1986,* at 56465 (Stanley Mailman ed. 1986)).

18. Immigration activists have pointed out that "[t]he 1986 Immigration Reform Act and the Immigration Marriage Fraud Amendment have combined to give the spouse applying for permanent residence a powerful tool to control his partner." Jorge Banales, Abuse Among Immigrants: As Their Numbers Grow So Does the Need for Services, *Wash. Post,* Oct. 16, 1990, at E5. Dean Ito Taylor, executive director of Nihonmachi Legal Outreach in San Francisco, explained that the Marriage Fraud Amendments "bound these immigrant women to their abusers." Deanna Hodgin, 'Mail-Order' Brides Marry Pain to Get Green Cards, *Wash. Times,* Apr. 16, 1991, at E1. In one egregious instance described by Beckie Masaki, executive director of the Asian Women's Shelter in San Francisco, the closer the Chinese bride came to getting her permanent residency in the United States, the more harshly her Asian-American husband beat her. Her husband, kicking her in the neck and face, warned her that she needed him, and if she did not do as he told her, he would call immigration officials. Id.

19. As Alice Fernandez, head of the Victim Services Agency at the Bronx Criminal Court, explained, " 'Women are being held hostage by their landlords, their boyfriends, their bosses, their husbands. . . . The message is: If you tell anybody what I'm doing to you, they are going to ship your ass back home. And for these women, there is nothing more terrible than that. . . . Sometimes their response is: I would rather be dead in this country than go back home.' " Vivienne Walt, Immigrant Abuse: Nowhere to Hide; Women Fear Deportation, Experts Say, *Newsday,* Dec. 2, 1990, at 8.

20. Immigration Act of 1990, Pub. L. No. 101-649, 104 Stat. 4978. The Act, introduced by Representative Louise Slaughter (D-N.Y.), provides that a battered spouse who has conditional permanent resident status can be granted a waiver for failure to meet the requirements if she can show that "the marriage was entered into in good faith and that after the marriage the alien spouse was battered by or was subjected to extreme mental cruelty by the U.S. citizen or permanent resident spouse." H.R. Rep. No. 723(I), 101st Cong., 2d Sess. 78 (1990), reprinted in 1990 U.S.C.C.A.N. 6710, 6758; see also 8 C.F.R. ß 216.5(3) (1992) (regulations for application for waiver based on claim of having been battered or subjected to extreme mental cruelty).

21. H.R. REP. NO. 723(I), supra note 20, at 79, reprinted in 1990 U.S.C.C.A.N. 6710, 6759.

22. Hodgin, supra note 18.

23. Id.

24. One survey conducted of battered women "hypothesized that if a person is a member of a discriminated minority group, the fewer the opportunities for socioeconomic status above the poverty level and the weaker the English language skills, the greater the disadvantage." M. Pagelow, supra note 12, at 96. The 70 minority women in the study "had a double disadvantage in this society that serves to tie them more strongly to their spouses." Id.

25. A citizen or permanent resident spouse can exercise power over an alien spouse by threatening not to file a petition for permanent residency. If he fails to file a petition for permanent residency, the alien spouse continues to be undocumented and is considered to be in the country illegally. These constraints often restrict an alien spouse from leaving. Dean Ito Taylor tells the story of "one client who has been hospitalized—she's had him arrested for beating her—but she keeps coming back to him because he promises

he will file for her. . . . He holds that green card over her head." Hodgin, supra note 18. Other stories of domestic abuse abound. Maria, a 50-year-old Dominican woman, explains that " 'One time I had eight stitches in my head and a gash on the other side of my head, and he broke my ribs. . . . He would bash my head against the wall while we had sex. He kept threatening to kill me if I told the doctor what happened.' " Maria had a "powerful reason for staying with Juan through years of abuse: a ticket to permanent residence in the United States." Walt, supra note 19.

26. One reporter explained that "Third-world women must deal with additional fears, however. In many cases, they are afraid of authority, government institutions and their abusers' threat of being turned over to immigration officials to be deported." Banales, supra note 18.

27. Incidents of sexual abuse of undocumented women abound. Marta Rivera, director of the Hostos College Center for Women's and Immigrant's Rights, tells of how a 19-year-old Dominican woman had "arrived shaken . . . after her boss raped her in the women's restroom at work." The woman told Rivera that "70 to 80 percent of the workers [in a Brooklyn garment factory] were undocumented, and they all accepted sex as part of the job. . . . She said a 13-year-old girl had been raped there a short while before her, and the family sent her back to the Dominican Republic." Walt, supra note 19. In another example, a "Latin American woman, whose husband's latest attack left her with two broken fingers, a swollen face and bruises on her neck and chest, refused to report the beating to police." She returned to her home after a short stay in a shelter. She did not leave the abusive situation because she was "an undocumented, illiterate laborer whose children, passport and money are tightly controlled by her husband." Although she was informed of her rights, she was not able to hurdle the structural obstacles in her path. Banales, supra note 18.

28. For example, in a region with a large number of Third-World immigrants, "the first hurdle these [battered women's shelters] must overcome is the language barrier." Banales, supra note 18.

29. There can be little question that women unable to communicate in English are severely handicapped in seeking independence. Some women thus excluded were even further disadvantaged because they were not U.S. citizens and some were in this country illegally. For a few of these, the only assistance shelter staff could render was to help reunite them with their families of origin.

M. Pagelow, supra note 12, at 96–97. Non-English speaking women are often excluded even from studies of battered women because of their language and other difficulties. A researcher qualified the statistics of one survey by pointing out that "an unknown number of minority group women were excluded from this survey sample because of language difficulties." Id. at 96. To combat this lack of appropriate services for women of color at many shelters, special programs have been created specifically for women from particular communities. A few examples of such programs include the Victim Intervention Project in East Harlem for Latina women, Jenessee Shelter for African American women in Los Angeles, Apna Gar in Chicago for South Asian women, and, for Asian women generally, the Asian Women's Shelter in San Francisco, the New York Asian Women's Center, and the Center for the Pacific Asian Family in Los Angeles. Programs with hotlines include Sakhi for South Asian Women in New York, and Manavi in Jersey City, also for South Asian women, as well as programs for Korean women in Philadelphia and Chicago.

30. For example, the Rosa Parks Shelter and the Compton Rape Crisis Hotline, two shelters that serve the African-American community, are in constant conflict with funding sources over the ratio of dollars and hours to women served. Interview with Joan Greer, Executive Director of Rosa Parks Shelter, in Los Angeles, California (April 1990).

31. One worker explained:

> For example, a woman may come in or call in for various reasons. She has no place to go, she has no job, she has no support, she has no money, she has no food, she's been beaten, and after you finish meeting all those needs, or try to meet all those needs, then she may say, by the way, during all this, I was being raped. So that makes our community different than other communities. A person wants their basic needs first. It's a lot easier to discuss things when you are full.

Nancy Anne Matthews, Stopping Rape or Managing its Consequences? State Intervention and Feminist Resistance in the Los Angeles Anti-Rape Movement, 1972–1987, at 287 (1989) (Ph.D. dissertation, University of California, Los Angeles) (chronicling the history of the rape crisis movement, and highlighting the different histories and dilemmas of rape crisis hotlines run by white feminists and those situated in the minority communities).

32. Typically, more time must be spent with a survivor who has fewer personal resources. These survivors tend to be ethnic minority women. Often, a non-assimilated ethnic minority survivor requires translating and interpreting, transportation, overnight shelter for herself and possibly children, and counseling to significant others in addition to the usual counseling and advocacy services. So, if a rape crisis center serves a predominantly ethnic minority population, the "average" number of hours of service provided to each survivor is much higher than for a center that serves a predominantly white population.

Id. at 275 (quoting position paper of the Southern California Rape Hotline Alliance).

33. Id. at 287–88.

34. The Director of Rosa Parks reported that she often runs into trouble with her funding sources over the Center's lower than average number of counselors accompanying victims to court. Interview with Joan Greer, supra note 30.

35. Even though current statistics indicate that Black women are more likely to be victimized than white women, Black women are less likely to report their rapes, less likely to have their cases come to trial, less likely to have their trials result in convictions, and, most disturbing, less likely to seek counseling and other support services.

Patricia Hill Collins, *Black Feminist Thought: Knowledge, Consciousness and the Politics of Empowerment* 178–79 (1990); accord Hubert S. Feild & Leigh B. Bienen, *Jurors and Rape: A Study in Psychology and Law* 141 (1980) (data obtained from 1,056 citizens serving as jurors in simulated legal rape cases generally showed that "the assailant of the black woman was given a more lenient sentence than the white woman's assailant"). According to Fern Ferguson, an Illinois sex abuse worker, speaking at a Women of Color institute conference in Knoxville, Tennessee, 10% of rapes involving white victims end in conviction, compared with 4.2% for rapes involving non-white victims (and 2.3% for the less-inclusive group of Black rape victims). UPI, July 30, 1985. Ferguson argues that myths about women of color being promiscuous and wanting to be raped encourage the criminal justice system and medical professionals as well to treat women of color differently than they treat white women after a rape has occurred. Id.

36. Most crime statistics are classified by sex or race but none are classified by sex and race. Because we know that most rape victims are women, the racial breakdown reveals, at best, rape rates for Black women. Yet, even given this head start, rates for other non-white women are difficult to collect. While there are some statistics for Latinas, statistics for Asian and Native American women are virtually non-existent. Cf. G. Chezia Carraway, Violence Against Women of Color, 43 *Stan. L. Rev.* 1301 (1993).

37. Shahrazad Ali, *The Blackman's Guide to Understanding the Blackwoman* (1989). Ali's book sold quite well for an independently published title, an accomplishment no doubt due in part to her appearances on the Phil Donahue, Oprah Winfrey, and Sally Jesse Raphael television talk shows. For public and press reaction, see Dorothy Gilliam, Sick, Distorted Thinking, *Wash. Post,* Oct. 11, 1990, at D3; Lena Williams, Black Woman's Book Starts a Predictable Storm, *N.Y. Times,* Oct. 2, 1990, at C11; see also Pearl Cleague, *Mad at Miles: A Black Woman's Guide to Truth* (1990). The title clearly styled after Ali's, *Mad at Miles* responds not only to issues raised by Ali's book, but also to Miles Davis's admission in his autobiography, *Miles: The Autobiography* (1989), that he had physically abused, among other women, his former wife, actress Cicely Tyson.

38. Shahrazad Ali suggests that the "[Blackwoman] certainly does not believe that her disrepect for the Blackman is destructive, nor that her opposition to him has deteriorated the Black nation." S. Ali, supra note 37, at viii. Blaming the problems of the community on the failure of the Black woman to accept her "real definition," Ali explains that "[n]o nation can rise when the natural order of the behavior of the male and the female have been altered against their wishes by force. No species can survive if the female of the genus disturbs the balance of her nature by acting other than herself." Id. at 76.

39. Ali advises the Blackman to hit the Blackwoman in the mouth, "[b]ecause it is from that hole, in the lower part of her face, that all her rebellion culminates into words. Her unbridled tongue is a main reason she cannot get along with the Blackman. She often needs a reminder." Id. at 169. Ali warns that "if [the Blackwoman] ignores the authority and superiority of the Blackman, there is a penalty. When she crosses this line and becomes viciously insulting it is time for the Blackman to soundly slap her in the mouth." Id.

40. Ali explains that, "[r]egretfully some Blackwomen want to be physically controlled by the Blackman." Id. at 174. "The Blackwoman, deep inside her heart," Ali reveals, "wants to surrender but she wants

to be coerced." Id. at 72. "[The Blackwoman] wants [the Blackman] to stand up and defend himself even if it means he has to knock her out of the way to do so. This is necessary whenever the Blackwoman steps out of the protection of womanly behavior and enters the dangerous domain of masculine challenge." Id. at 174.

41. Ali points out that "[t]he Blackman being number 1 and the Blackwoman being number 2 is another absolute law of nature. The Blackman was created first, he has seniority. And the Blackwoman was created 2nd. He is first. She is second. The Blackman is the beginning and all others came from him. Everyone on earth knows this except the Blackwoman." Id. at 67.

42. In this regard, Ali's arguments bear much in common with those of neoconservatives who attribute many of the social ills plaguing Black America to the breakdown of patriarchal family values. See, e.g., William Raspberry, If We Are to Rescue American Families, We Have to Save the Boys, *Chicago Trib.*, July 19, 1989, at C15; George F. Will, Voting Rights Won't Fix It, *Wash. Post,* Jan. 23, 1986, at A23; George F. Will, "White Racism" Doesn't Make Blacks Mere Victims of Fate, *Milwaukee J.*, Feb. 21, 1986, at 9. Ali's argument shares remarkable similarities to the controversial "Moynihan Report" on the Black family, so called because its principal author was now-Senator Daniel P. Moynihan (D-N.Y.). In the infamous chapter entitled "The Tangle of Pathology," Moynihan argued that

> the Negro community has been forced into a matriarchal structure which, because it is so out of line with the rest of American society, seriously retards the progress of the group as a whole, and imposes a crushing burden on the Negro male and, in consequence, on a great many Negro women as well.

Office of Policy Planning and Research, U.S. Department of Labor, The Negro Family: The Case for National Action 29 (1965), reprinted in Lee Rainwater & William L. Yancey, *The Moynihan Report and the Politics of Controversy* 75 (1967). A storm of controversy developed over the book, although few commentators challenged the patriarchy embedded in the analysis. Bill Moyers, then a young minister and speechwriter for President Johnson, firmly believed that the criticism directed at Moynihan was unfair. Some 20 years later, Moyers resurrected the Moynihan thesis in a special television program, The Vanishing Family: Crisis in Black America (CBS television broadcast, Jan. 25, 1986). The show first aired in January 1986 and featured several African-American men and women who had become parents but were unwilling to marry. Arthur Unger, Hardhitting Special About Black Families, *Christian Sci. Mon.*, Jan. 23, 1986, at 23. Many saw the Moyers show as a vindication of Moynihan. President Reagan took the opportunity to introduce an initiative to revamp the welfare system a week after the program aired. Michael Barons, Poor Children and Politics, *Wash. Post,* Feb. 10, 1986, at A1. Said one official, "Bill Moyers has made it safe for people to talk about this issue, the disintegrating black family structure." Robert Pear, President Reported Ready to Propose Overhaul of Social Welfare System, *N.Y. Times,* Feb. 1, 1986, at A12. Critics of the Moynihan/Moyers thesis have argued that it scapegoats the Black family generally and Black women in particular. For a series of responses, see Scapegoating the Black Family, *Nation,* July 24, 1989 (special issue, edited by Jewell Handy Gresham and Margaret B. Wilkerson, with contributions from Margaret Burnham, Constance Clayton, Dorothy Height, Faye Wattleton, and Marian Wright Edelman). For an analysis of the media's endorsement of the Moynihan/Moyers thesis, see Carl Ginsburg, *Race and Media: The Enduring Life of the Moynihan Report* (1989).

43. Domestic violence relates directly to issues that even those who subscribe to Ali's position must also be concerned about. The socioeconomic condition of Black males has been one such central concern. Recent statistics estimate that 25% of Black males in their twenties are involved in the criminal justice systems. See David G. Savage, Young Black Males in Jail or in Court Control Study Says, *L.A. Times,* Feb. 27, 1990, at A1; *Newsday,* Feb. 27, 1990, at 15; Study Shows Racial Imbalance in Penal System, *N.Y. Times,* Feb. 27, 1990, at A18. One would think that the linkages between violence in the home and the violence on the streets would alone persuade those like Ali to conclude that the African-American community cannot afford domestic violence and the patriarchal values that support it.

44. A pressing problem is the way domestic violence reproduces itself in subsequent generations. It is estimated that boys who witness violence against women are ten times more likely to batter female partners as adults. Women and Violence: Hearings Before the Senate Comm. on the Judiciary on Legislation to Reduce the Growing Problem of Violent Crime Against Women, 101st Cong., 2d Sess., pt. 2, at 89 (1991) [hereinafter Hearings on Violent Crime Against Women] (testimony of Charlotte Fedders). Other associated

problems for boys who witness violence against women include higher rates of suicide, violent assault, sexual assault, and alcohol and drug use. Id., pt. 2, at 131 (statement of Sarah M. Buel, Assistant District Attorney, Massachusetts, and Supervisor, Harvard Law School Battered Women's Advocacy Project).

45. Id. at 142 (statement of Susan Kelly-Dreiss) (discussing several studies in Pennsylvania linking homelessness to domestic violence).

46. Id. at 143 (statement of Susan Kelly-Dreiss).

47. Another historical example includes Eldridge Cleaver, who argued that he raped white women as an assault upon the white community. Cleaver "practiced" on Black women first. Eldridge Cleaver, *Soul on Ice* 14–15 (1968). Despite the appearance of misogyny in both works, each professes to worship Black women as "queens" of the Black community. This "queenly subservience" parallels closely the image of the "woman on a pedestal" against which white feminists have railed. Because Black women have been denied pedestal status within dominant society, the image of the African queen has some appeal to many African-American women. Although it is not a feminist position, there are significant ways in which the promulgation of the image directly counters the intersectional effects of racism and sexism that have denied African-American women a perch in the "gilded cage."

48. Alice Walker, *The Color Purple* (1982). The most severe criticism of Walker developed after the book was filmed as a movie. Donald Bogle, a film historian, argued that part of the criticism of the movie stemmed from the one-dimensional portrayal of Mister, the abusive man. See Jacqueline Trescott, Passions Over Purple; Anger and Unease Over Film's Depiction of Black Men, *Wash. Post,* Feb. 5, 1986, at C1. Bogle argues that in the novel, Walker linked Mister's abusive conduct to his oppression in the white world—since Mister "can't be himself, he has to assert himself with the black woman." The movie failed to make any connection between Mister's abusive treatment of Black women and racism, and thereby presented Mister only as an "insensitive, callous man." Id.

49. See, e.g., Gerald Early, Her Picture in the Papers: Remembering Some Black Women, *Antaeus,* Spring 1988, at 9; Daryl Pinckney, Black Victims, Black Villains, *N.Y. Review of Books,* Jan. 29, 1987, at 17; Trescott, supra note 48.

50. Trudier Harris, On the Color Purple, Stereotypes, and Silence, 18 *Black Am. Lit. F.* 155, 155 (1984).

51. The source of the resistance reveals an interesting difference between the Asian-American and African-American communities. In the African-American community, the resistance is usually grounded in efforts to avoid confirming negative stereotypes of African-Americans as violent; the concern of members in some Asian-American communities is to avoid tarnishing the model minority myth. Interview with Nilda Rimonte, Director of the Everywoman Shelter, in Los Angeles, California (April 19, 1991).

52. Nilda Rimonte, A Question of Culture: Cultural Approval of Violence Against Women in the Pacific-Asian Community and the Cultural Defense, 43 *Stan. L. Rev.* 1311 (1991); see also Nilda Rimonte, Domestic Violence Against Pacific Asians, in *Making Waves: An Anthology of Writings by and about Asian American Women* 327, 328 (Asian Women United of California ed. 1989) ("Traditionally Pacific Asians conceal and deny problems that threaten group pride and may bring on shame. Because of the strong emphasis on obligations to the family, a Pacific Asian woman will often remain silent rather than admit to a problem that might disgrace her family."). Additionally, the possibility of ending the marriage may inhibit an immigrant woman from seeking help. Tina Shum, a family counselor, explains that a " 'divorce is a shame on the whole family. . . . The Asian woman who divorces feels tremendous guilt.' " Of course, one could, in an attempt to be sensitive to cultural difference, stereotype a culture or defer to it in ways that abandon women to abuse. When—or, more importantly, how—to take culture into account when addressing the needs of women of color is a complicated issue. Testimony as to the particularities of Asian "culture" has increasingly been used in trials to determine the culpability of both Asian immigrant women and men who are charged with crimes of interpersonal violence. A position on the use of the "cultural defense" in these instances depends on how "culture" is being defined as well as on whether and to what extent the "cultural defense" has been used differently for Asian men and Asian women. See Leti Volpp, (Mis)Identifying Culture: Asian Women and the "Cultural Defense," (unpublished manuscript) (on file with the Stanford Law Review).

53. See, e.g., Hearings on Violent Crime Against Women, supra note 44, pt. 1, at 101 (testimony of Roni Young, Director of Domestic Violence Unit, Office of the State's Attorney for Baltimore City, Baltimore, Maryland) ("The victims do not fit a mold by any means."); Id. pt. 2, at 89 (testimony of Charlotte Fedders)

("Domestic violence occurs in all economic, cultural, racial, and religious groups. There is not a typical woman to be abused."); Id. pt. 2 at 139 (statement of Susan Kelly-Dreiss, Executive Director, Pennsylvania Coalition Against Domestic violence) ("Victims come from a wide spectrum of life experiences and backgrounds. Women can be beaten in any neighborhood and in any town.").

54. See, e.g., Lenore F. Walker, *Terrifying Love: Why Battered Women Kill and How Society Responds* 101–02 (1989) ("Battered women come from all types of economic, cultural, religious, and racial backgrounds. . . . They are women like you. Like me. Like those whom you know and love."); Murray A. Straus, Richard J. Gelles, Suzanne R. Steinmetz, *Behind Closed Doors: Violence in the American Family* 31 (1980) ("Wife-beating is found in every class, at every income level."); Natalie Loder Clark, Crime Begins At Home: Let's Stop Punishing Victims and Perpetuating Violence, 28 *Wm. & Mary L. Rev.* 263, 282 n.74 (1987) ("The problem of domestic violence cuts across all social lines and affects 'families regardless of their economic class, race, national origin, or educational background.' Commentators have indicated that domestic violence is prevalent among upper middle-class families.") (citations omitted); Kathleen Waits, The Criminal Justice System's Response to Battering: Understanding the Problem, Forging the Solutions, 60 *Wash. L. Rev.* 267, 276 (1985) ("It is important to emphasize that wife abuse is prevalent throughout our society. Recently collected data merely confirm what people working with victims have long known: battering occurs in all social and economic groups.") (citations omitted); Liza G. Lerman, Mediation of Wife Abuse Cases: The Adverse Impact of Informal Dispute Resolution on Women, 7 *Harv. Women's L.J.* 57, 63 (1984) ("Battering occurs in all racial, economic, and religious groups, in rural, urban, and suburban settings.") (citation omitted); Steven M. Cook, Domestic Abuse Legislation in Illinois and Other States: A Survey and Suggestions for Reform, 1983 *U. Ill. L. Rev.* 261, 262 (1983) (student author) ("Although domestic violence is difficult to measure, several studies suggest that spouse abuse is an extensive problem, one which strikes families regardless of their economic class, race, national origin, or educational background.") (citations omitted).

55. For example, Susan Kelly-Dreiss states:

> The public holds many myths about battered women—they are poor, they are women of color, they are uneducated, they are on welfare, they deserve to be beaten and they even like it. However, contrary to common misperceptions, domestic violence is not confined to any one socioeconomic, ethnic, religious, racial or age group.

Hearings on Violent Crime Against Women, supra note 44, pt. 2, at 139 (testimony of Susan Kelly-Dreiss, Executive Director, Pa. Coalition Against Domestic violence). Kathleen Waits offers a possible explanation for this misperception:

> It is true that battered women who are also poor are more likely to come to the attention of governmental officials than are their middle- and upper-class counterparts. However, this phenomenon is caused more by the lack of alternative resources and the intrusiveness of the welfare state than by any significantly higher incidence of violence among lower-class families.

Waits, supra note 54, at 276–77 (citations omitted).

56. However, no reliable statistics support such a claim. In fact, some statistics suggest that there is a greater frequency of violence among the working classes and the poor. See M. Straus, R. Gelles, & S. Steinmetz, supra note 54, at 31. Yet these statistics are also unreliable because, to follow Waits's observation, violence in middle- and upper-class homes remains hidden from the view of statisticians and governmental officials alike. See note 55 supra. I would suggest that assertions that the problem is the same across race and class are driven less by actual knowledge about the prevalence of domestic violence in different communities than by advocates' recognition that the image of domestic violence as an issue involving primarily the poor and minorities complicates efforts to mobilize against it.

57. On January 14, 1991, Senator Joseph Biden (D-Del.) introduced Senate Bill 15, the Violence Against Women Act of 1991, comprehensive legislation addressing violent crime confronting women. S. 15, 102d Cong., 1st Sess. (1991). The bill consists of several measures designed to create safe streets, safe homes, and safe campuses for women. More specifically, Title III of the bill creates a civil rights remedy for crimes of violence motivated by the victim's gender. Id. B 301. Among the findings supporting the bill were

"(1) crimes motivated by the victim's gender constitute bias crimes in violation of the victim's right to be free from discrimination on the basis of gender" and "(2) current law [does not provide a civil rights remedy] for gender crimes committed on the street or in the home." S. Rep. No. 197, 102d Cong., lst Sess. 27 (1991).

58. Letter of Diana M. Campos, Director of Human Services, PODER, to Joseph Semidei, Deputy Commissioner, New York State Department of Social Services (Mar. 26, 1992) [hereinafter PODER Letter].

59. The woman had been slipping back into her home during the day when her husband was at work. She remained in a heightened state of anxiety because he was returning shortly and she would be forced to go back out into the streets for yet another night.

60. PODER Letter, supra note 58 (emphasis added).

61. Id.

62. Id.

63. Said Campos, "it would be a shame that in New York state a battered woman's life or death were dependent upon her English language skills." PODER Letter, supra note 61.

64. The discussion in the following section focuses rather narrowly on the dynamics of a Black/white sexual hierarchy. I specify African Americans in part because given the centrality of sexuality as a site of racial domination of African Americans, any generalizations that might be drawn from this history seem least applicable to other racial groups. To be sure, the specific dynamics of racial oppression experienced by other racial groups are likely to have a sexual component as well. Indeed, the repertoire of racist imagery that is commonly associated with different racial groups each contain a sexual stereotype as well. These images probably influence the way that rapes involving other minority groups are perceived both internally and in society-at-large, but they are likely to function in different ways.

65. For example, the use of rape to legitimize efforts to control and discipline the Black community is well established in historical literature on rape and race. See Joyce E. Williams & Karen A. Holmes, *The Second Assault: Rape and Public Attitudes* 26 (1981) ("Rape, or the threat of rape, is an important tool of social control in a complex system of racial-sexual stratification.").

66. Valerie Smith, Split Affinities: The Case of Interracial Rape, in *Conflicts in Feminism* 271, 274 (Marianne Hirsch & Evelyn Fox Keller eds. 1990).

67. On April 18, 1989, a young white woman, jogging through New York's Central Park, was raped, severely beaten, and left unconscious in an attack by as many as 12 Black youths. Craig Wolff, Youths Rape and Beat Central Park Jogger, *N.Y. Times,* Apr. 21, 1989, at B1.

68. Smith, supra note 74, at 276–78.

69. Smith cites the use of animal images to characterize the accused Black rapists, including descriptions such as: " 'a wolfpack of more than a dozen young teenagers' and '[t]here was a full moon Wednesday night. A suitable backdrop for the howling of wolves. A vicious pack ran rampant through Central Park. . . . This was bestial brutality.' " An editorial in *The New York Times* was entitled "The Jogger and the Wolf Pack." Id. at 277 (citations omitted).

Evidence of the ongoing link between rape and racism in American culture is by no means unique to media coverage of the Central Park jogger case. In December 1990, the George Washington University student newspaper, *The Hatchet,* printed a story in which a white student alleged that she had been raped at knifepoint by two Black men on or near the campus. The story caused considerable racial tension. Shortly after the report appeared, the woman's attorney informed the campus police that his client had fabricated the attack. After the hoax was uncovered, the woman said that she hoped the story "would highlight the problems of safety for women." Felicity Banger, False Rape Report Upsetting Campus, *N.Y. Times,* Dec. 12, 1990, at A2; see also Les Payne, A Rape Hoax Stirs Up Hate, *Newsday,* Dec. 16, 1990, at 6.

70. Ian Ball, Rape Victim to Blame, Says Jury, *Daily Telegraph,* Oct. 6, 1989, at 3. Two months after the acquittal, the same man pled guilty to raping a Georgia woman to whom he said, "It's your fault. You're wearing a skirt." Roger Simon, Rape: Clothing is Not the Criminal, *L.A. Times,* Feb. 18, 1990, at E2.

71. See Barbara Kantrowitz, Naming Names, *Newsweek,* Apr. 29, 1991, at 26 (discussing the tone of several newspaper investigations into the character of the woman who alleged that she was raped by William Kennedy Smith). There were other dubious assumptions animating the coverage. One article described Smith as an "unlikely candidate for the rapist's role." Boy's Night Out in Palm Beach, *Time,* Apr. 22, 1991, at 82. But see Hillary Rustin, Letters: The Kennedy Problem, *Time,* May 20, 1991, at 7 (criticiz-

ing authors for perpetuating stereotypical images of who is or is not a "likely" rapist). Smith was eventually acquitted.

72. The *New York Times* pointed out that "[n]early all the rapes reported during that April week were of black or Hispanic women. Most went unnoticed by the public." Don Terry, In Week of an Infamous Rape, 28 Other Victims Suffer, *N.Y. Times,* May 29, 1989, at B25. Nearly all of the rapes occurred between attackers and victims of the same race: "Among the victims were 17 blacks, 7 Hispanic women, 3 whites, and 2 Asians." Id.

73. In Glen Ridge, an affluent New Jersey suburb, five white middle-class teenagers allegedly gang-raped a retarded white woman with a broom handle and a miniature baseball bat. See Robert Hanley, Sexual Assault Splits a New Jersey Town, *N.Y. Times,* May 26, 1989, at B1; Derrick Z. Jackson, The Seeds of Violence, *Boston Globe,* June 2, 1989, at 23; Bill Turque, Gang Rape in the Suburbs, *Newsweek,* June 5, 1989, at 26.

74. Robert D. McFadden, 2 Men Get 6 to 18 Years for Rape in Brooklyn, *N.Y. Times,* Oct. 2, 1990, at B2. The woman "lay, half naked, moaning and crying for help until a neighbor heard her" in the air shaft. Community Rallies to Support Victim of Brutal Brooklyn Rape, *N.Y. Daily News,* June 26, 1989, at 6. The victim "suffered such extensive injuries that she had to learn to walk again. . . . She faces years of psychological counseling. . . ." McFadden, supra.

75. This differential response was epitomized by public reaction to the rape-murder of a young Black woman in Boston on October 31, 1990. Kimberly Rae Harbour, raped and stabbed more than 100 times by eight members of a local gang, was an unwed mother, an occasional prostitute, and a drug-user. The Central Park victim was a white, upper-class professional. The Black woman was raped and murdered interracially. The white woman was raped and left for dead interracially. The Central Park rape became a national rallying cause against random (read Black male) violence; the rape of Kimberly Rae Harbour was written into a local script highlighted by the Boston Police Department's siege upon Black men in pursuit of the "fictional" Carol Stuart murderer. See John Ellement, 8 Teen-agers Charged in Rape, Killing of Dorchester Woman, *Boston Globe,* Nov. 20, 1990, at 1; James S. Kunen, Homicide No. 119, *People,* Jan. 14, 1991, at 42. For a comparison of the Stuart and Harbour murders, see Christopher B. Daly, Scant Attention Paid Victim as Homicides Reach Record in Boston, *Wash. Post,* Dec. 5, 1990, at A3.

76. Smith points out that "[t]he relative invisibility of black women victims of rape also reflects the differential value of women's bodies in capitalist societies. To the extent that rape is constructed as a crime against the property of privileged white men, crimes against less valuable women—women of color, working-class women, and lesbians, for example—mean less or mean differently than those against white women from the middle and upper classes." Smith, supra note 66, at 275–76.

77. "Cases involving black offenders and black victims were treated the least seriously." Gary D. Lafree, *Rape and Criminal Justice: The Social Construction of Sexual Assault* (1989). LaFree also notes, however, that "the race composition of the victim-offender dyad" was not the only predictor of case dispositions. Id. at 219–20.

78. Race Tilts the Scales of Justice. Study: Dallas Punishes Attacks on Whites More Harshly, *Dallas Times Herald,* Aug. 19, 1990, at A1. A study of 1988 cases in Dallas County's criminal justice system concluded that rapists whose victims were white were punished more severely than those whose victims were Black or Hispanic. The *Dallas Times Herald,* which had commissioned the study, reported that "[t]he punishment almost doubled when the attacker and victim were of different races. Except for such interracial crime, sentencing disparities were much less pronounced. . . ." Id.

79. Id. Two criminal law experts, Iowa law professor David Baldus and Carnegie-Mellon University professor Alfred Blumstein "said that the racial inequities might be even worse than the figures suggest." Id.

80. See G. Lafree, supra note 77, at 219–20 (quoting jurors who doubted the credibility of Black rape survivors); see also H. Feild & L. Bienen, supra note 35, at 117–18.

81. For example, Title I of the Violence Against Women Act creates federal penalties for sex crimes. See 137 *Cong. Rec.* S597, S599–600 (daily ed. Jan. 14, 1991). Specifically, section 111 of the Act authorizes the Sentencing Commission to promulgate guidelines to provide that any person who commits a violation after a prior conviction can be punished by a term of imprisonment or fines up to twice of what is otherwise provided in the guidelines. S. 15, supra note 57, at 8. Additionally section 112 of the Act authorizes the Sentencing Commission to amend its sentencing guidelines to provide that a defendant convicted of rape or

aggravated rape, "shall be assigned a base offense . . . that is at least 4 levels greater than the base offense level applicable to such offenses." Id. at 5.

82. Title I of the Act also creates new evidentiary rules for the introduction of sexual history in criminal and civil cases. Id. Sections 151 and 152 amend Fed. R. Evid. 412 by prohibiting "reputation or opinion evidence of the past sexual behavior of an alleged victim" from being admitted, and limiting other evidence of past sexual behavior. Id. at 39–44. Similarly, section 153 amends the rape shield law. Id. at 44–45. States have also either enacted or attempted to enact rape shield law reforms of their own. See Harriet R. Galvin, Shielding Rape Victims in the State and Federal Courts: A Proposal for the Second Decade, 70 *Minn. L. Rev.* 763 (1986); Barbara Fromm, Sexual Battery: Mixed-Signal Legislation Reveals Need for Further Reform, 18 *Fla. St. U. L. Rev.* 579 (1991).

83. See note 35 supra.

84. One can imagine certain trial-based interventions that might assist prosecutors in struggling with these beliefs. For example, one might consider expanding the scope of voir dire to examine jurors' attitudes toward Black rape victims. Moreover, as more is learned about Black women's response to rape, this information may be deemed relevant in evaluating Black women's testimony and thus warrant introduction through expert testimony. In this regard, it is worth noting that the battered women's syndrome and the rape trauma syndrome are both forms of expert testimony that frequently function in the context of a trial to counter stereotypes and other dominant narratives that might otherwise produce a negative outcome for the woman "on trial." These interventions, probably unimaginable a short while ago, grew out of efforts to study and somehow quantify women's experience. Similar interventions that address the particular dimensions of the experiences of women of color may well be possible. This knowledge may grow out of efforts to map how women of color have fared under standard interventions. For an example of an intersectional critique of the battered women's syndrome, see Sharon A. Allard, Rethinking Battered Woman Syndrome: A Black Feminist Perspective, 1 *U.C.L.A. Women's L.J.* 191 (1991) (student author).

85. See Smith, supra note 66 (discussing media sensationalization of the Central Park jogger case as consistent with historical patterns of focusing almost exclusively on Black male/white female dyads.); see also Terry, supra note 72 (discussing the 28 other rapes that occurred during the same week, but that were not given the same media coverage). Although rape is largely an intraracial crime, this explanation for the disparate coverage given to nonwhite victims is doubtful, however, given the findings of at least one study that 48% of those surveyed believed that most rape involved a Black offender and a white victim. See H. Feild & L. Bienen, supra note 35, at 80. Ironically, Feild and Bienen include in their book-length study of rape two photographs distributed to the subjects in their study depicting the alleged victim as white and the alleged assailant as Black. Given the authors' acknowledgment that rape was overwhelmingly intraracial, the appearance of these photos was particularly striking, especially because they were the only photos included in the entire book.

86. See, e.g., G. Lafree, supra note 77, at 237–39.

87. For a similar argument that race-of-victim discrimination in the administration of the death penalty actually represents the devalued status of Black victims rather than discrimination against Black offenders, see Randall L. Kennedy, McCleskey v. Kemp: Race, Capital Punishment, and the Supreme Court, 101 *Harv. L. Rev.* 1388 (1988).

88. The statistic that 89% of all men executed for rape in this country were Black is a familiar one. Forman v. Georgia, 408 U.S. 238, 364 (1972) (Marshall, J., concurring). Unfortunately, the dominant analysis of racial discrimination in rape prosecutions generally does not discuss whether any of the rape victims in these cases were Black. See Jennifer Wriggins, Rape, Racism, and the Law, 6 *Harv. Women's L.J.* 103, 113 (1983) (student author).

89. Race was frequently sufficient to fill in facts that were unknown or unknowable. As late as 1953, the Alabama Supreme Court ruled that a jury could take race into account in determining whether a Black man was guilty of "an attempt to commit an assault with an attempt to rape." See McQuirter v. State, 63 So. 2d. 388, 390 (Ala. 1953). According to the "victim's" testimony, the man stared at her and mumbled something unintelligible as they passed. Id. at 389.

90. Ida Wells, an early Black feminist, investigated every lynching she could for about a decade. After researching 728 lynchings, she concluded that "[o]nly a third of the murdered Blacks were even accused of

rape, much less guilty of it." Paula Giddings, *When and Where I Enter: The Impact of Black Women on Race and Sex in America* 28 (1984) (quoting Wells).

91. See Jacquelyn Dowd Hall, "The Mind That Burns in Each Body": Women, Rape, and Racial Violence, in *Powers of Desire: The Politics of Sexuality* 328, 334 (Ann Snitow, Christine Stansell, & Sharon Thompson eds. 1983).

92. Nine Black youths were charged with the rape of two white women in a railroad freight car near Scottsboro, Alabama. Their trials occurred in a heated atmosphere. Each trial was completed in a single day, and the defendants were all convicted and sentenced to death. See Dan T. Carter, *Scottsboro: A Tragedy of the American South* (1976). The Supreme Court reversed the defendants' convictions and death sentences, holding that they were unconstitutionally denied the right to counsel. Powell v. Alabama, 287 U.S. 45, 65 (1932). However, the defendants were retried by an all-white jury after the Supreme Court reversed their convictions.

93. Emmett Till was a 14-year-old Black boy from Chicago visiting his relatives near Money, Mississippi. On a dare by local boys, he entered a store and spoke to a white woman. Several days later, Emmett Till's body was found in the Tallahatchie River. "The barbed wire holding the cotton-gin fan around his neck had became snagged on a tangled river root." After the corpse was discovered, the white woman's husband and his brother-in-law were charged with Emmett Till's murder. Juan Williams, *Eyes on the Prize* 39–43 (1987). For a historical account of the Emmett Till tragedy, see Stephen J. Whitfield, *A Death in the Delta* (1988).

94. Crenshaw, supra note 7, at 159 (discussing how the generation of Black activists who created the Black Liberation Movement were contemporaries of Emmett Till).

95. Until quite recently, for example, when historians talked of rape in the slavery experience they often bemoaned the damage this act did to the Black male's sense of esteem and respect. He was powerless to protect his woman from white rapists. Few scholars probed the effect that rape, the threat of rape, and domestic violence had on the psychic development of the female victims.

Darlene Clark Hine, Rape and the Inner Lives of Black Women in the Middle West: Preliminary Thoughts on the Culture of Dissemblance, in *Unequal Sisters: A Multi-Cultural Reader in U.S. Women's History* (Ellen Carol Dubois & Vicki L. Ruiz eds. 1990).

96. Michael Madden, No Offensive from Defense, *Boston Globe,* Feb. 1, 1992, at 33 (hooks); Farrakhan Backs Calls for Freeing Tyson, UPI, July 10, 1992.

97. I follow the practice of others in linking antiessentialism to postmodernism. See generally Linda Nicholson, *Feminism/Postmodernism* (1990).

98. I do not mean to imply that all theorists who have made antiessentialist critiques have lasped into vulgar constructionism. Indeed, antiessentialists avoid making these troubling moves and would no doubt be receptive to much of the critique set forth herein. I use the term vulgar constructionism to distinguish between those antiessentialist critiques that leave room for identity politics and those that do not.

Reflection

KIMBERLE CRENSHAW

In the beginning, it was indeed personal. I was in college, managing an unlikely balance between my life rooted in Black radical politics, resident advising, and sorority life. My boyfriend took the notion of the liberation struggle literally, preparing himself to fight, first with fists, then with weapons, when and if "they" came calling in the morning. I had no notion that the only person he would ever use his fists on would be me; nor that when "they" did come, it would not be to suppress Black liberation, but to arrest him for assault. But it did happen, after a messy break-up, in my 10th floor dorm room with the plate glass window. I landed just a foot short of it, the first of many near misses that could have changed my life forever. What did change at that moment, though, was my political trajectory, for the trauma of the violence was nothing compared to the devastating response of my various communities. Sorors fell silent; the University punished us both; the revolutionaries lobbied for forgiveness. One sister whom I had admired and emulated persuaded me that the community could take care of the situation, that the police had no place in our lives, and cared little about us. This I knew to be true: campus security prepared to do nothing until they overheard my warning to a few friends that my ex-boyfriend had weapons. A week after I dropped the charges, my ex-boyfriend threatened my life. For months as the threats escalated, support came from unlikely sources, a few non-aligned male friends who escorted me everywhere, and one Black male administrator who saw to it that I graduated. The sorors remained silent, the University did nothing, and the Righteous Sister did not call again.

The opportunity finally came, many years later, to ask her about this routine deployment of racial rhetoric to protect batterers. My recounting of the event brought forward not even the slightest flicker of recognition. The painful sacrifice that she had implored me to make in the name of racial solidarity and trust had been completely forgotten.

This was a moment of reckoning for me, and it came at a time when the boundaries of antiracism and feminism were revealing in popular culture the ways that their narratives of oppression utterly marginalized women of color. The mind-numbing defenses of Mike Tyson and Clarence Thomas, along with the colorblind and counterproductive responses of many feminists, made it impossible to ignore the consequences of these mutually exclusive rhetorical politics on women of color. At the same time, standard critiques made by women of color of mainstream feminism were reaching a point where the form of the argument was outpacing the substance. It is of course one thing to say we are different—no political- or identity-based group isn't—including race-based political groups. To me the real challenge was the task of mapping, context by context, what difference our difference made. And it was in the arena of violence that experience indicated it was most acute. It seemed to me that only when we can articulate when and how difference matters can we effectively work to include our difference within the broader struggle to end the violence that circumscribes our lives.

The trajectory of this work has been surprising; it began simply as an effort to map what was happening on the ground, not as an indictment of feminism in particular, nor of identity politics more broadly. It was instead an attempt to strengthen the legitimate impulse to organize around our identities as women or as people of color while recognizing and addressing its multiple dimensions. While over-reading and under-reading the basic argument is to be expected in the academy, I've been interested and in fact delighted that women working in the trenches receive exactly the point I was offering, and have found the article useful in their practice. So it seems that the end is where it began, in the personal.

PART THREE

Perpetrators of Violence against Women

Early research on violence against women often focused on how battered women or rape victims were different from other women. Many of these early studies were rightfully criticized for their tendency to blame victims of violence for their difference rather than examining the role of perpetrators in assaults. Other early papers on domestic violence and sexual assault portrayed the perpetrators as mentally ill men at the margins of society. The papers presented in this section were some of the first and most important to challenge these assumptions by examining perpetrator behavior and suggesting that communities have a responsibility to intervene to stop the violence.

Diana Scully and Joseph Marolla's "Riding the Bull at Gilley's" is one of the earliest research studies to confront the myth that rape was the product of mentally ill men. Their paper clearly showed, in rapists' own words, how men purposefully used sexual assaults to dominate and control women. Diana Scully's reflection on her paper is also a powerful statement on how the personal and professional interact. Her personal experiences as a rape victim led her directly to this study. Consequently, the act of conducting the study again changed her life.

The next two papers in this section turn our attention to interventions with men who batter. What is the best way to intervene? What are the intended and unintended results of our interventions? Lawrence Sherman and Richard Berk's *The Specific Deterrent Effects of Arrest for Domestic Violence* spawned an entire generation of research and nationwide changes in laws, policies, and practices regarding police actions when responding to domestic assaults. The results of their experimental study of police responses in Minneapolis suggested that arresting a batterer was more effective than other actions commonly undertaken by police. The National Institute of Justice (NIJ) replicated this study in a number of cities. Richard Berk reflects on the original study, the NIJ replications, and how research findings are translated successfully and unsuccessfully into public policy and practice.

A surprise choice for inclusion in this book was Ed Gondolf's *The Effect of Batterer Counseling on Shelter Outcome.* Looking back, Gondolf felt that other works were perhaps more important. Our advisory board felt, however, that there was no avoiding the fact that one particular finding—that a batterer's involvement in treatment was a key reason for women to leave a shelter and return to him—created extensive discussion about the effectiveness of batterer intervention programs and women's reliance on men's involvement with these programs for their safety. Gondolf's reflection puts this finding in context and updates it with more recent findings from a multi-site study he is conducting.

Finally, no collection of classic papers would be complete without the inclusion of the "Duluth Model." Ellen Pence and her colleagues in Duluth, Minnesota, were some of the first to act on the notion that violence is a community problem and must be solved at a community level. Pence has written many papers on the topic and some slightly earlier than the chapter we included here. But this chapter seemed a particularly good and concise overview of the Duluth Model in its earliest stages. As Pence's reflection indicates, the Model has been replicated and adapted around the world.

Together, these four papers represent the beginnings of efforts to shift away from blaming victims for their situation to a clearer understanding of men's motivations for committing violence and of how communities can best intervene to decrease or stop it.

CHAPTER

20 "Riding the Bull at Gilley's"

Convicted Rapists Describe the Rewards of Rape

DIANA SCULLY AND JOSEPH MAROLLA

In this paper we argue that the popular image of rape, a nonutilitarian act committed by a few "sick" men, is too limited a view of sexual violence because it excludes culture and social structure as pre-disposing factors. Our data come from interviews with 114 convicted, incarcerated rapists. Looking at rape from the perspective of rapists, we attempt to discover the function of sexual violence in their lives; what their behavior gained for them in a society seeming prone to rape. Our analysis reveals that a number of rapists used sexual violence as a method of revenge and/or punishment while others used it as a means of gaining access to unwilling or unavailable women. In some cases, rape was just a bonus added to burglary or robbery. Rape was also a recreational activity and described as an "adventure" and an "exciting" form of impersonal sex which gained the offender power over his victim(s).

Over the past several decades, rape has become a "medicalized" social problem. That is to say, the theories used to explain rape are predicated on psychopathological models. They have been generated from clinical experiences with small samples of rapists, often the therapists' own clients. Although these psychiatric explanations are most appropriately applied to the atypical rapist, they have been generalized to all men who rape and have come to inform the public's view on the topic.

Two assumptions are at the core of the psychopathological model; that rape is the result of idiosyncratic mental disease and that it often includes an uncontrollable sexual impulse (Scully and Marolla, 1985). For example, the presumption of psychopathology is evident in the often cited work of Nicholas Groth (1979). While Groth emphasizes the non-sexual nature of rape (power, anger, sadism), he also concludes, "Rape is always a symptom of some psychological dysfunction, either temporary and transient or chronic and repetitive" (Groth, 1979:5). Thus, in the psychopathological view, rapists lack the ability to control their behavior; they are "sick" individuals from the "lunatic fringe" of society.

In contradiction to this model, empirical research has repeatedly failed to find a consistent pattern of personality type or character disorder that reliably discriminates rapists from other groups of men (Fisher and Rivlin, 1971; Hammer and Jacks, 1955; Rada, 1978). Indeed, other research has found that fewer than 5 percent of men were psychotic when they raped (Abel et al., 1980).

Evidence indicates that rape is not a behavior confined to a few "sick" men but many men have the attitudes and beliefs necessary to commit a sexually aggressive act. In research conducted at a midwestern university, Koss and her coworkers reported that 85 percent of men defined as highly sexually aggressive had victimized women with whom they were romantically involved (Koss and Leonard, 1984). A recent survey quoted in *The Chronicle of Higher Education* estimates that more than 20 percent of college women are the victims of rape and attempted rape (Meyer, 1984). These findings mirror research published several decades earlier which also concluded that sexual aggression was commonplace in dating relationships (Kanin, 1957, 1965, 1967, 1969; Kirkpatrick and Kanin, 1957).[1] In their study of 53 college males, Malamuth, Haber and Feshback (1980) found that 51 percent indicated a likelihood that they, themselves, would rape if assured of not being punished.

In addition, the frequency of rape in the United States makes it unlikely that responsibility rests solely with a small lunatic fringe of psychopathic men. Johnson (1980), calculating the lifetime risk of rape to girls and women aged twelve and over, makes a similar observation. Using Law Enforcement Assistance Association and Bureau of Census Crime Victimization Studies, he calculated that, excluding sexual abuse in marriage and assuming equal risk to all women, 20 to 30 percent of girls now 12 years old will suffer a violent sexual attack during the remainder of their lives. Interestingly, the lack of empirical support for the psychopathological model has not resulted in the demedicalization of rape, nor does it appear to have diminished the belief that rapists are "sick" aberrations in their own culture. This is significant because of the implications and consequences of the model.

A central assumption in the psychopathological model is that male sexual aggression is unusual or strange. This assumption removes rape from the realm of the everyday or "normal" world and places it in the category of "special" or "sick" behavior. As a consequence, men who rape are cast in the role of outsider and a connection with normative male behavior is avoided. Since, in this view, the source of the behavior is thought to be within the psychology of the individual, attention is diverted away from culture or social structure as contributing factors. Thus, the psychopathological model ignores evidence which links sexual aggression to environmental variables and which suggests that rape, like all behavior, is learned.

Cultural Factors in Rape

Culture is a factor in rape, but the precise nature of the relationship between culture and sexual violence remains a topic of discussion. Ethnographic data from pre-industrial societies show the existence of rape-free cultures (Broude and Green, 1976; Sanday, 1979), though explanations for the phenomena differ.[2] Sanday (1979) relates sexual violence to contempt for female qualities and suggests that rape is part of a culture of violence and an expression of male dominance. In contrast, Blumberg (1979) argues that in pre-industrial societies women are more likely to lack important life options and to be physically and politically oppressed where they lack economic power relative to men. That is, in pre-industrial societies relative economic power enables women to win some immunity from men's use of force against them.

Among modern societies, the frequency of rape varies dramatically, and the United States is among the most rape-prone of all. In 1980, for example, the rate of reported rape and attempted rape for the United States was eighteen times higher than the corresponding rate for England and Wales (West, 1983). Spurred by the Women's Movement, feminists have generated an impressive body of theory regarding the cultural etiology of rape in the United States. Representative of the feminist view, Griffin (1971) called rape "The All American Crime."

The feminist perspective views rape as an act of violence and social control which functions to "keep women in their place" (Brownmiller, 1975; Kasinsky, 1975; Russell, 1975). Feminists see rape as an extension of normative male behavior, the result of conformity or overconformity to the values and prerogatives which define the traditional male sex role. That is, traditional socialization encourages males to associate power, dominance, strength, virility and superiority with masculinity, and submissiveness, passivity, weakness, and inferiority with femininity. Furthermore, males are taught to have expectations about their level of sexual needs and expectations for corresponding female accessibility which function to justify forcing sexual access. The justification for forced sexual access is buttressed by legal, social, and religious definitions of women as male property and sex as an exchange of goods (Bart, 1979). Socialization prepares women to be "legitimate" victims and men to be potential offenders (Weis and Borges, 1973). Herman (1984) concludes that the United States is a rape culture because both genders are socialized to regard male aggression as a natural and normal part of sexual intercourse.

Feminists view pornography as an important element in a larger system of sexual violence; they see pornography as an expression of a rape-prone culture where women are seen as objects available for use by men (Morgan, 1980; Wheeler, 1985). Based on his content analysis of 428 "adults only" books, Smith (1976) makes a similar observation. He notes that, not only is rape presented as part of normal male/female sexual relations, but the woman, despite her terror, is always depicted as sexually aroused to the point of cooperation. In the end, she is ashamed but physically gratified. The message—women desire and enjoy rape—has more potential for damage than the image of the violence *per se.*[3]

The fusion of these themes—sex as an impersonal act, the victim's uncontrollable orgasm, and the violent infliction of pain—is commonplace in the actual accounts of rapists. Scully and Marolla (1984) demonstrated that many convicted rapists denied their crime and attempted to justify their rapes by arguing that their victim had enjoyed herself despite the use of a weapon and the infliction of serious injuries, or even death. In fact, many argued, they had been instrumental in making *her* fantasy come true.

The images projected in pornography contribute to a vocabulary of motive which trivializes and neutralizes rape and which might lessen the internal controls that otherwise would prevent sexually aggressive behavior. Men who rape use this culturally acquired vocabulary to justify their sexual violence.

Another consequence of the application of psychopathology to rape is it leads one to view sexual violence as a special type of crime in which the motivations are subconscious and uncontrollable rather than overt and deliberate as with other criminal behavior. Black (1983) offers an approach to the analysis of criminal and/or violent behavior which, when applied to rape, avoids this bias.

Black (1983) suggests that it is theoretically useful to ignore that crime is criminal in order to discover what such behavior has in common with other kinds of conduct. From his perspective, much of the crime in modern societies, as in pre-industrial societies, can be interpreted as a form of "self help" in which the actor is expressing a grievance through aggression and violence. From the actor's perspective, the victim is deviant and his own behavior is a form of social control in which the objective may be conflict management, punishment, or revenge. For example, in societies where women are considered the property of men, rape is sometimes used as a means of avenging the victim's husband or father (Black, 1983). In some cultures rape is used as a form of punishment. Such was the tradition among the puritanical, patriarchal Cheyenne where men were valued for their ability as warriors. It was Cheyenne custom that a wife suspected of being unfaithful could be "put on the prairie" by her husband. Military confreres then were invited to "feast" on the prairie (Hoebel, 1954; Llewellyn and Hoebel, 1941). The ensuing mass rape was a husband's method of punishing his wife.

Black's (1983) approach is helpful in understanding rape because it forces one to examine the goals that some men have learned to achieve through sexually violent means. Thus, one approach to understanding why some men rape is to shift attention from individual psychopathology to the important question of what rapists gain from sexual aggression and violence in a culture seemingly prone to rape.

In this paper, we address this question using data from interviews conducted with 114 convicted, incarcerated rapists. Elsewhere, we discussed the vocabulary of motive, consisting of excuses and justifications, that these convicted rapists used to explain themselves and their crime (Scully and Marolla, 1984).[4] The use of these culturally derived excuses and justifications allowed them to view their behavior as either idiosyncratic or situationally appropriate and thus it reduced their sense of moral responsibility for their actions. Having disavowed deviance, these men revealed how they had used rape to achieve a number of objectives. We find that some men used rape for revenge or punishment while, for others, it was an "added bonus"—a last minute decision made while committing another crime. In still other cases, rape was used to gain sexual access to women who were unwilling or unavailable, and for some it was a source of power and sex without any personal feelings. Rape was also a form of recreation, a diversion or an adventure and, finally, it was something that made these men "feel good."

Methods[5]

Sample

During 1980 and 1981 we interviewed 114 convicted rapists. All of the men had been convicted of the rape or attempted rape (n = 8) of an adult woman and subsequently incarcerated in a Virginia prison. Men convicted of other types of sexual offense were omitted from the sample.

In addition to their convictions for rape, 39 percent of the men also had convictions for burglary or robbery, 29 percent for abduction, 25 percent for sodomy, 11 percent for first or second degree murder and 12 percent had been convicted of more than one rape. The majority of the men had previous criminal histories but only 23 percent had a record of past sex offenses and only 26 percent had a history of emotional problems. Their sentences for rape and accompanying crimes ranged from ten years to seven life sentences plus 380 years for one man. Twenty-two percent of the rapists were serving at least one life sentence. Forty-six percent of the rapists were white, 54 percent black. In age, they ranged from 18 to 60 years but the majority were between 18 and 35 years. Based on a statistical profile of felons in all Virginia prisons prepared by the Virginia Department of Corrections, it appears that this sample of rapists was disproportionately white and, at the time of the research, somewhat better educated and younger than the average inmate.

All participants in this research were volunteers. In constructing the sample, age, education, race, severity of current offense and past criminal record were balanced within the limitations imposed by the characteristics of the volunteer pool. Obviously the sample was not random and thus may not be typical of all rapists, imprisoned or otherwise.

All interviews were hand recorded using an 89-page instrument which included a general background, psychological, criminal, and sexual history, attitude scales and 30 pages of open-ended questions intended to explore rapists' own perceptions of their crime and themselves. Each author interviewed half of the sample in sessions that ranged from three to seven hours depending on the desire or willingness of the participant to talk.

Validity

In all prison research, validity is a special methodological concern because of the reputation inmates have for "conning." Although one goal of this research was to understand rape from the perspective of men who have raped, it was also necessary to establish the extent to which rapists' perceptions deviated from other descriptions of their crime. The technique we used was the same others have used in prison research; comparing factual information obtained in the interviews, including details of the crime, with reports on file at the prison (Athens, 1977; Luckenbill, 1977; Queen's Bench Foundation, 1976). In general, we found that rapists' accounts of their crime had changed very little since their trials. However, there was a tendency to understate the amount of violence they had used and, especially among certain rapists, to place blame on their victims.

How Offenders View the Rewards of Rape

Revenge and Punishment

As noted earlier, Black's (1983) perspective suggests that a rapist might see his act as a legitimized form of revenge or punishment. Additionally, he asserts that the idea of "collective liability" accounts for much seemingly random violence. "Collective liability" suggests that all people in a particular category are held accountable for the conduct of each of their counterparts. Thus, the victim of a violent act may merely represent the category of individual being punished.

These factors—revenge, punishment, and the collective liability of women—can be used to explain a number of rapes in our research. Several cases will illustrate the ways in which these factors combined in various types of rape. Revenge-rapes were among the most brutal and often included beatings, serious injuries and even murder.

Typically, revenge-rapes included the element of collective liability. This is, from the rapist's perspective, the victim was a substitute for the woman they wanted to avenge. As explained elsewhere, (Scully and Marolla, 1984), an upsetting event, involving a woman, preceded a significant number of rapes. When they raped, these men were angry because of a perceived indiscretion, typically related to a rigid, moralistic standard of sexual conduct, which they required from "their woman" but, in most cases, did not abide by themselves. Over and over these rapists talked about using rape "to get even" with their wives or other significant woman.[6] Typical is a young man who, prior to the rape, had a violent argument with his wife over what eventually proved to be her misdiagnosed case of venereal disease. She assumed the disease had been contracted through him, an accusation that infuriated him. After fighting with his wife, he explained that he drove around "thinking about hurting someone." He encountered his victim, a stranger, on the road where her car had broken down. It appears she accepted his offered ride because her car was out of commission. When she realized that rape was pending, she called him "a son of a bitch," and attempted to resist. He reported flying into a rage and beating her, and he confided,

> I have never felt that much anger before. If she had resisted, I would have killed her . . . The rape was for revenge. I didn't have an orgasm. She was there to get my hostile feelings off on.

Although not the most common form of revenge rape, sexual assault continues to be used in retaliation against the victim's male partner. In one such case, the offender, angry because the victim's husband owed him money, went to the victim's home to collect. He confided, "I was going to get it one way or another." Finding the victim alone, he explained, they started to argue about the money and,

> I grabbed her and started beating the hell out of her. Then I committed the act,[7] I knew what I was doing. I was mad. I could have stopped but I didn't. I did it to get even with her and her husband.

Griffin (1971:33) points out that when women are viewed as commodities, "In raping another man's woman, a man may aggrandize his own manhood and concurrently reduce that of another man."

Revenge-rapes often contained an element of punishment. In some cases, while the victim was not the initial object of the revenge, the intent was to punish her because of something that transpired after the decision to rape had been made or during the course of the rape itself. This was the case with a young man whose wife had recently left him. Although they were in the process of reconciliation, he remained angry and upset over the separation. The night of the rape, he met the victim and her friend in a bar where he had gone to watch a fight on TV. The two women apparently accepted a ride from him but, after taking her friend home, he drove the victim to his apartment. At his apartment, he found a note from his wife indicating she had stopped by to watch the fight with him. This increased his anger because he preferred his wife's company. Inside his apartment, the victim allegedly remarked that she was sexually interested in his dog, which he reported, put him in a rage. In the ensuing attack, he raped and pistol-whipped the victim. Then he forced a vacuum cleaner hose, switched on suction, into her vagina and bit her breast, severing the nipple. He stated:

> I hated at the time, but I don't know if it was her (the victim). (Who could it have been?) My wife? Even though we were getting back together, I still didn't trust her.

During his interview, it became clear that this offender, like many of the men, believed men have the right to discipline and punish women. In fact, he argued that most of the men he knew would also have beaten the victim because "that kind of thing (referring to the dog) is not acceptable among my friends."

Finally, in some rapes, both revenge and punishment were directed at victims because they represented women whom these offenders perceived as collectively responsible and liable for their problems. Rape was used "to put women in their place" and as a method of proving their "manhood" by displaying dominance over a female. For example, one multiple rapist believed his actions were related to the feeling that women thought they were better than he was.

> Rape was a feeling of total dominance. Before the rapes, I would always get a feeling of power and anger. I would degrade women so I could feel there was a person of less worth than me.

Another, especially brutal, case involved a young man from an upper middle class background, who spilled out his story in a seven-hour interview conducted in his solitary confinement cell. He described himself as tremendously angry, at the time, with his girl friend whom he believed was involved with him in a "storybook romance," and from whom he expected complete fidelity. When she went away to college and became involved with another man, his revenge lasted eighteen months and involved the rape and murder of five women, all strangers who lived in his community. Explaining his rape-murders, he stated:

> I wanted to take my anger and frustration out on a stranger, to be in control, to do what I wanted to do. I wanted to use and abuse someone as I felt used and abused. I was killing my girl friend. During the rapes and murders, I would think about my girl friend. I hated the victims because they probably messed men over. I hated women because they were deceitful and I was getting revenge for what happened to me.

An Added Bonus

Burglary and robbery commonly accompany rape. Among our sample, 39 percent of rapists had also been convicted of one or the other of these crimes committed in connection with rape. In some cases, the original intent was rape and robbery was an after-thought. However, a number of the men indicated that the reverse was true in their situation. That is, the decision to rape was made subsequent to their original intent which was burglary or robbery.

This was the case with a young offender who stated that he originally intended only to rob the store in which the victim happened to be working. He explained that when he found the victim alone,

> I decided to rape her to prove I had guts. She was just there. It could have been anybody.

Similarly, another offender indicated that he initially broke into his victim's home to burglarize it. When he discovered the victim asleep, he decided to seize the opportunity "to satisfy an urge to go to bed with a white woman, to see if it was different." Indeed, a number of men indicated that the decision to rape had been made after they realized they were in control of the situation. This was also true of an unemployed offender who confided that his practice was to steal whenever he needed money. On the day of the rape, he drove to a local supermarket and paced the parking lot, "staking out the situation." His pregnant victim was the first person to come along alone and "she was an easy target." Threatening her with a knife, he reported the victim as saying she would do anything if he didn't harm her. At that point, he decided to force her to drive to a deserted area where he raped her. He explained:

> I wasn't thinking about sex. But when she said she would do anything not to get hurt, probably because she was pregnant, I thought, 'why not.'

The attitude of these men toward rape was similar to their attitude toward burglary and robbery. Quite simply, if the situation is right, "why not." From the perspective of these rapists, rape was just another part of the crime—an added bonus.

Sexual Access

In an effort to change public attitudes that are damaging to the victims of rape and to reform laws seemingly premised on the assumption that women both ask for and enjoy rape, many writers emphasize the violent and aggressive character of rape. Often such arguments appear to discount the part that sex plays in the crime. The data clearly indicate that from the rapists' point of view rape is in part sexually motivated. Indeed, it is the sexual aspect of rape that distinguishes it from other forms of assault.

Groth (1979) emphasizes the psychodynamic function of sex in rape arguing that rapists' aggressive needs are expressed through sexuality. In other words, rape is a means to an end. We argue, however, that rapists view the act as an end in itself and that sexual access most obviously demonstrates the link between sex and rape. Rape as a means of sexual access also shows the deliberate nature of this crime. When a woman is unwilling or seems unavailable for sex, the rapist can seize what isn't volunteered. In discussing his decision to rape, one man made this clear.

> All the guys wanted to fuck her . . . a real fox, beautiful shape. She was a beautiful woman and I wanted to see what she had.

The attitude that sex is a male entitlement suggests that when a woman says "no," rape is a suitable method of conquering the "offending" object. If, for example, a woman is picked up at a party or in a bar or while hitchhiking (behavior which a number of the rapists saw as a signal of sexual availability), and the woman later resists sexual advances, rape is presumed to be justified. The same justification operates in what is popularly called "date rape." The belief that sex was their just compensation compelled a number of rapists to insist they had not raped. Such was the case of an offender who raped and seriously beat his victim when, on their second date, she refused his sexual advances.

> I think I was really pissed off at her because it didn't go as planned. I could have been with someone else. She led me on but wouldn't deliver . . . I have a male ego that must be fed.

The purpose of such rapes was conquest, to seize what was not offered.

Despite the cultural belief that young women are the most sexually desirable, several rapes involved the deliberate choice of a victim relatively older than the assailant.[8] Since the rapists were themselves rather young (26 to 30 years of age on the average), they were expressing a preference for sexually experienced, rather than elderly, women. Men who chose victims older than themselves often said they did so because they believed that sexually experienced women were more desirable partners. They raped because they also believed that these women would not be sexually attracted to them.

Finally, sexual access emerged as a factor in the accounts of black men who consciously chose to rape white women.[9] The majority of rapes in the United States today are intraracial. However, for the past 20 years, according to national data based on reported rapes as well as victimization studies, which include unreported rapes, the rate of black on white (B/W) rape has significantly exceeded the rate of white on black (W/B) rape (La Free, 1982).[10] Indeed, we may be experiencing a historical anomaly, since, as Brownmiller (1975) has documented, white men have freely raped women of color in the past. The current structure of interracial rape, however, reflects contemporary racism and race relations in several ways.

First, the status of black women in the United States today is relatively lower than the status of white women. Further, prejudice, segregation and other factors continue to militate against interracial coupling. Thus, the desire for sexual access to higher status, unavailable women, an important function in B/W rape, does not motivate white men to rape black women. Equally important, demographic and geographic barriers interact to lower the incidence of W/B rape. Segregation as well as the poverty expected in black neighborhoods undoubtedly discourages many whites from choosing such areas as a target for house-breaking or robbery. Thus, the number of rapes that would occur in conjunction with these crimes is reduced.

Reflecting in part the standards of sexual desirability set by the dominant white society, a number of black rapists indicated they had been curious about white women. Blocked by racial barriers from legitimate sexual relations with white women, they raped to gain access to them. They described raping white women as "the ultimate experience" and "high status among my friends. It gave me a feeling of status, power, macho." For another man, raping a white woman had a special appeal because it violated a "known taboo," making it more dangerous, and thus more exciting, to him than raping a black woman.

Impersonal Sex and Power

The idea that rape is an impersonal rather than an intimate or mutual experience appealed to a number of rapists, some of whom suggested it was their preferred form of sex. The fact that rape allowed them to control rather than care encouraged some to act on this preference. For example, one man explained,

> Rape gave me the power to do what I wanted to do without feeling I had to please a partner or respond to a partner. I felt in control, dominant. Rape was the ability to have sex without caring about the woman's response. I was totally dominant.

Another rapist commented:

> Seeing them laying there helpless gave me the confidence that I could do it . . . With rape, I felt totally in charge. I'm bashful, timid. When a woman wanted to give in normal sex, I was intimidated. In the rapes, I was totally in command, she totally submissive.

During his interview, another rapist confided that he had been fantasizing about rape for several weeks before committing his offense. His belief was that it would be "an exciting experience—a new high." Most appealing to him was the idea that he could make his victim "do it all for him" and that he would be in control. He fantasized that she "would submit totally and that I could have anything I wanted." Eventually, he decided to act because his older brother told him, "forced sex is great, I wouldn't get caught and, besides, women love it." Though now he admits to his crime, he continues to believe his victim "enjoyed it." Perhaps we should note here that the appeal of impersonal sex is not limited to convicted rapists. The amount of male sexual activity that occurs in homosexual meeting places as well as the widespread use of prostitutes suggests that avoidance of intimacy appeals to a large segment of the male population. Through rape men can experience power and avoid the emotions related to intimacy and tenderness. Further, the popularity of violent pornography suggests that a wide variety of men in this culture have learned to be aroused by sex fused with violence (Smith, 1976). Consistent with this observation, recent experimental research conducted by Malamuth et al. (1980) demonstrates that men are aroused by images that depict women as orgasmic under conditions of violence and pain. They found that for female students, arousal was high when the victim experienced an orgasm and *no* pain, whereas male students were highly aroused when the victim experienced an orgasm and pain. On the basis of their results, Malamuth et al. (1980) suggest that forcing a woman to climax despite her pain and abhorrence of the assailant makes the rapist feel powerful, he has gained control over the only source of power historically associated with women, their bodies. In the final analysis, dominance was the objective of most rapists.

Recreation and Adventure

Among gang rapists, most of whom were in their late teens or early twenties when convicted, rape represented recreation and adventure, another form of delinquent activity. Part of rape's appeal was the sense of male camaraderie engendered by participating collectively in a dangerous activity. To prove one's self capable of "performing" under these circumstances was a substantial challenge and also a source of reward. One gang rapist articulated this feeling very clearly,

> We felt powerful, we were in control. I wanted sex and there was peer pressure. She wasn't like a person, no personality, just domination on my part. Just to show I could do it—you know, macho.

Our research revealed several forms of gang rape. A common pattern was hitchhike-abduction rape. In these cases, the gang, cruising an area, "looking for girls," picked up a female hitchhiker for the purpose of having sex. Though the intent was rape, a number of men did not view it as such because they were convinced that women hitchhiked primarily to signal sexual availability and only secondarily as a form of transportation. In these cases, the unsuspecting victim was driven to a deserted area, raped, and in the majority of cases physically injured. Sometimes, the victim was not hitchhiking; she was abducted at knife or gun point from the street usually at night. Some of these men did not view this type of attack as rape either because they believed a woman walking alone at night to be a prostitute. In addition, they were often convinced "she enjoyed it."

"Gang date" rape was another popular variation. In this pattern, one member of the gang would make a date with the victim. Then, without her knowledge or consent, she would be driven to a predetermined location and forcibly raped by each member of the group. One young man revealed this practice was so much a part of his group's recreational routine, they had rented a house for the purpose. From his perspective, the rape was justified because "usually the girl had a bad reputation, or we knew it was what she liked."

During his interview, another offender confessed to participating in twenty or thirty such "gang date" rapes because his driver's license had been revoked making it difficult for him to "get girls." Sixty percent of the time, he claimed, "they were girls known to do this kind of thing," but "frequently, the girls didn't want to have sex with all of us." In such cases, he said, "it might start out as rape but, then, they (the women) would quiet down and none ever reported it to the police." He was convicted for a gang rape, which he described as "the ultimate thing I ever did," because unlike his other rapes, the victim, in this case, was a stranger whom the group abducted as she walked home from the library. He felt the group's past experience with "gang date" rape had prepared them for this crime in which the victim was blindfolded and driven to the mountains where, though it was winter, she was forced to remove her clothing. Lying on the snow, she was raped by each of the four men several times before being abandoned near a farm house. This young man continued to believe that if he had spent the night with her, rather than abandoning her, she would not have reported to the police.[11]

Solitary rapists also used terms like "exciting," "a challenge," "an adventure," to describe their feelings about rape. Like the gang rapists, these men found the element of danger made rape all the more exciting. Typifying this attitude was one man who described his rape as intentional. He reported:

> It was exciting to get away with it (rape), just being able to beat the system, not women. It was like doing something illegal and getting away with it.

Another rapist confided that for him "rape was just more exciting and compelling" than a normal sexual encounter because it involved forcing a stranger. A multiple rapist asserted, "it was the excitement and fear and the drama that made rape a big kick."

Feeling Good

At the time of their interviews, many of the rapists expressed regret for their crime and had empirically low self-esteem ratings. The experience of being convicted, sentenced, and incarcerated for rape undoubtedly produced many, if not most, of these feelings. What is clear is that, in contrast to the well-documented severity of the immediate impact, and in some cases, the long-term trauma experienced by the victims of sexual violence, the immediate emotional impact on the rapists is slight.

When the men were asked to recall their feelings immediately following the rape, only eight percent indicated that guilt or feeling bad was part of their emotional response. The majority said they felt good, relieved or simply nothing at all. Some indicated they had been afraid of being caught or felt sorry for themselves. Only two men out of 114 expressed any concern or feeling for the victim. Feeling good or nothing at all about raping women is not an aberration limited to men in prison. Smithyman (1978), in his study of "undetected rapists"—rapists outside of prison—found that raping women had no impact on their lives nor did it have a negative effect on their self-image.

Significantly a number of men volunteered the information that raping had a positive impact on their feelings. For some the satisfaction was in revenge. For example, the man who had raped and murdered five women:

> It seems like so much bitterness and tension had built up and this released it. I felt like I had just climbed a mountain and now I could look back.

Another offender characterized rape as habit forming: "Rape is like smoking. You can't stop once you start." Finally one man expressed the sentiments of many rapists when he stated,

> After rape, I always felt like I had just conquered something, like I had just ridden the bull at Gilley's.

Conclusions

This paper has explored rape from the perspective of a group of convicted, incarcerated rapists. The purpose was to discover how these men viewed sexual violence and what they gained from their behavior.

We found that rape was frequently a means of revenge and punishment. Implicit in revenge-rapes was the notion that women were collectively liable for the rapists' problems. In some cases, victims were substitutes for significant women on whom the men desired to take revenge. In other cases, victims were thought to represent all women, and rape was used to punish, humiliate, and "put them in their place." In both cases women were seen as a class, a category, not as individuals. For some men, rape was almost an after-thought, a bonus added to burglary or robbery. Other men gained access to sexually unavailable or unwilling women through rape. For this group of men, rape was a fantasy come true, a particularly exciting form of impersonal sex which enabled them to dominate and control women, by exercising a singularly male form of power. These rapists talked of the pleasures of raping—how for them it was a challenge, an adventure, a dangerous and "ultimate" experience. Rape made them feel good and, in some cases, even elevated their self image.

The pleasure these men derived from raping reveals the extreme to which they objectified women. Women were seen as sexual commodities to be used or conquered rather than as human beings with rights and feelings. One young man expressed the extreme of the contemptful view of women when he confided to the female researcher.

> Rape is a man's right. If a women doesn't want to give it, the man should take it. Women have no right to say no. Women are made to have sex. It's all they are good for. Some women would rather take a beating, but they always give in; it's what they are for.

This man murdered his victim because she wouldn't "give in."

Undoubtedly, some rapes, like some of all crimes, are idiopathic. However, it is not necessary to resort to pathological motives to account for all rape or other acts of sexual violence. Indeed, we find that men who rape have something to teach us about the cultural roots of sexual aggression. They force us to acknowledge that rape is more than an idiosyncratic act committed by a few "sick" men. Rather, rape can be viewed as the end point in a continuum of sexually aggressive behaviors that reward men and victimize women.[12] In the way that the motives for committing any criminal act can be rationally determined, reasons for rape can also be determined. Our data demonstrate that some men rape because they have learned that in this culture sexual violence is rewarding. Significantly, the overwhelming majority of these rapists indicated they never thought they would go to prison for what they did. Some did not fear imprisonment because they did not define their behavior as rape. Others knew that women frequently do not report rape and of those cases that are reported, conviction rates are low, and therefore they felt secure. These men perceived rape as a rewarding, low risk act. Understanding that otherwise normal men can and do rape is critical to the development of strategies for prevention.

We are left with the fact that all men do not rape. In view of the apparent rewards and cultural supports for rape, it is important to ask why some men do not rape. Hirschi (1969) makes a similar observation about delinquency. He argues that the key question is not "Why do they do it?" but rather "Why don't we do it?" (Hirschi, 1969:34). Likewise, we may be seeking an answer to the wrong question about sexual assault of women. Instead of asking men who rape "Why?", perhaps we should be asking men who don't "Why not?"

NOTES

1. Despite the fact that these data have been in circulation for some time, prevention strategies continue to reflect the "lunatic fringe" image of rape. For example, security on college campuses, such as bright lighting and escort service, is designed to protect women against stranger rape while little or no attention is paid to the more frequent crime—acquaintance or date rape.

2. Broude and Green (1976) list a number of factors which limit the quantity and quality of cross-cultural data on rape. They point out that it was not customary in traditional ethnography to collect data on sexual attitudes and behavior. Further, where data do exist, they are often sketchy and vague. Despite this, the existence of rape-free societies has been established.

3. This factor distinguishes rape from other fictional depictions of violence. That is, in fictional murder, bombings, robberies, etc., victims are never portrayed as enjoying themselves. Such exhibits are reserved for pornographic displays of rape.

4. We also introduced a typology consisting of "admitters" (men who defined their behavior as rape) and "deniers" (men who admitted to sexual contact with the victim but did not define it as rape). In this paper we drop the distinction between admitters and deniers because it is not relevant to most of the discussion.

5. For a full discussion of the research methodology, sample, and validity, see Scully and Marolla (1984).

6. It should be noted that significant women, like rape victims, were also sometimes the targets of abuse and violence and possibly rape as well, although spousal rape is not recognized in Virginia law. In fact, these men were abusers. Fifty-five percent of rapists acknowledged that they hit their significant woman "at least once," and 20 percent admitted to inflicting physical injury. Given the tendency of these men to under-report the amount of violence in their crime, it is probably accurate to say, they under-reported their abuse of their significant women as well.

7. This man, as well as a number of others, either would not or could not, bring himself to say the word "rape." Similarly, we also attempted to avoid using the word, a technique which seemed to facilitate communication.

8. When asked towards whom their sexual interests were primarily directed, 43 percent of rapists indicated a preference for women "significantly older than themselves." When those who responded, "women of any age" are added, 65 percent of rapists expressed sexual interest in women older than themselves.

9. Feminists as well as sociologists have tended to avoid the topic of interracial rape. Contributing to the avoidance is an awareness of historical and contemporary social injustice. For example, Davis (1981) points out that fictional rape of white women was used in the South as a post-slavery justification to lynch black men. And LaFree (1980) has demonstrated that black men who assault white women continue to receive more serious sanctions within the criminal justice system when compared to other racial combinations of victim and assailant. While the silence has been defensible in light of historical racism, continued avoidance of the topic discriminates against victims by eliminating the opportunity to investigate the impact of social factors on rape.

10. In our sample, 66 percent of black rapists reported their victim(s) were white, compared to two white rapists who reported raping black women. It is important to emphasize that because of the biases inherent in rape reporting and processing, and because of the limitations of our sample, these figures do not accurately reflect the actual racial composition of rapes committed in Virginia or elsewhere. Furthermore, since black men who assault white women receive more serious sanctions within the criminal justice system when compared to other racial combinations of victim and assailant (LaFree 1980), B/W rapists will be overrepresented within prison populations as well as over-represented in any sample drawn from the population.

11. It is important to note that the gang rapes in this study were especially violent, resulting in physical injury, even death. One can only guess at the amount of hitchhike-abduction and "gang-date" rapes that are never reported or, if reported, are not processed because of the tendency to disbelieve the victims of such rapes unless extensive physical injury accompanies the crime.

12. It is interesting that men who verbally harass women on the street say they do so to alleviate boredom, to gain a sense of youthful camaraderie, and because it's fun (Benard and Schlaffer, 1984)—the same reason men who rape give for their behavior.

REFERENCES

Abel, Gene, Judith Becker, and Linda Skinner
1980 "Aggressive behavior and sex." Psychiatric Clinics of North America 3:133–51.

Athens, Lonnie
1977 "Violent crime: a symbolic interactionist study." Symbolic Interaction 1:56–71.

Bart, Pauline
1979 "Rape as a paradigm of sexism in society—victimization and its discontents." Women's Studies International Quarterly 2:347–57.

Benard, Cheryl and Edith Schlaffer
1984 "The man in the street: why he harasses." Pp. 70–73 in Alson M. Jaggar and Paula S. Rothenberg (eds.), Feminist Frameworks. New York: McGraw-Hill.

Black, Donald
1983 "Crime as social control." American Sociological Review 48:34–45.

Blumberg, Rae Lesser
1979 "A paradigm for predicting the position of women: policy implications and problems." Pp. 113–42 in Jean Lipman-Blumen and Jessie Bernard (eds.), Sex Roles and Social Policy. London: Sage Studies in International Sociology.

Broude, Owen and Sarah Greene
1976 "Cross-cultural codes on twenty sexual attitudes and practices." Ethnology 15:409–28.

Brownmiller, Susan
1975 Against Our Will. New York: Simon and Schuster.

Davis, Angela
1981 Women, Race and Class. New York: Random House.

Fisher, Gary and E. Rivlin
1971 "Psychological needs of rapists." British Journal of Criminology 11:182–85.

Griffin, Susan
1971 "Rape: the all American crime." Ramparts, September 10:26–35.

Groth, Nicholas
1971 Men Who Rape. New York: Plenum Press.

Hammer, Emanuel and Irving Jacks
1955 "A study of Rorschack flexnor and extensor human movements." Journal of Clinical Psychology 11:63–67.

Herman, Dianne
1984 "The rape culture." Pp. 20–39 in Jo Freeman (ed.), Women: A Feminist Perspective. Palo Alto: Mayfield.

Hirschi, Travis
1969 Causes of Delinquency. Berkeley: University of California Press.
Hoebel, E. Adamson
1954 The Law of Primitive Man. Boston: Harvard University Press.
Johnson, Allan Griswold
1980 "On the prevalence of rape in the United States." Signs 6:136–46.
Kanin, Eugene
1957 "Male aggression in dating-courtship relations." American Journal of Sociology 63:197–204.
1965 "Male sex aggression and three psychiatric hypotheses." Journal of Sex Research 1:227–29.
1967 "Reference groups and sex conduct norm violation." Sociological Quarterly 8:495–504.
1969 "Selected dyadic aspects of male sex aggression." Journal of Sex Research 5:12–28.
Kasinsky, Renee
1975 "Rape: a normal act?" Canadian Forum, September:18–22.
Kirkpatrick, Clifford and Eugene Kanin
1957 "Male sex aggression on a university campus." American Sociological Review 22:52–58.
Koss, Mary P. and Kenneth E. Leonard
1984 "Sexually aggressive men: empirical findings and theoretical implications." Pp. 213–32 in Neil M. Malamuth and Edward Donnerstein (eds.), Pornography and Sexual Aggression. New York: Academic Press.
LaFree, Gary
1980 "The effect of sexual stratification by race on official reactions to rape." American Sociological Review 45:824–54.
1982 "Male power and female victimization: towards a theory of interracial rape." American Journal of Sociology 88:311–28.
Llewellyn, Karl N., and E. Adamson Hoebel
1941 The Cheyenne Way: Conflict and Case Law in Primitive Jurisprudence. Norman: University of Oklahoma Press.
Luckenbill, David
1977 "Criminal homicide as a situated transaction." Social Problems 25:176–87.
Malamuth, Neil, Scott Haber and Seymour Feshback
1980 "Testing hypotheses regarding rape: exposure to sexual violence, sex difference, and the 'normality' of rapists." Journal of Research in Personality 14:121–37.
Malamuth, Neil, Maggie Heim, and Seymour Feshback
1980 "Sexual responsiveness of college students to rape depictions: inhibitory and disinhibitory effects." Social Psychology 38:399–408.
Meyer, Thomas J.
1984 " 'Date rape': a serious problem that few talk about" Chronicle of Higher Education, December 5.
Morgan, Robin
1980 "Theory and practice: pornography and rape." Pp. 134–40 in Laura Lederer (ed.), Take Back the Night: Women on Pornography. New York: William Morrow.
Queen's Bench Foundation
1976 Rape: Prevention and Resistance. San Francisco: Queen's Bench Foundation.
Rada, Richard
1978 Clinical Aspects of Rape. New York: Grune and Stratton.
Russell, Diana
1975 The Politics of Rape. New York: Stein and Day.
Sanday, Peggy Reeves
1979 The Socio-Cultural Context of Rape. Washington, DC: United States Department of Commerce, National Technical Information Service.

Scully, Diana and Joseph Marolla

1984 "Convicted rapists' vocabulary of motive: excuses and justifications." Social Problems 31:530–44.

1985 "Rape and psychiatric vocabulary of motive: alternative perspectives." Pp. 294–312 in Ann Wolbert Burgess (ed.), Rape and Sexual Assault: A Research Handbook. New York: Garland Publishing.

Smith, Don

1976 "The social context of pornography." Journal of Communications 26:16–24.

Smithyman, Samuel

1978 The Undetected Rapist. Unpublished Dissertation: Claremont Graduate School.

West, Donald J.

1983 "Sex offenses and offending." Pp. 1–30 in Michael Tonry and Norval Morris (eds.), Crime and Justice: An Annual Review of Research. Chicago: University of Chicago Press.

Weis, Kurt and Sandra Borges

1973 "Victimology and rape: the case of the legitimate victim." Issues in Criminology 8:71–115.

Wheeler, Hollis

1985 "Pornography and rape: a feminist perspective." Pp. 374–91 in Ann Wolbert Burgess (ed.), Rape and Sexual Assault: A Research Handbook. New York: Garland Publishing.

Reflection

DIANA SCULLY

It is an honor to have my and Joseph Marolla's paper, "Riding the Bull at Gilley's," included in *Violence against Women.* I accepted the editors' invitation to write a brief reflection on why I chose to research this problem because I have never written about the reasons for dedicating my career to issues related to violence against women.

It was during the early 1970s, while I was a graduate student at the University of Illinois, Chicago, ironically taking my first course in "Sex Roles" taught by Pauline Bart, when an unknown assailant broke into my apartment while I slept and raped me at knifepoint in an attack that lasted several hours and changed my life forever.

My recovery took many forms. I almost immediately became involved in the antirape movement that was just emerging in Chicago. In particular, I became a "public" victim willing to talk about my rape to any audience that I thought had the potential to help raped women. Understandably, in the early 1970s, most victims sought anonymity to avoid the stigma of rape. Perhaps most important, I redirected my scholarly interest to focus on sexual violence against women. My NIMH funded research, which involved face-to-face interviews with 114 incarcerated convicted rapists (and a contrast group of 75 other felons), publication of this paper among others and *Understanding Sexual Violence: A Study of Convicted Rapists* (Routledge, 1990), grew out of my personal experience and a deep desire to know why rape occurs.

At some point, I stopped speaking publicly as a victim because I was no longer effective in that role. In fact, my work as a feminist scholar on a topic of deep personal significance healed me and restored my sense of personal power—the thing that is taken from women when they are raped. It is important for raped women to know that despite what the medical model predicts, it is possible to emerge from rape an even stronger woman than you were before.

When I began my work on rape, the psychopathological model, which assumes that rape is the result of a mental illness and that it often includes an uncontrollable sexual impulse, dominated the field. According to this model, because men who rape cannot control their behavior, they are not responsible for it either. This also was the heyday of victim blaming and the assumption that women consciously or subconsciously precipitate, and consequently are the ones who are really responsible for, rape. Thus, much of the psychiatric literature focused on the behavior and motives of women and even girls rather than men.

I think the value of my work and that of many other feminists is the challenge it poses to those who would blame women for rape. Equally important is the contribution it made to the major paradigm shift that has taken place in our understanding of sexual violence from a psychopathological model to a feminist model and the assumption that rape is sociocultural in origin: men learn to rape and, as this paper demonstrates, many enjoy it as much as riding the bull at Gilley's!

CHAPTER 21

The Specific Deterrent Effects of Arrest for Domestic Assault

LAWRENCE W. SHERMAN AND
RICHARD A. BERK

with

42 PATROL OFFICERS OF THE MINNEAPOLIS POLICE DEPARTMENT, NANCY WESTER, DONILEEN LOSEKE, DAVID RAUMA, DEBRA MORROW, AMY CURTIS, KAY GAMBLE, ROY ROBERTS, PHYLLIS NEWTON, AND GAYLE GUBMAN

The specific deterrence doctrine and labeling theory predict opposite effects of punishment on individual rates of deviance. The limited cross-sectional evidence available on the question is inconsistent, and experimental evidence has been lacking. The Police Foundation and the Minneapolis Police Department tested these hypotheses in a field experiment on domestic violence. Three police responses to simple assault were randomly assigned to legally eligible suspects: an arrest; "advice" (including, in some cases, informal mediation); and an order to the suspect to leave for eight hours. The behavior of the suspect was tracked for six months after the police intervention, with both official data and victim reports. The official recidivism measures show that the arrested suspects manifested significantly less subsequent violence than those who were ordered to leave. The victim report data show that the arrested subjects manifested significantly less subsequent violence than those who were advised. The findings falsify a deviance amplification model of labeling theory beyond initial labeling, and fail to falsify the specific deterrence prediction for a group of offenders with a high percentage of prior histories of both domestic violence and other kinds of crime.

Sociologists since Durkheim ([1893] 1972:126) have speculated about how the punishment of individuals affects their behavior. Two bodies of literature, specific deterrence and labeling, have developed competing predictions (Thorsell and Klemke, 1972). Durkheim, for example, implicitly assumed with Bentham that the pains of punishment deter people from repeating the crimes for which they are punished, especially when punishment is certain, swift and severe. More recent work has fostered the ironic view that punishment often makes individuals more likely to commit crimes because of altered interactional structures, foreclosed legal opportunities and secondary deviance (Lemert, 1951, 1967; Schwartz and Skolnick, 1962; Becker, 1963).

Neither prediction can muster consistent empirical support. The few studies that allege effects generally employ weak designs in which it is difficult, if not impossible, to control plausibly for all important factors confounded with criminal justice sanctions and the rule-breaking behavior that may follow. Thus, some claim to show that punishment deters individuals punished (Clarke, 1966; F.B.I., 1967:34–44; Cohen and Stark, 1974:30; Kraut, 1976; Murray and Cox, 1979; McCord, 1983), while others claim to show that punishment increases their deviance (Gold and Williams, 1969; Shoham, 1974; Farrington, 1977; Klemke, 1978). Yet all of these studies suffer either methodological or conceptual flaws as tests of the effects of punishment (Zimring and Hawkins, 1973; Gibbs, 1975; Hirschi, 1975; Tittle, 1975), especially the confounding of incarceration with attempts to rehabilitate and the frequent failure to differentiate effects for different types of offenders and offenses (Lempert, 1981–1982).

Perhaps the strongest evidence to date comes from a randomized experiment conducted by Lincoln et al. (unpubl.). The experiment randomly assigned juveniles, who had already been apprehended, to four different treatments ranked in their formality: release; two types of diversion; and formal charging. The more formal and official the processing, the more frequent the repeat criminality over a two-year follow-up period. This study supports labeling theory for arrested juveniles, although it cannot isolate the labeling or deterrent effects of arrest per se.

In all likelihood, of course, punishment has not one effect, but many, varying across types of people and situations (Chambliss, 1967; Andenaes, 1971). As Lempert (1981–1982:523) argues, "it is only by attending to a range of such offenses that we will be able to develop a general theory of deterrence." The variables affecting the deterrability of juvenile delinquency, white-collar crime, armed robbery and domestic violence may be quite different. Careful accumulation of findings from different settings will help us differentiate the variables which are crime- or situation-specific and those which apply across settings.

In this spirit, we report here a study of the impact of punishment in a particular setting, for a particular offense, and for particular kinds of individuals. Over an eighteen-month period, police in Minneapolis applied one of three intervention strategies in incidents of misdemeanor domestic assault: arrest; ordering the offender from the premises; or some form of advice which could include mediation. The three interventions were assigned randomly to households, and a critical outcome was the rate of repeat incidents. The relative effect of arrest should hold special interest for the specific deterrence–labeling controversy.

Policing Domestic Assaults

Police have been typically reluctant to make arrests for domestic violence (Berk and Loseke, 1981), as well as for a wide range of other kinds of offenses, unless victims demand an arrest, the suspect insults the officer, or other factors are present (Sherman, 1980). Parnas's (1972) qualitative observations of the Chicago police found four categories of police action in these situations: negotiating or otherwise "talking out" the dispute; threatening the disputants and then leaving; asking one of the parties to leave the premises; or (very rarely) making an arrest.

Similar patterns are found in many other cities. Surveys of battered women who tried to have their domestic assailants arrested report that arrest occurred in 10 percent (Roy, 1977:35) or 3 percent (see Langley and Levy, 1977:219) of the cases. Surveys of police agencies in Illinois (Illinois Law Enforcement Commission, 1978) and New York (Office of the Minority Leader, 1978) found explicit policies against arrest in the majority of the agencies surveyed. Despite the fact that violence is reported to be present in one-third (Bard and Zacker, 1974) to two-thirds (Black, 1980) of all domestic disturbances police respond to, police department data show arrests in only 5 percent of those disturbances in Oakland (Hart, n.d., cited in Meyer and Lorimer, 1977:21), 6 percent of those disturbances in a Colorado city (Patrick et al., n.d., cited in Meyer and Lorimer, 1977:21) and 6 percent in Los Angeles County (Emerson, 1979).

The best available evidence on the frequency of arrest is the observations from the Black and Reiss study of Boston, Washington and Chicago police in 1966 (Black, 1980:182). Police responding to disputes in those cities made arrests in 27 percent of violent felonies and 17 percent of the violent misdemeanors. Among married couples (Black, 1980:158), they made arrests in 26 percent of the cases, but tried to remove one of the parties in 38 percent of the cases.

An apparent preference of many police for separating the parties rather than arresting the offender has been attacked from two directions over the last fifteen years. The original critique came from clinical psychologists, who agreed that police should rarely make arrests (Potter, 1978:46; Fagin, 1978:123–24) in domestic assault cases, and argued that police should mediate the disputes responsible for the violence. A highly publicized demonstration project teaching police special counseling skills for family crisis intervention (Bard, 1970) failed to show a reduction in violence, but was interpreted as a success nonetheless. By 1977, a national survey of police agencies with 100 or more officers found that over 70 percent reported a family crisis intervention training program in operation. While it is not clear whether these programs reduced separation and increased mediation, a decline in arrests was noted for some (Wylie et al., 1976). Indeed, many sought explicitly to reduce the number of arrests (University of Rochester, 1974; Ketternian and Kravitz, 1978).

By the mid-1970s, police practices were criticized from the opposite direction by feminist groups. Just as psychologists succeeded in having many police agencies respond to domestic violence as "half social work and half police work," feminists began to argue that police put "too much emphasis on the social work aspect and not enough on the criminal" (Langley and Levy, 1977:218). Widely publicized lawsuits in New York and Oakland sought to compel police to make arrests in every case of domestic assault, and state legislatures were lobbied successfully to reduce the evidentiary requirements needed for police to make arrests for misdemeanor domestic assaults. Some legislatures are now considering statutes requiring police to make arrests in these cases.

The feminist critique was bolstered by a study (Police Foundation, 1976) showing that for 85 percent of a sample of spousal homicides, police had intervened at least once in the preceding two years. For 54 percent of the homicides, police had intervened five or more times. But it was impossible to determine from the cross-sectional data whether making more or fewer arrests would have reduced the homicide rate.

In sum, police officers confronting a domestic assault suspect face at least three conflicting options, urged on them by different groups with different theories. The officers' colleagues might recommend forced separation as a means of achieving short-term peace. Alternatively, the officers' trainers might recommend mediation as a means of getting to the underlying cause of the "dispute" (in which both parties are implicitly assumed to be at fault). Finally, the local women's organizations may recommend that the officer protect the victim (whose "fault," if any, is legally irrelevant) and enforce the law to deter such acts in the future.

Research Design

In response to these conflicting recommendations, the Police Foundation and the Minneapolis Police Department agreed to conduct a randomized experiment. The design called for random assignment of arrest, separation, and some form of advice which could include mediation at the officer's discretion. In addition, there was to be a six-month follow-up period to measure the frequency and seriousness of domestic violence after each police intervention. The advantages of randomized experiments are well known and need not be reviewed here (see, e.g., Cook and Campbell, 1979).

The design only applied to simple (misdemeanor) domestic assaults, where both the suspect and the victim were present when the police arrived. Thus, the experiment included only those cases in which police were empowered (but not required) to make arrests under a recently liberalized Minnesota state law; the police officer must have probable cause to believe that a cohabitant or spouse had assaulted the victim within the last four hours (but police need not have witnessed the assault). Cases of life-threatening or severe injury, usually labeled as a felony (aggravated assault), were excluded from the design for ethical reasons.

The design called for each officer to carry a pad of report forms, color coded for the three different police actions. Each time the officers encountered a situation that fit the experiment's criteria, they were to take whatever action was indicated by the report form on the top of the pad. We numbered the forms and arranged them in random order for each officer. The integrity of the random assignment was to be monitored by research staff observers riding on patrol for a sample of evenings.

After police action was taken, the officer was to fill out a brief report and give it to the research staff for follow-up. As a further check on the randomization process, the staff logged in the reports in the order in which they were received and made sure that the sequence corresponded to the original assignment of treatments.

Anticipating something of the victims' background, a predominantly minority, female research staff was employed to contact the victims for a detailed face-to-face interview, to be followed by telephone follow-up interviews every two weeks for 24 weeks. The interviews were designed primarily to measure the frequency and seriousness of victimizations caused by the suspect after the police intervention.[1] The research staff also collected criminal justice reports that mentioned the suspect's name during the six-month follow-up period.

Conduct of the Experiment

As is common in field experiments, implementation of the research design entailed some slippage from the original plan. In order to gather data as quickly as possible, the experiment was originally located in the two Minneapolis precincts with the highest density of domestic violence crime reports and arrests. The 34 officers assigned to those areas were invited to a three-day planning meeting and asked to participate in the study for one year. All but one agreed. The conference also produced a draft order for the chief's signature specifying the rules of the experiment. These rules created several new situations to be excluded from the experiment, such as if a suspect attempted to assault police officers, a victim persistently demanded an arrest, or if both parties were injured. These additional exceptions, unfortunately, allowed for the possibility of differential attrition from the separation and mediation treatments. The implications for internal validity are discussed later.

The experiment began on March 17, 1981, with the expectation that it would take about one year to produce about 300 cases (it ran until August 1, 1982, and produced 330 case reports.) The officers agreed to meet monthly with the project director (Sherman) and the project manager (Wester). By the third or fourth month, two facts became clear: (1) only about 15 to 20 officers were either coming to meetings or turning in cases; and (2) the rate at which the cases were turned in would make it difficult to complete the project in one year. By November, we decided to recruit more officers in order to obtain cases more rapidly. Eighteen additional officers joined the project, but like the original group, most of these officers only turned in one or two cases. Indeed, three of the original officers produced almost 28 percent of the cases, in part because they worked a particularly violent beat, and in part because they had a greater commitment to the study. Since the treatments were randomized by officer, this created no internal validity problem. However, it does raise construct validity problems to which we will later return.

There is little doubt that many of the officers occasionally failed to follow fully the experimental design. Some of the failures were due to forgetfulness, such as leaving the report pads at home or at the police station. Other failures derived from misunderstanding about whether the experiment applied in certain situations; application of the experimental rules under complex circumstances was sometimes confusing. Finally, from time to time there were situations that were simply not covered by the experiment's rules.

Whether any officers intentionally subverted the design is unclear. The plan to monitor randomization with ride-along observers broke down because of the unexpectedly low incidence of cases meeting the experimental criteria. The observers had to ride for many weeks before they observed an officer apply one of the treatments. We tried to solve this problem with "chase-alongs," in which the observers rode in their own car with a portable police radio and drove to the scene of any domestic call dispatched to any officer in the precinct. Even this method failed.

Thus, we are left with at least two disturbing possibilities. First, police officers anticipating (e.g., from the dispatch call) a particular kind of incident, and finding the upcoming experimental treatment inappropriate, may have occasionally decided to void the experiment. That is, they may have chosen to exclude certain cases in violation of the experimental design. This amounts to differential attrition, which is clearly a threat to internal validity. Note that if police officers blindly decided to exclude certain cases (e.g., because they did not feel like filling out the extra forms on a given day), all would be well for internal validity.

Second, since the recording officer's pad was supposed to govern the actions of each pair of officers, some officers may also have switched the assignment of driver and recording officer after deciding a case fit the study in order to obtain a treatment they wanted to apply. If the treatments were switched between driver and recorder, then the internal validity was again threatened. However, this was almost certainly uncommon because it was generally easier not to fill out a report at all than to switch.

Table 21.1 shows the degree to which the treatments were delivered as designed.[2] Ninety-nine percent of the suspects targeted for arrest actually were arrested, while only 78 percent of those to receive advice did, and only 73 percent of those to be sent out of the residence for eight hours were actually sent. One explanation for this pattern, consistent with the experimental guidelines, is that mediating and sending were more difficult ways for police to control the situation, with a greater likelihood that officers might resort to arrest as a fallback position. When the assigned treatment is arrest, there is no need for a fallback position. For example, some offenders may have refused to comply with an order to leave the premises.

Such differential attrition would potentially bias estimates of the relative effectiveness of arrest by removing uncooperative and difficult offenders from the mediation and separation treatments. Any deterrent effect could be underestimated and, in the extreme,

TABLE 21.1 Designed and Delivered Police Treatments in Spousal Assault Cases

	Delivered Treatment			
Designed Treatment	*Arrest*	*Advise*	*Separate*	**Total**
Arrest	98.9%	0.0%	1.1%	29.3%
	(91)	(0)	(1)	(92)
Advise	17.6%	77.8%	4.6%	34.4%
	(19)	(84)	(5)	(108)
Separate	22.8%	4.4%	72.8%	36.3%
	(26)	(5)	(83)	(114)
Total	43.4%	28.3%	28.3%	100%
	(136)	(89)	(89)	(314)

artifactual support for deviance amplification could be found. That is, the arrest group would have too many "bad guys" *relative* to the other treatments.

We can be more systematic about other factors affecting the movement of cases away from the designed treatments. The three delivered treatments represent a polychotomous outcome amenable to multivariate statistical analysis. We applied a multinominal logit formulation (Amemiya, 1981:1516–19; Maddala, 1983:34–37), which showed that the designed treatment was the dominant cause of the treatment actually received (a finding suggested by Table 21.1). However, we also found that five other variables had a statistically significant effect on "upgrading" the separation and advice treatments to arrests: whether police reported the suspect was rude; whether police reported the suspect tried to assault one (or both) of the police officers; whether police reported weapons were involved; whether the victim persistently demanded a citizen's arrest; and whether a restraining order was being violated. We found no evidence that the background or characteristics of the suspect or victim (e.g., race) affected the treatment received.

Overall, the logit model fit the data very well. For well over 80 percent of the cases, the model's predicted treatment was the same as the actual treatment (i.e., correct classifications), and minor alterations in the assignment threshold would have substantially improved matters. Moreover, a chi-square test on the residuals was not statistically significant (i.e., the observed and predicted treatments differed by no more than chance). In summary, we were able to model the assignment process with remarkable success simply by employing the rules of the experimental protocol (for more details, see Berk and Sherman, 1983).

We were less fortunate with the interviews of the victims; only 205 (of 330, counting the few repeat victims twice) could be located and initial interviews obtained, a 62 percent completion rate. Many of the victims simply could not be found, either for the initial interview or for follow-ups: they either left town, moved somewhere else or refused to answer the phone or doorbell. The research staff made up to 20 attempts to contact these victims, and often employed investigative techniques (asking friends and neighbors) to find them. Sometimes these methods worked, only to have the victim give an outright refusal or break one or more appointments to meet the interviewer at a "safe" location for the interview.

The response rate to the bi-weekly follow-up interviews was even lower than for the initial interview, as in much research on women crime victims. After the first interview, for which the victims were paid $20, there was a gradual falloff in completed interviews with each successive wave; only 161 victims provided all 12 follow-up interviews over the six months, a completion rate of 49 percent. Whether paying for the follow-up interviews would have improved the response rate is unclear; it would have added over $40,000 to the cost of the research. When the telephone interviews yielded few reports of violence, we moved to conduct every fourth interview in person, which appeared to produce more reports of violence.

There is absolutely no evidence that the experimental treatment assigned to the offender affected the victim's decision to grant initial interviews. We estimated a binary logit equation for the dichotomous outcome: whether or not an initial interview was obtained. Regressors included the experimental treatments (with one necessarily excluded), race of the victim, race of the offender, and a number of attributes of the incident (from the police sheets). A joint test on the full set of regressors failed to reject the null hypothesis that all of the logit coefficients were zero. More important for our purposes, none of the t-values for the treatments was in excess of 1.64; indeed, none was greater than 1.0 in absolute value. In short, while the potential for sample selection bias (Heckman, 1979; Berk, 1983) certainly exists (and is considered later), that bias does not stem from obvious sources, particularly the treatments. This implies that we may well be able to meaningfully examine experimental effects for the subset of individuals from whom initial interviews were obtained. The same conclusions followed when the follow-up interviews were considered.

In sum, despite the practical difficulties of controlling an experiment and interviewing crime victims in an emotionally charged and violent social context, the experiment succeeded in producing a promising sample of 314 cases with complete official outcome measures and an apparently unbiased sample of responses from the victims in those cases.

Results

The 205 completed initial interviews provide some sense of who the subjects are, although the data may not properly represent the characteristics of the full sample of 314. They show the now familiar pattern of domestic violence cases coming to police attention being disproportionately unmarried couples with lower than average educational levels, disproportionately minority and mixed race (black male, white female), and who were very likely to have had prior violent incidents with police intervention. The 60 percent suspect unemployment rate is strikingly high in a community with only about 5 percent of the workforce unemployed. The 59 percent prior arrest rate is also strikingly high, suggesting (with the 80 percent prior domestic assault rate) that the suspects generally are experienced lawbreakers who are accustomed to police interventions. But with the exception of the heavy representation of Native Americans (due to Minneapolis' unique proximity to many Indian reservations), the characteristics in Table 21.2 are probably close to those of domestic violence cases coming to police attention in other large U.S. cities.

Two kinds of outcome measures will be considered. One is a *police-recorded* "failure" of the offender to survive the six-month follow-up period without having police generate a written report on the suspect for domestic violence, either through an offense or an arrest report written by any officer in the department, or through a subsequent report to the project research staff of a randomized (or other) intervention by officers participating in the experiment. A second kind of measure comes from the *interviews with victims,* in which victims were asked if there had been a repeat incident with the same suspect, broadly defined to include an actual assault, threatened assault, or property damage.

The two kinds of outcomes were each formulated in two complementary ways: as a dummy variable (i.e., repeat incident or not) and as the amount of time elapsed from the treatment to either a failure or the end of the follow-up period. For each of the two outcomes, three analyses were performed: the first using a linear probability model; the second using a logit formulation; and the third using a proportional hazard approach. The dummy outcome was employed for the linear probability and logit analyses, while the time-to-failure was employed for the proportional hazard method.[3]

TABLE 21.2 Victim and Suspect Characteristics: Initial Interview Data and Police Sheets

A. Unemployment		
Victims 61%		
Suspects 60%		
B. Relationship of Suspect to Victim		
Divorced or separated husband	3%	
Unmarried male lover	45%	
Current husband	35%	
Wife or girlfriend	2%	
Son, brother, roommate, other	15%	
C. Prior Assaults and Police Involvement		
Victims assaulted by suspect, last six months	80%	
Police intervention in domestic dispute, last six months	60%	
Couple in Counseling Program	27%	
D. Prior Arrests of Male Suspects		
Ever Arrested for Any Offense	59%	
Ever Arrested for Crime Against Person	31%	
Ever Arrested on Domestic Violence Statute	5%	
Ever Arrested on an Alcohol Offense	29%	
E. Mean Age		
Victims 30 years		
Suspects 32 years		
	Victims	*Suspects*
F. Education		
< high school	43%	42%
high school only	33%	36%
> high school	24%	22%
G. Race		
White	57%	45%
Black	23%	36%
Native American	18%	16%
Other	2%	3%

$N = 205$ (Those cases for which initial interviews were obtained)

Given the randomization, we began in traditional analysis of variance fashion. The official measure of a repeat incident was regressed on the treatment received for the subset of 314 cases (out of 330) that fell within the definition of the experiment. Compared to the baseline treatment of separation, which had the highest recidivism rate in the police data, the arrest treatment reduced repeat occurrences by a statistically significant amount ($t = -2.38$). Twenty-six percent of those separated committed a repeat assault, compared to 13 percent of those arrested. The mediation treatment was statistically indistinguishable from the other two. To help put this in perspective, 18.2 percent of the households failed overall.

The apparent treatment effect for arrest in this conventional analysis was suggestive, but there was a danger of biased estimates from the "upgrading" of some separation and advise treatments. In response, we applied variations on the corrections recommended by Barnow et al. (1980: esp. SS). In brief, we inserted instrumental variables in place of the delivered treatments when the treatment effects were analyzed. These instruments, in turn, were constructed from the multinomial logit model described earlier.[4]

Table 21.3 shows the results of the adjusted models. The first two columns report the results for the linear probability approach. Again, we find a statistically significant effect for arrest (t = –2.21). However, it is well known that the linear probability model will produce inefficient estimates of the regression coefficients and biased (and inconsistent) estimates of the standard errors. Significance tests, therefore, are suspect. Consequently, we also estimated a logit model, with pretty much the same result. At the mean of the endogenous variable (i.e., 18.2 percent), the logit coefficient for arrest translates into nearly the same effect (i.e., –.15) found with the linear probability model (t = –2.21).

One might still object that the use of a dummy variable outcome neglects right-hand censoring. In brief, one cannot observe failures that occur, after the end of the experimental period, so that biased (and inconsistent) results follow. Thus, we applied a proportional hazard analysis (Lawless, 1982: Ch. 7) that adjusts for right-hand censoring. In this model the time-to-failure dependent variable is transformed into (roughly) the probability at any given moment during the six-month follow-up period of a new offense occurring, given that no new offenses have yet been committed. The last two columns of Table 21.3 indicate that, again, an effect for arrest surfaces (t = –2.28). The coefficient of –0.97 implies that compared to the baseline of separation, those experiencing an arrest were less likely to commit a new battery by a multiplicative factor of .38 (i.e., be raised to the –0.97 power). If the earlier results are translated into comparable terms, the effects described by the proportional hazard formulation are the largest we have seen (see note 4). But the major message is that the arrest effect holds up under three different statistical methods based on slightly different response functions. Overall, the police data indicate that the

TABLE 21.3 Experimental Results for Police Data

	Linear		**Logistic**		**Proportional Hazard Rate**	
Variable	*Coef*	*t-value*	*Coef*	*t-value*	*Coef*	*t-value*
Intercept (separate)	0.24	5.03*	–1.10	–4.09*	–	–
Arrest	–0.14	–2.21*	–1.02	–2.21*	–0.97	–2.28*
Advise	–0.05	–0.79	–0.31	–0.76	–0.32	–0.88
	F = 2.01		Chi-square = 5.19		Chi-square = 5.48	
	P = .07		P = .07		P = .06	

N = 314

*p < .05, two-tailed test.

TABLE 21.4 Experimental Results for Victim Report Data

	Linear		Logistic		Proportional Hazard Rate	
Variable	*Coef*	*t-value*	*Coef*	*t-value*	*Coef*	*t-value*
Intercept (advise)	0.37	5.54*	–0.53	–1.70	–	–
Arrest	–0.18	–2.00*	–0.94	–2.01*	–0.82	–2.05*
Separate	–0.04	–0.35	–0.15	–0.10	–0.27	–0.09
	F = 2.31		Chi-square = 4.78		Chi-square = 4.36	
	P = .10		P = .09		P = .11	

N = 161 (Those cases for which *all* follow-up interviews were obtained)

*p < .05, two-tailed test.

separation treatment produces the highest recidivism, arrest produces the lowest, with the impact of "advise" (from doing nothing to mediation) indistinguishable from the other two effects.

Table 21.4 shows the results when self-report data are used. A "failure" is defined as a new assault, property destruction or a threatened assault. (Almost identical results follow from a definition including only a new assault.) These results suggest a different ordering of the effects, with arrest still producing the lowest recidivism rate (at 1990), but with advice producing the highest (37%).

Overall, 28.9 percent of the suspects in Table 21.4 "failed." Still, the results are much the same as found for the official failure measure. However, given the effective sample of 161, we are vulnerable to sample selection bias. In response, we applied Heckman's (1979) sample selection corrections. The results were virtually unchanged (and are therefore not reported).

An obvious rival hypothesis to the deterrent effect of arrest is that arrest incapacitates. If the arrested suspects spend a large portion of the next six months in jail, they would be expected to have lower recidivism rates. But the initial interview data show this is not the case: of those arrested, 43 percent were released within one day, 86 percent were released within one week, and only 14 percent were released after one week or had not yet been released at the time of the *initial* victim interview. Clearly, there was very little incapacitation, especially in the context of a six-month follow-up. Indeed, virtually all those arrested were released before the first follow-up interview. Nevertheless, we introduced the length of the initial stay in jail as a control variable. Consistent with expectations, the story was virtually unchanged.

Another perspective on the incapacitation issue can be obtained by looking at repeat violence which occurred shortly after the police intervened. If incapacitation were at work, a dramatic effect should be found in households experiencing arrest, especially compared

TABLE 21.5 Speed of Reunion and Recidivism by Police Action

	Time of Reunion					
Police Action	*Within One Day*	*More Than One Day but Less Than One Week*	*Longer or No Return*	**(N)**	**New Quarrel within a Day**	**New Violence within a Day**
Arrested (and released)	38%	30%	32%	(N = 76)	(2)	(1)
Separated	57%	31%	10%	(N = 54)	(6)	(3)
Advised	–	–	–	(N = 72)	(4)	(1)

N = 202 (Down from the 205 in Table 21.2 due to missing data)

to the households experiencing advice. Table 21.5 shows how quickly the couples were reunited, and of those reunited in one day, how many of them, according to the victim, began to argue or had physical violence again. It is apparent that *all* of the police interventions effectively stopped the violence for a 24-hour period after the couples were reunited. Even the renewed quarrels were few, at least with our relatively small sample size. Hence, there is again no evidence for an incapacitation effect. There is also no evidence for the reverse: that arrested offenders would take it out on the victim when the offender returned home.

Discussion and Conclusions

The experiment's results are subject to several qualifications. One caution is that both kinds of outcome measures have uncertain construct validity. The official measure no doubt neglects a large number of repeat incidents, in part because many of them were not reported, and in part because police are sometimes reluctant to turn a family "dispute" into formal police business. However, the key is whether there is *differential* measurement error by the experimental treatments; an undercount randomly distributed across the three treatments will not bias the estimated experimental effects (i.e., only the estimate of the intercept will be biased). It is hard to imagine that differential undercounting would come solely from the actions of police, since most officers were not involved in the experiment and could not have known what treatment had been delivered.

However, there might be differential undercounting if offenders who were arrested were less likely to remain on the scene after a new assault. Having been burned once, they might not wait around for a second opportunity. And police told us they were less likely during the follow-up period (and more generally) to record an incident if the offender was not present. For example, there would be no arrest forms since the offender was not available to arrest. If all we had were the official outcome measures, there would be no easy way to refute this possibility. Fortunately, the self-report data are *not* vulnerable on these grounds, and the experimental effects are found nevertheless.

It is also possible that the impact for arrest found in the official outcome measure represents a reluctance of *victims* to call the police. That is, for some victims, the arrest may have been an undesirable intervention, and rather than face the prospect of another arrest from a new incident, these victims might decide not to invoke police sanctions. For example, the arrest may have cost the offender several days' work and put financial stress on the household. Or the offender may have threatened serious violence if the victim ever called the police again. However, we can again observe that the self-report data would not have been vulnerable to such concerns, and the experimental effects were found nevertheless. The only way we can see how the self-report data would fail to support the official data is if respondents in households experiencing arrest became more hesitant to admit to *interviewers* that they had been beaten a second time. Since there was no differential response rate by treatment, this possibility seems unlikely. If the arrested suspects had intimidated their victims more than the other two treatment groups, it seems more likely that such intimidation would have shown up in noncooperation with the interviews than in differential underreporting of violence in the course of the interviews.

This is not to say that the self-report data are flawless; indeed there is some reason to believe that there was undercounting of new incidents. However, just as for the official data, unless there is differential undercounting by the experimental treatments, all is well. We can think of no good reasons why differential undercounting should materialize. In summary, internal validity looks rather sound.

The construct validity of the treatments is more problematic. The advice and separation interventions have unclear content. Perhaps "good" mediation, given consistently, would fare better compared to arrest. The more general point is that the treatment effects for arrest are only relative to the impact of the other interventions. Should their content change, the relative impact of arrest could change as well.

Likewise, we noted earlier that a few officers accounted for a disproportionate number of the cases. What we have been interpreting, therefore, as results from different intervention strategies could reflect the special abilities of certain officers to make arrest particularly effective relative to the other treatments. For example, these officers may have been less skilled in mediation techniques. However, we re-estimated the models reported in Tables 21.3 and 21.4, including an interaction effect to capture the special contributions of our high-productivity officers. The new variable was not statistically significant, and the treatment effect for arrest remained.

Finally, Minneapolis is hardly representative of all urban areas. The Minneapolis Police Department has many unusual characteristics, and different jurisdictions might well keep suspects in custody for longer or shorter periods of time. The message should be clear: external validity will have to wait for replications.

Despite these qualifications, it is apparent that we have found no support for the deviance amplification point of view. The arrest intervention certainly did not make things worse and may well have made things better. There are, of course, many rejoinders. In particular, over 80 percent of offenders had assaulted the victims in the previous six months, and in over 60 percent of the households the police had intervened during that interval. Almost 60 percent of the suspects had previously been arrested for something. Thus, the counterproductive consequences of police sanction, if any, may for many offenders have already been felt. In labeling theory terms, secondary deviation may already have been established, producing a ceiling for the amplification effects of formal sanctioning. However, were this the case, the arrest treatment probably should be less effective in households experiencing recent police interventions. No such interaction effects were found. In future analyses of these data, however, we will inductively explore interactions with more sensitive measures of police sanctioning and prior criminal histories of the suspects.

There are, of course, many versions of labeling theory. For those who theorize that a metamorphosis of self occurs in response to official sanctions over a long period of time, our six-month follow-up is not a relevant test. For those who argue that the development of a criminal self-concept is particularly likely to occur during a lengthy prison stay or extensive contact with criminal justice officials, the dosage of labeling employed in this experiment is not sufficient to falsify that hypothesis. What this experiment does seem to falsify for this particular offense is the broader conception of labeling implicit in the prior research by Lincoln et al. (unpubl.), Farrington (1977) and others: that for every possible increment of criminal justice response to deviance, the more increments (or the greater the formality) applied to the labeled deviant, the greater the likelihood of subsequent deviation. The absolute strength of the dosage is irrelevant to this hypothesis, as long as some variation in dosage is present. While the experiment does not falsify all possible "labeling theory" hypotheses, it does at least seem to falsify this one.

The apparent support for deterrence is perhaps more clear. While we certainly have no evidence that deterrence will work in general, we do have findings that swift imposition of a sanction of temporary incarceration may deter male offenders in domestic assault cases. And we have produced this evidence from an unusually strong research design based on random assignment to treatments. In short, criminal justice sanctions seem to matter for this offense in this setting with this group of experienced offenders.

A number of police implications follow. Perhaps most important, police have historically been reluctant to make arrests in domestic assault cases, in part fearing that an arrest could make the violence worse. Criminal justice sanctions weakly applied might be insufficient to deter and set the offender on a course of retribution. Our data indicate that such concerns are by and large groundless.

Police have also felt that making an arrest was a waste of their time: without the application of swift and severe sanctions by the courts, arrest and booking had no bite. Our results indicate that only three of the 136 arrested offenders were formally punished by fines or subsequent incarceration. This suggests that arrest and initial incarceration alone may produce a deterrent effect, regardless of how the courts treat such cases, and that arrest makes an independent contribution to the deterrence potential of the criminal justice system. Therefore, in jurisdictions that process domestic assault offenders in a manner similar to that employed in Minneapolis, we favor a *presumption* of arrest; an arrest should be made unless there are good, clear reasons why an arrest would be counterproductive. We do not, however, favor *requiring* arrests in all misdemeanor domestic assault cases. Even if our findings were replicated in a number of jurisdictions, there is a good chance that arrest works far better for some kinds of offenders than others and in some kinds of situations better than others.[5] We feel it best to leave police a loophole to capitalize on that variation. Equally important, it is widely recognized that discretion is inherent in police work. Simply to impose a requirement of arrest, irrespective of the features of the immediate situation, is to invite circumvention.

NOTES

1. The protocols were based heavily on instruments designed for an NIMH-funded study of spousal violence conducted by Richard A. Berk, Sarah Fenstermaker Berk, and Ann D. Witte (Center for Studies of Crime and Delinquency, Grant #MH-34616–01). A similar protocol was developed for the suspects, but only twenty-five of them agreed to be interviewed.
2. Sixteen cases were dropped because no treatment was applied or because the case did not belong in the study (i.e., a fight between a father and son).
3. In addition to the linear probability model, the logit and proportional hazard formulations can be expressed in forms such that the outcome is a probability (e.g., the probability of a new violent incident). However, three slightly different response functions are implied. We had no theoretical basis for selecting the proper response function, and consequently used all three. We expected that the substantive results could be essentially invariant across the three formulations.
4. We did *not* simply use the conditional expectations of a multinomial logit model. We used an alternative procedure to capitalize on the initial random assignment. The details can be found in Berk and Sherman (1983).
5. Indeed, one of the major policy issues that could arise from further analysis of the interaction effects would be whether police discretion should be guided by either achieved or ascribed relevant suspect characteristics.

REFERENCES

Amemiya, Takeshi
1981 "Qualitative response models: a survey." Journal of Economic Literature 19:1483–1536.
Andenaes, Johannes
1971 "Deterrence and specific offenses." University of Chicago Law Review 39:537.
Bard, Morton
1970 "Training police as specialists in family crisis intervention." Washington, D.C.: U.S. Department of Justice.
Bard, Morton and Joseph Zacker
1974 "Assaultiveness and alcohol use in family disputes—police perceptions." Criminology 12:281–92.
Barnow, Burt S., Glen G. Cain and Arthur S. Goldberger
1980 "Issues in the analysis of selectivity bias. Pp. 53–59 in Ernst W. Stromsdorfer and George Farkas (eds.), Evaluation Studies Review Annual, Volume 5. Beverly Hills: Sage.
Becker, Howard
1963 The Outsiders. New York: Free Press.

Berk, Richard A.
1983 "An introduction to sample selection bias in sociological data." American Sociological Review, 48:386–98.
Berk, Richard A. and Lawrence W. Sherman
1983 "Police responses to family violence incidents: an analysis of an experimental design with incomplete randomization." Unpublished manuscript, Department of Sociology, University of California at Barbara.
Berk, Sarah Fenstermaker and Donileen R. Loseke
1981 "Handling family violence: situational determinants of police arrest in domestic disturbances." Law and Society Review 15:315–46.
Black, Donald
1980 The Manners and Customs of the Police. New York: Academic Press.
Chambliss, William
1967 "Types of deviance and the effectiveness of legal sanctions." Wisconsin Law Review 1967:703–19.
Clarke, Ronald V. G.
1966 "Approved school boy absconders and corporal punishment." British Journal of Criminology: 6:364–75.
Cohen, Lawrence E. and Rodney Stark
1974 "Discriminatory labeling and the five-finger discount." Journal of Research in Crime and Delinquency 11:25–39.
Cook, Thomas D. and Donald T. Campbell
1979 Quasi-Experimentation: Design and Analysis Issues for Field Settings. Chicago: Rand McNally.
Durkheim, Emile
[1893] 1972 Selected Writings. Edited with an Introduction by Anthony Giddens. [Selection from Division of Labor in Society, 6th edition, 1960 (1893)] Cambridge: Cambridge University Press.
Emerson, Charles D.
1979 "Family violence: a study by the Los Angeles County Sheriff's Department." Police Chief 46(6):48–50.
Fagin, James A.
1978 "The effects of police interpersonal communications skills on conflict resolution." Ph.D. Dissertation, Southern Illinois University Ann Arbor: University Microfilms.
Farrington, David P.
1977 "The effects of public labeling." British Journal of Crininology 17:112–25.
Federal Bureau of Investigation
1967 Uniform Crime Reports. Washington, D.C.: U.S. Department of Justice.
Gold, Martin and Jay Williams
1969 "National study of the aftermath of apprehension." Prospectus 3:3–11.
Gibbs, Jack P.
1975 Crime, Punishment and Deterrence. New York: Elsevier.
Heckman, James
1979 "Sample selection bias as a specification error." Econometrica 45:153–61.
Hirschi, Travis
1975 "Labeling theory and juvenile delinquency: an assessment of the evidence." Pp. 181–203 in Walter R. Gove (ed.), The Labeling of Deviance. New York: Wiley.
Illinois Law Enforcement Commission
1978 "Report on technical assistance project—domestic violence survey." (Abstract). Washington, D.C.: National Criminal Justice Reference Service.

Ketterman, Thomas and Marjorie Kravitz
Police Crisis Intervention: A Selected Bibliography. Washington, D.C.: National Criminal Justice Reference Service.
Klemke, Lloyd W.
1978 "Does apprehension for shoplifting amplify or terminate shoplifting activity?" Law and Society Review 12:391–403.
Kraut, Robert E.
1976 "Deterrent and definitional influences on shoplifting." Social Problems 23:358–68.
Langley, Richard and Roger C. Levy
1977 Wife Beating: The Silent Crisis. New York: E. P. Dutton.
Lawless, Jerald F.
1982 Statistical Models and Methods for Lifetime Data. New York: Wiley.
Lemert, Edwin M.
1951 Social Pathology. New York: McGraw-Hill.
1967 Human Deviance, Social Problems and Social Control. Englewood Cliffs, NJ: Prentice-Hall.
Lempert, Richard.
1981–1982 "Organizing for deterrence: lessons from a study of child support." Law and Society Review 16:513–68.
Lincoln, Suzanne B., Malcolm W. Klein, Katherine S. Teilmann and Susan Labin
unpubl. "Control organizations and labeling theory: official versus self-reported delinquency." Unpublished manuscript, University of Southern California.
Maddala, G. S.
1983 Limited, Dependent and Qualitative Variables in Econometrics. Cambridge: Cambridge University Press.
McCord, Joan
1983 "A longitudinal appraisal of criminal sanctions." Paper presented to the IXth International Congress on Criminology, Vienna, Austria, September.
Meyer, Jeanie Keeny and T. D. Lorimer
1977 Police Intervention Data and Domestic Violence: Exploratory Development and Validation of Prediction Models. Report prepared under grant #RO1MH27918 from National Institute of Mental Health. Kansas City, Mo., Police Department.
Murray, Charles A. and Louis A. Cox, Jr.
1979 Beyond Probation. Beverly Hills: Sage.
Office of the Minority Leader, State of New York
1978 Battered Women: Part I (Abstract). Washington, D.C.: National Criminal Justice Reference Service.
Parnas, Raymond I.
1972 "The police response to the domestic disturbance." Pp. 206–36 in Leon Radzinowicz and Marvin E. Wolfgang (eds.), The Criminal in the Arms of the Law. New York: Basic Books.
Police Foundation
1976 Domestic Violence and the Police: Studies in Detroit and Kansas City. Washington, D.C.: The Police Foundation.
Potter, Jane
1978 "The police and the battered wife: the search for understanding." Police Magazine 1:40–50.
Roy, Maria (ed.)
1977 Battered Women. New York: Van Nostrand Reinhold.

Schwartz, Richard and Jerome Skolnick
1962 "Two studies of legal stigma." Social Problems 10:133–42.

Sherman, Lawrence W.
1980 "Causes of police behavior: the current state of quantitative research." Journal of Research in Crime and Delinquency 17:69–100.

Shoham, S. Giora
1974 "Punishment and traffic offenses." Traffic Quarterly 28:61–73.

Thorsell, Bernard A. and Lloyd M. Klemke
1972 "The labeling process: reinforcement and deterrent." Law and Society Review 6:393–403.

Tittle, Charles
1975 "Labeling and crime: an empirical evaluation." Pp. 157–79 in Walter R. Gove (ed.), The Labeling of Deviance. New York: Wiley.

University of Rochester
1974 "FACIT—Family Conflict Intervention Team Experiment—Experimental Action Program." (Abstract). Washington, D.C.: National Criminal Justice Reference Service.

Wylie, P. B., L. F. Basinger, C. L. Heinecke and J. A. Reuckert
1976 "Approach to evaluating a police program of family crisis interventions in sex demonstration cities." (Abstract). Washington, D.C.: National Criminal Justice Reference Service.

Reflection

RICHARD A. BERK

I had already been doing applied research on law enforcement responses to domestic violence (Berk et al., 1980; 1982) when I was contacted by Lawrence Sherman. Larry had proposed to do a randomized experiment on police interventions in domestic violence incidents in part because there was little good research at the time on what law enforcement strategies might work best. The agency approached for funding suggested that he might benefit from some technical assistance. I had been involved in large-scale randomized experiments before (Rossi et al., 1980) and more generally had experience with the kinds of statistical tools that might be necessary. I was also on record arguing that randomized trials were by far the best way to advance public policy when "what works" was a key question. In short, the project seemed potentially useful and consistent with my existing interests. I readily agreed to help. A useful division of labor followed capitalizing on our different comparative advantages. Basically, Larry was to administer the experiment and I was to analyze the data that resulted.

I was quite excited when I first saw that arrest looked to be the most effective intervention. I was also well aware of the experiment's limitations. Larry shared many of the same concerns, which we expressed perhaps most forcefully in the second publication coming out of the research (Berk & Sherman, 1988). A key issue was how well the findings would generalize to new settings. In other cities, the nature of *each* intervention could be different. All arrests are not the same and can depend on training and policies that can differ across police departments. Equally important, and too often unappreciated, is that the nature of the interventions to which arrest is compared can also differ. Both the "separation" intervention and the "restore-order-and-leave" intervention were even more vaguely defined than arrest. Did either include, for example, referrals to social service agencies or threats about what might happen if the police were called back to the same address in the near future? It is critical to appreciate that the estimated impact of the arrest treatment was necessarily relative to the other interventions. If those differed across cities, even if the impact of arrest was the same, the estimated impact of arrest would differ. An additional complication was that the impact of arrest could depend on what happened to the offender subsequently. Would the offender be held awaiting a bail hearing or simply released? Would there be a serious effort to prosecute the case? Would support services be available for the victim if the case went forward? Should these factors vary across cities, the estimated impact of arrest would likely vary as well.

In retrospect, I think it is fair to say that caveats we offered were soon lost in the excitement surrounding the findings. It was a time when law-and-order sentiments were on the rise. So, getting tough on crime—any crime—was popular. Moreover, there were strong statements from feminist spokespersons that domestic assault should be treated the same as any other form of assault. For these and other reasons, many police departments across the country soon implemented mandatory arrest policies that went beyond the findings of the Minneapolis experiment.

Follow-up experiments in several new cities then failed to replicate in a convincing fashion the earlier results (Berk et al., 1992). Some studies seemed to suggest that a failure to replicate was the result of two opposing effects that could cancel each other out; arrest would deter offenders who had a "stake in conformity," but would make more violent those who did not. However, measures of this "stake in conformity" were at best indirect and "stake in conformity" was not randomly assigned. So, any conclusions necessarily rested on statistical models whose credibility was easily and quite properly challenged.

Where are we today? To my knowledge, there have been no new randomized experiments in the United States on police interventions in domestic violence incidents. What this means is that to date, no police interventions have been shown to work better than arrest. Therefore, if arresting offenders in domestic violence incidents is a desirable intervention on *other* grounds, there is no scientific reason to oppose it. For example, one might favor a policy of presumptory (not mandatory) arrest on the grounds that all assaults should be treated alike regardless of the relationship between the perpetrator and the victim. But like with any kind of intervention, one must be prepared for it to work better for some individuals than others and perhaps for it even to be harmful at times. That is just a painful fact of public policy. There are rarely any risk-free interventions.

As for my own activities, I have continued working on a wide variety of policy-related research in criminal justice and a number of other areas. I also have continued to mount randomized experiments whenever possible. But I have also become far more circumspect about what can be learned in the short run about the effectiveness of various public policy interventions. One-shot studies are not likely to be sufficient. What is needed is a long-term research initiative of the sort more commonly found in the biomedical sciences. Various interventions for preventing and treating heart disease, for instance, have been subjected over several decades to a large number of randomized experiments. The same should hold for important matters of public policy.

REFERENCES

Berk, R. A., Loeske, D. R., Berk, S. F., & Rauma, D. (1980). Bringing the cops back in: A study of efforts to make the criminal justice system more responsive to incidents of family violence. *Social Science Research 9*(3), 193–215.

Berk, R. A., Loeske, D. R., Berk, S. F., & Rauma, D. (1982). Throwing the cops back out: The decline of a local program to make the criminal justice system more responsive to incidents of domestic violence. *Social Science Research 11*(3), 245–279.

Berk, R. A., & Sherman, L. (1988). Police responses to family violence incidents: An analysis of an experimental design with incomplete randomization. *Journal of the American Statistical Association 83*(401), 70–76.

Berk, R. A., Campbell, A., Klap, R., & Western, B. (1992). The differential deterrent effects of an arrest in incidents of domestic violence: A bayesian analysis of four randomized field experiments. *American Sociological Review,* 5, 689–708.

Rossi, P. H., Berk, R. A., Lenhhan, K. (1980). *Money, Work and Crime: Experimental Evidence.* New York: Academic Press.

CHAPTER 22

The Effect of Batterer Counseling on Shelter Outcome

EDWARD W. GONDOLF

Despite the strong support for shelter care, relatively little research empirically assesses the impact of shelter service on battered women. The handful of shelter assessments, moreover, do not identify the specific services obtained during shelter that contribute to the outcome. Shelters remain therefore a kind of "black box" that women pass through on their way to safer living arrangements.[1]

This study attempts to shed more light on the services related to a shelter resident's decision not to return to the batterer.[2] The role of eight service-related variables that operationalize economic independence and intervention decisions are examined using discharge interviews from Texas shelters statewide (1984–1985). Whether the batterer is in counseling is considered in this analysis and proves to have a particularly strong influence on the shelter outcome.

Previous Assessments of Shelter Outcome

Previous shelter assessments have employed varied "predictors" and outcome measures. Outcome is generally measured in terms of the women's living arrangements at discharge or at some follow-up period. Actuarial data (background and abuse variables), the total services obtained, the number of intervention decisions, and the women's evaluation of the shelter have been considered as predictors. The relationship of specific services to leaving the batterer has yet to be examined, however. This omission seems useful to address, since the service predictors are variables that shelter staff can most readily influence.

Outcome Measures

Previous shelter studies have used the following measures for outcome: the woman's living arrangements upon leaving the shelter, her living arrangements at some follow-up point, or the reported level of violence at follow-up. The clinical and empirical literature on shelter outcome suggests that about one-third of the residents return to their batterer upon leaving the shelter (Aguirre, 1985; Martin, 1976; Snyder & Scheer, 1981; Walker 1979). One follow-up study found that while only 14% intended to leave the batterer at shelter admission and

33% at discharge, 55% were living with the batterer two months after shelter (Snyder & Scheer, 1981). Of these returnees, 12% reported having been physically abused, and an additional 15% verbally abused. A study of a Michigan shelter showed that 30% terminated the relationship directly after shelter and another 43% within two years (Okum, 1986), for a follow-up total of 73% not living with the batterer and 27% still living with batterer. These findings demonstrate that many women eventually return to their batterer, despite their initial intent not to return. As Strube and Barbour (1983) document, the women often return because of economic dependence or psychological commitment.

Nevertheless, there is some indication that the living arrangements at discharge represent an important step toward greater safety. For one, the discharge decision not to return to the batterer may be an important next step toward final separation. Okum (1986) found that most women in a Michigan shelter went through a progression of separations in the process of terminating the relationship. In total, 74% of the Texas shelter sample had, in fact, previously left the batterer (Gondolf, Fisher, & McFerron, in press). Also, the discharge living arrangements are a sign of assertive decision making for women often considered to be victimized with a sense of learned helplessness (Walker, 1979). The mere decision to leave can afford the woman increased leverage if she does resume the relationship (Bowker & Maurer, 1985).

The discharge living arrangements are, moreover, a more practical measure than the outcome measure of postshelter violence. It is difficult to control for the many extraneous factors related to this ideal follow-up outcome. Also, the cost and difficulty of locating subjects for an extensive follow-up of our sample would make it prohibitive. This study, therefore, uses the "planned" living arrangements as a measure of shelter outcome.

Predictors

The previous assessments suggest that shelter outcome may be best predicted by the degree of economic independence and intervention decisions, along with select background variables. "Economic independence," in this case, refers to whether a battered woman had a personal income that enabled her not to depend on the batterer for support. Aguirre (1985), using the Texas intake data from 1980 (n = 1,024), produced a logistic model with the following variables: husband's source of income, violence as a child, number of issues related to battering, and number of injuries from abuse. However, only "husband as sole source of income" was statistically significant. Snyder and Scheer (1981) found the following background variables to be significant predictors in their discriminant function for follow-up living arrangements: length of marriage, occurrence of previous separations, and religious affiliation of the resident (80% classification rate).

The limited investigation of service-related predictors suggests that the extent of shelter service coupled with other interventions, such as obtaining legal assistance or court injunction, is also important. Aguirre (1985), in another part of her study, examined the influence of several service-related variables: number of intervention decisions made during shelter stay, number of shelter services used, the woman's evaluation of shelter care, and whether the batterer was in counseling. The "number of decisions" was the only variable that proved to be statistically significant.[3] Berk, Newton, and Berk (1986) further demonstrated the interactive effect of shelter stay and other help-seeking in reducing the number of violent episodes.[4] In sum, the effects of shelter care appear to be related to a woman's actively taking control of her life.

Only Okum's (1986) study has noted a relationship between batterers' counseling and living arrangements. In total, 83% of the batterers in counseling with a shelter-sponsored batterers program resumed living with their partners, and 65% of the batterers not entering counseling returned within one year of discharge.

The obvious shortcoming of these assessments is that they do not indicate the specific kinds of independence or interventions that relate to shelter income. This study, therefore, uses specific service-related variables that operationalize economic independence and intervention decisions. It is expected that the discharged women are more likely not to return to their batterers if they had acquired their own income, transportation, and child care and thus lessened their dependence on their batterer. Their tendency to separate is also likely to be influenced through specific interventions, such as legal assistance and calling the police, that suggest to the batterer that the woman "means business."

Method

Sample

The sample (n = 6,612) consists of all those women who entered the 51 Texas shelters during an 18-month period in 1984–1985.[5] The sample may be characterized as having experienced life-threatening abuse. Over 40% of the women had weapons used on them, and 70% of their batterers have threatened to kill them. The majority of the Texas shelter women also suffer from poverty. Over half (58%) have no personal income and 44% have not completed high school. (A summary of the background characteristics and abuse variables for the sample appear in Tables 22.1 and 22.2.)

The status of the Texas sample is further evident in contrasts with other shelter samples and with a random sample of Texas women. The Texas shelter sample has a lower average income than the samples from a California (Pagelow, 1981) and Michigan shelter (Okum, 1986). Also, the Texas income is much lower than the recruited samples of battered women in the Bowker (1983) and Walker (1984) studies, although the latter samples may be skewed upward by their self-selection process. The Texas shelter sample is, furthermore, lower in occupational status, higher in severity of abuse, and higher in help-seeking than the abused women identified in a statewide survey derived from driver's license holders (n = 2,000 with a response rate of 60.5%; Teske & Parker, 1983).

Variables

The variables used in the analysis were drawn from structured interviews administered by shelter staff to each client in the sample at intake and discharge. The outcome measure used, as mentioned above, was "planned living arrangements"—that is, the woman's intention at discharge to return to the batterer or not return to him. Overall, 8% of the total sample who indicated that they were "undetermined" about their plans were deleted from the analysis. The predictor variables include service-related variables associated with economic

TABLE 22.1 Frequencies for Background Characteristics (in Percentages)

Income (Woman only)	
none	58
$5,000 or less	20
$5,000–$10,000	12
$10,001–$15,000	7
$15,001–$20,000	4
Occupation	
homemaker	55
unskilled labor	15
student	2
clerical	9
skilled labor	10
manager/professional	6
other	5
Education	
less than 12 years	44
high school grad./GED	37
vocational training	4
college	15
Number of Children	
none	11
one	27
two	29
three	20
four	9
five or more	5
Length of Relationship	
less than one year	16
1 to 5 years	48
more than 5 years	36

independence, intervention decisions, and shelter service. Several background and abuse variables were also used in the analysis (see Tables 22.1 and 22.2).

Three dichotomous variables operationalized economic independence: the woman's having her "own home," "own transportation," and "child care" at discharge. Three additional dichotomous variables were used to operationalize intervention decisions: "legal assistance sought during shelter," "previous contact with the police," and "batterer in counseling at the time of discharge."

Shelter services were measured as followed. The "total number of shelter services obtained" and the "total number of services to be continued after discharge" were coded as interval responses for 1 through 8 possible different kinds of service. The possible shelter services included referral, transportation, medical care, child services, counseling, legal assistance, employment assistance, crisis phone counseling. The logarithmic

TABLE 22.2 Frequencies for Abuse Variables (in Percentages)

Physical Abuse	
things thrown	46
held against will	69
woman thrown around	83
slapped	81
pulled hair	61
choked	57
burned	9
punched	75
kicked	60
weapon used	43
Verbal Abuse	
personal insult	93
threaten physical harm	77
threaten sexual abuse	20
threaten to use weapons	47
threaten to kill	70
threaten to harm child	42
Injury	
none	5
bruises	16
cuts	8
internal bleeding	20
sprains/dislocations	5
teeth out or broken	1
burns	1
head injury/concussion	29
broken bones	8
miscarriage	6
permanent injury	2
Duration of Abuse	
first time	3
1 to 4 weeks	7
1 to 12 months	25
1 to 5 years	41
more than 5 years	24
Frequency of Abuse (during last 6 months)	
only once	11
once/month or less	24
2 to 3/month	20
once/week	12
2 to 6/week	18
daily	15

transformations of these two variables were used in the analysis in order to approximate a normal distribution.

Lastly, twenty-four background and abuse variables ("actuarial" variables) were selected from the shelter intake interview (see Table 22.3 for the full listing). The background variables, such as women's income amount, education level, age, and number of children are used in typical ordinal response form. The principal abuse variables (verbal abuse, physical abuse, and injury) are the total kinds of abuse or injury mentioned. "Previous help-seeking" and "care for injuries" were also measured as the total number of help-sources contacted. These "total number" variables serve as normally distributed indicators for the severity of abuse or extent of help-seeking.[6] As shown in Table 22.3, several related

TABLE 22.3 Stepwise Discriminant Function of Background, Abuse, and Service-Related Variables (32 Variables Entered)

Predictor Variables	Standardized Coefficient
Service Related	
batterer in counseling[a]	–.54
own transportation[a]	.44
child care[a]	.44
own income source at discharge[a]	.33
shelter services continued	.15
police contacted[a]	–.11
Abuse and Background	
emergency room care[a]	.29
batterer threatened to harm child[a]	.27
verbal abuse	–.25
witnessed abuse as child	.24
weapons used[a]	–.21
child abuse[a]	.15
batterer threatened to kill[a]	.15
racial minority[a]	–.13
alcohol abuse related to abuse[a]	–.11
income amount prior to shelter	–.11
Not Significant	
service related: shelter services obtained (total), legal assistance	
background: woman's age, woman's income amount, woman's education, number of children	
abuse: physical abuse, abused in previous relationship,[a] frequency of abuse, duration of abuse, injuries, broken bones,[a] total issues related to abuse, general violence, batterer employed,[a] batterer arrested,[a] previous help-seeking	

Note: eigen value = .30; canonical corr. = .48; lambda = .77; $\chi^2 = 125.52(16)$; $p < .00001$ (n = 800).

[a]Dichotomous variable.

dichotomous variables were also used to further indicate the kind or severity of abuse; the frequency and duration of abuse were measured as five- and six-level ordinal variables (as in Table 22.2).

Analysis

A stepwise discriminant analysis was used to investigate the relationship of the eight service-related and twenty-four actuarial variables to outcome.[7] This operation was also used to ascertain whether the actuarial variables would substantially supersede the service-related variables as predictors. A cross-classification test to assess the predictive power of the discriminant function was conducted with random subsamples of 800. Lastly, the service variables were cross-tabulated with outcome (n = 1,000) to describe further the influence of the predictors.

Findings

About a quarter of our Texas sample (24%) planned to return to the batterer at discharge, according to the frequency distribution of the outcome measure (see Table 22.4). This is less than the 33% return rate for the 1980 partial Texas sample (Aguirre, 1985) and a Detroit shelter sample (Snyder & Scheer, 1981). However, if the "undetermined" category is included as "not returning," the percentage of those returning for our sample becomes more comparable to the others (31%).[8]

The discriminant function shows that batterer-in-counseling (–.54) and the variables associated with economic independence—transportation (.44), child care (.44), and own income (.33)—are the most influential predictors of the shelter outcome (see Table 22.3). At the other extreme, the background variables, on the whole, appear to have very little predictive power. In fact, those background variables related to class and those related to physical abuse are not significant, contrary to Gelles's (1976) hypothesis. We might assume, therefore, that the service-related variables are relatively sufficient in themselves for predicting shelter outcome.

TABLE 22.4 Frequencies for Living Arrangements

Category	Percentage	
Return to Batterer		24
Not Return		76
Live with relatives	30	
Live with friends	17	
Clients live on own	29	
Total		100

The classification rate for the function was an impressive 79% (see Table 22.5). A discriminant function using only the eight service-related variables had an equivalent classification rate (78%). This verifies that the actuarial background and abuse variables contribute little to the prediction.[9]

Cross-tabulations of "batterer-in-counseling" with "planned living arrangements" (the shelter outcome measure) illustrate further the strong influence of batterer-in-counseling as a predictor. In total, 19% of the women *without* batterers in counseling planned to return to their batterers, as opposed to 53% of the women *with* batterers in counseling—almost three times the proportion (see Table 22.6).

The overriding effect of batterer counseling is evident in the cross-tabulations controlling for income. Only 16% of the women *with an income* returned to their batterers, while as many as 38% of the women *with an income* were planning to return to the batter if he was *in counseling* (χ^2 = 18.68 [1]; $p \leq .00001$). Controlling for "violence against others," "previously arrested" or "physical abuse" did not appreciably alter the "return to batterer" percentage for the batterer-in-counseling variable. This latter finding suggests that the counseling predictor holds regardless of the level of violence generally or in the relationship.[10]

TABLE 22.5 Classification of Actual and Predicted Outcome (in Percentages)

	Predicted Group Membership	
Actual Group	*Return*	*Not Return*
Return	37	63
Not Return	7	93
Cases Correctly Classified	79	

TABLE 22.6 Cross-Tabulation of Living Arrangements by Batterer-in-Counseling (in Percentages)

	Batterer-in-Counseling		
Living Arrangements	*No*	*Yes*	**Total**
Return to Batterer	19	53	24
Not Return	81	47	76
	84	16	100

Note: $\chi^2 = 85.17(1)$; $p < .00001$ (n = 1000).

Discussion

The discriminant functions revealed three major findings: the predominant influence of batterer-in-counseling, the influence of economic independence, and the lack of influence of the actuarial background and abuse variables. The three service variables associated with independence (transportation, child care, and own income), along with the batterers *not* being in counseling, were the best predictors of a woman's planning to live separately from the batterer. These findings bear out the previous research indicating the importance of economic independence in separating from the batterer (Aguirre, 1985; Strube & Barbour, 1983). Services that specifically assure personal income, transportation, and child care appear to have a substantial impact on living arrangements and need to accompany shelter care.

The importance of intervention decisions, suggested by Aguirre (1985) and Berk et al. (1986), is somewhat contradicted, however. Furthermore, the total of shelter services obtained does not appear to be influential in itself, as Aguirre (1985) previously showed. It may be that our intervention variables need to consider more the nature or quality of the intervention or services. Also, the range of available services could vary from shelter to shelter in a way that negates their influence as a predictor variable.

One outstanding finding nevertheless remains—that is, the inordinate influence that the batterer's counseling has on the women's decision to return to the relationship. The influence of batterers counseling raises important theoretical and programmatic implications. In terms of theory, this finding supports the hypothesis that women stay in an abusive relationship because they expect their batterers will change (Frieze, 1979; Pfouts, 1978). In fact, nearly three-quarters (73%) of one shelter sample reportedly returned because "the batterer repented" or "they believed he would change" (Pagelow, 1981). Batterer counseling, most probably, offers the hope that "this time he *is* really going to change," and thus makes returning to the batterer a rational option in many women's minds.

Unfortunately, batterers often use counseling as a form of manipulation, rather than as a means of change. As many clinical studies observe, most batterers initially attend counseling to get their wives back, dropping out as soon as the threat of separation is over (see Gondolf, 1985). The high drop-out and recidivism rates in batterer programs appear to bear this out (Priog-Good & Stets-Kealey, 1986).

There are two further problems with the association between batterer counseling and returning to the batterer. One, counseling programs vary widely and many are simply not equipped to deal with the serious nature of abuse and therefore present "false hopes" (Gondolf, 1987a). Two, as many as a third of the batterers of shelter women may be considered severely antisocial men who are likely to be unresponsive to counseling (Gondolf, 1987b).

The programmatic implication is that shelter services are likely to be offset by batterer counseling. That is, even after provision of child care, personal income, or transportation, a woman is likely to be drawn back to her batterer by the fact that he is in counseling. Shelter staff, therefore, need to better apprise the women of the limitations of batterer counseling. Moreover, it is obviously in the shelter staff's interest to monitor batterer programs closely. In light of these findings, it may even be their right to supervise counseling programs, given the tremendous influence they have on battered women's decisions (see Hart, 1987). These implications deserve particular attention given the rapid expansion of batterer programs and the advent of court-mandated counseling for batterers.

NOTES

1. The research in fact has been focused primarily on the battered woman and her abuse rather than on her help-seeking and the response of interventions. This is unfortunate for two reasons. One, it has left policymakers with little evidence to base their decisions about appropriate intervention [on] (Berk et al., 1986). Two, shelters are left with little evidence of their effectiveness amidst the stiff competition for funds (Bowker & Maurer, 1985).

2. Independent living remains the goal of most shelters, since it has been considered the surest way to end the violence (NiCarthy, 1986). The cycle of violence will continue and escalate unless it is decisively interrupted (Walker, 1979). Separation in itself, however, does not guarantee safety, since the woman may still be beaten when the batterer comes to visit her or his children (Loseke & Berk, 1982). In fact, several of the shelter assessments indicated that separation did not reduce violence, unless it was accompanied by other assistance or interventions (Aguirre, 1985; Berk et al., 1986; Bowker, 1983).

3. The "number of intervention decisions" refers, here, to the number of different kinds of interventions sought by battered women during their shelter stay. The options included obtaining a protective order, pressing assault charges, obtaining a restraining order, or filing for divorce.

4. Berk et al. (1986) developed a logistic regression for reduced violent episodes using shelter or prosecutor cases. Their covariates included a "propensity score" that controls for treatment effects. "Days at risk" and previous help-seeking were also controlled. Their outcome measure is the only one to consider the recurrences of violence at follow-up, instead of living arrangements.

5. Those women who were under 16 years of age and not physically abused (i.e., not battered women) were deleted from the total sample (n = 9,076), along with duplicate and incomplete questionnaires. Also omitted are incomplete questionnaires from women who were referred elsewhere, or who were from two shelters that did not comply with the instructions. The distribution on the general background and abuse questions of Part One of these questionnaires was comparable to the remaining sample. This suggests that the deleted incomplete questionnaires did not particularly bias the results.

6. For example, the variable used to represent physical abuse is the total number of different categories of abuse mentioned by each woman. This "total" variable is highly correlated ($r > .8$) with the most severe category mentioned and with a weighted score derived from summing the rank order of all the categories mentioned. The categories used for physical abuse were those appearing in the following multiresponse question: "If you were physically abused which of the following happened?" The batterer (1) threw things, (2) held you against your will, (3) pushed you around, (4) slapped you, (5) pulled your hair, (6) choked you, (7) burned you, (8) punched you, (9) kicked you, (10) used a weapon or object against you. These response categories reflect those of the widely used Conflict Tactics Scale.

7. Discriminant functions were used, despite the categorical nature of the data, because they offer classification rates that serve as a convenient measure of prediction and they allow for the exploratory stepwise procedure like that presented in Table 22.3. Moreover, the findings of the discriminant analysis were replicated in a logistic model.

8. It is estimated in a related Texas survey of shelter directors and residents that 40%–50% of the residents eventually returned to the batterer (cited in Aguirre, 1985).

9. This classification rate is comparable to that derived from a discriminant function for a series of background variables (80%) (Snyder & Scheer, 1981).

10. As mentioned, batterer-in-counseling was not statistically significant in Aguirre's (1985) multivariate study of the 1980 partial Texas sample. This may be a reflection of the relatively few counseling programs available at the time of this particular sample.

REFERENCES

Aguirre, B. E. (1985). Why do they return? Abused wives in shelters. *Social Work, 30,* 350–354.

Berk, R. A., Newton, P. J., & Berk, S. F. (1986). What a difference a day makes: An empirical study of the impact of shelters for battered women. *Journal of Marriage and the Family, 48,* 481–490.

Bowker, L. H. (1983). *Beating wife beating.* Lexington, MA: Lexington Books.

Bowker, L. H., & Maurer, L. (1985). The importance of sheltering in the lives of battered women. *Response, 8*(1), 2–8.

Frieze, I. H. (1979). Perceptions of battered wives. In I. H. Frieze., D. Bar-tal, & J. S. Carroll (Eds.), *New approaches to social problems: Applications of attribution theory.* San Francisco: Jossey-Bass.

Gelles, R. J. (1976). Abused wives: Why do they stay? *Journal of Marriage and the Family, 38,* 659–668.

Gondolf, E. W. (1985). *Men who batter: An integrated approach to stopping wife abuse.* Holmes Beach, FL: Learning Publications.

Gondolf, E. W. (1987a). Evaluating programs for men who batter. Problems and prospects. *Journal of Family violence, 2,* 95–108.

Gondolf, E. W. (1987b). *Who are those guys? A typology of men who batter based on shelter interviews.* Paper presented at Third National Family Violence Research Conference, Durham, NH.

Gondolf, E. W., Fisher, E. R., & McFerron, J. R. (1990). The helpseeking behavior of battered women: An analysis of 6,000 shelter interviews. In E. Viano (Ed.), The victimology handbook: Research findings, treatment and public policy. New York: Garland.

Hart, B. (1987). *Safety for women: Monitoring batterers programs.* Harrisburg: Pennsylvania Coalition Against Domestic Violence.

Loseke, D. R., & Berk, S. F. (1982). The work of shelters: Battered women and initial calls for help. *Victimology, 7,* 35–48

Martin, D. (1976). *Battered wives.* San Francisco: Glide.

NiCarthy, G. (1986). *Getting free: A handbook for women in abusive relationships.* Seattle, WA: Seal.

Okum, L. (1986). *Woman abuse: Facts replacing myths.* Albany: State University of New York Press.

Pagelow, M. D. (1981). *Woman-battering: Victims and their experiences.* Beverly Hills, CA: Sage.

Pfouts, J. S. (1978). Violent families: Coping responses of abused wives. *Child Welfare, 57,* 101–111.

Pirog-Good, M., & Stets-Kealey, J. (1986). Programs for abusers: Who drops out and what can be done. *Response, 9*(2), 17–19.

Snyder, D. K., & Scheer, N. S. (1981). Predicting disposition following brief residence at a shelter for battered women. *American Journal of Community Psychology, 9,* 559–566.

Strube, M. J., & Barbour, L. S. (1983). The decision to leave an abusive relationship: Economic dependence and psychological commitment. *Journal of Marriage & the Family, 45,* 785–793.

Teske, R., & Parker, M. L. (1983). *Spouse abuse in Texas: A study of women's attitudes and experiences.* Huntsville, TX: Criminal Justice Center Publication, Sam Houston State University.

Walker, L. (1979). *The battered woman.* New York: Harper & Row.

Walker, L. (1984). *The battered woman syndrome.* New York: Springer.

Reflection

EDWARD W. GONDOLF

This study of shelter outcome grew out of a larger research project on the help-seeking of battered women in Texas shelters. Ellen Fisher of the Texas Council of Family Violence initiated the project. Texas shelters had been collecting standardized data from battered women entering their 51 shelters. In the process, they had amassed an exceptional database on battered women—one of the largest at the time. Ellen saw a great opportunity to substantiate some of the characteristics of women entering the shelters and document the initial shelter outcomes. At the time of the study in the mid-1980s, few shelter studies had been published, and those studies focused on a single shelter with a narrow set of variables.

Given the suspicions of research and researchers at the time, and the uncertain results and information, Ellen and her co-workers were taking a risk in releasing the data and supporting its analysis. The opportunity and success of the research, eventually summarized in the book *Battered Women as Survivors* (Sage, 1988), grew from a trusting collaborative relationship between Ellen and me. There was a lot of talking and listening and some mutual experience in each other's world. I had been involved in shelter work and batterer counseling work previously, and Ellen had exposure to research in her graduate study and as a former employee of the Texas Department of Human Services.

We were especially eager to explore the reasons for shelter outcome. One of the main objectives of the shelters was to help move battered women away from dangerous men. The principal discharge question was, therefore, whether a woman was planning to return to her partner on leaving the shelter. Nearly a quarter of the Texas shelter women professed that they did. We attempted to explain the outcome in terms of economic dependency or resource theory. This sort of explanation was basic to the advocacy viewpoint that prevailed at most of the shelters. As shelter staff were able to help battered women gain more resources and support, the women were more likely to be "empowered" to leave an abusive and violent relationship behind. The resource-related variables, such as "own transportation," "child care," and "own income," were significantly associated with not returning to one's partner. The one surprise was finding the strong influence of "the batterer being in counseling" on returning to the partner.

This latter finding has been widely cited as a caution against batterer counseling and even objection to it. The implication is that batterer counseling may help men to lure their partners back to continue their abuse. This concern is, of course, a legitimate one as we discuss in the article. It is especially of note given the optimistic view of battered women that their partners will complete batterer counseling to which they are court-ordered. Our recent multi-site study of batterer programs found that 90 percent of the women thought their batterers would complete the counseling, whereas the completion rate was closer to 65 percent (see *Batterer Intervention Systems,* Sage, 2002). The Texas women admittedly may have been over-estimating more the court's power to keep men in counseling than the men's willingness to participate.

At the same time, there are naturally some limitations to the "batterer counseling" finding. The finding applies only to the small percentage of the batterers of shelter women actually in batterer counseling, and not necessarily battered women in general. In our multi-site study of batterer programs, only a small portion (7 percent) of the partners of batterer program participants had previously been in shelters or was currently in them. Nearly half of the women were not living with their partners and the contact with partners varied over time. In other words, "returning to the partner" was not a fixed outcome but evolved and changed with a number of circumstances.

The most striking, and somewhat reassuring, in our multi-site evaluation was that the vast majority of the women with batterer program participants felt safe, and this perception was highly correlated with the batterer's behavior. The judgment of most of the women appeared, in other words, to be well-grounded. Moreover, the majority of men did eventually stop their physical violence and lower other forms of abuse during the four-year follow-up. It could be, therefore, that some of the shelter women returning to their partners in counseling will experience "safety." In the Texas study, they may have been less severe cases to begin with.

The greatest contribution of the article may be its early consideration of women's decision-making and exposing the impact of resource and service circumstances on that process. The foundations for a rationale adaptation were documented in the Texas study. There has been increasing attention to how women make decisions about safety and help-seeking in the subsequent work of Cris Sullivan, Jackie Campbell, Mary Ann Dutton, and Lisa Goodman; their findings seem to reinforce the importance of advocacy and emotional support. As we argued in a recent study on women's perceptions from our multi-site evaluation, we need to go deeper and further on how women make informed decisions, and how especially to help some avoid making dangerous ones.

CHAPTER

23 Batterer Programs

Shifting from Community Collusion to Community Confrontation

ELLEN PENCE

A Picture of an Abusive Relationship

Nancy was 19 years old, 3 months pregnant and married only 6 months when her husband first hit her. She was stunned. In their 2 years of dating, Bill had talked many times about how his father had hit his mother, so she felt particularly safe with him. His disgust for that kind of violence was somehow reassuring.

He didn't beat her, he slapped her and shoved her down. He left the house crying. She was afraid for him, for her unborn child, and for herself. What was going wrong? Why so soon? This was not supposed to happen.

She went to her mother. She needed to figure this out. Her mother saw the signs of a new marriage under stress, her daughter struggling with the challenge of being a wife to a man, a boy really, with the worries of a man not yet secure with who he was in the world. She cautioned her daughter against a rash decision. It's a hard world out there for a single woman with a child—welfare, the stigma of a divorce, the type of man who would now be attracted to her. She advised that Nancy's best bet was to work it out, to figure out what she could do to restore a sense of balance to the relationship. It was the first big test; she should be cautious.

Nancy adjusted. She hashed and rehashed that single blow until it made sense, until it no longer represented a threat to everything she was building.

Bill adjusted, too. He made excuses for his violence. He explained it to her. He talked about why they both had to work it out. He took responsibility, sort of, but mostly he blamed the outside world. He believed himself. It made it easier. He swore he'd never touch Nancy again, but he knew she was changed by the episode. She was more compliant, more tuned into his moods, but also more distant—and something he wanted from her was being withheld. She had taken a piece of herself away from him and put it somewhere he couldn't reach.

He obsessed over that piece.

Their baby was born. She was a mother. He was a father. Another piece of her was taken from him and given to their daughter, another piece that didn't belong to him.

He obsessed over that piece.

A phase of their relationship was over, the phase in which she had centered her life around him, his phone calls, their dates, his dreams. They lived together now. There was the baby. There was a renewed tie with her mother and her sister, who also had a baby. There were pieces of her that were separate from him.

He obsessed over those pieces.

He had become more moody, more demanding. He wasn't violent toward her, but he knew that certain outbursts of anger drew her total attention to him.

Sara was Nancy's best friend. He hated that relationship. One night at a Halloween party, he made a pass at Sara. Suddenly that relationship wasn't so threatening. Now he was in it. In fact, he was in the middle of it. He felt Nancy's jealousy, and he felt the split between Sara and Nancy. He knew he had succeeded. He could stop obsessing about one thing.

On their daughter's first birthday, it happened again. The room was filled with guests—her mother, her sister, her friends and their kids. He came into the room and told her to fix him a sandwich. He had been working on the car, and he was hungry. She put him off, telling him, "I'll fix it later."

He grabbed her by the arm and threw her into the kitchen. "You'll fix it now. I'm hungry now." The party broke up. The tension stayed on. That night when she screamed at him in outrage, he hit her first with an open hand and then with a fist. He walked out.

She was pregnant again, but she hadn't told anyone. Her world was shrinking. Her friend was gone; her sister and her mother were disappointed in her withdrawal from them.

He came home drunk. He decided to tell her the truth about how he was jealous of the baby, her mother, her friend, how he didn't deserve her, how he was scared of being a father like his own. She comforted him. She told him the news, and they held each other and committed themselves once again to love each other above all else. He became preoccupied about how she would react to his last act of violence. He wanted to know her every thought. Had she talked to her mother? Her sister? Was she attracted to other men? Of course she was. Was she sleeping with someone? He hated the power she had over him. She was making him feel this way on purpose.

He told himself he would never hit her again, but she would have to see how life would be without him. She's stupid, she wouldn't make it without him, she'd never get custody of the kids if she left him. He reminded her of these truths daily.

She wanted things to be different. She feared him, she fought with him, she told him what he wanted to hear, she begged him, she screamed at him, she ignored him, she got drunk with him, she started to slip. She started to merge with him. His thoughts and opinions became hers, his truths became hers. She was losing herself, and she knew it. She hated herself.

She had no real friends, and her relationships with her mother and sister were strained. She had tried going back to school, but he put a stop to that. She was trapped.

In the spring, he beat her again. This time she was afraid as she had never been before. She called the police. She was bleeding from her mouth, and the kids were crying. He was meaner than she'd ever seen him. As the police pulled up to the house, he grabbed her by the hair, pulled her face up to his, and whispered, "Someday I know I'm going to have to kill you."

The police came. "What happened? Why did you hit her?" "What do you want, lady?" "Is this your husband?" "If you want to press charges, call the city attorney." They warned him, "Another trip out to this address tonight will land you in jail." They left.

The next night he comes home, kicks off his shoes, throws his paper down. He is angry. She doesn't know why, and she really doesn't care. She tells him to leave if he's going to bring all that shit in the house. The kids leave the room. They know when to leave the room now. They're old enough to figure these things out but not old enough to know why—why the constant fear, the hatred, the names, the attacks.

She backs off when she sees the danger signs. He tells her to make his dinner, she complies. He tells her he wants her to go out with him to a party. She declines the offer.

It isn't an offer.

She doesn't have a babysitter. "Get one."

She doesn't feel good. "You never do for me. You must save it for someone else." She senses what's about to happen. She picks up the phone, he grabs it.

"Forget it. Maybe you would rather go out with your boyfriend."

She tries to change the subject.

He wants to know who "he" is.

"There isn't anyone."

"You're lying. Tell me who he is."

She's fed up. She's sick of the whole thing. She's exhausted, she's scared, she tries to gather her energy to find the right words, as she has so many other times. Words that will divert his attention, change his energy. Her mind is racing but she senses the futility. She keeps talking, talking, talking.

Finally he leaves the house.

A reprieve—something worked, she doesn't really know what it was.

Grabbing her out of a sound sleep, he grasps her neck hard. "Tell me who he is."

She can't breathe. What's going on? There's that familiar smell. Booze and rage. It's 2, maybe 3 A.M. She struggles to free herself, but she can't move under the weight of his body.

"Tell me who he is."

She's shaking her head. Gasping for air. "There isn't anyone."

The veins in his neck are bulging. His eyes are burning with hatred. "Tell me who he is."

She's grabbing at him, scratching at his face. With one hand he holds her down, with the other he pushes his fingers into her rectum as hard as he can.

She screams in pain and humiliation. "Whoever he is, he can have you." She pleads with him to stop.

He pulls himself up and leans over her. "You wanted it to come to this. You always wanted it to come to this."

She's sobbing.

He still doesn't have those pieces of her that she's kept for herself, but at this point she doesn't either.

The Response to Abusive Men

To have even a remote chance of stopping the violence of millions of Bills in this country, we must first ask ourselves, "Who is he? Where did he come from? Why does he do these terrible things to a woman he claims to love?"

Since the first battered women's shelters opened in 1974, activists in this social movement have been asked, "What about the men? What are you doing for them?" It was asked by reporters, judges, police officers, community board members, members of countless audiences, funders, and more and more often through the years by battered women.

For years that question was answered by some with a cold stare, by others with a cynical quip, by still others with a return question: "What would you suggest?" But many programs worked to offer real solutions: arrest, detention, prosecution, expulsion from the home. From the mid-1970s to the present, women's organizations in all 50 states have struggled to provide concrete tools for communities to answer constructively the question "What about the men?"

Most states now have arrest laws that provide police officers with expanded powers of arrest in domestic abuse cases. These laws were passed in response to the repeated claims of police officers that their hands were tied in these cases when the officer doesn't see the assault and the woman won't press charges. A few states mandate that officers arrest in certain domestic situations, such as those involving felony assaults, assaults resulting in injury to the victim, or threats with a weapon. But the overwhelming majority of police officers legally empowered to make arrests still failed to do so, now arguing that arrest without successful prosecution is meaningless.

Prosecutors, on the other hand, claimed that placing immediate legal sanctions on wife beaters was difficult in the cumbersome and painfully slow criminal court system. Still recovering from legislative battles around arrest, advocates for battered women, many of whom were battered themselves, were again in the halls of state legislatures seeking and in many states winning civil court orders of protection. These new laws provided a speedy remedy to exclude batterers from the homes of those they abused. But as the violence continued, women now legally entitled to police protection waived their civil court orders in front of apathetic officers.

More laws were passed to close the loopholes and tend to the more technical aspects of the legal system. Specialized criminal justice reform projects cropped up in cities such as Minneapolis, Seattle, San Francisco, and Miami. As these projects successfully pushed for more effective court and police intervention, thousands of "Bills" came into the courts, with an equal number of "Nancys" asking for a just and safe resolution.

By 1980 there was a sinking feeling across the country that the question, "What about the men?" was bigger than the solution of arrest and jail. Judges and probation officers asked, "How are you going to help them?" They meant "rehabilitate." Suddenly the battered women's movement was asked to fix batterers in exchange for women's protection.

Before 1980 there were only a handful of programs working on developing counseling/educational interventions for batterers. Most of those were operating with primarily volunteer labor. As the courts began to mandate batterers into chemical dependency programs, counseling agencies, and self-help groups, the mental health profession responded to the "new client on the horizon." As group, individual, and couples' counseling involving batterers spread across the nation, young Ph.D. candidates worked tirelessly for more established researchers, picking apart and analyzing these acts of hitting, biting, slapping, kicking, gun waving, hair pulling, stabbing, and killing. A national debate ensued. Is Bill the problem, or is it alcohol, or is it his background, or is it his anger, or is it the relationship? After all, two out of three women don't get beaten. Why was Nancy one of the ones who did? Who or what should we study?

Battered women's programs spanned the range of reaction to the growing number of programs. Some ignored them completely, others engaged in a time-consuming monitoring process. Still others, hoping to ensure that the men's programs in their communities were run properly, started their own.

And so the question of what to do with the men became a more immediate question: "What are we doing with the men?"

It was at this point in 1980 that the Domestic Abuse Intervention Project (DAIP) was organized by women in Minnesota who had for the past 5 years been actively involved in the shelter movement. Its goal was to test an emerging theory that coordinating police and human service agencies' responses to domestic assault cases, through developing uniformly applied procedures, would drastically reduce the acts of violence against women seeking help from the system. Simply put, if everyone did his or her job well, most women wouldn't keep getting beaten. Of course, this forced the community to ask some basic questions: "What is the job of the police when intervening in a case of wife beating? What is the role of a therapist or any representative of a community institution when confronted with this issue? What does it mean to collude with batterers?"

The Duluth Response

The Duluth response, like all other efforts, is limited in its total vision. This program has, however, made some key contributions to the national search for an intervention and prevention strategy. First, the goal of the project is the protection of battered women, not the fixing of batterers. The rehabilitation of abusers is a component of a much larger intervention strategy beyond the DAIP. Second, the project assumes that battering is not an individual pathology or a mental illness but rather just one part of a system of abusive and violent behaviors to control the victim for the purposes of the abuser.

In 1980 and 1981 the DAIP negotiated written agreements with the police, prosecutors, probation officers, family and criminal court judges, jailers, and the women's shelter, all designed to place increasingly harsh legal sanctions on abusers who continue to threaten or harm their former or current partners. A rehabilitation program is offered as an alternative to jail for offenders who are convicted for the first time and to second-time offenders after serving some jail time.

The following is a synopsis of how a typical assault case would be handled in this system.

The intervention process begins when the police are called to the home of the victim and the assailant. An assault has occurred during the evening, and police have been called by the victim. Upon arrival, the officers take statements from both the assailant and the victim. The officers learn (for the sake of this illustration) that the couple are married, and the wife states that her husband hit her in the face following an argument that occurred an hour earlier. Officers observed bruises on the victim's face. The assailant is informed that he is being arrested for fifth-degree assault. The victim is told that a women's advocate from the intervention project will be contacting her. The assailant is then transported by police to the county jail.

At the jail an officer calls the shelter to inform shelter staff of the arrest and provide information on the assailant and victim. Shelter staff use a beeper system to contact the on-call women's advocate. Women's advocates work alone or in teams of two. Information on the assailant and victim is given to the advocates, and they immediately visit the victim at her residence.

Meanwhile, the assailant has been jailed and is held until court, normally the following day. During the early morning, the shelter calls the volunteer on duty and informs him of the arrest. At 8:00 A.M. the volunteer visits the assailant in jail. He explains the intervention program and informs the assailant that a counseling/educational program is available for stopping violent behavior.

At the arraignment, the assailant enters his plea. In this illustration, the assailant pleads guilty to a misdemeanor assault. Had a not-guilty plea been made, the trial process would have begun, and until the case was resolved, there would have been no further DAIP-initiated contact with the assailant.

A pre-sentence investigation is next completed by a probation officer. The probation officer interviews the assailant and consults with the on-call advocate or the victim and anyone else thought necessary in arriving at a sentencing recommendation to the judge. The probation officer, following the agreed-upon sentencing guidelines, recommends (1) a jail sentence, (2) a jail sentence partially served and participation in counseling, or (3) a stayed jail sentence with counseling. The recommendation is based on the assailant's (1) prior convictions, (2) willingness to follow through on counseling, (3) past record in following through on counseling, and (4) the appropriateness of the counseling to the individual. In this case, the judge accepts the probation officer's recommendation and sentences the assailant to 30 days in the county jail. The jail sentence is stayed, and the assailant is placed on probation for 1 year. Probation conditions mandate the assailant to comply with the DAIP and frequently require completion of a chemical dependence program prior to entering DAIP.

Following sentencing, the assailant meets with a DAIP staff member who explains the assailant's obligation to the DAIP and assigns him to a group. If the assailant re-offends or does not meet DAIP obligations, the assailant is reported to the probation officer. The result is normally a violation of probation charge and an imposition of a portion of the original jail sentence with an order to once again participate in the DAIP.

A DAIP staff member interviews the partners of men mandated to groups, preferably in person. Women are encouraged to attend two DAIP-sponsored groups that explain the theory and process of abusers' groups and the process for reporting new violence. In addition, a shelter advocate keeps in contact with the women, offering childcare and transportation to enable them to attend one of three weekly neighborhood-based groups. Counselors, probation officers, advocates, and DAIP staff all encourage women to report further acts of violence.

Today the primary functions of the DAIP are to monitor the compliance of professionals in the community with agreed-upon protocols and to monitor individual batterers' compliance with court orders. Monitoring the response of police, prosecutors, and other agencies involved is done through a continual review of their records, attendance at all civil protection order hearings, and periodic interviews with victims. Monitoring individual batterers is similarly done by monitoring the records of counseling agencies and frequent contacts and interviews with their partners. Bimonthly meetings are facilitated by DAIP staff for probation officers, counselors, and shelter advocates.

In order to allow for communication among intervening agencies and to comply with confidentiality laws, all abusers court ordered to a rehabilitation program are ordered directly to the DAIP, which enters into specific agreements with assailants and assigns them on a rotating basis to one of eight ongoing groups conducted by three community mental health agencies.

The Importance of Community-Wide Coordination

The monitoring and coordinating role of the DAIP is intended to prevent community collusion with abusers. First, it ensures that individual police officers, probation officers, therapists, prosecutors, judges, advocates, or jailers are not screening cases out of the system based on misinformation provided by the abuser, lack of information, or race, sex, or class biases. Such screening is one of the most prevalent ways communities collude with batterers. Since the establishment of closely monitored procedures and protocols in 1981, annual arrests are 10 times higher than those of prepolicy years, the percentage of minority males arrested has dropped from 33% to 11%, and the arrest of women has increased from 0% to 8%. The number of women filing and following through on protection orders has tripled. Conviction rates in domestic assault cases have significantly increased, and the number of assailants brought back to court for failure to comply with civil or criminal court orders has risen tenfold.

A second form of community collusion is the victim blaming that permeates our thinking, our language, and our reactions to victims of domestic violence. Perhaps no issue has caused as much tension and conflict within the network of agencies in Duluth as that of eliminating victim-blaming practices and acknowledging the relationship of these practices to collusion with barterers. One of the most important functions of the DAIP is to maintain open communication among the many intervening agencies and individuals connected with these cases. To coordinate a community effort that involves a paramilitary, male-dominated police force and a nonhierarchical female-dominated shelter staff with nine other agencies is no easy task. But no sustained change will take place if such an effort is merely based on having the political power to enact policies and protocols. At some point, those practices must reflect each agency's intervention role.

For example, an advocacy group can use the media, contacts with community leaders, public opinion, and friends in the court system or city government to secure a mandatory arrest policy. Such a policy forces police officers to act otherwise than they would if given personal discretion. However, unless officers eventually accept the need for these policies, such policies will be sabotaged by a disgruntled front line at the police department. Many communities have seen their police departments' arrest policies used against women and minorities by officers resisting commands from above. In the state of Washington, for example, where all departments were mandated by law to arrest abusers, entire departments resisted, resulting in scores of women being arrested, emergency meetings, and, finally, amendments to the law.

In addition, the DAIP offers participating agencies a constant forum for reflection. Everything a community does—naming groups, developing an intake process, using jail, excluding abusers from their homes, implementing a group rehabilitation process—communicates a message to those battering and those being battered. An independent organization strongly influenced by formerly battered women that provides a forum for open discussion greatly reduces collusion with batterers. If collusion is the secret cooperation with something questionable or wrong, then the intervention process used in the Duluth program is its opposite. When the project functions properly, each case is open to scrutiny. Each case can be held up for examination and approval. This creates a context that is not conducive to collusion.

In the first 3 years of organizing the DAIP, a series of agreements were reached. Most notably, police and court administrators and participating therapists agreed with victim advocates that the act of violence must be made the sole responsibility of the person using it. In other words, the police would no longer base the decision to arrest an assailant on what the victim said or did to contribute to the argument that preceded the assault. The judge would not order a woman to counseling with her abuser to learn how she could communicate with him differently to avoid his beatings. A probation officer would not rest easy that a client was not being violent simply because he has been ordered not to have contact with the woman he was convicted of assaulting. A therapist would not provide marriage counseling to a couple when violence was present. The collective community message to batterers must be clear: When you beat your partner, you are not the victim, you are the aggressor. Either stop it or lose increasing amounts of your personal freedom.

Second, the agencies agreed that their contact with batterers was to be a part of a community effort to confront their use of violence and not to advocate for them. When batterer counseling programs are not tied to a much larger community system of controls and accountability, they are used by abusers to get back into their homes, to win court and custody battles, to avoid criminal and civil court sanctions and proceedings, and to convince their partners that they are changing when, in fact, there has been no true altering of the power dynamics in the relationship.

General agreements or statements must ultimately be applied to real people's lives. In many ways, Bill is very much like the majority of men who are mandated to the DAIP. His acts of violence, if analyzed as separate and unrelated events removed from the context of all his other abusive and controlling behaviors, may appear to be uncontrolled bursts of anger releasing days or months of built-up tension. He may be seen as impulsive, having poor stress or anger control skills, insecure, codependent. Surely there is a piece of the truth in each of these observations, but from another view he is very much in control of his anger. After all, he chose when and where and how severely to hurt Nancy. At times it seems that he felt very secure. For example, when the police arrived, Nancy was intimidated enough by Bill's threat to kill her that she protected him from the law enforcement officer. His threat served to mobilize her to get the police to back off. The DAIP has attempted to build a coordinated community-wide program that involves literally hundreds of people, each with his or her own biases and perspectives on battering. The primary function of the DAIP is to draw those separate perspectives together under a common intervention strategy.

It is in a community utilizing its institutional powers to confront batterers that the DAIP conducts the men's groups discussed below. To conduct such classes without first insisting on police and court reforms is not only shortsighted but can also be, in the long run, dangerous to battered women. Ninety-two percent of the abusers in Duluth convicted of assaulting their partners are court mandated to the DAIP. Twelve percent also serve some jail time. Ninety-seven percent of all civil protection orders granted in cases where there are minor children involved also carry a requirement that the abuser participate in educational classes conducted by the DAIP. Approximately 92% of abusers mandated to the DAIP are male, and 8% are female.

The Rehabilitative Process

The Duluth court requires abusers who have been convicted or who have had orders for protection issued against them to participate in a 26-week counseling and educational program coordinated by the DAIP. The first 2 weeks consist of orientation sessions teaching men the rules and concepts of group process and the underlying assumptions of the program.

The next 12 sessions are conducted by therapists in one of three community mental health/counseling programs. These groups focus on confronting men's minimization and denial of their violence, with the goal of stopping the violence through anger management training. Following 12 weeks of counseling, the men enter a 12-week course taught by community activists trained by DAIP staff. Facilitators use a curriculum designed by the DAIP staff. Men are encouraged to remain in the program beyond the total 26 weeks of required sessions. They may choose to remain in the classes or to join an ongoing support group. In addition to court-required groups, voluntary relationship counseling is offered by participating therapists, but only if the batterer has completed the initial 12 weeks of the program and has remained nonviolent.

The description below focuses on the 12-week curriculum developed by the DAIP, because it best demonstrates the integration of theory with practice.

Assumptions of the Curriculum

Men who batter use a system of abusive tactics to control their partners. Violence is rarely used to the exclusion of other controlling and abusive tactics. Figure 23.1 presents a chart developed by the DAIP based on interviews and discussions with over 200 battered women,

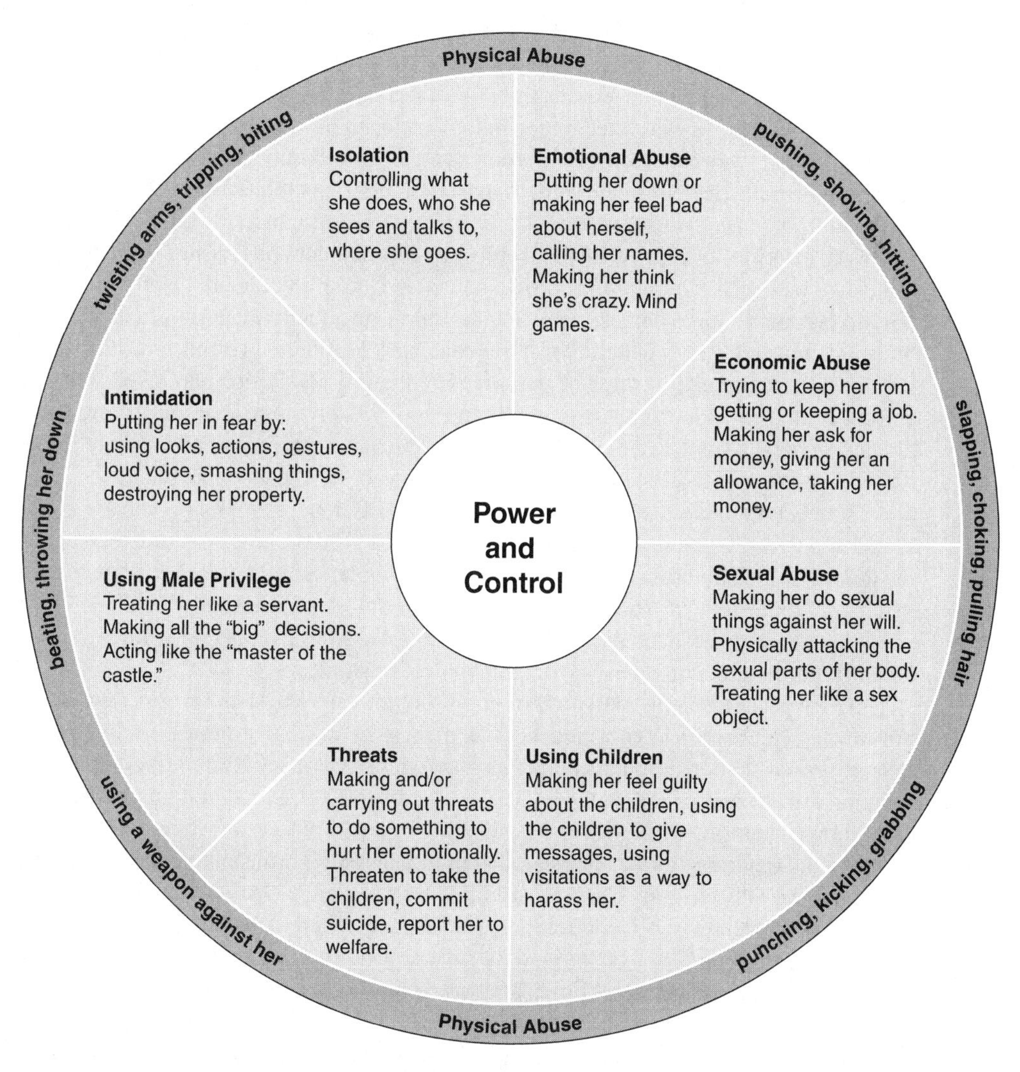

FIGURE 23.1 Abuser's Most Controlling and Abusive Tactics

which depicts nine of their abusers' most controlling and abusive tactics. The use of physical attacks, whether frequent or sporadic, reinforces the power of other tactics such as emotional abuse, isolation, sexual abuse, and threats of taking the children.

These behaviors are not unintentional. Each abusive act can be traced back to an intention of the abuser's. For example, an abuser will frequently increase his use of degrading names prior to an assault in order to depersonalize his partner. Once he has objectified her, he hits the object he has created rather than the person he lives with. The tactics used by abusers reflect tactics used by many groups or individuals in positions of power in our culture. These men mirror the worst of our society's norms. Each of the tactics depicted on the chart is typical of behaviors used by groups of people who dominate others. They are the tactics employed to sustain racism, ageism, classism, heterosexism, anti-Semitism, and many other forms of group domination. The men learn these tactics not only in their families of origin but also in their experience of the dominant culture in this society.

They, like those who intervene to help, have been immersed in the consciousness of oppressiveness. This consciousness is rooted in the assumption that, based on differences, some people have the legitimate right to master others. This relationship is seen as beneficial to both the master and the one who is "guided" by the master. Afrikaners dominating South African blacks claim that the technical advancements of that nation resulted from this relationship; Southern whites proclaimed segregation to be God's plan carried out in the interest of Southern blacks; the Soviet Union invades Afghanistan, and the United States, Grenada, for the "benefit" of those countries. Elaborate systems are constructed to legitimize various relationships of mastery. Community institutions are used by those in control to shape the consciousness of all within the system. Extensive efforts are made to obtain a general acceptance of the premises that the hierarchy is natural and that those who are at the bottom of it are there because of their own deficiencies or defects.

The consciousness of separateness prevails. Differences among people are not celebrated and treasured but used as a reason to dominate. The dominant culture then becomes the norm to which all others are forced to assimilate unless they prefer to exist on the fringe of a more "sophisticated" society. Individuals mirror these national and global relationships in their own interpersonal dealings with the world. Abusers operate from deeply held beliefs regarding their gender-based rights in relationships.

Consciousness is the sum total of one's thoughts, feelings, and world view. To be in this world with a critical consciousness, one must be allowed to question, to enter into debate, and to challenge much of the "mystical thinking" this culture promotes. Mystical thinking fails to distinguish between the laws and forces of nature and human-made laws and forces of culture.

Men, operating from a submerged consciousness, vigorously defend their beliefs as absolute truths: "Somebody has to be in charge"; "You can't have two captains to one ship"; "If I don't control her, she'll control me"; "God made man first, which means men are supposed to rule women."

The consciousness of both men and women in this society is shaped by their experiences of this system and all of the forces that work within it. Yet not all men batter women, even though all men have been socialized in a society that grants them certain gender privileges. Likewise, not all white people commit violent acts of racism, yet all whites have been exposed to powerful socializing experiences that tell them they are superior to people of color.

There are different reasons why men feel the need to control the women they live with. Each man brings to a group his own history. It is often a history that has included abuse as a child, exposure to men who have demonstrated hateful attitudes toward women, exposure to a myriad of woman-hating environments, alcoholism, racial and class oppression, or the denial of love and nurturance as a child. These individual experiences become both an explanation of why he batters and his excuse to continue his violence. To change long-held patterns, men must acknowledge the destructive nature of their present behaviors and accept responsibility for their actions. They are not, however, responsible for creating the many forces that have shaped their consciousness. While men are not victims of sexism as are the women they beat, they are dehumanized by their socialization.

Not all batterers are the same. Some are mentally ill, some have seemingly no remorse for their violence, and others are, if not motivated to change, at least miserable enough to want their situations to change. Still others are truly appalled at their behavior. The rationalizations of abusers for their behaviors, like those of other individuals and groups who dominate through force, often result in the men's not only portraying but also in some sense believing themselves to be the victims of the women they beat. This delusion is reinforced by the practices of police, judges, social workers, clergy, educators, reporters, and other representatives of society's institutions, who collude with an abuser's claim of being the victim.

Batterers are capable of personal transformation, and many men will make very powerful changes if certain conditions exist. These include a community that holds them fully accountable for their use of violence by making and enforcing consequences of continued acts of abuse and by providing an environment that is nonviolent, respectful of women, and nonjudgmental in which to make those changes. In addition to these conditions, the individual must be willing to work on a long process involving self-reflection, self-respect, painful honesty, and accountability to his victim. Men who batter do not often reflect about how they are living their lives and frequently are guided by mystical thinking. Such thinking prevents a critical consciousness and contributes to men's engaging in self-destructive behavior and, even more intensely, in behavior with brutal and terrorizing effects on the women and children they dominate.

The use of these tactics results in the abuser's domination of his partner physically, sexually, emotionally, and spiritually. Women subjected to these acts of terror experience severe physical, psychological, and spiritual trauma. When a battered woman manifests characteristics of being traumatized or fights back, she is labeled defective by the abuser and by the system that colludes with him. The victim is labeled by the abuser as provocative, a whore, a drunk or junkie, a bitch, a bad mother, violent, a liar, a man hater, a thief, out to get him, clinging, and a host of other negative things. She is labeled by the community as an enabler, codependent, nonassertive, a poor mother, a drug or alcohol abuser, violent, self-destructive, and provocative. Like any person or group at the bottom of an abusive hierarchical order, she is thought to be there because of some defect or weakness. He defines her this way, and the system backs him up in both subtle and blatant ways. She is studied by countless Ph.D. candidates in her postvictimized state and is typically judged to be lacking. She's compared to "nonbattered women" in test after test, and the difference between the two is defined as the cause of her problem. The question of why this woman is the one who gets hit is answered by academic and professional theories that sound suspiciously like the claims of her batterer. She lacks certain skills, certain attitudes, and her behavior is not quite right. He is reinforced; she is revictimized. He becomes a more cooperative client; she becomes more problematic. In such a system, he is no longer challenged to change.

A system that attempts to help batterers change and avoid these victim-blaming practices is difficult to establish. It is, however, possible to create a supportive environment in which men can make changes without our collusion with them, without abandoning the goal of establishing a community safe for women.

Finally, the DAIP and its curriculum are based on the assumption that there is no such thing as a neutral educational or change process for men who batter or for the women they abuse. Every aspect of the class, from the seating arrangement to the evaluation form, either supports or challenges the consciousness of domination. To teach a man who has beaten his wife how to get what he wants without violence without ever asking him, "Is what you want fair?" is neither neutral nor moves toward a more just and non-violent relationship. The implication of this assumption is far-reaching. It calls for each teacher to join with the men in the process of self-reflection. It brings the facilitator into process with the men, because it ultimately acknowledges that the consciousness of the abuser, which presupposes a right to impose his values and needs on his partner, is a consciousness shared by most people in this culture. With this recognition and a commitment to making personal change, the facilitator can stand in process with him, without judgment and without collusion, while standing equally in the process of liberation with the women he has hurt.

Curriculum Design

Each of the nine tactics of control depicted on the chart in Figure 23.1 is discussed over a 2- or 3-week period for a total of 18 weeks. The first stage of discussion of each topic focuses on six aspects of the use of a particular tactic. The group examines these aspects by answering a series of questions relative to their last or most powerful use of a certain tactic. These questions are

1. Exactly how do I use this tactic and how does my use of this tactic interact with other abusive tactics?
2. What is my intent in using this tactic, and specifically, what did I want to have happen the last time I used it?
3. What are some underlying belief statements that seem to be in operation when I use this tactic or feel justified to obtain the goal I've set with abusive tactics?
4. How have I minimized or denied my use of this tactic and the effects of my using this abusive behavior on others?
5. What effects has my use of this tactic had on me, on my partner, on my children, on my relationship, and on others?
6. What is the relationship of my past use of violence to continuing incidents in which I still use this tactic of control or abuse?

During the second stage of discussion on a particular tactic, the group explores noncontrolling and nonviolent behavior they could have used in situations in which they have previously been abusive. The facilitator teaches skills lacking in some of the men, for example, assertiveness rather than aggressiveness, letting go of needing to win, negotiating, fighting fairly, anger management, relaxation, empathizing, compassion, and expression of feelings. If, for example, Bill, whose story was told earlier, was a class participant in the 2- or 3-week period covering physical abuse, the following would occur: The group begins by watching a short videotape depicting physical abuse. Bill is then asked to role play or discuss in detail with one of the other group members a situation in which he used physical violence. He chooses the day of the Halloween party. The facilitator assists in getting as real a reenactment or description of Bill's emotions and behaviors in that situation as possible. Bill's experience and the short videotape are now group experiences. They become "codes" or a common framework for the class. The class now decodes the scenes step by step.

Week 1 of Each Tactic

Naming Actions. First, the men name each controlling or abusive tactic Bill used in this situation or that they viewed in the videotape. Although the scene involved physical abuse as the primary tactic, Bill also used gestures and language that employ other tactics (i.e., emotional abuse, threats, isolation).

The men are asked to examine the relationship of various tactics to one another. They observe not only which tactics were used but also how Bill shifted tactics throughout the scene. This discussion dispels the myth of the "blown fuse." The men are able to see the skillful use of different tactics at different times for different results. Although it is acknowledged that Bill felt out of control, he also faces the reality of how much control he was intuitively using.

Intentions and Beliefs. Next, the discussion moves to an examination of Bill's intent—what did he want in this situation? What did he think would be different if he employed these tactics? If the men are going to stop thinking of themselves as victims and therefore powerless to change, they must face the reality that each of their abusive behaviors is intended to change how their partners act, think, or feel. This realization comes and goes from week to week as the men come face to face with themselves in these scenes.

Why did Bill do this in front of her family? Why didn't he just fix himself a sandwich? Why did he get so angry? What did he gain by this? Intent is rooted in belief. If, for example, his intention was to keep her from being with her family, then he must believe something about that. "If she hangs around with her sister and mother, she will leave me." "She's supposed to take care of me first." "If she has other interests outside of me, it means she doesn't care about me." A major goal of this educational process is to help the men act in the world in a reflective way. Most of the men hold strong opinions about whose role it is to do the money-making, the housework, the childcare, the decision making. These long-held beliefs are reported by the men as laws of nature, as God's way. The men are continually confronted in these discussions with the possibility that these "truths" are perhaps created by people. They are cultural, not laws of physics, and therefore, they are alterable situations. This discussion frequently traces the source of these "truths" in the individual and collective cultural experiences of the men.

Feelings. After exploring the tactics of power used by Bill, along with his intentions and his underlying beliefs, the group goes on to examine the relationship of Bill's feelings to his actions. Bill first identifies how he was feeling (for example, hurt, jealous, angry, lonely). Next, Bill and the group make the connections between what he wanted, what he believed, and how he felt. In this phase of the discussion, the group comes to understand that feelings are not free-floating entities separate from who we are; they are extensions of how we see ourselves in the world. Many of an abuser's negative, hostile, and angry feelings are inextricably tied to who he believes he is and who he believes his partner is in the world. For example, through the reflective group process, Bill may articulate that Nancy was with her family, or her children. They were having a birthday party, and he didn't fit in. He wasn't central to that activity; therefore, he felt excluded.

The curriculum is not designed to teach men that by expressing their feelings to their partners, they will be less abusive. In fact, quite the opposite may be true. If an abuser's perceived right to control his partner, to shape who she is, what she does, and how she feels, is not first challenged, then teaching him to talk about or express his feelings may only increase the pressure on his partner to comply to his wishes. Now, not only does he feel jealous, but he has also shared this feeling with her. He has become more vulnerable to her and may expect her to respond by fixing his feelings. For example, if Bill is told that an alternative to his abuse would have been to come in the house and call Nancy aside and say, "I feel excluded," what does that mean Nancy should do? Ask her mother and sister to leave? Try to bring him into the group? Go outside and be with him? He must first give up the expectation that she must make all his negative feelings go away before the expression of these feelings to her will be healthy for either of them.

Minimizing and Denying. From this discussion, Bill, again with help from the group, lists methods he used to minimize and deny his actions or to blame Nancy or others for the abusive behavior. The group looks at the intents and effects of his denial. Once again, this discussion counters the almost universal claim of the abusers that they are victims of the women that they batter. This discussion will often focus on the self-talk practices of the men. It is the almost universal experience of the men that they turn everything around in their minds so much that a simple phone call to her friend is seen as total disloyalty to him. During this self-talk, many belief statements come pouring out. Getting Bill to role play all his self-talk aloud to the group sets the stage for a meaningful discussion of this aspect of abuse.

Effects of Behaviors. In order to motivate the men to change these behaviors, the discussion focuses on the effects of Bill's behaviors on himself, his partner, and their relationship. This discussion clearly demonstrates that these acts of abuse often work to gain her compliance to what he wants. However, the men also see that these behaviors have the long-term effect of alienating them from their partners, their children, their friends, and their families.

Past Use of Violence. The first phase of discussion of this topic ends with the group's naming the ways in which Bill's past use of violence affected Nancy in this situation. The group may also discuss how men's violence and aggression toward women in general affects Nancy. Each group ends with a brief acknowledgment that the effect of past violence toward women in relationships and in society is always there and provides a foundation for a woman's response to an abuser.

Week 2 of Each Tactic—Alternatives to Abusive Behaviors

The next week the men each bring to group a personal log that analyzes their own use of physical abuse to control a woman's behavior. Bill, with the help of other group members, once again role plays the situation in which he used violence. This time he uses noncontrolling behavior in the same situation. Several men role play or discuss alternatives to the abusive behaviors recorded on their logs during that week. The group explores concrete steps a participant can take to alter these behaviors. What can each man do in the situation that is nonabusive? What must he do in the long run to stop engaging in these behaviors? This is the time to teach men nonviolent relationship skills, including anger control techniques, positive self-talk, and time-out and relaxation techniques. In this part of the discussion, many of the commonly used cognitive-behavioral therapy techniques used in other batterer programs are employed. It is not enough for men to come to the realization that they are using abusive tactics to control their partners. They must be given specific and obtainable tasks and goals to start doing something different.

Figure 23.2 is a control log that each of the men complete by analyzing a specific form of control that they used against their partners. The log is completed and brought to the second phase of the discussion. Four or five members of the group may role play their nonviolent alternatives.

The use of the logs and highly structured group process help facilitators keep the focus of the group on the central issue—the use of abusive tactics to exercise power and control over women.

Evaluation

Since 1980 the DAIP has attempted to measure its successes and failures in a number of ways. Three methods have consistently provided meaningful feedback and have been incorporated in the overall program design.

The first process uses a participant research method to review the effectiveness of policies, procedures, and protocols in protecting women and reducing institutional victim-blaming practices.

In 1984 and 1985, 11 formerly battered women worked with Dr. Melanie Shepard of the University of Minnesota to design two instruments to measure program effectiveness. The first instrument is an extensive questionnaire administered anonymously to a random sampling of women who contacted the police, the shelter, or the courts because of physical abuse. These questionnaires are mailed to women 2 years after their initial contact with the

No Log—No Credit
Instructions: Complete each section. Be specific.

Topic: ____________________ Date: __________ Name: ________________________

1. Briefly describe the situation and the action *you* used to control (statements, gestures, tone of voice, physical contact, facial expressions). ____________________________________

2. Intent: What did you want to happen in the situation? ______________________________

3. What feelings were you having? ______________________________

4. In what ways did you minimize or deny your actions or blame her? ____________________

5. Effects: what was the result of your action? Include results of blaming or minimizing.

(on you) ______________________________

(on her) ______________________________

(on the relationship and others) ______________________________

6. It would have been better if I . . . ______________________________

7. How did your past use of violence affect this situation? ______________________________

FIGURE 23.2 Controlling Behavior: Weekly Logs—Educational Groups

system. They ascertain the women's satisfaction with seven aspects of community intervention: initial police calls, the prosecution of criminal cases, the civil court process, the legal advocacy provided by the shelter, educational groups for women, probation officers' and judicial involvement in criminal cases, and the counseling and education groups for abusers. The questionnaire is designed to measure women's satisfaction with the actions and attitudes of whomever they called upon for protection. The final section of the survey asks women to rate the overall effectiveness of the combined community response in protecting her from further abuse.

A community meeting is called to analyze the results of these surveys. Invitations are sent to all women to whom surveys are sent, as well as to current and former shelter residents, members of neighborhood-based education groups, and DAIP and shelter staff. The results of each section of the surveys are thoroughly discussed, and a series of recommendations are made to improve the system's response. Committees composed of DAIP or shelter staff and battered women are formed to follow up with agency meetings on each recommendation.

The results of this survey in Duluth showed that a majority of the 65 respondents reported that they had had favorable experiences with the police, the shelter, and the court system. They reported less favorable experiences with probation officers and prosecutors. All of the respondents thought that their assailants should have been ordered to attend counseling and education groups, and most felt safer when the assailant was doing so. Eighty-eight percent reported that the combined response of the police, the courts, the shelter, and the counseling and education groups had been helpful or very helpful.

Half of the respondents attended the follow-up community meeting forum, in addition to 25 women who were currently participating in women's groups. The 55 women broke into five groups, each group reviewing the results of a section of the survey and reporting back to the larger group with a list of recommendations. Thirty-one recommendations were made for altering procedures or policies. Forty-two women volunteered to serve on four committees formed to implement the recommendations. Eventually, 23 of the recommendations were implemented.

This evaluation process did more than provide DAIP with an agenda for further work. It pointed out the importance of battered women's organizing on their own behalf. The women's recommendations and their effort to implement them brought the project back to the grass roots, where the battered women's movement began.

The second set of questionnaires is administered at three different intervals to men court mandated to groups and to their partners. This "behavior checklist" was designed by formerly battered women and Dr. Shepard. It is designed to measure the change in the frequency of use of all of the abusive and controlling tactics depicted in Figure 23.1 by abusers over a 12-month period.

The same process was used to design a survey for women to measure the degree to which their freedoms are restored over a 1-year period. This questionnaire attempts to assist women in evaluating how free they are to act without control or restraints from their abusers.

The results of the questionnaire in Duluth showed significant reductions in rates of abuse being reported, particularly during the first 3 months of the intervention process

(Novak & Galaway, 1983; Shepard, 1985). Shepard (1986) found that approximately 70% of the victims reported experiencing no recent physical abuse at a 1-year follow-up. Although significantly less psychological abuse was reported, 60% of the women did report having experienced some form of psychological abuse. Evaluation efforts have been limited by the unavailability of comparison groups and difficulty in locating subjects at follow-up. The extent to which different components of the project contributed to program outcomes is unclear. Police and court intervention, as well as the counseling and education program, are important elements of the program. Novak and Galaway (1983) did find that fewer victims reported experiencing violence from DAIP court mandated participants than from those who were not mandated. Studies of other programs have reported a range from 32% to 81% of program participants remaining nonviolent at follow-up periods from 3 months to 1 year. Diversity in treatment and research methods makes it difficult to compare findings.

Finally, DAIP staff and shelter staff collect data on a continuing basis to determine if the procedures, protocols, and policies are consistently applied. Through examination of police, court, shelter, and DAIP records and telephone interviews with women, a fairly accurate assessment of when and how the system breaks down can be determined.

The results of the data show that the level of compliance with the procedures, protocols, and policies varies with the agency. If the role of the agency is very concrete, it is more likely to adhere to the agreements than an agency whose role is more subjective.

These three processes are neither exhaustive nor adequate to evaluate fully this community's response to battering. They do, however, provide three important pieces of information: Are the community agencies doing what they say they are doing? How do battered women experience this system? Does the community response reduce women's vulnerability to continued abuse?

Conclusion

Every aspect of the program, from the police arrest to the group structure, is designed to focus on the batterer as a person in control of his partner, acting in what he perceives to be his best interest at the expense of his partner and children. This does not mean he is in control of himself. In fact, most men feel very out of control on a personal level. To focus literally hundreds of people in a community toward that end is a long process, but one we owe to battered women.

This work begins with commitment. It starts with a commitment to women who are beaten, kicked, pushed, stabbed, held hostage, called names, and subjected to constant attack on their very essence as human beings. It involves a commitment to these men—not to the part of them that unfairly uses another person but to the part of them that is capable of giving and receiving love. Our work must be personal. This work offers each of us the opportunity to examine some of our most basic beliefs about who we are in relationship to our partners, our friends, and our communities. Our culture and society encourage us to see power as the ability to control. The extent to which one is able to influence events, to acquire and control increasing amounts of resources, and to influence the behavior and actions of others is the measure of one's power. Those of us intervening in these cases, as well as the abuser, share in that cultural perspective.

To move from a society in which individuals seek power and its corresponding ability to control to a society in which its members seek collective and personal empowerment and its creative power is a complex process. But what is the role of the individual batterer in the overall scheme of things? If we see him as only the victim of a larger system in which he has no say and as merely a pawn of a sexist society, we take away his individual responsibility, making it difficult for him to change. This program in all its aspects rejects the notion of men as victims of sexism. Any system that gives one group power over another group dehumanizes both those with too much power and those without enough power. However, that does not make those who abuse their access to power innocent victims of the system. Ultimately, each of us must be held accountable for the choices we make. This project challenges men to see their use of violence as a choice—not an uncontrolled reaction to their past, their anger, or their lack of skills, but a choice.

The socialization of men and women in this society teaches us to adhere to rigidly defined roles that in the end separate us from one another. A community confrontation challenges much of what the men believe and in the process challenges those of us who orchestrate the confrontation.

A non-victim-blaming community response to abusers is all about power and can lead to true empowerment in men. It challenges men to take the risk to stop controlling, to stop having all the power. Above all else, it is respectful to each man because it believes that at each man's core is the ability to act in a loving and caring way. It gives men control of themselves and asks them to be in a world as a whole person—a person who feels pain, who sometimes loses, and who doesn't always get to decide. It asks men to give women the choice to love them. Finally, it asks men to respect women, to give up the privileged status our society has given them.

As a community, our ability to successfully intervene with a batterer is directly tied to our understanding of him as a manifestation of a part of all of us. He mirrors the worst in our culture. He is changed by our responding not in collusion with him, not by seeing him as different than us or as mentally ill, but by acknowledging the need for our own personal and institutional transformation to be a part of his.

REFERENCES

Novak, S., & Galaway, B. (1983). Independent evaluation conducted for the Domestic Abuse Intervention Project.

Shepard, M. (1985). Independent evaluation conducted for the Domestic Abuse Intervention Project.

Shepard, M. (1986). Unpublished doctoral dissertation conducted at the University of Minnesota.

Reflection

ELLEN PENCE

It seemed like a simple task. I get an email from Jeff Edleson asking if I would be willing to write a short reflective piece on a book chapter I wrote 18 years ago. A few days later the chapter arrived in the mail. As I read it I was flooded with memories and feelings. It was a description of how a small group of activists had organized the Duluth Domestic Abuse Intervention Project (DAIP). The chapter was written to discuss how such efforts either collude with or confront men's violence toward women. As I read it I was surprised at how direct I was about batterers, men, gender. Back then I didn't use the words offenders, victims, perpetrators—an ideological shift I've made over the years that I must rethink. Looking back I am awed by the impact we had in the United States and even globally. At the same time I know that had we done some things differently we could have, perhaps, helped to avoid some of the negative consequences of criminal justice reform efforts.

I wrote the article when people were just starting to come to Duluth to check out this so-called Coordinated Community Response. Our project was at its most exciting and energetic period. A lot of agency administrators had taken a chance on the changes we had proposed—from the police chief to the court clerks, roles were changed. Many battered women risked retribution by actively participating in planning meetings and open community evaluation sessions. The women's shelter had turned its programming upside down to accommodate our notion that most of the women who need help would never enter their doors. Neighborhood educational groups replaced in-house support groups and an advocacy program was organized for women seeking protection orders who would never move into the shelter. Every groundbreaking project has a period like this, when resistance to change starts to give way to a spirit of cooperation.

In just five years we had gone from a police and court system response that literally turned its back on women to one that turned its scrutiny and powerful control mechanisms toward the batterer. When we started, those men who had hospitalized or killed their partners were arrested and jailed. Men who were arrested for less violent attacks were almost all poor men and men of color. We created a dual track civil and criminal approach that women could count on for at least some basic protections: enforcement of protection orders, consequences for repeat assaults, mandated rehabilitation programs, and an immediate response to calls for help. Basic, but for some women, life saving. It was a response that included businessmen, doctors, and teachers who batter; for the first time they were not excluded from the grasp of state intervention.

Many things that we did were new and groundbreaking. We introduced the power and control wheel and its accompanying theoretical framework, which tried to shift away from seeing violence against women as the problem of a few psychologically distorted men and lots of bad marriages, by linking men's violence toward their partners to other forms of domination—class, race, gender, and colonization. We built on the work of previous projects that held individual agencies responsible to protect women and proposed a fairly bold notion of linking agencies together and forming a community-based advocacy program. We took the lead at the negotiating table. Policy makers had never had to deal so directly with a public group asking questions, reading documents, and watching cases grind through a system not designed with battered women in mind. We had established a tracking system that focused as much attention on tracking practitioners' compliance with agreed on practices as it did on individual men's compliance with court orders. We moved the collective agenda of the battered women's movement a big step forward because we showed that the strategy worked for women, for children, for men, and for the system.

But for every breakthrough we were able to accomplish, we also planted the seeds of new practices that reactive forces would eventually grab onto and use to undermine our vision of a legal system that promotes a woman's safety, acknowledges that her children's destinies are inextricably linked to hers, and subverts one of the pillars of men's historic ability to dominate women in marriage—the ability to use physical and sexual violence without consequence. Scarce space reduces me to listing some hindsights that I would love to explain.

First, we had incomplete thinking about how legal interventions individualize the social and require individual women to stop the violence men use against them. I guess we were thinking something like this: "Look, we created him; it's our responsibility to stop his use of violence." But we still saw as our goal stopping an individual man's violence against his individual partner. We saw violence harming women and their relationships with their children, but we were less clear on how the violence harmed us as a society. And so we held men accountable to individual women rather than to their community. To date we have failed to articulate the social nature of men's violence and the impact of that violence on our entire community.

Second, although we acknowledged that turning to the criminal justice system to protect women was a limited strategy, we focused all of our skills, analysis, resources, and energy on changing that one institutional response. This approach may not have been such a problem had we not simultaneously entered the Reagan and post-Reagan era. The DAIP reached its programmatic high just as conservatives were using the criminal justice system to cover up the evidence of an unjust economic order. To our surprise, Ronald Reagan was not a four-year accident. By the end of the decade his presidency ushered in, there was a 700 percent increase in the rate of imprisonment for poor men, mainly men of color; a shift in the wealth in this country unparalleled during any other presidency; and a fundamental erosion of social programs and economic protections that most battered women depended on for economic autonomy from their abusers. Although the battered women's movement had a far larger vision for community protection of women and children than reforming the police and court responses, it was unable to even come close to reaching that vision. The DAIP was in too many ways compatible with the conservative view that social problems are due to a criminal element in society and that its offenders were products of dysfunctional families and neighborhoods. The call to criminalize batterers came at a time when the newly empowered right wing found it an acceptable, fundable, tolerable feminist project.

Third, as organizers of what we thought would be a model for institutional advocacy in Minnesota, our work became a standard against which others measured effective interventions. We were unprepared in many ways for such a role. First, our community was predominantly white working class and Native American. We were a small, urban town. While I wouldn't paint us as pollyannaish about the repressive nature of the criminal justice system, we did organize the project in a community with a police and sheriff's department that has relatively few complaints against them for brutality, at a time when the bench was quite progressive, and there was agreement that jail, prisons, and punishment were really last resorts when other forms of intervention failed. The local conditions that made our approach work in Duluth did not always exist in other communities that took up the "model." Nor did we know how to insist on or encourage a reinvention of that model for each community in which it would be considered. Many who came to observe and learn the approach did in fact reinvent it. But for too many, that was not the case. I have personally been to dozens of communities that use the "Duluth model," but I rarely recognize its essential elements. It so often seems off to me. Rather than teaching about what we accomplished, we needed to teach about how we organized locally and carved out a role for activists in public policies.

Yet in other places I see the Duluth model tailored for the community. In Hamilton, New Zealand, for example, the leadership of the Maori domestic violence community reinvented our educational curriculum and our concepts of cultural adaptation. In Guam, the link between the batterer's program and the court system resulted in a tracking system far superior to ours. In San Diego, the leadership of the City Attorney's office created a prosecution project we cannot match. In many places, projects have developed the skills of their men's and women's group facilitators far deeper than our project. In London, Ontario, the inclusion of educational, medical, and child protection agencies in their community response, and in Chicago, the inclusion of neighborhood groups in their response, comes closer to our original vision of community than our own project's configuration.

In the end I think the DAIP's greatest contribution was its demonstration of how a local advocacy group could reshape institutional responses to male violence. In our case, that meant that we were able to create new boundaries around acceptable interventions to protect women and children. It redefined police action, it integrated women's safety into all court interventions, it created a way to focus rehabilitation on the abuser instead of the relationship, it demonstrated how to create interventions based on different levels of dangerousness and the context of the violence, it insisted on a system that intervened beyond the incident and understood the whole context of the violence, and finally it showed a way for activists and their allies in the system to work together. We made gender visible in a justice system that purported to be blind to all of the privileges it so routinely maintained.

INDEX

CREDITS

Chapter 1

p. 5: Reprinted with the permission of Simon & Schuster Adult Publishing Group, from *Against Our Will: Men, Women and Rape,* by Susan Brownmiller. Copyright © 1975 by Susan Brownmiller.

Chapter 2

p. 9: Republished with the permission of the *American Journal of Psychiatry,* from "Rape Trauma Syndrome," by Ann Wolbert Burgess and Lynda Lytle Holmstrom, 131, pp. 981–986. Copyright © 1974; permission conveyed through Copyright Clearance Center, Inc.

Chapter 3

p. 21: From "Father-Daughter Incest," by Judith Herman and Lisa Hirschman, in *Signs 2*(4), pp. 735–756. Copyright © 1977 by University of Chicago Press. Reprinted by permission.

p. 40: Reprinted by permission of the publisher from *Father-Daughter Incest,* by Judith Lewis Herman, Cambridge, Mass.: Harvard University Press. Copyright © 1981, 2000 by the President and Fellows of Harvard College.

Chapter 4

p. 42: Reprinted with permission of The Free Press, a Division of Simon & Schuster Adult Publishing Group, from *Sexually Victimized Children,* by David Finkelhor. Copyright © 1979 by David Finkelhor.

Chapter 5

p. 57: Reprinted from *Child Abuse and Neglect, 9,* Gail Wyatt, "The Sexual Abuse of Afro-American and White-American Women in Childhood," pp. 507–519, copyright © 1985, with permission of Elsevier.

Chapter 6

p. 75: Reprinted by permission of the publisher from *Sexual Harassment of Working Women,* by Catharine MacKinnon. Copyright © 1979 by Yale University Press.

p. 77: The line from "Cartographies of Silence." Copyright © 2002 by Adrienne Rich. Copyright © 1978 by W. W. Norton Company, Inc. *The Fact of a Doorframe: Selected Poems 1950–2001* by Adrienne Rich. Used by permission of W. W. Norton and Company.

Chapter 7

p. 98: Reprinted by permission of the publisher from *Rape in Marriage,* by Diane E. H. Russell. Copyright © 1990 by Indiana University Press.

Chapter 8

p. 110: From the *Journal of Consulting and Clinical Psychology,* "The Scope of Rape: Incidence and Prevalence of Sexual Aggression and Victimization in a National Sample of Higher Education Students," by Mary P. Koss, Christine A. Gidycz, and Nadine Wisniewski, *55,* pp. 162–170. Copyright © 1987 by the American Psychological Association. Reprinted with permission.

Chapter 9

p. 130: Marie Marshall Fortune, *Sexual Violence, The Unmentionable Sin: An Ethical and Pastoral Perspective,* (The Pilgrim Press: Cleveland, 1993), pp. 125–139. Copyright © 1993 by Marie Marshall Fortune. Used by permission.

Chapter 10

p. 140: Reprinted by permission of the publisher from *Female Sexual Slavery,* by Kathleen Barry. Copyright © 1979 by New York University Press.

Chapter 11

p. 155: Reprinted by permission of the publisher from *Battered Wives,* by Del Martin. Copyright © 1976 by Volcano Press.

Chapter 12

p. 168: From *Victimology: An International Journal,* "Wives: The 'Appropriate' Victims of Marital Violence," *2*(3–4). Copyright © 1978 by the authors. Reprinted by permission.

Chapter 13

p. 187: Republished with the permission of the National Council on Family Relations, from the *Journal of Marriage and the Family,* "Measuring Intrafamily Conflict and Violence: The Conflict Tactics (CT) Scales," by Murray A. Straus, *41*(1), pp. 75–88. Copyright © 1979; permission conveyed through Copyright Clearance Center, Inc.

Chapter 14

p. 198: Reprinted by permission of the publisher from *Women and Male Violence: The Visions and Struggles of the Battered Women's Movement,* by Susan Schechter. Copyright © 1982 by South End Press.

Chapter 15

p. 220: Pages 42–54 from *The Battered Woman* by Lenore E. Walker. Copyright © 1979 by Lenore E. Walker. Reprinted by permission of HarperCollins Publishers, Inc.

Chapter 16

p. 229: Reprinted with the permission of The Free Press, a Division of Simon and Schuster Adult Publishing Group, from *When Battered Women Kill,* by Angela Browne. Copyright © 1987 by The Free Press.

Chapter 17

p. 244: From the *International Journal of Health Services,* "Women and Children at Risk: a Feminist Perspective on Child Abuse," by Evan Stark and Anne H. Flitcraft, *18*(1), pp. 97–118. Copyright © 1988 by Baywood Publishing Company, Inc. Reprinted with permission.

Chapter 18

p. 268: From the book *Naming the Violence: Speaking Out About Lesbian Battering,* by Kerry Lobel. Copyright © 1986 by the National Coalition Against Domestic Violence. Reprinted by permission of the publisher, Seal Press.

Chapter 19

p. 282: Copyright © 1994 by Kimberle Crenshaw. Reprinted by permission of the author.

Chapter 20

p. 317: "'Riding the Bull at Gilley's': Convicted Rapists Describe the Rewards of Rape," by Diana Scully and Joseph Marolla, in *Social Problems 32*(3), pp. 251–263. Copyright © 1985 by the Society for the Study of Social Problems. Reprinted by permission.

Chapter 21

p. 335: "The Specific Deterrent Effects of Arrest for Domestic Assault," by Lawrence W. Sherman and Richard A. Berk, in *American Sociological Review, 49,* pp. 261–272. Copyright © 1984 by the American Sociological Association. Reprinted by permission.

Chapter 22

p. 355: Edward Gondolf, "The Effect of Batterer Counseling on Shelter Outcome," *Journal of Interpersonal Violence, 3*(3), pp. 275–289. Copyright © 1988 by Sage Publications, Inc. Reprinted by permission of Sage Publications, Inc.

Chapter 23

p. 368: From *Treating Men Who Batter,* by P. Lynn Caesar and L. Kevin Hamberger, eds. Copyright © 1989 by Springer Publishing Company, 536 Broadway, New York, NY, 10012. Used by permission.